The
Birth
of
Vietnam

The
Birth
of
Vietnam

Keith
Weller
Taylor

University of California Press
Berkeley · Los Angeles · London

University of California Press
Berkeley and Los Angeles, California
University of California Press, Ltd.
London, England
© 1983 by
The Regents of the University of California
Composition in Hong Kong by Asco Trade Typesetting Ltd.
Printed in the United States of America

1 2 3 4 5 6 7 8 9

Library of Congress Cataloging in Publication Data
Taylor, Keith Weller.
  The birth of Vietnam.
  Revision of thesis (Ph.D.)—University of Michigan,
1976.
  Bibliography: p.
  Includes index.
  1. Vietnam—History—To 939.   I. Title
DS556.6.T39 1982   959.7′03   81-11590
ISBN 0-520-04428-2   AACR2

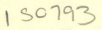

To my parents,
Weller Herbert
and
Clara Vander Vlucht
Taylor

Contents

Tables

Maps

Preface

As an American soldier in Vietnam, I could not help being impressed by the intelligence and resolve of the Vietnamese who opposed us, and I asked: "Where did these people come from?" This book, the revised and expanded version of a doctoral thesis completed at the University of Michigan in 1976, is my answer to that question.

Many investigators have preceded me into early Vietnamese history. French scholarship on this subject has been accumulating for nearly a century and contains much that is stimulating and useful. The work of Chinese and Japanese scholars is particularly valuable, for it is generally based on a firm knowledge of classical literature and of traditional historiography. Japanese scholars of early Vietnam have especially distinguished themselves through several fine studies. The work of modern Vietnamese scholars is immense. Archeological efforts of the past quarter century have yielded discoveries that have revolutionized our understanding of Vietnamese prehistory and forced reevaluations of subsequent historical eras.

In the English-speaking world, we are beginning to realize the significance of Vietnam's deep heritage. This heritage has been shaped by a history going back more than two thousand years. I hope this book will encourage a greater understanding of how this long national experience has contributed to the outlook of the Vietnamese people today.

I have relegated Vietnamese diacritics and Chinese characters to the glossary to avoid expensive composition. It is impossible to identify and pronounce Vietnamese words without diacritics, so readers familiar with Vietnamese are encouraged to consult the glossary for the correct spelling of a Vietnamese word upon its first occurrence in the text. Likewise, a Chinese word cannot be identified without its character, so readers familiar with Chinese are encouraged to consult the glossary as needed.

I owe a debt of gratitude to Professor Paul G. Fried of Hope College for encouraging me to again take up formal academic work after a period of military service.

At the University of Michigan, it was my good fortune to study under Dr. John K. Whitmore, a pioneer in the field of premodern Vietnamese history in the United States. I also acknowledge my debt to the other members of my graduate and thesis committees at the University of Michigan: Professor Chun-shu Chang, Professor John V. A. Fine, Jr., Professor Charles O. Hucker, and Professor Thomas R. Trautmann, all of whom inspired my efforts to study history.

I am expecially grateful to Professor O. W. Wolters of Cornell University for his comments during the revision process, which not only held me back from error but also set me on the way toward serious reevaluations.

I am also indebted to Professor Chi-yun Chen of the University of California, Santa Barbara, Professor David G. Marr of the Australian National University, Professor Alexander B. Woodside of the University of British Columbia, and Professor Ying-shih Yü of Yale University for their evaluations during the revision process; their comments played a large part in correcting confusion, developing my ideas, and giving the manuscript its present shape.

Professor William H. Nienhauser, Jr., of the University of Wisconsin, kindly offered valuable insights into the poem by P'i Jih-hsiu discussed in Appendix N.

John K. Musgrave of the University of Michigan Library and Ikuta Shigeru of the Tōyō Bunko Library in Tokyo gave timely assistance in locating materials.

Sadako Ohki, my friend and spouse, translated Japanese books and articles and helped identify obscure characters.

A grant from the Social Science Research Council allowed me to put this manuscript into publishable form.

I am grateful to Grant Barnes, Phyllis Killen, and their colleagues at the University of California Press for their encouragement, guidance, and professional expertise.

This book has benefited from the editorial skill of Helen Tartar. I appreciate her thorough attention to detail and sure sense of correct grammar and good style.

All the mistakes are mine.

Introduction

This book is about Vietnam from the beginning of recorded history in the third century B.C. to the tenth century, when Chinese control ended and an independent Vietnamese kingdom was established. During these twelve centuries, the Vietnamese evolved from a preliterate society within a "south-sea civilization" into a distinctive member of the East Asian cultural world. This long process was the birth of historical Vietnam.

Chinese historians and French sinologists have treated this period of Vietnamese history as a branch of Chinese history. They have seen Vietnam as little more than a refractory frontier province of the Chinese empire, blessed with China's "civilizing" influence. Vietnamese historians, on the other hand, look at this era as a time when their ancestors struggled under alien rule, a time when their national identity was tested and refined. To gain a balanced view, it is important to consider both the information about Vietnam recorded by Chinese historians and the historical traditions that preserve what the Vietnamese have remembered from this time.[1]

It is sometimes imagined that an indigenous core of "Vietnameseness" survived unscathed through the fire of Chinese domination. To a certain extent this is true, for the Vietnamese language survived, as did mythical traditions from the pre-Chinese period. But both the Vietnamese language and the mythical traditions were transformed through intimate contact with China.

Tenth-century Vietnamese were very different from their ancestors of twelve centuries before. They had grown to understand China as only a slave can know its master; they knew China at its best and at its worst. They could enjoy composing poetry in T'ang-style verse, but they could also be fierce in their resistance to Chinese soldiers. They had become experts at surviving in the shadow of the mightiest empire on earth.

Vietnamese independence did not suddenly appear in the tenth century solely as a result of Chinese weakness. China never renounced its presumed right to rule the Vietnamese and has more than once tried to reconquer Vietnam. But, by the tenth century, the Vietnamese had developed a spirit and intelligence capable of resisting Chinese power. This spirit and intelligence matured during centuries of Chinese rule; it was

1. See Appendix O.

rooted in a conviction held by Vietnamese that they were not, and did not want to be, Chinese.

It has been thought that Vietnamese independence was the result of Chinese influence, that the stimulation of Chinese concepts of government and society galvanized the Vietnamese into reaching the level of modern statehood. But the ancestors of the Vietnamese had their own kings and cultural symbols before the arrival of Chinese armies, and presumably their continued existence would have been assured even if they had never heard of China.[2]

The experience of Chinese rule affected the Vietnamese in two ways. First, it fostered a receptivity to Chinese cultural leadership among ruling-class Vietnamese. As a result of the admission of numerous Chinese words to their vocabulary and of many centuries' experience as a Chinese province, the Vietnamese came to possess a political and philosophical idiom that has something in common with China. Intellectual trends in China, whether Taoist, Buddhist, Confucianist, or Marxist, are easily understood by the Vietnamese.

On the other hand, Chinese rule bred an instinctive resistance to Chinese and, by extension, to all foreign political interference. Over the past one thousand years, the Vietnamese have no less than seven times defeated attempts by China to assert its influence by armed force. No theme is more consistent in Vietnamese history than the theme of resistance to foreign aggression.

The Vietnamese concept of kingship became increasingly encrusted with Sinitic theories and formalities as the centuries passed, but it had its origin in a peculiar quality reflecting the perspective of a stubborn, intelligent peasant who has mastered the art of survival. The founder of the independent Vietnamese monarchy in the tenth century was not reared within the Chinese imperial tradition. He was a rustic peasant warrior whose two achievements, of uniting the Vietnamese and of providing for national defense, have remained the indispensable qualifications for political leadership in Vietnam to the present day.

This book ends with the assassination of the man who founded the new Vietnamese kingdom in the tenth century. China took advantage of this to attempt to reassert its ancient hegemony in Vietnam. Such a crisis, calling for strong leadership to meet invaders, became a common theme in Vietnamese history, and Vietnamese kings were expected to know how to rally mass participation in resistance efforts. In the nineteenth century, Vietnamese leaders grew so dependent on Chinese concepts of government that they alienated themselves from their own people and failed to effectively resist French aggression. Contemporary Vietnam grew out of this failure.

2. See my "An Evaluation of the Chinese Period in Vietnamese History."

The birth of Vietnam was a prolonged process of adjustment to the proximity of Chinese power. It may be more correct to speak of the "births" of Vietnam, for in their long history the Vietnamese have more than once experienced the transformation of consciousness that can be associated with "birth." A prominent Vietnamese scholar recently offered a new synthesis of Vietnamese history, suggesting that the nation has been "established" three times: once during the prehistoric era culminating in the Dong-son civilization that predates Chinese influence, again in the tenth century when Chinese rule ended, and once more now in the twentieth century.[3] This book focuses on the birth of Vietnam in the tenth century, although the story begins with Dong-son.

This birth can be analysed in six phases, each one of which contributed to defining the limits within which the Vietnamese were able to grow. These limits were largely determined by the degree and nature of Chinese power felt in Vietnam.

In the first phase, which can be called the Dong-son or Lac-Viet period, Chinese power had not yet reached Vietnam. The Vietnamese were important members of a prehistoric Bronze Age civilization oriented toward the coasts and islands of Southeast Asia. The cultural and political frontier between the Vietnamese and the Chinese was well defined.

In the second phase, which can be called the Han-Viet period, Chinese military power arrived, and a new ruling class of mixed Sino-Vietnamese ancestry emerged. Chinese philosophy appeared, and Vietnamese Buddhism began. Vietnamese culture experienced an initial realignment toward China, while countering this trend with a Buddhist religion preached by missionaries that arrived directly from India by sea. The cultural and political frontier during this phase was drawn through the midst of Vietnamese society.

The third phase can be called the Giao-Viet period, for it was a time when the province of Giao was firmly established in the Vietnamese lands and a new concept of cultural and political frontiers was enforced by men owing allegiance to northern dynasties. Lin-i, the Cham kingdom on the southern coast, ceased to be a factor in domestic Vietnamese politics and instead became a foreign enemy. The Lin-i wars are the most distinctive characteristic of this period. This phase began in the late third century, after the violence of the Chin intervention, when T'ao Huang, a popular Chinese governor, pushed back the borders and reorganized provincial administration. The cultural and political frontier was now between the Vietnamese and their southern neighbors.

In the fourth phase, which spanned most of the sixth century, Chinese power momentarily withdrew from Vietnam, and local heroes attempted to enforce a new concept of frontiers that set the Vietnamese off, not only from

3. Pham Huy Thong, "Ba lan dung nuoc."

their southern neighbors, but also from China. This was a time of self-discovery as the Vietnamese experimented with different forms of national expression, from an effort to imitate the dynastic institution of China to an attempt to return to the mythical traditions of the pre-Chinese past and, finally, to a Buddhist rendition of national authority that foreshadowed the establishment of Vietnamese independence in the tenth and eleventh centuries.

The fifth phase, the T'ang-Viet phase, found the Vietnamese firmly within the northern empire. The pressure to conform to Chinese patterns of behavior was relatively intense, and the Vietnamese responded with acts of resistance, inviting their non-Chinese neighbors to intervene on their behalf. But all resistance and all attempts to ally with neighboring peoples were crushed by T'ang's military power. The most serious challenge to T'ang rule came in the mid-ninth century, when anti-T'ang Vietnamese allied with the mountain kingdom of Nan-chao in Yün-nan. But the Vietnamese discovered that they could tolerate T'ang misgovernment easier than they could the undisciplined habits of their "barbarian" neighbors. The T'ang-Viet period saw the cultural and political frontiers of Vietnam severely drawn, not only separating the Vietnamese from their coastal and upland neighbors, but also dividing the Vietnamese from the Muong, who inhabited peripheral areas beyond the direct control of T'ang officials and who preserved a form of Vietnamese culture that shows little Chinese influence.

In the tenth century, the final phase was reached when Vietnamese leaders drew a political frontier between themselves and the Chinese. Defining and enforcing this frontier has played a large role in subsequent Vietnamese history.

Each of these phases modified the Vietnamese perception of themselves in relation to their neighbors. The modifications made in the second, third, and fifth phases, when strong Chinese dynasties asserted their power in Vietnam, drew the Vietnamese closer to China and cut them off from their non-Chinese neighbors. Only in the sixth and tenth centuries, when the Vietnamese were able to take the initiative, did the frontiers reflect an effective native power. And even then there is little evidence of backsliding, of the Vietnamese reverting to an earlier outlook.

By the tenth century, the Vietnamese knew that their national destiny was unavoidably entangled with China. They could never pretend that China did not pose a continual potential threat to the unhindered development of their national life. Whatever they did would have to be done with one eye on China. They had no time to indulge any primeval longing to become more like their Southeast Asian neighbors.

This does not mean that the Vietnamese are not "Southeast Asian," whatever that may mean. First and foremost, they are Vietnamese. They have asserted their distinctive view of the world against both China and their Southeast Asian neighbors. Vietnam's non-Chinese neighbors have little understanding of the price paid by the Vietnamese for their national survival and of the depth of the Vietnamese resolve to resist China's historical pressure. The Vietnamese have accepted the perspective imposed on them by history. They see themselves standing alone between a threatening giant and a circle of relatively self-absorbed realms. In fact, the Vietnamese revel in their Southeast Asian identity, though not for its own sake, but rather for the refreshment and reinforcement it provides in the grim business of maintaining the northern border.

From a broader perspective, Vietnam stands on the frontier between East and Southeast Asia. The question of whether Vietnam "belongs" to Southeast Asia or to East Asia is probably one of the least enlightening in Vietnamese studies. Although everything from the Vietnamese language to Vietnamese eating habits reflects a distinctive blend of the two cultural worlds, literature, scholarship, and government administration clearly show that the Vietnamese have been participating members of the classical civilization of East Asia. This stems from the success of Chinese dynasties in enforcing a cultural and political frontier between the Vietnamese and their Southeast Asian neighbors for several centuries.

The birth of Vietnam described in this book was the birth of a new consciousness within the East Asian cultural world that had its roots outside that world. Within the context of East Asia as a whole, this was a frontier consciousness, but for the Vietnamese it was simply what they happened to be. They had learned to articulate their non-Chinese identity in terms of China's cultural heritage. Given the constraints imposed by Chinese power during long periods of their history, the survival of this identity is as significant as the cultural form in which it came to be expressed.

I
Lac
Lords

The Earliest Traditions

The earliest traditions of the Vietnamese people, as revealed in the *Linh-nam chich quai*, an accumulation of lore edited in the fifteenth century, are associated with the Hung kings who ruled the kingdom of Van-lang.[1] The Hung kings claimed descent from Lac Long Quan, "Lac Dragon Lord," a hero who came to the Hong River plain in what is now northern Vietnam from his home in the sea; he subdued all evil demons in the land and civilized the people, teaching them to cultivate rice and to wear clothes. Lac Long Quan returned to the sea after instructing the people to call on him if they were ever in distress. Eventually, a monarch from the north, China, entered the land and, finding it without a king, claimed it for himself. When the people cried out to Lac Long Quan for deliverance from this alien ruler, he heard them and came back from the sea; he kidnapped Au Co, the wife of the intruder, and took her to the top of Mount Tan-vien, which overlooks the Hong River as it enters the plains. Failing to retrieve his wife, the northern king departed in despair. Au Co eventually gave birth to the first of the Hung kings, and Lac Long Quan returned to his home in the sea after again promising to return if needed. Lac Long Quan, a prince of the sea, and Au Co, a princess of the mountains, are regarded by the Vietnamese as the progenitors of their race.

The mythical traditions surrounding Lac Long Quan and the origin of the Hung kings reveal a sea-oriented culture coming to terms with a continental environment. Civilization arrived with a culture hero from the sea who foiled a continental power by seizing his foe's wife and making her the mother of his heirs. This theme of the local culture hero neutralizing a northern threat by appropriating its source of legitimacy foreshadowed the historical relationship between the Vietnamese and the Chinese. The mythical origin of the Hung kings reflects a maritime cultural base with political accretions from continental influences. This idea was later elaborated by Vietnamese literati into a genealogy of Lac Long Quan and Au Co that brought together the southern aquatic line and the northern continental line

---

1. *LNCQ*, 5–7. On the *Linh-nam chich quai*, see Appendix O. On Hung and Van-lang, see Appendix B.

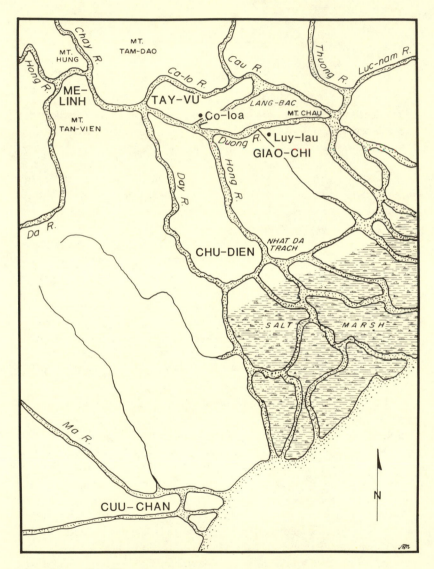

Map 1. Lac Vietnam

of a single royal family, of which the founder was selected to predate the first mythical Chinese emperor.[2]

According to a recent Vietnamese study, the name *Hung* derives from an Austroasiatic title of chieftainship that has persisted up to the present time in the languages of Mon-Khmer-speaking peoples living in the mountains of Southeast Asia, as well as in Muong, the upland sister language of Vietnamese; the title is also found among the Munda of northeast India, who speak the most western of the surviving Austroasiatic languages.[3] A modern Vietnamese linguist has associated *Van-lang*, the traditional name of the Hung kingdom, with phonetically similar words in the languages of minority peoples throughout the region bounded by the Yangtze and Mekong rivers that mean "people" and, by extension, "nation."[4] According to oral tradition, the totem of the Hung kings was a large mythical bird; the name of this bird is thought to have been the origin of the toponym given by the Chinese to the region from which the Hung kings ruled: Me-linh.[5]

Me-linh was in the northwest corner of the plain, where the Hong River emerges from the mountains and is joined by its two great tributaries, the Da and the Chay. The confluence of these three rivers is at an altitude of about 30 to 35 feet above sea level, approximately one hundred miles from the sea. Me-linh is dominated by Mount Tan-vien to the southwest and Mount Tam-dao to the northeast. The three rivers join their waters at the foot of Mount Hung, where the ancestral temple of the Hung kings is located.[6]

The earliest event recorded as historical in a Vietnamese source comes from the *Viet su luoc* and is dated in the reign of a Chinese king, Chuang of Chou, who reigned from 696 to 682 B.C. Eighteen generations separated Chuang of Chou from the end of his dynasty. Vietnamese historians seem to have inherited a tradition of eighteen generations of Hung kings, coming to an end simultaneously with the Chinese house of Chou; that they dated the first Hung king to Chuang of Chou on the basis of this tradition is a reasonable supposition. According to the *Viet su luoc*, Vietnamese history began when an "extraordinary man" of Me-linh used magical arts to unite all the tribes under his authority; he took the title of Hung king and named his realm Van-lang. The origin of this account is obscure, and its authenticity

2. See Appendix A.

3. Tran Quoc Vuong, "Ve danh hieu 'Hung Vuong,'" pp. 353–55.

4. Hoang Thi Chau, "Nuoc Van-lang qua tai lieu ngon ngu," pp. 39–42. Tran Quoc Vuong, "Ve danh hieu," p. 353, conjectured that *Van-lang* derived from the ancient Vietnamese name for the mythical bird believed to have been the clan totem of the Hung kings.

5. Tran Quoc Vuong, "Ve danh hieu," p. 353.

6. Le Tuong and Nguyen Dinh Ai, "Qua trinh hinh thanh khu di tich lich su thoi Vua Hung tren Nui Hung," pp. 66–72; Le Tuong and Nguyen Loc, "Ve kinh do Van-lang," pp. 34–45; Van Lang, "Dat to den Hung," pp. 76–77.

is open to serious question.[7] However, the date it assigns to the rise of the Hung kings coincides with archeological evidence indicating that, about the seventh century B.C., the different cultures of northern Vietnam became united under the influence of the oldest bronze-using culture, which had its origins in the Me-linh area; this marked the beginning of what is generally called the Dong-son culture.[8]

The archeological progression culminating in the Dong-son culture began near the end of the third millennium B.C. with the appearance of late Neolithic, early Bronze Age cultures in the valleys of the Hong and Ma rivers. These two cultural centers continued a parallel yet distinct development until they were united in the Dong-son culture around the seventh century B.C. The Dong-son culture is known for its ornamented bronze drums, which have been found in many parts of Southeast Asia and in southern China; the designs on these drums reflect a sea-oriented culture.[9]

Vietnamese scholars associate the Hung kings with the Dong-son culture. They consider this to have been the formative period in establishing their national tradition;[10] thus they can view the subsequent period of Chinese rule as a temporary intrusion into an already established national life. This perspective explains Vietnamese independence in the tenth century A.D. as the reappearance of a preexisting tradition; it denies the conventional view of Chinese and French scholars, according to which the Vietnamese heritage has its roots in the Chinese provincial experience, a view increasingly difficult to maintain as archeological, linguistic, and historical work progresses.

From their center in Me-linh, the Hung kings extended their influence eastward to include the region of Tay-vu. The name *Tay-vu* came from later centuries and derived from contact with Chinese-oriented peoples further north. This region lay between the Cau and Hong rivers at the foot of Mount Tam-dao. It was a fertile region of lakes, rivers, hills, and plains, bounded by mountainous terrain on one side and soggy delta lands on the other; it was heavily populated from a very early time.[11] The highlands north of Tay-vu are drained by rivers whose valleys communicate with southern China through low passes. Consequently, Tay-vu was vulnerable to attack from the north, and the earliest legends from this region are about defending the land against invaders from the north.

The best known of these legends is about Ong Giong, a three-year-old boy who grew miraculously into a giant by eating vast amounts of rice; after

7. See Appendix C.

8. See Appendix D.

9. Chikamori Masashi, "Don Son Seiōki Bunka no Kigen ni kansuru Ichi Shiron," p. 90.

10. Pham Huy Thong, "Ba lan dung nuoc," pp. 64–67.

11. Dinh Van Nhat, "Vung Lang-bac ve thoi Hai Ba Trung," p. 49.

sweeping the invaders from the land, he disappeared into the heavens.[12] Ong Giong has been interpreted as an incarnation of Lac Long Quan returning to succor his people;[13] he is similar to heroes in Indonesian lore.[14]

One of the most powerful figures of Vietnamese mythology is the Great King of Mount Tan-vien, also known as the Spirit of Mount Tan-vien or simply the Mountain Spirit. He was a son of Lac Long Quan and Au Co, who followed his father to the sea but later returned to dwell on Mount Tan-vien, the "Olympus" of Vietnamese mythology. One legend about the Mountain Spirit is virtually identical to a folk tradition from northern Borneo.[15]

The most famous legend of the Mountain Spirit is about his battle with the Water Spirit,[16] which has been differently interpreted as symbolizing the monsoon rain season,[17] a sudden rise in sea level,[18] or invaders from the sea.[19] While a plausible case can be made for each of these

12. According to Dinh Van Nhat, "Vung Lang-bac," p. 49, the legend of Ong Giong (variously Ong Dong), which in later centuries received official recognition, was simply one of several similar legends from the area of ancient Tay-vu. The fullest version of the legend is found in *LNCQ*, 13–15, from which the account in *TT*, 1, 3b–5a, is apparently derived. *CL*, 26, contains a short notice giving the barest outline of the legend. The *VDULT* and *VSL* do not contain the legend.

13. According to *LNCQ*, 33–35, in the invasion crisis the Hung king was advised to seek the aid of Lac Long Quan. After performing sacrifices for three days, the Hung king was visited by Lac Long Quan in the form of an old man who promised deliverance. Ong Giong subsequently rose to defend the land. On Ong Giong as a reincarnation of Lac Long Quan, see Cao Huy Dinh, "Hinh tuong khong lo va tap the anh hung dung nuoc, giu nuoc trong truyen co dan gian Viet Nam," pp. 87–91, and Yamamoto Tatsurō, "Myths Explaining the Vicissitudes of Political Power in Ancient Viet Nam," pp. 85–86.

14. The notion of a baby boy's consuming prodigious amounts of rice and growing miraculously to heroic proportions is found in the folk traditions of many areas of Southeast Asia. One example can be found in the preliminary draft of a translation of *Temelak Mangan*, "a folk epic from Lombok telling of the origin of the Sasak people," by Ma'sum Ahmod, Hunsi A. Hatid, and A. L. Becker (manuscript; Malang, East Java, 1970–71).

15. The legend consists of a confrontation between the Mountain Spirit and the Tree Spirit on Mount Tan-vien, in which an ancient tree is miraculously restored after being chopped down by the Mountain Spirit. After the third such episode, the Mountain Spirit hides and observes the White Star Spirit restore the tree at the break of dawn. The Mountain Spirit captures the White Star Spirit and reaches an agreement on the use of the land and the trees on it. See Gustave Dumoutier "Étude historique et archeologique sur Co-loa, capital de l'ancien royaume de Au Lac," pp. 261–62. In the Borneo legend, a tree is similarly restored after being cut down; the spirit who restores the tree is captured and in return for the use of the trees and the land demands sacrifice and veneration. See Henry Ling Roth, *The Natives of Sarawak and British North Borneo*, 1: 177–78. Both of these legends can be compared with the victory of Lac Long Quan over the thousand-year-old demon-tree in Me-linh (*LNCQ*, 9–10).

16. *VDULT*, 36–37, and *LNCQ*, 26–27. Also see Yamamoto, "Myths," p. 87.

17. Gustave Dumoutier, "Choix de legendes historique de l'Annam et du Tonkin," pp. 159–91.

18. Nguyen Duy, "Cu dan o Viet Nam truoc, trong, va sau thoi Hung Vuong," p. 22.

19. Claude Madrolle, "Le Tonkin ancien," pp. 308–21.

interpretations, they do not take into account all elements of the legend as it has been preserved in the *Viet dien u linh tap*, our earliest source.

Far from being an alien invader, the Water Spirit was originally a good friend of the Mountain Spirit; both dwelt in seclusion in Me-linh. The cause of their enmity was courtship of a Hung princess. The Hung king and his advisors considered both to be acceptable consorts for the royal bride and invited each to compete for the honor of her hand. The Mountain Spirit won the contest and took his bride to Mount Tan-vien; the Water Spirit, however, refused to accept defeat and assaulted the Mountain Spirit with great ferocity, but little success. This legend appears to explain the preeminence of Mount Tan-vien over the adjacent lowlands as resulting from its possession of the princess. This is supported by popular folklore, in which the political importance of Mount Tan-vien in ancient times is a recurring theme.[20]

The legend of Nhat Da Trach, "One Night Marsh,"[21] comes from the southern part of the Hong River plain, a low swampy area near the sea. According to this legend, a Hung princess named Tien Dung was exploring the river channels of the deltaic plains when she met a naked young man named Chu Dong Tu. She married the lad, and the couple established themselves near the sea in a palace filled with the luxury wares of seaborne merchants. Hearing of this, the Hung king sent an army against the upstarts; however, as the army approached, the palace disappeared in a single night and nothing remained but a vast impenetrable swamp: Nhat Da Trach. This legend contains elements similar to the founding myth of what the Chinese called Fu-nan, in the lower Mekong.[22]

Legends of Lac Long Quan, Ong Giong, the spirit of Mount Tan-vien, and Nhat Da Trach were incorporated into Ngo Si Lien's court history in the fifteenth century. All of these legends were by that time encrusted with elaborations stemming from the cultural currents of later centuries.[23] These legends were remembered by the Vietnamese because they expressed their earliest identity as a people.

Beyond the details of these legends lies a basic psychological truth of ancient Vietnamese society: sovereign power came from the sea. Lac Long Quan belonged to the watery realm. As we have seen, certain elements of

20. Tan Vu, "Tu tuong chu yeu cua nguoi Viet thoi co qua nhung truyen dung dau trong than thoai va truyen thuyet," p. 110; Nugyen Loc, "Buoc dau tim hieu moi quan he Hung Vuong va Thuc Vuong," pp. 54–60.

21. *LNCQ*, 11–13; Dumoutier, "Choix," pp. 172–74; Maurice Durand, "La Dynastie des Ly anterieurs d'après le *Viet dien u linh tap*," p. 448, n. 2. *TT*, 4, 17b.

22. In the Fu-nan myth, the Brahman Kaundinya encounters a naked woman in the Mekong delta whom he marries, thereby founding a kingdom (Georges Coedès, *The Making of Southeast Asia*, p. 37).

23. Tran Quoc Vuong, "Tu tu duy than thoai den tu duy lich su," p. 404.

these legends are similar to legendary themes found in the island and coastal world of Southeast Asia. The idea of an aquatic spirit's being the source of political power and legitimacy, which attended the formation of the Vietnamese people in prehistoric times, is the earliest hint of the concept of the Vietnamese as a distinct and self-conscious people.[24] This idea was given clear visual form in the art of the Dong-son bronze drums, where sea birds and amphibians surround boats bearing warriors.

Lac Society

Vietnamese archeologists date the beginning of their civilization to the Phung-nguyen culture of the late third millennium B.C., which flourished in the region later called Me-linh.[25] They regard Phung-nguyen as an advanced Neolithic, early Bronze Age culture. Phung-nguyen sites covered tens of thousands of square meters and accommodated thousands of inhabitants. This has been seen as evidence of a communal life built up from aggregations of clans and tribes.[26]

As the use of bronze developed during the next two millennia, this primitive communalism broke up into a more hierarchical society based on relatively small village or family groups.[27] This trend culminated in the Dong-son civilization, which Vietnamese archeologists date from the seventh century B.C. to the first century A.D.[28] The graves of ruling-class people from the Dong-son period are rich with bronze burial goods.[29] They show that ruling-class people had by this time established a clear distance between themselves and the people they ruled. Vietnamese scholars identify this as the time of the legendary Hung kings and their kingdom of Van-lang.[30]

A Vietnamese linguist has pointed out, in a study of terms found in traditions associated with the Hung kings, that words for "headman" (*phu-dao*), "lady or princess" (*mi-nuong*), and "gentleman or prince" (*quan-lang*) are shared with a number of Austroasiatic and Austronesian languages in

24. Jean Pryzluski ("La Princesse a l'odeur de poisson et la Nagi dans les traditions de l'Asie oriental") pointed out that the idea of sovereignty's issuing from the sea is directly opposed to the continental cultures of the Indo-Aryans and Chinese and attributed it to a prehistoric maritime civilization in Southeast Asia. For more on this, see my "Madagascar and the Ancient Malayo-Polynesian Myths."

25. Hoang Xuan Chinh and Bui Van Tien, "Van hoa Dong-son va cac trung tam van hoa trong thoi Dai Kim Khi o Viet Nam," pp. 40–41.

26. Nguyen Phuc Long, "Les nouvelles recherches archéologiques au Vietnam," p. 46.

27. Ibid., p. 6.

28. Nguyen Duy Ty, "Nien dai van hoa Dong-son," p. 84.

29. Nguyen Phuc Long, pp. 7 and 83, n. 2.

30. Pham Huy Thong and Chu Van Tan, "Thoi Dai Kim Khi o Viet Nam va 'Van Minh Song Hong,'" pp. 37–44.

Southeast Asia, and he theorizes that these words entered Chinese from these southern languages.[31] A word for "maidservant or slave" (*xao*) is shared with Thai, a word for "people or subjects" (*hon*) is shared with both Thai and Cham, and a word for "assistant headman" (*bo-chinh*) is shared with Jarai, an Austronesian language in the mountains of central Vietnam.[32] The precise linguistic origins of these titles and terms are not yet clear, but their distribution suggests that ancient Vietnam was a meeting place of different linguistic cultures.

An ancient Vietnamese word for "village or locality" (*ke*) seems to be indigenous to the Hong River plain, and the geographical sphere of its survival in contemporary village names suggests an origin in Neolithic and Bronze Age paddy society.[33]

The Vietnamese word for "river" (*song*), which is shared with many neighboring linguistic groups and was borrowed by Chinese (*chiang*),[34] has recently been shown to have derived from Austroasiatic.[35] Likewise, as noted earlier, there is reason to believe that the term *Hung* derives from an Austroasiatic title of chieftainship. Modern scholars tend to see Austroasiatic and Austronesian as continental and maritime branches of an older Austroasian group. The Austronesian influence left the mainland for the islands of Southeast Asia, while the Austroasiatic presence moved overland through mainland Southeast Asia; Mon-Khmer is a major language family within Austroasiatic.[36] Vietnamese is, according to a recent investigator, "an undoubted Mon-Khmer language" with clearly recognizable loans from Austronesian.[37]

The opposition of mountain and sea in Vietnamese mythology[38] thus has a linguistic base. In northern Vietnam during prehistoric times, we can assume that the Mon-Khmer, or Austroasiatic, linguistic world thrived on land adjacent to the sea-based Austronesians, and eventually absorbed them; the Vietnamese language accordingly developed from Mon-Khmer in a cultural world deeply indebted to contact with Austronesian peoples. Con-

---

31. Hoang Thi Chau, "Nuoc Van-lang qua tai lieu ngon ngu," pp. 41, 46. Refer to Chinese *fu-t'ou*, *niang*, and *lang*. On *phu-dao*, see also Nguyen Dinh Chien and Ngo The Long, "Tam bia doi Tran Du Tong moi phat hien o Ha-Tuyen," p. 69.

32. Hoang Thi Chau, pp. 46–47.

33. Ibid., p. 45; Le Tuong and Nguyen Loc, p. 41.

34. Hoang Thi Chau, p. 39.

35. Jerry Norman and Tsu-lin Mei, "The Austroasiatics in Ancient South China," pp. 280–83. Other Austroasiatic words identified as having been borrowed by Chinese during the first millennium B.C are: "the housefly insect," "tiger," "tooth, tusk, ivory," and "crossbow" (Norman and Tsu-lin Mei, pp. 284–94).

36. Nguyen Phuc Long, pp. 12–13.

37. H. L. Shorto, "The Linguistic Protohistory of Mainland South East Asia," pp. 276–77.

38. See Appendix A.

tact with Thai peoples and, in historical times, the Chinese has also left conspicuous marks.

Dong-son art reveals a ruling-class perspective heavily influenced by Austronesian culture. The rectangular stone axe, which is generally associated with Stone Age Austronesian culture, has been found in large quantities in northern Vietnam, while the stone-shouldered axe, thought to be characteristic of Austroasiatic culture, is relatively scarce.[39]

A distinctive Dong-son weapon, the bronze pediform axe, is thought to be a development of the rectangular stone axe.[40] The pediform axe was superior to other bronze axes because it could be used both for chopping and for thrusting; furthermore, it could easily be disengaged by rolling it loose against its heel, enabling the delivery of more strokes in a given period of time.[41]

This weapon, depicted in the hands of warriors on the Dong-son drums, bears witness to the grim strategic position of the Hong River plain as a point of demographic pressure in ancient times. This plain lay astride the only lowland corridor between the Tibetan highlands and the sea; it was consequently in the path of peoples moving between East and Southeast Asia. Those who chose to make this place their home faced frequent challenges from all directions. They, of necessity, had to arm themselves with weapons equal to these challenges. Other bronze weaponry uncovered from Dong-son sites includes blades for daggers, halberds, and swords; points for javelins and lances; arrowheads; and crossbow triggers.[42]

Today, we can find the bronze pediform axe depicted in an artistic tradition inspired by Austronesian peoples. According to Vietnamese historical tradition, this axe was wielded in the name of a line of kings who bore an Austroasiatic title. Dong-son civilization was a cultural synthesis achieved by peoples inhabiting a single geopolitical environment. These peoples came from both the mountains and the sea. The society they shared eventually superseded their mutual differences. We can surmise that the Vietnamese people originated in a concerted human response by diverse peoples to a particular geographical setting, the plains of northern Vietnam.

The origin and significance of the bronze Dong-son drums has been

39. Nguyen Phuc Long, pp. 44–45.

40. Ibid., p. 64 and fig. 144. Jeremy Davidson, "Archeology in Northern Vietnam since 1954," p. 104, reported that the bronze pediform axe was inspired by the stone-shouldered axe, but this seems to be a misunderstanding. For a comparison of a Dong-son bronze pediform axe with a similar axe found in Indonesia, see Trinh Sinh, "Vai net ve giao luu van hoa a thoi Dai Kim Khi trong boi canh lich su Dong Nam A," p. 56. On the "originality" of the Dong-son pediform axe, see Diep Dinh Hoa, "Tinh doc dao cua nguoi Viet co qua viec khao sat nhung luoi riu Dong-son."

41. Nguyen Phuc Long, p. 65.

42. L. Bezacier, *Manuel d'archéologie d'Extrême-Orient*, p. 104, fig. 35; Nguyen Phuc Long, pp. 57–62.

discussed by several scholars, but no consensus of opinion has yet emerged.[43] While traditionally it has been thought that bronze casting spread into Southeast Asia from China,[44] recent research suggests the opposite.[45] According to ancient Chinese texts, bronze drums were used by southern peoples as symbols of wealth and influence.[46] The most convincing explanation of their origin is that they evolved from the rice mortar, for "pestle music" was cited by early Chinese writers as an important part of social life among southern peoples,[47] and modern Vietnamese anthropologists have found a remarkable similarity between depictions of drumlike vessels being pounded, found in Dong-son art, and scenes of rice pestling observed among both Vietnamese peasants and upland minority peoples in Vietnam.[48]

According to the oldest descriptions of ancient Vietnamese economy and society, which survive in quotations from nonextant Chinese sources dating from the third to the fifth centuries A.D.,[49] the economy of the Hong River plain before the arrival of Chinese administration included paddy fields that were irrigated by taking advantage of the change in the level of the rivers in accordance with the tides. These fields were called Lac fields. We have seen that *Lac* is also the name of the culture hero to whom Vietnamese tradition ascribes the introduction of agriculture. Japanese scholars have suggested that the name *Lac* derives from the Vietnamese word *lach* or *rach*, which means "ditch, canal, waterway."[50] The construction of drainage ditches was certainly the first step toward making the swampy plains of northern Vietnam suitable for agriculture. Canals and ditches with water gates would have been essential for using the tides to control water. The Lac fields, as described in the texts, were surely dependent on some kind of water-control system. We must nevertheless bear in mind that the Chinese texts cite the practice of tidal irrigation by way of explaining the name *Lac* and that Lac society may well have been based on a diversity of agricultural methods, of which tidal irrigation was but one.

Lac is the earliest recorded name for the Vietnamese people. We can appropriately refer to the society of the Dong-son period as Lac society, for

43. Nguyen Phuc Long, pp. 77–80.

44. Chikamori, pp. 65–96.

45. Clark D. Neher, "Area News," p. 186.

46. Matsumoto Nobuhiro, "Religious Thoughts of the Bronze Age Peoples of Indochina," pp. 141–46. As late as the fourth century, Chinese merchants were illegally selling copper cash to aboriginal tribes in southern China, who melted it down to make bronze drums; see Yang Lien-sheng, "Notes on the Economic History of the Chin Dynasty," p. 181.

47. Matsumoto, "Religious Thoughts," pp. 152–53.

48. Nguyen Khac Tung, "Nghien cuu van hoa vat chat cac dan toc o nuoc ta," pp. 80–81.

49. Émile Gaspardone, "Champs Lo et Champs Hiong," pp. 467–68.

50. Gotō Kimpei, *Betonamu Kyūgoku Kōsō Shi*, p. 62.

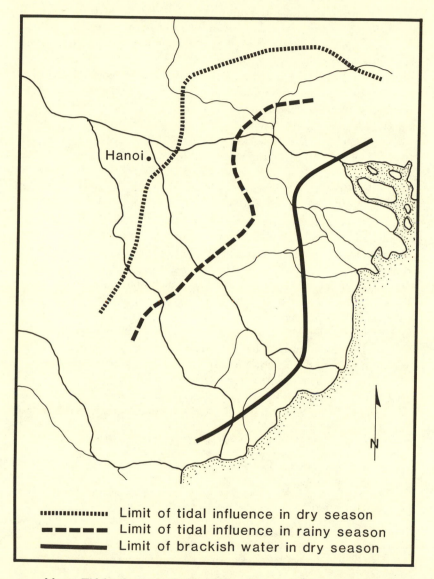

Hanoi

N

▪▪▪▪▪▪▪▪▪▪▪▪▪ Limit of tidal influence in dry season
▬ ▬ ▬ ▬ ▬ Limit of tidal influence in rainy season
▬▬▬▬▬▬ Limit of brackish water in dry season

Map 2. Tidal Influence in the Hong River Plain in Modern Times. Based on P. Gourou, *Les Paysans du Delta Tonkinois*, p. 78.

the one factor that united the legendary traditions of the Hung kings and the early historical period down to Eastern Han was the dominant position of the Lac lords as a regional ruling class.

The practice of tidal irrigation, as described in the texts that mention Lac fields,[51] reveals a relatively advanced agricultural technology. Map 2 shows tidal influence in the Hong River plain in the 1930s. Two thousand and more years ago, we can assume that tidal influence penetrated even deeper than shown here, for alluvial deposits have extended the deltaic coast into the sea as much as ten miles during historical times.[52] Tidal influence was greatest in the Tay-vu area, which lay outside the path of the Hong River.[53] A recent study of the ancient geography of this area suggests that this was where the Lac-field society was based.[54] Grains of the earliest strain of rice found in Asia, *Oryza fatua*, have been excavated from the oldest neolithic cultures in all parts of modern Vietnam.[55] Archeology has revealed that the ancient Vietnamese worked the land with hoes of polished stone; as early as the Go-mun archeological level, dating to the second half of the second millennium B.C., sickles and other reaping implements had bronze blades, and by the Dong-son period, hoes, plowshares, and scythe blades were made of bronze.[56] The skills of the farmers were sufficient to support a clearly defined ruling class.

The earliest surviving Chinese text to mention the Hung kings, from the fifth century A.D., explains the title *Hung* in terms of the Chinese word used to render it phonetically.[57] The Chinese word means "strong, virile," and the text develops this meaning by describing a fierce tropical climate and fertile soil. We can surmise that the Chinese explanation of the term *Hung* was prompted by the penetration into Chinese literature of oral lore from Vietnam about the legendary Hung kings.

According to tradition, the Hung kings were in direct control of the Me-linh area.[58] Beyond this area they were to some degree dependent upon

51. See Appendix B. Yumio Sakurai has recently conjectured that the description of Lac fields as tidal is simply a contrived elaboration to explain the name *Lac* and that ancient agriculture in Vietnam was based on agronomic expertise, not water-control engineering; this view deserves more study.

52. H. Maspero, "Le Protectorat general d'Annam sous le T'ang," pp. 674–80. See the map in Dinh Van Nhat, "Dat Me-linh," 190: 37.

53. Gotō, p. 68.

54. Dinh Van Nhat, "Vet tich cua nhung ruong Lac dau tien quanh bo Ho Lang-bac va tren dat que huong cua Phu-dong Thien Vuong," pp. 24–37.

55. Ha Van Tan and Nguyen Duy Hinh, "Kinh te thoi Hung Vuong," pp. 145–46; Nguyen Duy Hinh, "Nghe trong lua nuoc thoi Hung Vuong," pp. 173–76; Chu Van Tan, "Cay lua va nghe trong lua xua o Viet Nam," pp. 43–51.

56. Nguyen Phuc Long, pp. 71–73. On the Go-mun blades, see Nguyen Viet, "Buoc dau nghien cuu phuong thuc gat lua thoi Hung Vuong."

57. Gaspardone, "Champs Lo," pp. 469–77.

58. Le Tuong and Nguyen Loc. On the Me-linh area in ancient times, see Dinh Van Nhat, "Dat Me-linh."

the cooperation of the Lac lords. The Hung kings seemingly protected the Lac lords against raids and invasions from the mountains, while the Lac lords supported the Hung kings with their manpower and wealth.

Henri Maspero, conjecturing from the upland society of northern Vietnam in his day, described this as a hierarchical society based on hereditary privilege, mutual obligation, and personal loyalty.[59] The people lived in villages or small kinship communities under the rule of Lac lords. The Lac lords enjoyed different levels of privilege and authority, from village headmen up to regional leaders who personally advised the Hung kings. The Hung kings maintained their prestige with a prosperous court life that facilitated peaceful relations with neighboring mountain peoples. Legendary traditions and excavated Dong-son tombs tend to confirm this picture of Lac society.

Women enjoyed a relatively high status in Lac society. As we shall presently see, when the Lac lords eventually rose up against increasing Chinese influence, they were led by women. According to Vietnamese tradition, the children of Lac Long Quan and Au Co were divided into two groups, with half following their father back to the sea and half going into the mountains with their mother. This division of the children into two groups appears to reflect a bilateral family system in which inheritance rights could be passed on through both maternal and paternal lines.[60]

Lac society was relatively advanced and apparently self-contained. It had developed far from the expanding political centers of northern China and northern India and was equal to any threat arising from surrounding territories. This situation came to an end, however, with the arrival of Chinese power on the South China Sea.

Prologue to a New Age

In the last half of the third century B.C., the ancient Vietnamese entered a new era. For the first time in memory, their king fell before an invader, King An Duong, the first authentic historical figure in Vietnam. This was related to events occurring in the north, where the state of Ch'in was eliminating its rivals and treading the path of empire, scattering a host of disinherited princes ambitious for fresh thrones. To better understand this situation, it may be profitable to review its antecedents.

As is well known, the center of ancient Chinese civilization was in the valley of the Yellow River in what is now northern China. In the Yangtze River basin of central China, three major powers appeared among non-

---

59. H. Maspero, "Études d'histoire d'Annam," 18: 9.

60. Yamamoto, "Myths," p. 83, A Dong-son bronze drum unearthed in Yün-nan depicts a "chieftainess enthroned," according to Richard Pearson, "Dong-son and Its Origins," p. 28.

Chinese populations with ruling classes in the process of adopting Chinese culture. The state of Shu was located in Ssu-ch'uan, a fertile valley surrounded by mountains, where the Yangtze emerges from the highlands. The state of Ch'u lay along the central Yangtze, a land of lakes and plains. The state of Yüeh occupied the coast, where the Yangtze enters the sea. Shu was separated from the south by the rugged terrain of Kuei-chou, though the Yangtze led up to the Yün-nan Plateau, with routes going in all directions from there. Ch'u was by far the largest and most important of these semi-Chinese states; it was separated from the Hsi River valley of southern China by a chain of mountains pierced by five famous passes. Yüeh was in certain respects under the influence of Ch'u, yet it benefited from the many contacts made possible by its location on the sea. South of Yüeh lay the coastal enclaves of Wen-chou (Yung-chia), in southern Che-chiang, and Fu-chien; these were separated from the Yangtze and Hsi River systems by mountains.

Little is known of southern China before the third century B.C. The Hsi River valley had important trading connections both with the state of Ch'u to the north and with seaborne peoples. Trade was well established between the coasts of the South China Sea and northern China as early as the second millennium B.C.[61] These commercial contacts became an increasingly important part of the Chinese economy during the Chou dynastic period (1122–255 B.C.).[62] Evidence suggests that Malayo-Polynesian peoples carried cinnamon by sea from southern China to East Africa, whence it found its way to the Mediterranean as early as the end of the second millennium B.C.;[63] when Ch'in eventually entered southern China, one of the three prefectures originally established there was named Kuei-lin, "Cinnamon Forest," in modern Kuang-hsi. The political situation undoubtedly revolved around the mouth of the Hsi River, where in modern times Canton, Hong Kong, and Macao continue to reflect an environment comprising both continental and seaborne influences. Five hundred miles to the southwest, the Hong River plain was separated from the expanding Chinese world by distance and terrain. In the last half of the fourth century B.C., this situation began to change with the destruction of two of the three Yangtze states.

In 333 B.C., Ch'u conquered Yüeh. Eighteen years later, the northern state of Ch'in conquered Shu. While a portion of the Shu ruling class eventually took refuge in Ch'u, the Yüeh ruling class scattered southward along the coast, where it established many small kingdoms and principalities that became known to the Chinese as the "Hundred Yüeh." [64]

61. Charles O. Hucker, *China's Imperial Past*, p. 65.

62. Cho-yun Hsu, *Ancient China in Transition*, p. 120.

63. J. Innes Miller, *The Spice Trade of the Roman Empire*, pp. 42–47 and 153–79.

64. Leonard Aurousseau, "Le Premièr Conquête chinoise des pays annamites," pp. 181 and 254, n. 3; Jao Tsung-i, "Wu Yüeh wen-hua," p. 625.

Four of these realms are known to history. The Chinese called the largest of them Nan Yüeh, "Southern Yüeh"; it was centered on the mouth of the Hsi River in the vicinity of modern Canton.[65] Second in size was Min Yüeh in Fu-chien.[66] Eastern Ou, also called Yüeh of the Eastern Sea, was located in southern Che-chiang at modern Wen-chou (Yung-chia).[67] Western Ou lay in the upper basin of the Hsi River in modern Kuang-hsi.[68]

Thus, after 333 B.C., the inhabitants of southeastern China fell under the rule of people bearing the name and the heritage of the state of Yüeh. Nan Yüeh was the center of this new order; Min Yüeh was of secondary importance. These were flanked by Eastern and Western Ou. The Ou realms are of particular interest, for, in the Hong River plain, the kingdom of Van-lang was superseded by the kingdom of Au Lac, and *Au* is simply the Vietnamese pronunciation of *Ou*.

The relationship between Eastern and Western Ou is not revealed in historical records, yet the names imply a common frame of reference.[69] This was apparently the world of the "Hundred Yüeh" with Nan Yüeh at its center; such, at least, was the view of later Chinese historians.[70] However, this does not explain the significance of the name *Ou* within the Yüeh realm.

The name appears to have originated in southern Che-chiang, where the capital of Eastern Ou was located on the banks of a river that has carried the name *Ou* into modern times.[71] This area was an early center of the Yüeh culture that had contributed to the political state of Yüeh, and it had older and firmer ties with the traditions of that now defunct kingdom than did the larger centers of Min Yüeh and Nan Yüeh further south. Many small principalities that sprang up beyond the reach of the two major centers apparently chose to associate themselves with the venerable traditions of the Ou in order to increase their prestige with the more powerful kingdoms. The name *Ou* was recorded in reference to peoples on Hai-nan Island;[72] there may have been other instances of which knowledge has not been preserved.

65. Aurousseau, p. 259.

66. Ibid., pp. 257–59.

67. Ibid., pp. 255–57.

68. Jao Tsung-i, "Wu Yüeh," p. 625. The sole mention of Western Ou in the sources occurs in connection with events that could only have taken place in what is now Kuang-hsi between 219 and 214 B.C. (see the passage from the *Huai nan tzu* in Aurousseau, p. 172). Confusion of the kingdom of Western Ou with the kingdom of Western Au Lac, which appeared in the year 180 B.C. (see the passage from the *Shih chi* in Aurousseau, p. 196) and was located in northern Vietnam, is a common error in the secondary literature (Aurousseau, pp. 176, 280; Sugimoto Naojirō, *Tōnan Ajiashi Kenkyū*, 1: 42; Wang Gung-wu, "The Nan-hai Trade," pp. 8–10; C. Ch'en, "An Yō Ō no Shutsuji ni tsuite," p. 9). See Morohashi Tetsuji, *Dai Kanwa Jiten*, 10: 282.

69. C. Ch'en, "An Yō Ō," p. 11; Jao Tsung-i, "Wu Yüeh," p. 625.

70. Chang Shou-chieh's eighth-century commentary on the *Shih chi*; see Aurousseau, p. 248.

71. Aurousseau, p. 255.

72. Ibid., p. 248, n. 6, and 255.

If the name *Ou* spread among the smaller and more isolated centers of the "Hundred Yüeh" in this way, it is conceivable that *Ou* signified a particular style of political leadership that had evolved along the frontier of the Yüeh realm. We might conjecture that *Ou* held the meaning of "border-land," and that the lord of Western Ou who resisted Ch'in's invasion of what is modern Kuang-hsi in 219 B.C. was a kind of march lord associated with Nan Yüeh.[73]

The idea that the origin of the Vietnamese people lay in the arrival of migrating Yüeh people during the third century B.C.[74] is not supported by the sources.[75] During the course of the third century B.C., the peoples of what is now southeastern China became known to the Chinese as the "Yüeh," but this does not mean that the local peoples were overwhelmed by a migration from the old state of Yüeh. Geopolitical obstacles made such an event improbable. There were formidable mountains and rivers to be crossed; this was not a natural migration route as were, for example, the steppes of Inner Asia. The lowland indigenous peoples were not nomads organized in migratory tribes capable of maneuvering around newcomers; in the plains, settled peoples would have forced outsiders to compromise their identity.

From what is known of comparable migrations in historical times, we can assume that, when Yüeh was conquered by Ch'u in 333 B.C., most of the Yüeh population remained where it was, and only the ruling class with its servants and retainers fled south, perhaps as bands of armed fugitives rather than as a conquering army. Such small, predatory groups were able to impose their rule and name over the southern peoples because they were experienced in war and possessed prestigious symbols of authority related to the political traditions of northern China. A similar process is documented during the seventh century A.D. in the Balkan Peninsula, a region of mountains and valleys comparable to southeastern China, when Iranian Serb and Croat princes with personal armies asserted their authority over the indigenous Slavic peoples, drawing on the prestige of Byzantium to legitimize their rule.[76]

The concept of migrations in ancient times has been reevaluated in recent years, and it is increasingly clear that many so-called migrations involved a relatively small group of ruling-class people, whose mastery of

73. According to the passage from the *Huai nan tzu* in Aurousseau, p. 172, the Chinese killed the lord of Western Ou after Ch'in armies dug a canal through the mountains to assure supplies during their penetration of the Yüeh lands; this was the Hsing-an Canal in the westernmost of the five traditional passes into the south, which entered directly into Kuang-hsi (Aurousseau, p. 175, n. 3; P. A. Lapique, "Note sur le canal de Hing-ngan," pp. 425–28).

74. Aurousseau, pp. 245–64.

75. See Appendix E.

76. Francis Dvornik, *The Making of Central and Eastern Europe*, pp. 268–304.

political and military affairs was felt throughout the linguistic and cultural scene. The most significant evidence of this comes from linguistic studies that suggest the current distribution of languages in mainland Southeast Asia resulted not from mass migrations but from the response of indigenous peoples, governed by political expediency, to small but influential groups of upper-class immigrants. A recent investigator envisages the spread of Thai into Southeast Asia as the result of "a migration into northern Thailand consisting only of a royal court and small standing army."[77]

This brings to mind the arrival of King An Duong with his army of thirty thousand that, according to historical sources, brought the line of the Hung kings to an end late in the third century B.C.[78] As we will presently see, this was the opening wedge for "Yüeh" influence in the Hong River plain. But there is no evidence that the rise of King An Duong left any mark on the Vietnamese language, and it is clear that there was no major demographic change. Recent studies in physical anthropology reveal a remarkable continuity of racial evolution in northern Vietnam from earliest prehistoric times to the present. A marked racial connectedness from one era to another rules out any large-scale, sudden migration of sufficient magnitude to account for the origin of a people.[79]

King An Duong

In 222 B.C., Ch'in conquered Ch'u, and in the following year, Ch'in Shih Huang Ti, the "First Emperor of Ch'in," ordered half a million soldiers into the Yüeh lands. The earliest surviving record of the campaign was written less than a century after it occurred and is worth quoting:

> Ch'in Shih Huang Ti was interested in the rhinoceros horn, the elephant tusks, the kingfisher plumes, and the pearls of the land of Yüeh; he therefore sent Commissioner T'u Sui at the head of five hundred thousand men divided into five armies. . . . For three years the sword and the crossbow were in constant readiness. Superintendent Lu was sent; there was no means of assuring the transport of supplies so he employed soldiers to dig a canal for sending grain, thereby making it possible to wage war on the people of Yüeh. The lord of Western Ou, I Hsü Sung, was killed; consequently, the Yüeh people entered the wilderness and lived there with the animals; none consented to be a slave of Ch'in; chosing from among themselves men of valor, they made them their leaders and attacked the Ch'in by night, inflicting on them a great defeat and killing Commissioner T'u Sui; the dead and wounded were many. After this,

77. D. T. Bayard, "Comment," pp. 279–80.
78. Gaspardone, "Champs Lo," p. 473.
79. Nguyen Duy, p. 23.

the emperor deported convicts to hold the garrisons against the Yüeh people.[80]

The five armies marched south in 221 B.C. One army sufficed to subdue Eastern Ou and Min Yüeh; two armies marched against Nan Yüeh. The remaining two armies entered Kuang-hsi, where Superintendent Lu was sent to solve the problem of supply. The canal he built was the Hsing-an Canal through the westernmost of the five passes into the south; it linked the river system of the Yangtze with that of the Hsi.[81]

Ch'in attacked Western Ou after the completion of the canal, in 219 B.C., and gained initial success with the death of I Hsü Sung, lord of Western Ou. But there followed several years of warfare, culminating in a serious defeat and the death of T'u Sui, the Ch'in commander. These events were remembered by the Chinese as follows:

> The Yüeh people fled into the depths of the mountains and forests, and it was not possible to fight them. The soldiers were kept in garrisons to watch over abandoned territories. This went on for a long time, and the soldiers grew weary. Then the Yüeh came out and attacked; the Ch'in soldiers suffered a great defeat. Subsequently, convicts were sent to hold the garrisons against the Yüeh.[82]

The Ch'in advance thus bogged down in the mountains and forests of Kuang-hsi. It was in 214 B.C. that convicts were deported to hold the garrisons; with them went "all the inveterate vagabonds, the lazy, and shopkeepers" to settle in the occupied lands.[83] Commissioner Chao T'o was sent to impose a military occupation;[84] he requested that thirty thousand maidens and widows be sent south as wives for his men.[85]

In the next few years, the Chinese and the Yüeh bitterly contended for the south. Officially, the Chinese divided the Yüeh lands into prefectures, and it is recorded that "the princes of the Hundred Yüeh, their heads bowed and with ropes about their necks, delivered their fates to the subordinate Ch'in officials."[86] These words were probably too optimistic, for a Chinese historian writing about a century later affirmed that the Ch'in

> remained at loggerheads with the Yüeh. Soldiers were stationed at worthless locations; having advanced, they were unable to retreat. During more than

80. This passage is from the *Huai nan tzu* of Liu An, a grandson of the founder of the Han dynasty, who died in 123 B.C. See Aurousseau, pp. 169–72. All translations in this book are mine.

81. Lapique, pp. 425–28.

82. From the *Huai nan tzu*; see Aurousseau, p. 206.

83. From the *Shih chi*; see Aurousseau, p. 180.

84. Ibid.; see Aurousseau, p. 207.

85. Ibid.; see Aurousseau, p. 201.

86. Ibid.; see Aurousseau, p. 181.

ten years, the men carried the sword while the women saw to provisions. Along the routes could be seen those who were unable to endure their suffering and hanged themselves from the trees. Then, it happened that the Emperor of Ch'in died and the empire fell prey to great rebellions.[87]

Ch'in Shih Huang Ti died in 210 B.C. His imperial ambitions had fallen on the Yüeh lands like an angry beast, sending a wave of violence that shattered the prehistoric solitude of the ancient Vietnamese.

The last of the Hung kings was dethroned by a man who imposed his authority over the Lac lords, founded the kingdom of Au Lac, and took the title King An Duong. King An Duong's antecedents are cloudy; the only clue provided by historical records is that his family name was Thuc, which is Vietnamese for Shu, and his personal name was Phan.

Who Thuc Phan was and where he came from are major problems in early Vietnamese history.[88] His family name suggests that he was related to the old ruling class of the state of Shu in Ssu-ch'uan; this was the traditional view of Chinese and Vietnamese historians. But even if this were the case, Ssu-ch'uan had been under Ch'in control for a century, and Thuc Phan's family must have been established in some other place during this time.

An oral tradition, but recently recorded, links the Thuc family with the strategic valley of Cao-bang, where the Hsi River system of southern China communicates with the Hong River plain.[89] According to this account, which is of doubtful authenticity, at the end of the time of the Hung kings, the Thuc family ruled over a kingdom named Nam Cuong, meaning "Southern Border," comprising Cao-bang and adjacent portions of Kuang-hsi to the north. When his father died, Thuc Phan was still a boy;

87. Ibid.; see Aurousseau, p. 186.

88. King An Duong is identified in Chinese sources as "Son of the King of Shu" (*Chiao chou wai yu chi* in Aurousseau, p. 211, and *Kuang chou chi* in Aurousseau, p. 213); Vietnamese sources agree, adding the detail of his personal name Phan (*VDULT*, 36; *LNCQ*, 22; *TT*, 1, 7b; *VSL*, 1, 1a). This appears to link him with the state of Shu in Ssu-ch'uan, which was conquered by Ch'in in 315 B.C. Yet nearly a century had elapsed between 315 B.C. and the time of King An Duong. Dao Duy Anh has made the most strenuous attempt to associate King An Duong with the defunct state of Shu; his theory has been reviewed by C. Ch'en, "An yŏ Ō," p. 2, who faulted it for "excessive conjecturing." Dao Duy Anh's idea is that remnants of the Shu ruling class found refuge first in Ch'u and then, after Ch'u's demise, with a king in Yün-nan; from there, King An Duong presumably followed the Hong River down to the sea. The connection with Yün-nan seems to be strengthened by a theory put forward by Nguyen Linh, who cited a reference in the *Hou Han shu* to the land of "Western Shu" in Yün-nan. Perhaps the strongest objection to this line of reasoning has been made by Nguyen Duy Hinh, who argued that, in ancient times, Yün-nan was the route to India, not China, and King An Duong's kingdom of Au Lac was oriented toward the north (Tran Quoc Vuong and Do Van Ninh, "Ve An Duong Vuong," p. 373).

89. The source of this tradition is Le Dinh Su, an inhabitant of Cao-bang of Thai ancestry born in 1916 (Pham Nhu Ho and Do Dinh Truat, "Vai y kien quanh truyen thuyet 'Cao Chua Cheng Vua,'" pp. 395, 396).

however, his unusual cleverness enabled him to retain his father's throne. As Nam Cuong grew in strength, Van-lang became weak; subsequently, Thuc Phan conquered Van-lang and founded the kingdom of Au Lac.

That the Thuc family was established on the frontier of Van-lang for several generations is supported by a detail in the legend of the battle between the Mountain Spirit and the Water Spirit as recorded in a fourteenth-century quotation from a ninth-century source.[90] According to this source, a forebear of Thuc Phan had asked to marry a Hung princess; although the Hung king was willing, the Lac lords refused, saying, "He only intends to spy on our land." Another fourteenth-century source cites this episode to explain that Thuc Phan later conquered Van-lang to gain revenge for his rebuffed ancestor.[91] A poem written about the Me-linh area by a fourteenth-century Vietnamese official contains the line: "Ah! Van-lang's radiance, shining upon Thuc's mountains and rivers."[92] This suggests a remembrance of the Thuc family as ancient neighbors of the Vietnamese realm.

That the Thuc family ruled a kingdom named Nam Cuong is supported by circumstantial evidence. Geographically, Cao-bang and neighboring areas comprised the natural "southern border" of the Western Ou (Kuang-hsi) realm. As a family, the Thuc may have traced their lineage back to the state of Shu in Ssu-ch'uan, but the political realities of their time and place surely forced upon them some association with the Ou Yüeh lords of Kuang-hsi.

When Ch'in armies entered Kuang-hsi, killed the lord of Western Ou, and sent the people fleeing into the wilds, the Thuc domain was a natural place of refuge. As the Ch'in occupation progressed, the Thuc family probably attracted dispossessed Ou lords anxious to recoup their fortunes, and through their influence the Thuc grew strong and bellicose toward their southern neighbor in the fertile Hong River plain. The ensuing conquest produced a fusion of the invading Ou (Au) lords and the resident Lac lords, thereby forming the kingdom of Au Lac.[93]

Our knowledge of the kingdom of Au Lac is a mixture of legend and history. King An Duong is the first figure in Vietnamese history documen-

90. *VDULT*, 36.

91. *LNCQ*, 22.

92. O. W. Wolters, "Assertions of Cultural Well-Being in Fourteenth-Century Vietnam," 11: 74.

93. This is the general interpretation suggested by Tran Quoc Vuong and Do Van Ninh, p. 370. C. Ch'en, "An Yō Ō," p. 11, also points in this direction. The *VSL*, 1, 1a, says that Thuc Phan "expelled and replaced" the Hung king at the end of the Chou dynasty; this is apparently what prompted the *TT*, 1, 6a, to assign this event to the year 257 B.C., one year before the abdication of the last Chou king.

ted by reliable sources,[94] yet most of what we know about his reign has survived in legendary form. Me-linh remained a center of Lac power. The new Au overlords established their headquarters in Tay-vu, where they built a large citadel, known to history as Co-loa or Co-loa Thanh, "Old Snail City"; this name comes from the fact that the walls were laid out in concentric rings reminiscent of a snail shell. The archeological remains at Co-loa reflect heavy northern influence in architecture, yet the pottery and the large stores of bronze arrowheads are simply developments of local industries.[95] The events associated with the building of Co-loa have been remembered in the legend of the golden turtle.[96]

According to this legend, construction of the citadel was stalled because each day's work was mysteriously undone during the night by the spirits of the land; these spirits were assisting the son of the previous king to gain revenge for the loss of his inheritance. The local spirits were led by a thousand-year-old white chicken perched on nearby Mount Tam-dao. A golden turtle appeared, subdued the white chicken, and remained with King An Duong until the citadel was completed. When he departed, he gave one of his claws to be used as the trigger of the king's crossbow, with the assurance that with it he could destroy any foe. King An Duong commissioned a man named Cao Lo to construct the crossbow and christened it "Saintly Crossbow of the Supernaturally Luminous Golden Claw."

The crossbow, along with the word for it, seems to have been introduced into China from Austroasiatic peoples in the south during the third or fourth century B.C.[97] This weapon quickly became part of the Chinese arsenal; its trigger mechanism was capable of withstanding high pressure and of releasing an arrow with more force than any other type of bow.[98] Two bronze trigger mechanisms have been excavated in Vietnam; most mechanisms were probably made of bamboo.[99] The turtle claw used as a trigger mechanism indicates the military nature of King An Duong's conquest and suggests that his rule was based on force or the threat of force.

94. The earliest surviving source for King An Duong is the Chin dynasty *Kuang chou chi*. C. Ch'en, "An Yō Ō," p. 7; Aurousseau, p. 213; Gaspardone, "Champs Lo," p. 473.

95. Nguyen Duy Chiem, "Tim dau vet cua An Duong Vuong tren dat Co-loa," pp. 387–88, and Do Van Ninh, "Ve mot vai khia canh cua van hoa vat chat thoi ky An Duong Vuong," pp. 389–94. One problem in the archeology of Co-loa is that it was rebuilt in Later Han times; this, along with subsequent renovations, has clouded evidence from the earliest levels (Trans Quoc Vuong and Do Van Ninh, pp. 375–79; Truong Hoang Chau, "Phat bieu them ve nien dai Co-loa," pp. 383–86).

96. *LNCQ*, 22–24.

97. Norman and Tsu-lin Mei, pp. 293–94.

98. Homer Dubs, "A Military Contact between Chinese and Romans in 36 B.C.," pp. 70–71.

99. Bezacier, *Manuel*, p. 128; Nguyen Phuc Long, p. 62.

The building of Co-loa and the legend of the golden turtle are reminiscent of the building of Ch'eng-tu in Ssu-ch'uan by Ch'in after the conquest of Shu, a century earlier.[100] Efforts to rule from Ch'eng-tu during the third century were also remembered in connection with the power of water spirits.[101]

The underlying theme of King An Duong's legend is the test of strength between the white chicken and the golden turtle. The chicken is an indigenous symbol of great antiquity. A bronze statue of a chicken dating from the turn of the first millennium B.C. was excavated in Me-linh.[102] On the other hand, the turtle is a symbol of the Chinese god of war, Chen Wu.[103] These totemic associations reflect shifting political fortunes. In a separate legend from this period, King An Duong is depicted as a golden chicken spirit and the Lac lords as white monkey spirits.[104] Having subdued the white chicken with the assistance of the golden turtle, King An Duong is here portrayed as having appropriated the chicken spirit to himself, changing its color to that of the turtle; the color white remained symbolic of indigenous power, although it had become descriptive of monkeys.

The perspective of the golden turtle legend belongs to the conqueror King An Duong; it is about the building of Co-loa and the suppression of forces bent on preventing its construction. The golden turtle was borrowed from the imperial juggernaut to the north as a symbol of military supremacy. Yet, as this legend has been handed down, the golden turtle appears to be an incarnation of Lac Long Quan, with its home in the waters of the Hong River plain.[105] This represents the perspective of the Lac lords as they fitted the new political order into older themes of their mythology. Similarly, the name *Au Co* was probably introduced into Lac mythology at this time to symbolize the political union of Au and Lac as the marriage of Au Co, who arrived with a northern intruder, and Lac Long Quan, the local culture hero. The original Au Co, mother of the Hung kings, may perhaps more correctly be associated with Ngu Co, the celestial deer in the version of the myth that has been passed down by the Muong, upland cousins of the Vietnamese.[106]

The legend of Ly Ong Trong is the only indication of contact

100. Cheng Te-k'un, *Archeological Studies in Szechuan*, p. 9.

101. *HYKC*, 3, 4–6.

102. Uy Ban Khoa Hoc Xa Hoi Viet Nam, *Lich su Viet Nam*, 1: 43; Nguyen Phuc Long, figs. 127, 148; Trinh Sinh, p. 56. Wolfram Eberhard, *The Local Cultures of South and East China*, p. 423, reported an ancient cult of a divine chicken that lived in a cave in southern Kuang-hsi.

103. Tran Quoc Vuong, "Tu tu duy than thoai," p. 404, and Gustave Dumoutier, *Le Grand Buddha de Hanoi*.

104. *VDULT*, 29.

105. Yamamoto, "Myths," p. 90.

106. Nguyen Linh and Hoang Xuan Chinh, p. 103, and Jean Cuisinier, *Les Muong*, p. xii.

between King An Duong and the Ch'in empire. Ly Ong Trong was a Vietnamese giant supposedly sent as tribute from King An Duong to Ch'in Shih
Huang Ti; after a distinguished career fighting the Hsiung-nu on the
empire's northern frontier, he returned to his native village and died there.
However, Ly Ong Trong's cult was established by a ninth-century Chinese
governor in Vietnam, so it probably had little to do with events in the time
of King An Duong.[107]

The career of King An Duong reflects an era of transition. He came
from the north and built a great citadel. Although he subdued the Lac lords,
he did not disinherit them. He was absorbed into the legendary traditions of
the people he had conquered. Eventually, he fell prey to stronger forces
coming from the north.

Chao T'o

In the brief moment of Ch'in hegemony, the kings
of Eastern Ou and Min Yüeh were reduced to vassalage. But after the death
of Ch'in Shih Huang Ti and the dissolution of his dynasty, they regained a
measure of independence under Han suzerainty. Further south, affairs
evolved differently.

When Ch'in Shih Huang Ti died and the empire collapsed, the
Chinese sent to occupy the Yüeh lands in the Hsi River basin were stranded
in hostile territory. In the words of an ancient writer, they "suffered
insupportable misfortunes" and their leaders "doubted among themselves."[108]

According to surviving records, when the governor at Canton was on
his deathbed, he summoned the only man he trusted, Commissioner Chao
T'o. He cautioned Chao T'o against getting involved in the civil wars taking
place in the north, and stressed the remoteness of Canton, saying, "With the
many Chinese people here, one has the means to become an independent
sovereign and to found a kingdom." After the governor's death, Chao T'o
assumed command. He sealed the mountain passes leading north and eliminated all officials not personally loyal to him. He gained control of the entire
Hsi River basin and proclaimed himself King of Nan Yüeh.[109]

Chao T'o's success rested not only on his ability to rally the Chinese
immigrants in the south, but also on his popularity among the non-Chinese

107. The *VDULT*, 15–16, account of Ly Ong Trong does not mention King An
Duong; it only cites an unnamed local king, Ch'in Shih Huang Ti, and two Chinese governors
who later patronized the giant's cult. The *LNCQ*, 18–19, cites both a Hung king and King An
Duong; this version is more detailed than the *VDULT*.

108. From the *Shih chi*; see Aurousseau, p. 185.

109. Ibid.; see Aurousseau, p. 188. The same information is found in abbreviated form in
VSL, 1, 1b, and *TT*, 1, 9b.

population. In 196 B.C., an envoy of the newly established Han Empire arrived with a seal recognizing Chao T'o as King of Nan Yüeh;[110] Chao T'o received the envoy according to the manner of the local people, "hair in chignon and squatting." The envoy accused Chao T'o of forgetting his true ancestry and of daring to stand apart from the empire. Chao T'o excused himself by saying that after so many years of living in the south he no longer remembered the proper usages of the north.[111]

In fact, Chao T'o won the loyalty of the local peoples of the south by his resistance to Han. This was demonstrated in 185 B.C. when Empress Lü of Han grew fearful of Chao T'o's power and forbade the sale of iron, gold, weapons, horses, and cattle to Nan Yüeh. Chao T'o responded by seizing two Han provinces in what is now Hu-nan. He furthermore took the title of emperor, thereby ending the recognition of Han suzerainty implicit in his acceptance of the royal seal in 196 B.C. Empress Lü sent an army against him, but it was ravaged by a cholera epidemic. When she died in 180 B.C., the soldiers sent against Nan Yüeh were recalled. It is recorded that "with his military power, Chao T'o inspired fear on the frontier; with rich presents, he gained Min Yüeh and Au Lac as vassals."[112]

Au Lac and Min Yüeh temporarily acknowledged the suzerainty of Nan Yüeh, but rather than meaning that Nan Yüeh had any real control over them, this simply represented anti-Han solidarity. In 179 B.C., when peaceful relations with Han were restored, Nan Yüeh's influence over Au Lac and Min Yüeh lapsed. Both Nan Yüeh and Min Yüeh again recognized Han suzerainty; thus, their mutual relations were under the watchful eye of Han. However, if Nan Yüeh chose to enforce its suzerainty over Au Lac, there would be no response from the north, for Au Lac lay beyond Han influence. This was apparently what prompted Chao T'o to march his armies against King An Duong. Having mobilized his forces for war with Han and having gained success without serious battle, Chao T'o found the conquest of Au Lac both tempting and feasible.[113]

110. From the *Shih chi*; see Aurousseau, p. 202.

111. Ibid. See Aurousseau, p. 184; Gustave Dumoutier, "Étude historique sur Trieu-vo-de (Tchou-wou-ti) et sa dynasty," pp. 417–18; *TT*, 2, 1a–2b.

112. From the *Shih chi*; see Aurousseau, p. 196. Dumoutier, "Trieu-vo-de," pp. 414, 420–21, 424; *CL*, 82–83; *TT*, 2, 3a–b. According to an eighth-century commentator, Au Lac was called Western Au Lac in the *Shih chi* because it was west of Nan Yüeh (Aurousseau, p. 248.)

113. Dumoutier, "Trieu-vo-de," pp. 421–22; *TT*, 2, 3b–6a; *CL*, 40, 82–83. If the conquest of Au Lac by Nan Yüeh took place prior to 180 B.C., according to the dating of *TT*, 1, 8b–10b, and the interpretation of Aurousseau, pp. 232–44, then Nan Yüeh would not have gained the vassalage of Au Lac in 180 B.C. by means of "rich gifts" unless we theorize that sometime after the conquest and before 180 B.C. Au Lac regained its independence, for which there is no evidence. We know that the dating of the *TT* for this early period is arbitrary and often in error (Cao Huy Giu and Dao Duy Anh, *Dai Viet su ky toan thu*, p. 317, n. 9). Aurousseau, pp. 196–99, accepted the *TT* date only by rejecting the *Shih chi* date; this is

The details of the campaign are not authentically recorded.[114] However, they inspired a legend whose theme is the transfer of the turtle-claw-triggered crossbow from King An Duong to Chao T'o. According to this legend, possession of the crossbow conferred the right and power to rule. In the words of Cao Lo, the man who constructed it, "He who is able to hold this crossbow rules the realm; he who is not able to hold this crossbow will perish."[115]

Unsuccessful on the battlefield against the supernatural crossbow, Chao T'o asked for a truce and sent his son Shih Chiang to the court of his foe; Shih Chiang won the confidence of King An Duong and the heart of An Duong's daughter My Chau. Gaining entrance to the armory with the aid of My Chau, Shih Chiang stole the turtle claw, rendering the crossbow useless. Then he returned to his father. Chao T'o renewed hostilities and was victorious. King An Duong fled to the sea, where he was greeted by the golden turtle, who guided him into the watery realm.[116]

The practical effect of this legend was to legitimize Chao T'o's rule. The ancient Vietnamese entered the world of kingdoms and empires with the reign of King An Duong. Before this time, in the view of one ancient Chinese writer, the Vietnamese lived "beyond the hellish wilderness."[117] Now the long prehistoric era of relative isolation was over; the Chinese were at the door. The legend of the turtle claw made into a magic crossbow as a symbol of political ascendancy was a way to grasp conceptually a shifting world.

Chao T'o divided the conquered lands of Au Lac into the two

---

conceivable only in the context of his overall interpretation of the period, about which see H. Maspero, "Bulletin critique." If the absorption of Au Lac by Nan Yüeh did not involve armed conflict but was instead effected peacefully, according to the interpretation of H. Maspero, "Bulletin," p. 392, then we must ignore the *Kuang chou chi* ("Chao T'o, King of Nan Yüeh, attacked and vanquished King An Duong"; Aurousseau, p. 213, and Gaspardone, "Champs Lo," p. 473) and the *Chin T'ai K'ang ti chi* ("the King of Nan Yueh attacked [King An Duong]"; Jao Tsung-i, "An Yō Ō," p. 38).

114. The *TT*, 1, 8b–10b, account, derived from *LNCQ*, 23–24, appears to draw on the details of Ma Yüan's expedition in A.D. 42 (Gaspardone, "Champs Lo," p. 466, n. 1a), as well as on the events of the sixth century, when the Hong River plain was divided by agreement between two local lords (Durand, "La Dynastie," pp. 444, 451). By dating this narrative to 210–8 B.C. the *TT* wished to associate the incorporation of Au Lac into Nan Yüeh with the initial formation of the kingdom of Nan Yüeh; this served the traditional perspective of official Vietnamese historiography, which emphasized Nan Yüeh as the first national kingdom to successfully resist northern pressure..

115. This quotation is from the *Chiao chou wai yu chi*, as cited in *SCC*, 37, 7a. *CL*, 25, contains an abbreviated version of the quotation. The only other source in which this quotation appears is the *Chin Liu hsin ch'i Chiao chou chi* (Jao Tsung-i, "An Yō Ō," p. 38).

116. See Appendix F.

117. *SCC*, 37, 4a.

prefectures Giao-chi and Cuu-chan. Giao-chi was located in the Hong River plain, and Cuu-chan lay in the smaller plain of the Ma River to the south. The name *Giao-chi* was plucked from the *Li chi* (Records of Rituals), an early Chinese text, where it appears as a term used to describe the communal sleeping habits of "southern barbarians." *Giao-chi* means "intertwined feet" and refers to the custom of sleeping in groups with each person's head extending outward, while all feet came together in the center.[118]

This does not mean that the ancient Vietnamese practiced such a custom, for the term appears under the Cheng family in the *Li chi*, and the Cheng ruled in Ho-nan from 774 to 500 B.C. In that time and place the "southern barbarians" would have been the people in the Yangtze basin or, at furthest, the Hsi basin, but not in a place so remote as the Hong basin. Nevertheless, as the *Li chi* came to be included among the classics of Chinese literature, its phraseology gained a special authority that was indiscriminately applied by later generations to conditions in their day.

The origin of the name *Cuu-chan* is more obscure, for no literary precedent survives. It can be translated as "the nine verities" and probably derived from some philosophical term.

Thus, these two names originally derived from the intellectual heritage of Chinese civilization. Yet, as fixtures of Vietnamese political geography for centuries after, they assumed new, more localized meanings and gave rise to newer usages. For example, in the sixteenth century, *Giao-chi* was rendered *Cochin* in the Portugese tongue, thereby producing the term *Cochinchina*.

Chao T'o sent two legates to oversee his Vietnamese prefectures.[119] The traditional Lac order remained intact, for a royal court continued to exist at Co-loa, under which the Lac lords ruled as before, only now as vassals of Nan Yüeh; the legates appear to have presided over developing commercial centers that were the focus of Chinese interest.[120]

For the first time in their history, the Vietnamese people were part of a kingdom encompassing all of southern China. This kingdom was stamped with the personality of its founder Chao T'o; it is recorded that Chao T'o ruled for more than seventy years and died in 136 B.C. at the exceedingly ripe age of one hundred and twenty-one years. He was succeeded by a seventy-year-old grandson named Hu.[121]

Chao T'o was remembered by later Vietnamese historians as a king

---

118. *LC*, 4, 10b; Asami Shōzō, "Kōshi to iu Koshō," pp. 64–67.

119. From the *Chiao chou wai yu chi* in *SCC*, 37, 4a, and the *Kuang chou chi*; see Aurousseau, p. 213.

120. Gotō, pp. 59–60; Ying-shih Yü, *Trade and Expansion in Han China*, pp. 7–8.

121. Dumoutier, "Trieu-vo-de," p. 427; *VSL*, 1, 2a; *TT*, 2, 7b–8a, 8b–9a.

who defended their lands against Chinese aggression.[122] His spirit cult was eventually honored in many parts of northern Vietnam.[123] His kingdom of Nan Yüeh stimulated imaginations for centuries. The memory of Nan Yüeh provided inspiration to local rebels, who were unable to resist proclaiming themselves king of Nan Yüeh.[124] At the same time, Chinese scholars visiting the south often dedicated a line or two of poetry to the memory of Chao T'o, the first Chinese ruler of this remote region.[125] The popular image of Chao T'o as a great ruler in antiquity survived in the Canton area well into T'ang times.[126]

Chao T'o had a foot in both worlds, the expanding empire and the shrinking frontier. The Chinese remembered him as a maverick imperial official, and the Vietnamese remembered him as a great anti-Han king. He was the last ruler to find a place in ancient Vietnamese mythology. His possession of the magic turtle claw signified his legitimacy in the minds of the Vietnamese and explained his ascendancy over King An Duong. But, after his death, Nan Yüeh fell increasingly under Han influence.

The Coming of Han

As Han influence spread southward, survivors of the old Yüeh ruling class felt increasingly endangered. At the time of Chao T'o's death, the kingdom of Min Yüeh in Fu-chien was responding to the threat of extinction with growing belligerency. Fear of Min Yüeh prompted the less bellicose people of Eastern Ou in southern Che-chiang to migrate, between 138 and 135 B.C., to a safer location within the Han empire. In 135 B.C. Min Yüeh attacked Nan Yüeh, hoping to shake it out of its passively pro-Han policy. But Nan Yüeh did not dare to raise an army in its own defense and, instead, simply informed Han in the capacity of a loyal vassal.[127] The dependence of Nan Yüeh's King Hu on Han in the Min Yüeh crisis was characteristic of Nan Yüeh's developing relationship with Han.

In 124 B.C., Hu died and was succeeded by his son Yung Ch'i. As a young man, Yung Ch'i had served at the Han court, where he had married a

---

122. O. W. Wolters, "Historians and Emperors in Vietnam and China," pp. 73–74, 77–78.

123. Nguyen Khac Dam, "Cuoc noi day chong nha Han cua La Gia," p. 58.

124. See, for example, *TCTC*, 213, vol. 11, 870–71.

125. For example, see *CL*, 157.

126. Edward Schafer, *The Vermilion Bird*, p. 97.

127. The Han army dispatched against Min Yüeh was recalled when the king of Min Yüeh was killed by a brother; Min Yüeh was thereafter partitioned between this brother and a son of the assassinated king until the final Han conquest in 110 B.C. (Aurousseau, pp. 256, 257–58; *CL*, 50, 57; *TT*, 2, 9a–11b).

Chinese courtesan named Ku. Upon Yung Ch'i's accession, Ku became his queen; upon his death in 113 B.C., she became the queen regent and ruled in the name of her young son Hsing.[128]

It is recorded that after Yung Ch'i's death, Han sent a former lover of Ku's as ambassador to the Nan Yüeh court; the ambassador resumed his liaison with Ku, and she fell under his influence. The pro-Han faction then moved to enforce Han laws in Nan Yüeh and proposed sending the young king to the Han court. However, the army remained in the hands of Lü Chia, a "Yüeh person" whose family had served Chao T'o from the founding of the kingdom and had intermarried with the royal family in each succeeding generation; it is recorded that the "Yüeh people" trusted and loved the Lü family more than they did the king.[129] As Lü Chia stood up against the growing Chinese presence, the court split into two armed camps. Han responded by sending two thousand soldiers to protect the pro-Han faction gathered around the queen regent and young King Hsing.[130]

Hearing of the Han expedition, Lü Chia mobilized his forces and killed all the Chinese he could lay his hands on, including King Hsing. He then raised to the throne his son-in-law, an elder half-brother of Hsing. He sent his soldiers to man the frontiers, but Han answered with five armies under the command of Lu Po-te, bearing the title "Wave-Calming General." The year was 111 B.C., and it saw the end of Nan Yüeh.[131] Lü Chia's resistance to Han expansion was remembered by the Vietnamese, and a temple was later built for his spirit in Me-linh.[132]

When Lu Po-te arrived in the vicinity of Giao-chi, he was met by the two legates who had been appointed by Nan Yüeh; they reportedly presented him with one hundred head of cattle, one thousand measures of wine, and the population registers of their jurisdictions. Lu Po-te recognized the legates and confirmed their authority with the title of prefect; the Lac lords continued to rule the people as before.[133]

The information about cattle, wine, and population registers should

128. Dumoutier, "Trieu-vo-de," p. 428; VSL, 1, 2a; CL, 112–14; TT, 2, 11b–12b.
129. CL, 141–42.
130. Dumoutier, "Trieu-vo-de," p. 429; VSL, 1, 2b.
131. Dumoutier, "Trieu-vo-de," pp. 430–34; VSL, 1, 3a; TT, 2, 13a–17b; CL, 114.
132. Nguyen Khac Dam, pp. 65–68.
133. SCC, 37, 5b. CL, 57, cites a Giao chau ky (Chinese Chiao chou chi) as the source of a quotation that speaks of three lords in place of two prefects. The third lord is from Nhat-nam, a prefecture organized at this time, or shortly after, south of Cuu-chan. The quotation ends with: "The Lac king and the Lac lords ruled the people as before." This source may be the Chiao chou chi written by Liu Hsin-ch'i in the late fourth or early fifth century (O. W. Wolters, Early Indonesian Commerce, p. 81), or perhaps it is the Chiao chou wai yu chi, which the SCC cites for the same information. TT, 2, 17a, also speaks of Nhat-nam and three, rather than two, legates in this context.

be treated carefully.[134] Cattle and wine pose no problem, for there is no reason to doubt Giao-chi's ability to supply these things. Meeting an advancing army with food and drink is a venerable method of initiating an accommodation. But the mention of population registers implies some kind of stable administrative control. Whatever this control may have been, we can be sure that it did not have a very wide application over Lac society, for the Lac lords largely remained in control of the land and people during this time.

The Nan Yüeh legates appear to have been chiefly interested in overseeing the trade routes and presiding over commercial centers.[135] Their administrative sphere of action was almost certainly confined to the immediate vicinity of the market towns where they resided. Perhaps the legates' authority extended to some of the surrounding fields, and the population of that area may have been formally identified in some way. But we should bear in mind that the possession of population registers was a kind of legitimizing credential for ancient Chinese officials; consequently, their value as an indication of effective control over the population must be treated with caution, particularly in the context of events such as those just discussed, where local officials sought to legitimize their position in the eyes of an invader.

Behind the legates, the Lac lords also had an interest in preserving the prevailing state of affairs, and we can assume that the meeting of the legates with Lu Po-te was part of a common policy pursued by the Lac lords and the legates toward the Han expeditionary force. This is clear from the information that, after submitting to Han, "the Lac lords ruled the people as before."[136]

The transfer of suzerainty from Nan Yüeh to the Han empire was not entirely peaceful, for in 110 B.C. a certain "General of the Left of Old Au Lac" received a title from Han as a reward for his having killed the "King of Tay-vu."[137] This king was apparently a monarch established at Co-loa as a vassal of Nan Yüeh; with the demise of Nan Yüeh, he may have resisted overtures from Han and attempted an uprising. The "General of the Left" was perhaps a high-ranking lord who foiled this attempt with the support of the legates, or he may have killed the king on Han instructions simply to get him out of the way. The life of the people was undisturbed by these events, however, and the position of the Lac lords remained unchallenged.

The brief mention of the "King of Tay-vu" in 110 B.C. is the first

---

134. Gotō, p. 59, says this reference is "doubtful" but does not explain.
135. Ibid., pp. 59–60; Khong Duc Thien, "Tu su tham gia cua nhan dan Vu-ninh vao cuoc khoi nghia Hai Ba Trung," p. 59; Ying-shih Yü, pp. 181–82.
136. *SCC*, 37, 5b.
137. H. Maspero, "Études," 18: 11.

instance of the name Tay-vu in Vietnamese history. We have already used this name as a toponym for the region where Co-loa was built. After 111 B.C., Han referred to this area as Tay-vu District. In A.D. 43, when the Lac lords were dispossessed, it was divided into two new districts, and the name Tay-vu was suppressed. It seems reasonable to associate the name Tay-vu with the heritage of the kingdom of Au Lac. It was a lord of "Old Au Lac" who killed the king of Tay-vu, and the name endured only as long as did the political posterity of Au Lac, for it finally disappeared when the Lac lords were subdued by Han soldiers. Although the exact origin of the name is not known,[138] it can be associated with a royal tradition established at Co-loa by King An Duong, and it probably had some connection with the Western Ou.

The shift in overlords from Nan Yüeh to the Han Empire left no mark on the legendary traditions of the Vietnamese people; unlike the fall of Au Lac, the fall of Nan Yüeh did not loom in the collective memory of the Vietnamese. The traditional date of 111 B.C. as the beginning of Chinese rule does not accurately reflect the continuing authority of the Lac ruling class up to A.D. 42, a date that more properly represents the arrival of direct Chinese rule.

Han organized the old lands of Nan Yüeh into seven prefectures.[139] Nan-hai, Ts'ang-wu, Yü-lin, and Ho-p'u were located in modern Kuang-tung and Kuang-hsi; the other three were in Vietnam. In addition to Giao-chi and Cuu-chan, Nhat-nam was established further south, beyond the Hoanh-son massif. *Nhat-nam* means "south of the sun," and the prefecture was so named because it was in fact south of the sun during the summer months.

The five passes that had marked the northern border of Nan Yüeh were placed under the jurisdiction of provinces to the north, thereby depriving the south of its strategic frontier.[140] The seven prefectures in the south were organized into Chiao-chih (Vietnamese Giao-chi) Circuit, which was placed under the authority of a governor.[141] The governor's residence was initially at Luy-lau in Giao-chi Prefecture, but in 106 B.C. it was moved to the more central location of Ts'ang-wu in modern Kuang-hsi.[142]

138. On theories about the etymological origins of *Tay-vu*, see C. Ch'en, "An Yō Ō," pp. 9–10.

139. Two additional prefectures were theoretically established on Hai-nan Island but were later abolished (Cao Huy Giu and Dao Duy Anh, p. 318, n. 1; Émile Gaspardone, "Materiaux pour servir a l'histoire d'Annam," p. 82, n. 4, nos. 1–3; Aurousseau, p. 204; Rolf Stein, "Le Lin-i," pl. 3).

140. Aurousseau, p. 242.

141. Cao Huy Giu and Dao Duy Anh, p. 318, n. 2; Ozaki Yasushi, "Gokan no Kōshi Shishi ni tsuite," pp. 140–43.

142. Gaspardone, "Materiaux," p. 32, n. 4, no. 4.

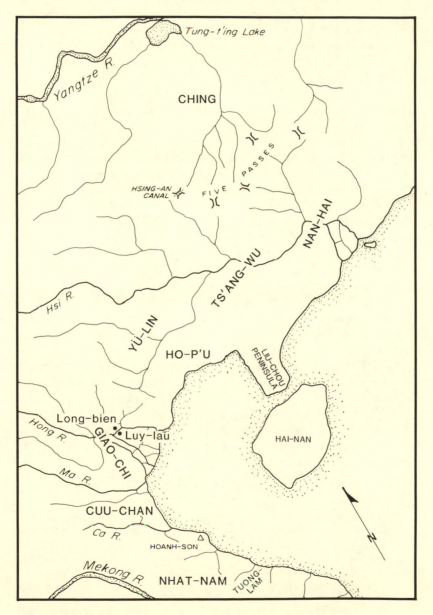

Map 3. Chiao-chih Circuit

The removal of the governor's seat from Luy-lau, in the middle of a heavily populated plain, to Ts'ang-wu, in a narrow upland valley, was apparently a recognition that Chinese administration would be quickly swallowed up by Vietnamese society unless it was located in a relatively isolated spot. The names of only three governors have been preserved from the Former Han period: one each from the reigns of Han Wu Ti (140–87 B.C.) and Han Chao Ti (86–74 B.C.),[143] and one from the Wu-feng reign period (57–54 B.C.).[144]

Luy-lau became the administrative center of Giao-chi Prefecture. Unlike the earlier political centers of Me-linh and Tay-vu, whose importance derived from their proximity to the mountains, Luy-lau lay well within the plains. This reflected the spread of settlement deeper into the plains, as well as the developing political importance of the riverine and coastal route to China. Luy-lau seems to have been the legate's residence from the beginning of Giao-chi under Nan Yüeh and was important primarily as a trading center.[145]

In addition to the prefectural seat at Luy-lau, Han established a military outpost under a commandant in Me-linh,[146] probably to oversee the routes leading into the mountains. Small garrisons of Han soldiers were established at Luy-lau and Me-linh, but their sphere of action was apparently limited to protecting Han property and personnel.[147]

Ten districts are recorded for Giao-chi Prefecture, all concentrated in the northern and western part of the plain.[148] Further south, Cuu-chan Prefecture consisted of seven districts and included the residence of a commandant; Nhat-nam Prefecture was composed of five districts.[149] Rather than implying direct administrative control, these districts should be understood as representing areas familiar to the Chinese with which some form of commercial and tributary relationship existed.

The early Han outposts were primarily commercial centers. Han was not yet interested in establishing a full-scale administration in this remote, isolated place but, rather, wanted only to secure the southern trade routes and to gain access to the tropical luxury goods of the south seas. There would

143. *VSL*, 1, 3a–b; *TT*, 3, 1a.

144. *CL*, 85.

145. Khong Duc Thien, p. 59. On the commercial activities of Han outposts, see Ying-shih Yü, pp. 92–99.

146. Gaspardone, "Materiaux," p. 82, n. 4, no. 2. On the probable location of this outpost, see Dinh Van Nhat, "Dat Me-linh," 191: 47–48.

147. H. Maspero, "Études," 18 : 11–12.

148. Gaspardone, "Materiaux," p. 82, n. 4, no. 2a; Madrolle, map opposite p. 272; Jennifer Holmgren, *Chinese Colonisation of Northern Vietnam*, pp. 23–53; Dinh Van Nhat, "Dat Me-linh," vol. 190, map on p. 37.

149. Gaspardone, "Materiaux," p. 82, n. 4, nos. 2b–c.

have been no profit in trying to change the prevailing pattern of life. Sending soldiers was too costly.[150]

Although the Lac lords continued to rule as they had in the past, their status nevertheless underwent a subtle, yet significant change. Han "established" prefectures and districts in Lac society, which meant that the Lac lords were formally recognized as prefectural and district officials. By payment of regular tribute, they received "seals and ribbons," which legitimized their authority in the eyes of Han and enhanced their prestige in the eyes of their peers. The old aristocratic hierarchy under a monarchy, whether of the Hung kings, of King An Duong, or of the "King of Tay-vu," was officially replaced by bureaucratic relationships based on the theory of prefectural and district administration. So while Han informally allowed the Lac lords to rule in their accustomed manner, the principle of prefectural and district administration was established as an official policy.[151]

No information about political events in Vietnam survives from the first century B.C., but we can assume that the Lac lords accepted their designated role in the theoretical context of Han prefectural and district administration. This assumption is supported by the census of A.D. 2, according to which the three Vietnamese prefectures contained 143,643 households and 981,755 people; this represented 67 percent of all households and 72 percent of all people registered in Chiao-chih Circuit for that year (see table 1). These statistics are an indication of the extent to which the Lac lords participated in Han administration, for this registration of households and people was surely accomplished through the assistance of the Lac lords and can be taken as a reflection of Lac society at that time.

This census coincides with the tenure of Hsi Kuang as prefect of Giao-chi. He served during the reign of Emperor P'ing (A.D. 1–5) and is reported to have opened schools, enforced Chinese-style marriage rites, prescribed the wearing of hats and sandals, and "instructed the people in justice and ritual." [152] Hsi Kuang's reforms show that Han officials were beginning to pursue a more aggressive policy toward the indigenous way of life. This policy gained momentum in the following years with the arrival of a large number of Han refugees in the south.

In A.D. 9, a high minister named Wang Mang usurped the Han throne. Wang Mang's unsuccessful administrative and economic reforms provoked a vast peasant rebellion that led to restoration of the Han in A.D. 23. During this brief but violent interlude, many refugees fled into southern China,

150. Gotō, pp. 59–60; Hans Bielenstein, "The Census of China during the Period 2–742 A.D.," pp. 141–42.

151. Gotō, pp. 62–63; Ying-shih Yü, pp. 71–72, 79–80.

152. *HHS*, 76, 6b, from which are derived *CL*, 85, and *TT*, 3, 1b. Also the *T'ung tien* as cited by H. Maspero, "Études," 18: 12, n. 5.

where conditions remained peaceful. The governor of Chiao-chih, Teng Jang, refused to recognize Wang Mang and closed his borders against the anarchic situation in the north.[153] Large numbers of Han ruling-class people found refuge in the south; these newcomers strengthened the position of local Han officials and encouraged a less tolerant attitude toward the local society.

The most famous Han official in Vietnam during the Wang Mang era was Jen Yen, who was appointed prefect of Cuu-chan in A.D. 25. According to his biography,[154] Jen Yen found that the people of Cuu-chan did not use draft animals for agriculture. As a result, productivity was very low, and grain had to be purchased from Giao-chi. The local economy was based on hunting and fishing, and Jen Yen presumably found it difficult to collect taxes. He therefore ordered the production of iron field implements and supervised the opening up of new lands for farming. The land under cultivation was expanded year after year, and the life of the people became more secure. Jen Yen also found that there was no stable family system in Cuu-chan. Men and women joined at random, and there was no concept of husband and wife, parent and child. He therefore ordered all men between the ages of twenty and fifty and all women between the ages of fifteen and forty to pick a partner. Local officials were ordered to pay the wedding expenses of those too poor to afford them. Jen Yen introduced Chinese-style marriage observances and is reported to have married one thousand couples on a single occasion. Many children of these marriages were named after Jen Yen, and, after his return north, the people were said to have erected a shrine to his memory.

All of this information comes from Jen Yen's official biography, so we must bear in mind that it is a one-sided view that almost certainly gives an exaggerated estimation of his accomplishments.[155] Furthermore, it was common for officials to paint as meritorious a picture as possible of their administrative skills as a means of advancing their careers. This would especially have been the case in Cuu-chan, an extremely remote place where the claims of officials were nearly impossible to verify and where resident Han officials were very anxious to be promoted elsewhere.

Jen Yen's biography is often cited as evidence that the use of iron implements and draft animals for agriculture was introduced into Vietnam at this time. This is a hasty judgment, for Jen Yen's activities were confined to Cuu-chan, a relatively backward locale. If Giao-chi could produce a surplus of grain sufficient to supply Cuu-chan, agriculture in the Hong River plain must have been well developed.

153. *CL*, 85.
154. *HHS*, 76, 6a–7a.
155. Gotō, p. 72.

Bronze Dong-son plowshares have been uncovered in the Me-linh area,[156] and the bones of water buffalo have been excavated at sites in the Me-linh area dating from the second millennium B.C.[157] We have already seen that one hundred head of cattle, probably water buffalo, were presented to the Han army in 111 B.C. Two bronze objects from the Dong-son period uncovered in the Me-linh area appear to be models of plows that could have been pulled by draft animals.[158] While this evidence is not strong enough to support the assertion that water buffalo were used to pull bronze plows in the pre-Han period, it nevertheless shows that the use of draft animals at such an early date was not impossible. Plows can be pulled by people, but common sense suggests that draft animals will be used if they are available in sufficient quantities.[159]

The use of draft animals becomes more certain with the introduction of iron agricultural implements, for iron plows are too heavy to be easily pulled by people. We have seen how in 185 B.C. Empress Lü of Han forbade the export of iron and cattle, among other things, to Nan Yüeh. This is the earliest textual evidence of iron in the south. Presumably, if the iron trade was stopped at this time, it had been going on for some time before. Gotō Kimpei has conjectured that iron was first brought into the south by merchants, who traded it for the rare tropical luxury goods that were coveted by ruling-class Chinese.[160]

Circumstantial evidence strongly suggests that iron plows and draft animals were used in the Hong River plain prior to 111 B.C. Here, the Lac fields supported a society that was sufficiently advanced to apply technical improvements in agricultural methods. Any technique that would increase agricultural productivity, and thereby produce a larger surplus, would have been to the advantage of the Lac lords.[161] It is hard to believe that, with representatives of Nan Yüeh residing in their midst, the Lac lords would not have heard of iron plows and, furthermore, that they would not have taken advantage of this new implement once they had heard of it.

The texts that mention Lac fields do not seem to apply to Cuu-chan. There, the development of agriculture was apparently slower than in Giao-chi. The information about Jen Yen's reforms implies that his primary aim was to collect taxes. A subsistence economy of hunting and fishing produces no surplus. By encouraging the use of iron plows and draft animals and by bringing more land under cultivation, Jen Yen was aiming at a more stable

156. Nguyen Phuc Long, pp. 71–72.

157. Nguyen Duy Hinh, p. 181.

158. Nguyen Phuc Long, p. 72; Bezacier, *Manuel*, pp. 174–75.

159. Nguyen Duy Hinh, pp. 181–82.

160. Gotō, p. 71. See also Ying-shih Yü, pp. 7–8.

161. Gotō, p. 72. On the development of iron agricultural implements and the spread of new methods of cultivation on the Han frontiers, see Ying-shih Yü, pp. 21–22, 24–26.

source of tax revenue. His efforts to reform the family system served the same purpose, for the people could not be registered and taxed unless they could be identified as members of what the Chinese recognized as a clearly defined kinship group.

We must nevertheless remain skeptical of the claim in Jen Yen's biography that he introduced agriculture to Cuu-chan, for the census of A.D. 2 records a registered population of 35,743 households and 166,013 people for Cuu-chan. Registered households imply a settled agrarian life. The truth may be that Jen Yen increased the amount of land under cultivation and tried to make farming more efficient by manufacturing iron implements, thereby making them more readily available.

The marriage reforms of Hsi Kuang and Jen Yen reveal a great difference between the family systems of ancient Vietnam and China. A society's concept of marriage is a direct reflection of its family system. The Vietnamese family, with its loose authority, its individualistic tendencies, and its bilateral character, was an early target of Chinese administrative policy. The Chinese concept of political authority was based on a tightly controlled patriarchal family system. The Vietnamese family was by its nature inhospitable to the Chinese concept of government, for it lacked the disciplined relationships that made the Chinese family system the cornerstone of Chinese government and political authority. Only to the extent that the Vietnamese could be made to conform to the Chinese family system could they be ruled according to orthodox concepts of government and thereby be fully incorporated into the Chinese world. The Chinese sought to encourage stable, monogamous marriage as a basis for their type of government.[162] The failure of China's efforts to change the Vietnamese family system during several centuries of political control ultimately meant the failure of China's effort to rule Vietnam.

Chinese policy in Vietnam during the early decades of the first century A.D. had two aims. One was to develop the agrarian economy as a stable source of tax revenue. The other was to establish a patriarchal society based on monogamous marriage that would be capable of responding to Han-style government. These two aims were related. Raising agricultural productivity meant increasing the role of men in agriculture, which encouraged Chinese concepts of marriage and society; with the use of iron plows and draft animals, the role of men in agriculture increased, as did productivity.[163] Furthermore, clearly defined monogamous family units were easier to register and tax.

These policies represented a change in the Chinese attitude toward Vietnam. Instead of simply collecting rare goods and letting the Lac lords

162. Miyakawa Hisayuki, "The Confucianization of South China," p. 32.
163. Ibid., loc. cit.

carry on as before, Han now tried to develop agriculture and collect taxes. This new point of view seems to have been the result of a growing Han awareness of Vietnam's agricultural potential. This awareness was probably aroused by the success of the Lac lords in gathering a sizable surplus from the Lac fields. This success can reasonably be accounted for by the political stability of the Han peace, as well as by improvements in agricultural technology stimulated by contact with the Chinese.[164]

The reforms of the Wang Mang era posed a challenge to the Lac lords. If local officials were in fact required to pay for the Chinese-style marriage observances of those unable to do so, as reported by Jen Yen's biographer, it would mean that the Lac lords were being forced to subsidize the extension of Chinese influence over their own people, for the Lac lords were themselves local officials by virtue of the "seals and ribbons" given to them by Han.[165] As Chinese concepts of marriage and etiquette spread through Lac society, cultural supports for the traditional authority of the Lac lords began to crumble. Lac lords and Han officials competed for control of the Lac fields and of the people who tilled them. As discrepancies between the old principle of aristocratic hierarchy and the new principle of prefectural and district administration became increasingly evident, the Lac lords were faced with the choice of becoming subordinate officials in Han government or of taking their case to the battlefield.

The Trung Sisters

In A.D. 29, after the Han restoration, Teng Jang, the governor who had kept Chiao-chih loyal to Han during the Wang Mang era, led the prefects of his jurisdiction to the Han court to be recognized and rewarded.[166] Many, perhaps most, of the Han refugees appear also to have returned north at this time. The reforms of the Wang Mang era in Vietnam had been carried out by talented officials, who probably would not have been in the south except for the disorders in northern China. With the Han restoration, men of ability were eager to go back north to pursue their careers near the centers of Han power, and the south was left in the hands of lesser men. Su Ting, the new prefect of Giao-chi, was reportedly greedy and inept;[167] he was thus portrayed according to the traditional Chinese historiographical stereotype of the bad official who provokes a rebellion. During his tenure the Lac lords began to test Chinese authority, and in doing so grew increasingly bold.

164. Gotō, p. 74.
165. Ibid., pp. 73–74.
166. *HHS*, 76, 7a; *CL*, 85; *TT*, 3, 1a.
167. *CL*, 86; *TT*, 3, 1b.

The Lac lord of Me-linh had a daughter named Trung Trac; her husband was Thi Sach, the Lac lord of Chu-dien, a short distance down-river.[168] According to Chinese records, Thi Sach was "of a fierce temperament," and Su Ting attempted to restrain him with legal procedures, literally "tied him up with the law." Trung Trac, "of a brave and fearless disposition," stirred her husband to action and became the central figure in mobilizing the Lac lords against the Chinese.[169]

Su Ting was in no position to cross swords with the Lac lords. According to a later report on the uprising, "Su Ting opened his eyes to money but closed them when it came to punishing rebels; he feared to go out and attack them."[170] In the spring of A.D. 40, the Chinese settlements were overrun, and Su Ting fled. Cuu-chan, Nhat-nam, and Ho-p'u joined the uprising. Trung Trac established a royal court in Me-linh and was recognized as queen by sixty-five strongholds. It is recorded that for two years she "adjusted the taxes" of Giao-chi and Cuu-chan.[171]

The information that Trung Trac "adjusted" the taxes for two years should be understood to mean "abolished." She ruled from her ancestral estates, and it is unlikely that her authority was exercised by means of Chinese-style taxes. Her fellow aristocrats recognized her as queen and undoubtedly showered her with gifts that could be interpreted as tribute. But the movement she led was a restoration movement, an effort to bring back a simpler state of affairs more congenial to traditional values. The "taxes" she abolished were apparently tribute exactions levied on the Lac lords by Han in return for formal recognition of traditional rights. From what little is known of taxation in Vietnam during the Former Han, we can surmise that these exactions were mainly in the form of corvée and tropical luxury products; there is specific mention of officials appointed to collect oranges.[172] The Lac lords resisted the tax-collector mentality that lay at the heart of Chinese government. Rather than taxes enforced by legalistic notions, the Lac lords preferred the exchange of gifts based on hereditary rights and mutual benefit.

Trung Trac and her younger sister Nhi, who gained fame as the queen's constant companion, have been remembered with affection by the Vietnamese, and through the centuries much popular lore has grown up

168. On the location of Chu-dien, see Appendix H.

169. *HHS*, 24, 12a.

170. From Ma Yüan's report following his suppression of the uprising; see Bui Quang Tung, "Le Soulevement des Soeurs Truong," p. 76.

171. *SCC*, 37, 6a.

172. Katakura Minoru, "Chugoku Shihaika no Betonamu," pp. 21–22. On the exchange of "tributary products" and "imperial gifts" in sino-barbarian relations, see Ying-shih Yü, pp. 36–39.

around them.[173] Later Vietnamese historians favored the idea that Thi Sach was killed by Su Ting, thus provoking his wife to rebellion.[174] There is no evidence for this idea; surely it came from the patriarchal bias of later centuries, which could not countenance a woman leading a rebellion and being recognized as queen so long as her husband still lived. The Chinese sources make it clear that Thi Sach followed his wife's leadership.[175] The matriarchal flavor of the time is further attested by the fact that Trung Trac's mother's tomb and spirit temple have survived, although nothing remains of her father.[176] The names and biographies of over fifty leaders of Trac's uprising are recorded in temples dedicated to her cult; a large percentage of these were women.[177]

At the beginning of A.D. 41, one of the empire's best generals, Ma Yüan, fresh from suppressing a rebellion in An-hui, was appointed, at the age of fifty-six, to march to the far south.[178] He was given the title "Wave-Calming General," which had been held by Lu Po-te during his conquest of Nan Yüeh a century and a half earlier. With eight thousand regular troops and twelve thousand militiamen from the eastern prefectures of Chiao-chih Circuit, he marched to the port in Ho-p'u where the maritime route to Giao-chi originated. When the fleet commander died, it was discovered that the two thousand ships available were insufficient to transport the army. Ma Yüan thereupon began an arduous advance along the coast, building a road as he went and depending on the fleet for supply.

Ma Yüan's advance was unhindered until he entered the strategic region of Tay-vu, where the ancient Vietnamese traditionally met their enemies in battle.[179] His progress was checked before Co-loa, and he withdrew to the heights of Lang-bac, a short distance to the east, where he established a base camp. The heights of Lang-bac overlooked the southern shore of an ancient lake of that name; Lake Lang-bac was a natural reservoir

173. See Appendix K.

174. *TT*, 3, 2a; Bui Quang Tung, pp. 76, 83.

175. H. Maspero "Études," 18: 13, n. 1.

176. Nguyen Ngoc Chuong, "Buoc dau gioi thieu mot so nguon tu lieu xung quanh de tich lich su thuoc ve cuoc khoi nghia Hai Ba Trung," pp. 23–25.

177. Vu Tuan San, "Cuoc khoi nghia Hai Ba Trung tai thu do Ha-noi," pp. 41–50; Nguyen Khac Xuong, "Ve cuoc khoi nghia Hai Ba Trung qua tu lieu Vinh-phu," pp. 41–49.

178. *HHS*, 8, 9, and 24, 12. H. Maspero's confused dating led him to assign Ma Yüan's appointment to A.D. 42. Although the correct year, A.D. 41, appears in his "Études," 18: 14, n. 1, he miscorrects it to A.D. 42 in the "erratum" at the end of fasc. 3 to accord with the dates and conclusions found elsewhere in his text. He concludes: "It was necessary to wait nearly two years before it was possible to organize an expedition" (18: 18). Although it was two years before the expedition reached its destination, it was apparently organized within a year of the uprising. Maspero's article contains several genuine or typographical errors in dating.

179. Dinh Van Nhat, "Vung Lang-bac ve thoi Hai Ba Trung," pp. 50–54.

attached to the Cau River. Ma Yüan's supply fleet probably ascended the Cau River and anchored in the lake.[180]

It was now the spring of A.D. 42, and the wet season had begun. Unaccustomed to the heat and the monsoon humidity, the Chinese paused, perhaps intending to wait for the dry season before returning to the offensive. In Ma Yüan's words: "When I was between Lang-bac and Tay-vu and the rebels were not yet subdued, rain fell, vapors rose, there were pestilential emanations, and the heat was unbearable; I even saw a sparrowhawk fall into the water and drown."[181]

However, with a Chinese army in their midst, the Lac lords, according to the interpretation of a fifteenth-century Vietnamese source,[182] began to lose heart. Apparently realizing that inaction would only encourage disaffection among her followers, Trung Trac gave battle to the Chinese. She was badly defeated; several thousand of her partisans were captured and beheaded, while more than ten thousand surrendered to the Chinese. Trac and her most loyal retainers retreated to the foot of Mount Tan-vien in Me-linh, where her ancestral estates were located;[183] others fled to Cuu-chan. Ma Yüan proceeded to Me-linh and, by the end of the year, succeeded in capturing Trung Trac and her sister Nhi; in the first month of the new year, their heads were sent to the Han court at Lo-yang.[184]

The nature of Trung Trac's authority is clearly shown in these events. So long as she could maintain a momentum of success, her followers stood by her. When she suffered a reverse, she was quickly abandoned. She was forced into a hasty battle simply to keep her partisans in the field. She did not have a disciplined army. Rather, she was followed by a collection of Lac lords with their retainers, each looking to his or her own best interests and as ready to go over to the Chinese as to stay with her if it should be to their advantage. This reveals that the century and a half of Han overlordship had seriously eroded the moral authority of traditional values. One element of disaffection with Trung Trac's leadership was undoubtedly the growing influence of the patriarchal values preached by the Chinese. The fifteenth-century *Dai viet su ky toan thu* interpreted these events as follows: "Trung

180. Khong Duc Thien, pp. 55–56.

181. *HHS* 24, 13a–b; *CL*, 25; H. Maspero, "Études," 18: 16, n. 1.

182. *TT*, 3, 26.

183. See Dinh Van Nhat, "Dat Cam-khe, can cu cuoi cung cua Hai Ba Trung trong cuoc khoi nghia Me-linh nam 40–43."

184. *HHS*, 8, 9b–10a, and 24, 12b–13a. According to *VDULT*, 11, and *TT*, 3, 3a–b, the sisters were abandoned by their followers and "died in battle." *VSL*, 1, 3b, says that Trac was "killed by Ma Yüan." *CL*, 58 and 148, follows the *HHS* and says that the sisters were "beheaded" by Ma Yüan. There are several popular traditions according to which the sisters committed suicide by drowning themselves in a river, died of illness, or disappeared into the clouds (Bui Quang Tung, pp. 75, 82–83).

Trac, seeing that the enemy was strong and that her own followers were undisciplined, feared that she could not succeed . . . her followers, seeing that she was a woman, feared she could not stand up to the enemy and consequently dispersed."[185] The mentality of fifteenth-century ruling-class Vietnamese may be reflected in these words, but they probably contain a core of truth.

Ma Yüan spent most of the year 43 laying the foundations for direct Han rule in the Hong River plain. We will look at his reforms in detail at the beginning of the next chapter. Near the end of the year, he loaded his two thousand ships with men and supplies and set out for Cuu-chan, where recalcitrant Lac lords had taken refuge.[186] Following the major river channels of the Hong River plain, he arrived at its southern extremity and advanced into the plain of the Ma River. There, he swept his enemies before him. Some fled up the river valleys into the mountains; others fled south along the coast. Ma Yüan divided his command and sent half in each direction. The army sent south went as far as modern Nghe-an Province, at that time southern Cuu-chan. Between three and five thousand persons were captured and beheaded; several hundred families were deported to southern China.[187] In the spring of A.D. 44, Ma Yüan departed Giao-chi for the north; in the following autumn he arrived at the Han capital to a hero's welcome.[188]

Yüeh and Viet

The expedition of Ma Yüan was a major event in Vietnamese history. With it, Dong-son culture came to an end, and the Lac lords, who had prospered with that culture, are not heard of again.[189] The ancient Vietnamese had to learn new ways of doing things from foreign officials. The Vietnamese had long been familiar with the Chinese, but suddenly Chinese rule was made more direct, while traditional barriers to Chinese power were removed. The Vietnamese were deprived of their traditional ruling class, and the struggle for cultural survival became closely identified with the more basic problem of physical survival under an exploitative, alien regime. Unlike Japanese culture, for example, which

185. *TT*, 3, 2b. J. Holmgren used ethnographic data to argue that Ma Yüan can be associated with a "reduction of female power in Yüeh society" (pp. 18–21).

186. *SCC*, 37, 9a.

187. H. Maspero, "Études," 18: 22–23.

188. *HHS*, 24, 14a; H. Maspero, "Études," 18: 27.

189. Nguyen Duy Ty, p. 84; Le Thanh Khoi, *Le Viet-Nam*, p. 103; Le Van Lan, "Tai lieu khao co hoc va viec nghien cuu thoi ky Hai Ba Trung," pp. 35–40; H. Maspero, "Études," 18: 18.

grew up beyond the reach of external threats, Vietnamese culture has preserved very little that is not directly related to national survival.

The Chinese assumed that the different "barbarian" peoples who were fortunate enough to have been conquered would eventually be "civilized"—in other words, would become Chinese. Any name expressing a people's distinctive identity, such as *Lac*, was diluted with broader terms, such as *Yüeh*, which were employed as synonyms of "barbarian." Chinese historians writing of Ma Yüan's expedition referred to the ancient Vietnamese as the "Lac Yüeh" or simply as the "Yüeh"; one Chinese scholar, commenting on Ma Yüan's biography, went so far as to write: "Lac is another name for Yüeh." [190]

"Yüeh" had become a category of Chinese perception designating myriad groups of non-Chinese peoples in the south. It began with the Yüeh culture of Che-chiang and Fu-chien and the heritage it bequeathed to realms along the southeastern coast of China. This heritage was political. It provided a tradition of kingship on the southern frontier of the Chinese imperial world; the name *Ou* (*Au*) simply represented a militant fringe of this tradition. Although Yüeh culture itself never extended south of Fu-chien, elements of its political heritage reached as far as northern Vietnam in the baggage of ruling-class refugees. [191]

According to Chinese historical tradition, the Yüeh were not completely barbarian. The *Shih chi* declares that King Kou Chien (505–465 B.C.), who ruled the state of Yüeh during the time of its greatest power, was a descendent of Yü, the founder of the mythical Hsia dynasty, through a concubine of Shao K'ang (2079–58 B.C.), a great-great-grandson of Yü. [192] The Yüeh were thus regarded as a degenerate branch of the civilized world, a people who had fallen into barbarism through long residence among barbarians.

With the Chinese conquest of the south, "Yüeh" was applied indiscriminately to all conquered peoples along the south coast. Thus, the category "Yüeh" came to express the conquered peoples' place in the conceptual world of Chinese empire and civilization. Naturally, it was but a temporary category for those peoples destined to become Chinese, but for those whose connection with China would eventually be broken, it became a permanent identity expressing both their place within the Chinese world view and their distinctness from it.

The Chinese considered the Lac to be a "Yüeh" people, and it was customary to attribute certain clichéd cultural traits to the Lac in order to identify them as "Yüeh." These traits, with the exception of tattooing, were

190. *HHS*, 24, 14a.
191. Eberhard, p. 432.
192. *SC*, 41, 1.

simply hackneyed opposites of what the Chinese considered proper civilized usage; thus, they were no more than a literary elaboration of the concept "barbarian."[193]

As Chinese rule became a long-term affair, the ancient Vietnamese imbibed the terminology of their overlords and came to regard themselves as one of the "Yüeh" peoples. *Yüeh* was a term that the Chinese understood; they could accept it as a legitimate cultural designation even if, for them, it designated those who had slipped beyond the realm of civilization. *Lac* had no meaning for the Chinese; Chinese writers using the name *Lac* had to couple it in hybrid fashion with *Yüeh*, as in *Lac Yüeh*, or else explain that *Lac* was merely "another name for Yüeh."

In coming to terms with their imperial masters, the ancient Vietnamese found that the name *Lac* was of no account, whereas the name *Yüeh* carried some weight. As the ancient Vietnamese became increasingly aware of the empire that had conquered them, their sense of identity shifted to take account of their new position. The legend of Lac Long Quan and Au Co was revised to make their progeny the Hundred Yüeh, thereby enhancing the status of the ancient Vietnamese in Chinese literature.[194]

This does not mean that there was no cultural or linguistic relationship between the ancient Vietnamese, or Lac, and the peoples of southeastern China that were known to the Chinese as Yüeh. Recent linguistic research suggests that all the Yüeh peoples of ancient southeastern China, along with the ancient Vietnamese, were Austroasiatic speakers, and that the Chinese term *Yüeh* may have referred to a language group.[195] For example, the following non-Chinese words in the Min dialect of Fu-chien are shared with Vietnamese and other Austroasiatic languages: "shaman" (Vietnamese *dong*), "child" (*con*), "damp, wet moist" (*dam*), "a type of crab" (*sam*), "to know, to recognize" (*biet*), "scum, froth" (*bot*), "duckweed" (*beo*), "a kind of small fish" (*ke*).[196] Furthermore, the earliest references to the Vietnamese language, in Chinese sources of the second century A.D., identify the Vietnamese word for "to die" (*chet*) as a "Yüeh" word and the Vietnamese word for "dog" (*cho*) as a "Nan Yüeh" word.[197]

Considering this evidence, we can reasonably assume that the ancient Vietnamese were part of a broad linguistic-cultural world that included so-called Yüeh peoples in southeastern China. The name *Yüeh* arrived in northern Vietnam as a Chinese perception of the ancient Vietnamese as members of this larger world; the term was not indigenous to Vietnam.

---

193. Aurousseau, p. 247, n. 1, and 248, n. 2; Gaspardone, "Champs Lo," p. 461, n. 3, and 462, n. 2; Jao Tsung-i, "Wu Yüeh," pp. 620–25.

194. Yamamoto, "Myths," p. 84.

195. Norman and Tsu-lin Mei, p. 295.

196. Ibid., pp. 296–99.

197. Ibid., pp. 277–80.

"Viet" is the Vietnamese pronunciation of *Yüeh* and thus was derived the name of a people. The modern name of Vietnam dates from 1803, when envoys from the new Nguyen dynasty went to Peking to establish diplomatic relations. They claimed the name *Nam Viet* (*Nan Yüeh*). But the Chinese objected to this invocation of Chao T'o's rebellious realm in antiquity and changed the name to *Viet Nam*. This Chinese adherence to the formalities of imperial theory was resented at the time, but in the twentieth century the name *Vietnam* has acquired general acceptance among the Vietnamese.[198]

198. Alexander Woodside, *Vietnam and the Chinese Model*, pp. 120–21.

2

The Han-Viet Era

Ma Yüan's Legacy

After the Trung sisters were dead, Ma Yüan spent most of the year 43 building up Han administration in the Hong River plain and preparing the local society for direct Han rule. His activities followed three steps. First, he suppressed what remained of the pre-Han political heritage. Second, he firmly rooted Han officialdom at prefectural and district administrative levels. Third, he bound the local people to this new state of affairs with a personal covenant.

Ma Yüan found that Tay-vu District contained 32,000 households. This was more than a third of all households registered for the Hong River plain in the census of A.D. 2. Tay-vu district surrounded the ancient royal seat of Co-loa and had been an important political center since the days of King An Duong. A "King of Tay-vu" had been killed in 110 B.C., when Han authority was first established in Giao-chi. Furthermore, the Trung sisters had made their first stand in Tay-vu. Ma Yüan, noting that it was disproportionately large in comparison with other districts, suppressed Tay-vu and divided it to make two new districts.[1] In addition to equalizing the size of districts, this measure was aimed at erasing any memory of the political heritage of the area.[2]

It is recorded that "wherever he passed, Yüan promptly established prefectures and districts to govern walled towns and their environs, and ditches were dug to irrigate the fields in order to benefit the people living in those places."[3] This information contains two points worth considering.

One is the implication that Han soldiers were settled to protect Han officials. The mention of walled towns and their environs and of newly dug irrigation ditches suggests soldier-farmers. A wall is of little use without soldiers to man it, and soldiers unable to grow their own food would have been a fiscal burden beyond the means of this isolated administration.

---

1. *HHS*, 24, 13b–14a; H. Maspero, "Études d'histoire d'Annam," 18: 18.
2. Gotō Kimpei, *Betonamu Kyūgoku Kōsō Shi*, p. 80.
3. *HHS*, 24, 14a.

Garrisons of Han soldiers could conceivably have been provisioned by exactions from the local peasantry. But, considering that this had never been attempted before, that the area had but recently been in a state of open rebellion, and that the number of soldiers necessary to man all the walls implied in the establishment of prefectures and districts must have been relatively large, it is more reasonable to imagine that at least some of the soldiers were given land to support both themselves and the new administration struggling to establish itself. Giving the soldiers land would have been an incentive for keeping them "in place." Garrisoned soldiers far from home are unavoidably a potential source of disaffection. If given land, soldiers will settle down and take an interest in local affairs. This seems to be implied in the reference to irrigation ditches dug to benefit the people living in the walled towns and their environs, where prefectural and district administration was established.

The second implication from the information about irrigation ditches is that Han administrators were now taking direct control of what had been called the Lac fields. If some ditches were dug by Han, we must assume that all ditches were under their care, for water-distribution systems cannot function properly without coordinated supervision. This means that Ma Yüan did not lose the chance, offered by his victory, of taking the rice fields away from the Lac lords.[4]

Finally, it is recorded that Ma Yüan "reported more than ten discrepancies between Viet statutes and Han statutes. He clearly explained the old regulations to the Viet people in order to bind them. Henceforth, the Lac Viet carried on what had been established by General Ma."[5] The statutes (*lü*) refer to criminal and customary law and should not be confused with the more politically oriented imperial law (*fa*) that Su Ting had attempted to force on Thi Sach, thereby igniting the Lac uprising.[6] Ma Yüan simply reported discrepancies between Han and Viet statutes; there is no indication that he attempted to rectify these discrepancies. This indicates that ancient Vietnam was not shattered or utterly demoralized by Ma Yüan's conquest, but continued to exist as an organized society with its own patterns of marriage, inheritance, and public order.

Although the Lac lords are not heard of again, this does not mean that they were all killed or chased out. As we have seen, several thousand Vietnamese were captured and beheaded at the battle of Lang-bac, and between three and five thousand more were later captured and beheaded in Cuu-chan. But it is recorded that ten thousand surrendered to Ma Yüan at Lang-bac. Since only several hundred families were reported to have been

4. Gotō, pp. 80–81.
5. *HHS*, 24, 14a.
6. Katakura Minoru, "Chūgoku Shihaika no Betonamu," pp. 24–25.

deported north to China, it seems that a rather large number of Trung Trac's followers remained alive and in Vietnam after submitting to Han. These people were almost certainly used by Ma Yüan as local officials, for there would have been no other way for him to staff prefectural and district administrations large enough to directly rule the people.[7]

This clarifies why Ma Yüan "clearly explained" the old regulations. The expression "to clearly explain" is severe and implies that those who disobey will be beheaded.[8] Lac lords who had submitted would be spared; they would not be beheaded as imperial law demanded. In return for this mercy, they must henceforth obey the law. Ma Yüan was undoubtedly moved to show such mercy because he needed these people to maintain order at the lowest levels of Han administration.

The "old regulations" (*chiu chih*) that Ma Yüan "clearly explained" apparently refer to the rule of prefectural and district administration that had prevailed in theory since 111 B.C., when Han first "established" prefectures and districts in Vietnam.[9] We can assume that the "old regulations" were given substance and shape by such officials as Hsi Kuang.[10] The reforms of the Wang Mang era suggest an effort to put the theory of prefectural and district administration into practice. The outcome of this effort was perhaps embodied in these "old regulations," which affirmed basic rules of Han government in the context of ancient Vietnamese society.

The term "to bind," in the phrase "he clearly explained the old regulations to the Viet people in order to bind them," implies a covenant or agreement between Ma Yüan and the conquered Lac lords that included a formal promise or oath on their part to obey the "old regulations." The term "to carry on," in the phrase "henceforth the Lac Viet carried on what had been established by General Ma," means to carry on something in response to an order from a superior, which is further evidence of a clearly defined legal relationship imposed on the defeated Lac lords by Ma Yüan. The expression "what had been established by General Ma" implies a standard of behavior established as a rule for later generations.

The personal impact of Ma Yüan upon the collective memory of the Vietnamese people was large. A ninth-century T'ang governor with the surname Ma found this memory sufficiently potent in his day to make it expedient to claim Ma Yüan as an ancestor in order to increase his own prestige among the Vietnamese.[11] Much legendary lore grew up around the great deeds and superhuman feats Ma Yüan is supposed to have performed in

7. Gotō, p. 83, argues in this direction.
8. Ibid., loc. cit.
9. Ibid., p. 82.
10. Katakura, pp. 24–25.
11. *CL*, 100.

Vietnam.[12] Ma Yüan was a man of unusual ability and a hardy old warrior; it is not difficult to imagine that the reputation he left in Vietnam was itself an important factor in establishing the new Han regime of direct rule through prefectural and district administration.

One of the deeds attributed to Ma Yüan by later folklore was the erection of a pair of bronze pillars to mark the southern limit of the Han empire. Certain accounts attach to this legend a story of Chinese settlers left by Ma Yüan in the vicinity of the pillars. These settlers reportedly took the surname Ma and maintained their linguistic identity for several genera-tions.[13] While this story cannot be accepted at face value, it seems to reflect a memory of the settlement of Han people in Vietnam by Ma Yüan.[14]

Ma Yüan's legacy was twofold. First, he established some kind of prefectural and district administration. Second, he established Han immi-grants in Vietnamese society. Both of these accomplishments were shortly transformed by the local society's response. Han administration was eventu-ally overshadowed by the rise of great families that grew from a process of Han-Viet intermarriage.

The Great Han-Viet Families

In the wake of Ma Yüan's expedition, a new ruling class emerged. It grew from both Chinese immigrants and local Vietnamese families. We have seen that a large number of upper-class Han people entered the south during the Wang Mang disorders. Many of these returned north after the Han restoration, but it is clear that some remained in the south, particularly in the area of modern Kuang-tung and Kuang-hsi, but also, to a lesser extent, in northern Vietnam.

The Shih family, which rose to prominence at the end of Han, came from Shan-tung and settled in Ts'ang-wu during the Wang Mang period. The Ly family, which produced Ly Bi, the sixth-century Vietnamese in-dependence leader, came from northern China at the same time.[15] The Trung sisters' uprising must have sent most of the Han immigrants in Vietnam fleeing back north, although some of them undoubtedly returned to Vietnam in the wake of Ma Yüan's expedition. The initial immigration of the Wang Mang era probably included women and children, so that the upper-class Chinese community in Vietnam was able to maintain its Han character for a generation or two.

Ma Yüan's expedition brought a new class of immigrants. His army

12. Rolf Stein, "Le Lin-i," pp. 147–202.
13. H. Maspero, "Études," 18: 23–27; Stein, pp. 153–64.
14. Gotō, p. 114.
15. See Appendix G.

included eight thousand men from northern China and twelve thousand militiamen from Kuang-hsi and eastern Kuang-tung. It is recorded that Ma Yüan deported several hundred families from Vietnam to the north, and we can confidently assume that he conversely settled many of his soldiers in Vietnam as a base for Han administration. Some of these newcomers may have subsequently sent for women from the north, and some probably married daughters of the immigrants of the Wang Mang era, but it is likely that most of them eventually took wives from the local population. When Ch'in Shih Huang Ti invaded southern China nearly three centuries before, Chao T'o had requested thirty thousand women from the north as wives for his men, but there is no evidence of any similar attempt to provide Han soldiers in Vietnam with northern brides.

The soldiers of Ma Yüan were not educated men, as the immigrants of the Wang Mang era had been. They carried swords and crossbows rather than books and writing brushes. They would have found it easy to adjust to the indigenous society and to be influenced by it. If they had land, they would have had little incentive to return north. Many of them may have been of mixed parentage to begin with, children of Chinese immigrants and the indigenous peoples of the Kuang-tung and Kuang-hsi area. Their interest in Han culture and their loyalty to Han authority was maintained by opportunities to serve as middle- and low-level officials of Han government, especially in police and military affairs.

The settlement of Han soldiers had long-term implications for patterns of land ownership. During the Later Han period in general, prevailing patterns of land ownership encouraged the rise of a powerful landlord class. Government exactions tended to drive peasants to sell their lands to rich merchants or officials and to become tenant farmers. This trend in China proper may have had its counterpart in the provincial environment of Vietnam.

The indigenous pattern of land ownership in Vietnam seems to have been communal.[16] The Lac lords appear to have enjoyed certain rights that were satisfied by the village or community as a whole in the form of manpower, comestibles, and craft goods. The Lac lords, in turn, supplied their suzerain with tribute goods. It is reasonable to assume that these tribute goods were the major form of revenue collected by the Former Han.

After Ma Yüan's expedition, the concepts of private property and state revenue were given a more general application, at least in areas surrounding the major Han administrative centers. Settled Han soldiers were the direct means of building a new socioeconomic foundation for Han-style patterns of land ownership and revenue collection. Beyond this, it would have been a simple matter for Han officials to tax Vietnamese peasants

16. Katakura, pp. 25, 29–30.

into debt, then buy their communal lands and turn them into private estates. Another possibility is that Han soldiers may have been given confiscated communal lands, and the local people then sent to open up new land assigned to them on the basis of individual holdings. In any case, the concept of private property began to develop in Vietnam as the economic basis of the Han-Viet ruling class. Certainly not all, and probably not even most, of the communal lands were changed into private property in this way, but enough were to support the new ruling class. These changes most affected areas in the vicinity of major Han centers, which were generally located in a few places that were at that time most suitable for wet rice agriculture. These are the places where Han-style brick tombs have been unearthed.[17]

Approximately one hundred and twenty Han-style brick tombs, dating from the last half of the first century through the second century, and possibly as late as the fourth or fifth centuries, have been excavated in northern Vietnam,[18] These tombs, and the burial goods found in them, offer many clues for analyzing the new Han-Viet ruling class.

Stylistically and structurally, the tombs show universal Han characteristics. Furthermore, with few exceptions the items found in them show nothing distinctively Vietnamese; the kinds of burial goods discovered are typical of those found in Han tombs south of the Yellow River plain.[19] This suggests that ruling-class people in Vietnam formally accepted Han culture with few or no reservations.

The material culture reflected by the burial goods found in the tombs is high. Not only are there glass ornaments, bronze and earthenware vessels, iron swords, and coins of the Wang Mang and Later Han periods, but there are also game boards, musical instruments, mirrors, inkstones, and lampstands.[20] This shows that the people buried in these tombs were literate and that they cultivated a varied social life.

Although no Dong-son bronze drums have been found in the tombs, a number of items, particularly lampstands, can be interpreted as a mixture of Han and local influence. The most famous of these is the lampstand portraying a kneeling human figure found in Lach-truong tomb number three. This lampstand shows a servant with indeterminate non-Chinese facial features accompanied by ten dwarfish musicians. It appears to be the product of a local artistic tradition.[21] The fact that lampstands were vulnerable to local influence may reflect no more than regional fashion, or it

17. See the map in Gotō, p. 133.

18. Ibid., pp. 125, 129–30.

19. Ibid., p. 129.

20. Ibid., p. 127.

21. L. Bezacier, *Manuel d'archéologie d'Extrême-Orient*, pp. 263, 270; Nguyen Phuc Long, "Les Nouvelles Recherches archéologiques au Vietnam," pp. 100–101; Gotō, pp. 127, 131–32. J. Hejzlar, *The Art of Vietnam*, figs. 28–31.

may indicate that the use of leisure time, with nighttime entertainment and amusements, was heavily influenced by the local culture.

The tombs also contain model ceramic farms, which show that these people were landowners whose wealth derived from agriculture. Model houses, granaries, wells, and kilns were arranged in fortresslike compounds with many buildings perched atop walls and accessible only by ladder.[22] These models resemble ones found in China and strongly suggest that the great landlord families that came to dominate Later Han life had their counterparts in Vietnam. Much is known of these great Han families. They originated from wealthy merchants or powerful officials who accumulated land, reducing the peasants to a serflike status as tenants or indentured servants. These great families supported a private community of "guests" that included scholars, technical experts, spies, and assassins; they also maintained personal armies of fighting men.[23] Such families seem to have appeared in the wake of Ma Yüan's expedition as the custodians of Han prefectural and district administration in Vietnam.

Evidence for this has been found at Tam-tho, a site near the modern city of Thanh-hoa in what was Cuu-chan, where eight kilns contemporary with the brick tombs were unearthed. The bricks and earthenware in the Han tombs are the same as those found at the Tam-tho kilns. At one kiln was found a stamp for impressing three characters (*chun-i-kuan*) into tiles used along the eaves of a house's roof. The first of the three characters can be translated "lord" or "gentleman." The second character can be translated as "should be" or "is rightfully" and refers to the last character, which means "public official." This stamp connects two terms of status, one social and the other administrative, and reveals that upper-class members of Han-Viet society, probably those buried in the tombs, filled administrative positions.[24]

The presence of this stamp at the kiln suggests that the kiln was owned or controlled by the ruling-class people of the area. It may have been an "official kiln" under government license, or it may have been under the collective ownership of ruling-class families.[25] It may, in fact, have been both if the trend of Later Han society toward the domination of prefectural and district administration by great landowning families is any indication.

The tombs, mostly located in fertile lowlands, have been found in groups of as many as thirty in one necropolis. A necropolis presupposes a stable regional society and implies that ruling-class people viewed themselves as members of that society. They apparently did not want to be buried

22. Bezacier, *Manuel*, pp. 268–69; Nguyen Phuc Long, figs. 273–77.
23. Charles O. Hucker, *China's Imperial Past*, pp. 176–77.
24. Gotō, pp. 136–38.
25. Ibid., p. 138.

elsewhere.[26] Some scholars have imagined that these ruling-class people were either Han immigrants who became local leaders or else native ruling-class people who adopted Han-style burial. A more reasonable interpretation is that they were not wholly one or the other, but rather a mixture.[27] The grouping of the tombs into regional necropolises is strong evidence that the people who were buried there shared a common regional viewpoint.

The ruling-class people buried in these tombs were established in the local economy and society. They had come to settle in the rich plains of northern Vietnam and had no intention of returning north. The fact that they were buried in Vietnam reveals that they considered it to be their home, for the bones of ruling-class Han Chinese were as a rule returned to their homes for burial, no matter where they died.[28]

The great distance between Vietnam and northern China, as well as periodic political violence, would certainly have discouraged the repatriation of remains northward. A pair of tombs in what was Cuu-chan has nevertheless stimulated speculation about this. The two tombs seem to belong to a husband and wife. The larger tomb, presumably the husband's, is empty, while the smaller tomb was found intact. This has been interpreted as a case of a Chinese husband's remains being repatriated, while his local wife's remains were left in place. If so, this would be archeological proof of intermarriage; however, there is some indication that the larger tomb was broken into by grave robbers, so the evidence is inconclusive.[29]

The picture of a well-organized regional ruling-class society emerges from the tombs and kilns. These people lived in fortified compounds, where they accumulated wealth gained from their ownership or control of the fertile plains of northern Vietnam. The necropolises strongly imply that this Han-Viet ruling class was firmly planted in the regional society. The model compounds suggest large economic, social, and political units, which were surely dependent upon local people for manpower and basic skills. Literati and technical experts may have been immigrants from the north, and military officers may have been sons of Ma Yüan's soldiers, but the peasants who tilled the land, the common soldiers, the cooks, the house servants, the slaves, and the concubines were surely Vietnamese. And with the passing of each generation, with sons and daughters of concubines, and perhaps of wives, strengthening blood ties with the local society, the Han character of the great families was progressively eroded.

Judging from the brick tombs and the kind of society they represent, it would appear that if Ma Yüan did indeed settle soldiers on the land, as

26. Ibid., p. 135.
27. Ibid., p. 131.
28. Ibid., p. 123.
29. Ibid., pp. 133–34.

evidence suggests, this state of affairs did not long endure, but quickly evolved in favor of great landowning families who consolidated large estates. These families became the focus of regional politics when Han began to decline in the second century.

Aside from the immigrants of the Wang Mang era and Ma Yüan's soldiers, there is no direct evidence of Han immigration to Vietnam. We can nevertheless assume that there were other immigrants. Upper-class scholars and officials who settled in Vietnam probably maintained a relatively strong Han character, and it is their cultural influence that dominates the brick tombs. We can assume that some of these people sent their sons north to be educated and that some of those sons returned with northern brides. The Han character of this upper class was certainly reinforced to some extent by exiles and other members of the Han ruling class who decided to settle in Vietnam.

On the other hand, exiles probably held views critical of Han official-dom and were to some degree psychologically prepared to cut their ties with the north.[30] Furthermore, those who deliberately chose to settle in Vietnam undoubtedly included disaffected officials attracted by a remote frontier, far from the centers of Han power.

Not all Han immigrants were ruling-class people. Only about 120 brick tombs have so far been unearthed in northern Vietnam. Many immigrants were soldiers, laborers, and technicians. These were even less likely than the people who left tombs to maintain their Han character. Lower-class immigrants would have tended to join the mixed world formed by the human residue of Ma Yüan's expedition. Many Han immigrants were ready and willing to compromise their Han orthodoxy by associating with the local society, and we can assume that they did this through intermarriage and by standing forth as representatives of the regional society during the rebellions that broke out in the second century.[31]

Generally speaking, we can say that Han immigrants became members of the regional society and, strictly speaking, were no longer Chinese. They developed their own perspective on Chinese civilization. They brought Chinese vocabulary and technology into Vietnamese society, but they developed a regional point of view that owed much to the indigenous heritage. The Vietnamese language survived, and it is reasonable to assume that after the first or second generation Han immigrants spoke Vietnamese. Vietnamese society as a whole remained separate from Chinese civilization, and Han-Viet society existed as a wing of this autonomous cultural world. Han immigrants were more effectively "Vietnamized" than the Vietnamese were sinicized.

30. Ibid., p. 144.
31. Ibid., pp. 145–46.

We can surmise that Lac ruling-class families who had submitted to Ma Yüan were used as local functionaries in Han administration; these people were natural participants in the process of intermarriage. Men and women of old Lac ruling-class families with Chinese son-in-laws, nephews, or husbands were well placed to spread indigenous sensibilities to Han officials. Vietnamese women were accustomed to voicing their opinions and exercising leadership, in both the family and society. The shadow of the Trung sisters lies over the rebellions of the second century; Vietnamese grandmothers, mothers, and wives prevailed over lingering respect for the Han loyalties of grandfathers and fathers. This also helps explain why some of these rebellions were calmed by persuasion; talented Han officials appealed to these lingering loyalties. The Han-Viet officers who played central roles in these uprisings were caught between the Han allegiance of their fathers and the regional outlook of their mothers and wives. The effects of inter-marriage could not help but be felt on the political stage.

Han-style brick tombs have been uncovered only in what was Giao-chi, Cuu-chan, and northern Nhat-nam along the Giang River. No tombs have been found in southern Nhat-nam. This suggests that in southern Nhat-nam there were not enough Han immigrants to form a distinct social class.[32] There seems to have been only a handful of Han officials in southern Nhat-nam, and, in 192 or thereabouts, as we will presently see, the son of one of them founded the breakaway kingdom of Lin-i.

Han immigration into Vietnam was not overwhelming. This is clear from a study of census statistics, which indicate that there were no abnormal demographic changes in northern Vietnam during Han. There were apparently enough immigrants to form a coherent Han-Viet ruling-class society throughout most of northern Vietnam, but not enough to administratively or culturally dominate the indigenous society. The effective influence of Han immigration was spent before reaching the southern military frontier.

To clarify this point, it is useful to consult Han census records. Table 1 contains Han census statistics from Chiao-chih Circuit. This jurisdiction stretched along the South China Sea for a thousand miles, from Canton to Hue, and in A.D. 2 it contained a registered population of approximately one and one-third million. More than half of the registered population was in the Hong River plain. This explains why Giao-chi (Chinese Chiao-chih) Prefecture gave its name to the entire circuit; it was the demographic hub of the South China Sea. This also explains why the Chinese took such pains to conquer the Vietnamese, for they could not control the economy of the South China Sea and secure unrestricted access to the southern trade routes unless they ruled the Vietnamese, who demographically dominated the

32. Ibid., p. 143.

Table 1. Han Census Statistics for Chiao-chih Circuit

Prefectures	Former Han (A.D. 2)		Later Han (140)	
In Modern China	*Hearths*	*Heads*	*Hearths*	*Heads*
Nan-hai	19,613	94,253	71,477	250,282
Ts'ang-wu	24,379	146,160	111,395	466,975
Yü-lin	12,415	71,162	....	....
Ho-p'u	15,398	78,980	23,121	86,617
Subtotal:	71,805	390,555		
In Modern Vietnam				
Giao-chi	92,440	746,237	....	....
Cuu-chan	35,743	166,013	46,513	209,894
Nhat-nam	15,460	69,485	18,263	100,676
Subtotal:	143,643	981,755		
Total:	215,448	1,372,290		

SOURCE: *HS*, 28b, 10a–11b, and *HHS*, 33, 20a–22a.

region. Only after the Canton area had been built up by Chinese immigration as a counterweight to the Vietnamese did the urgent necessity of ruling Vietnam diminish. This did not occur until the T'ang period.[33]

A comparison of census statistics from A.D. 2 and 140 illuminates demographic changes in China during Han and the extent to which the Vietnamese prefectures participated in these changes.[34] Table 2 summarizes these statistics and reveals that Vietnam remained virtually unaffected by population movements that changed the face of China.

The Wang Mang disorders in northern China from A.D. 9 to 23 sent a great wave of humanity fleeing southward. The number of registered households in northern China decreased by 50 percent, and the number of persons by 40 percent; remaining households absorbed lingering portions of fleeing households, causing an increase in average household size. In the Yangtze basin of central China, registered households increased 102 percent, and the number of persons increased 84 percent; the influx of small refugee households caused a decrease in average household size. In the northern prefectures of Chiao-chih, in the Hsi basin of southern China, the flood of

33. See Tsang Wah-moon, *T'ang-tai Ling-nan fa-chan ti heh-hsin hsing.*
34. Gotō, pp. 116–19; Hans Bielenstein, "The Census of China during the Period 2–272 A.D.," pp. 142–43.

Table 2. Han Census Statistics (A.D. 2 and 140)

	Percentage Increase or Decrease from A.D. 2 to 140		Average Number of People per Household		Increase or Decrease in Average Number of People per Household
	Hearths	Heads	A.D. 2	140	
Northern China					
Yellow Basin	− 50	− 40	4.7	5.5	+ .8
Central China					
Yangtze Basin	+ 102	+ 84	4.7	4.2	− .5
Southern China					
Nan-hai, Ho-p'u, and Ts'ang-wu	+ 247	+ 152	5.4	3.9	− 1.5
Northern Vietnam					
Cuu-chan and Nhat-nam	+ 27	+ 31	4.6	4.8	+ .2

refugees caused tremendous changes in the population; registered house-holds increased 247 percent, the number of persons increased 152 percent, and the average size of households decreased severely, reflecting the impact of fragmented refugee families.

Unfortunately, census figures from the Hong River plain for 140 have not survived. We can nevertheless assume that statistics from the southern prefectures, Cuu-chan and Nhat-nam, generally reflect the experience of Vietnamese society; these statistics show a normal rate of growth for regis-tered households, 27 percent, and for persons, 31 percent, as well as a slight increase in average household size. It is clear from these statistics that, although central and southern China were experiencing abnormal popu-lation growth as a result of incoming refugees, Vietnamese society main-tained a normal pattern of growth.

This, of course, does not mean that no Han immigrants came to Viet-nam, for surely they did. But it could mean that not many came, and it does mean that Vietnamese society was stable enough to absorb what immigrants did arrive without experiencing abnormal growth. This is not so surprising when we bear in mind that the three Vietnamese prefectures accounted for nearly three-fourths of the total population of Chiao-chih Circuit in A.D. 2. At that time, Lac society was the dominant demographic feature of the Han

Empire on the South China Sea. Not even the expedition of Ma Yüan, with its decisive political consequences, disturbed the pattern of normal population growth. The strength of Vietnamese society rested on firm prehistoric foundations and was equal to the pressures of Chinese immigration.

Ma Yüan's legacy was inherited by a new regional ruling class that emerged as the custodian of Han administration in Vietnam. Comparing the types of societies reflected in the Dong-son tombs and the Han-style brick tombs, strong threads of continuity appear between the Lac lords and the great Han-Viet landlord families. Both derived their status and wealth from the control of land. Both cultivated a way of life that sharply distinguished them from the people they ruled. Both accumulated wealth that they took with them to the grave. Both were recognized by Han as representatives of the local society. The Lac lords ruled prefectures and districts by virtue of "seals and ribbons"; the great Han-Viet families ruled prefectures and districts by virtue of character seals applied to the tiles in the roofs of their houses.

Whereas prefectural and district administration seems to have been largely theoretical under the Lac lords, and they apparently controlled land according to traditional concepts of privilege based on communal ownership, the great Han-Viet families presided over a more functional administrative organization and controlled land through clearly defined rights of private ownership. While the cultural outlook of the Lac lords was inhospitable to Han government, the Han-Viet families formally accepted Han culture. Ma Yüan made Han rule an inescapable fact in Vietnam, but the regional ruling-class people who emerged as a result of this fact were too far from the centers of Han power and too compromised by association with a vigorous local society to be totally committed to Han civilization.

When, in the second century, Han began to decline and was no longer able to protect these people from frontier violence, the Han-Viet families began to take affairs into their own hands. Han attempts to rule Vietnam became more aggravating than stabilizing, and the Han-Viet families were unavoidably caught up in the spirit of insurrection.

The Second-Century Rebellions

After Ma Yüan departed Giao-chi, he took nearly six months to return to the Han capital at Lo-yang.[35] The land route between Lo-yang and Giao-chi covered approximately one thousand eight hundred miles. Cuu-chan stretched for two hundred miles south of Giao-

35. H. Maspero, "Études," 18: 27. Eight centuries later, T'ang officials spent between three and six months traveling from Lo-yang to Canton (Edward Schafer, *The Vermilion Bird*, pp. 22–24).

chi, and Nhat-nam extended beyond that. In ancient times, these were formidable distances. Han officials in the south were both physically and psychologically isolated from what Chinese considered to be the civilized world. Many arrived in disgrace and took up their posts as exiles. Others came to accumulate personal wealth on a lawless frontier.

Ozaki Yasushi studied Later Han administration in Chiao-chih and concluded that Han never devised a successful method of ruling this place.[36] The rate of turnover in the administration was extremely high, for officials generally returned north as soon as they had made a fortune, and that usually did not take long, for there were few restraints on their activities. The emerging class of immigrant Chinese collaborated closely with corrupt administrators, placing the burden of bribery and extortion on the indigenous inhabitants. This state of affairs incited rebellions, which led to the arrival of able officials, but their talents were in great demand, and they soon returned north. During most of the second century, the central government was itself in turmoil, and the cycle of rebellion and repression gained momentum as periodic military expeditions replaced regular administration. It was under these conditions that local families of immigrant Chinese assumed power as Han collapsed.

Gotō Kimpei, in his study of this period, reached a similar conclusion.[37] Moreover, he cautioned against accepting at face value the historical record of "good officials" and "bad officials."[38] For example, a prefect of Ho-p'u during the reign of Emperor Huan (147–67) reportedly collected pearls from the people and amassed a private fortune; the people subsequently died in the roads of starvation, for it had been their custom to exchange pearls for rice from Giao-chi. But this information comes from the biography of Meng Ch'ang,[39] the prefect who came after this and who reportedly grieved over the situation. Likewise, the biography of Chia Tsung,[40] a governor in the 180s portrayed as an exemplary official full of concern for the people, records that his predecessor's greed had reduced the people to starvation and rebellion.

The information in these biographies was taken from inscriptions on memorial stele composed to praise the deceased, so it would certainly contain nothing derogatory about Meng Ch'ang and Chia Tsung. Furthermore, we can expect that, in order to emphasize the good qualities of these men, the bad qualities of their predecessors were exaggerated. Since officialdom was generally so bad during this period, the historiographical trend was to take special notice of good officials; as a result, the contrast between good

36. Ozaki Yasushi, "Gokan no Kōshi Shishi ni tsuite," pp. 151–52.
37. Gotō, pp. 87–108; Ying-shih Yü, *Trade and Expansion in Han China*, pp. 81–84.
38. See Miyakawa Hisayuki, "The Confucianization of South China," pp. 29–30.
39. *HHS*, 106.
40. *HHS*, 61.

and bad officials was made even sharper. Consequently, we must take the accomplishments of so-called good officials with a grain of salt.[41]

Two officials during the reign of Emperor Ming (A.D. 58–75) epitomize the two types of men reflected in Later Han historiography. Li Shan, prefect of Nhat-nam, "governed with benevolence and was tolerant of strange customs"; he was subsequently promoted to a position further north.[42] On the other hand, Chang Hui, prefect of Giao-chi, "used the law to extort bribes" and filled a storehouse with the possessions he had seized; he was eventually executed and the booty he had amassed was distributed among members of the metropolitan court.[43]

The mention of Li Shan's tolerating "strange customs" as a measure of his administrative success is instructive. It shows that, in order to govern the Vietnamese, the Chinese had to adjust their habits to the local culture; they were in no position to force their way of life on the local people. But while the Chinese could not change the local culture, they dominated the regional economy and extracted material wealth. Chang Hui's corruption was recorded because it was sufficiently excessive to attract the attention of the distant imperial court. In fact, the general impact of Han administration in the south was exploitative, and a certain amount of corruption was standard procedure. But as the punitive effect of Ma Yüan's expedition gradually wore off, exploitative policies were less taken for granted, and resistance to them became more open. In the year 89, Emperor Ho ordered an end to the sending of fresh fruit from Chiao-chih to the capital in consideration of the expense in men and horses bringing the perishables at breakneck speed day and night;[44] we can assume that ending such extravagant practices reflects pressure from the south.

In spite of the many shortcomings of the Han regime in Chiao-chih, it was nonetheless remarkably stable for nearly a century. When Han power began to decline, the first symptom in the south was not rebellion, but rather a deteriorating frontier. A series of invasions and frontier uprisings strained the administration beyond its capacity; this stimulated internal unrest and encouraged a spirit of insubordination.

As early as A.D. 2, it is recorded that a certain kingdom of Huang Chih, located "south of Nhat-nam," sent rhinoceroses to the Han court. According to one theory, Huang Chih was Kāñcī, near Conjeeveram in southern India.[45] If so, this is evidence of well-established seaborne contact with the

41. Gotō, p. 98.

42. *TT*, 3, 4a; *CL*, 7, 86.

43. *CL*, 86.

44. *CL*, 69.

45. *HS*, 11, 4b; *HHS*, 116, 9a; Wang Gung-wu, "The Nan-hai Trade," p. 30; O. W. Wolters, *Early Indonesian Commerce*, pp. 33–34; Ying-shih Yü, pp. 173–174.

coasts of South and Southeast Asia.[46] Commerce in tropical luxury goods was a major preoccupation of local administrators, and seaborne contacts became a strong alternative to the declining Han economy. As Chinese civilization pushed south in the wake of imperial armies, the Hinduized civilization of India spread along the trade routes of Southeast Asia. Nhat-nam, where the two civilizations met, became an international entrepôt and a cultural battleground.

Oc Eo, an archeological site on the lower Me-kong in what is now southern Vietnam, has yielded abundant evidence of contact with the West. In addition to numerous items of Indian origin, Roman coins have been found. One of these bears the effigy of Antoninus Pius (138–61). The generals of Antoninus Pius's successor, Marcus Aurelius (161–80), con-quered part of Mesopotamia in 162–65; this apparently stimulated contact with the trade routes leading east, for in 166 a group of merchants claiming to be ambassadors of Marcus Aurelius arrived in Chiao-chih by sea on their way to the Han court.[47] The maritime route between eastern and western Asia was at this time a well-worn commercial thoroughfare.

The cultural frontier of this thoroughfare was Tuong-lam, the south-ernmost district of Nhat-nam, located in the vicinity of modern Hue.[48] Here, Han officials encountered Hinduized currents of Indian civilization as they flowed along the trade routes of Southeast Asia. Around the year 192, the son of a district official in Tuong-lam, named Ou Lien,[49] killed the district magistrate and proclaimed himself a king, thereby founding the Cham kingdom of Lin-i, which endured into the seventeenth century as an important neighbor of the Vietnamese. Lin-i aligned itself with the civili-zation of India. It nevertheless grew from within the structure of Han administration and clung to the edge of the Chinese political world for three centuries before broadening its power base to include areas further south. This rapidly evolving frontier had a destabilizing influence on Chiao-chih from the beginning of the second century.

In the year 100, at the beginning of summer, more than two thousand inhabitants of Tuong-lam District attacked, plundered, and burned the Han

46. Ptolemy, the ancient Greek geographer, used information from the dawn of the second century to locate commercial centers along the coasts of modern Vietnam (G. E. Gerini, *Researches on Ptolemy's Geography of Eastern Asia*, pp. 265–81, 739; Ying-shih Yü, p. 175).

47. Georges Coedès, *The Indianized States of Southeast Asia*, p. 60; Edouard Chavannes, "Les pays d'Occident d'après le *Heou Han Chou*," p. 185.

48. Stein, pp. 54–107.

49. *SCC*, 36, 24a, says Ou K'uei. *LS*, 54, 53a, says Ou Ta. *CS*, 97, 9a, says Ou Lien. Coedès, *Indianized States*, p. 43, proposed the equation of *Ou Lien* with *Ch'ü-lien*, which appears as a tribal or ethnic name in the year 136 (*HHS*, 116, 11a); *Ch'ü* is pronounced *Ou* as a surname. Stein, pp. 209–40, postulated that *Ch'ü* is the Chinese transcription of a term indigenous to the frontier.

centers in their district. The Chinese responded by raising an army from districts further north. After the leaders of the uprising were captured and beheaded, their followers submitted to the Chinese. Han thereafter established a special military command in Tuong-lam to guard against future trouble.[50] In 102, Tuong-lam was exempted from three categories of taxes for two years in an effort to reconcile the refractory district to Han rule.[51]

For the next few decades, the frontier was outwardly peaceful. In 124, "barbarians from beyond the frontier of Nhat-nam" arrived and submitted to Han authorities; this seems to have been a migration, perhaps a group of refugees from political struggles occurring beyond the frontier, although details are lacking.[52] On the other hand, Rolf Stein has presented a convincing case for interpreting the expression "barbarians from beyond the frontier of Nhat-nam" to mean people within the geographical sphere of Nhat-nam but beyond the administrative control of Han officials.[53] A reference to peaceful contact with "barbarians from beyond the frontier of Nhat-nam" also occurs in the year 85.[54]

In 136, the frontier erupted in violence, sending a shock through prefectures further north from which Han authority never fully recovered. Several thousand people called Ch'ü-lien came from "beyond the frontier" and attacked Tuong-lam; they burned down the Han centers and killed resident Han officials. Chia Ch'ang, a censor, led an army into Nhat-nam, but soon found himself hopelessly surrounded. As the invaders marched north, the governor of Chiao-chih, Fan Yen, raised an army of more than ten thousand men from the prefectures of Giao-chi and Cuu-chan. However, the recruits feared the distant frontier and not only refused to march south but, rising in rebellion, attacked and destroyed the Han centers in their home prefectures.[55]

When news of the disaster reached the Han capital, the court at first decided to raise an army of forty thousand from four provinces in northern and central China and to send it south. This plan was abandoned, however, on the advice of an official named Li Ku. Li Ku listed seven reasons why an

---

50. *HHS*, 4, 19b, and 116, 10b.

51. Katakura, pp. 24–25.

52. *HHS*, 116, 10b–11a; Stein, p. 136. It is further recorded that in 131 a certain king of Yeh-t'iao from beyond Nhat-nam sent tribute to Han and received a gold seal with purple ribbons as a symbol of imperial investiture (*HHS*, 116, 11a); however, this information is open to interpretation, and Stein, pp. 136–42, suggested that it may in fact pertain to Yün-nan rather than to the southern coast.

53. Stein, pp. 130–47.

54. *HHS*, 3, 15b, and 116, 10a.

55. The most complete account of these events is in *HHS*, 116, 11a, which is closely followed by *TT*, 3, 4b. *CL*, 69 and 86, contains two brief notices of the Ch'ü-lien uprising and of Fan Yen's unsuccessful attempt to suppress it.

army should not be sent to Chiao-chih.[56] First, the areas proposed as recruitment grounds for the expedition were already in a state of rebellion and disorder. Second, attempting to send an army so far south would result in mutiny and desertion. Third, the southern climate would cause disease and death among the soldiers. Fourth, marching the army for such a distance would reduce it to exhaustion. Fifth, the cost of supplying such an expedition would be too great. Sixth, such an expedition would require reinforcements and would be a source of disaffection. Seventh, the soldiers in Giao-chi and Cuu-chan refused to fight, and how could soldiers sent thousands of miles be expected to do what they would not? Li Ku went on to recommend the use of Chu Liang and Chang Ch'iao, whom he described as able officials with spirit and courage, to go and calm the rebellion with bribery and persuasion.[57]

Li Ku's seven points reveal Han's attitude toward the south at this time. The situation was quite different from what it had been a century earlier, when Ma Yüan was ordered south with no official misgivings. The Han court was now dominated by harem politics and influential eunuchs; the emperor was little more than a pawn. Furthermore, Han was at this time occupied with a more serious threat on its western frontier. Beyond this, the choice of diplomacy over coercion was a recognition of the geopolitical realities of that time and place. Chiao-chih was never more than a frontier outpost of the Han Empire, and Han officials there were isolated in a sea of "southern barbarians."[58] When the imperial house began its irreversible decline, this change in the political wind was quickly felt there, and the consequences were soon apparent.

Li Ku's cautious advice was heeded. Rather than an army, two men were sent. Chang Ch'iao was appointed governor of Chiao-chih and Chu Liang was named prefect of Cuu-chan. These men were members of Li Ku's clique, and their appointments represented an effort by Li Ku to raise the status of his group. He was gambling the abilities of his protégés against the recalcitrance of the rebels; at stake in this gamble was his influence at court.[59]

When Chang Ch'iao entered Giao-chi in 138, he published conciliatory words, and the population responded with interest. Chu Liang audaciously rode his chariot into the midst of the rebel camp in Cuu-chan and spoke with "imposing majesty," prompting several tens of thousands of the rebels to return to Han allegiance. Ch'iao sent envoys to Nhat-nam with

56. Li Ku's memorial is in *HHS*, 116, 11b–13a. Slightly abridged versions are in *CL*, 69–70, and *TT*, 3, 5a–b.

57. For a full translation, see Appendix L.

58. Miyakawa, pp. 28–29.

59. Gotō, p. 92.

"soothing and enticing words" and won back the loyalty of the people there. By force of personality, a handful of men pacified Chiao-chih.[60]

The peace thus achieved was fragile, and the prefect of Giao-chi, Chou Ch'ang, requested that Chiao-chih be promoted from a circuit to a province to reinforce Han prestige in the south. The request was denied, but soon after Ch'ang was promoted to the governorship when Chang Ch'iao returned north.[61] At the same time, the seat of Giao-chi Prefecture was moved from Luy-lau to Long-bien.[62] The site of Long-bien was apparently easier to defend.

In 144, a new wave of rebellion rolled in from the south. This episode was nearly identical to that of eight years earlier. Beginning in Nhat-nam, rebels seized the Han centers, inciting similar uprisings in Cuu-chan and Giao-chi; the governor, Hsia Fang, published a pledge of clemency and persuaded the rebels to return to Han allegience.[63]

After this incident, the situation was relatively quiet for more than a decade. Han authority was nevertheless weakening, and the spirit of rebellion only waited for an opportune moment.

The events just narrated raise a number of questions. In 100, an uprising by the inhabitants of Tuong-lam was put down with soldiers recruited from jurisdictions further north, presumably in northern Nhat-nam, Cuu-chan, and Giao-chi. A special military command was immediately established in Tuong-lam. Thirty-six years later, when Nhat-nam again erupted in violence, soldiers recruited in Cuu-chan and Giao-chi refused to march south and, instead, turned against Han authority in their home districts. As a result, Han officials dared not enter the area for two years, and when they did return, they came with conciliatory gestures and hastened to remove their headquarters to a more secure location. What caused such a difference in the reaction of Cuu-chan and Giao-chi to events in Nhat-nam separated by little more than one generation?

This question leads us to consider who exactly were the people in Cuu-chan and Giao-chi that in 100 made the decision to go with Han and in 136 decided to resist Han. No details survive of how local military units were recruited and organized, but this task was probably entrusted to persons with some visible mark of allegiance to Han, most likely to those who

---

60. *TT*, 3, 6a, duplicates *HHS*, 116, 13a–b. *CL*, 86, contains biographical notices for Chang Ch'iao and Chu Liang. *VSL*, 1, 4a, contains a sketch of Chang Ch'iao.

61. *CS*, 15, 9a–b; *CL*, 86; Ozaki, 152. *TT*, 3, 4a–b, erroneously dates Ch'ang's request to 136. *VSL*, 1, 4a, simply identifies Ch'ang as governor during the reign of Emperor Shun (126–44).

62. Dang Van Lung, "Thanh Co Long-bien," p. 73; H. Maspero, "Le Protectorat general d'Annam sous le T'ang," p. 569.

63. *HHS*, 116, 13b; *TT*, 3, 6a; *CL*, 86.

carried northern blood in their veins. The bulk of the soldiers were un-doubtedly men of local origin, who would serve as long as Han leadership remained united and confident. But the class of officers who mediated between these soldiers and the highest officials were probably descendents of Ma Yüan's soldiers in the service of the great Han-Viet families who controlled the local administration.

In the emergency of the year 100, it must have been the sons of Ma Yüan's soldiers who led recruits from Giao-chi, Cuu-chan, and northern Nhat-nam down to suppress the uprising at Tuong-lam and who sub-sequently served in the special military command established there. Their mothers may have been local women, but their fathers had fought for Han, and it seems to have been natural for them to do the same.

In the emergency of 136, however, the sons of the men of the year 100 were called upon, and they found mutiny more natural than service. Of course, in 136 throughout the entire empire the sense of allegiance to Han was much less than it had been in 100.[64] However, of more direct signifi-cance was the fact that, by this time, the crucial class of middle- and low-level Han officials in Vietnam may have had three grandparents of indige-nous stock and only one grandfather of northern origin. The Han character of these people had been seriously compromised by intermarriage.

The rebellions of 136 and 144 are similar in that both were calmed by persuasion. This suggests that, while rebel leaders may have been prompted to rise against Han through the influence of their grandmothers, mothers, and wives, the loyalties of their fathers and grandfathers were sufficiently palpable to encourage their return to Han allegiance under certain circum-stances, particularly when able Han officials appeared.

Chang Ch'iao and Chu Liang, in 138, and Hsia Fang, in 144, probably regained the allegiance of local rebels by appearing to take their side against hated prefects and magistrates, whose oppressive behavior may have con-tributed to the disturbances. They issued conciliatory proclamations and pledges of clemency, "soothing and enticing words," which must have given local people reason to believe that past injustice would be corrected. This became a typical response of Han officials sent to deal with disaffection and insurrection in Chiao-chih. As we will presently see, Chou Ch'eng and Chia Tsung, later in the century, also gained reputations for calming down resentment and open rebellion by dismissing corrupt officials, reforming the administration, and promising honest government to the local people. It seems, however, that men such as these were exceptions to a rule of rapacity.

The next uprising began in Cu-phong District, located in the uplands separating the plains of the Ma and Ca rivers in Cuu-chan. In 157, a particularly odious district magistrate in Cu-phong aroused popular anger.

64. Hucker, p. 132.

An inhabitant of Cu-phong named Chu Dat attacked and killed the magistrate; then he marched north with a rebel army of between four and five thousand. The prefect of Cuu-chan, Ni Shih, was killed in battle. The military overseer of Cuu-chan, Wei Lang, eventually succeeded in gathering an army and attacking the rebels, capturing and beheading two thousand of them. He subsequently employed threats and coercion to regain control of Nhat-nam, which had also taken the opportunity to rebel.[65]

This was a new kind of uprising, provoked by an "odious Han magistrate" rather than by violence on the Tuong-lam frontier. Chu Dat, who killed the magistrate and led the brief but bloody rebellion, was never cited by Vietnamese historians. He appears only in Chinese records, which suggests that he may have been of Chinese origin.[66] If this was the case, his uprising reveals that the local character of the Han-Viet class was growing. Chu Dat marched against the Han centers in Cuu-chan with an army of between four and five thousand. He was finally defeated by another locally recruited army, which implies that the Han-Viet class had been polarized after the events of 138 and 144, with some resisting Han and others standing with the empire.

Chu Dat's uprising was confined to Cuu-chan and Nhat-nam, which suggests that the development of Han-Viet society was conditioned by geography. Areas furthest from the principal Han centers became openly anti-Han rather early. Chu Dat's success in killing not only a local Han magistrate but also the prefect of Cuu-chan in battle suggests that he was familiar with military affairs. Cu-phong, the district where he began his movement, was on an upland frontier. Before his rebellion, he may have been in charge of defending that frontier. Frontier duty, as subsequent history demonstrates, was often a radicalizing experience, as unreliable or corrupt officials were frequently sent to the frontier as a form of demotion. Frontier duty was hazardous and entailed constant contact with so-called barbarians. Therefore, it was natural for members of the Han-Viet class sent to watch the frontiers to be the first to raise the standard of revolt. The frontier was a chronic source of disaffection, both because officials sent there were often already disaffected and because the cultural outlook of the peoples indigenous to the frontier contradicted the assumptions of Han civilization, from the family system to the concept of political authority. On the other hand, the men who led soldiers against Chu Dat were probably from the settled agricultural communities near the main Han centers in the Hong and Ma river plains.

Chu Dat and two thousand of his followers were beheaded. This temporarily took the recalcitrant edge off the Han-Viet class. Three years

---

65. *HHS*, 116, 13b–14a; *CL*, 86–87; There is no mention of Chu Dat's rebellion in either the *VSL* or the *TT*.

66. Gotō, p. 93.

later, in 160, Cuu-chan and Nhat-nam again rebelled, but the leaders of this uprising were persuaded to return to Han allegiance by the man who had calmed rebel nerves in 144, Hsia Fang. Fang followed a policy of "kindness and majesty," and in Nhat-nam alone it is recorded that more than twenty thousand rebels returned to Han allegiance.[67]

The 136 and 144 uprisings were in response to events on the Tuong-lam frontier. The 157 and 160 uprisings were confined to the southern areas of Cuu-chan and Nhat-nam and were probably inspired by developments on the Han frontier. The Han presence in this remote border zone was more provocative than it was stabilizing. It brought new concepts of political authority without sufficient military power to enforce them. Consequently, the peoples along the central coast of what is now Vietnam were stimulated by Han without being effectively conquered.

A prime motive of the Han-Viet people who led these rebellions, aside from the aggravation of greedy Han officials, was very likely the conviction that they could protect themselves against frontier violence more effectively if they were in control of their own affairs. It was becoming increasingly clear that Han could not guarantee their security. For them, it was a choice between the anarchy of a disintegrating Han administration and a stability fashioned by their own hands without the interference of Han officials from the north.

The southern frontier was not the only trouble spot in Chiao-chih. There was also a long history of rebellion in the mountain valleys of what is now Kuang-hsi and Kuei-chou.[68] This unrest affected Vietnam, for it lay between it and the administrative center of Chiao-chih Circuit at Ts'ang-wu. In 162, a rebellion forced the governor of Chiao-chih, Hou Fu, and the prefect of Ts'ang-wu, Kan Ting, to flee.[69] In 163, a general named Ko Ch'i was sent against the rebels but was captured.[70] The manner in which this situation was resolved is not recorded, but the personality of Governor Chou Ch'eng may have been an important factor. Our knowledge of Chou Ch'eng is confined to a notice in the *An-nam chi luoc*.[71] Although this information is undated, it appears to fit most reasonably at this time.[72]

As an imperial censor, Chou Ch'eng had argued against the will of the emperor and was consequently exiled to be governor of Chiao-chih. After arriving in the south, he reported to the throne:

> Chiao-chih is a distant land; greed and corruption are customary practice; powerful families connive in deceit; local officials are reckless and oppressive;

67. *HHS*, 116, 14a; *CL*, 86; *VSL*, 1, 4a; *TT*, 3, 6a.
68. *HHS*, 116, 3b–7a.
69. *HHS*, 7, 18a.
70. *CL*, 87.
71. *CL*, 87–88.
72. Ozaki, p. 153.

the people are plundered and exploited. I have received great kindness and am pleased to be an imperial servant; my desire is that the throne allow me to clean up this one place.[73]

He proceded to dismiss more than thirty officials. It is recorded that he earned the reputation of having "pacified" Chiao-chih.

We must treat the information about Chou Ch'eng with caution, for it fits into the historiographical pattern of "good officials" following "bad officials." Important changes were nevertheless taking place in the local administration of Chiao-chih. Previously, prefects had been sent down from the north. But as the court became absorbed in palace intrigues and able officials grew scarce, any available person was used, regardless of his background. Thus, local people began to fill the office of prefect. Rather than being agents of empire, the prefects gradually became representatives of local interests; in this way there appeared in Chiao-chih a strong regional movement supported by the population. It was in this context that the fortunes of the Shih family began to rise.[74]

During the reign of Emperor Huan (147–67), Shih Ssu was appointed prefect of Nhat-nam. Five generations earlier, his forebears had fled from their ancestral home in Shan-tung to escape the disorders of Wang Mang's usurpation; they settled in Ts'ang-wu Prefecture, the administrative seat of Chiao-chih Circuit in modern Kuang-hsi. The Shih family and others like it were recognized by Han as local arbiters of power; they in turn developed patron-client relationships with the indigenous population. In this way they became the focus of regional politics as the empire faded away.

One of Shih Ssu's sons, named I, was a prefectural military official at this time. Ting Kung, a Chiao-chih governor during the reign of Emperor Huan, was so impressed with I's diligence that when he was later transferred to a position at the Han court he summoned I to join him in the capital. The association of the Shih family with a man of Ting Kung's caliber suggests the quality of its members and helps explain its subsequent rise to power.[75]

In 178, the prefect of Nan-hai (Canton) rebelled, stimulating an uprising in Ho-p'u and Giao-chi under the leadership of a certain Luong Long. This uprising spread to Cuu-chan and Nhat-nam and was joined by tribal peoples in modern Kuang-hsi.[76] This was the first time that all the prefectures of Chiao-chih had been inflamed by a single rebellion. It was also

73. *CL*, 87–88.

74. Ozaki, p. 153.

75. By the time I arrived at the captial, Ting Kung had already been dismissed. Kung's replacement graciously sponsored I, but I became embroiled in a feud between his patron and the powerful general Tung Cho; when Tung Cho openly rebelled, I fled back south (*SKC*, 49, 9b). The dating of Ting Kung's governorship to the reign of Emperor Huan is per *CL*, 87. See also Ozaki, pp. 152–53.

76. See *HHS*, 86.

the first time anti-Han initiative was taken by a man identified as an appointed Han official. And it was also the first time the Vietnamese were stimulated to rebel by events to their north. The governor, Chou Yung, was helpless.

In 181, Chu Chüan was sent against Chiao-chih. Chu Chüan was one of the powerful, semi-independent generals who were making their presence felt as the enfeebled Han court lost its hold on the countryside. On his way south, he passed through his home district and added his personal army to the five thousand imperial troops under his command. Splitting his forces, he advanced along two routes. Ahead of the army he sent envoys to admonish the rebels and learn the true state of affairs. After arriving in the south, he rallied pro-Han elements and attacked the rebels. Luong Long was captured and beheaded; thereafter, resistance ceased.[77] Chu Chüan was a particularly able general.[78] The peace he enforced, however, seems not to have lasted any longer than the time he spent in the south.

Three years later, in 184, military colonists joined with local rebels and killed the governor, Chou Yung. The situation is recorded as follows:

> Chiao-chih had many rare and precious goods; from first to last, the governors all kept unscrupulous accounts; the officials and the people harbored resentment and rebelled.[79]

This kind of situation was not new in Chiao-chih; corruption and oppression had been part of Han rule from the start. What was new, however, was that now local forces were successfully testing their strength against unpopular officials. This rebellion is the only direct reference to military colonists in the south during Han. These colonists were probably in Ts'angwu, for that is where the governor's residence was located.

Following the well-worn pattern of conciliation, the court appointed Chia Tsung, a man of reputed integrity, to be governor of Chiao-chih. On his arrival, he issued a written proclamation with the following five points: first, all would be allowed to pursue their livelihood in peace; second, the homeless and scattered would be received and cared for; third, taxes would be remitted for those in distress; fourth, bullies and exploiters would be executed; fifth, good people would be selected to serve as officials. With this policy, peace was quickly restored, and, if Chia Tsung's biographer can be trusted, the people sang a popular song with the following words:

> Father Chia arrived late,
> Which is why we formerly rebelled;

77. *HHS*, 116, 14a; *TT*, 3, 6a–b; *CL*, 87; *VSL*, 3, 4b.
78. Gotō, p. 94.
79. *CL*, 87; *TT*, 3, 6b–7a.

Now we see good officials and live in peace,
We do not dare betray a friend.[80]

Chia Tsung's reputation as a benevolent administrator rests to a large degree on a historiographical mentality that attributed all the virtues of a good official to those who were successful in collecting taxes and maintaining order in their jurisdictions. Looking behind the rhetoric of his reforms, we can say that he remitted taxes and killed rebel leaders in order to restore order. This was a common method of pacification. Of course his personal character was a factor, but his intention was simply to restore prefectural and district administration, which means returning the tax collection system to normal. By removing unlawful exactions and improper taxation, he may have earned a reputation like that expressed in the song cited above, but in doing so he was also making it easier to collect lawful revenue. According to Gotō Kimpei, Chia Tsung gained fame as a result of his success in collecting taxes in Chiao-chih, and this achievment was an important stepping-stone in advancing his career. After three years, he obtained promotion to a better post in the north. It is not impossible that his achievements were falsely reported to further his career, and we may assume that the politics of the prefectural and district control system are reflected in the sources.[81]

Chia Tsung's success in Chiao-chih was based on policies that were bound to stimulate greater participation by local people in the Han system of government. His policy of selecting officials from local families was surely a boon to immigrant Chinese who had a classical education and a gift for leadership. According to Vietnamese records, Chia Tsung was succeeded as governor by a local man named Li Chin. One Vietnamese source cites a letter of Li Chin to the imperial court recommending that more southerners be appointed to positions throughout the empire and contains anecdotes about two sons of Chiao-chih who made a reputation at the Han court.[82]

The information about Li Chin is doubtful because it is not found in Chinese sources. Furthermore, it was against Han policy to appoint a man to govern his home jurisdiction. On the other hand, Han government in Chiao-chih during the last quarter of the second century was not a regular administration in the orthodox sense, and, as an outcome of Chia Tsung's policy of selecting officials from local families and of Han's desire to maintain the peace, a local man may have been appointed governor.

In any case, by the late 180s Han influence in Chiao-chih was largely nominal; by the time Tuong-lam District had become the center of the independent Lin-i kingdom in 192, jurisdictions further north had resolved

80. *CL*, 87; *VSL*, 1, 4b; *TT*, 3, 7a.
81. Gotō, pp. 99–101.
82. *CL*, 87; *VSL*, 1, 4b; *TT*, 3, 7b, 8b–9a.

their political difficulties under the leadership of the Shih family. The post-Han order emerged rather quickly in the south and was remarkably stable. While the Shih family system is generally considered an aspect of the Chinese political realm, in more practical terms it belonged to the momentarily more vigorous world of maritime Southeast Asia, of which Lin-i was a less ambiguous member.

The prosperity of Chiao-chih under the Shih family resulted in part from its position on the southern maritime frontier of China. This prosperity gave economic strength to the Shih family's political position and enabled it to deal effectively with the rapidly changing situation in the north. The Han-Viet class had developed a taste for politics during the rebellions of the second century. As Han authority disappeared, this class naturally took affairs into its own hands and, under the leadership of the Shih family, established a stable regional power center in northern Vietnam. Upper-class Han immigrants maintained a formal acknowledgment of Chinese civilization, particularly in using the Chinese classics to educate their youth, but Han-Viet society as a whole turned toward Buddhist influences arriving by sea from India. Thus, in the late second century, Indian civilization became an attractive alternative to the ebbing Han tide, inspiring Lin-i kingship and Vietnamese Buddhism.

The outcome and glory of Han-Viet society was the age of Shih Hsieh, when, for forty years, the great Han-Viet families were free of external control. This became a memorable age in the formation of Vietnamese civilization.

Shih Hsieh

Shih Hsieh was the eldest son of Shih Ssu, who served as prefect of Nhat-nam during the reign of Emperor Huan (147–67). Earlier, we saw that the Shih family immigrated from Shan-tung during the Wang Mang era. Hsieh was born in 137 at Ts'ang-wu in modern Kuang-hsi; in his youth he traveled north to Ying-ch'uan (in modern Ho-nan), where he studied the classics under Liu Tzu-ch'i. He eventually received an appointment at the Han court as a state secretary. When his father died, he returned to his home district in Ts'ang-wu. After observing the prescribed mourning period, he was examined and received a *mao-ts'ai* degree. He was then appointed magistrate of Wu District in eastern Ssu-ch'uan. It seems to have been during the governorship of Chia Tsung, in the 180s, when local men of ability were reportedly selected to implement a new humanitarian policy, that Hsieh was promoted to be prefect of Giao-chi.[83]

In his contacts with Han, Shih Hsieh posed as a loyal administrator of

83. See Shih Hsieh's biography in *SKC*, 49. The date of Hsieh's promotion is not provided in the sources, but circumstantial evidence favors this particular time (Ozaki, p. 153).

the prefectural and district system. It is, nevertheless, clear from events following his death that he presided over an aberrant regional power arrangement based on great Han-Viet families that could field private armies. The mixed perspective of the Han-Viet environment became an important element of the Vietnamese historical experience. From the Chinese side, Shih Hsieh stood as a frontier guardian; from the Vietnamese side, he was the head of a regional ruling-class society. It was relatively easy for people to shift back and forth between these two perspectives. Thus, the man of Chinese or mixed ancestry playing a mixed role or, in some cases, an unambiguously Vietnamese role is a common figure in early Vietnamese history. Shih Hsieh was the first of many such people to emerge as strong regional leaders who nurtured the local society in the context of Chinese civilization.

Chu Chüan, the general who had pacified Chiao-chih in 181, helped suppress the Yellow Turban Rebellion that broke out in northern China in 184. Under the protection of his family, many upper-class refugees entered Chiao-chih to escape the fury of the rebellious peasants. Chüan's son Chu Fu was accordingly named governor of Chiao-chih. The relationship between the governor, Chu Fu, and the prefect, Shih Hsieh, was irregular. Fu was an outsider dependent on his personal army and upper-class refugees. Hsieh was a local man standing at the head of the great families of the regional ruling-class society. The territory under Hsieh's jurisdiction was peaceful and increasingly prosperous. Fu was in no position to assert his authority over Hsieh; the lands he was attempting to rule in modern Kuang-tung and Kuang-hsi were infested with bandits and disaffected officials.

Chu Chüan died in 195, and the fortunes of his family thereafter declined. In 196, Chu Fu was "tracked down and killed" by a "local strongman."[84] It is reasonable to see the hand of Shih Hsieh in the background, for upon Fu's death Hsieh quickly took control of coastal Chiao-chih. Hsieh named his three younger brothers, I, Yü, and Wu, to be prefects in Ho-p'u, Cuu-chan, and Nan-hai, respectively. Approximately one hundred scholars who had come south under the protection of the Chu family were welcomed by Shih Hsieh and found refuge with him.[85]

By this time, the empire was in the process of being partitioned by three families, who shortly would inaugurate the "Three Kingdoms" period of Chinese history. Han nevertheless made one last attempt to recover its waning fortunes with an administrative reform that delegated wide powers to provincial viceroys. Chiao-chih Circuit was not included in this new system, however, and the court sent Chang Chin to replace Chu Fu as governor.

Chang Chin was an eccentric who, according to Chinese historians,

84. *CL*, 88. *SKC*, 49, 9b, simply says that Fu was killed by "barbarian bandits."
85. *SKC*, 49, 9b; *TT*, 3, 8a–b; *CL*, 88; *VSL*, 1, 5a; Ozaki, pp. 153–57.

"ignored the teachings of the ancient sages and abolished the laws of the Han dynasty." He wore a red turban, played the lyre, burned incense, and read "false, vulgar" books.[86] In fact, Chang Chin was very interested in Taoism and, since Taoism had been an important element of the Yellow Turban Rebellion, we can assume he was disliked by Han ruling-class people, which may explain his appointment to Chiao-chih.

Real power in most of Chiao-chih, however, was in Shih Hsieh's hands. Chang Chin's influence was limited to the landlocked prefectures of Ts'ang-wu and Yü-lin in the upper Hsi basin. His position was very unsafe, for it lay in the path of the ambitions of Liu Piao, viceroy of Ching Province, directly to the north. Chang Chin and Liu Piao were soon engaged in constant warfare. Hsieh properly supported Chin in this contest, for the Liu family was considered to be in rebellion by the Han court. The court was too feeble and too far away to assist Chin, but in 203 it raised Chiao-chih to provincial status, thereby promoting Chin to the rank of viceroy. From that time, Chiao-chih Circuit was officially called Chiao Province. In spite of this moral support, Chin was treacherously killed two years later by one of his own generals. Liu Piao immediately sent Lai Kung, one of his generals, to Ts'ang-wu, where officials loyal to the Liu family were installed.[87]

When news of Chang Chin's death reached the Han court, the following imperial proclamation was sent to Shih Hsieh:

> Chiao-chih is a distant land in the south along rivers and the sea; imperial favor has not been displayed from above and factual information has been obstructed from below. We know that the rebel Liu Piao has sent Lai Kung to watch the southern lands. Now we name Shih Hsieh South-Soothing General with authority over the seven prefectures and confirm him as prefect of Giao-chi as before.[88]

From this it is clear that the Han court was now cut off from affairs in the south. It was reduced to conferring titles in the hope of influencing the course of events.

Hsieh responded to this proclamation by sending envoys with tribute to the imperial court. Considering the turmoil of the time, this was a notable accomplishment; the court recognized this demonstration of loyalty by conferring on Hsieh an imperial mandate as Remote Tranquillity General and a title of nobility.

Hsieh's peaceful realm was effectively outside the empire; it belonged instead to the developing commercial world of the South China Sea with maritime routes leading south and west. This enabled Hsieh to stand aside from the factional struggles further north and to maintain his legitimacy in

86. Miyakawa, p. 34.
87. Ozaki, pp. 157–60.
88. SKC, 49, 10b; TT, 3, 10b; CL, 88–89; VSL, 1, 5a.

terms of a powerless imperial court. Only when the question of the empire's future was nearing its resolution did Hsieh ally himself with the winner in the south; this was Sun Ch'üan, founder of the Wu dynasty.

The alliance of Shih Hsieh and Sun Ch'üan blocked Liu Piao's southern ambitions. Liu Piao died in 208, and two years later Sun Ch'üan sent a general named Pu Chih to oversee Chiao Province. Chih was content to clean up the residue of Liu Piao's intervention at Ts'ang-wu, leaving the rest of the south to Shih Hsieh. Hsieh and his brothers greeted Chih, recognized his nominal overlordship, and showered him with gifts. Ch'üan named Hsieh General of the Left in recognition of his effective control over the south.[89]

In 220, the Ts'ao family forced the last Han emperor to abdicate in its favor, thus founding the Wei dynasty in northern China. The Liu family in Ssu-ch'uan thereupon founded the Shu Han dynasty, and Sun Ch'üan in Nanking proclaimed the Wu dynasty. Hsieh immediately sent his son Hsin to Nanking as a pledge of his loyalty. Ch'üan named Hsin to a prefectural seat along the Yangtze. At the same time, Hsieh, his brother I, and their sons were given new titles by Wu. When Hsieh persuaded the leaders of mountain tribes in Kuei-chou to submit to Ch'üan, he received an additional rank of nobility.

Hsieh flooded the Wu court with luxury goods: perfumes, pearls, shell, coral, amber, fruits of all kinds, peacocks, rhinoceroses, elephants, drugs, and other rare and exotic goods. His brother I sent hundreds of horses. Not a year passed without a fresh wave of tribute. This liberality was an important source of revenue for Wu, and it guaranteed the position of the Shih family in Chiao Province.[90]

Shih Hsieh's capital was at Luy-lau, which was by this time a very old political center. Chao T'o had established a legate there about four hundred and fifty years before. It had been abandoned in the 140s, when unrest had rendered it insecure, and the site of Long-bien, which lay in the midst of hills near the northern edge of the plain, had been used as the prefectural administrative center from then until Hsieh gained power in the 180s. Hsieh's return of the capital to Luy-lau shows that his rule rested on firm local support.

Hsieh was a model ruler; in the words of his biographer:

> Hsieh's studies were wide and excellent; furthermore, he was superb in matters of government. He was modest toward subordinates, respectful of scholars, of a spacious and liberal character. During the time of great rebellion [at the end of Han], he protected an entire region; for more than twenty years

89. *SKC*, 49, 11a; *TT*, 3, 11a; *CL*, 89.
90. *SKC*, 49, 11a; *TT*, 3, 11a–b; *CL*, 89; *VSL*, 1, 5a. See also Ying-shih Yü, pp. 177–78.

he prevented trouble in the area, and all the people could pursue their livelihood in happiness. He went forth to the sound of bells, musical stones, drums, and whistles; horses and chariots filled the road; wherever he went he was accompanied by scores of Hu people bearing lighted incense; scores of wives and concubines rode in curtained wagons; his brothers and sons rode on horseback escorted by soldiers. His prestige was without equal; all the southern barbarians were shaken and submitted. Commissioner T'o was not greater than this.[91]

The comparison with Chao T'o is significant. Shih Hsieh's realm occupied the same geographical area as the old kingdom of Nan Yüeh, though Hsieh ruled from northern Vietnam rather than southern China; an important difference, however, was that in the intervening centuries a new civilization had developed on the coasts to the south. The flourishing of Chiao Province under Shih Hsieh was closely related to the rise of this new pole of attraction.

One French scholar went so far as to compare Shih Hsieh to Alcuin, under whose leadership Charlemagne's palace school was established and Latin culture propagated in northern Europe.[92] Shih Hsieh's reputation as a Confucianist was naturally enhanced by his patronage of refugee Han scholars, for some of these scholars were first-rank luminaries, eclectic scholars grounded in the classics, typical of the Han period. Yet the impact of these men on the Vietnamese was negligible. In fact, it appears that much of the sinicizing activity recorded by Han officials had little substance and was simply a means of career advancement through publicizing cultural accomplishments on this remote frontier.

Far from viewing Chiao-chih as a place worthy of their labors, refugee Han scholars were eager to return north as soon as political conditions allowed. When Shih Hsieh allied himself with Sun Ch'üan, many of these scholars departed for Ssu-ch'uan and northern China; having come south as clients of the Chu family, they were hostile to the Sun, who rose to power at the expense of the Chu. Other scholars were less particular and eventually attached themselves to the Wu court.[93]

The most vivid source for this period comes from the brush of Hsüeh Tsung. He had come south in his youth to escape the turmoil of Han's collapse and was educated in Giao-chi under a refugee scholar named Liu Hsi, who dwelt under Shih Hsieh's umbrella for several years. Hsüeh Tsung himself served Shih Hsieh and made his career in the south; after Shih Hsieh's death, he received an appointment from Wu as prefect of Ho-p'u, in western

91. The original passage is in *SKC*, 49, 10a. Abridged versions appear in *TT*, 3, 10a–b; *CL*, 88–89; and *VSL*, 1, 5a.

92. Émile Gaspardone, "L'Histoire et la philologie indochinoise," p. 8.

93. Ozaki, pp. 162–65.

Kuang-tung. In 231, five years after Shih Hsieh's death, he wrote a long memorial to the Wu throne in which he summarized his experiences as an administrator.[94]

Hsüeh Tsung's basic theme is that it was nearly hopeless to try to civilize the people in the south. The heterogeneity of the different ethnic groups was enough to daunt most administrators: "Customs are not uniform and languages are mutually unintelligible so that several interpreters are needed to communicate." To an educated Chinese, the cultural level of the people was appalling: "The people are like birds and beasts; they wear their hair tied up and go barefoot, while for clothing they simply cut a hole in a piece of cloth for their head or they fasten their garments on the left side [in barbarian style]." It was useless to place local administrators among them: "If district-level officials are appointed, it is the same as if they were not."

Hsüeh Tsung reviewed the civilizing measures taken by officials in earlier generations as recorded in the history books. He mentioned the criminals sent south by Ch'in Shih Huang Ti and especially the famous reforms of the officials of the Wang Mang era, Hsi Kuang, prefect of Giao-chi, and Jen Yen, prefect of Cuu-chan: they "taught the people to plow, established schools for instruction in the classics, and made everyone follow proper marriage ceremonies with designated matchmakers, public notification of officials, and parental invitations to formal betrothals." But, in fact, those who studied books gained only "a rude knowledge of letters," and the impact of Chinese culture on the local way of life was essentially passive: "Those who came and went at the government posts could observe proper ways of doing things."

These efforts had left virtually no mark on the local cultures as they existed in Hsüeh Tsung's day: "According to the records, civilizing activities have been going on for over four hundred years, but, according to what I myself have seen during many years of travel since my arrival here, the actual situation is something else." Hsüeh Tsung then elaborated on local customs that had proven impervious to Chinese influence:

> Concerning marriage in Chu-yai [Hai-nan Island], where all administration has been abandoned, in the eighth month family leaders assemble the people and men and women on their own volition take one another and become husband and wife with the parents having nothing to do with it. In the two districts of Me-linh in Giao-chi and Do-long in Cuu-chan, when an elder brother dies, a younger brother marries his widow; this has been going on for generations, thereby becoming an established custom, so district officials give

---

94. *CL*, 90, contains a short biographical sketch of Hsüeh Tsung. The text of the memorial is found in Hsüeh Tsung's biography, *SKC*, 53, 8b–11a; an abridged version is in *TT*, 4, 2b–3b.

in and allow it, not being able to stop it. In Nhat-nam Prefecture, men and women go naked without shame. In short, it can be said that these people are on the same level as bugs.[95]

The Chinese reserved a special disgust for unorthodox marriage customs that denied the strong patriarchal authority lying at the heart of their political system, if not of their entire civilization. The mention of levirate among the Vietnamese is particularly significant, for it is strong evidence of the bilateral character of ancient Vietnamese society. As we have already noted, Me-linh was the prehistoric political center of the Hong River plain; it was the home of the Hung kings and the Trung sisters. As Me-linh lay at the head of the Hong River plain, so Do-long lay at the head of the Ma River plain. These are the most venerable hearths of Vietnamese civilization, with deep neolithic roots.

Levirate was once thought to be a "relic of matriarchy," but in recent years this view has lost favor among anthropologists because there is no consensus on how a given practice could become a "relic" of some earlier pattern and, moreover, there is currently little inclination to use the term *matriarchy* for lack of a generally accepted evaluation of its significance in early societies. Perhaps a useful way to apprehend levirate is to compare it with sororate. Levirate can be thought of as related to polyandry as sororate is related to polygamy. Levirate gives a woman the right to her husband's younger brothers, while sororate gives a man the right to his wife's younger sisters. But while sororate endured into historical times as a genuinely polygamous practice, levirate appears in history as a form of polyandry in the process of transformation under the influence of an ascending male status.

Levirate, as it has been practiced in historical times, gives a woman the right to her husband's younger brother only after her husband's death. This, in effect, was a denial of the seemingly polyandrous origins of the practice and implies that the custom survived a sexual reorientation of society. Furthermore, an offspring of a levirate marriage was considered to be a child of the deceased husband. This unpopular provision, based on patriarchal concepts, probably hastened the demise of the custom in a male-dominated environment, for we can assume that most men were reluctant to sire another man's heir.[96]

Originally, and more logically, in a polyandrous society children gained their hereditary rights through their mothers, but levirate reflects a rising male status and attributes the transmission of rights to the father's side. Levirate consequently appears to be an adaptation of a polyandrous practice

95. *SKC*, 53, 9a–b.
96. For example, see the story of Onan and Tamar in Genesis 38: 7–9.

to a patriarchal society; a patriarch who died childless could thereby gain an heir to legally carry on his bloodline.

If we take the basic definition of matriarchy to be a stage in the evolution of a society in which descent is traced in the female line with all children belonging to the mother's clan, it is not difficult to see an affinity between matriarchy and levirate, provided the matriarchy also be polyandrous. This definition of matriarchy is sometimes called a matrilineal society to distinguish it from what is, strictly speaking, a matriarchate, or a society ruled by women. In fact, we need not use the term *matriarchy* to appreciate the significance of levirate in the evolution of a society towards increasingly patriarchal values. The term *bilateral* seems to be most appropriate for describing Vietnamese society in early historical times.[97] The law codes of Vietnamese dynasties in later centuries reflect a relatively high status for women, indicating resistance to patriarchal influence from China. Ancient Vietnamese society may not have been controlled by women, but it is clear that women enjoyed hereditary rights that allowed them to assume roles of political leadership.

Hsüeh Tsung's teacher, Liu Hsi, also commented on the freedom of women in the south. Liu Hsi considered the people in Giao-chi to be "incorrigible barbarians" and returned to northern China as soon as conditions permitted.[98] He later wrote a book entitled *Shih ming* (Explaining the Names of Things). In the section on "Explaining the Names of Female Ornaments" he wrote:

> To display pearls by piercing the ear: such are called earrings. This originally came from the usage of southern barbarians. Southern Barbarian women are untrustworthy and promiscuously wander about. For this reason they are made to wear tinkling pendants to keep them at home. Nowadays people in the Central Kingdom imitate this.[99]

While nothing in this passage explicitly relates it to the Vietnamese, we know that Liu Hsi lived among the Vietnamese for about ten years, and we can imagine that his firsthand knowledge of "southern barbarians" came directly from his contact with the Vietnamese. We cannot be sure how accurately Liu Hsi evaluated the reasons Vietnamese women wore earrings, but his comments can be taken as an indication that sexual roles in Vietnamese society were changing. This passage suggests an aspect of the imposition of patriarchal values on Vietnamese society. Women were seemingly accustomed to enjoying strong rights that included certain sexual prerogatives. Aspiring patriarchs appeared to have kept track of their proud

97. A. Thomas Kirsch, "Kinship, Genealogical Claims, and Societal Integration in Ancient Khmer Society," pp. 198–201.

98. Gotō, p. 160.

99. *SM*, 2, 33a.

women by weighing them down with tinkling earrings. This is possibly an example of a custom arising among "barbarians" as a means of adopting Chinese values that was then adopted by the Chinese, presumably to reinforce these values.

Not only were the Vietnamese culturally intransigent, but they were politically volatile. Hsüeh Tsung leads his readers to wonder why the Chinese were interested in such a place, and then provides some reasons:

> They easily become rebellious and are difficult to pacify; district officials act dignified but are careful not to provoke them. What can be obtained from field and household taxes is meager. On the other hand, this place is famous for precious rarities from afar: pearls, incense, drugs, elephant tusks, rhinoceros horn, tortoise shell, coral, lapis lazuli, parrots, kingfishers, peacocks, rare and abundant treasures enough to satisfy all desires. So it is not necessary to depend on what is received from taxes in order to profit the Central Kingdom.[100]

Such normal functions of Chinese administration as education and tax collection were stymied by the strength of prevailing indigenous patterns. But the Chinese interest in Vietnam was not a normal administrative one; rather, it was extractive and exploitative.

The lure of tropical luxury goods first brought Ch'in Shih Huang Ti's armies into the south, and quick profits remained the fundamental attraction of the region for the Chinese. As a result, Chinese officials were not administrators so much as get-rich-quick artists. Hsüeh Tsung recognized this:

> It must be admitted that, outside of the imperial heartland [in northern and central China], men selected to be district officials are not carefully examined. Under Han, law was lax and many officials were self-indulgent and debauched. Consequently, many illegal acts occurred.[101]

Hsüeh Tsung elaborated with a few examples. He wrote that Han had to abandon Hai-nan Island after an uprising provoked by greedy officials who forcibly cut off the people's hair to sell for wigs. A prefect named Huang Kai arrived in Nhat-nam and killed local leaders at random when he decided that they had not welcomed him with large enough gifts; he was chased back north by the people. Officials in Cuu-chan were so lawless that on one occasion soldiers sent by Shih Hsieh to restore order were forced back.[102]

How could this region be governed? Hsüeh Tsung advised that those selected as officials must be

> wise and cautious men with the ability to devise resourceful methods for keeping the loyalty of the people; only then can there be peaceful adminis-

100. *SKC*, 53, 9b.
101. Ibid., 53, 9b.
102. *CL*, 88, identifies Huang Kai as a Wu man, apparently because Hsüeh Tsung's memorial was addressed to the Wu throne.

tration. If men of ordinary talent are used, governing according to the usual way without shrewdness or unorthodox measures, then day by day rebellion and banditry will increase.[103]

From this it is clear that the Vietnamese were beyond the realm of normal government. Chinese officials in Vietnam could not succeed by simply following the rules. Governing the Vietnamese required special skill.

Considering what Hsüeh Tsung tells us, we must be skeptical of the well-worn tendency to exaggerate the impact of Han culture on the Vietnamese and of Shih Hsieh's supposed role in consolidating this impact.

Shih Hsieh was an astute leader who understood his time and place. He was a beneficiary of powerful political currents flowing from the indigenous society. He stood at the head of a Han-Viet class that had become firmly embedded in the local society after several generations of intermarriage. This class was awakening to a more confident awareness of political power when Han administration began to falter. The long era of unrest and rebellion that characterized most of the second century came to an end with the rise of Shih Hsieh.

It is doubtful that one man's personality could have accounted for such a dramatic change of affairs. The advent of Shih Hsieh coincided with the final disappearance of Han government from the south. As events following his death reveal, his family was distinct from the regional ruling class. The Shih family stood forth as imperial representatives and mediators between the local powers and the political situation in the north. Shih Hsieh's imperial appointments gave formal legitimacy to the emergence of a regional ruling class with strong ties to the local society. We can assume that this class drew on traditions of authority inherited from Lac lords as well as from Han officials, for both were among its ancestors.

The Shih family, and others like it, maintained a strong Han character. Nearly all the young men of the Shih family were educated in the north, and their principal wives were probably northerners. But Shih Hsieh's biography speaks of "scores of wives and concubines," and many, if not most, of these were probably local women, whose influence was in some way felt in the Shih household. Behind the Shih family, the Han-Viet class exemplified the full spectrum of cultural outlooks governed by marital vicissitudes. Undoubtedly, while some Han-Viet people, out of pride and a desire for prestige or because of personal taste, aspired to a more perfect conformity to the patterns of Han civilization despite their mixed ancestry, others, because of an aversion to the claims of Han civilization or because of personal taste, eagerly embraced the local way of life.

Shih Hsieh's spirit later occupied an honored place in the pantheon of Vietnamese national heroes. His success lay not so much in anything he did, but rather in what he did not do. He did not go against the grain of

103. *SKC*, 53, 10b–11a; *TT*, 4, 3b.

indigenous sensibilities. He did not enforce alien concepts of government or squeeze the economy into his pockets. He allowed the local way of life to prosper.

Buddhism

One aspect of Vietnamese culture that prospered during Shih Hsieh's rule was Buddhism. As we have seen, it is recorded that Shih Hsieh's retinue included many Hu people. *Hu* was a name applied by the Chinese to different foreign peoples, including those from India and Central Asia. There were, in fact, a large number of Indians and Central Asians in Chiao Province for reasons of commerce and religion. At this time, the Kushana Empire of northern India was stimulating trade and the spread of Buddhism to all parts of Asia. Chiao Province was very receptive to these contacts with the West.[104]

One Hu person in Chiao was K'ang Seng Hui, literally "Sogdian Buddhist Priest Hui," whose biography was recorded by the Chinese.[105] Seng Hui's family was originally from Sogdiana in Central Asia, but for several generations it had been established in India; his father settled in Giao-chi as a merchant and died there. After his father's death, Seng Hui was ordained as a Buddhist monk at the age of ten. He studied the classical learning of both Buddhism and Confucianism and translated many Buddhist scriptures from Sanscrit into Chinese. Later in his career he traveled north, founding numerous stupas and temples. In 247, he converted Sun Ch'üan to Buddhism, thereby introducing the new religion to the Wu court. He died in 280. His biography says that he was "the first Buddhist monk seen in the land of Wu."

Giao-chi was at this time a center for the diffusion of Buddhism into China. An Indo-Scythian named Kalyāṇaruci translated Buddhist scriptures in Giao-chi in the third century. About this same time, an Indian named Jīvaka sailed to Fu-nan and then walked up the coast performing miracles and stirring interest in the Buddha as he went; he reached Lo-yang near the end of the century.[106] These men, commented on in Chinese records, were only the most noteworthy of many such religious men of Indian or Central Asian origin, scores of whom found a place in Shih Hsieh's entourage.

At the same time that holy men were arriving from the south, men with similar interests were coming from the north. The preface of the *Mou tzu*, a Buddhist treatise, describes conditions in Vietnam during Shih Hsieh's

104. Tran Van Giap, "Le Bouddhisme en Annam des origins au XIII siècle," p. 206.
105. For a translation of Seng Hui's biography, see Edouard Chavannes, "Seng Houe," pp. 199–211.
106 Tran Van Giap, "Bouddhisme," pp. 211–14.

rule.[107] This preface tells of Mou Po, who seems to have been born between 165 and 170 in Ts'ang-wu; he dwelt in Giao-chi in his youth, returning to Ts'ang-wu around 195.[108] The classical education of his youth gave way to Taoism, and he was finally converted to Buddhism.[109] The preface contains precious information on the cultural atmosphere of that time:

> At that time, after the death of Emperor Ling [189], the empire was in disorder; only Chiao Province was relatively calm, and unusual men from the north came to live there. Many occupied themselves with the worship of gods and spirits, abstinence from cereals, and immortality. Many people of that time devoted themselves to these studies. Mou Po unceasingly proposed objections based on the five classics; none of the Taoists and spiritualists dared argue with him.[110]

Vietnamese Buddhism took root in the midst of this religious and intellectual experimentation.

The introduction of Buddhism to Vietnam is associated with the founding of four temples in the environs of Luy-lau during the rule of Shih Hsieh. These were temples dedicated to the Buddha of Clouds (Phap-van), the Buddha of Rain (Phap-vu), the Buddha of Thunder (Phap-loi), and the Buddha of Lightning (Phap-dien). The tradition about the origin of these temples[111] is as follows.

In the time of Shih Hsieh, a holy man named Tu Dinh from Fu-nan, on the lower Mekong, established himself in a village near Luy-lau, where he practiced asceticism; he was a simple man who violated all the norms of propriety. He took the name Man, meaning "barbarian," and had a daughter named Man Nuong, "barbarian lady."

Toward the end of the reign of Emperor Ling (168–89), a man of the Brahman caste from western India named Khau-da-la (Kṣūdra) arrived

---

107. K. Ch'en, *Buddhism in China*, p. 37

108. Paul Pelliot, "Meou-tseu ou les doutes leves," pp. 257, 288, 329–30, nn. 9–10.

109. Tran Van Giap, "Bouddhisme," pp. 214–15.

110. *MoT*, l; Pelliot, "Meou-tseu," p. 287.

111. Vietnamese texts state that Khau-da-la arrived in Giao-chi with Jīvaka toward the end of the reign of Emperor Ling. Chinese texts date Jīvaka's arrival at Lo-yang in 294, after which he returned to India. Either there were two different men named Jīvaka or else Jīvaka lived to a very old age (Tran Van Giap, "Bouddhisme," pp. 219–20). My narrative of this tradition is drawn from four Vietnamese sources. Two of them, cited by Tran Van Giap "Bouddhisme," pp. 217–19, are about the history of the four temples Phap-van, Phap-vu, Phap-loi, and Phap-dien and date from before 1313. The third is the biography of Man Nuong found in *LNCQ*, 25–26. The fourth is a work cited by Claude Madrolle, *Le Tonkin ancien*, pp. 293–95, who unfortunately provided no information on its date; it is apparently a work of Buddhist hagiography. According to another tradition referred to by Gustave Dumoutier, "Choix de legendes historique de l'Annam et du Tonkin," pp. 176–78, Man Nuong was regarded as the "Mother of Buddha," and the day of her death was celebrated as the day of Buddha's birth.

from the south, performing miracles and preaching the Buddhist way. Tu Dinh worshipped him as a living Buddha and constrained him to tarry as his guest. Tu Dinh's daughter, Man Nuong, became a disciple of Khau-da-la and learned from him the wisdom of the Buddha as well as the art of making rain. Eventually, her reputation reached the ears of Shih Hsieh after she ended a drought with her spiritual powers.

On one occasion a typhoon uprooted a gigantic banyan tree and deposited it at the front gate of Shih Hsieh's palace. The efforts of three hundred men were to no avail in moving the tree out of the way. When Man Nuong easily lifted the tree, it was recognized as a sacred object. Four statues were carved from it, representing the Buddhas of clouds, rain, thunder, and lightning; temples were then built for each of the statues. Shih Hsieh further dedicated Man Nuong's retreat as the Phuc-nhan Temple, "Temple of the Blessed Grotto."

From this tradition, it appears that Buddhism spread among the people, at least in part, as a new method of controlling the vagaries of nature in the interests of agriculture. By dedicating temples to manifestations of the monsoon season and identifying them with incarnations of the Buddha, the Vietnamese were reinforcing old values with the authority of new ideas. The tradition associated with Man Nuong is further evidence of the important role played by women in ancient Vietnamese culture and society.

The legend of Nhat Da Trach contains Buddhist elements that led one nineteenth-century Vietnamese scholar to write of "Buddhist priests from India in the time of the Hung kings." [112] Whatever the earlier version of this legend may have been, it appears to have received its final form during the time of Shih Hsieh, for the Buddhist details reflect conditions at that time. According to the legend, [113] Tien Dung, the Hung princess, and Chu Dong Tu, her consort, presided over a market thronged with foreign merchants. Apprised of the opportunities for profit, Dong Tu took gold and accompanied a merchant on a voyage into the sea. They stopped to rest at a certain mountain on the coast; while the merchant gathered a supply of fresh water, Dong Tu climbed to the top of the mountain. There he found a hut inhabited by a Buddhist priest from India named Phat Quang, "Brilliant Buddha." Dong Tu decided to remain with the priest; he gave his gold to the merchant, instructing him to buy merchandise for him and to stop for him on his return journey.

On the top of the mountain, Phat Quang taught Dong Tu the wisdom of the Buddha and gave him a staff and a straw hat, symbolic of a royal scepter and crown. When Dong Tu eventually returned to Tien Dung, he told her what he had learned; they subsequently abandoned the merchant's

112. Tran Van Giap, "Bouddhisme," p. 216, n. l.
113. *LNCQ*, 11–13.

life and traveled from place to place searching for masters of the Buddhist way. On one occasion they were late in returning home and spent the night beside the road in the shelter of the staff and straw hat. When they awoke the next morning, the staff and straw hat had been transformed into a magnificent palace full of treasure.

This connection between seaborne merchants and the arrival of Buddhism describes a situation documented in the time of Shih Hsieh. Of particular interest, however, is the notion of Buddhist kingship exemplified by the miraculous appearance of the palace from the symbolic staff and straw hat, as if devotion to the Buddha were associated with commercial wealth and royal authority. There was a strong Buddhist flavor to the culture of Shih Hsieh's realm; he patronized Buddhist priests, thereby legitimizing his rule in the eyes of all who trusted the new religion. The founding of Buddhist temples for guardian deities of agricultural fertility reveals that Buddhism had significantly penetrated the peasantry. Thus, in the eyes of the people, Shih Hsieh's authority was reinforced by his posture as a Buddhist ruler.[114]

This was a period of cultural realignment in Vietnam. Buddhism, Confucianism, and Taoism all flourished in varying degrees. Buddhism in particular captured the imagination of the common people by attaching itself to the indigenous spirit cults associated with the worship of trees and aquatic powers.[115] Ruling-class people were predominantly Confucianist by virtue of their education. Taoism lay between Buddhism and Confucianism. Many public Confucianists were private Taoists, and many Taoists found Buddhism but a short step away.

Near the end of the Han dynasty, Taoism acquired a tendency toward politicization and was often subversive of the established order; this tendency remained alive in central China for several centuries.[116] Taoist traditions in the south, however, centered on the search for immortality rather than on politics; drugs used by Taoists in preparing their elixir of life were readily available in the south, and many southern mountain peaks were famous as sites where Taoist immortals had soared into the clouds. Local spirit beliefs greatly modified the influence of both Taoism and Buddhism.[117]

In spite of Vietnam's political attachment to the Chinese empire, important cultural currents continued to be felt from the south seas. As late as T'ang times, the primary Buddhist influence was by sea from southeast India rather than overland from north India; Buddhist images from the

114. Ozaki, p. 157.

115. Dumoutier, "Choix," pp. 176–78.

116. Anna K. Seidel, "The Image of the Perfect Ruler in Early Taoist Messianism," pp. 215–47.

117. Schafer, *Vermilion Bird*, pp. 87–114.

T'ang period excavated in Kuang-hsi display resemblances to the Javanese style of Borobudur and are very different from the Gandharan-style images found in northwest China.[118] The great era of prosperity in Giao-chi under Shih Hsieh was contemporaneous with the first flowering of Indian civilization in Southeast Asia and is most intelligible as a beneficiary of that development.

118. Ibid., p. 91.

3
Regionalism and the Six Dynasties

The Han-Viet Legacy

By the turn of the third century, a regional ruling class had emerged in Vietnam based on the great Han-Viet families. According to a Vietnamese source, the ancestors of Ly Bi, a sixth-century independence leader, came to Vietnam from China during the Wang Mang era and, after seven generations, "became southerners." Since Shih Hsieh was in the sixth generation from his ancestors who migrated during the Wang Mang era, we can assume that it was during his lifetime that the Ly became conscious of their identity as Vietnamese.[1]

The experience of the Ly family was probably not unique, but rather was part of a broad reorientation of the regional ruling class away from dependence on northern dynasties and toward a more self-reliant acceptance of local society and culture. The fall of Han and the division of China surely encouraged Han-Viet families to strengthen their ties with the local society and to identify their interests more completely with a regional concept of political power. This is what seems to have happened under the guidance of Shih Hsieh. An important part of this transformation of outlook among regional ruling-class families was the spread of Buddhism as an alternative to Han civilization.

By the late fifth century, a score of Buddhist edifices had been erected at Luy-lau, and the local monkhood numbered over five hundred.[2] Although this is the only direct information on Vietnamese Buddhism between the time of Shih Hsieh and the sixth century, we can assume that monastic life was developing steadily during this time. The monks were undoubtedly members of local ruling-class families. Monasteries and temples would have been not only centers of learning and culture, but also places of economic and political importance. Chinese dynasties periodically sought to supervise the monasteries, but their efforts were few and relatively brief.[3] Some monks probably retained an interest in political affairs, and the contacts of Vietnamese monks with Buddhist institutions in the north must

---

1. Gotō Kimpei, *Betonamu Kyūgoku Kōsō Shi*, p. 115. See Appendix G.
2. Tran Van Giap, "Le Bouddhisme en Annam des origins au XIII siècle," pp. 208–11.
3. Ibid., p. 210.

have been an important source of information for local leaders in their attempts to challenge imperial authority.

During the three centuries following Shih Hsieh's death in 226, ruling-class families in Vietnam repeatedly resisted the authority of Chinese dynasties. The events of this time reveal a stable regional ruling class that was capable of handling its own affairs; the authority of Chinese dynasties was a destabilizing intrusion that invited Lin-i aggression across the southern frontier and provoked open resistance from the Vietnamese. The times of peace and prosperity in Vietnam were times of dynastic weakness or transition in China. The times when new Chinese dynasties attempted to rule Vietnam were times of violence and war.

The people who emerged as Vietnamese leaders during this time were of mixed ancestry and, to varying degrees, saw themselves as members of a larger imperial world, but it is misleading to call them "Sino-Vietnamese": most of their families had already been in Vietnam for several generations; they undoubtedly spoke Vietnamese; and their political outlook was based on the regional interests of Vietnamese society.

When we speak of provincial administration in Vietnam during this time, whether it be in times of relatively strong dynastic control or of autonomy and effective independence, we are speaking of a system of rule by powerful landowning families. Administrative records from this period (table 3) show that the registered population in Vietnam was down to little more than twenty-five thousand households in the fourth century and that this had dropped to around ten thousand households by the fifth century. This means that tax-paying farmers were losing their land to great estates and disappearing from the tax rolls.

As we will see, prominent families in Vietnam staffed local government and, in times of dynastic weakness, elected their own regional leadership. Harsh or inept dynastic rule often polarized this regional leadership, with some families resisting northern officials and others welcoming them.

The regional ruling class that appeared during the Han-Viet era passed through many transformations under the six so-called southern dynasties that ruled at Nanking from the third to the sixth centuries. These transformations appear to be repetitious at first glance, but they provide many clues for understanding the evolution of Vietnamese society toward autonomy and independence.

Wu

In 210, when Sun Ch'üan sent Pu Chih south to receive the homage of the Shih family, the nominal capital of Chiao Province was moved from Ts'ang-wu to Nan-hai (Canton). Chih resided at Nan-hai and, after the founding of the Wu dynasty in 221, led an army of ten thousand from Chiao to resist Liu Pei, founder of the Shu Han dynasty in Ssu-ch'uan, who was marching down the Yangtze. After defeating Pei, Chih remained in Hu-nan to track down bandits and pacify the population. Lü Tai was sent to replace Chih in Nan-hai.[4]

It is recorded that Lü Tai was an honest man with a deep concern for public affairs, and that wherever he went his reputation endured.[5] His career nonetheless revealed a smallness of spirit that surfaced when he set out to destroy the Shih family.

Shih Hsieh died at the age of ninety in 226. The Wu court immediately named his son Shih Hui Remote Tranquillity General, a title Han had given to Hsieh. Then, in an attempt to curb the power of the Shih family, Hui was appointed prefect of Cuu-chan, while a certain Ch'en Shih was sent from Nanking to be prefect of Giao-chi. Lü Tai recommended that, in view of the distance between Nan-hai and Giao-chi, Chiao Province should be divided, with the four northern prefectures being detached to form Kuang Province. This was done; Tai was appointed governor of Kuang, and one Tai Liang was appointed governor of Giao (Chinese Chiao), which comprised the prefectures in modern Vietnam. Ch'en Shih and Tai Liang proceeded to Giao-chi, but when they arrived at the border, they found it closed against them and were forced to wait in Ho-p'u.[6]

Shih Hui had decided that the time had come to rid his family of Wu suzerainty. The Han Empire had been partitioned into three kingdoms; there was no reason to believe that a fourth kingdom might not succeed, particularly in the case of the Shih family, which was popular among the people, prosperous, talented, and geographically remote.

However, Shih Hui faced stiff local resistance to a scheme sure to invite invasion and the misery of war. Hoan Lan, who had been a prominent official under Hsieh, admonished Hui to renounce his ambitions and to welcome Tai Liang and accept his authority. Hui angrily ordered that Lan be flogged to death. Hui's cruel reaction suggests that Lan's point of view was shared by others and that Hui wished to make an example of him. Lan's son and his elder brother, Hoan Tri, responded by raising their family warriors and attacking Hui. Hui shut the gates of the city and defended himself within its walls. Hoan Tri attacked for several months, but was unable to take the city; finally, he made peace with Hui and withdrew his soldiers.[7] The Hoan family seems to have represented local interests, people who saw only danger in supporting the ambitions of the Shih family. This suggests that

4. *CL*, 89.

5. Ibid., 90.

6. *SKC*, 49, 11b; *TT*, 4, 1a; *CL*, 89; *VSL*, 1, 5a; Achilles Fang, trans. and annotator, *Chronicle of the Three Kingdoms*, pp. 205–6.

7. *SKC*, 49, 11b; *TT*, 4, 1a–b; Fang, pp. 206, 220; Gotō, pp. 173–74.

powerful local families were committed to a concept of regional stability larger than the ambitions of any one man or family. These families were apparently confident of their ability to cope with Wu officials.

Though reduced to defending the walls of their capital, the Shih were able to outwait their besiegers. This suggests that some of the local families, with their private armies, may have favored the Shih experiment in independence. The test of wills between the Shih and Hoan families was a standoff and was soon transcended by the arrival of Wu soldiers.

Lü Tai, having gained permission to launch a punitive expedition against Shih Hui, sailed from Nan-hai with three thousand soldiers and joined Ch'en Shih and Tai Liang in Ho-p'u. One of his advisors cautioned: "Hui can depend on the good will his family has earned for generations; the whole province obeys him. It will not be easy to trifle with him." Lü Tai replied:

> Hui does not anticipate my coming. If I keep my troops concealed, move lightly, and take him by surprise, I am certain to defeat him. Should I tarry and move slowly, putting him on the alert to defend himself solidly within walled cities, then the hundred barbarian tribes of the seven prefectures will echo and respond to him, and not even the wisest man will then be able to cope with him.[8]

Tai realized that the only way to defeat Hui was to take him by surprise. In order to do this, he procured the cooperation of Shih family members willing to accept Wu sovereignty, for the Shih family, imbued through education with the ideal of imperial authority, was not of one mind in challenging Wu.

A son of Shih I named K'uang happened to be in Ho-p'u. He and Tai were old friends from their student days; Tai made him his assistant and sent him to Hui, a cousin, with a guarantee of personal safety if Hui submitted peacefully. Hui was greatly shaken upon hearing of Tai's unexpected approach. Unprepared to resist and trusting the sincerity of Tai's assurance, Hui led his brothers and sons, six men in all, to meet him, with their shoulders bared in submission. Tai pardoned them, told them to cover their shoulders, and sent them to a suburb of Luy-lau. But the next morning a tent was set up, and Tai summoned the six men to appear. Before an audience of officials, Tai read an accusation of treason against them; they were forthwith beheaded.[9]

Although the arrival of the six heads at the Wu court contributed to Tai's reputation there, this act of bad faith provoked bitter resistance in Giao-chi. Hoan Tri joined one of Hui's generals named Cam Le in leading

8. *TCTC*, 70, vol. 3, 2231 (Shanghai, 1956).
9. *SKC*, 49, 11b–12b; *TT*, 4, 1b–2a; *CL*, 89; Fang, p. 207.

the local officials and people against Tai, for Tai appeared to them to be a harsh and treacherous man. Tai was a relentless foe, however, and with energetic attacks he dispersed his opponents. After pacifying Giao-chi, he moved against Cuu-chan, where he killed or captured ten thousand persons. Surviving members of the Shih family were subsequently executed.[10]

Lü Tai remained in Giao-chi for five years. Under his regime, Kuang and Giao were combined into Chiao Province as before. One of his first acts was to send messengers beyond the frontier to announce the power of Wu to neighboring foreign kingdoms; in response, the kings of Lin-i, Fu-nan (in the lower Mekong), and T'ang-ming (north of modern Cambodia) sent envoys bearing gifts.[11] An important motive in Tai's conquest of Giao-chi was a desire to control the international markets established there. For example, in 226, a Roman envoy arrived in Giao-chi and was hastened to the Wu court.[12] The commercial profits that had formerly accrued to the Shih family now went directly into Wu coffers. In 229, Wu sent envoys to Fu-nan, where merchants from India and beyond gathered. Wu cultivated relations in the southern seas to compensate for its isolation from the overland route through Central Asia.[13]

In 231, Lü Tai was summoned to deal with a rebellion elsewhere in the Wu kingdom. His narrow pursuit of Wu's interests had alienated the Vietnamese and had set the stage for a major rebellion. He had never succeeded in stabilizing a border with the rising kingdom of Lin-i in the old prefecture of Nhat-nam. And although he had temporarily conquered Cuu-chan, Wu rule was not established there; soon after his departure, Wu sent a general named Chu Chih to "exterminate and pacify the barbarous Yüeh" in Cuu-chan.[14]

Since the turmoil of the Ch'ü-lien uprising a century earlier, Cuu-chan had been in a nearly constant state of ferment.[15] This was related to the growing power of Lin-i. Having originated in the old frontier district of Tuong-lam, Lin-i was extending its influence northward. In 248, Lin-i invaded what remained of Nhat-nam, annexing most of it and fighting a battle with the Chinese near the Cuu-chan border.[16]

10. *SKC*, 60, 9a; *TT*, 4, 2a–b; Fang, p. 207.

11. *SKC*, 60, 9a.

12. Edouard Chavannes, "Seng Houe," p. 202, n. 2.

13. Sugimoto Naojirō, *Tōnan Ajiashi Kenkyū*, pp. 417–526; Rafe de Crespigny, "Prefectures and Population in South China in the First Three Centuries A.D.," pp. 150–51.

14. *CL*, 88, dates this in 202, which is impossible because Sun Ch'üan, who sent Chu Chih, was not active in the south until 210 and would not have made appointments in Cuu-chan until after Lü Tai's suppression of the Shih family in 226. Since Hsüeh Tsung does not mention this incident, it must have occurred after 231, when Lü Tai departed the area.

15. Nguyen Dinh Thuc, "Cuoc khoi nghia Ba Trieu," pp. 153–54.

16. *SCC*, 36, 18a, 22b.

The people of Cuu-chan seized the opportunity to rebel, and Giao-chi followed suit; several walled towns fell. Wu sent Lu Yin to deal with the situation. Yin used a combination of threats and persuasion to calm the insurrection. By a proclamation of good faith and the distribution of gifts, Yin won over three thousand families who had followed the rebel leader Hoang Ngo; then he moved his troops further south and with the same tactics gained the surrender of a hundred rebel leaders and over fifty thousand families.[17]

A hard core of resistance nevertheless remained in Cuu-chan's Cu-phong District, where Chu Dat had initiated the uprising of 157. Here a young woman remembered as Lady Trieu rallied the rebels and led them in a fresh march northward. After several months of warfare, Lady Trieu was defeated and killed.[18]

Chinese records do not mention Lady Trieu; our knowledge of her comes only from Vietnamese sources. From this it is evident that the events of 248 were remembered differently by the two sides. The Chinese only recorded their success in buying off certain rebel leaders with bribes and promises. The resistance led by Lady Trieu was for them simply a kind of stubborn barbarism that was wiped out as a matter of course and was of no historical interest. On the other hand, the Vietnamese remembered Lady Trieu's uprising as the most important event of the time. Her leadership appealed to strong popular instincts. The traditional image of her as a remarkable yet human leader, throwing her yard-long breasts over her shoulders when going into battle astride an elephant, has been handed down from generation to generation. After Lady Trieu's death, her spirit was worshipped by the Vietnamese. We owe our knowledge of her to the fact that she was remembered by the people.

The events of 248 show the multilayered perspectives of the regional ruling class at that time. Wu oppression made the entire class ripe for rebellion, and Lin-i aggression provided an opportunity. Wu was chased out. There was a host of rebel leaders, but the name of only one was

17. *SKC*, 61, 13a–b. His name is recorded as Lu I in *CL*, 90, and as Lu Yun in *VSL*, 1, 5b.

18. *TT*, 4, 4a, cites a *Giao-chi ky* as its source for Lady Trieu; this could conceivably be the *Giao-chi ky* cited by Do Thien's *Su ky* in the *VDULT* (Émile Gaspardone, "Bibliographie annamite," pp. 127 and 55, n. 2). Lady Trieu's posthumous cult flourished, and many details of doubtful authenticity can be found in temple documents, including the exploits of her brother and her personal name; these details are summarized by Tran Trong Kim, *Viet Nam su luoc*, 1: 44–47, and by Uy Ban Khoa Hoc Xa Hoi Viet Nam, *Lich su Viet Nam*, pp. 109–10. Nguyen Dinh Thuc, p. 50, pointed out that the traditional designation, Trieu Au, in fact means "Lady Trieu," for *Au* was a respectful term of address for women. The only surviving source besides the *TT* to mention Lady Trieu is *CL*, 148, where she is listed under the heading "Rebels" along with Trung Trac, Ly Bi, and Duong Thanh. The *CL* account is identical with the citation in the *TT*, and I believe it is based on Vietnamese documentation familiar to Le Tac.

recorded: Hoang Ngo, with a following of over three thousand families. Hoang Ngo was the first of the rebel leaders to respond to Wu persuasion; his base of power was apparently furthest north, and he was probably most susceptible to imperial appeals. Further south were a hundred leaders followed by over fifty thousand families.

This disunity was an effect of Wu's harsh regime. The suppression of the Shih family in 226 had provoked resistance by the old Han-Viet leadership and the general population; ten thousand were killed or captured. The brutal Wu regime undoubtedly fragmented the supralocal Han-Viet leadership. Thus, in 248, there was no single rebellion united under a common leader, but rather a multitude of local leaders who could be individually bribed and intimidated.

After the Han-Viet class had been neutralized, popular indigenous leaders carried on the struggle. Lady Trieu was the last woman to lead a rebellion in Vietnamese history. Her defeat may well have ended a late blossoming of political ideals inherited from the Lac lords, a blossoming stimulated by the relaxed atmosphere of Shih Hsieh's rule.

The Wu regime traumatized the regional ruling class that had developed during Han and prospered under Shih Hsieh. Twice this class had risen against Wu with the support of the local population. But, whereas the uprising of 226 was put down by force, the Han-Viet leadership of 248 was won over to Wu by bribes and threats; only the most intransigent rebels, under indigenous leadership decidedly not Han-Viet, held strubbornly for battlefield martyrdom.

In the generation separating the two rebellions, new people more congenial to Wu had arrived among the Vietnamese and were making their influence felt. We can assume that they were part of the post-Han immigration of upper-class refugees from the disorders in northern China. The old Han-Viet class and the new protégés of Wu seem to have been irreconcilable. In the 260s, the ruling class in Vietnam broke apart in a civil war. This civil war was related to events in China that brought the era of the Three Kingdoms to an end.

Chin Intervention

The Wu court in Nanking was an extravagant affair. The luxury goods of the south and the skills of fine craftsmen were in great demand. In the Yung-an period (258–63), the prefect of Giao-chi, Sun Hsü, drafted over a thousand master craftsmen and sent them to Nanking. Unfortunately, we do not know what kind of craftsmen these were. Hsü was reportedly hated by the people for deeds such as this, as well as for his greed and cruelty. In 263, the Wu court sent an official named Teng Hsün to Giao-chi, apparently to investigate the unrest provoked by Hsü. As soon as he arrived, however, Hsün levied thirty peacocks to be sent to Nanking; this aroused new fear that more people would be conscripted for service in distant places.[19] The situation might have gone no further had it not been for events in Ssu-ch'uan that offered hope of expelling Wu.

In 263, Wei conquered the Shu Han dynasty in Ssu-ch'uan, thereby threatening Wu from the west. Anti-Wu leaders in Vietnam hoped to take advantage of this situation. Lu Hung, a prefectural official in Giao-chi, gained the support of the local soldiers and people; he killed both Sun Hsü and Teng Hsün, then sent envoys to Wei requesting a prefect and military assistance. Cuu-chan and Nhat-nam joined Giao-chi in going over to Wei.[20]

In 264, the Wei court appointed Lu Hung commander-in-chief of all armed forces in Chiao Province. Huo I, a general stationed in Ssu-ch'uan, was named governor of Chiao, with authority to appoint all subordinate officials. One year later, a powerful family in control of the Wei court founded its own dynasty of Chin. Intervention in Giao-chi consequently got off to a slow start in the midst of this dynastic change, peaceful though it was.

Huo I supervised the operation from Ssu-ch'uan. The first two men he named to be prefect of Giao-chi died of illness before they were able to assume their duties. Furthermore, Lu Hung was killed by one of his subordinates before Chin arrived on the scene.[21]

During this time, Wu was occupied with more direct threats to its borders in the north and west; the only action it took in the south was to divide Chiao Province as had been done for a short time in 226, establishing Kuang Province in the north, where its authority remained intact.[22]

The situation in Giao-chi during this time is obscure. Whether Lu Hung's assassin was a Wu partisan is not known, but some local officials undoubtedly remained loyal to Wu, and political life was probably tentative until the arrival of Chin soldiers. Finally the Chin prefect, Yang Chi, and seven military commanders with their men arrived, having traveled over six hundred miles through mountainous terrain. Before leaving Ssu-ch'uan they swore an oath to Huo I that if in the end they should be trapped and besieged they would resist for one hundred days before surrendering or face execution upon their return; if no help arrived within one hundred days, Huo I would assume responsibility for their defeat.[23] Considering the

19. SKC, 48, 12a; CL, 90; VSL, 1, 5b; Fang, pp. 402, 419–20.

20. SKC, 48, 12a–b; TT, 4, 4a; CL, 90; VSL, 1, 5b; Fang, pp. 402, 419–20.

21. CS, 57, 4b; SKC, 48, 14a–b; TT, 4, 4b; CL, 91; Fang, p. 466. Wei named Lu Hung "An-nam General," which, to my knowledge, is the earliest use of the term An-nam in an official title in connection with Vietnam.

22. SKC, 48, 13a.

23. CS, 57, 5a.

nature of this oath, the expedition was more an adventurous gamble than a well-planned intervention.

In 268, Wu sent two generals, Liu Chün and Hsiu Tse, to reconquer Giao. Three times they attempted to advance into Giao-chi, and each time Yang Chi forced them back. Then, taking the offensive, Chi sent two of his commanders into Ho-p'u to attack Wu headquarters. Liu Chün and Hsiu Tse were both killed, and their army was sent fleeing in confusion. The Chin were assisted in this victory by local military units; in addition to Giao-chi, the prefectures of Cuu-chan and Yü-lin actively supported the Chin.[24]

One year later, five Wu generals gathered their men in Ho-p'u for a new offensive. However, these generals could not agree on a common plan, and their efforts were plagued with dissention. In 270, two of the generals were put to death for unilaterally withdrawing their troops in the midst of a campaign.[25]

In 271, Chin and Wu forces clashed at Fen-shui in Ho-p'u. One of the Wu generals, T'ao Huang, lost two commanders and was forced to withdraw. He was accordingly blamed by his colleagues, one of whom threatened to abandon the campaign. Huang was eager to rally the Wu cause, so he immediately took several hundred men by night and raided the encampment of Tung Yüan, one of the Chin generals, seizing Yüan's boats and valuables. This deed led to his appointment as commander-in-chief of the Wu armies.[26]

T'ao Huang was the son of a former Wu governor of Chiao. Before Chin's intervention, he had been prefect in Ts'ang-wu.[27] He was therefore familiar with affairs in the south and moved quickly to resolve the situation in favor of Wu. He caught the Chin off guard by advancing directly into Giao-chi by sea. Tung Yüan prepared an ambush and pretended to retreat. Huang, however, anticipated this tactic and routed his foe.[28] Thus gaining the initiative, Huang contacted Luong Ky, commander of the local military units collaborating with Chin. Huang gave Ky the treasure previously captured from Tung Yüan, and Ky brought more than ten thousand men over to Huang's side.[29]

24. *SKC*, 48, 17b–18a; *CS*, 57, 4b; *TT*, 4, 5a; *CL*, 90.

25. *SKC*, 48, 18a–b.

26. *CS*, 57, 4b; *TT*, 4, 5b. *CL*, 91, mixes up Huang's night attack with his later invasion of Giao-chi.

27. *SKC*, 48, 18a; *CS*, 57, 4b.

28. *TT*, 4, 5b, and *VSL*, 1, 6a, say that Tung Yüan was killed in the battle. T'ao Huang's biography in *CS*, 57, 5a, says only that Yüan suffered a great defeat. *CL*, 91–92, follows Huang's biography on this point but says that it was at this time that Huang seized Yüan's valuables and boats; the *CL* combines the earlier night attack and this battle into a single engagement.

29. *CS*, 57, 5a; *TT*, 4, 5b–6a; *CL*, 92. These sources identify Luong Ky as the "rebel commander at Phu-nghiem"; I do not know where Phu-nghiem was, but I interpret his being a

After this, the Chin no longer trusted their erstwhile allies, and Yang Chi beheaded the local commander of Long-bien on suspicion that he was preparing to defect.[30] Before long, the Chin were besieged at Long-bien. They ran out of supplies before the hundred days stipulated in their oath. Realizing that no help would come, for Huo I had already died, the Chin contingent surrendered.[31] The Chin generals were sent to Nanking; although Yang Chi died enroute, most of his colleagues were eventually sent back to Chin. One of them, Meng Kan, subsequently helped devise the strategy for conquering Wu and was later appointed prefect of Nhat-nam.[32]

The Chin adventure in Giao-chi was not a superficial episode on the surface of local politics. Those who remained unreconciled to Wu gathered in Cuu-chan under the leadership of a local official named Ly To. T'ao Huang sent an army against To; after some difficulty it eventually succeeded in besieging him. To's maternal uncle, Le Hoan, was with T'ao Huang's army and tried to persuade To to surrender. To replied: "You are a general of Wu; I am a general of Chin. There is nothing for us to do but test our strength." After an hour of fighting, the stronghold fell.[33]

To's diehard loyalty earned him the praise of a later Vietnamese historian,[34] but there may have been more to his last stand than simple loyalty. The Chin intervention was possible only with the support of local anti-Wu elements. It can be assumed that these elements were seeking to displace more entrenched interests allied with Wu. Thus, beneath the dynastic conflict between Chin and Wu may have lain a local power struggle between an emerging group aspiring to power and a more conservative group seeking to maintain its position. To's last stand appears somewhat strange if it is understood as loyalty to Chin, for the Chin generals had already surrendered; furthermore, the Chin were not in Giao-chi long enough to foster deep loyalties among local people. Instead, To's declaration of loyalty to Chin is comprehensible only in terms of a local power struggle in which anti-Wu forces claimed legitimacy as vassals of Chin.

It appears that the warfare of these years eventually alienated the population from both contenders. Wu partisans in Vietnam never did have sympathetic links to the local society. The anti-Wu side, by turning to a rival

---

"rebel commander" to mean that he was a local man who aided Chin against Wu; the large number of men under his command suggests that he was probably the commander in chief of local forces.

30. CS, 57, 5a; TT, 4, 6a; CL, 92. The Long-bien commander must have been a local leader, for his younger brother was in Huang's camp; it was by means of a letter from this younger brother that Huang planted suspicion in Yang Chi's mind.

31. CS, 57, 5a.

32. CS, 57, 5b; CL, 91.

33. CS, 57, 5b; TT, 4, 6a–b.

34. TT, 4, 6b.

Chinese dynasty for help, ended by cutting itself off from the local society as well. The significance of this is amplified by comparison with the events of 248. In 248, local anti-Wu forces rose in response to an expanding power in the south and were led by a popular heroine whose career left a mark in the memory of the people. In 263, local anti-Wu forces rose in response to an expanding power in the north and were led by officials who attached their ambitions to the rising star of Chin, a dynasty in northern China. With the ebbing of Chin, these officials were isolated, for apparently they had not gained broad popular support. What began amid popular anti-Wu senti-ment ended as an affair between rival officials.

The Ly To affair suggests that blood ties had given way to broader symbolic associations in forming political loyalties. Ly To stubbornly held out for Chin, even after the war was, in effect, over. His uncle stood up for Wu. Perhaps this final act was as much a conflict of generations as anything else. The older men, sobered by experience, wanted peace, even if it meant the return of Wu. The younger men, idealistic and reckless, could not release the object of their youthful devotion. For a decade, violence had dominated the political scene. This could not help but have an unsettling effect on impressionable youth. During these years, the regional ruling class grew preoccupied with the conflicting claims of competing Chinese dynasties and lost its footing in the indigenous society. The pro-Wu people never did have a secure footing in the local society, and the pro-Chin people lost what footing they had by bringing in foreign soldiers.

In 268, the Wu offensive was defeated with popular support. Three years later, however, Wu was successful after large-scale defections of local forces to its side. Popular resentment of Wu must have dissipated after its departure; with the passing of year after year of seemingly pointless warfare between glory-seeking generals, the bulk of the population was ready to accept a leader who stood above the crowd and offered prospects of peace. T'ao Huang was such a man.

T'ao Huang

T'ao Huang was more than a talented strategist; he became genuinely popular among the Vietnamese. It is recorded that he relieved the distress of those in need and won the hearts of the people. When he was called away to new duties by the Wu court, more than a thousand local leaders requested that he return, and Wu prudently sent him back.[35]

In 280, when Chin finally conquered Wu and the defeated Wu monarch sent a letter ordering Huang to submit to Chin, it is recorded that

35. *CS*, 57, 5a–b; *TT*, 4, 6b. *CL*, 92, erroneously says thirty persons requested that he remain.

Huang wept for several days before sending his seal of office to the Chin court. Chin was too distant to be concerned with the south and confirmed Huang in his position, giving him new titles in recognition of his merit.[36] Huang was in Giao for many years, and when he died it is recorded that the people mourned for him as if for a parent.[37]

What was left of the regional ruling class after the events of 226, 248, and the Chin intervention apparently united in favor of T'ao Huang. Like Shih Hsieh, Huang ruled at a time when no Chinese dynasty was strong enough to control the south. He cultivated a regional power base while maintaining correct relations with the imperial world. After the rebellions and wars of the preceding half century, Huang initiated a policy of reconstruction that strengthened the indigenous society, placing it on a firm administrative basis without threatening its local character.

T'ao Huang rebuilt Long-bien several miles west of its old location; for the next three centuries, this city remained the capital of Giao Province.[38] Huang's most urgent problem was to secure the frontiers. To this end he established three new prefectures in marginal jurisdictions. The district of Me-linh, with adjacent mountainous regions, became the prefecture of Tan-hung, changed to Tan-xuong after the fall of Wu. The northern edge of the Hong River plain and the highlands beyond became Vu-binh Prefecture. The southern half of Cuu-chan in the Ca River plain became Cuu-duc Prefecture. Huang pacified the peoples "who hindered civilization" in these areas and established thirty new districts in the new prefectures and in Cuu-chan.[39] The extreme south, however, was a persistent source of trouble.

T'ao Huang was initially unsuccessful in entering Nhat-nam by force. He thereupon turned to other means: "If we cut off the salt and iron trade with the southern coast and cause the ruination of their markets, then after two years they can be crushed in a single battle."[40] This policy was successful. But as miscellaneous "rebels" were cleared away, Huang came face to face with the king of Lin-i, a man known to the Chinese as Fan Hsiung.

Fan Hsiung was in league with someone identified as the king of Fu-nan, and together they pursued a policy of incessant raids across the frontier. In 280, in his first report to the Chin throne, Huang stated that out of more

---

36. CS, 57, 5b–6a; TT, 4, 6b–7a; CL, 92; VSL, 1, 6a.

37. CS, 57, 6b; TT, 4, 7a.

38. H. Maspero, "Le Protectoral general d'Annam sous les T'ang," p. 569.

39. CS, 57, 5b; TT, 4, 6b; CL, 92.

40. CS, 67, 5a. I assume that in this passage the "southern coast" and the "rebels in the south" refer to Nhat-nam, or what was left of it after the rise of Lin-i. Elsewhere T'ao Huang's biography speaks of pacifying rebels to establish Cuu-duc in what was southern Cuu-chan; in a third instance it discusses the troubles with Lin-i on the frontier.

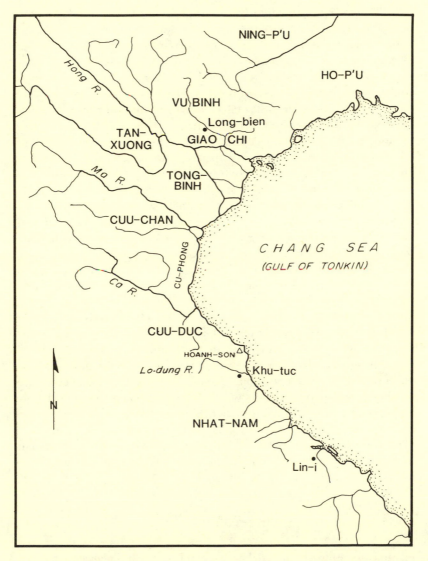

Map 4. Giao Province

than seven thousand men he originally had on the frontier, only two thousand four hundred and two remained alive; the rest had succumbed to disease or had died in battle. Chin responded by sending Meng Kan, one of the generals who had surrendered to Huang in 271, to be prefect of Nhat-nam.[41]

There is no further information on relations with Lin-i during this period. T'ao Huang's campaigns, however, indicate that there was no fixed border and that this was a time of chronic warfare. During the confusions of the Chin intervention, a number of local power centers had risen in Nhat-nam, perhaps loosely associated with Lin-i. Huang's strategy for over-coming the resistance of these areas reveals the importance of commerce in the fortunes of these small coastal powers. By simply imposing a trade embargo, Huang succeeded in bringing them to their knees. This means that the leaders of these areas were dependent on market-produced wealth and its distribution to keep the loyalty of their followers. Lin-i was clearly in a different category from these petty frontier chiefs, for Chin felt constrained to send one of its best generals to stabilize the border with Lin-i.

It appears that local upper-class families were reformed under the leadership of Huang into a more effective ruling class with a greater aware-ness of the importance of established frontiers and a greater skill in defending them. This implies that regional leaders, isolated from the centers of dynastic politics in northern China, learned to rely increasingly on themselves and developed a self-confidence that allowed them to take regional affairs into their own hands.

T'ao Huang's rule was formative in the administrative history of Vietnam. The ancient prefectures of Giao-chi and Cuu-chan were for the first time subdivided to distinguish the agricultural regions from the less secure frontier lands. After the exploitation of the Wu regime and the violence of the Chin intervention, T'ao Huang initiated an era of peace and stability. The Wu had passed away, and the Chin had not yet arrived. Sur-viving families of the old Wu aristocracy transferred their allegiance to Chin and enjoyed a generation of relative independence in the south, far from the Chin court in northern China. The cultivation of regional government under T'ao Huang was continued by his successors and inspired resistance to the Chin when they eventually appeared in the south.

Chin Comes South

Chin Wu Ti, founder of the Chin dynasty, labored manfully to restore the imperial heritage of Han. He momentarily reunited

---

41. Exerpts from Huang's report, as recorded in CS, 57, 6a, are quoted in the TT under the year 353 (4, 8b); the TT changes the first figure from "more than seven thousand" to "eight thousand." On Meng Kan, see CS, 57, 5b, and CL, 91.

China, but, after his death in 290, his realm was divided by warring princes. China subsequently became easy prey for marauding nomadic peoples of the northern frontier. In the second decade of the fourth century, these peoples conquered northern China. Vast throngs of Chinese refugees fled south, and the Chin dynasty reestablished itself at Nanking. This brought the center of Chinese imperial power closer to Vietnam and forced a realignment of the regional ruling class closer to northern interests. This realignment was accompanied by many years of intrigue and violence.

Until the fall of northern China, the south continued on the political momentum of defunct Wu and was hardly touched by the distant Chin court. When T'ao Huang died, Chin appointed Wu Yen, another old Wu official, to replace him. Wu Yen arrived in Giao to find soldiers of the Cuu-chan garrison in open rebellion. They had mutinied and chased out the prefect. Nothing is known of their leader except his name, Trieu Chi, and that Yen quickly captured and beheaded him.[42]

Trieu Chi's uprising shows an affinity with many uprisings of the preceding two centuries that sprouted in Cuu-chan and drew inspiration from the adjacent frontier. Trieu Chi was certainly an official of some kind, for he led a mutiny of regular soldiers. He may well have been the last echo of the old anti-Wu faction of the Chin intervention that went to defeat in Cuu-chan with Ly To's last stand. Although T'ao Huang's death may have been sincerely mourned by the less adventurous populace of the Hong River plain, embittered leaders in Cuu-chan may have taken it as an opportunity to reclaim a lost cause. Chin was distant and feeble. The only obstacle between these people and power was the great old Wu families who still dominated the south.

Unfortunately for Trieu Chi, Wu Yen was a man of considerable ability. After crushing Trieu Chi's rebellion, Yen governed for many years. It is recorded that he displayed both mercy and majesty and that the province was peaceful during his rule. The "mercy and majesty" formula indicates that he was stern without being cruel.

When Wu Yen eventually requested a replacement, the court appointed Ku Pi, the son of an old Wu general.[43] The Chin court in northern

---

42. *CS*, 57, 6b–7b; *CL*, 92; *TT*, 4, 7a.

43. *CS*, 57, 6a; *TT*, 4, 7a; *CL*, 92. T'ao Huang's biography (*CS*, 57, 6b) says he was "in the south for thirty years." Before being sent to retake Giao Province from Chin in 269, T'ao Huang had been prefect in Ts'ang-wu; his thirty years "in the south" probably include that assignment. Wu Yen's biography (*CS*, 57, 7b) says he was "on duty for more than twenty years" in the south. It is unclear whether or not this refers only to his time in Giao Province. T'ao K'an's biography (*CS*, 66, 7a) says that at the beginning of the T'ai-hsing period (318–21) he was named "P'ing Nan General" and shortly thereafter was given authority over military matters in Giao Province. From the time of Ku Pi's appointment until T'ao K'an was given military authority over Giao Province, aside from Pi and his two sons, three members of T'ao Huang's family held the office of governor of Giao Province; we know that the first of them governed for three years (*CS*, 57, 6b). All of these members of the Ku and T'ao families except

China was by now on the verge of collapse, and it is likely that Ku Pi was raised up as a protégé of Wu Yen. The ascendance of the old Wu families was thus assured. But with the fall of northern China and the arrival in the south of upper-class northern refugees, the old Wu aristocracy was in grave danger. The newcomers were anxious to accumulate land and power, all, of course, at the expense of the old Wu people. Local leaders in Vietnam sensed this change of affairs rather quickly and turned it to their own, albeit short-lived, advantage.

When Ku Pi died, provincial leaders asked his son Ts'an to take authority over provincial affairs. There was no imperial appointment, for northern China had fallen and the empire was in chaos; rather, powerful local families simply agreed that Ku Ts'an should stand at their head. The regional ruling class seems to have been unprepared to deviate from the established pattern in its nominal relation to the empire.

Furthermore, the Ku family commanded a considerable following, for when Ts'an died, his younger brother Shou temporarily prevailed against the wishes of so-called "provincial officials." In attempting to consolidate his power, he killed the senior clerk, Ho Trieu, and others of Trieu's party.[44]

In imperial administration, the senior clerk was the governor's deputy. He supervised the day-to-day activities of provincial government. In Giao, this position seems to have evolved to represent prevailing provincial interests as interpreted by the regional ruling class. The conflict between Ho Trieu and Ku Shou was, more broadly speaking, between powerful local families and those posing as representatives of a distant, enfeebled imperial court.

After Ho Trieu's death, resistance to Shou gathered around Luong Thac, identified as a field commander.[45] Shou attempted to kill Thac, but Thac escaped and mobilized his soldiers. Shou was captured, and Thac forced him to drink poison.[46]

For the next several years, Luong Thac ruled Giao. It is recorded that he took the title prefect of Tan-xuong. Tan-xuong was old Me-linh, home of the Hung kings and the Trung sisters. It was the oldest political center in

---

Ku Pi were placed in office by local powers or by their own ambitions; only Pi received an imperial appointment. For this reason I surmise that Pi's appointment was prior to 311, the date of the fall of Lo-yang; after this the Chin Empire was in turmoil, and Giao Province was left to itself for several years.

44. CS, 57, 6b; TT, 4, 7a–b; CL, 92. Ho Trieu's family name is not a Chinese surname; it is a term used to designate foreign peoples and as such appears in the sources as descriptive of men in Shih Hsieh's retinue.

45. CS, 57, 6b, identifies Luong Thac as a common soldier, literally a "tent dweller."

46. CS, 57, 6b; TT, 4, 7b; CL, 92.

Vietnam. Because it was strategically located at the head of the Hong River plain, many soldiers were stationed there to guard the mountain frontier. It is conceivable that the title prefect of Tan-xuong, recorded in Chinese sources, camouflaged some more indigenous form of authority related to the venerable traditions of this place. In any case, Luong Thac proved to be one of the most persistent and successful of the anti-imperial leaders during the Chinese provincial era, which suggests that he led a relatively united regional ruling class.

Thac nevertheless realized that he lacked the personal pedigree and prestige necessary to present a facade of legitimacy to the empire. He accordingly invited the prefect of Ts'ang-wu, T'ao Wei, a son of T'ao Huang, to be governor. T'ao Wei stood as a symbol of imperial obedience in relations with the Chin dynastic system as it penetrated the south, but in terms of actual control over affairs in Giao, he was but a figurehead for Luong Thac. It is recorded that T'ao Wei was popular among the people. He undoubtedly benefited from his father's reputation in Giao. But he died after only three years.[47]

By now, the new Chin court at Nanking was making its presence felt in the south, and a rebellious clique of old Wu families was forming in Kuang to resist the southward expansion of the Chin political system. In Giao, after T'ao Wei's death, both Wei's younger brother and his son claimed the title of governor.[48] But actual power remained in the hands of Luong Thac, and the T'ao family faded from the scene, perhaps drawn north by events in Kuang.

In Kuang, resistance to Chin gathered behind Wang Chi. He was a member of an old Wu family, and both his father and elder brother had been governors of Kuang. The Wang family had been in the south for several generations and had reportedly established a good reputation among the indigenous people there. When refugees from northern China arrived in the name of Chin, Wang Chi was shouldered aside. In resentment, he assembled an army of one thousand, and it is recorded that the soldiers and people of Kuang "turned their backs" on the Chin appointee and "invited" Wang Chi to be governor.[49]

Wang Chi believed in the legitimacy of the empire, but he could not fulfill his ambition. A social revolution was underway that gave precedence to refugee officials from the north and to their protégés. The frustration of the old Wu families found expression in Chi's indecisive leadership. He resisted Chin authority, but shrank from outright treason.

After gaining control of Kuang, Wang Chi feared Chin retaliation.

---

47. *CS*, 57, 6b, and 89, 14a; *TT*, 4, 7b; *CL*, 92.
48. *CS*, 57, 6b; *TT*, 4, 7b; *VSL*, 1, 6a–b.
49. *CS*, 100, 11a–12a.

Hoping to demonstrate his loyalty and also to put distance between himself and Chin forces, he requested the governorship of Giao. His request was approved, and Chin ordered him to attack Luong Thac.[50]

Hearing of Chi's appointment, Luong Thac sent his son to meet with Chi near the border at Yü-lin. When Thac's son arrived late, Chi angrily rebuked him and issued veiled threats against Thac. His arrogant manner alerted Thac's son, who hastened back and reported the encounter to his father. Thac is reported to have said: "This fellow of the Wang family has already ruined Kuang Province; with what pretext does he now come to destroy Giao Province?" He thereupon closed the border against Chi and forbade anyone in the province to have dealings with him.[51]

Unable to enter Giao, Wang Chi drifted into a state of rebellion and was eventually forced to flee into the mountains, where he died of illness. Order was restored in Kuang by the Chin general T'ao K'an. In the autumn of 318, K'an was given a new title in recognition of his control of Kuang. Shortly after, he was assigned nominal authority over military affairs in Giao.[52]

Meanwhile, in Giao, Luong Thac dealt forcefully with repercussions from the Wang Chi affair. A faction in Giao was sympathetic to Wang Chi; it for the most part comprised recent arrivals to the province, "sojourners," who considered Chi the legitimately appointed governor. These "sojourners" may have been merchants who anticipated prosperity once Giao was reintegrated into the imperial order; they may also have included the vanguard of Chin immigration into the south, prominent northern families with their armed retainers. A military commander named Tu Tsan championed the cause of this faction and led his soldiers against Thac. Thac easily defeated Tsan; then, still suspicious of the "sojourners," he ordered the execution of all their retainers. Finally, he proclaimed himself prefect of Giao-chi.[53]

By naming himself prefect of Giao-chi, Thac revealed his growing confidence as leader of the province. However, the resistance of the "sojourners" to his rule reveals that he had a problem in presenting himself as a legally acceptable ruler in the context of imperial politics. Consequently, he felt the need for a figurehead, so he invited Hsiu Chan to represent provincial interests. Chan was a son of Hsiu Tse, who had been appointed commander-in-chief of Giao by Wu and had lost his life attempting to wrest the province from Chin in 268. One of Chan's brothers had accompanied

50. CS, 100, 11b; CL, 92–93.
51. CS, 100, 11b; CL, 93.
52. CS, 6, 5a, and 66, 6b–7a, and 100, 11b–12a; CL, 93; VSL, 1, 6b.
53. CS, 100, 11b; CL, 93.

T'ao Huang's advance into Giao in 271 and later served as prefect of Ho-p'u, so the family was well known in Giao.[54] Using Hsiu Chan as a screen, Luong Thac continued to pursue an independent course.

The situation remained stable for the next few years, as T'ao K'an was fully occupied with consolidating Chin's position in Kuang. Then, in 322, T'ao K'an's patron, a Chin general in control of the central Yangtze, appointed one of his protégés, Wang Liang, governor of Giao.[55] Wang Liang was instructed that "Hsiu Chan and Luong Thac are traitorous rebels; when you arrive, behead them at once."

Wang Liang's arrival in Giao was uncontested. Luong Thac, hoping to avoid crossing swords with T'ao K'an, whose military reputation was considerable, chose to welcome the new governor and to see how things would go. His position was too strong for Wang Liang to challenge directly, and since he did not call himself governor, there were no conflicting claims between them.

Hsiu Chan, on the other hand, was in perilous straits, for, having no personal base of power, he was dependent on the men who had invited him to take the governor's seat; these same men now found it expedient to deal with Wang Liang, whose gubernatorial credentials carried the threat of northern intervention. Chan withdrew to the relative safety of Cuu-chan.

T'ao K'an closely watched events in Giao, for it was his responsibility to enforce Wang Liang's authority. He sent an envoy to Cuu-chan and persuaded Hsiu Chan to return and meet with Liang at Long-bien. However, as Chan entered the provincial hall he was seized by Liang's men; Liang intended to behead him.

Witnessing this, Luong Thac objected, saying, "Chan is the son of a former general of this province; if he has committed a crime he can be banished but he cannot be killed." Liang replied, "The fact that a man has virtue on account of his ancestors has nothing to do with my business." From this exchange we can perceive the clashing perspectives of the old Wu aristocratic world and the new Chin order. Liang beheaded Chan, making clear the hostility of Chin toward the regional ruling class.

Thac prepared for war. Liang sent an assassin to kill him, but the plot failed. Thac soon had Liang under siege in Long-bien. T'ao K'an sent soldiers, but they were too late. The city fell, and as Thac came face to face with Liang he demanded the governor's flag. Liang clung to the imperial pennon and refused to let go; Thac thereupon severed Liang's right arm

54. *CS*, 57, 5a, 5b; *CL*, 93.

55. *TT*, 4, 7b; *VSL*, 1, 6b. *CL*, 93, follows Wang Liang's biography (*CS*, 89, 14a) in dating his appointment in the third year of Yung-hsing (304–5), which is impossible; perhaps this is a confusion of T'ai-hsing (318–21) or Yung-ch'ang (322). The *TT* and *VSL* apparently obtained the year 322 from *CS*, 6, 8a.

with his sword and took the flag. Liang reportedly said, "I am not afraid to die, so what is the loss of an arm?" But ten days later, he died, groaning with indignation.[56]

Regional leadership in Vietnam was finding it increasingly difficult to ignore the advent of Chin. One Chin-appointed governor had been turned back at the border, and another had been killed. But Chin pressure was growing all the time. Newcomers were clamoring for full integration with the Chin system, and each confrontation brought more Chin soldiers into the province.

After the death of Wang Liang, Luong Thac's problems multiplied. It is recorded that he was vindictive and tyrannical and that he provoked a distressing situation; this view is certainly colored by the perspective of Chinese historians. Luong Thac, and the local families he led, resisted change. But there was no way to turn back the tide of restless Chin officers and adventurers entering Giao. T'ao K'an sent Kao Pao, one of his generals, into Giao. Within a year, Pao captured Thac and sent his head north.[57]

Luong Thac stands out as a typical figure in Vietnamese history. Of humble origins, identified as a "tent dweller," or common soldier, he appeared as the leader of local interests at a time when imperial forces were in a state of shock. He was willing to compromise, if necessary, as long as he was not pushed too far. He died in the midst of a bitter struggle between local and foreign interests that has continued to the present day.

T'ao K'an was named governor of Giao, but he was occupied with a rebellion in the north and left Giao in the hands of Kao Pao. In 325, K'an was promoted to a position further north. The following year, Yüan Fang, a high minister of the Chin court, requested and received the governorship of Giao; he was apparently motivated by a desire to avoid the intrigues that were then swirling about the Chin throne. As he neared the Giao border, he invited Kao Pao to a banquet and prepared to ambush him when he came. Pao learned of the plot and attacked first. Fang escaped and fled into Giao, where he suddenly died, complaining of an unquenchable thirst.[58]

Events in Giao are unclear after this, but could conceivably have had some connection with the Taoist Ch'eng Han dynasty that arose in Ssu-ch'uan in reaction to the social upheaval provoked by Chin's regime. In 328,

56. These events are recorded in: CS, 66, 7a, and 89, 14a–b; TT, 4, 8a; VSL, 1, 6b; CL, 93.

57. CS, 66, 7a, and 89, 14b; TT, 4, 8a. The CS dates Thac's rebellion in the tenth month of 322 (6, 8a) and his death in the sixth month of 323 (6, 9b).

58. Fang was vice-president of the Board of Civil Office. TT, 4, 8a, says he was appointed governor of Giao "not long after" Pao vanquished Thac. CL, 94, says it was "when Emperor Ch'eng was a minor and the Yü family seized power." The Yü family gained control over the Chin court around 325. Ch'eng's reign began in 326. Considering that in 328 Truong Lien was governor, I surmise that Fang was appointed in 326, after the promotion of T'ao K'an in 325.

as the Ssu-ch'uan dynasty was attacking Chin, a certain Truong Lien mysteriously appeared as governor of Giao; he invaded Kuang and got as far as Shih-hsing before he was vanquished by a Chin general. Lien's rise from obscurity was clearly a reaction to the new forces pressing down from the north. The fact that he was not content simply to pursue a policy of local resistance but actually began a march on the Chin capital suggests that his movement was inspired by broader strategic considerations related to the Ch'eng Han campaign of that year. There are indications that Lien was moved by Taoist sentiments, which were common among anti-Chin Chinese in central and southern China at the time.[59]

A common thread of resistance to Chin runs through all the events in the south during this period. All of the resistance movements, whether comprising upper-class remnants of Wu under Wang Chi, low-level provincial officials under Luong Thac, or a broad last-ditch coalition under Truong Lien, shared a strong antipathy to the new Chin order, although they seem to have shared little else. The south had become a last refuge for all manner of Chin dissidents.

The way the Chin court finally established its authority over Giao has not been recorded, but the situation was clarified by 336. In that year the governor of Kuang sent an army against the tribal peoples of Kuei-chou. The prefect of Tan-xuong, a certain T'ao Hsieh, assisted this campaign by leading an army into Yün-nan and taking a city on the route to Ssu-ch'uan.[60] This was probably part of an effort to seal Giao off from the contaminating influence of the Ch'eng Han dynasty in Ssu-ch'uan, which was not conquered until 347.

---

59. *CS*, 7, 3a. *CL*, 93, cites the information from the *CS*, then adds: "The *Memoirs* of Wang Hsü say: 'Lien was governor of Giao Province and held the title of High Marquis; he traveled past Mount Cu and loved the scenery so he remained there.' This is not in agreement with the imperial records; I do not know which is correct." Mount Cu is perhaps Mount Nua in the old district of Cu-phong, "Cu wind," in Cuu-chan Prefecture (see Nguyen Dinh Thuc, p. 42). *HHS*, 23, 21b, quotes the following from a certain *Chiao chou chi* about Cu-phong District: "There is a mountain where a golden buffalo frequently comes out at night and shines with a dazzling brilliance that can be seen for ten *li*; the slopes of the mountain are often windy." Thus, the name of the district derived from a famous windy mountain named Cu. It is reasonable to conjecture that Truong Lien's rebellion was somehow related to the Taoist movement of Li Hsiung in Ssu-ch'uan, for the information that Lien entered the province as a traveler and decided to stay after viewing its unusual scenery sounds like a description of a Taoist adept with a geomancer's itch. In 328, the Li of Ssu-ch'uan were attacking the Chin frontier (*CS*, 7, 2a–3a); this may have encouraged a similar eruption in the south. Chu Dat in 157 and Lady Trieu in 248 both began their northward march from Cu-phong District; Chang Lien may have blown on the ashes of these old rebellions and raised a new fire. On Taoism and the Ch'eng Han dynasty, see Seidel, p. 233. On the social and economic impact of Chin's arrival in the south, see Yang Lien-sheng, "Notes on the Economic History of the Chin Dynasty," pp. 169–73.

60. *CS*, 7, 5b.

Chin wrought a significant change in central and southern China. Formerly, Chinese civilization was concentrated in a few places of political importance where the literate class throve; henceforth, Chinese values increasingly spread to the countryside through the medium of northern refugees. Of all places in the south, Giao was the least affected by this, for it was the most distant, and few immigrants went so far south. Giao, however, did become a haven for some upper-class families and officials who tried to avoid the troubles attending the arrival of Chin. The quality of immigrants into Giao was relatively high. The prime example of this is the Do (Chinese Tu) family that gradually rose to prominence in Giao during the fourth century.

Chin's arrival forced the south to define itself more strictly in terms of its position within the empire. The first crowd of Chin appointees to arrive in Giao followed the old Han and Wu tradition of making a quick fortune and then retiring north. This holiday of greed extended to foreign relations and contributed to provoking war with Lin-i. The Lin-i wars of the fourth and fifth centuries helped to place the Vietnamese psychologically more firmly within the Sinitic sphere.

Chin and Lin-i

After the death of Fan Hsiung, the king who had battled with T'ao Huang in the 270s, Lin-i prospered under the long and peaceful reign of his son Fan I. In 284, Fan I sent the first official embassy from Lin-i to the Chin court; the only prior diplomatic contact had been with Lü T'ai after T'ai's suppression of the Shih family in 226.[61] As friendly contacts with China developed, Lin-i experienced important social changes, for when Fan I died in 336, his throne was usurped by a former slave of Chinese origin named Wen.

Wen was reportedly born on the lower Yangtze. Sold into slavery as an infant, he eventually served a Lin-i prince. As a teenager, he escaped and joined a Lin-i merchant engaged in long-distance commerce. Sometime during the reign of Emperor Min (313–16), he traveled in China, going as far north as Lo-yang.[62] At this time northern China was being conquered by northern tribal peoples; Wen's sojourn in Lo-yang was after that capital had fallen.

One can only surmise what impression these events left in Wen's mind, but it seems he concluded that the Chinese imperial world was falling into ruin and that the greatest opportunities lay with imaginative leaders along the frontiers. After witnessing the conquest of northern China by the

61. G. Maspero, *Le Royaume de Champa*, p. 55, n. 5.
62. Ibid., p. 55, nn. 8 and 9, and 56, n. 2

peoples of the north, perhaps he envisioned a comparable event in the south. Shortly thereafter he entered the service of the king of Lin-i.

Wen built a palace for Fan I in the Chinese style; more important, he built fortifications and supervised the manufacture of weapons. Winning the confidence of the king, he was made commander in chief of the army. As the king grew old, Wen's influence increased. When the king died, Wen disposed of the legitimate heirs and took the throne.[63]

After conquering some small neighboring chiefdoms, Wen turned his attention northward. In 340 he sent gifts to the Chin emperor and requested that the border be fixed at Hoanh-son; he was in effect asking for the formal cession of Nhat-nam. Chin naturally refused, for even if it was unable to rule Nhat-nam, it would never relinquish its formal claim. In 344, Wen responded by raiding through Nhat-nam, Cuu-duc, and Cuu-chan; this was a reconnaissance mission in anticipation of a full-scale invasion.[64]

In addition to Wen's ambitions, Chin misgovernment contributed to instability on the frontier. The position of Lin-i and Nhat-nam made them natural centers of international commerce on the sea route between China and points south and west. Chin officials in Nhat-nam took advantage of this to extort bribes from foreign merchants. According to one source:

> All the kingdoms beyond the border brought valuable goods from the sea routes for trade; the governor of Giao Province and the prefect of Nhat-nam were unquenchably avaricious and insultingly extorted bribes between twenty and thirty percent of the value of the merchandise.[65]

The situation grew worse during the governorship of Chiang Chuang; he appointed a relative of his named T'ao Chi prefect of Nhat-nam. Chi raised the bribes to more than half the value of the merchandise. After Chi's death, the prefect Hsieh Cho returned to the old level of bribery, but this less inflammatory policy was abandoned by his successor, Hsia-hou Lan.[66] Lan was so debauched and corrupt that he provoked a wave of disaffection that invited intervention; Wen took the opportunity.

In 347, as the Lin-i army marched north, drummers fanned out before it, announcing to the population: "The reason for this invasion is the anger and exasperation of the different kingdoms." Wen thus posed as a protector of the international commercial community. It is also recorded that "Lin-i had few fields and coveted Nhat-nam's land."[67] Whether as a result of

63. A myth has been preserved that explains Wen's rise to power in terms of folk themes recorded for peoples in Southeast Asia and southeastern China from antiquity; see Rolf Stein, "Le Lin-i," pp. 241–312.

64. *CS*, 7, 6b; *SCC*, 36, 25b; G. Maspero, pp. 56–57.

65. *CS*, 97, 9b.

66. *CS*, 97, 9b–10a; *LS*, 54, 3a; *CL*, 94; G. Maspero, p. 58.

67. *CS*, 97, 10a.

population pressure or, more likely, simply from a desire for territorial aggrandizement, Lin-i was in an expansionist mood. Seizing Hsia-hou Lan, Wen reportedly sacrificed him to Heaven as expatiation for the sins he had committed against the people. After occupying Nhat-nam, he proposed to Chu Fan, governor of Giao, that the border be fixed at Hoanh-son.[68]

Chu Fan replied by sending an army south under the command of Governor General Liu Hsiung. Wen attacked and defeated Hsiung. Then, in 348, he invaded Cuu-duc and Cuu-chan, overwhelming the Chin forces garrisoned there; between five and six thousand men were killed, comprising between eighty and ninety percent of the Chin soldiers in those two prefectures. In 349, the combined forces of Kuang and Giao marched south under the command of Governor General T'eng Chün. Chün and Wen met in battle at Lo-dung, a major seaport on what is today called the Giang River, in northern Nhat-nam. Chün was defeated and withdrew to Cuu-chan; Wen was mortally wounded and died within the year.[69]

Wen's son, Fan Fu, continued the policy of aggression. He marched north and besieged the prefect of Cuu-chan, Kuan Sui. In 351, T'eng Chün and a new governor named Yang P'ing led an army down to Sui's relief; as it approached, Sui launched a surprise attack on his besiegers and sent them fleeing. Chün and P'ing pursued and defeated Fan Fu in southern Nhat-nam. As the Chin army neared the capital of Lin-i, Fan Fu submitted, begged forgiveness, and swore and oath of good conduct.[70]

Intermittent hostilities continued, however, as Fan Fu continued to contest the frontier. In 353, Governor Yüan Fu attacked Lin-i and destroyed more than fifteen fortified encampments.[71] But as the urgency of the situation receded, the willingness of provincial leaders to fight for Chin declined. A war of defense was being transformed into a war for glory and profit by ambitious Chin officials.

In 358, preparations for a large-scale campaign against Lin-i were being made under the supervision of T'eng Han, the governor of Kuang, and Wen Fang-chih, the governor of Giao. The project was opposed by Do Bao, the prefect of Giao-chi, and Nguyen Lang, a provincial judicial officer. Fearing that these men would spread dissension among the other officials, Fang-chih had them executed. In 359, Fang-chih led an army south; he succeeded in besieging Fan Fu in his capital city and forcing him to swear an

68. CS, 8, 1b, and 97, 9b; CL, 94.

69. CS, 8, 2a–b, and 97, 9b–10a; LS, 54, 3b; CL, 94. Lo-dung was an ancient name for the Giang River just south of the Hoanh-son massif. SCC, 36, 20b–21a, cites K'ang T'ai's Fu-nan chi on the Lo-dung River: "Proceeding southward from [this river's] port [one arrives at] Fu-nan; [to go to] all [other] countries [in the south seas, one] usually goes out from this port."

70. SCC, 36, 20b; LS, 54, 3b; CL, 94; G. Maspero, p. 59.

71. CS, 8, 4a; CL, 94; TT, 4, 8a–b.

oath of loyalty. Thereafter, the frontier was peaceful. In the 370s, Fan Fu sent several diplomatic missions to the Chin court; he died in 380.[72]

The war with Lin-i reveals the developing cultural and political perspective of ruling-class people in Giao. When Lin-i seized Nhat-nam in 248, the people of Cuu-chan and Giao-chi responded by rising in rebellion. However, in 348, when Lin-i took Nhat-nam and ravaged as far north as Cuu-chan, there was no echoing reaction from the Vietnamese. The regional ruling class joined with Chin officials in pushing Lin-i back across the frontier. It was only after the worst was over and desultory hostilities were used as a pretext for enforcing the imperial court's authority that local leaders attempted to resist further demands. We can surmise that this relative willingness to cooperate with the north was to some extent an effect of Chin immigration on the regional ruling class.

Chin control over Giao, however, did not long survive the peace. The tide of Chin influence that rose to meet the threat in the south receded as quickly as that threat began to fade.

The Do Family

At this time, the Tibetan Fu Chien (357–85) was uniting northern China; in 383 he invaded southern China. While the Chin throne survived this challenge, it continued a prisoner of powerful families. At the end of the century, a Taoist-inspired peasant rebellion consumed vast territories, including Kuang Province. The man who distinguished himself in suppressing this uprising, Liu Yü, went on to seize the throne in 420, founding the Sung dynasty. Throughout this turbulent era, Giao enjoyed relative peace and quiet under the leadership of the Do family.

By the 370s, Chin control in Giao had relaxed significantly. In 377, the governor of Ching Province, in modern Hu-nan, held military authority over five other provinces; two were in Ssu-ch'uan, one was in Kuei-chou, and the remaining two were Kuang and Giao; a few months later a seventh province to the east was added to this vast ceremonial command.[73] The Chin court lay powerless before a powerful minister who deposed and

---

72. *SCC*, 36, 23b, and the imperial records of the *CS* (8, 6a) speak only of Wen Fang-chih. The *CS* notice on Lin-i (97, 10a), however, speaks only of T'eng Han. *CL*, 94, speaks of both but makes Han a governor of Giao and implies that there were two separate campaigns; the *CL* simply copies the different sources without attempting to integrate them. G. Maspero, p. 60, n. 10, rejected the citation of T'eng Han as an error. However, the imperial records of the *CS* (8, 6b) say that in the second month of 361, T'eng Han, South-Pacifying General and governor of Kuang Province, died. Han's military title tends to confirm the idea that he was involved in the Lin-i campaign. On Do Bao and Nguyen Lang, see also *SCC*, 36, 26b.

73. *CS*, 9, 5b.

appointed emperors at will; only his premature death prevented him from taking the throne for himself. Under these circumstances, the local political life of Giao flourished.

Wen Fang-chih, who chastised Lin-i in 359, was succeeded as governor by a certain Chu Fu, of whom nothing is known. Thereafter, the position of governor fell vacant, and the prefect of Cuu-chan, Ly Ton, gained control of the province. Ton and a son of his were known for their courage and determination; together, their power and influence dominated Giao.[74]

In 380, news reached Giao of the imminent arrival of T'eng Tun-chih, a newly appointed governor. Ly Ton decided to resist. Perhaps he reasoned that Chin was too busy in the north to pay any attention to Giao. In this he may have been right, but he neglected to take into account potential rivals in the province eager to use his insubordination as a pretext for attacking him. Ton sent two of his sons to guard the land and sea routes into the province and to prevent Tun-chih's arrival. This act of rebellion occurred in the tenth month of 380; nine months later, Ton was beheaded by Do Vien, the prefect of Giao-chi.[75]

The Do family was originally from Ch'ang-an. Sometime between the fall of Wu in 280 and the fall of Lo-yang in 311, Vien's grandfather had been appointed prefect in Ning-p'u, a prefecture just across the northern border of Giao created by Wu from portions of Yü-lin and Ho-p'u.[76] It was probably to avoid the troubles of Wang Chi's rebellion that the Do family moved to Giao-chi and settled in Chu-dien District. Do Bao, the prefect of Giao-chi executed by Wen Fang-chih before the 359 campaign against Lin-i, could conceivably have been Do Vien's father.[77]

Do Vien began his career as an official of the central provincial government. He subsequently served as prefect in Nhat-nam, Cuu-duc, and

74. VSL, 1, 6b, cites Chu Fu as governor during the time of Fu Chien (357–85), the Tibetan conquerer who invaded Chin in 385 and died shortly thereafter. Why this governor is dated to a northern ruler is unclear. Sometime before 380, the Ly family gained control of the province. Chu Fu was governor before then. On the Ly family, see SS, 92, 4a, the biography of Do Tue Do, the most important source for this period. An abridged version appears in VSL, 1, 7a; the CL reproduces nearly the entire biography under the names of the principal figures in it: Ly Ton (94), Do Vien, Do Tue Do, and Do Hoang Van (143). CL, 94, cites Ko Hung in this period; he was an old man who wanted to prepare the elixir of immortality to prolong his life. Hearing that cinnabar, a prime ingredient of the elixir, was produced in Giao-chi, he asked to be appointed a district magistrate there.

75. CS, 9, 6a–b; TT, 4, 8b.

76. CS, 15, 9b; SS, 38, 38a.

77. This conjecture is wholly circumstantial. The official careers of both Vien and his grandfather suggest that Vien's father was also a prefect; in terms of chronology, Do Bao could easily have been Vien's father.

finally Giao-chi. When Ly Ton set a course of rebellion in 380, Do Vien gathered a following and, disposing of Ton, welcomed Governor T'eng Tun-chih. The court named Vien "Prancing Dragon General." [78]

The relationship between Vien and Tun-chih was apparently cordial, for it lasted nearly two decades, until Tun-chih returned north. Tun-chih was barely out of the province, however, before Lin-i broke a peace of forty years.

Fan Fu's death in 380 had been followed by a regency during the minority of his son Fan Hu Ta. When T'eng Tun-chih departed Giao at the beginning of 399, Hu Ta, now an adult, took the opportunity to renew the ambitions of his father and grandfather. He marched north, seizing the prefects of Nhat-nam and Cuu-duc as he went; catching the province by complete surprise, he had the provincial capital under siege before a response could be organized. [79]

Do Vien and his third son led the inevitable reaction. In the words of their biographer:

> Using all their strength with careful and persistent efforts, they multiplied the deaths of the enemy utilizing an irregular strategy of expediency; accumulating battlefield victories, they pursued and attacked the enemy in Cuu-chan and Nhat-nam; success followed success until Hu Ta returned to Lin-i. [80]

Here is an early example of the guerrilla warfare that became second nature to Vietnamese leaders. The Do family was unquestionably the most Vietnamese of all the imperial clans to govern Vietnam. Born and raised among the Vietnamese, Do Vien nevertheless distinguished himself as a loyal and capable leader in the eyes of the Nanking court. After defeating Fan Hu Ta, he was appointed governor of Giao. [81]

In 405, Hu Ta began attacking Nhat-nam once again; in response, Vien sent a fleet that ravaged the coast of Lin-i in 407. [82] After this, the southern frontier settled down for a few years, and the attention of provincial leaders was drawn northward, where rebellions were shaking the empire.

In 410, the governor of Kuang, Lu Hsün, rebelled. He sent an envoy to Do Vien in anticipation of collaborating in an independence movement. Vien was now eighty-four years old; he had made his career as a faithful imperial servant and was not about to connive with a traitorous adventurer. He promptly beheaded Hsün's envoy. Vien died the same year, and provin-

78. SS, 92, 4a.
79. G. Maspero, p. 61.
80. SS, 92, 4b. This campaign is briefly mentioned in LS, 54, 3b.
81. SS, 92, 4b.
82. LS, 54, 5a; G. Maspero, p. 62.

cial officials prevailed upon his fifth son, Tue Do, to take responsibility for the province.[83]

Do Tue Do had begun his official career as keeper of the provincial account books and population registers; later, he served as prefect of Cuu-chan. Even before his father's death, Tue Do had established a close relationship with the officials of the province. His election by local officials was endorsed at the beginning of 411 by imperial appointments as governor of Giao, "Special Viceroy" with authority over all military affairs in Giao, and "Martial General of Kuang."[84] The last appointment was undoubtedly intended to solicit Tue Do's assistance in putting down Lu Hsün's rebellion. As it turned out, Tue Do had little choice in the matter, for, even before the arrival of the imperial appointments, Hsün's rebellion spilled into Giao.

Defeated by Liu Yü, Lu Hsün turned south and invaded Ho-p'u Prefecture, then proceeded towards Giao-chi. Tue Do led an army of six thousand and met Hsün in battle at Thach-ky, somewhere in Giao-chi.[85] Hsün was defeated, and his senior advisor was captured. Nevertheless, he still had three thousand veteran soldiers eager for more adventure and was not yet ready to give up.

The sons of Ly Ton, Ly Nhiep and Ly Thoat, had apparently sided with Lu Hsün at the battle of Thach-ky; it is recorded that they were "routed" and subsequently fled among the tribal peoples of the nearby mountains. Knowing of the resentment harbored by the Ly family against the Do family, Hsün sent envoys to Nhiep and Thoat proposing an alliance. The Ly brothers led between five and six thousand "Li" tribesmen out of the mountains and accepted Hsün's leadership.

In the face of this formidable coalition, Tue Do distributed his personal wealth among provincial officials to encourage their loyalty. He sent a younger brother to be prefect of Cuu-chan, the old center of the Ly family's power. He exhorted the people and prepared military units. When Hsün led his followers against Long-bien on a summer morning in 411, Tue Do was ready to meet him.[86]

Hsün and his main force advanced upriver in war boats. Tue Do mounted a high-decked war boat and joined battle; his foot soldiers soon appeared on both sides of the river. All of Hsün's boats were set ablaze with flaming arrows, and his followers scattered in confusion. Wounded by an arrow and seeing that all was lost, Hsün leaped into the water and drowned.

Tue Do gained a complete victory. Hsün's father, two of his sons, two

---

83. *CS*, 10, 6a; *SS*, 92, 4b.

84. *SS*, 92, 4b–5a.

85. Ton Nu Thuong Lang, trans. and Ta Quang Phat, annotator, *Kham dinh Viet su thong giam cuong muc*, part 1, 3, 24, identifies Thach-ky as "a town southwest of the capital of Giao Province."

86. *SS*, 92, 5a–b.

of his commanders, the Ly brothers, and other leaders of the rebellious clique
were all captured and beheaded. In recognition of this accomplishment, the
imperial court named Tue Do "Marquis of Long-bien," with an assignment
of the revenue from one thousand households.[87]

Two years later, Tue Do scored a similar success against Lin-i. In 413,
Fan Hu Ta again invaded Giao. After prolonged fighting in Cuu-chan, two
of Hu Ta's sons, one of his generals, and a hundred of his officers were
captured or killed; Hu Ta himself was not heard of again.[88]

Although the disappearance of Hu Ta occasioned a succession problem in Lin-i that lasted several years, it did not end the chronic raiding and
plundering, against which Tue Do sent a general in 415.[89] In 420, Tue Do
led an army of ten thousand against Lin-i and gained a great success. More
than half the enemy forces were killed, and all that had been plundered by
Lin-i over the preceding years was recovered. When Lin-i begged to submit,
Tue Do generously halted the campaign and released the prisoners he had
taken.

In the same year, Liu Yü took the Chin throne and founded the Sung
dynasty. Tue Do sent an official to hail the new emperor with gifts of
war booty from Lin-i. Liu Yü reciprocated by promoting Tue Do to
"Kingdom-Sustaining General."[90]

Once again, Giao had weathered a dynastic transition under strong
regional leadership. When the Han Empire fell into anarchy, Shih Hsieh
gave the south forty years of peace and prosperity. When the Wu kingdom
was extinguished, T'ao Huang provided continuity in Giao. When northern
China fell and the Chin dynasty was sent reeling southward, Luong Thac
delayed and softened the transition on the frontier. And now Do Tue Do
stood immune to the vicissitudes of dynastic politics. From this it is clear that
Giao possessed a political momentum of its own, independent of the empire.
In fact, it was when the empire was in deepest trouble that the south
prospered most. Whenever the imperial court was strong enough to dominate the region, as under Han and Wu, rebellion and political instability
ensued. When the court was weak, local forces rose, and stability followed.
This became an enduring pattern of Sino-Vietnamese relations; a strong,
united China has traditionally posed a political problem to the Vietnamese.

87. *CS*, 10, 6b; *SS*, 92, 5b. *TT*, 4, 9b, contains a more dramatic account of Hsün's death.
After administering poison to his wife and children, Hsün asked his servants, "Is there anyone
able to follow me in death?" One answered: "Even birds and mice are greedy for life; to follow
you in death is very difficult." Another said, "The lord must die, but we still desire to live." But
Hsün killed them all, then leaped into the water and drowned. This information clearly did not
come from firsthand witnesses.

88. *CS*, 10, 7b; *LS*, 54, 5a; *SCC*, 36, 22a; *TT*, 4, 9b; G. Maspero, pp. 62–63.

89. *TT*, 4, 9b; G. Maspero, pp. 64–67.

90. *SS*, 92, 5b; *TT*, 4, 9b–10a.

In 420, Do Tue Do had loyally sent his eldest son Hoang Van at the head of a three-thousand-man army, composed of convicts, to assist the tottering Chin throne. Hoang Van got only as far as Kuang before hearing that the matter was already settled, so he returned. One of Hoang Van's titles was "Minister of Irregular Cavalry beyond the Border,"[91] which suggests that the Do family patrolled the northern border and beyond against the arrival of rebels and adventurers. The Lu Hsün episode had alerted the Do to the unsettled conditions in the north. With vigilance, such unwanted influences could be intercepted before they reached the border.

Judging from his military exploits against rebels in the north and Lin-i in the south, Do Tue Do was a gifted leader. But beyond these martial accomplishments, he was a remarkable man. In the words of his biographer:

> [Tue Do] wore cotton garments in the way of the common people; he ate only vegetables; he lived frugally and was simple mannered; he could play the lute rather well; he was correct in his behavior. He prohibited licentious rituals and built schools. In years of famine, when the people were hungry, he used his personal salary to aid those in distress. He governed with astuteness and intimacy, as if regulating a family; he was both stern and kind. Debauchers and bandits dared not show their faces. The gate of the city was not closed at night; items dropped along the road were not stolen.[92]

This description reads like a propaganda tract on the ideal ruler; he combined virtues extolled by both Confucianists and Buddhists. Perhaps in the austerity of this remote frontier the ideals of Chinese government were easier to realize than in the compromised dynastic power centers. However that may be, there must have been some justifying substance beneath the hagiographical fervor. In this man we see the best that Chinese civilization had to offer, yet he is also a tribute to Vietnamese culture. Although he was a loyal imperial servant, he nonetheless was born and grew to manhood in Giao. While his allegiance to northern dynasties was largely a formality, he nevertheless epitomized the complexity of the relationship between Giao and the empire. Yet it is significant that the Do family did not consider Giao to be its permanent home. Tue Do's son and successor took the first chance he had to escape the provincial setting, with fatal haste.

When Do Tue Do died in 423 at the age of fifty, his son Hoang Van was prefect of Cuu-chan. Hoang Van succeeded to the governorship, gained the support of the people, and received the imperial title "Marquis of Long-bien," which had been held by his father.[93]

In 427, Hoang Van received an imperial summons to fill a high position at the Sung court. This fulfilled his greatest ambition, and he

91. SS, 92, 6a.
92. Ibid., 92, 5b–6a.
93. Ibid., 92, 6a.

immediately set out for the capital, in spite of the fact that he had suddenly taken ill. When it was suggested that he wait until he recovered his health, he replied: "Our family has borne imperial favor for three generations; we have always desired to present ourselves at the imperial court and report that for which we have been responsible; now, having been personally summoned, can I tarry for my ease?" Hoang Van was eager to reap the metropolitan recognition that his family had earned in this rustic corner of the empire. As his carriage went forth, his aged mother could not bear to see him go in such a weak condition and hurried to join him. While traveling through Kuang, his health faltered, and he died.[94] Thus, after nearly half a century, the Do family's rule over Giao came to an end.

During the tenure of the Do family, the regional ruling class recovered its composure after the disruptions of Chin's arrival in the south. The option of independence, championed by the Ly family, was rejected because the residue of Chin prestige and personnel in the wake of the Lin-i wars was strong enough to enforce the imperial connection, formality though it became. But, as the Lu Hsün affair revealed, the Ly family remained unreconciled to this situation and could count on allies in the mountains to support independence movements. The Do family clearly achieved a working consensus with the regional ruling class. But alienated families, such as the Ly, continued to pose a threat of separatism. Successive Chinese regimes would discover that this threat was ineradicable. Through many vicissitudes, it eventually blossomed into Vietnamese independence.

Sung and Lin-i

When the Sung court took responsibility for Giao, its first concern was to secure the frontier against Lin-i. The young king of Lin-i, Fan Yang Mai, was charting a course of aggression. In 424, he seized what remained of Nhat-nam and raided Cuu-duc. Do Hoang Van was just getting around to organizing an expedition in 427 when he was promoted and replaced by Wang Hui.[95] The expedition never materialized, for Wang Hui, a senior minister at court prior to his appointment,[96] appears to have been preoccupied with putting the Sung stamp on provincial government.

During this time, Yang Mai built up the fortress of Khu-tuc. Located near the mouth of the Giang River,[97] Khu-tuc was first fortified by Fan Hu Ta,[98] probably during his campaign of 399. A major international trading

94. Ibid., 92, 6b.
95. Ibid., 97, 1a–b; *LS*, 54, 4b–5a; *SCC*, 36, 27b.
96. *SS*, 92, 6a; *CL*, 94; *VSL*, 1, 7b; *TT*, 4, 10a; G. Maspero, p. 69, n. 1.
97. Stein, pp. 1–53.
98. *SCC*, 36, 19a.

center, standing guard at the northern border of old Nhat-nam, Khu-tuc was the key to Lin-i's frontier defenses.

In 430, Yang Mai sent envoys to the Sung court with an apology for his unfriendly acts toward Giao.[99] Apparently, the real purpose of this mission, however, was to gather information on Sung determination to defend the frontier. Yang Mai must have gained the impression that he had little to fear, for in 431 he sent more than a hundred ships to pillage the coast of Cuu-duc. Yüan Mi-chih, Wang Hui's successor, sent an army and a fleet against Khu-tuc, but difficult sailing weather and an inconclusive nighttime naval battle prevented the fleet from joining the army, and the campaign was called off.[100]

Thereafter, Yang Mai grew bolder. He first asked the king of Fu-nan for soldiers to help him conquer Giao, but was refused. Then, in 433, he sent envoys to Sung requesting the cession of Giao; Sung naturally refused. Thereafter, in 435, 438, 439, and 441, he sent tribute to Sung, all the while increasing his raids into Giao.[101]

The Sung response was slow in coming, but was well planned and mercilessly executed. The dynasties ruling at Nanking were generally too weak to have much of an impact on local affairs in Giao; yet when a serious threat from the frontier materialized in the form of Lin-i aggression, considerable momentum could be generated for an expedition into the distant south. In this case, the task was facilitated by a blossoming interest in the south among the merchant- and gentry-class families of Sung society. After a prolonged period of inconclusive warfare in the north, it was with relief and enthusiasm that imperial attention turned south.

In 443, the governor of Giao, T'an Ho-chih, was ordered to recruit soldiers and officials for the Lin-i campaign.[102] Three years later, after careful preparation, he marched south with an ample army commanded by two talented officers. Tsung Ch'üeh, a gifted battle leader, had volunteered for the expedition and was named field marshal, with the title "War-Rousing General."[103] Hsiao Ching-hsien, a cavalry commander

99. SS, 97, 1b.

100. SS, 97, 1b, and LS, 54, 5a, mention only the land action; SCC, 36, 23a–b, mentions only the sea action. CL, 95, contains a creative combination of the two accounts. While the SS and the LS speak of an army of three thousand under Hsiang Tao-sheng, the CL speaks of an army of seven thousand under Yüan Wu-chih. While the SCC speaks of a fleet under Yüan Ch'ien-chih, the CL has Yüan Mi-chih himself in command of the fleet. Both the SCC and the CL are in agreement on the details of the nighttime naval battle in which Yang Mai's helmsman was wounded, causing the vessel to drift dangerously crosswise and forcing Yang Mai to escape in a small boat.

101. SS, 97, 1b.

102. SCC, 36, 19b–20a.

103. SS, 76, 3b–4a; VSL, 1, 7b; TT, 4, 11a.

with a reputation for ably handling tough frontier assignments, led the vanguard.[104]

When Yang Mai learned of Ho-chih's approach, he lost his nerve and sent messengers offering to return captured people and territory and to pay a large indemnity in gold and silver. Ho-chih informed the court, and the emperor decided to accept Yang Mai's proposal. The Sung army thereupon advanced into Nhat-nam, and a delegation was sent to Yang Mai with the emperor's answer.[105]

Meanwhile, Yang Mai had regained his composure. He seized the Sung delegation and sent a general to hold Khu-tuc. Khu-tuc was promptly besieged by the Sung army. A Lin-i relief army was routed, and Khu-tuc fell. All the adult inhabitants of the city were beheaded. The palace chambers were awash with blood, and corpses were piled in heaps as the city's vast stores of gold, silver, and precious objects were plundered.[106]

From Khu-tuc the Sung army proceeded south to the capital of Lin-i. Yang Mai drained his realm of men and fielded a formidable army led by an array of armored elephants. It is recorded that the Sung nearly lost heart at the sight of this great host. But Tsung Ch'üeh reportedly counseled: "I have heard that the lion inspires fear in all other animals." He ordered the construction of bamboo and paper lions. Advancing with these pseudolions in the van, the Sung are said to have sown panic among the elephants, which turned and scattered through the Lin-i army, melting it into confusion.[107]

Yang Mai's army was massacred, and he fled into the mountains. Ho-chih entered the capital in triumph and gathered a fabulous booty, including fifty tons of gold from the palaces and temples; he remained in Lin-i for nearly a year. When the Sung army returned north in 447, Yang Mai ventured back and surveyed his devastated and depopulated kingdom; it was said that he died of chagrin.[108]

T'an Ho-chih's conquest of Lin-i ended a century of intermittent warfare. Thereafter, the frontier was generally peaceful. The old capital of Lin-i, in the vicinity of modern Hue, was abandoned, and Yang Mai's successors ruled further south at Tra-kieu, in the vicinity of modern Danang.[109]

Nhat-nam nevertheless fell gradually under the sway of Lin-i. After the brief moment of Sung hegemony on the frontier, the Hoanh-son massif

104. *SS*, 97, 2a; *LS*, 54, 5b; *CL*, 95.

105. *SS*, 97, 2a; *LS*, 54, 5b.

106. *SS*, 76, 4a, and 97, 2a–b; *LS*, 54, 5b; *SCC*, 36, 20a; *VSL*, 1, 7b; *TT*, 4, 11a–b.

107. *SS*, 76, 4a–b.

108. *SS*, 97, 2b; *LS*, 54, 5b; *SCC*, 36, 23b–24a and 27a–b; *VSL*, 1, 7b; *TT*, 4, 11b–12a; *CL*, 95.

109. Stein, pp. 71, 111, 129.

gradually came to be the cultural and political boundary of the northern empire.[110]

The era of Nhat-nam was drawing to a close. Originally the southernmost outpost of the Han Empire, Nhat-nam gave birth to a new kingdom when that empire passed away. For three centuries this kingdom of Lin-i had clung to the edge of the imperial world; the ambitions of its kings were defined by their perceptions of imperial power. During this time, Nhat-nam was a cultural and political battlefield; as northern influence was increasingly endangered, the warfare became increasingly bitter, culminating in the grim events of 446.

In spite of 446, Nhat-nam was lost to the northerners. The very ferocity of this war unmasked the underlying weakness of the northerners' position. The Sung army was conquering a foreign kingdom, not liberating an imperial prefecture. Not until the fifteenth century did the Vietnamese finally overrun this old region of Nhat-nam. Once the possession of Nhat-nam was decided in the fifth century, not by war but by the logic of geography, the kingdom of Lin-i became more involved with regions further south and developed along a broader cultural and political front.[111]

The Empire Fades

As Giao's southern border contracted to a more natural geographical frontier, a similar process occurred in the north. After the victorious return of the Sung army from Lin-i, Hsiao Ching-hsien was named governor of Giao, with military authority over the prefectures of Yü-lin and Ning-p'u in Kuang. Yü-lin and Ning-p'u were frontier prefectures located in the mountains separating the Hong and Hsi river basins. They were separated from the sea by Ho-p'u, while in the other direction lay the untamed uplands of Yün-nan and Kuei-chou. Ching-hsien's appointment was made in recognition of his ability "to overawe the barbarians of the wilderness."[112] This began a policy of opening up previously neglected lands, which in 471 culminated in the formation of the province of Yüeh, comprising Ho-p'u and its hinterland between Kuang and Giao.[113] In this

110. Paul Pelliot, "Deux Itineraires de Chine en Inde a la fin du VIIIe siècle," pp. 183–92.

111. Later administrative use of the name *Nhat-nam*, along with the names of the districts in Nhat-nam, refers to locations north of Hoanh-son, so designated to perpetuate in theory the existence of the famous old prefecture (Pelliot, "Deux Itineraires," pp. 190–91). Furthermore, dynastic histories continued to list Nhat-nam and its districts in the geographical records to maintain the historical claim to these regions; for example, *NCS*, 14, 25a, lists Nhat-nam and seven districts, including Tuong-lam, which since 192 had comprised the kingdom of Lin-i.

112. *SS*, 97, 3a.

113. *SS*, 38, 43b–44b.

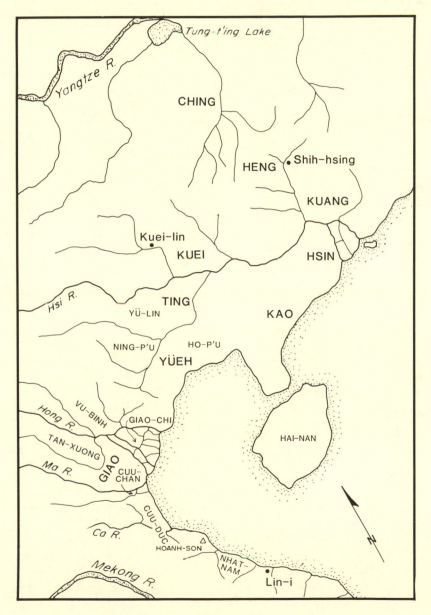

Map 5. The South during the Six Dynasties

Table 3. Administrative Records from Chin, Sung, and Ch'i

Number of Districts

	Chin (265–419)	Sung (420–78)	Ch'i (479–501)
Kuang	68	136	188
Yüeh	....	7	55
Giao	53	53	52

Hearth Counts
(none available from Ch'i)

	Chin	Sung
Kuang	43,120	49,726
Yüeh	....	938
Giao	25,600	10,453

Giao Hearth Counts
(none available from Ch'i)

Prefecture	Chin	Sung
Ho-p'u	2,000	....
Giao-chi	12,000	4,233
Tan-xuong	3,000	....
Vu-binh	5,000	1,490
Cuu-chan	3,000	2,328
Cuu-duc	....	809
Nhat-nam	600	402

SOURCE: *CS*, 15, 8b–9b; *SS*, 38, 23b–44b; *NCS*, 14, 20a–28b.

way, the northern border of Giao contracted as Ho-p'u was detached to form the nucleus of the new province.

Internally, one administrative change occurred in Giao under Sung. Giao-chi Prefecture was divided to establish the prefecture of Tong-binh south of the Hong River in the region of modern Hanoi.[114] This was the first significant administrative adjustment in Giao since the 270s. It indicates the extension of water-control systems along the Hong River, facilitating the development of paddy fields and a denser population. As the geographical center of the Hong River plain, this region's importance increased as the southern part of the plain was progressively brought under cultivation.

114. H. Maspero, "Le Protectorat general," p. 551, n. 2.

Tsung Ch'üeh, the Sung field marshal, refused to partake of the spoils plundered from Lin-i.[115] Other men were less chivalrous, however, and the distribution of war booty from the campaign of 446 was an economic inspiration to the south.[116] The fifth century was a time of phenomenal growth in population and administration; yet this growth was confined to Kuang and the new province of Yüeh.

Table 3 shows administrative and census records from the three dynasties of the fifth century. While the number of districts in Kuang nearly tripled and the figure for Yüeh grew prodigiously, the figure for Giao decreased slightly. Population statistics from Chin and Sung consist only of hearth counts, and they are very meager. (One modern writer has estimated that the actual population of Giao was at least ten times what is recorded here.)[117] Moreover the Chin figures are obviously estimates. While these figures are worthless for arriving at an accurate idea of the population, they do tell another story. As a product of imperial administration, they clearly show that in the last half of the fifth century that administration was disappearing from Giao.

As Chin power in Giao had ebbed after the conclusion of the wars with Lin-i in the fourth century, so did the power of Sung in the fifth century. The imperial court sank into drunkenness, licentiousness, and violence. In 479 the Hsiao family seized the throne and founded the Ch'i dynasty; in 502 a royal prince usurped the throne and founded the Liang dynasty. There was nearly constant fighting with the Toba empire of northern China, and the far south was neglected.

During the reign of Emperor Hsiao Wu (454–64), Huan Hung obtained appointment as governor of Giao after paying a huge sum of money; he then sold prefectural appointments and was obliged to pay a percentage of his profits to the court.[118] By the time these officials arrived in Giao, we can assume that they were mainly interested in making good their investment.

Two Sung officials who served in Giao during this time seem to stand out as exceptions to the rule of greed. A governor named Yüan Yen was a noted calligrapher famous for his cursive script. A minister at court named Chang Mu-chih "saw calamity coming," and requested the post of Giao-chi prefect; "there were signs and wonders while he governed."[119]

As corruption and a "get rich quick" mentality came to dominate court appointees, the regional ruling class, led by powerful local families,

---

115. *SS*, 76, 4a.
116. Ibid., 5, 14b.
117. Lü Shih-p'eng, *Pei shu shih-chi ti Yüeh-nan*, p. 14. Also see Hans Bielenstein, "The Census of China during the Period 2–272 A.D.," p. 145.
118. *CL*, 95.
119. Ibid., loc. cit.

looked for a chance to reclaim control of provincial affairs. In 468, Governor Liu Mu died of illness, prompting a local man named Ly Truong Nhan to kill resident officials from the north and name himself governor. A few months later, the court sent Liu Po to be Mu's replacement. However, imperial authority was very weak in the south; the governor of Kuang had been killed by rebels at the same time as Truong Nhan had gained control of Giao. Truong Nhan managed to seal the border and to prevent Po from entering the province. Po died shortly thereafter, and the court formally recognized Truong Nhan's possession of Giao.[120]

Sometime between 468 and 471, Truong Nhan died and was succeeded by his nephew Ly Thuc Hien. However, Thuc Hien had difficulty enforcing his authority, so he requested the appointment of a governor. Sung responded by naming the prefect of Nan-hai, Shen Huan, governor of Giao and appointing Thuc Hien prefect of Tan-xuong and Vu-binh. Meanwhile, probably because of his recognition by the court, Thuc Hien's position in the province had improved; he was able to raise soldiers, man the border, and prevent Shen Huan's arrival. Huan waited in Yü-lin and died there of illness.[121]

In 471, Yüeh Province was organized from portions of Kuang and Giao.[122] The immediate reason for this was to recognize those portions of Giao that were still under imperial authority, most important being the prefecture of Ho-p'u, which became the headquarters of the new province. Yüeh Province, in effect, became the new frontier of the empire.

Attempts, albeit futile, to reassert control over Giao continued. In 473, the governor of Yüeh, Ch'en Po-shao, was appointed governor of Giao in anticipation of his being able to enforce his authority there. In 477, a general named Shen Liang-te was appointed governor of Giao; his failure to enter

---

120. *TCTC*, 132, vol. 7, 572; *SS*, 8, 16b–17a. *TT*, 4, 12a–b, is based on the *SS* except for information that Truong Nhan requested and received imperial recognition at the end of 468, which is derived from *TCTC*, 132, vol. 7, 573. *VSL*, 1, 7b–8a, simply lists the names of Liu Mu, Liu Po, and Ly Truong Nhan as governors during the reign of Emperor Ming (465–72). *CL*, 95, names only Liu Po and erroneously identifies him as a governor under the Ch'i dynasty.

121. *VSL*, 1, 8a; *TT*, 4, 12b. The *TT* places these events in the seventh month of 479, the date under which Ly Thuc Hien is mentioned in *NCS*, 2, 6a, and in *TCTC*, 135, vol. 7, 683. The *VSL* and the *TT* follow the *TCTC* regarding Shen Huan; the *TCTC* prefaces this information with "in the beginning." I date the episode prior to 471, the date of the organization of Yüeh Province, for it seems to me that if Yüeh Province had already been organized, it would have figured in these events; Shen Huan was sent from the Canton area, which, until 471, was the Sung administrative center nearest to Giao. Furthermore, 479 was the year of Sung's demise and of the new Ch'i emperor's proclamation recognizing Thuc Hien; the Shen Huan episode occurred at the beginning of Thuc Hien's regime, while the Ch'i proclamation implies that Thuc Hien had been in power long enough to establish a reputation.

122. *SS*, 8, 22a, and 28, 43b–44b.

the secessionist province was recognized six months later when he was appointed governor of Kuang.[123]

In 479, when the Sung dynasty passed away and the Ch'i dynasty began, Ly Thuc Hien was still in control of Giao. In that year, the new emperor issued a proclamation about the Giao problem. The proclamation noted that Giao stood apart from the empire, failed to send taxes, and refused all communication; yet Ly Thuc Hien kept the land peaceful and reports from civil and military officials in the region praised his ability. The proclamation ended by appointing Thuc Hien governor of Giao.[124]

If the emperor had hoped to gain Thuc Hien's cooperation by this proclamation, his hopes were vain. According to one Ch'i official named Yang Hsiung-chen:

> Giao Province has gone its own way. It is located at the edge of the horizon and is joined to the Southern Barbarians beyond. It produces valuable merchandise; incomparably strange and curious things are gathered from the mountains and the sea. The people trust in their remoteness and the dangers of the road; they often rise in rebellion.[125]

Another Ch'i official named Liu Shan-ming wrote that Giao had to be dropped from the official list of imperial jurisdictions because it was "remote and inaccessible." He explained that in the later years of the Sung dynasty, Giao had been governed harshly and consequently grew resentful and rebellious; he thereby put the blame for the situation on the preceding dynasty. He recognized that administrative weakness on the frontier invited disturbances and declared that the Ch'i dynasty was trying a new policy of "mercy and virtue";[126] this was a euphemism for "issue proclamations, wait, and see," a policy dictated by weakness. From a practical point of view, Shan-ming affirmed that Giao was good only for obtaining treasure.

Ch'i's policy of "mercy and virtue" had no effect on Giao. At the end of 484, an edict noted that Giao refused to pay taxes, ignored orders, and intercepted tribute coming from foreign countries; the decision was then published to attack the recalcitrant province.[127] Significantly, this decision came during one of the few years of relative stability enjoyed by the ephemeral Ch'i dynasty.

In 485, Liu K'ai was appointed governor of Giao by Ch'i and given a large army as escort. Learning of the approaching army, Thuc Hien made a belated attempt to establish contact with the court; he sent messengers with

---

123. Ibid., 9, 3b–4a, 12b, and 10, 3b.
124. *NCS*, 2, 6a; *TCTC*, 135, vol. 7, 683.
125. *NCS*, 14 (Katakura Minoru, "Chūgoku Shihaika no Betonamu," p. 31).
126. *NCS*, 28 (Katakura, p. 31).
127. *TCTC*, 136, vol. 7, 733; *TT*, 4, 13a.

rich tribute, promising to disband his soldiers and pay regular taxes. The emperor turned a deaf ear. As K'ai neared the border, Thuc Hien personally hastened to the capital in a final, futile effort to demonstrate loyalty.[128]

The Ly family that held Giao during the dynastic transition from Sung to Ch'i bears a strong resemblance to the Ly family that attempted to seal the provincial border in 380. At that time, the Do family rose up in favor of the imperial connection. Now, however, there were no effective pro-imperial interests in the province. The Do had acted out of ambition, certainly, but also with an idealistic sense of loyalty to the empire. There seems to have been no such idealism in Giao a century later.

When Ly Truong Nhan died, Ly Thuc Hien sought a court appointment to quiet fears of northern reprisals. The fact that his appointment comprised but two prefectures did not matter; the official recognition was enough to rally the province against three would-be governors sent by the imperial court. Only after the dynastic crisis was well over and an imperial army was on its way did Thuc Hien admit the end of the road. The Ly families of the fourth and fifth centuries were anti-imperial in outlook and rebellious by inclination; it is reasonable to see in them the first stirrings of the urge toward independence that would dominate much of the sixth century.

It is recorded that as Liu K'ai prepared to depart for Giao he sought out Huan Shen, the son of former Giao governor Huan Hung, and ordered him to join the expedition; Shen was known as a "polished scholar."[129] Shen died soon after arriving in Giao, yet his participation in the project suggests that scholars as well as soldiers played important roles in imperial policy toward Giao. This was particularly true in the case of Liu K'ai's successor, Fang Fa-ch'eng.

Fang Fa-ch'eng seems to have been a sickly man who loved to read books and neglected government affairs. On his own initiative and without Fa-ch'eng's knowledge, the senior clerk, Phuc Dang Chi, was able to fill major civil and military positions with men loyal to himself. When a minor clerk informed Fa-ch'eng of what was happening, the governor angrily arrested Dang Chi and imprisoned him. Ten days later, however, Dang Chi gained his freedom by paying a large bribe to Fa-ch'eng's brother-in-law; he subsequently raised soldiers and captured Fa-ch'eng.

The presence of Fa-ch'eng's brother-in-law in a position of trust and responsibility reveals the importance of family associations in political life. Men sent to be governors of distant provinces such as Giao were accom-

128. NCS, 3, 9a; VSL, 1, 8a; TT, 4, 13a. The NCS simply announces K'ai's appointment; the VSL says he was sent to attack Thuc Hien; the TT names three prefectures in the lower Yangtze where his army was mobilized. The VSL and the TT are based on TCTC, 136, vol. 7, 736.

129. CL, 95.

panied by many members of their extended families, along with servants and armed retainers, who served as their base of power. In this case, however, family loyalty was weaker than avarice.

Dang Chi confined the governor to his home, saying, "You are ill and should not exert yourself." When Fa-ch'eng complained of nothing to do and requested books to read, Dang Chi refused, saying, "You must rest quietly to avoid exciting your illness." Dang Chi reported that Fa-ch'eng was mentally ill and incapable of performing his duties; in 490, the court appointed Dang Chi governor. Fa-ch'eng was sent back north, but died enroute.[130]

Whether Phuc Dang Chi was a provincial leader of local origin or a northerner is not clearly revealed in the records. Circumstantial evidence suggests that he was a local man, since he held the position of senior clerk. When Ku Shou attempted to gain control of the province early in the fourth century, his first move had been to kill the senior clerk, Ho Trieu. In traditional Chinese provincial administration, the senior clerk was second only to the governor in power, for day-to-day matters of government were in his hands. In Giao, where imperial authority rested upon a non-Chinese society, the senior clerk was apparently a prominent provincial leader through whom local interests were represented and imperial policy implemented. Dang Chi was able to maneuver his partisans into high office under the nose of an inattentive governor; when that governor took measures against him, he had the means to buy his way out of prison and raise an army. If he were simply a northern appointee, it is unlikely that he could have accomplished this.

In 494 the empire was ravaged by civil war, and three emperors occupied the throne in rapid succession. The three appointments to the governorship of Giao recorded in this year were only ceremonial rewards given during the course of the struggles for the throne; none of the appointees went to Giao.[131]

Sometime during the reign of Emperor Ming (494–98), Ly Khai, who was a member of a local family, replaced Phuc Dang Chi as governor. The increasing feebleness of the throne encouraged the emergence of powerful provincial families in a more active political role.

The most difficult question for ruling-class people in Vietnam at that

---

130. *NCS*, 3, 19b, simply identifies Dang Chi as a general and announces his appointment as governor in the eleventh month of 490. *TT*, 4, 13a–b, is based on *TCTC*, 137, vol. 7, 775; *CL*, 95, and *VSL*, 1, 8a–b, contain shorter versions (the *VSL* has Fang Fa-sung).

131. In the first month of 494, Senior Imperial Clerk Shen Hsi-tzu was appointed governor of Giao (*NCS*, 4, 3a). In the fourth month of 494, Tsang Ling-chih was appointed governor of Giao; he is differently recorded as the prefect of Tung-kuan (*NCS*, 4, 4b) or "Excelling Army Cavalry Commander" (*NCS*, 5, 2b). In the ninth month of 494, "former prefect of Cuu-chan" Sung Tz'u-ming was appointed governor of Giao (*NCS*, 5, 3a).

time was whether or not to continue to recognize imperial authority. Those who dared to ignore the imperial world were faced with the problem of legitimacy; by what right could they claim to challenge the throne, and with what appeal could they gain the support of the province? Without effective answers to these questions, revolutionary leaders were vulnerable to rivals willing to accept imperial overlordship.

Thus, when Ly Khai refused to recognize the new Liang dynasty in 502, Senior Clerk Ly Tac saw his opportunity. In 505, Tac mobilized his family army and killed Khai in the name of Liang; the Liang court promptly recognized him as governor.[132]

Factional strife continued, however, and eleven years later, in 516, Tac beheaded a leader of Ly Khai's old clique and gained imperial approval of his deed.[133] How much longer Tac controlled the province is unknown, but he apparently opened the way to a more direct imperial presence, for in 523 Liang effected an organizational reform that included Giao, which brings us to the story of the next chapter.

Imperial Administration and Regional Leadership

During the period covered in this chapter, imperial administration in Vietnam was neither permanent nor wholly Chinese. It came and went with the tides of dynastic power to which frontiers were so sensitive. Even at its strongest it was no more than an expedient compromise with the local society. We have seen how the census-taking abilities of imperial administration withered away in Giao after the fall of Han. Imperial taxation followed a similar course.

From the beginning of Chinese interest in the south at the time of Ch'in Shih Huang Ti, its chief motivation was a desire to possess the tropical luxury goods available there. This, in addition to the strategic concern of frontier security, remained the basic attraction for the Chinese throughout their long involvement with the Vietnamese. As Hsüeh Tsung and other writers noted, taxes were difficult to collect, but this was no cause for concern, because valuable goods and rare treasures were readily obtainable. It is not surprising, then, that very little information survives about taxation.

132. *VSL*, 1, 8b, dates Khai to the reign of Emperor Ming. No source mentions Dang Chi's death or Khai's appointment, yet *TT*, 4, 14a, says that Khai replaced Dang Chi. From this I surmise that it was a peaceful transition within the context of provincial politics; the imperial court was too weak to influence events in Giao at this time. The *TT* gives Ly Khai a middle name: Nguyen. On Ly Tac, see: *LS*, 2, 11b; *CL*, 95–96; *VSL*, 1, 8b; *TCTC*, 146, vol. 8, 273; *TT*, 4, 14a.

133. *LS*, 2, 27b; *TCTC*, 148, vol. 8, 374; *TT*, 4, 14a. The *LS* and the *TCTC* say that Tac beheaded the rebel Nguyen Tong Lao and sent his head to the capital. The *TT* identifies the dead man as Ly Tong Lao, a member of Ly (Nguyen) Khai's faction.

The only specific information on Han taxation comes from an edict of 102 that exempted Tuong-lam District in Nhat-nam from three taxes for a period of two years following an uprising there.[134] We can assume that the three taxes listed in the Tuong-lam exemption were applied throughout Chiao-chih, for Tuong-lam, where Lin-i shortly arose, was the most distant and remote Han outpost on the southern frontier.

The first tax was a "household tax" levied in place of "frontier corvée." "Frontier corvée" was a labor tax exacted by Han in frontier jurisdictions where such public works as roads, dikes, and fortifications were of special strategic importance. It was mandatory by law in border regions and could be avoided only through the payment of a "household tax," which enabled wealthy families to escape physical labor. Another tax included in the Tuong-lam exemption was a "grass-cutting tax." What exactly this was is unclear; perhaps it was a special corvée to clear new land for agriculture. The third tax listed in the Tuong-lam exemption was a "field tax." There is no further information about Han taxation in Giao except for an observation that the rebellion of 184 was in part the result of heavy taxation.[135]

The decline of Han meant the end of effective imperial taxation in Giao. Shih Hsieh sent wagonloads of luxury goods to Han and Wu as tribute in place of the imperial revenue-gathering system, which was by then extinct.

Wu eschewed the thankless task of tax collection in favor of outright confiscations and levies, as, for example, the drafting of over one thousand master craftsmen for service in Nanking or the demand for thirty peacocks to be sent to the court. This arbitrary form of exploitation lay behind the Chin intervention.

In contrast to Wu's provocative policy of extraction, the Chin interventionists came with a rational tax policy. In 271, at the height of its intervention, Chin published an edict abolishing the "cloth tax" in Giao for one year. Of course, Chin never collected any taxes from Giao during the intervention because of distance and wartime conditions. This edict was a form of propaganda. By abolishing the tax, Chin affirmed its legal right to collect it as well as its decision not to. Furthermore, the edict informed the Vietnamese that Chin intended to give them the benefit of an established tax system that would protect them from the kinds of arbitrary exactions that had become customary under Wu. Chin's "cloth tax" was specific about what was required from whom. It was graded according to distance from the Chin capital and from local administrative centers. Agriculturists in the lowlands of Giao would be required to pay a "border jurisdiction rate" set at

134. *HHS*, 4, the year 102.
135. Katakura, p. 24.

one-third the rate in China proper; silk and cotton were paid in prescribed amounts by household, with households headed by women or younger brothers paying a half rate. In addition to this "border jurisdiction rate" there were two "barbarian rates," for more remote areas, that were applied at varying distances from the provincial capital.[136]

There is no evidence that this Chin "cloth tax" was eventually collected after the fall of Wu. The only Chin taxes mentioned in the sources are the exorbitant commercial taxes that invited Lin-i aggression in the mid-fourth century. While the exorbitance of these taxes was in the well-worn tradition of greed and corruption, we can assume that the taxes themselves were part of an official revenue system designed to control the lucrative international markets on the Vietnamese coast. These markets were the main focus of Chinese interest in the south, and Chinese dynasties regarded them as an important source of enrichment.

No specific information has survived about land taxation during the period covered in this chapter, but it probably followed an aberrant system peculiar to Giao. Land taxation under the Chinese dynasties was dependent upon land systems devised in northern China to regulate the ownership and distribution of land. While these land systems and their corresponding tax systems were theoretically applied in Giao, Katakura Minoru concluded that it was not possible to put them into practice for three reasons.[137] First, Chinese dynasties before T'ang were not strong enough to enforce their land systems in Giao. Second, Chinese land systems were based on private ownership and were not uniformly applicable to Giao, where communal ownership was still strong. Third, imperial land-distribution systems were not uniformly applicable in Giao because traditional Vietnamese distribution systems based on communal ownership were still effective. Katakura may have overemphasized the importance of communal ownership while neglecting the great estates, which were beyond the effective reach of imperial revenue-gathering capabilities.

Theoretically, land taxes were applied according to three categories that depended on distance from administrative centers. According to Katakura, land taxation by Chinese in Giao was not according to any theory or law; rather, it was a specialized skill developed by the Chinese for extracting revenue in the particular circumstances of Vietnamese society; imperial land taxation in Giao was unorthodox and underwent more or less constant evolution.[138]

The theory of imperial rule and the reality of government in Giao posed a problem to Chinese dynasties, particularly when events in Giao passed beyond the control of imperial officers. In practical terms, the gap

136. Ibid., p. 29.
137. Ibid., pp. 29–30.
138. Ibid., p. 25.

between theory and reality was bridged by liberal doses of "treasure" extracted from the stubbornly un-Sinitic province. But court officials were still uncomfortable about their irregular relationship with Giao and felt a need to make some legal provision for it. This was done by invoking a "special amnesty" (*ch'ü-she*).

This term was originally coined by Chin for the specific circumstance of its intervention in Giao. The Chin generals and officials who arrived in Giao in 269 came bearing a "special amnesty," the first use of the term in Chinese history. This "special amnesty" theoretically signified the extension of imperial law over Giao; prior "foolishness" was forgiven, and future obedience was expected. In practical terms, it was a recognition of the local power situation while at the same time being an attempt to impose formal legal authority over the Vietnamese.[139]

In the late fifth and early sixth centuries, weak Chinese dynasties resorted to "special amnesties" as a means of recognizing local leaders in Giao while maintaining the fiction of imperial rule. Ch'i issued a "special amnesty" in 479 recognizing Ly Thuc Hien's control of Giao. Liang issued a "special amnesty" in 505 recognizing Ly Tac's ascendance over Ly Khai and in 516 issued another one acknowledging Ly Tac's defeat of a challenge from the Ly Khai faction.[140]

These "special amnesties" reveal that even in the realm of legal theory some adjustment was felt necessary to account for the unique situation of Giao in the imperial world. Not only was there no permanent Chinese administration in a practical sense, there was also no permanent Chinese administration in a theoretical sense. The legal status of Giao in the empire was irregular and required periodic remedial legislation. This is further illustrated by the shifting legal status of the title *governor of Giao*; in the appointments of 494, it had been reduced to an honorific.

The ineffectiveness of imperial administration in Giao was both a cause and an effect of the rising class of local families who led Giao steadily toward autonomy and independence. Heirs of the ancient Lac lords, these powerful landowning families controlled the revenues from the rich farm-lands of northern Vietnam. The inability of imperial tax collectors to benefit from these lands was partially due to the skill of these people in protecting their source of livelihood.

The character of this landowning class underwent more or less constant change in response to the vicissitudes of dynastic fortunes. Not only were ruling-class people in Giao on the fringe of imperial civilization, but their distinctive regional identity was reinforced by Vietnamese society and culture, in which they became increasingly embedded through successive generations of intermarriage.

139. Ibid., pp. 28–29.
140. *NCS*, 2, 6a; *LS*, 2, 11b, 27b.

Like Japan, Korea, and other, more transitory, realms on the periphery of China, Vietnam received Chinese civilization without losing its own personality. From the Chinese point of view, such areas comprised a particular cultural world of "Sino-Barbarian thought." [141] After a generation or more of residence in Vietnam, Chinese immigrants, no matter how outwardly loyal they may have remained to the imperial ideals of China, could not help being influenced by the values and patterns of Vietnamese society.

Vietnamese society frequently contradicted the values of Chinese society. We have already discussed the survival of levirate as late as the third century and other evidence showing the relatively high status of women in traditional Vietnamese society. The law code of the Le dynasty (fifteenth to eighteenth centuries) reveals strong female rights in marriage and inheritance that Chinese law never countenanced. [142] The role of women in Vietnamese society has always been important, and the relative freedom women enjoyed greatly ameliorated the pressures of China's patriarchal values. Chinese immigrants were certainly influenced by Vietnamese culture as much as they were able to influence it, particularly after several generations of residence and intermarriage among the Vietnamese.

It is significant that Chinese immigrants who settled permanently in Vietnam during this time were for the most part from upper-class backgrounds. They did not come as common immigrants simply looking for a place to live. They often came with books and education and imperial appointments, and sometimes with the sense of a duty to bring their civilization to a benighted frontier. They were different from the general crowd of officials, who temporarily resided among the Vietnamese with the idea of making a quick fortune before returning north. The Shih family, the T'ao family, and the Do family were all loyal imperialists; at the same time they put down roots in Vietnamese society.

Closer to the Vietnamese themselves stood men such as Luong Thac, Ly Ton, Ly Truong Nhan, Ly Thuc Hien, Phuc Dang Chi, and Ly Khai; they ignored the imperial world when they could. Through intermarriage and long residence, the regional ruling class at one end merged with Vietnamese society while at the other end, through education and imperial ambitions, it was linked to the imperial world.

The great families first appeared in a political role to stop the slide toward chaos in the south as Han collapsed. The Shih family gave the south peace as long as unresolved conflicts in the north allowed the maintenance of a locally based system of power. But when Wu was strong enough to challenge the Shih family, a contradiction appeared between imperial au-

141. Yamamoto Tatsurō, *Betonamu Chūgoku Kankei Shi*, p. 4.
142. Yu Insun, "Law and Family in Seventeenth and Eighteenth-Century Vietnam." pp. 87–174.

thority and regional tranquillity. The unrest provoked by Wu's exploitative policies and the Chin intervention that resulted from this unrest were aspects of the post-Han disorders, which finally reached Giao in the form of conflicting dynastic claims.

The fourth and fifth centuries saw the flowering of a political system congruent with a more clearly defined Vietnamese society. The effects of the upheaval caused by the fall of northern China were cushioned in Giao by distance as well as by the innate strength of Vietnamese society. The appearance of Luong Thac demonstrated the vitality of Vietnamese society and its ability to respond to changing conditions in the empire.

The new era of the Southern Dynasties, however, did bring changes to Giao, particularly under the pressure of periodic wars with Lin-i. New families took root in Giao; among them the Do, who ruled Giao for fifty years as Chin declined. The Do family was remarkable for its loyalty to the empire, its ability to rule, and its integrity to the people. It was prominent in Vietnam for five generations. This was a formative time for the regional ruling class. Under the Do, the province grew increasingly self-sufficient and confident in running its own affairs.

The brief interlude in which Sung took a particular interest in the south, culminating in the devastation of Lin-i in 446, stimulated prodigious administrative growth everywhere except in Giao. The strength of the regional ruling class in Giao was now equal to the pressure of imperial administration. Thereafter, Giao moved toward autonomy as a succession of strong local leaders gave continuity to the concept of regional leadership.

It was at this time that Giao's northern border was adjusted to the modern border between China and Vietnam in recognition of the natural frontier dividing the indigenous Vietnamese political system from imperial administration. The Vietnamese were no longer part of an amorphous frontier jurisdiction as they had been under Han and Wu, a jurisdiction based on concepts of empire rather than on the indigenous culture. By detaching Ho-p'u and establishing Yüeh Province, late in the fifth century, the Chinese realized that the Vietnamese lands were too far away and too un-Chinese to rule in the usual way. Thereafter, the Vietnamese were recognized administratively in a province of their own.

On the other hand, the Lin-i wars eventually fixed the southern border at the Hoanh-son massif. The most insistent imperial demand was that Lin-i be kept at arm's length, for no tampering with the cultural frontier would be tolerated. This imperative was a powerful influence on the formation of Vietnamese identity. The Vietnamese learned to live with it while exploring the limits of imperial control over them. They belonged to a northern empire, but they were of a southern culture. The cultural and political contradictions of their position encouraged an instinctive understanding of the use of power that became an enduring feature of their national character.

4
Local
Rule
in
the
Sixth
Century

The Liang System Penetrates the South

In the sixth century, Vietnamese identity was tested by the relaxation of Chinese power and by a search for indigenous forms of political legitimacy. The Liang political system entered the south slowly, and its penetration was cut short by the rebellion of Ly Bi in the 540s. Although Ly Bi was defeated by the redoubtable Ch'en Pa-hsien, the independence movement he began continued to develop when Pa-hsien returned north to found his own dynasty and the south fell prey to anarchy. Not until the end of the century, when the Sui dynasty extended its power into the south, was this movement brought to an end.

While Emperor Wu of Liang enjoyed a long reign (502–49) and became famous as a patron of Buddhism and literature, the business of government was largely left to his court clique. The main problem confronting Liang was the ineffectiveness of court-appointed governors in the face of powerful local families. In the south, this political problem was reinforced by an economy directed toward the south seas.

In 522, the court ordered the minting of new coins, noting that in Kuang and Giao gold and silver, rather than the official currency prevailing in all other provinces, were used as a medium of exchange. When another minting of coins was ordered more than two decades later, it was noted that the situation had not changed, and Kuang and Giao continued to use gold and silver rather than imperial coinage.[1] This is not surprising, considering the geographical isolation of the south from the rest of the empire. Kuang

---

1. *TCTC*, 149, vol. 8, 434, and 159, vol. 9, 17.

and Giao were "beyond the passes," and their economies were more naturally a part of the maritime world of Southeast Asia.

As Liang attempted to integrate the economy of the empire by issuing new currency regulations, it also sought to gain more direct control over local areas by increasing the number of governors. The governors may have been less effective than in earlier eras, but if their numbers were increased, it was hoped that the hold of the court on the countryside could be maintained. Thus, as Liang gradually extended its authority into the south, the old provinces were subdivided to form a host of new ones. While on the surface this new system might appear to have increased imperial control over these localities, in fact it was simply a recognition of emerging local power centers.

As early as 507, Kuei Province was established in western Kuang. It was in 523, however, that a significant reorganization of the south took place. Kuang was at that time further subdivided to form four new provinces, while the southern prefectures of Cuu-chan and Cuu-duc were separated from Giao to form Ai Province. Many additional provinces were subsequently created as the Liang political system was consolidated; Liang eventually established no less than thirteen new provinces in what had formerly been the provinces of Kuang and Yüeh. In 535, Hoang Province was formed along the barren coast north of the Hong River plain. Further south, Duc Province was formed out of old Cuu-duc Prefecture, while two obscure provinces named Ly and Minh were formed on the Lin-i frontier.[2]

Under the Liang system, new provinces were formed in insecure regions to give these areas recognition and to encourage their participation in the imperial order. There was no comparison in terms of territory and population between Giao Province on the one hand and Ai and Duc on the other, to say nothing of Hoang or of the nondescript provinces Ly and Minh. The provinces were not conceived as units of equal importance.

The most strategic provinces were given to members of the imperial family. In 541, two nephews of the emperor were governors of the key provinces Giao and Kuang. Provinces of less importance were given to men of lower status, including members of powerful local families. The end result of the Liang system was that the conflict of interest between local families and the court was institutionalized by recognizing local leaders as governors of small provinces. The old arena in which a court-appointed governor faced a potentially rebellious family or alliance of families was transformed into a contest between little governors and big governors.

The creation of many small provinces was intended to deflect and contain the urge toward independence, and local men were encouraged to find their place in the imperial order. Inevitably, however, there were not

2. *LS*, 2, 15b, and 3, 4b; *SuiS*, 31, 9a–13a; *YHCHC*, 1087, 1088.

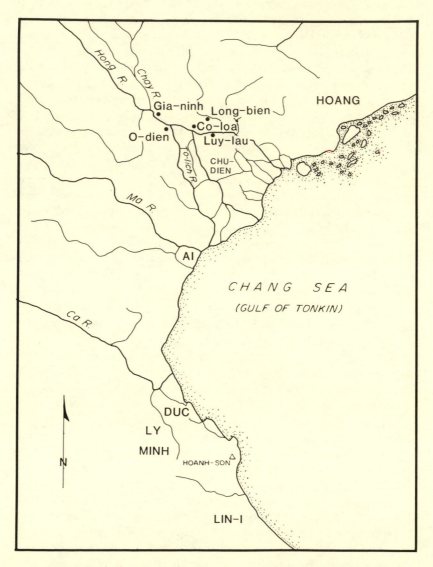

Map 6. Sixth–Century Vietnam

enough positions to absorb local ambitions. Far from closing the gap between the court and local areas, the new system simply raised the stakes of rebellion. As their familiarity with the imperial system increased, local leaders lost their fear of it and were tempted to replace it with one of their own making.

To counter this danger, special military jurisdictions were established for generals charged with enforcing the authority of the court. At first, the governor of the most important province in an area concurrently held this military post. In 509, for example, one man was appointed governor of Kuang with military authority for all four provinces that at that time comprised the south: Kuang, Kuei, Yüeh, and Giao.[3] But this military post soon evolved into a separate command held by generals of proven ability.

These generals were often protégés of the imperial princes who were appointed to the most important governorships. One such general, Ch'en Pa-hsien, arrived in the south with Hsiao Yung, son of a younger brother of Emperor Wu; Yung became governor of Kuang, and Pa-hsien became Hsi River protector general, with his headquarters in modern Kuang-hsi.[4] Pa-hsien was a man of ability and ambition; from a successful career in the south he later rose to the throne and founded the last of the southern dynasties.

Ly Bi

Ly Tac, who gained control of Giao in 505 and defeated a rival clique in 516, apparently cultivated close and friendly relations with the empire. Men of prominent local families were encouraged to seek careers as imperial officials. One such person was Tinh Thieu, a man of some literary talent who went to the Liang court in search of an official position. The president of the Board of Civil Office, Ts'ai Tsun, denied Thieu the sort of job he was looking for on the grounds that his family had never before produced a scholar; Tsun instead appointed him to oversee one of the gates in the wall of the capital city. Thieu resented this disregard for his ability and subsequently returned to Giao with another disappointed office seeker named Ly Bi. They probably returned to Giao around 523, when new provinces were being formed there.[5]

Ly Bi's ancestors were among the Chinese who fled south to escape the disorders of Wang Mang's usurpation (A.D. 9–23). In the sixth century, the Ly family was established on the north bank of the Hong River in Vu-binh near Tan-xuong, in the shadow of Mount Tam-dao. This was a strategic

---

3. *LS*, 21, 20a.

4. *ChS*, 1, 2a; *TCTC*, 158, vol. 8, 745.

5. *TCTC*, 158, vol. 8, 738–39; *TT*, 4, 15a. Ts'ai Tsun died in 523; judging from his biography, he was president of the Board of Civil Office sometime between 510 and 520 (*LS*, 21, 21b).

area on the upland frontier of the Hong River plain, and the Ly were known as a family of "military assistants." At the beginning of his career, Bi went north and held an official position at the Liang court but was "unable to attain his ambition." So he returned to Giao, where he was appointed military overseer of Duc Province. There, he eventually "joined with the heroes of several provinces" and rose in rebellion.[6]

Ly Bi's ambitions were favored by the political situation in Giao. The governor of Giao was a nephew of the emperor named Hsiao Tzu; it is recorded that he had alienated the population with acts of extortion and cruelty. In 541, Bi gained the support of Trieu Tuc, a man identified as the "leader" of Chu-dien. It is recorded that Tuc "yielded to the talent and virtue" of Bi and led an army into Bi's service. When Hsiao Tzu saw this, he purchased his own life with a bribe and hastened to Kuang, where his cousin Hsiao Yung was governor.[7]

The location of Chu-dien is discussed in Appendix H. In Han times it lay between the Day and Hong rivers, probably near the place where these two rivers divide their waters; Trung Trac's husband, Thi Sach, was from there. Through the centuries, however, the name *Chu-dien* seems to have shifted downriver until, by the sixth century, it lay near the coast, where the Hong River met the tides. Much of the land was swampy and uncultivated, for the diking system had not yet been extended so far. Ancient traditions that were but a lingering, albeit potent, memory among the more settled districts further north probably remained alive in Chu-dien, and spokesmen of this region seem to have wielded a latent moral authority capable of awakening a response in all parts of the plain.

Chinese records are ignorant of Trieu Tuc. The Chinese saw, understood, and recorded Ly Bi and his advisor Tinh Thieu as two former imperial servants who had become rebels. But Tuc's authority was apparently based on cultural assumptions outside Chinese perception. According to

---

6. *ChS*, 1, 2a; *TCTC*, 158, vol. 8, 138, 139; *TT*, 4, 14b–15a. For a discussion of textual problems related to Ly Bi's background, see Appendix G.

7. *TT*, 4, 15a; *TCTC*, 158, vol. 8, 739; *CL*, 96. *LS*, 3, 26a, says Tzu fled to Yüeh Province, which is on the way to Kuang. Chinese records and the *CL* do not mention Trieu Tuc; they simply record that Tzu bought his freedom and fled after Ly Bi and his followers rose in rebellion. *VSL*, 1, 8b, merely says that Ly Bi rebelled and occupied Long-bien, the capital of Giao, without mentioning either Tuc or Tzu. The *TT*'s introduction of Trieu Tuc and its elaboration of his role in the uprising is the beginning of a divergence between the Chinese and Vietnamese sources on the events of the sixth century. The considerable amount of information about the sixth century that is peculiar to the *TT* is derived from the *Su ky* of Do Thien, a work of the first half of the twelfth century, which remains only in citations preserved in the *VDULT*, the *LNCQ*, and the *TT* (Émile Gaspardone, "Bibliographie annamite," pp. 55, 127). Do Thien's *Su ky* was apparently based on records from the many temples erected to the memory of the Vietnamese heroes of this era; for example, see Nguyen Van Huyen, "Contribution a l'étude d'un génie tutelaire annamite Lí Phuc Man."

Vietnamese records, the rise of Tuc was the immediate event that prompted Hsiao Tzu to flee the province.

This is understandable if we recall that Ly Bi's rebellion began in Duc, where he was a military official. Bi probably advanced north from Duc into Ai. Chu-dien bordered on Ai and was consequently Bi's key for entering the Hong River plain. When Tuc opened Chu-dien, and thereby the Hong River plain, to Bi, the Chinese saw their position was hopeless; the response to Tuc was so overwhelming that Hsiao Tzu had to bribe his way out of the province. While the Chinese recognized the strategic implications of Tuc's leadership, they preferred to officially ignore him in favor of Ly Bi, who could easily be identified in terms of established categories of imperial political thought.

Liang's response was organized with alacrity. Sun Ch'iung, the governor of Kao, and Lu Tzu-hsiung, the governor of Hsin, were ordered to march against Ly Bi. Kao and Hsin were among the provinces created by Liang in old Kuang, west of modern Canton. Ch'iung and Tzu-hsiung were local men, now suddenly thrust into the unenviable position of being forced to demonstrate their loyalty by undertaking a hazardous frontier assignment.

It was springtime, 542, and the rainy season was about to begin. Ch'iung and Tzu-hsiung requested that the enterprise be postponed until autumn, when the danger of malaria and other monsoon afflictions would be reduced. The request was denied by Hsiao Yung, and Hsiao Tzu urged the army forward. The reluctant army advanced as far as Ho-p'u, where it stalled; between sixty and seventy percent of the men were reported dead, whether from disease or from ambush by Ly Bi's men is unclear.[8] The Liang army was scattered and straggled back in confusion.

Ch'iung and Tzu-hsiung seem to have been victims of the hasty preparations forced upon them by their superiors. Perhaps to ease his pricked dignity, Hsiao Tzu reported that the two men were in league with the rebels and had, in loitering, occasioned the disaster; he forthwith obtained an imperial order for their execution. Ch'iung and Tzu-hsiung were summoned to Kuang and put to death.[9]

This act of imperial pique provoked a violent reaction. The sons and nephews of Sun Ch'iung and Lu Tzu-hsiung gathered a large following and, capturing the local protector general, invaded Kuang Province with the intention of killing Hsiao Tzu and Hsiao Yung in revenge for the deaths of

8. Maurice Durand, "La Dynastie des Ly anterieurs d'aprés le *Viet dien u linh tap*", p. 440, surmised that the Liang army was struck by an epidemic. Modern Vietnamese historians (Uy Ban Khoa Hoc Xa Hoi Viet Nam, *Lich su Viet Nam*, 1: 114) prefer to posit an ambush sprung by Ly Bi.

9. *TCTC*, 158, vol. 8, 739, 745; *ChS*, 1, 2a; *TT*, 4, 15a–b; *CL*, 96. The *CL* observes that Tzu's accusation was false.

their kinsmen. However, the imperial princes were saved by the timely arrival of Ch'en Pa-hsien, Hsi River protector general, with three thousand handpicked soldiers, who succeeded in restoring order.[10]

Pa-hsien was rewarded with new titles and emerged as the dominant figure in the south when Hsiao Yung died shortly thereafter. Hsiao Tzu disappears from the records. The fragile situation throughout the south in the wake of these events insured that no major campaign against Ly Bi could be contemplated for some time. Small local forces were nonetheless sent to probe Giao's border and to observe the situation.[11]

In early summer of 543, the king of Lin-i invaded Duc. It is not known whether or not this aggression was prompted by Liang diplomacy; it may simply have been a natural response to the opportunity presented by political turmoil in the empire. Ly Bi sent a general named Pham Tu against the invaders; the Lin-i army was defeated and withdrew.[12]

After this, Ly Bi's prospects looked brighter; threats from both the north and the south had been disposed of, and it was now possible for him to think of organizing his realm. At the beginning of 544, Ly Bi proclaimed himself the emperor of Nam Viet. *Nam Viet* is Vietnamese for Nan Yüeh; Bi was thus invoking the precedent of Chao T'o, who seven centuries earlier had defied the Han Empire by taking the title emperor of Nan Yüeh. Bi published the name of his realm as Van Xuan, "Ten Thousand Spring-times," and took the reign title Thien-duc, "Heavenly Virtue." He established a court hierarchy and built a palace named Van Tho, "Ten Thousand Life Spans." Tinh Thieu was designated Bi's chief civil official, Pham Tu became the chief military official, and Trieu Tuc was named "Great Master."[13]

The title "Great Master" (*thai-pho*) originated during the Chou dynasty of antiquity, when it was held by one of the three dukes who advised

10. *ChS*, 1, 2a–b; *TCTC*, 158, vol. 8, 745.

11. *LS*, 3, 26b. The *LS* ignores the unsuccessful campaign of 542 and the resulting uprising against Kuang. It is, however, the only source to record that late in 542 the governor of Yüeh, Ch'en Hou, the governor of Lo, Ning Chu, the governor of An, Li Chih, and the governor of Ai, Yüan Han, were ordered to attack Ly Bi. Yüeh, Lo, and An were all on the Giao border; Yüan Han's appointment as governor of Ai may have been in recognition of his role on the border.

12. *TCTC*, 158, vol. 8, 751; *LS*, 3, 26b; *TT*, 4, 15b.

13. *TCTC*, 158, vol. 8, 755, says "Emperor of Viet." *TT*, 4, 15b, and *VSL*, 1, 8b, both say "Emperor of Nam Viet"; Chinese historians would not have countenanced the name Nam Viet because of Chao T'o's rebellious precedent. *LS*, 3, 27a, says Bi usurped imperial authority by changing the reign title. *TCTC*, 158, vol. 8, 755, gives the reign title as Thien-duc. *TT*, 4, 15b, and *VSL*, 1, 8b, give not only the reign title but the name of the kingdom as well: Van Xuan. The *LS* (3, 27a), the *TCTC* (158, vol. 8, 755), and the *VSL* (1, 8b), state that Bi established an imperial court hierarchy. *TT*, 4, 15b, adds the information about the Van Tho Palace and the names and titles of Ly Bi's appointees.

the king about auspicious and inauspicious portents.[14] In the Later Han period, only one such duke was appointed, and he held the title "Great Master." The Chin dynasty returned to the classical practice of appointing three dukes, and this was followed by all the succeeding southern dynasties.[15] The appearance of this title in sixth-century Vietnam suggests that Trieu Tuc was perceived as a kind of royal mentor.

Ly Bi stood at the head of a group of people who began their careers as frontier guardians. Many of them seem to have visited the Liang capital as office seekers and to have returned in disappointment to take up frontier assignments. Considering their familiarity with the Liang court and imperial government, it was natural for them to look at independence as merely the duplication of Chinese forms. The idea of an emperor, of a reign title, and of a literary name for the kingdom were all Chinese in inspiration.

On the other hand, Trieu Tuc came from the lowland culture of the Hong River plain. There is no evidence of his being an official in the Liang system of government. He undoubtedly stood at the head of a powerful, influential family. Chu-dien was on the southern fringe of the agricultural heartland, but it was nevertheless encompassed by the Buddhist culture of Vietnam. The Do family that ruled Vietnam for half a century in the late fourth and early fifth century had settled in Chu-dien. As we will see later in this chapter, the most prominent Vietnamese Buddhist monk of the sixth century came from Chu-dien and bore the surname Do.[16] We can reasonably conjecture that Trieu Tuc represented the agrarian Buddhist culture of the Hong River plain.

As "Great Master," Trieu Tuc may have fostered Buddhist influence at Ly Bi's court. There is evidence to suggest that a Buddhist temple with an eight-foot seated Amitabha carved of stone was erected by Ly Bi. The style of the Amitabha, which still exists, closely resembles that of the carvings found at Lung-men in northern China, which belong to the sixth century. Nguyen Phuc Long has surmised that people such as Tinh Thieu, who served in the Liang capital at Nanking, brought this style back to Vietnam and that the giant Amitabha was carved to celebrate the opening of Ly Bi's reign. The Amitabha exists in a temple of undated origin named Van Phuc, "Ten Thousand Happinesses," and Nguyen Phuc Long has proposed that this temple was built in conjunction with Ly Bi's palace, Van Tho, "Ten Thousand Life Spans," for *phuc*, "happiness," and *tho*, "longevity," are words that often appear together in Chinese and Vietnamese literature.[17]

14. Morohashi Tetsuji, *Dai Kanwa Jiten*, 3, 540.

15. Ibid., 3, 532.

16. Tran Van Giap, "Le Bouddhisme en Annam des origines au XIIIe siècle," p. 236.

17. Nguyen Phuc Long, "Les Nouvelles Recherches archéologiques au Vietnam," pp. 26–27.

However that may be, the use of Buddhism to buttress an independent monarchical tradition is an important theme in later Vietnamese history, particularly from the tenth through the fourteenth centuries. This theme seems to owe its origins to the independence movements of the sixth century, and perhaps it may be possible to trace it back to the time of Shih Hsieh.

Ly Bi's court was organized along traditional Chinese lines, and he may have patronized the Buddhist religion. There is also evidence that he honored a popular spirit cult. According to one tradition preserved in temple documents, Ly Bi erected a shrine to the memory of Lady Trieu, the leader of the 248 uprising, and honored her with a posthumous title.[18] The shrine still exists in what was Cuu-chan, or Ai. Since Ly Bi marched north through Ai when he raised the standard of revolt, perhaps he built the shrine at that time. Lady Trieu had also led a rebel army north through Ai against the Chinese, and Ly Bi may have tried to invoke the memory of this popular folk heroine to spur the enthusiasm of his followers.

In his few years of rule, Bi's principal concern was to guard the frontiers and keep the peace. The only information on this is the following brief notice about one of Bi's commanders named Ly Phuc Man:

> He assisted Ly the Southern Emperor as a general and became famous for his loyalty and heroism; he was entrusted with the two valleys of Do-dong and Duong-lam; the Lao barbarians feared him and dared not make trouble; he kept the peace throughout the entire region.[19]

Ly Phuc Man became the object of a spirit cult after his death and was posthumously honored by a Vietnamese king in the eleventh century.[20]

Do-dong and Duong-lam appear in Vietnamese sources from the tenth century and refer to an area along the right bank of the Hong River west and north of modern Hanoi. This was directly across the river from Ly Bi's home estates. The importance of Ly Phuc Man's role can be understood if we bear in mind that he guarded the southern bank of the Hong while Ly Bi, from his home district, guarded the northern bank; together they sealed the strategic routes leading into the mountains and shielded the Hong River plain from the depredations of mountain tribes. These tribes were called Lao by the Chinese and Vietnamese of that time; their exact ethnic identification is unclear, though they were presumably related to Thai-speaking peoples.

Ly Bi's capital is not identified in the sources, but we can surmise that his main citadel was Gia-ninh. Gia-ninh lay close to Bi's home estates, near the place where the Hong is joined by its tributaries. This is the region where

18. Tran Trong Kim, *Viet Nam su luoc*, 1: 47.
19. *VDULT*, 25, quoted from Do Thien's *Su ky*.
20. Nguyen Van Huyen.

the Hung kings supposedly ruled; it was a natural political center at the head of the Hong River plain.[21]

While Ly Bi and his assistant Ly Phuc Man watched the mountains and kept peace in the Hong River plain, other trusted generals, such as Pham Tu, watched the frontiers with Liang and Lin-i. Actual administration in the agricultural lands of the Hong River plain, whatever that may have been, was probably supervised by Tinh Thieu, perhaps from the traditional provincial seat of Long-bien. The Trieu family undoubtedly dominated the lowlands.

This first gesture of the Vietnamese toward independence was aborted by the martial skill and imperial ambitions of Ch'en Pa-hsien. Yet the forces it unleashed continued to run their course for several decades, arousing a heightened consciousness among the Vietnamese of their distinctive identity as a people and contributing to the eventual realization of Vietnamese independence.

By 545, Liang had stabilized the situation in the south and was prepared to move against Ly Bi. Yang P'iao was appointed governor of Giao, and Ch'en Pa-hsien was given responsibility for military affairs in the secessionist province. An army of seasoned veterans was organized in Kuang and marched west to rendezvous with Hsiao Po, the governor of Ting, in what is modern Kuang-hsi.

Hsiao Po's father was a cousin of the emperor; as a member of the imperial family, his words carried some weight. Furthermore, as governor of Ting, he was presumably in a position to be best informed of the situation further south. Po echoed the fears of military officials who dreaded the thought of a campaign in the far south and advised Yang P'iao to forgo the projected expedition in favor of more subtle stratagems. P'iao thereupon convened a conference of his generals to decide what to do. The energy and determination of Ch'en Pa-hsien dominated the discussion, as he expostulated with the vigor of a man destined to be emperor:

> Giao-chi has risen in criminal rebellion and transgressed against the imperial family, sending confusion and turbulence into several provinces and escaping punishment year after year. Ting Province wants to use clandestine means to resolve this situation and shrinks from a direct attack. We have received an imperial order to punish a crime, and we should carry it out even if we die in the attempt. How can we loiter about and not advance, thereby increasing the advantage of the rebels and demoralizing our own troops?[22]

This rhetoric had its desired effect. P'iao gave Pa-hsien command of the vanguard, and the army proceeded.

---

21. On Gia-ninh, see H. Maspero, "Le Protectorat general d'Annam sous les T'ang," pp. 666–67.

22. *ChS*, 1, 2b–3a; *TCTC*, 159, vol. 9, 3; *TT*, 4, 16a; *CL*, 96.

Near the end of summer in 545 the Liang expedition penetrated Ly Bi's kingdom. Ly Bi led an army of thirty thousand men to meet the Chinese as they entered the Hong River plain; the route of the Liang army is not revealed in the sources, but the details of the campaign imply that it came by sea.

Pa-hsien defeated Bi in the lower plain at Chu-dien. Bi then retreated to the mouth of the To-lich River, in the environs of modern Hanoi, where he waited behind a system of hastily constructed fortifications. However, he was defeated a second time and withdrew to his citadel at Gia-ninh at the head of the plain, where he was promptly besieged by the Liang army.[23]

At the beginning of 546, Gia-ninh fell to the Chinese, Ly Bi neverthe-less managed to escape into the nearby mountains among Lao tribesmen. He rallied his scattered forces, along with a number of Lao chieftains, and, in the autumn of the year, emerged from the mountains with an army of twenty thousand men.[24]

Bi camped on the shore of Dien-triet Lake on the border of Tan-xuong Prefecture, where the mountains meet the plains. The lake was a natural reservoir that emptied into the rivers during times of low water and filled when the rivers were high. Bi had his men construct boats, and he filled the lake with them. The Chinese were camped at the mouth of the lake and observed Bi's host with increasing trepidation.

Sensing that the moment of truth had arrived, Pa-hsien called together his generals and said:

> I have already been in command for a long time and the soldiers are utterly weary in body and spirit; moreover, we are a solitary army, without support, entering into the very heart of the enemy; if we do not gain victory with one more battle, how can we hope to get out alive? Now, in view of the fact that our enemy has repeatedly run away, and the feelings of the people are not firmly fixed, and the Lao barbarians are undisciplined and unreliable, it will be easy to exterminate our foe. The proper course of action is to pursue our task to the death, concentrating all our strength on attaining success; there is no reason for delay; now is the time to act![25]

His dispirited generals were stunned and made no reply. Although Bi had lost every battle, his genius for survival threatened to outlast the strength of his enemy.

Pa-hsien's assertion that "the feelings of the people are not firmly fixed" was based on his own severe sense of loyalty and discipline. But even

23. The details of the campaign to this point come from *TCTC*, 159, vol. 9, 3, from which are derived the accounts of the *TT* (4, 16a) and the *VSL* (1, 8b–9a). *ChS*, 1, 3a, mentions only the battle at the mouth of the To-lich River. On the location of Chu-dien and the probable route of the Liang army, see Appendix H.

24. *TCTC*, 159, vol. 9, 15; *LS*, 3, 29a; *TT*, 4, 16b; *VSL*, 1, 9a.

25. *ChS*, 1, 3b.

allowing for this, it is clear that Ly Bi's rule had been too short to engender deep feelings of loyalty among the people. The idea of independence from the empire was probably difficult for many people to grasp. Nearly a year had passed since Bi had gone into the mountains. His return from the mountains, however, undoubtedly raised the spirits of all Vietnamese and threatened to rally a new uprising capable of sweeping away the isolated Liang army.

The above quotation reveals to what extent the success of the Liang expedition depended upon the personality of one man, and to what extent it crossed the prevailing tide of affairs in the south. Ly Bi's so-called "defeats," recorded in Chinese sources, may in fact have been strategic withdrawals designed to draw the Chinese ever deeper into his realm and away from their supply bases, wearing them out through attrition. If this was indeed Bi's plan, Ch'en Pa-hsien's extraordinary stubbornness brought it to naught.

The night after Pa-hsien's exhortation to his generals, the level of the river abruptly rose, causing the water to flow precipitantly into the lake. Seizing the advantage of this strong and unexpected current, Pa-hsien embarked his army and sent it rushing into the lake amidst a tumultuous clamor; Bi was unprepared for this assault, and his army scattered in confusion.

Bi escaped once more into the mountains among the Lao; he established himself at Khuat-lieu Valley, somewhere along the upper Hong. He was apparently attempting to organize further resistance when the Lao, responding to Chinese bribes, killed him and sent his head to the Chinese.

In 547, after the death of Ly Bi, Bi's elder brother Ly Thien Bao escaped to the southern coast in Duc, where he raised an army of twenty thousand men with the assistance of a local leader named Ly Thieu Long. After killing Ch'en Wen-chieh, the newly appointed Liang governor of Duc, Thien Bao advanced and besieged the citadel of Ai. However, Pa-hsien soon arrived with reinforcements and drove him back into the mountains. Pa-hsien's determined energy had swept away the nascent kingdom of Van Xuan, but the troubles that immediately broke out in the north prevented the Chinese from reestablishing their control over the Vietnamese.[26]

26. On the battle at Dien-triet Lake, see *ChS*, 1, 3b; *TCTC*, 159, vol. 9, 18–19; *TT*, 4, 16b–17a; *VSL*, 1, 9a. On Ly Thien Bao's campaign, see *ChS*, 1, 4a (the only source to mention Ly Thieu Long and Ch'en Wen-chiai); *VSL*, 1, 9a (the only source to identify Thien Bao as a son of Ly Bi); *TT*, 4, 19a–b (which makes the Vietnamese army thirty thousand strong and introduces Ly Phat Tu as a kinsman and companion of Thien Bao); and *TCTC*, 161, vol. 9, 65 (which cites the *LS* for dating Bi's death and Thien Bao's campaign in 548). The *LS* ignores the battle on the lake, as well as Bi's death and Thien Bao's campaign; it simply records a "special amnesty" granted to the three provinces of Giao, Ai, and Duc in the fifth month of 548 (*LS*, 3, 33b). The *TCTC* dates Bi's death and Thien Bao's campaign on the basis of this "special amnesty." However, the *ChS*, which is the most detailed and contemporary source, embeds

The View from Chinese Records: 548–89

Chinese and Vietnamese sources take different paths through the sixth century, and before turning to the Vietnamese sources we must look carefully at the Chinese side to determine how far the Vietnamese side of the story can be trusted. We need to examine the crumbling edge of Chinese power and to discuss the extent to which its decay made space for the Vietnamese to pursue a political life of their own.

By 548, Ch'en Pa-hsien had returned to his post as Hsi River protector general in modern Kuang-hsi. At this time, the Toba Empire (Northern Wei dynasty), which had dominated northern China for a century and a half, was disintegrating under the pressure of ambitious generals who controlled much of the countryside. One such general was Hou Ching, a governor in the area of modern Ho-nan. In 547, he proclaimed allegiance to Liang, but in the following year, with the collaboration of some Liang princes and officials, he openly invaded Liang. In 549 he seized the Liang capital and put Emperor Wu to death.

These events aroused in Ch'en Pa-hsien the utmost eagerness to march north and test his ability against the northern usurper. In 548, he was on the point of leading an army to the emperor's assistance when he learned that the governor of Kuang, Yüan Ching-chung, was secretly preparing to join Hou Ching's clique. The situation quickly evolved into open hostilities between Pa-hsien and Ching-chung. In 549, Ching-chung was defeated, and Pa-hsien invited Hsiao Po to be governor of Kuang.[27] With Kuang secure in his rear, Pa-hsien prepared to go north, but he found further difficulties barring the way.

Between Kuang and the mountains to the north separating the Hsi and Yangtze basins lay Heng Province. When Pa-hsien marched against Ly

---

these events in the narrative of Ch'en Pa-hsien's biography, which follows the chronology of his career. After describing the battle on the lake in 546 and Bi's escape to Khuat-lieu Valley, *ChS*, 1, 4a, says: "Khuat-lieu beheaded Bi and sent his head to the capital. In the same year, being Tai-ching the first [547], Bi's elder brother Thien Bao escaped." Durand's interpretation ("La Dynastie," p. 444) fails to account for the word "escape" and its relationship to Ly Bi's death, or for the presence of Liang forces in Duc and Ai prior to Thien Bao's arrival there. Durand ("La Dynastie," pp. 443–44) locates Khuat-lieu north of the Hong, while modern Vietnamese historians (Cao Huy Giu, trans. and Dao Duy Anh, annotator, *Dai Viet su ky toan thu*, p. 322, n. 45) believe it was south of the Hong. *CL*, 96, agrees with the *ChS* that Bi was beheaded by the mountain tribes; *VSL*, 1, 9a, and *TT*, 4, 18a, claim that he died a natural death. The thirteenth-century Vietnamese historian Le Van Huu lamented Ly Bi's misfortune in having to face a man of such unusual ability as Ch'en Pa-hsien. The fifteenth-century historian Ngo Si Lien added to this the sad thought that the will of Heaven was not yet prepared to countenance Vietnamese independence and so caused the waters to rise, to the advantage of the Chinese (*TT*, 4, 18a–b).

27. *ChS*, 1, 4a; *LS*, 4, 3b.

Bi in 545, the governor of Heng, Lan Ch'in, went along; accompanying Ch'in was his trusted assistant Ou-yang Wei. When Ch'in died of illness enroute to Giao, Wei obtained permission to return with his patron's body. Wei was subsequently left in charge of Heng when senior officials of the province hastened north to fight Hou Ching.

When Hou Ching killed Emperor Wu, local officials in many parts of the south usurped authority and seized territory; among these was Lan Yü, the younger brother of Wei's deceased patron Lan Ch'in and now the governor of Kao Province. Yü was trying to organize a clique of his own and invited Wei to join him; when Wei refused, Yü attacked him. Pa-hsien had just finished securing Kuang, so he moved north to Wei's assistance and defeated Yü. Wei subsequently aided Pa-hsien when he prepared to move north through the mountains against Hou Ching.[28]

Although Hsiao Po again cautioned restraint, as he had before the expedition against Ly Bi, Ch'en Pa-hsien could not be held back. In 550, he won his first important battle north of the mountains, in modern Chiang-hsi; it was in recognition of this victory that he was named governor of Giao by the Liang prince in whose name he was campaigning.[29] In the chaos of that time, gubernatorial appointments were used as a means of recognizing loyalty and merit and were not necessarily connected with the actual province in question.

In 551 Pa-hsien gained new victories, and in 552 Hou Ching was driven from the capital and killed. Emperor Yüan, who now came to the throne, was a prince with roots in the central Yangtze; he left the eastern half of the empire, including the capital, in the hands of two powerful generals, one of whom was Ch'en Pa-hsien, and personally ruled from the city now called Wu-han (Hankow).[30]

With the empire partitioned in this manner, the south was left in the hands of Hsiao Po. Po's first order of business was to put down a new rebellion in Kuang. The general decay of authority in the south is recognized in the records, which state that the area under Po's command extended for less than one thousand Chinese miles and that the population registers did not add up to thirty thousand.[31]

A Chinese mile was usually reckoned at 360 paces, so one thousand Chinese miles might be calculated as approximately three hundred and fifty English miles, a distance that, if measured from Po's headquarters at Canton, falls short of the Giao border. But the phrase "one thousand miles" in

28. *ChS*, 1, 4b, and 9, 6b–7b; *NS*, 66, 15b; *TCTC*, 161, vol. 9, 82, and 162, vol. 9, 117, 125.

29. *TCTC*, 163, vol. 9, 139. *TT*, 1, 19a, assumes that Ch'en Pa-hsien was still in Giao at this time and that his appointment as governor was in recognition of his victory over Ly Bi.

30. *TCTC*, 163, vol. 9, 140, and 164, vol. 9, 175, 203.

31. *TCTC*, 164, vol. 9, 206, 209.

Chinese sources was as rhetorical and psychological in intent as it was geographical, and in particular the expression "less than one thousand miles" meant that Po's sphere of authority was extremely limited.

As an old associate of Pa-hsien, Hsiao Po was not particularly trusted by Emperor Yüan; Po contributed to this distrust by raising and training a large army. Hoping to allay the emperor's suspicions, Po boldly offered to go to the court and answer any charges against him. The emperor ignored him, however, and, in 554, sent Wang Lin, a general who was becoming too popular in the north, to replace Po. Wang Lin was in the south for less than a year and spent that time in what is now Kuang-hsi. One immediate result of his southern sojourn was to force Ou-yang Wei into Hsiao Po's increasingly rebellious clique.[32] Ou-yang Wei was at that time in command of Shih-hsing, strategically located on the route north from Canton. However, the potentially explosive situation developing between Wang Lin and Hsiao Po was abruptly terminated by more serious events in the north.

Ever since the time of Hou Ching's usurpation, the Toba successor state in the northwest, known as the Western Wei dynasty, had been encroaching on the northern and western borders of Liang. Finally, a full-scale invasion captured the Liang emperor's capital in 555; large portions of the central Yangtze region were thereafter controlled by the Western Wei, which became known as the Northern Chou dynasty after 557. It was to resist this invasion that Wang Lin suddenly returned north late in 554.[33]

As soon as Wang Lin had returned north, Hsiao Po renewed his military preparations. Late in 555, as Po consolidated his position in the south, one of Wang Lin's men, named Liu Yüan-yen, returned north with his dependents, numbering several thousand persons, and joined Lin; when Lin returned north, Yüan-yen had apparently remained in modern Kuang-hsi, where Lin's influence was fairly strong. Yüan-yen held the honorific title governor of Giao;[34] he could not have been in the south for much more than a year, and it is very unlikely that he set foot in Giao during that time.

In 556, both Hsiao Po and his colleague Ou-yang Wei received titles from Ch'en Pa-hsien. At the beginning of the following year, however, when Pa-hsien took the throne for himself, Po, a scion of the Liang imperial family, openly challenged him. Po remained at Shih-hsing and sent Wei north against the new emperor. Wei's army was defeated, and he himself was captured. When this news reached Shih-hsing, Po's followers looked to their own safety; one of them, named Ch'en Fa-wu, attacked and killed Po. (Fa-wu, a former governor of Heng, held the honorific title governor of Duc in 557,[35] although he was probably never in Duc, unless it was during Pa-hsien's campaign against Ly Bi.)

32. ChS, 9, 8a; TCTC, 165, vol. 9, 238, and 167, vol. 9, 298.
33. LS, 5, 29a; TCTC, 164, vol. 9, 209.
34. Ibid., 166, vol. 9, 260, 267–68, 269.
35. LS, 6, 6a, 7b–8a; TCTC, 166, vol. 9, 289, and 167, vol. 9, 298, 299–300.

After Po's death, the south was in disorder. Aware that Ou-yang Wei enjoyed a certain reputation in the south, Pa-hsien set him free and appointed him governor of Heng and governor general with military authority over the nineteen provinces that in theory now comprised the old provinces of Kuang and Giao. Ou-yang He, Wei's son, was already in the south, and he assisted his father in securing the submission of Po's old clique, which had withdrawn to Kuang Province.[36]

One month later, however, Wang Lin, in the central Yangtze, rose in rebellion, and the south labored under his shadow for three years. Until 557, when he accepted an appointment from the new Ch'en emperor, Wang Lin had remained loyal to the surviving remnant of the Liang imperial household.[37] Lin attracted the support of some officials in the south, and in 558 he attempted to rally their active participation on his behalf. In that year Wei was appointed governor of Kuang by Ch'en Pa-hsien, perhaps to encourage his loyalty. When Ch'en Pa-hsien died in 559, the governor of Kuei, in modern Kuang-hsi, went over to Lin, but Wei remained loyal to Ch'en and was rewarded with a series of new titles and a more prestigious rank. Finally, in 560, Lin was defeated and forced to seek refuge in northeastern China.[38] For the next decade there was relative stability in the south under the Ou-yang father and son.

Sometime during the rebellion of Wang Lin, Ou-yang Wei secretly received a quantity of gold from a certain Yüan T'an-huan, who bore the title governor of Giao. Wei sent a portion of this gold to the prefect of Ho-p'u and gave the rest to his son. This obscure episode was probably related to Wang Lin's rebellion and the demonstration of, and the rewarding of, loyalty. When T'an-huan died, the title governor of Giao was given to Wei's younger brother Ou-yang Sheng.[39]

Sheng's title as governor of Giao was clearly an honorific, for his only recorded activities come from helping his elder brother suppress rebels north of Kuang.[40] This recalls the appointment of Ch'en Pa-hsien as governor of Giao in 550 after he had already left the south, the departure of Liu Yüan-yen, governor of Giao, northward to join Wang Lin in 555, and the title of Ch'en Fa-wu, governor of Duc, who killed Hsiao Po at Shih-hsing in 557. These men may indeed have had some connection with Giao, perhaps as participants in the expedition against Ly Bi, but all the evidence suggests that the titles they held were merely honorifics.[41]

In 563, Ou-yang Wei died and was succeeded by his son He. It is

36. *ChS*, 9, 8b; *NS*, 66, 16b; *TCTC*, 167, vol. 9, 301.

37. *TCTC*, 166, vol. 9, 278, 281–82, 285, 286, 288, and 167, vol. 9, 298.

38. *ChS*, 9, 8b–9a; *NS*, 66, 16b; *TCTC*, 167, vol. 9, 320–22, 336, and 168, vol. 9, 361, 383.

39. *ChS*, 9, 9a; *NS*, 66, 16b.

40. *ChS*, 35, 8a.

41. Gotō Kimpei, *Betonamu Kyūgoku Kōsō Shi*, pp. 218–20.

recorded that He "displayed majesty and kindness to those dwelling among the Hundred Yüeh."[42] The term *Hundred Yüeh* is here used as a blanket designation for the indigenous peoples of the south; "those dwelling among the Hundred Yüeh" means the Chinese and their clients in the south. From this we can gather that the Ou-yang family had achieved a relative amount of tranquillity in the area under its influence, which clearly did not extend beyond modern Kuang-tung and Kuang-hsi.

In 567, the governor of Hsiang Province, in modern Hu-nan, rebelled and invited He to join him. Although He played no active role in this rebellion and it was soon crushed, he was thereafter distrusted by the Ch'en court. When he was summoned to appear before the court in 569, He refused and openly rebelled; in 570 he was captured and beheaded.[43]

The year 570 marked a minor turning point in the south. Ever since Ly Bi's uprising in 541, the south had been in constant turmoil; what small measure of stability did exist was enforced by local strong men whose chief preoccupation was either staying clear of the political troubles in the north or profiting from them. Beginning with Ch'en Pa-hsien, leading figures in the south followed one another in open rebellion.

In 570, the Ch'en court imposed a new measure of central authority over the south. After the death of Ou-yang He, it is recorded that "the Lao barbarians of Giao-chi often assembled for plunder," and Yüan Cho was commissioned to "beckon and pacify" them. Furthermore, Giao-chi was in communication with Lin-i, and there was a brisk trade in "gold, kingfishers, pearls, shells, precious gems, and unusual goods; from first to last, all the messengers [despatched to Giao-chi] sent [these items]; only Cho steeled himself and returned."[44]

This precious information throws light on the relationship between the empire and the far south. It appears that men who actually did go to Giao tended to abandon the thankless task of government for the more lucrative occupation of commerce. The term *messenger* used here implies that these were low-ranking officers without personal authority. Although Yüan Cho resisted the temptation of profit and returned, the main effect of his sojourn on the frontier was to place the Ch'en court in communication with the thriving markets of the south seas, for in the year of Cho's expedition, envoys from Fu-nan and Lin-i, the first in many years, arrived at the Ch'en court.[45]

Aside from stimulating commercial contacts, Cho's expedition had

42. *ChS*, 9, 9b; *TCTC*, 169, vol. 9, 414, and 170, vol. 9, 490. *CL*, 96, reads "displayed majesty to the Hundred Yüeh."

43. *ChS*, 5, 4b–5a, and 9, 9b–10a; *TCTC*, 170, vol. 9, 466, 490, 496.

44. *ChS*, 34, 24a. I interpret "Nhat-nam, Tuong Prefecture" to mean Lin-i. Ch'en-liu, which H. Maspero, "Études d'histoire d'Annam," 16: 22, takes to be the name of a man who accompanied Yüan Cho, is the name of Cho's home prefecture (*ChS*, 34, 23a, and 35, 17a).

45. *ChS*, 5, 8a.

little effect on the frontier. Shortly after this, a certain Ts'ai Ning was temporarily exiled to Giao-chi; however, there is no indication of his occupying an official position there.[46] About this same time a Tai Huang appeared on a list of officials as the governor of Minh, one of the two obscure provinces established by Liang on the Lin-i frontier.[47] Perhaps Tai Huang had gone with Yüan Cho's expedition and received this title as recognition of his good service; it is also possible that he received the title without ever stirring from the Ch'en court. As for Ts'ai Ning, although his exile could conceivably imply some formal relationship between the Ch'en court and local powers in Giao-chi, there is no clear evidence of such a relationship.

For two years after Yüan Cho's expedition, until 572, a general named Shen K'o was the dominant figure in the south as governor of Kuang. K'o was succeeded by Fang T'ai, a prince who was a nephew of Ch'en Pa-hsien's mother; he was given the old command of governor general that had been held by the Ou-yang family. He departed in 574 and was succeeded in 575 by another imperial prince who was then promoted elsewhere the following year.[48] There was little continuity of leadership in these years.

In 576, Shen Chün-kao was appointed governor general at Kuang. It is recorded that "the Li and Lao were continually attacking each other; Chün-kao was a literary man without military skill; he exhausted his heart soothing and arguing to gain harmony among the people." In 578, Chün-kao died at the age of forty-seven after two years in office.[49]

Lao, as we have seen, referred to inhabitants of the southern mountains; *Li*, a term used in the fifth century for mountain tribespeople, was a name used during the sixth century for non-Chinese peoples leading a settled existence in the lowlands. The Vietnamese were considered to be among the Li. Judging from Chün-kao's experience in the south, local powers were shaking off any semblance of imperial control; he was reduced to being an ineffectual mediator.

The troubles that wore down the energy of Chün-kao and seem to have led to his early death resulted in the breaking up of his vast southern command and the appearance of a number of governor generals with greatly reduced spheres of responsibility. According to the *An-nam chi luoc*, based on Chinese sources, a Yang Chin held the position of governor general for the two provinces of Giao and Ai sometime after the death of Chün-kao, and when the Ch'en dynasty fell in 589, a Yang Hsiu-p'u was governor general of Giao.[50]

In contrast with these governor generals, who may have resided in the

46. Ibid., 34, 22a.
47. Ibid., 35, 17a.
48. Ibid., 5, 5b, 10a, 18a, 18b–19a, and 14, 4a, 6a–b; *NS*, 65, 4b.
49. *ChS*, 23, 3b; *NS*, 68, 12b.
50. *CL*, 96; the "Chin dynasty" cited in reference to Yang Hsiu-p'u is probably a mistake for "Ch'en dynasty."

south as representatives of the throne, was a certain Ly Huu Vinh, recorded as the governor of Giao. In 583, he sent trained elephants to the Ch'en court as tribute.[51] Trained elephants were a common form of tribute from Lin-i; the curious arrival of trained elephants from the "governor of Giao" implies that the "governor of Giao" was following non-Chinese diplomatic usage.

This brief review of information on the south for the forty-odd years from Ch'en Pa-hsien's victory over Ly Bi to the demise of his dynasty is derived entirely from Chinese records. Information on Giao is virtually nonexistent, save for a few scattered references to titles and even fewer comments of substance, nearly all of which suggest commercial rather than political contacts. The details we have reviewed could conceivably be interpreted as supporting the view that Chinese control of Giao continued unabated throughout this period, inasmuch as nothing directly contradicts such an idea. However, two considerations indicate otherwise.

First of all, the information we have examined amply demonstrates the feebleness of imperial authority in the south during this time. As Ch'en Pa-hsien progressed northward during the years 548–52, the spirit of the empire went with him. In 552, Hsiao Po's authority did not extend beyond the limits of modern Kuang-tung. Between 554 and 560, the area of modern Kuang-hsi was largely under the influence of Wang Lin. For the next ten years, the Ou-yang family at Canton maintained a system built on nepotism and personal loyalty; their system was linked to Giao and beyond by the single thread of trade. The fall of this family in 570 was followed by Yüan Cho's frontier expedition, which attracted envoys from the kingdoms of Lin-i and Fu-nan but was otherwise so lacking in results that the most memorable detail recorded is astonishment that Cho was ever heard from again. The local conflicts that were the despair of Shen Chün-kao (576–78) led to the disintegration of imperial authority as the ailing Ch'en dynasty lived out its last years in the growing shadow of Sui. The maintenance of trade may have motivated the sending of trained elephants to the Ch'en court in 583 by a local leader in Giao. Thus, the Chinese sources do not contradict the idea that during these years Giao was autonomous, if not effectively independent.

The second consideration is that a great deal of information from the sixth century has been preserved in Vietnam. In the wake of Ly Bi's death, several popular leaders arose; after their deaths they were venerated by the people with shrines and temples and the maintenance of spirit cults. Information about the lives of these heroes was recorded and preserved in their temples. In the first half of the twelfth century, this information passed into a historical work that is no longer extant, by means of which it passed

51. *ChS*, 6, 7a–b.

into surviving works.[52] As one might expect of information derived from hagiography, what remains contains a good bit of legend; although this obscures our view of actual events, it nevertheless lays bare the cultural environment in which those events took place or in which they were remembered. Thus, we see that at this time, after more than five centuries of Chinese influence, ancient themes from the pre-Chinese period remained potent.

Trieu Quang Phuc

When Ly Bi withdrew to Khuat-lieu Valley after the battle on the lake in 546, Trieu Quang Phuc, son of "Great Master" Trieu Tuc, became the leader of resistance in the Hong River plain. He established his headquarters on an island in the midst of a vast swamp in Chu-dien that the popular mind identified as Nhat Da Trach, from which the supernatural palace of the Hung princess Tien Dung and her consort Chu Dong Tu had ascended into heaven.[53]

The swamp was an ideal refuge. An army unfamiliar with its innumerable channels would become hopelessly lost there, while native warriors could issue from its depths without warning and strike as opportunity permitted. Quang Phuc reportedly had some twenty thousand men under his command. Resting by day, he would embark his men at night and sally forth to seize the supplies of the Liang army, killing and capturing many Chinese soldiers and withdrawing into the security of the swamp before the enemy forces could concentrate against him.[54]

These guerrilla tactics, according to Vietnamese sources, provoked Ch'en Pa-hsien to exclaim: "In ancient times this was the marsh of the ascension of one night [meaning the ascension of the palace into heaven]; now it is the marsh of the bandits of one night."[55] While Pa-hsien may have considered Quang Phuc a mere bandit chief, Quang Phuc was a hero among

52. The earliest known Vietnamese source for the sixth century is the nonextant *Su ky* of Do Thien from the twelfth century. The *VDULT*, the *LNCQ*, and the *TT* all derive their information from this work. The principal citations about Trieu Quang Phuc and Ly Phat Tu (*VDULT*, 7–10) have been translated by H. Maspero, "Études," 16: 14–15, and Durand, "La Dynastie," pp. 447–52; in addition, Trieu Quang Phuc's two generals, the brothers Truong Hong and Truong Hat, are the subject of a separate notice (*VDULT*, 24–25). The *LNCQ* (13) appends a notice about the rise of Trieu Quang Phuc to the legend of Nhat Da Trach and contains a separate notice on the Truong brothers (27–28). All of this information in the *VDULT* and *LNCQ* is reproduced in *TT*, 4, 17a–23a, except for that about the Truong brothers, which is briefly cited in *TT*, *Ban ky*, 3, 9b. Information about Ly Bi's general Ly Phuc Man also comes from Do Thien and survives in *VDULT*, 25–26, and *TT*, *Ban ky*, 2, 7b–8a.

53. *LNCQ*, 13; *TT*, 4, 17a–b.

54. *VDULT*, 8; *LNCQ*, 13; *TT*, 4, 17a–b.

55. *LNCQ*, 13.

the people, and his association with the locale of the ancient legend was of more than symbolic importance. Quang Phuc proclaimed himself king of Da Trach, "King of Night Marsh." [56]

Two events contributed to the rise of Trieu Quang Phuc: first, the death of Ly Bi turned the hopes of many of his followers toward Quang Phuc; second, the departure of Ch'en Pa-hsien to attend to the usurpation of Hou Ching was followed by a deterioration of Chinese strength in the region. Equally important, perhaps, was the way Quang Phuc legitimized his authority.

According to tradition, Quang Phuc raised an altar in the marsh, lit incense, and prayed to the spirits; his faith was answered by the appearance of Chu Dong Tu descending from heaven astride a yellow dragon. The immortal said to Quang Phuc: "Although I long ago ascended into heaven, spiritual power still remains in this place; since you have prayed with sincerity, I have come to assist you in the task of calming disorder." Taking a claw from the dragon and presenting it to Quang Phuc, the immortal continued: "Place this on your helmet and your path will lead to success." The apparition disappeared into the clouds, and Quang Phuc went on to proclaim himself king of Viet. [57]

In this tradition, Quang Phuc invests himself with a concept of kingship that draws on indigenous notions of political legitimacy. The blessing of Chu Dong Tu associates Quang Phuc with the concept of a king who protects the Buddhist religion, which appeared in the time of Shih Hsieh. This strain of thought may not have been contemporary with Trieu Quang Phuc, but may rather have been elaborated in later centuries under Buddhist and Taoist influence, for by the fifteenth century Chu Dong Tu had become an important figure in the spirit pantheon of popular Vietnamese Taoism. In fact, the earliest source for this legend does not mention the immortal, but contains only a yellow dragon. [58] The use of a dragon claw as the symbol of military invincibility and political sovereignty is an echo of the turtle claw that accounted for the power of King An Duong seven and a half centuries earlier. [59] Quang Phuc was drawing on ancient pre-Chinese traditions of the Vietnamese people.

Yang P'iao, who had been appointed governor of Giao and who accompanied Ch'en Pa-hsien into the separatist province, is not heard of again. Vietnamese records speak of a general named Yang Ch'an, whom Ch'en Pa-hsien left behind when he returned north. It is possible that Yang

---

56. *VDULT*, 8; *TT*, 4, 17b.

57. *LNCQ*, 13; *VDULT*, 8; *TT* 4, 18b–19a.

58. *LNCQ*, 13, speaks only of an immortal, although it is clear that Chu Dong Tu is meant, and the *TT* (4, 18b–19a) explicitly identifies him as such, citing oral tradition as evidence. The *VDULT* ignores the immortal and speaks only of a "yellow dragon" (8).

59. Yamamoto Tatsurō, "Myths Explaining the Vicissitudes of Political Power in Ancient Viet Nam," p. 91.

P'iao and Yang Ch'an are but different renderings of a single man's name. After Pa-hsien had departed from the south and was absorbed in the Hou Ching affair, Quang Phuc attacked, defeated, and killed Yang Ch'an; surviving Liang troops escaped north as Quang Phuc took possession of Long-bien and brought peace to the Hong River plain, naming himself king of Nam Viet.[60]

Meanwhile, Ly Thien Bao, the elder brother of Ly Bi, whose siege of Liang forces in Ai had been thwarted by Pa-hsien in 547, took refuge in the mountains. According to Vietnamese sources, he arrived at Da-nang Valley, at the source of the Dao River, a place blessed with fertile soil and prosperous inhabitants. There, Thien Bao proclaimed the kingdom of Da-nang and took the title king of Dao-lang. After his death in 555 from natural causes, he was succeeded by a kinsman named Ly Phat Tu.[61]

In 557, Ly Phat Tu led an army out of the mountains against Trieu Quang Phuc. Phat Tu laid claim to Ly Bi's succession by proclaiming himself "Emperor of the South." After prolonged fighting in the home district of the Ly family, Phat Tu recognized Quang Phuc's greater power and requested a truce. Considering that Phat Tu was a kinsman of Ly Bi, Quang Phuc agreed, and the Hong River plain was partitioned between them. Phat Tu acquired Tan-xuong Prefecture, as well as the lands west of the Hong River; he established his capital at O-dien, west of modern Hanoi. Quang Phuc retained the agricultural heartland of eastern Giao.[62]

How these events related to the situation further north is not difficult to imagine. Ch'en Pa-hsien crossed the mountains northward into the Yang-tze basin in 550, though he had left Giao no later than 548. At that time, Trieu Quang Phuc defeated what Liang forces remained in Giao and gained possession of the Hong River plain. Hsiao Po, at Canton, was too weak and too absorbed in his own intrigues to have had any influence in Giao. In 554, however, Wang Lin briefly entered what is now Kuang-hsi, and one of his

60. *VDULT*, 8, says that after gaining possession of Long-bien, Quang Phuc governed from the two locations of Loc-loa, another name for Co-loa, west of Long-bien, and Vu-ninh, east of Long-bien; Quang Phuc then proclaimed himself "King of the Nam Viet Kingdom." The *LNCQ* says that after the deaths of Ly Bi and Yang Ch'an, Quang Phuc proclaimed himself King Trieu and established his capital on Mount Chau in Vu-ninh. The association of Quang Phuc with Vu-ninh is possibly a confusion with Chao T'o (Vietnamese Trieu Da), king of Nan Yüeh (Vietnamese Nam Viet), who, according to Vietnamese tradition, had his headquarters at this place during his campaign against King An Duong (*TT*, 1, 9a). According to *CL*, 22, a "King Trieu of Viet" is buried on Mount Chau, but inasmuch as Le Tac ignored Quang Phuc, this would seem to refer to Chao T'o; on the other hand, Chao T'o was buried at Canton, so Le Tac may have inadvertantly reproduced a tradition originating with Quang Phuc. Temples to both Chao T'o and Trieu Quang Phuc survive at Vu-ninh; see Dinh Van Nhat, "Vung Lang-bac ve thoi Hai Ba Trung," p. 47. *TT*, 4, 19a, simply says that Quang Phuc entered Long-bien and dates this event in 550, apparently because this is the year the author of the *TT* believed Pa-hsien to have returned north. *VDULT*, 9, dates the beginning of Quang Phuc's reign in 551.

61. *VDULT*, 8; *TT*, 4, 19b. On the "Kingdom of Da-nang" see Appendix M.

62. *VDULT*, 8; *TT*, 4, 19b–20a.

clients, named Liu Yüan-yen, was named governor of Giao. Quang Phuc
and Yüan-yen may have been in contact, but Yüan-yen's focus of attention
remained in the north, and in 555 he led his entourage northward to assist
Wang Lin in the crisis overtaking the Liang imperial house.

The year 557 was one of political change throughout China. Pa-hsien
proclaimed the Ch'en dynasty, provoking Hsiao Po's ill-fated uprising. Po
was killed by Ch'en Fa-wu, a former governor of Heng bearing the
honorific title governor of Duc. Then, no sooner had the Ou-yang family
returned south than Wang Lin's rebellion broke out. From 557 to 560, Ou-
yang Wei, at Canton, was occupied with combating the influence of Wang
Lin, which was strongest in modern Kuang-hsi, on the Giao border. Quang
Phuc was in a position to feel the influence of both sides, and it may have
been the uncertainty of events in the north that prompted him to tolerate Ly
Phat Tu's presence in the lowlands; likewise, it may have been the chaos in
the north that encouraged Phat Tu to emerge from the mountains.

The secret transfer of gold from Yüan T'an-huan, governor of Giao,
to Ou-yang Wei might conceivably be interpreted as a result of Quang
Phuc's desire to secure the good will of Wei against the influence of Wang
Lin, whose rebellion may have inspired the hopes of Phat Tu. T'an-huan
may have been Wei's representative at Quang Phuc's court and the means of
contact between Quang Phuc and Wei. After the Wang Lin affair was over,
T'an-huan's successor, Ou-yang Sheng, may have continued in this capacity, although his only recorded deed while governor of Giao occurred in
the north. It is also possible that the Yüan T'an-huan episode had nothing
whatever to do with the situation in Giao.

In the 560s, "messengers" were sent to Giao, settled there, and engaged in commerce. One might reasonably conclude that Quang Phuc was
in some way allied with the Ou-yang family, for, according to Vietnamese
sources, he fell from power at the time of Ou-yang He's rebellion and death
and of Yüan Cho's frontier expedition.

The fall of Trieu Quang Phuc was remembered by the same myth that
had explained the passing of King An Duong; the two myths are identical
except for the names of the protagonists and the dragon claw that replaced
the turtle-claw-triggered crossbow. In the sixth-century version, a son of
Phat Tu named Nha Lang became the husband of Cao Nuong, a daughter of
Quang Phuc. Nha Lang gained access to the dragon claw with Cao Nuong's
assistance; after taking the claw and replacing it with a counterfeit, he
returned to his father, who thereupon renewed hostilities. Defeated on every
side, Quang Phuc fled to the sea and was received by the "Yellow Dragon
Spirit King," who escorted him into the depths of the watery kingdom.[63]

63. *VDULT*, 8–9; *TT*, 4, 20a–21a. Only the *VDULT* mentions the "Yellow Dragon
Spirit King"; the *TT* version has Quang Phuc entering the sea without spiritual assistance. On
the geographical distribution of spirit cults for the figures in this legend, see the map in Nguyen
Van Huyen.

The resurrection of this ancient myth to explain the rise and fall of Trieu Quang Phuc signals a revival of pre-Chinese values and the indigenous cultural symbols that represented them. It is significant that Quang Phuc took the title of king, which had indigenous roots, rejecting the more sinitic appellation of emperor used by Ly Bi. Quang Phuc's reign can be interpreted as a prolonged revolt that left a mark on Vietnamese folk memories. Ly Bi and Ly Phat Tu were mentioned by Chinese historians, but Quang Phuc was not. The Ly family was visible to the Chinese because they claimed Chinese ancestry and had served the imperial government as "frontier assistants." The Trieu family appears to have been more closely associated with the popular Buddhist culture of Giao.

The actual manner in which Quang Phuc's reign came to an end was probably related to Yüan Cho's expedition of 570.[64] Quang Phuc would have had to deal with any incursion from the north, whereas Phat Tu would have stood to benefit from such an event. Phat Tu may even have allied himself with Yüan Cho against Quang Phuc, or he may simply have moved in after Quang Phuc and Cho had put each other into difficult situations. The Lao, who, according to Chinese records, were gathering for plunder in Giao at the time of Cho's expedition, may in fact be a reference to Phat Tu, for the Lao had at one time been allied with Phat Tu's kinsman Ly Bi, and he may have subsequently enlisted their assistance against Quang Phuc. In such a case, one might conclude that Cho's expedition was intended to aid Quang Phuc, but the evidence is too sparse for any firm conclusion.

Ly Phat Tu and Vinītaruci

Whereas indigenous traditions of antiquity seem to have been revived and proclaimed by Trieu Quang Phuc, the cultural direction of Giao under Ly Phat Tu was toward a Vietnamized form of Buddhism. A century before, Emperor Kao of Ch'i (479–82), a fervent patron of Buddhism, had announced his intention of sending missionaries to spread the religion in Giao. However, T'an Ch'ien, a Buddhist master of Central Asian origin, advised the emperor that

> the land of Giao Province is in contact with India; the teaching of Buddha had not yet arrived at Chiang-tung [where the Ch'i capital was located] when a score of Buddhist edifices were already erected at Luy-lau and more than five hundred monks recited fifteen sacred scrolls . . . missionaries are not necessary, but officials should be sent to inspect the monasteries.[65]

64. According to *VDULT*, 9, Quang Phuc reigned for nineteen years, from 551 to 569, while Phat Tu's reign did not begin until 571. *TT*, 4, 21a, lengthens Quang Phuc's reign to 571, thereby avoiding a gap in the chronology.

65. Tran Van Giap "Bouddhisme," pp. 208–11. This information comes from a twelfth-century Vietnamese source. Tran Van Giap discusses the textual problems of the quotation.

This is virtually the only information surviving on the state of Vietnamese Buddhism between the time of Shih Hsieh and the sixth century. Yet it is clear from later events that Buddhism found a firm foothold among the Vietnamese during this time.

The sixth century was an especially vigorous period for the growth of Buddhism in Giao. The ease and alacrity with which Buddhist trends in China were picked up and developed in Vietnam at this time bear witness to the maturity and energy of Vietnamese Buddhism. We have already mentioned the Lung-men style of Buddhist sculpture and evidence suggesting its arrival in Vietnam at the time of Ly Bi. There are other, more direct, examples of contact between Chinese and Vietnamese Buddhism in the sixth century.

During the Ch'en dynasty (557–89), the third patriarch and virtual founder of the T'ien T'ai sect, Chih I (538–97), was preaching and writing, systematizing the literature of Buddhism. Eclectic in intent and syncretic in method, the doctrines of the T'ien T'ai sect spread quickly into Vietnam.[66] These doctrines, however, were never as influential among ruling-class Vietnamese as the meditational school of Buddhism, called *Dhyāna* in Sanskrit, *Ch'an* in Chinese, *Zen* in Japanese, and *Thien* in Vietnamese.

The introduction of Dhyāna into China is attributed to an Indian named Bodhidharma, who traveled to China and resided at the Shao-lin monastery of Lo-yang in the first half of the fifth century; most of the surviving information about this man is legendary. A disciple of his named Hui K'o passed on his teachings to a monk named Seng Ts'an. During the Buddhist persecutions initiated by Emperor Wu (561–77) of the Northern Chou dynasty, Seng Ts'an found refuge on a mountain in Ho-nan.[67]

In 574, a Brahman from southern India named Vinītaruci arrived in northern China. He had spent his youth studying Buddhism in western India and was searching for a teacher. In due course, he arrived at Seng Ts'an's mountain retreat and became his disciple. Seng Ts'an advised Vinītaruci to go south; Vinītaruci subsequently established himself in Kuang, where he translated two Buddhist texts. In 580, he went to Giao and resided at the temple dedicated to the Buddha of the Clouds (Phap-van) in Luy-lau, one of the four temples built in the time of Shih Hsieh; there he translated a third text. He died in 594 after transmitting the teachings of Seng Ts'an to his favorite disciple, Phap Hien.[68]

Phap Hien was from Chu-dien and bore the surname Do. Whether or

66. Vietnamese Buddhist texts use the term *Giao-ton*, which is based on the Chinese transcription of the Sanskrit word *agama*, meaning "doctrine." Tran Van Giap, "Bouddhisme," pp. 207–8, 227–29, identifies this "School of the Doctrine" with T'ien T'ai.

67. Pelliot, "Artistes des Six Dynasties et des T'ang," pp. 252–65; Tran Van Giap, "Bouddhisme," pp. 230–31.

68. Tran Van Giap, "Bouddhisme," pp. 235–36.

not his was the same Do family that ruled Vietnam in the fourth and fifth centuries is a matter of conjecture. Thien Buddhism was already established in Vietnam before Vinītaruci's arrival, for Phap Hien studied under and was ordained by Quan Duyen, a Thien master at Phap-van Temple. But Phap Hien received the "essence" of Thien from Vinītaruci. After Vinītaruci's death, Phap Hien built the Temple of Chung-thien at Mount Tu, about twenty miles northwest of Luy-lau. He died in 626 after instructing more than three hundred disciples in the teachings received from Vinītaruci.[69]

Seng Ts'an had advised Vinītaruci to go south because of the unsettled conditions in northern China and the hostility towards Buddhism that prevailed there. Vinītaruci found safety under the protection of the governor general at Kuang. Shen Chün-kao, governor general from 576 to 578, seems to have been a man of culture. His death and the resulting disintegration of his command opened an era of anarchy. It was at this time that Vinītaruci found refuge in Giao; there he remained, writing and teaching, for the fourteen remaining years of his life. After his death, his principal disciple founded a new temple, which attracted hundreds of monks.

The appearance of a new religious sect in this manner, involving the arrival of a foreign teacher, the building of a new temple, and the gathering of monks, could not have occurred without a religious community of sufficient stature to attract the foreign teacher and of sufficient maturity to respond to his guidance. There also must have been a powerful patron able to enforce conditions of peace in the land. Ly Phat Tu was such a patron. His personal name, Phat Tu, means "Son of Buddha." He may, in fact, not have used this appellation until late in his life. It is reasonable to assume that Ly Huu Vinh, the "governor of Giao Province" who in 583 sent trained elephants to the Ch'en court, was Ly Phat Tu; Huu Vinh may have been his name at that time, or he may have chosen not to reveal his true name to the Chinese, considering the uncertainty of the times and the devious nature of diplomatic intercourse. Likewise, in the chaos that marked the transition from Ch'en to Sui in 589–90, Phat Tu is known in Chinese records as Ly Xuan; Ly Bi had named his kingdom Van Xuan, and in those troubled times Phat Tu's surname may have been combined with the name of his deceased kinsman's realm.[70]

The long reign of three decades that Vietnamese sources attribute to Phat Tu clarifies the political background of the rise of the Vinītaruci sect. Vinītaruci traveled to southern China in quest of a peaceful environment friendly to Buddhism. As in previous times of dynastic change in China, the

---

69. Ibid., p. 236.

70. This is the traditional Vietnamese interpretation. H. Maspero, "Études," 16: 2, characterized it as "a hypothesis more ingenious than convincing," but he believed the Chinese and Vietnamese sources for the sixth century were irreconcilable, so he entirely rejected the Vietnamese side.

Vietnamese enjoyed peace and prosperity under the leadership of a local man. This attracted Vinītaruci and made possible the founding of the Vietnamese Buddhist sect that bore his name. The Vinītaruci sect was the first of three historical Thien Buddhist sects. These sects played important roles in the early independence period and endured into the thirteenth century.

Sui Comes South

Ly Phat Tu's relationship with the Ch'en dynasty was probably friendly, but, considering the feebleness of the Ch'en throne, not close. The most important means of contact was trade. In the early 570s, as we have already noted, a dismissed Ch'en official, Ts'ai Ning, temporarily resided in Giao as a political exile; about this same time, one Tai Huang appeared on a list of officials as the governor of Minh. These two items may have been related to Yüan Cho's expedition of 570, but are otherwise too obscure to warrant further comment. In the 580s, however, one source records two governor generals for Giao, Yang Chin and Yang Hsiu-p'u.[71] Some formal relationship may have existed between these men and Ly Phat Tu, but the paucity of information prevents any firm conclusion. Their titles may well have been merely honorifics dispensed by the faltering Ch'en court to encourage loyalty.

Meanwhile, events in the north were moving rapidly toward a conclusion. In 581, Yang Chien founded the Sui dynasty in north China; in 589, Sui armies forced the submission of the Ch'en dynasty, and China was reunited for the first time in two and a half centuries. The first Sui army to venture into the south, "beyond the passes," was stalled by the resistance of surviving Ch'en forces. Only after the captured Ch'en emperor ordered his followers to surrender was the Sui army able to advance and take possession of Kuang.[72]

After a governor general in the south failed in an attempt to rally support behind a Ch'en prince, Sui consolidated its hold on Kuang and gained the submission of neighboring provinces; the resistance of the governor of Ting in modern Kuang-hsi was crushed by force.[73] But the Sui were not yet equal to their conquests, and after the initial shock of their success had dissipated, the south erupted in resistance. In 590, according to Chinese records:

> The old [southern] frontier of Ch'en broke out in great resistance and rose up in mutually supporting rebellions; the big rebels had armies of several tens of

71. *CL*, 96, is the only source for these two men.
72. *TCTC*, 177, vol. 10, 10.
73. Ibid., 177, vol. 10, 20, 28.

thousands, the little rebels had armies of several thousands. They seized the district magistrates; some they disemboweled, others they chopped up and ate.[74]

Three men claimed to be "sons of heaven" and established imperial courts. Seven others claimed the title of "great governor general" and ruled different localities; among these was listed Ly Xuan of Giao Province, surely a reference to Ly Phat Tu.[75]

The Sui general Yang Su led an army into the south. He fought "more than seven hundred battles; from the mountains to the sea he attacked and destroyed strongholds, several he could not overcome." The Sui court recalled Su on account of his physical exhaustion, but he asked to remain, saying that the rebels were not yet subdued and he feared even greater trouble would arise if he were to depart. After a series of new campaigns undertaken by Su, the situation momentarily quieted down, then exploded afresh, with a "barbarian king" besieging the Sui forces in Kuang. A new Sui army was sent to the rescue, and this final uprising was put down.[76]

There is no indication that Yang Su ever penetrated as far south as Giao. For several years, Sui was fully occupied in securing the lands of modern Kuang-tung and Kuang-hsi. As the authority of Sui gradually consolidated in this region, Ly Phat Tu recognized Sui overlordship.

In 595, Sui influence on the frontier was sufficient to attract envoys from Lin-i.[77] Nevertheless, Sui's position in the south remained fragile. After sweeping away the old Ch'en ruling class, Sui came face to face with non-Chinese indigenous leaders, whom they called Li. Sui identified Ly Phat Tu as a Li leader; many such regional figures were tolerated by Sui, whose policy was to gradually absorb them into the emerging imperial system.

In 597, Li Kuang-shih, the Li leader of Kuei Province in modern Kuang-hsi, rebelled. Sui sent an army from the north to assist a locally recruited army, and the rebellion was put down. A second rebellion broke out in Kuei later in the same year, however, and demonstrated the necessity of some new initiative. An official named Ling-hu Hsi was accordingly given charge of Kuei Province and entrusted with a military command that theoretically encompassed the entire south, including Giao.[78]

Hsi was given discretionary authority to act first and report later. He quickly established a reputation for clemency and sincerity. It is recorded

74. Ibid., 177, vol. 10, 41.

75. Ibid., 177, vol. 10, 41; *SuiS*, 2, 6b.

76. *SuiS*, 2, 6b–7a; *TCTC*, 177, vol. 10, 41–43, 44. See also Arthur Wright, *The Sui Dynasty*, pp. 150–56.

77. *SuiS*, 2, 10a.

78. *TCTC*, 178, vol. 10, 81, 86.

that local leaders took counsel together: "Before, all the officials used soldiers to terrify and coerce us; this man appeals to reason and issues proclamations." In this way, Hsi won the trust and cooperation of the people. He gathered the educated men of the region and sent them to "establish towns, build schools, and civilize the population." The moral appeal of Hsi's new policy was so overwhelming that local leaders inclined toward rebellion refrained out of respect for him. One Li leader, Ning Meng-li, became famous for his loyalty to Hsi, a circumstance that occasioned favorable comment at the Sui court about Hsi's ability to inspire the loyalty of a barbarian.[79]

The relationship between Ly Phat Tu and Ling-hu Hsi was outwardly correct but remained rudimentary. Hsi was an old man with a strong desire to retire; his energies were consumed by his immediate activities, and he had neither the inclination nor the means to encroach on the prerogatives of a man as firmly entrenched on an isolated frontier as was Phat Tu.

Hsi, however, did take an interest in the formalities of administrative nomenclature. Finding that many of the provincial and district names in the south were identical to toponyms elsewhere in the Sui Empire, he made it his business to change all such names under his official jurisdiction.

During his career in the south, Ch'en Pa-hsien had raised Tan-xuong Prefecture to provincial status under the name of Hung. In 598, Ling-hu Hsi changed the name of this province to Phong. In the same year, he changed the name of Hoang Province, created in 535 on the northern coast of Giao, to Luc, and the name of Duc Province to Hoan. The names of many districts were changed, but the only innovation of substance was the suppression of Vu-binh Prefecture, placing its districts directly under the jurisdiction of Giao Province.[80] The provincial names Phong, Luc, and Hoan would endure until the end of the Chinese provincial period.

Hsi's renaming of provinces and districts implies no actual control over the localities in question. His contribution was literary; he was bringing the toponyms under his theoretical jurisdiction into line with those already existing elsewhere in the empire.

In the year 600, Hsi was sixty-one years old and requested retirement. He wrote: "My strength allows but light duties and of this I am ashamed; I often have a heartfelt desire to make an end of my foolishness . . . . I am an official of advanced age, destitute of comfort." He also wrote of the difficulty

79. Ibid., 178, vol. 10, 81–82, 87–88; SuiS, 56, 4a–b.

80. YHCHC, 1083–86, 1087, 1088; SuiS, 31, 12b–13a, and 56, 4b. If the discontinuation of Vu-binh Prefecture occurred in 590, as the records indicate, one might associate it with Yang Su's campaigns in the south of that year. A more likely explanation, however, is that when Sui first learned of the existing toponyms in 590, Vu-binh had already disappeared, having been abandoned sometime during the reigns of Trieu Quang Phuc and Ly Phat Tu.

in changing the barbarous customs of the people and that he was sick and weary and wished to return north. The court rejected his appeal and, instead, sent him medicine.[81] It was at this time that the inevitable clash between Ly Phat Tu and the empire began to take shape.

As Hsi sank wearily toward the grave, Phat Tu took the empire less seriously. But, as the most powerful and enduring Li leader on the frontier, he had attracted the concerned attention of the Sui court itself. In 601, Hsi forwarded an imperial summons for Phat Tu to appear at the Sui capital. Resolved to resist this demand, Phat Tu sought delay by requesting that the summons be postponed until after the new year. Hsi approved the request, believing that he could keep Phat Tu's allegiance by exercising restraint. Someone, however, accused Hsi of taking a bribe from Phat Tu, and the court grew suspicious. When Phat Tu openly rebelled early in 602, Hsi was promptly arrested; he died en route north.[82]

Ly Phat Tu signaled his independence by moving his capital to the ancient citadel of Co-loa. He left his old capital, O-dien, in the hands of a general named Ly Pho Dinh and sent Ly Dai Quyen, a nephew, to occupy Long-bien.[83]

Phat Tu's move to secure Co-loa and Long-bien at this time is significant. Co-loa and Long-bien lay in the provincial heartland of Giao, the area of maximum Chinese influence. An early Vietnamese source refers to this region as the land of Co-loa and Vu-ninh; Vu-ninh was a jurisdiction in the northeastern part of the Hong River plain. This source says that Trieu Quang Phuc governed from the two "places" Co-loa and Vu-ninh, and, furthermore, that Ly Phat Tu signaled his rebellion by moving his capital to the "places" Co-loa and Vu-ninh.[84] This topographical formula is probably meant to include all the land lying between these two places, for the region so defined is a coherent geographical and cultural unit.[85] Luy-lau and Long-bien both lay in this area, as well as the temples associated with Vinītaruci and his disciple Phap Hien.

For thirty years, then, from the fall of Quang Phuc until Phat Tu's

81. *SuiS*, 56, 4b.

82. Ibid., 56, 4b–5a.

83. Ibid., 53, 9a; *TCTC*, 179, vol. 10, 159; *VSL*, 1, 9a. These sources identify Co-loa as the "ancient city of the Viet kings." The *VDULT* mistakenly uses the name Xuong Ngap for Dai Quyen; Xuong Ngap was the name of a Vietnamese prince of the Ngo family in the tenth century. *TT*, 4, 22a, unaccountably declares that at this time Phat Tu moved his capital to Phong Province. Phat Tu's rebellion must have begun upon the expiration of the postponement of the Sui summons, in the second month of 602, for Hsi's successor was appointed in that month (*SuiS*, 2, 15b, and 55, 11a–b).

84. *VDULT*, 9.

85. Dinh Van Nhat, "Vung Lang-bac" and "Vet tich cua nhung ruong Lac dau tien quanh bo Ho Lang-bac va tren dat que huong cua Phu-dong Thien Vuong."

rebellion against Sui, this region, the traditional center of imperial influence, enjoyed some special status while Phat Tu governed from his capital of O-dien southwest of the Hong River. Yüan Cho's expedition of 570 may have left a residue of merchants and adventurers; this and a lingering loyalty of the people to Quang Phuc's memory may have discouraged Phat Tu from moving his capital there. Also, the Buddhist church was growing in this area and may have performed some functions of local government. Representatives of Ch'en, then of Sui, may have resided here as commercial agents and political observers. The area became in effect a political and cultural buffer zone, where the Buddhist church prospered under the watchful eyes of Vietnamese leaders and imperial officials. By openly taking control of this region, Phat Tu signaled his independence in unmistakable terms.

The Sui court's first move was to consult Yang Su, who had earned a reputation as the senior military expert on the southern frontier by virtue of his campaigns in 590. Su praised the abilities of a general named Liu Fang and recommended him for the present task. Su further helped to plan the projected expedition, and it was apparently his idea to send Fang into Giao through Yün-nan.[86] The reason for this was to gain the advantage of surprise. An army marching south along the traditional route through modern Kuang-tung and Kuang-hsi would be subject to the scrutiny of spies at every step of the way, but an army hidden in the mountains until the moment of attack could expect to throw panic into the foe.

Liu Fang set out from Ch'ang-an in northern China with an army of twenty-seven battalions. Although a strict disciplinarian, Fang is reported to have been popular among his officers and men because of his consideration for the ill and wounded. After marching through Ssu-ch'uan, Fang led his army up to the Yün-nan plateau. There the senior civil official accompanying the army fell gravely ill and could not proceed. Anxious to reach Giao before Phat Tu learned of his whereabouts, Fang left the bulk of the army with the ailing official and hastened forward with his best troops.

At Do-long Pass, on the watershed between the Hsi and Chay Rivers, Fang met two thousand of Phat Tu's men.[87] Brushing aside this unsuspecting frontier garrison, Fang descended the Chay River and penetrated into the heart of Phat Tu's realm. Unprepared to resist an assault from such an unexpected quarter, Phat Tu heeded Fang's admonition to surrender and was sent to the Sui capital at Ch'ang-an. Phat Tu's advisors and subordinates, "cruel and crafty ones" according to Fang's biographer, were beheaded to preclude future trouble.[88]

86. SuiS, 53, 9a; TCTC, 179, vol. 10, 159.

87. SuiS, 53, 9b. TCTC, 179, vol. 10, 159, says ten thousand men. On the location of Do-long, see H. Maspero, "Études," 16: 25.

88. SuiS, 2, 16b–17a, and 53, 9b; TCTC, 179, vol. 10, 159; TT, 4, 22a, and 5, 1a; VSL, 1, 9a.

The Sixth Century in Perspective

In earlier chapters we followed the rise of powerful local families in Giao. By the beginning of the sixth century, these families had achieved virtual autonomy from the imperial court. The political stability resulting from the long reign of Emperor Wu of Liang, however, fostered a trend of imperial interference in regional affairs that in due course provoked the uprising of Ly Bi.

Ly Bi represented the logical development of the regional ruling class up to that time. Such a class could do no better than to emulate its metropolitan overlords; Ly Bi did this when he proclaimed himself emperor, established a reign title, and organized an imperial court. The experiment lasted for only a few years, but it opened a vista that inspired Vietnamese for centuries.

Ch'en Pa-hsien's expedition drove a wedge between Vietnamese leaders who fled into the mountains and those who found refuge in the swamps. The Ly family, which took to the mountains, made itself conspicuous by its imperial claim and its leadership in the war with Ch'en Pa-hsien. The Trieu family, not even noted by Chinese historians, seems to have been screened by the society of the densely populated lowlands, in typical guerrilla fashion. Trieu Quang Phuc's cultivation of local concepts of kingship contrasted Ly Bi's emulation of northern political ideals.

But even as mere imitation of Chinese forms could not satisfy the deeper feelings of the Vietnamese people, so a purely indigenous attitude took ill account of the centuries of imperial influence. The synthesizing agent was the Buddhist religion, which had a foot in each world.

Vietnamese Buddhism had already seen more than three centuries of indigenous development; on the other hand, it was highly receptive to contacts with Buddhism elsewhere, particularly with Chinese Buddhism. The reign of Ly Phat Tu and the founding of the Vinītaruci sect came at the end of a particularly creative century in Vietnamese history and foreshadowed the resolution in the tenth and eleventh centuries of the gradual growth toward independence.

The sixth century poses problems to historians, both in evaluating sources and in broader terms of interpretation. The absence of information from the Chinese side forces us to look at the Vietnamese sources, but it is clear that the Vietnamese sources provide a kind of information different from that in the Chinese sources. Rather than rejecting the Vietnamese sources because there is no collaborating information from the Chinese side, we should try to understand what these sources are saying, realizing that there can be no collaborating information from the Chinese side because Chinese historians did not know what happened in Vietnam from the time Ch'en Pa-hsien went north until Liu Fang went south.

The information in Vietnamese sources was passed on through three more centuries of Chinese rule before emerging in the independence period. It was preserved in shrines and temples dedicated to such men as Trieu Quang Phuc, Ly Phat Tu, and others of lesser stature. These men were heroes in Vietnamese culture. Their biographies survived and were elaborated because they exemplified a native conception of power.

In searching for the meaning of the sixth century in Vietnamese history we must look both at the past and at the future. The events of this time stand as a pylon by which the ancient pre-Chinese heritage of Vietnam was transmitted over the centuries to the independence period. The theory of political power ascribed to Trieu Quang Phuc and Ly Phat Tu came from the prehistoric Lac culture. Lac Long Quan returned from the sea and gave his people a claw as a symbol of his power to protect the land. Possession of a claw explained the successive rise of Trieu Quang Phuc and Ly Phat Tu. The transfer of the claw from one to the other followed an established mythical pattern of marriage alliance and betrayal.

Looking in the other direction, the three-step political evolution of the Vietnamese in the sixth century was a portent of the tenth and eleventh centuries, when independence was eventually achieved and consolidated. In the first step, the great upper-class families reached for independence, severing formal ties with the empire, although retaining its cultural and political assumptions. In the second step, the upper-class world was challenged by the eruption of indigenous forces, which upheld traditional Vietnamese symbols of authority. In the third step, the Buddhist community emerged as a mediator between the two points of view. This three-step sequence was repeated in the initial phase of the independence period and represents a process of adjusting to the removal of Chinese power.

Undoubtedly, the lack of firm information from the sixth century has enhanced its ability to mirror both its past and future and has made it malleable in the hands of later historians. Yet we cannot deny that a core of actual experience lies beneath the collective Vietnamese memory of that time. It would be strange to assume that during more than half a century of freedom from Chinese rule nothing memorable happened. The Vietnamese sources certainly must reflect actual events in their general outline, if not in detail.

Closing this period of experimentation was an episode that has delighted moralizers for centuries. Yang Chien, the founder of the Sui dynasty, had heard of the fabulous wealth seized in the 446 Lin-i campaign and was eager to adorn his empire with the treasures of this exotic southern kingdom. After Liu Fang secured Giao, Yang Chien ordered him to proceed to the conquest of Lin-i. Yang Chien never savored this anticipated conquest, for he died in 604, before the expedition set out.

Nevertheless, in 605, Fang led his army south and, after the usual battle with the elephants, gained possession of the capital city, located at modern Tra-kieu near Da-nang. The immense booty included eighteen golden tablets dedicated to the memory of the eighteen preceding kings of Lin-i, a Buddhist library comprising 1,350 works in the local language, and an orchestra from a kingdom in the Mekong basin.

After erecting an inscribed tablet celebrating his victory, Fang started back north loaded with plunder. En route, an epidemic utterly destroyed the Sui army; death did not even spare Fang.[89] Thus, fate appeared to have justly punished an unprovoked conquest motivated solely by greed.

The most poignant moralizing on this incident has come from the learned but ineffectual Vietnamese monarch Tu Duc (1847–83). As his realm was being conquered by France, he wrote:

> The army is a cruel instrument that the wise man uses only under duress to resist tyranny or to insure that the people can live in peace; considering this, how can one submit to a sordid love of wealth, seeking only one's self-gratification while pitilessly causing the people to suffer and undermining the strength of the nation? In the words of the ancients: "Once the deed is done, thousands of bones bleach in the sand!" There is no need to say more about this, not to mention that the Sui general did not escape death and the Sui dynasty also disappeared soon after. This affair is a worthy lesson for the student to ponder concerning the proper use of the army.[90]

Tu Duc's reaction is rather severe. Perhaps he recognized in this episode the kind of greed that had caused his people so much difficulty throughout their long history. Tu Duc's scholarly admonition became the swan song of upper-class Vietnamese as they retreated into their libraries in the nineteenth century. It was nevertheless based on the solid experience underlying Vietnam's heritage. What Tu Duc said about the Sui conquest of Lin-i applied equally to the imperial policies of the different Chinese dynasties toward the Vietnamese; it also applied to the French colonial policy of his own time.

The promise of the sixth century was cut short by a resurgence of Chinese power. From the Chinese point of view this was a revival of civilization; for the Vietnamese, it was a revival of greed. In the long run the promise of the sixth century was kept. But it was not kept by great upper-class families. Tu Duc preferred his library to his army.

89. *SuiS*, 53, 9b–10a, and 82, 2b; *TCTC*, 180, vol. 10, 195–96; *VSL*, 1, 9a–b; *TT*, 5, 1a–b.

90. Ton Nu Thuong Lang, trans., and Ta Quang Phat, annotator, *Kham dinh Viet su thong giam cuong muc*, part 1, 4, 15.

5
The
Protectorate
of
An-Nam

Ch'iu Ho

The Sui dynasty, like the Ch'in of eight centuries before, was the harbinger of a greater imperial house. Emperor Yang, who ascended the throne in 604, literally wore out his young empire with wars, costly construction projects, and an extravagant life-style. In 615, he narrowly escaped capture by the Turks. Thereafter, his authority declined, and the empire broke up into numerous independent domains. In 618, the Li family captured the capital, Ch'ang-an, and founded the T'ang dynasty. As in previous eras of imperial collapse and dynastic change, the Vietnamese enjoyed peace under able leadership. The man who gave peace to the southern frontier at this time was Ch'iu Ho.

Ch'iu Ho was born and raised in Lo-yang. His father was a general, and in his youth he cultivated the martial arts. In his later years, however, he grew interested in civil administration. He was born in 551 and began his career under the Chou dynasty. Under Sui he governed several prefectures in northern China, gaining a reputation for lenient adminstration and the absence of trouble in his jurisdiction.

Near the end of Emperor Yang's reign, rebellions broke out in the south in reaction to the exploitative activities of officials there. The court decided to send honest officials of tested integrity to replace the corrupt administrators and thereby to calm things down. Although in his sixties, Ch'iu Ho was selected to go to Giao-chi.[1]

Sui reduced all provinces to the rank of prefectures, and after 604 the Vietnamese lands were organized into three prefectures comprising a single province. Giao-chi Prefecture included the entire Hong River plain; Ai Province was once again called Cuu-chan Prefecture; and Duc Province, which had been renamed Hoan in 598 by Ling-hu Hsi, became Nhat-nam

---

1. *CTS*, 59, 4b.

Table 4. Sui Census Statistics for Giao Province

Prefecture	Hearths
Giao-chi (Hong River plain)	30,516
Cuu-chan (Ma River plain)	16,135
Nhat-nam (Ca River plain)	9,915
Total	56,566

SOURCE: *SuiS*, 31, 12b–13a.

Prefecture. Further south, three ephemeral prefectures were organized in territories conquered from Lin-i in 605.

Although this administrative organization did not survive the Sui dynasty, it clarifies the Sui census figures in table 4. These figures represent the extent to which Sui administrators were able to register households for purposes of taxation. A comparison of the census statistics in tables 3 and 4 shows that the arrival of Sui marked the beginning of relatively more effective administrative control. What this administration comprised, however, is hard to say. Sui undoubtedly tried to curb the great landowning families. The higher census figures may reflect an effort to introduce the so-called "equal-field" land reform into Vietnam; this reform was intended to assign land to tax-paying farmers, who might otherwise become tenants on great private estates and thereby be lost from the tax rolls.

The only surviving information about taxation under Sui is that special titles were given to local "leaders" who helped the Chinese collect slaves, pearls, kingfishers, elephant tusks, and rhinoceros horn.[2] This seems to have been a form of taxation collected through local leaders or powerful landowners.

While the administrative center of Giao-chi Prefecture remained at Long-bien, a Giao Province governor general was established at Tong-binh, in the vicinity of modern Hanoi, with authority over the entire southern frontier,

> to control the barbarians of all the kingdoms south of the sea, those south and southwest of Giao Province, and those who dwell on the islands of the great sea . . . arriving in boats after traveling unknown distances . . . bringing goods by the Giao-chi route as they have done from the time of Emperor Wu of Han.[3]

2. Katakura Minoru, "Chūgoku Shihaika no Betonamu," p. 31.
3. *CTS*, 41, 43a.

It is recorded that when Ch'iu Ho arrived in Giao-chi, he "soothed all the local heroes and gained the loyalty of the barbarians. . . . all the kingdoms west of Lin-i sent Ho gifts of clear pearls, rhinoceros horn, gold, and precious goods worthy of a king."[4] The success of Ho's rule is a tribute to his reputation as a benevolent administrator, but it is also a reflection of the vital maritime commercial world of the south seas that underlaid the prosperity of Shih Hsieh's time and had dominated the local economy ever since.

As the Sui dynasty lost its hold on the empire, regional leaders appeared. In the central Yangtze, a descendent of the Liang imperial family, Hsiao Hsien, claimed the title of emperor and established an imperial court. Further east, Lin Shih-hung usurped imperial authority and gathered a following of miscellaneous adventurers, among whom was a certain Feng Ang.[5]

Feng Ang's father had come south with the Sui armies, and he himself had been born of a local woman on what is now the central coast of Kuang-tung. He was an official in northwestern China when Sui collapsed. He then returned to his natal region and gained control of modern Kuang-tung and eastern Kuang-hsi. Western Kuang-hsi was retained by a local official named Ning Ch'ang-chen, who placed himself under the protection of Hsiao Hsien.[6]

Ch'iu Ho remained aloof from these emerging political relationships. When envoys from both Hsiao Hsien and Lin Shih-hung arrived soliciting his collaboration, he refused to deal with them, not being satisfied in his own mind that the Sui dynasty was actually finished.

News of Ch'iu Ho's wealth, however, provoked envy in the north, and Hsiao Hsien ordered Ning Ch'ang-chen to lead an army against him. Ho was prepared to submit peacefully, but one of his officials, Kao Shih-lien, argued for resistance:

> Although Ch'ang-chen has many soldiers, he must travel far to get here, and considering the problems of supply he cannot campaign for long; on the other hand we have trained soldiers within fortifications and plenty of supplies; what kind of business is it to submit after hearing nothing but rumors?[7]

Ho thereupon appointed Shih-lien to prepare the defense, and Ch'ang-chen's army was easily defeated. Later, when Ho learned that Emperor Yang had died and that the Sui dynasty was in fact ended, he recognized the suzerainty of Hsiao Hsien.[8]

4. Ibid., 59, 4b–5a.
5. Ibid., 56, 1a–3a, 9a–b; TCTC, 184, vol. 10, 433, 465.
6. HTS, 110, 1a–2b; TCTC, 185, vol. 10, 465; TT, 5, 2b; CL, 96.
7. CTS, 59, 5a.
8. TCTC, 185, vol. 10, 466; TT, 5, 2b–3a; CL, 96–97.

In 622, Hsiao Hsien was defeated by T'ang and Ho immediately submitted to the new imperial house. T'ang appointed Ho administrator of Giao Province, and Kao Shih-lien traveled to the T'ang court to formalize Ho's submission. Ho was seventy-one years old at this time. Soon after, he returned north, where he lived to the age of eighty-six.[9]

Ch'iu Ho led the Vietnamese into the T'ang Empire under conditions of peace and prosperity. Thus, early T'ang administrators had an excellent foundation to build on. They came, not among a sullen, conquered population, but among a prosperous people with a high level of culture and a stable political system sufficiently advanced to be integrated into the empire without violence.

The peaceful extension of T'ang rule into Vietnam was largely a result of Ch'iu Ho's leadership and of the stability of Vietnamese society. It was also in accord with the pacifist mood of the early T'ang court.

Ch'iu Ho's role in Vietnam during the breakup of Sui and the advent of T'ang differs significantly from the earlier pattern of local family initiative under such conditions. We can surmise that the Sui regime imposed after Ly Phat Tu's submission had neutralized local leadership. An undisclosed number of Ly Phat Tu's officials were executed, and surviving members of the local ruling class were probably cowed into submission with threats and promises. The chief consideration, however, is that China was now united and was experiencing a historic outward projection of its power. This was the beginning of a new age.

The Organization of the Protectorate

T'ang began, in 622, by dividing the Vietnamese lands into numerous small provinces and placing over them two central administrations. The most important of these central administrations was located in the vicinity of modern Hanoi, with authority over the ten provinces in the plains of the Hong and Ma rivers.[10] A second central administration was established in the Ca River plain, with authority over the provinces on the extreme southern frontier. Although Ai Province was under the northern central administration, it was in a position of preeminence over the other provinces of the Ma River plain.[11]

9. *CTS*, 59, 5a; *TCTC*, 190, vol. 10, 607, 711; *TT*, 5, 3a; *CL*, 97.

10. H. Maspero, "Le Protectorat general d'Annam sous les T'ang," p. 552, calls this the "Protectorate of Giao Province" (Giao Chau Do ho phu), while the sources he cites in reference call it the "Central Administration of Giao Province" (Giao Chau Tong quan phu); see *TPHYC*, 170, 2b, and *CTS*, 41, 42b. *HTS*, 43c, 9b, merely says Giao Chau. *YHCHC*, 1081–82, not cited by Maspero, says Giao Chau Tong quan phu.

11. *CTS*, 41, 44b–45a, 45b–46a.

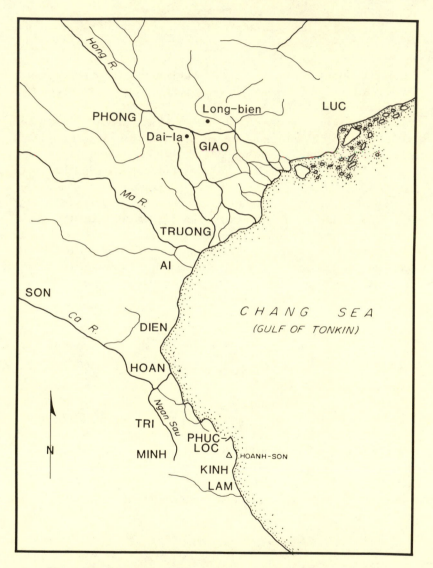

Map 7. The Protectorate of An-nam

The initial proliferation of provinces was apparently intended to identify population centers. In following years, this organization was greatly modified as T'ang officials grew more intimately acquainted with local conditions, and their position became more secure.

Beginning in 627, in response to administrative reforms initiated by the new emperor, T'ai Tsung, the number of provinces was greatly reduced. In 628, the central administrations were changed to general governments presided over by governor generals,[12] an administrative category designed for use in areas outside the imperial heartland. During the next fifty years, a process of administrative experimentation and development culminated in the organization of the Protectorate of An-nam in 679.

The protectorate, under the authority of a protector general, was an administrative category used by T'ang to rule "barbarian," or non-Chinese, peoples in frontier areas. In 678, the empire had suffered a serious defeat in Central Asia at the hands of the Tibetans; the appearance of the Protectorate of An-nam at this time reflected a concern for frontier organization stimulated by the Central Asian setback.

The Protectorate of An-nam, "Pacified South," was simply one of several protectorates on the T'ang frontiers, which included the Protectorates of the "Pacified West" in the Tarim Basin, the "Pacified North" in Mongolia, and the "Pacified East" on the Korean border.

The type and number of provinces under the protectorate varied from time to time, but eight are worth mention as being the most important, as well as comprising the lands that would become the nucleus of independent Vietnam.

The southern border was anchored in Hoan Province, which lay in the lowlands of the Ca River. Hoan had jurisdiction over a number of "halter provinces" (*co mi chau*) set up to "restrain" tribal populations in the neighboring mountains.[13] "Halter provinces" were little more than titles given to tribal leaders in the mountains as a way of encouraging their cooperation.

The administrative reform of 627 did not immediately affect Hoan, except for the changing of a few provincial names and the elimination of two districts; here the process of instituting the T'ang system of government lagged behind the reforms effected further north. New provinces were still being established in Hoan after 627, when the number of provinces was

12. Ibid., 41, 45b, dates the establishment of the southern general government (*do doc phu*) to 628, while 41, 42b, says that in 679 the Giao Chau Do doc phu was changed to the "Protectorate of An-nam" (An-nam Do ho phu); I assume that the "Giao Chau Central Administration" (Tong quan phu) was changed to the Giao Chau Do ho phu at the time this reform took place in the southern jurisdiction.

13. YHCHC, 1087; CTS, 41, 45b–46a.

being reduced elsewhere.[14] The reason for this was the time-consuming procedure of defining and consolidating the frontier.

In 628, it is recorded that Lin-i was "soothed and comforted," resulting in the establishment of Kinh Province on the southern border of Hoan. In 635, Lin-i was again "soothed and comforted," and a second province, named Lam, was established on Hoan's southern border. These two border provinces, located in the vicinity of the Hoanh-son massif, were discontinued later in the century;[15] they were apparently an experiment in observing and testing the Lin-i frontier.

Administration on the Lin-i frontier was eventually formalized with the establishment of Phuc-loc Province.[16] The area had reportedly been appropriated by migrating "uncivilized Lao" during the sixth century. Beginning in 663, these "uncivilized Lao" were "beckoned and soothed," resulting in the establishment of Phuc-loc Province in 669. Phuc-loc Province was created by combining a new Phuc-loc District with an already existing Duong-lam Province; Duong-lam Province had been formed but a short time before by combining a new Duong-lam District with an older district, dating from Sui, that had been detached from Hoan. With this process of administrative expansion, T'ang achieved firm control over the strategic coastal frontier.

In 635, Son Province was established along the upper Ca River on the edge of the Tran-ninh Plateau (Plain of Jars); it included a frontier garrison outpost with a population of more than five thousand.[17] Dien Province was originally located along the coast north of Hoan. Around 650 it was discontinued and incorporated into Hoan. In 764, it reappeared as a separate province. At that time, Son Province was discontinued, and its territory

14. In 622, the provinces of Minh and Ly, first proclaimed under the Liang dynasty a century before, were restored in the area drained by the Ngan Sau, a tributary of the Ca extending south parallel to the seacoast. Ly was now known as Tri Province, a name change made by Ling-hu Hsi in 598. In 639, Minh Province was discontinued and its territory placed under Tri; later, Tri was also discontinued and the entire area became a single district of Hoan Province. A similar process of consolidation occurred simultaneously along the coast as centralized administration became more effective. According to surviving administrative data from the first half of the seventh century, Hoan Province comprised four fundamentally distinct areas identified as the districts of Cuu-duc, Hoai-hoan, Pho-duong, and Viet-thuong (HTS, 43a, 10b; CTS, 41, 46a; TPHYC, 171, 6a). It is clear that Cuu-duc contained the major portion of the Ca River plain, including the coastal zone. Hoai-hoan lay to the north and was subsequently detached to form Dien Province. Pho-duong was the same as Son Province, on the upper Ca; it was detached with Hoai-hoan and became part of Dien Province in 764. Viet-thuong, which consisted of old Minh and Ly (Tri) provinces, must have lain along the Ngan Sau, the only significant remaining geographical area.

15. HTS, 43a, 10b; CTS, 41, 46b; TPHYC, 171, 13b–15a.

16. On the location of Phuc-loc, see Appendix I.

17. HTS, 43a, 10b; YHCHC, 1090; Émile Gaspardone, "Materiaux pour servir a l'histoire d'Annam," p. 101, n. 3.

added to Dien. Dien thus comprised the coast north of Hoan, along with the entire upland area drained by the Ca.[18]

Ai Province lay in the Ma River plain. In 622, Ai was one of eight provinces established in this plain and its hinterland; in 627, these were consolidated into two provinces; and in 636, Ai absorbed the remaining one.[19] Situated in the center of the protectorate, Ai escaped the full impact of the Chinese influence pressing upon the Hong River plain to the north; at the same time, Hoan shielded Ai from the more volatile influences of the frontier in the south. This seems to have enabled Ai to be more selective about what it absorbed from external influence and perhaps explains why Ai emerged in the tenth century as the original and most persistent center of the politics of independence.

Truong Province lay along the uplands north of Ai and included the southern extremities of the Hong River plain. The portion of the plain included in Truong was not suitable for agriculture because the diking system had not yet been extended this far down the Hong River, so the relatively sparse population of Truong lived mainly by fishing and hunting. The date of Truong's formation has not been preserved; it is not mentioned in the reforms of the first half of the seventh century, but appears in the census of 740.[20] We may conjecture that Truong appeared contemporaneously with Phuc-loc in the 660s as part of an effort to gain firm control of coastal lands adjacent to the lowland population centers. The strategic importance of Truong was that it commanded the coastal route out of the Hong River plain toward the south.

Phong Province occupied the region where the Hong River and its tributaries emerge from the mountains. It contained the headquarters for overseeing the entire mountainous hinterland of the Hong and Ma river plains; not less than twenty-eight "halter provinces" were under its jurisdiction, which extended as far as Yün-nan.[21] When, in the ninth century,

18. *HTS*, 43a, 11a; *TPHYC*, 171, 13a; *YHCHC*, 1090. According to *TPHYC*, 171, 13b, Dien was 250 *li* south of Ai, 150 *li* north of Hoan, and 600 *li* "southwest of the sea." *YHCHC*, 1089, says Dien lay "west of the sea on the route from the Middle Kingdom to Lin-i and Funan"; the same source, 1090, locates one of Dien's districts four *li* west of the sea, but this may be an error, for the district in question seems to be the same as Son Province, which was on the upper Ca.

19. *CTS*, 41, 44b–45a; *HTS*, 43a, 10a–b.

20. H. Maspero, "Le Protectorat general," pp. 668–80, reviewed salient information on this province. *YHCHC*, 1090, lists Truong as a "tributary province," indicating that the population retained control of local affairs while tendering tribute. *TPHYC*, 171, 12a, and *HTS*, 43a, 10b, list gold as an item of tribute from Truong. *YHCHC*, 1091, lists six other "tributary provinces" in Annam, most of them in the mountains.

21. *YHCHC*, 1087–88. H. Maspero, "Le Protectorat general," pp. 665–68, reviewed surviving geographical and administrative information on this province, including historical and legendary traditions localized there.

T'ang administrators antagonized the tribal populations of the mountains, Phong became the scene of prolonged hostilities. The strategic role of Phong during T'ang was to protect Giao from the tribal peoples of the mountains.

The demographic and administrative center of the protectorate was Giao Province. Here a large agricultural population occupied the heart of the Hong River plain. Chinese influence was naturally most effective in Giao; the area it comprised had been the arena of Sino-Vietnamese contact from earliest times. During the T'ang period, Giao received an unprecedented lesson in Chinese civilization. Chinese provincial regimes had never before been so strong and enduring. While in other provinces, resistance to Chinese influence was reinforced by regional geographies, Giao was firmly under the imperial thumb and grew accustomed to Chinese ideas and social organization by force of habit. The demands of administrators shaped the behavior of villagers; schools were built; and ambitious families acquired a Chinese education with an imperial point of view.

In the temples, however, ancient beliefs survived, sheltered by the Buddha and a host of native spirits who stood as guardians of the indigenous cultural heritage. Giao was the center of Vietnamese Buddhism. The popular cultural outlook of Giao, based on spirit cults in the context of an elastic Buddhism, was eventually the source of the dominant cultural outlook of independent Vietnam as it evolved from the tenth century on.

Giao did not experience a "regular Chinese administration," for it remained a frontier jurisdiction populated by non-Chinese people; yet it came closer to such an experience than any other of the provinces we have examined. In 622, eight provinces were proclaimed there; in 627, these were all consolidated into Giao Province, comprising eight districts.[22]

Sui had established its central government in the vicinity of modern Hanoi. In 618, during the crisis of Ning Ch'ang-chen's invasion, Ch'iu Ho erected a small citadel nine hundred paces in circumference at this location. A citadel of this size erected inside a larger metropolitan area was called a *tzu-ch'eng* by the Chinese; Ch'iu Ho's citadel was accordingly known as Tu-thanh (Chinese Tzu-ch'eng).[23] This was where Ly Bi had built fortifications to resist Ch'en Pa-hsien in the second battle of 545. It lay on the right bank of the Hong River just beyond the dry-season influence of the tides. Appearing for the first time as a separate administrative jurisdiction in the mid-fifth century, this area rose to political prominence under Sui and T'ang because

22. *CTS*, 41, 42b; *HTS*, 43a, 9b. H. Maspero, "Le Protectorat general," pp. 551–84, wrote a reasonably good study of this province, including a long discourse on the early history of Hanoi (555–63).

23. *TT*, 5, 3a. H. Maspero, "Le Protectorat general," p. 555, erroneously dated its construction in 621.

of its central location and because dikes had by this time been built along the Hong there. The broadening perspective of imperial administration is revealed in the positioning of the central government south of the Hong River.

Finally, Luc Province lay along the coast north of the Hong River plain. First established as the province of Hoang in 535, its name was changed to Luc in 598 by Ling-hu Hsi. In 622, Luc was organized as a province by T'ang, but it was discontinued and placed under a province to the north in 628; in 650 it reappeared as a separate province.[24]

The name *Luc* means "dry land" and derived from the fact that the province consisted of a "dry land road" that connected the coasts "north of the sea," Kuang-tung, with the coasts "south of the sea," Vietnam. It is recorded that this province was "located on an impoverished coast where grain and vegetables would not grow and silk and cotton were unknown, so the people lived from the sea."[25] Luc was on the border between the protectorate and the empire proper; consequently, it was often more directly under the control of jurisdictions to the north.

This geographical and administrative review of the protectorate shows that there was great disparity among the provinces in terms of population and function. The provinces were in fact parts of a whole, and their individual peculiarities reflected the role they played within the unity of the protectorate.

Giao, Phong, Ai, and Hoan occupied fertile lowland areas where dense, settled populations were concentrated. Giao, the largest, experienced the most intimate relationship with T'ang. Phong was characterized by its proximity to the mountains and its role as a protective frontier screen for Giao. Ai was relatively sheltered from disturbing external forces and is thus less easy to stereotype. In the tenth century, Ai responded vigorously to the idea of Vietnamese independence; from this, we might surmise that, of all areas in Vietnam, Ai remained most traditional during T'ang. Hoan, small and isolated, was in close contact with the foreign kingdoms to the south and west and experienced the unruly forces peculiar to a cultural frontier. Dien and Phong secured the mountainous hinterland of the three plains; Phuc-loc, Dien, Truong, and Luc secured the coasts that separated the plains from each other, from Lin-i, and from the empire to the north.

In 742, all of these provinces were reduced to prefectural status, but just sixteen years later, in 758, the old provincial organization was restored. This was the last administrative change before the rebellion of An Lu-shan unleashed disorder throughout the empire.

24. *HTS*, 43a, 10a.
25. *YHCHC*, 1088.

Table 5. T'ang Census Statistics for the Protectorate of An-nam

| | "Old Census" (ca. 700) | | 726 | 740 | | 742 | | 807 |
	Hearths	Heads	Hearths	Hearths	Heads	Hearths	Heads	Hearths
Giao	17,523	88,788	25,690	24,730	99,660	24,230	99,652	27,135
Phong	5,444*	6,435	3,561*	1,920	5,119	1,920	....	1,483
Ai	9,080	36,519	14,056	40,700*	135,030*	14,700	....	5,379
Hoan	6,579	16,689	6,649	9,629	53,818	9,619	50,818	3,843
Luc	....	....	1,934*	490	2,710	494	2,674	231
Truong	....	....	....	630	3,040	....	....	648
Dien				(included in Hoan)		....		1,450
Phuc-loc	....	....	....	....	....	....	....	317
Total		148,431				40,963		40,486

* Obvious errors

SOURCE: CTS, 41, 42b–46b; HTS, 43a, 9b–11a; YHCHC, 38; T'T, 174, 50a–51a; TPHYC, 171, 11b.

Census Records

Table 5 shows five sets of census figures for the protectorate that have survived from the T'ang period. The earliest is simply identified as the "old census" and probably dates from the turn of the eighth century.[26] The second is from the K'ai-yüan period (713–41) and possibly dates from 726.[27] The census statistics from 740 and 742 are naturally very similar and probably derive from a single enumeration. The 742 census was ordered on the occasion of publishing a new reign title and undoubtedly made use of the figures compiled two years earlier. Omissions and variations can be attributed to clerical mistakes and separate traditions of preservation.[28] The last census is from 807.[29]

The decrease in the 807 figures for Ai and Hoan reflects a war with Huan-wang (Lin-i) that ravaged portions of these two provinces in the years 803–9. Dien was now a separate province, and this also reduced Hoan's total.

Because of gaps and apparent inaccuracies, a statistical comparison can be made for only two provinces. Table 6 shows a comparison of the "old census" with the census of 742 for Giao and Hoan, the only provinces whose figures are complete and free from detectable error.

This comparison suggests that major demographic changes produced abnormal growth in the registered population of the eighth century. At this time, unlike the stable pre-T'ang centuries, Chinese immigration was clearly of sufficient magnitude to cause basic changes in certain portions of Vietnamese society. The impact of immigrants in Giao is revealed by the number of households, which grew three times faster than the population, causing a significant decline in the average number of persons per household.

At the other end of the protectorate, the figures for Hoan show a

---

26. *CTS*, 41, 42b–46b.

27. *YHCHC*, 38. On the date 726, see H. Maspero, "Le Protectorat general," p. 547, n. 5, and *TCTC*, 213, vol. 11, 863.

28. The 740 census comes from *T'T*, 174, 50a–51a, a contemporary source. The 742 census comes from *CTS*, 41, 42b–46b, and *HTS*, 43a, 9b–11a. The *TPHYC* also uses the 742 figures, but records 24,232 hearths for Giao.

29. *YHCHC*, 38. The three figures for Truong, Dien, and Phuc-loc from this census also appear in the *HTS* (43a, 10b–11a), which otherwise uses figures from the census of 742. Likewise, the *CTS* (41, 45b) and the *TPHYC* (171, 11b) both include the figure 648 for Truong Province, while otherwise using the census of 742. The contemporary source is the *YHCHC*, completed in the Yüan-ho period (806–20), which does not use the figures from the 742 census, but rather provides figures from the so-called K'ai-yüan census (probably 726) and the Yüan-ho census (807). The figure for Dien must certainly belong to the Yüan-ho census, for Dien was part of Hoan prior to 764. I conjecture that later sources used figures from the 807 census to fill what were perceived to be gaps in the earlier census. In the case of the *HTS*, it is redundant and incongruous to include a figure for Dien with census statistics dating prior to 764.

Table 6. T'ang Census Statistics from the "Old Census" and the
Census of 742 for the Provinces of Giao and Hoan

Province	Percentage Increase		Average Number of People per Household:		Increase or Decrease in Average Number of People per Household
	Hearths	Heads	"Old Census"	742	
Giao	38	12	5.1	4.1	− 1
Hoan	46	204	2.5	5.3	+ 2.8

different situation. Here the population grew over four times faster than the
number of households, more than doubling the average number of persons
per household. This shows the impact of immigration, too, but it is not the
kind of pattern caused by Chinese immigration.

Chinese immigrants came as individuals or in relatively small nuclear
family groups. Most of the Chinese immigrants arrived as soldiers or
merchants, then took a local wife and settled down. There are also a fairly
large number of exiles, who arrived alone or with a few family members.
Furthermore, some officials grew to like the area and decided to stay. This
kind of immigration caused a decline in average household size in Giao. In
Hoan, however, where average household size more than doubled, the
immigrants clearly arrived in large kinship groups of extended families,
clans, and tribes. So, while Chinese immigrants were modifying Vietnamese
society in the north, immigrants of a different kind were modifying
Vietnamese society in the south.

The eighth century was a particularly unstable time on the southern
frontier. In 722, as we will shortly see, a man from Hoan led a large army of
foreigners that temporarily swept T'ang power out of the protectorate.
These newcomers came from many areas of Southeast Asia, having been
uprooted by a series of migrations not yet fully understood.

Beginning in 758, Chinese records cite Huan-wang in place of Lin-i,
and in 877 they speak of Chan-ch'eng, the Chinese transcription of
Champapura, "City of Champa." During the "Huan-wang era," the Cham
kingdom was based in the vicinity of modern Nha-trang and Phan-rang, far
to the south of old Lin-i. Beginning in 875, a new dynasty appeared in the
vicinity of modern Da-nang, near the T'ang border. This instability south of
the border had a strong demographic impact on Hoan. Many of the clans
and tribes that came across the frontier in 722 probably stayed on and settled
down in Hoan. As the Cham kingdom evolved down, then back up the
coast, many groups undoubtedly sought security behind the T'ang frontier.

Many of the immigrants into Giao from the Chinese side, as reflected in census statistics, may have been T'ang soldiers who were settled after the events of 722.

A comparison of tables 4 and 5 shows that Sui census figures were slightly higher than those from T'ang. This may be due in part to different methods of computation. However, there is a more basic reason for this variation. Sui conquered the Vietnamese without a battle and took immediate control of a society that had been developing autonomously for over half a century. Sui eventually provoked unrest among the Vietnamese that resulted in the sending of Ch'iu Ho, but the Sui census dates from early in the Sui regime, before this unrest produced demographic effects. The T'ang census records, however, date from after major rebellions in 687 and 722, and a period of anarchy and quasi-independence in the late eighth century. We can assume that the lower T'ang figures reflect the demographic effects of political violence.

T'ang census statistics, like those of earlier dynasties, represent that portion of the population most firmly under administrative control. During the first century and a half of T'ang, only the top three of six categories of taxpaying subjects were included in the census.[30] The percentage of the actual population included in the census can only be roughly surmised. I estimate that these census figures represent somewhere between 10 and 30 percent of the actual population of the protectorate.

T'ang census records show that Giao Province contained well over half the total registered population of the protectorate. In the "old census," Giao comprised 64.2 percent of the registered population. In 742, Giao accounted for 47.5 percent of registered households; by 807, this figure was up to 67 percent, although this increase can be attributed in part to warfare in Ai and Hoan. The four provinces of Giao, Phong, Ai, and Hoan account for virtually the entire registered population; they were all located in the lowlands and consisted of settled agricultural communities. The census figures from the other provinces can be taken as representative of agricultural settlements in the midst of mountainous or coastal terrain more conducive to a nomadic, or less governable, existence. All of this tends to confirm the idea that the economy and social life of the protectorate rested, not only on commerce, but more fundamentally on a fully developed peasant class chiefly occupied with the seasonal pursuit of growing rice.

But we must also bear in mind that the registered population was not coterminous with Vietnamese society. A significant portion of the Vietnamese chose to live in upland regions or in marginal areas of the lowlands where imperial authority was relatively weak. The ancestors of the Muong, who lived in the uplands between the Hong and Ca rivers, did not experi-

30. *T'T*, 6 (Katakura, pp. 33–34).

ence the cultural and linguistic impact of T'ang that their lowland kinsmen did. Moreover, they were never included in any T'ang census.

A comparison of Han and T'ang census figures offers a clue to the origin of the Muong. Han statistics are disproportionately large in comparison with statistics preserved from later centuries. For example, the census of A.D. 2 records over 950,000 persons for Vietnam, whereas T'ang figures eight centuries later do not exceed 150,000. Yet it is difficult to assume that the Han statistics are inflated, for officials had to provide tax receipts equal to the population reported in their jurisdictions. Officials often reported numbers lower than the actual population, but it was to their disadvantage to report a greater population than they could account for in tax revenue.

In fact, Chinese census figures as a whole show that the total population recorded in A.D. 2 was not equaled again for over a thousand years. This was partially a result of the many wars, invasions, and rebellions that periodically swept China during and after the fall of Han, but a more basic explanation lies in the ascendance of great landowning families; independent farmers became tenants or "serfs" on private estates and were no longer registered with the taxpaying population.

In Vietnam, the decline in census figures after Han is relatively sharp. The rise of great landowning families is an important consideration in evaluating these statistics. Another factor is the growing power of the Lin-i people on the southern coast. The frontier between the kingdom of Lin-i and the Vietnamese jurisdictions of the different Chinese dynasties fluctuated greatly in the centuries after Han. This political instability was accompanied by demographic instability as well, and during this time there were significant population movements away from Chinese control, for Lin-i itself sprang from within the Han frontier.

The social and political pressures caused by the prolonged presence of Chinese dynastic power in Vietnam and, in particular, the chronic political violence provoked by these pressures must have had great demographic effects. Many people surely escaped from the provincial regime imposed in the plains and settled in the surrounding highlands, where Chinese authority was diluted by geography as well as by prevailing social and economic conditions. This helps to explain the origins of the Muong, an upland people whose language and culture is closely related to Vietnamese.

The Muong are concentrated in the highlands south of the Hong River. Modern Vietnamese scholars believe that separate development of the Muong and Vietnamese languages did not begin until T'ang or later, when Chinese control was thrown off.[31] Until then, it was relatively easy

31. Nguyen Linh and Hoang Xuan Chinh, "Dat nuoc va con nguoi thoi Hung Vuong," pp. 103–4. On the demographic impact of Chinese rule on the indigenous peoples of southern China, see Rafe de Crespigny, "Prefectures and Population in South China in the First Three Centuries A.D.," p. 148.

for plains dwellers to migrate to the hills and enter the culture there. This was a form of Vietnamese culture that reflected a tribal society, without the intellectual patterns that became mandatory under Vietnamese dynasties of the later independence period.

The rise of the Muong helps explain the decline of census figures after Han, for people in the uplands were never registered. The Tay and Nung of the northern Vietnamese mountains on the Chinese border, who played important roles in Vietnamese history from earliest times, and the Mon-Khmer and Malayo-Polynesian peoples of the southern mountains and coasts were also beyond the reach of direct T'ang rule, as was the large floating population in the lower plains beyond the dikes, who subsisted from the sea or maritime trade.

The focus of Vietnamese history nevertheless rests on the lowland peasantry. Although registered and taxed by Chinese officials, the Vietnamese remained true to themselves. They never lost their language, with the distinctive emotions and thoughts it evokes. They never broke faith with their past and its heritage. By preserving this heritage, they have left their mark, not only in census records found among old books, but also in the continuing reality of an independent Vietnam.

Census statistics from Han through T'ang show that, in comparison with Vietnam, the area of modern Kuang-tung and Kuang-hsi was demographically transformed. In A.D. 2, 67 percent of the registered households in the Kuang-tung, Kuang-hsi, Vietnam region were in Vietnam; this figure dropped to only 13 percent in the "old census" of T'ang. Registered households in Kuang-tung and Kuang-hsi were 71,805 in A.D. 2 and 274,696 in the "old census" of T'ang, an increase of nearly 400 percent; on the other hand, registered households in Vietnam were 143,643 in A.D. 2 and less than 40,000 in the "old census" of T'ang.[32]

These statistics suggest that the pattern of Chinese immigration in Vietnam was very different from what it was in the Kuang-tung and Kuang-hsi area.[33] They further suggest that the response of Vietnamese society to Chinese rule placed relatively severe limitations on the ability of Chinese dynasties to register and tax the population. These limitations appear to have been imposed by powerful local families and by a porous upland frontier.

Pilgrims and Merchants

During the seventh and early eighth centuries, the political stability that the T'ang Empire imposed over much of Asia stimulated an era of pilgrimage by Buddhists from East Asia to the holy lands of India and Ceylon. The Protectorate of Annam was an important point of

---

32. *CTS*, 41.
33. See Tsang Wah-moon, *T'ang-tai Ling-nan fa-chan ti heh-hsin hsing.*

embarkation for pilgrims following the sea route. Vietnamese Buddhism benefited from and participated in this desire to travel.

Information on some of the Chinese pilgrims has survived.[34] Ming Yüan, a native of Ssu-ch'uan, embarked from the protectorate and sojourned in Ho-ling (Java) on his way to Ceylon and India. Wu Hsing, from Hu-pei, likewise embarked from the protectorate, stopping in Śrīvijaya (Sumatra) on his way to India, where he became a companion of the well-known pilgrim I Ching (635–713). Another pilgrim from Hu-pei, named Hui Ming, was less fortunate. His voyage was cut short by a storm off Lin-i, and he was forced to return north through the protectorate.

In addition to Chinese pilgrims who merely passed through the protectorate were others who stayed long enough to contribute to the Buddhist life there. The pilgrim Chih Hung, a native of Lo-yang, resided in the protectorate for one year before continuing his journey to India via Śrīvijaya. Similarly, T'an Jun, also from Lo-yang, passed a monsoon season in the protectorate and was honored by the local people for his "upright behavior." When he finally set sail, Van Ki, a native of Giao, accompanied him.

T'an Jun died en route, somewhere in the vicinity of Java, and Van Ki remained in the islands, where he became fluent in both Sanskrit and the local Malay language (K'un-lun). Later, a Chinese pilgrim in Java named Hui Ning and a Javanese monk named Jñānabhadra translated a portion of Buddhist scripture into Chinese, and Van Ki was entrusted with the task of bearing it to China.

Van Ki arrived in the protectorate in the 670s; from there he traveled directly to the T'ang capital and presented the new scripture to the emperor. On his return, he tarried in the protectorate and preached to the Buddhist community and among the people before proceeding to Java to convey a message of imperial gratitude to the translators. Hui Ning, however, had meanwhile departed for India; Van Ki subsequently settled in Śrīvijaya.

Also in the last half of the seventh century, a Sogdian (native of Central Asia) named Saṃghavarma, who had traveled the pilgrim route through India, was sent by the T'ang court to the protectorate to make drugs. His acts of mercy during a famine there earned him the veneration of the people, who regarded him as a bodhisattva.

The spirit of pilgrimage, encouraged by the lives and deeds of such men as these, was picked up by many Vietnamese Buddhists. A native of Giao known as Moc-xoa-de-ba (Mokṣadeva) followed the pilgrim route through the south sea islands to India. The pilgrim Khuy Sung, also from Giao, accompanied the Chinese pilgrim Ming Yüan to Java, Ceylon, and India. A third native of Giao, Hue Diem, followed his spiritual teacher to

34. On the pilgrims discussed in this section, see Tran Van Giap, "Le Bouddhisme en Annam des origins au XIIIe siècle," pp. 221–27.

Ceylon. A native of Ai Province, Tri Hanh, traveled through the south sea islands and on to India. Dai-thang-dang, also from Ai, traveled to Dvāravatī (Thailand) in his youth and lived in the T'ang capital before taking the pilgrim route through the south sea islands and Ceylon to India, where he became a companion of I Ching.

These pilgrims sailed from the protectorate in the vessels of merchants. There could not have been an era of pilgrimage had there not been lively international commerce, for the pilgrims simply followed the trade routes. What, from the religious point of view, was an age of pilgrimage is, from a more prosaic point of view, an age of wide-ranging commercial contacts.

Once again we are reminded how closely the Vietnamese were associated with the maritime world of Southeast Asia. The cultural frontier between India and China was ameliorated by the common heritage of the Buddha, especially during the cosmopolitan age of T'ang. Chinese and Vietnamese Buddhists traveled to the kingdoms in the islands of Southeast Asia to study Sanskrit and to prepare themselves for the holy land. The ships on which they sailed were owned by merchants and filled with merchandise.

This age of pilgrims and merchants underlines a basic theme of Southeast Asian history shared by the Vietnamese, a theme of maritime contact and of this contact as a source of civilization.

Exiles

The most persistent contacts, however, remained with the north, and from the north came a steady stream of soldiers, great mandarins, imperial princes, and exiled officials.

One of the earliest governor generals of Giao was a member of the imperial house named Li Shou. In the wake of Emperor T'ai Tsung's accession in 627 and the reforms ordered by him, Shou was dismissed on a charge of corruption. The emperor then summoned Lu Tsu-shang, an official of talent and reputation, and said: "Giao is a large frontier region and it is necessary to have good officials to look after it; up to now, none of the governor generals has been equal to his responsibilities. You have the ability to pacify this frontier; go and defend it for me, and do not refuse on account of its being far away."

Tsu-shang thanked the emperor and accepted the appointment, but later he refused to go south on the pretext of illness. After the urgings of one imperial messenger failed to move him, the emperor sent Tsu-shang's own brother-in-law to reason with him. Tsu-shang listened as his kinsman spoke of honor and duty, then replied, "In the south there is much malaria; if I go there I shall never return." Tsu-shang's stubbornness so angered the emperor that he was forthwith beheaded.[35]

35. *TCTC*, 193, vol. 10, 880–81; *TT*, 5, 3b; *CL*, 97.

The choice between the executioner's sword and disappearing into the pestilential vapors of the south confronted many officials as demotion and banishment became a prime means of staffing the administration there. For example, in 635, Li Tao-hsing, a member of the imperial family who was appointed governor general of Giao as punishment for some unrecorded offense, died of illness within a year of his arrival.[36]

The list of exiles on the southern frontier is long and includes several men of prominence. Tu Cheng-lun had been appointed by Emperor T'ai Tsung as an assistant to crown prince Ch'eng-ch'ien. When Ch'eng-ch'ien conspired to seize the throne in 643, Cheng-lun was demoted to governor general of Giao.[37]

The Fang I-ai conspiracy of 652 produced new exiles. Wan Pei's elder brother and Ch'ai Che-wei's younger brother had been involved in this conspiracy; consequently, both men were under suspicion and were exiled to the south. Later, Che-wei was pardoned and given a chance to rehabilitate himself as governor general of Giao.[38]

After 655, Li I-fu rose as a powerful minister at court, and Tu Cheng-lun, recovering from his demotion of 643, again became influential.[39] As they and their party prospered under the patronage of Empress Wu, they recognized the great calligrapher Ch'u Sui-liang as a serious obstacle to their plans.

In 656, Sui-liang was accused of disloyalty and demoted to governor general of a province in modern Hu-nan. Early in 657, he was further demoted to governor general of Kuei Province in modern Kuang-hsi.[40] Four months later, I-fu accused Sui-liang of using Kuei Province as a base for plotting sedition, and the hapless official was further demoted to the governorship of Ai Province. Sui-liang arrived in Ai and immediately sent a letter to the throne protesting his innocence, but to no avail.[41] When Sui-liang died at the end of 658, his two sons, who had been exiled with him, were killed.[42]

Court politics were fickle, however, and in the same year, 658, I-fu and Cheng-lun were charged with conspiracy and exiled to modern Kuang-hsi. Only a few months earlier, Cheng-lun had counseled that too many men were being exiled; now, although I-fu would return north and again enjoy power, Cheng-lun himself was destined to die in the south.[43]

---

36. *TT*, 5, 3b; *CL*, 97. On T'ang exiles in the south, see Edward Schafer, *The Vermilion Bird*, pp. 37–44.

37. *TCTC*, 197, vol. 11, 51; *CL*, 98.

38. *TCTC*, 197, vol. 11, 164, 168–69; *CL*, 98.

39. *TCTC*, 200, vol. 11, 189, 193.

40. Ibid., 200, vol. 11, 196, 201.

41. Ibid., 200, vol. 11, 202.

42. Ibid., 200, vol. 11, 212; *CL*, 98.

43. *TCTC*, 200, vol. 11, 205, 211, 219.

As a general rule, the more odious a person's offense, the further south he was sent. Thus, Li Yu, a kinsman of I-fu and retainer of Cheng-lun, who was especially hated by the emperor for his devious role as a conspiratorial go-between, was exiled to Hoan Province. In 628, P'ei Ch'ien-t'ung, an old lieutenant of Emperor Yang of Sui, had been sent to Hoan after it was decided that he could not be trusted. Later, Li Ch'ien-yu, a governor in modern Ho-pei, was exiled to Hoan after writing satirical letters about court politics. Late in the seventh century, Yen Shan-ssu, once a powerful but corrupt censorate official, was sent to Hoan.[44]

The censorate was a particularly sensitive apparatus, and many conscientious officials who could not adjust to its convolutions found themselves heading south. Lang She-ch'ing was appointed governor of Giao after demonstrating an excess of zeal in the censorate.[45] A respected censorate official named Li Ch'ao was appointed keeper of the records at Long-bien in Giao after arguing against the will of the emperor.[46]

Then, there is the case of Han Ssu-yen, a highly regarded censorate official who ventured to warn Emperor Kao against the rising influence of Empress Wu. He retired from public life under pressure from Li I-fu. In 675, long after I-fu's death, Emperor Kao remembered Ssu-yen and summoned him with the intention of giving him an official position. Ssu-yen had been away from the capital for so many years that he had forgotten the details of court etiquette. When he appeared before the emperor, he failed to perform the ritualized steps mandatory on such an occasion. Consequently, he was exiled as district magistrate of Chu-dien in Giao and died there.[47]

Many of the exiles sent south were men of letters, who were influential in developing cultural life on the frontier. One such man was Wang Fu-shih, who came from an old literati family of Shan-hsi. During the reign of Emperor Kao, he was exiled as district magistrate in Giao-chi after his son had been disgraced. His son, the somewhat famous Wang Po, was traveling to join his father when he was shipwrecked and drowned. It is recorded that Fu-shih built schools and was respected by local gentry families.[48]

In 705, in the wake of Empress Wu's forced abdication, two scholar-officials were temporarily exiled in the protectorate. Tu Shen-yen was sent to Phong Province, and Shen Ch'üan-ch'i was sent to Hoan.[49] Both men have left poems written during their exile.[50] Here is one of Ch'üan-ch'i's poems:

> I have heard it said of Giao-chi
> That southern habits penetrate one's heart.

44. *CL*, 109–10.
45. Ibid., 98.
46. Ibid., 109.
47. Ibid., loc. cit.
48. *HTS*, 201, 6b; *CL*, 109. Lü Shih-p'eng, *Pei-shu shih-chi ti Yüeh-nan*, pp. 135–36.
49. *TCTC*, 207, vol. 11, 583–86; *HTS*, 201, 5a, and 202, 2a; *CL*, 109.
50. Lü Shih-p'eng, pp. 136–37.

Winter's portion is brief;
Three seasons are partial to the brightly wheeling sun.
Here Commissioner T'o obtained a kingdom;
Shih Hsieh has long been roaming the nether world.
Village dwellings have been handed down through generations;
Fish and salt have been produced since ancient times.
In remote ages, the people of Yüeh sent pheasants as tribute;
The Han general pondered the sparrowhawk.
The Northern Dipper hangs over Mount Ch'ung;
The south wind pulls at the Chang Sea.
Since I last left home, the months have swiftly come and gone;
My hairline shows that I have grown old.
My elder and younger brothers have yielded to their fates;
My wife and children have departed to reap their destinies.
An empty path, a ruined wall, tears;
It is clear that my heart has not echoed Heaven's will.[51]

The allusion to the people of Yüeh (Viet) sending pheasants as tribute goes back to the reign of King Cheng of Chou (1115–1078 B.C.), who, according to Chinese historical tradition, received white pheasants as tribute from the "Yüeh-shang Clan" in the year 1110 B.C. Since this was the earliest recorded mention of contact between the ancient Chinese and the "Yüeh," it became a cornerstone of classical lore about the beginning of Vietnamese history.[52] In the minds of the Chinese, this ancient episode connoted the subordinate position of the Vietnamese, embodied in the sending of tribute. For later Vietnamese scholars, the episode was proof that their nation was of great antiquity. Of course, as chapter 1 makes clear, the "Yüeh-shang Clan" of 1110 B.C. certainly had nothing to do with the ancient Vietnamese.

The reference to the Han general pondering the sparrowhawk is to Ma Yüan's written account of his expedition of A.D. 42–43. The general described how he was temporarily halted in the Hong River plain by the monsoon season. After observing a sparrowhawk fall into a river and drown while trying to fly through the rain, he mused on the purpose of life and the reason for his efforts in worldly affairs. The poetic allusion to the sparrowhawk is meant to evoke a feeling of melancholy caused by being far from home in a strange and potentially fatal environment.

Mount Ch'ung was a high mountain in southern Hu-nan. The idea of a stellar constellation of the northern sky positioned over a southern mountain was symbolic of being unnaturally far to the south, beyond the normal conception of the world for an educated Chinese in T'ang times. The Chang Sea was what we now call the Gulf of Tonkin.

In this poem, Ch'üan-ch'i blends an informed appreciation of the

51. CL, 157.
52. VSL, 1, 1a; TT, 1, 4a; LNCQ, 17–18. Ton Nu Thuong Lang, trans., and Ta Quang Phat, annotator, Kham dinh Viet su thong giam cuong muc, part 1, 1, 6a–b.

peculiar heritage of the south with the pain of his personal tragedy. His feelings of disorientation, rejection, and confusion were common afflictions of exiles.

However, not all T'ang officials came south under coercion, nor did they all regard their residence there as a purgatorial unhappiness. Many found the habits of the south to their liking and settled there permanently. As we will see, one protector general in the ninth century founded a family in Giao that became prominent in Vietnamese government in later centuries.

The Rebellion of 687

A tradition preserved in Vietnam from the Yung-hui period (650−55) suggests that some T'ang officials utilized the indigenous culture to legitimize their authority among the people. According to this tradition, there was a governor general named Li Ch'ang-ming. Seeing that the land was peaceful and contented, he erected a shrine in Phong containing the image of a "kingdom-protecting spirit." After burning incense, he called out, "Now may the powerful spirits of this land announce their presence in the likeness of this image for the comforting of simple hearts!" That night, two spirits appeared to him in a dream; both looked like the image. One announced himself as Local Magistrate, the other as Great Lord.

Ch'ang-ming proposed that they test their magical skills to see who should be first. The Great Lord declared that he would leap across the Hong River, but when he did so he found that the Local Magistrate was already there waiting for him. The same thing happened when the Great Lord leaped back, so the Local Magistrate was recognized as the most powerful spirit.[53]

The spectacle of a governor general presiding over a competition of the spirits of the land to determine which one should be honored as the regional guardian spirit suggests some interaction between imperial authority and the indigenous culture. The fact that the spirit Local Magistrate prevailed over the spirit Great Lord appears to indicate the dominant social perspective of the regional ruling class.

This tradition comes from the honeymoon period of T'ang rule, when the blessings of empire had not yet faded before the inevitable corruption of power. Prior to the formation of the protectorate in 679, the only recorded trouble was with refractory Lao tribesmen of Minh Province in 638; they were pacified by Governor General Li Tao-yen, and, soon after this, Minh Province was incorporated into Hoan.[54] However, as the weight

---

53. Li Ch'ang-ming is unknown in Chinese records according to H. Maspero, "Le Protectorat general," p. 667. This is from Chao Ch'ang's *Chiao chou chi* as cited in *VDULT*, 39.
54. *CL*, 97; *HTS*, 222c, 18b.

of T'ang power settled more firmly on the frontier, arbitrary and oppressive government became feasible. As the potential for abuse was realized, the people resisted.

In 676, an order went out for the governor generals of Kuang (Kuang-tung), Kuei (Kuang-hsi), and Giao to establish a method of selecting local men for administrative positions. Every four years, in what was to be called the "southern selection," "aboriginal leaders" were to be appointed to fill positions of the fifth degree and above.[55] The flow of regular appointees and exiles from the north was insufficient to staff the growing administration, so local men were to be recruited.

With the growth of officialdom went a corresponding decline in public morality. At this time, Empress Wu was gaining control of the T'ang court, stimulating political intrigue and a general feeling of uncertainty among officials. In Kuang Province, the governor general at Canton withdrew from the bother of government and averted his eyes as corrupt officials filled their pockets. When, in 684, these officials seized the ship of a foreign merchant, Malay (K'un-lun) boatmen killed the governor general and fled to the sea.[56]

In the same year, a serious rebellion broke out in eastern China under the leadership of Li Ching-yeh, grandson and heir of the former great minister Li Chi.[57] After Ching-yeh was defeated, all officials who had advanced under the patronage of his family were purged; some were executed, others exiled. One of those exiled was Liu Yen-yu.

When he entered officialdom in 668, Yen-yu had respectfully received the advice of Li Chi: "You are young and have a good name; you should restrain yourself and do nothing to surpass your superiors."[58] Now, however, Yen-yu found himself traveling south to be protector general of An-nam as a result of Chi's grandson's treason. Perhaps Chi had detected a hint of brashness in the young Yen-yu; in any case, Yen-yu met his death in An-nam for lack of caution.

Until Liu Yen-yu became protector general, taxation was more moderate in An-nam than within the empire proper; the harvest tax was one-half the standard rate. This was a recognition of the political problems inherent in ruling a non-Chinese population. For reasons that are no longer clear, Yen-yu attempted to enforce the full tax; in effect, he doubled the taxes.

The people, under the leadership of a certain Ly Tu Tien, resisted. Rather than resolving the situation peacefully, Yen-yu provoked open rebellion by killing Tu Tien. Dinh Kien, one of Tu Tien's compatriots, led the people against Yen-yu and besieged him in Tu-thanh. The T'ang

55. *TCTC*, 202, vol. 11, 308.
56. Ibid., 203, vol. 11, 358.
57. Ibid., 201, vol. 11, 282, and 203, vol. 11, 362–67.
58. *HTS*, 201, 3b; *TCTC*, 201, vol. 11, 275.

garrison was too small to do more than man the walls and wait for help.

The governor general of Kuang at this time was Feng Yüan-ch'ang, a man with a checkered career who had once earned the hatred of Emperor Kao for his devious behavior. Ordered to go to Yen-yu's rescue, Yüan-ch'ang embarked an army at Canton and sailed to An-nam, where he established a fortified camp and sent envoys to harangue the rebels. Hoping to gain influence in An-nam at Yen-yu's expense, he encouraged the rebels to kill their leaders and accept his authority, while making no move to rescue the besieged protector general. Finally, at the end of summer in 687, the rebels took Tu-thanh and put Yen-yu to death. Yüan-ch'ang then slunk back to Kuang when Ts'ao Hsüan-ching, a general from Kuei, marched into An-nam and put down the rebellion, capturing and beheading Dinh Kien.[59]

In the absence of more information, it is difficult to fully evaluate this rebellion. It was a peasant uprising led by men of whom absolutely nothing is known save their names. It was not led by upper-class people in defense of their prerogatives or in search of supreme power, as so frequently had been the case in earlier centuries. It rose in response to a specific administrative act and thereby bears witness to the revolutionary impact of T'ang administration on peasant society in An-nam.

An administrative act could not have provoked such a violent reaction unless it embodied a serious threat to the existing way of life. The doubling of taxes may or may not have been a significant act, depending on the government's ability to enforce it. The peasants' perception that exploitative taxation was administratively possible lay behind their resistance. If the administrative system had not been equal to the task of oppression, peasants could have lived with it in peace.

The rebellion of 687 is obscure in some ways but very clear in others. It showed that after more than sixty years of T'ang rule the Vietnamese rose up and besieged the Chinese for an extended period of time before eventually taking the capital and putting imperial officials to death. This uprising was not stimulated by external aggression or assisted by the collaboration of mountain tribesmen. It was a peasant movement based on the politics of peasant life in reaction to a single administrative measure. Vietnamese peasant society was capable of successfully fielding its own leaders against oppressive government. This indicates the strength, cohesion, and positive spirit of Vietnamese society even under the shadow of T'ang.

It might be argued that Ly Tu Tien and Dinh Kien were members of

---

59. The primary sources for the events of 687 are the biographies of Liu Yen-yu (*HTS*, 201, 3b–4a) and Feng Yüan-ch'ang (*CTS*, 185a, 11a–b). The imperial annals of the *HTS* (4, 3b) contain a brief notice that attributes Yen-yu's death to Ly Tu Tien and does not mention Dinh Kien. *TCTC*, 204, vol. 11, 388, is based on the biographies, as is *TT*, 5, 4a–b; whereas the *TCTC* appends the information about Yüan-ch'ang in a comment, the *TT* integrates it into the narrative. *VSL*, 1, 9b–10a, and *CL*, 98, contain brief notices based on Yen-yu's biography.

powerful local families and that the rebellion of 687 was a test of strength between great landowning families and T'ang tax collectors, but Liu Yen-yu's biography specifically identifies the rebels as "low-class people" (*li hu*).[60] Furthermore, the incredible stubbornness of the rebels, impervious to all threats and persuasion, suggests that they did not share the ruling-class values of T'ang.

We can assume that, in the case of some grievance against T'ang, powerful local families would have had means short of insurrection for voicing their complaints and negotiating a compromise. The doubling of taxes would not have been a likely cause of rebellion for the great landowning families, for they would simply have passed the tax burden on to their tenants; in such a situation, they would have been more likely to identify with the tax collector against the peasants. The rebellion of 687 suggests that the great families in Vietnam had in some way been absorbed into the T'ang system of government, leaving the peasantry vulnerable to administrative acts.

Mai Thuc Loan

There is little reliable information about An-nam for the next thirty-five years. In 693, an obscure rebellion broke out in the south; it was largely confined to Kuang, however, and appears not to have affected An-nam. In the following year, Lao tribesmen in modern Kuang-hsi rebelled.[61] Both uprisings were quickly put down, yet they demonstrated a weakening of authority in the south.

In 690, Empress Wu proclaimed her own "Chou dynasty," theoretically bringing the T'ang dynasty to an end. She was not deposed until 705; until then the empire was in a state of malaise. The only protector general known from this period is a certain Liu Yu. It is recorded that he was from a wealthy family and ate a whole chicken at every meal. It is further recorded that "for every chicken killed he ordered his servants to replace it with two more; there was not a moment when he was not enjoying good food."[62]

If this spectacle of the protector general endeavoring to consume as many of An-nam's chickens as possible is accurate, one might infer that with the crushing of the rebellion of 687 the regime became openly oppressive, perhaps out of the belief that such was the only way to keep the peasants in their place. The standard of official morality so deteriorated that, during the reign of Chung Tsung (705–9), Protector General Ch'ü Lan was killed by one of his subordinates, who was provoked by Lan's avarice and cruelty.[63]

60. *HTS*, 201, 3b.
61. *TCTC*, 205, vol. 11, 457, 466.
62. *CL*, 98.
63. *VSL*, 1, 10a.

At the end of the Ching-lung period (707–9), Tu Ming-chü was appointed protector general. He seems to have cultivated a good reputation among the people, for a tradition survives that his appointment as protector general was first announced to him in a dream by an inhabitant of An-nam.[64]

Nevertheless, in these years T'ang authority in An-nam seems to have come to depend more and more on coercion as the bulk of the population grew sullen and alienated by arbitrary acts of exploitation. This situation, aided by events occurring elsewhere in Southeast Asia, moved rapidly toward a new crisis.

We have spoken of the pilgrims and merchants who circulated through the seas between China and India during the seventh and eighth centuries. At this time the political life of these seas was entering a new era. Political centers along the lower Mekong, which for several centuries had controlled the maritime route between China and India, had disappeared. On Java and Sumatra, new kingdoms were vying for supremacy.

As the eighth century began, the Sumatran kingdom of Śrīvijaya was in control of the maritime routes through Southeast Asia. The lower Mekong fell prey to divisions and general anarchy. Lin-i was in a process of transformation, with its center of gravity shifting southward.[65] This fluid situation on the T'ang frontier combined with the combustible situation inside An-nam and ignited a spectacular attempt to push T'ang power out of the region.

Mai Thuc Loan was an inhabitant of a coastal village in southern Hoan, southeast of the modern city of Ha-tinh; this village has specialized in the production of salt since ancient times. Nearby mountains and valleys contain the tombs of Mai Thuc Loan's parents, as well as a citadel that he built.[66] Inscribed in a temple located in the midst of this area are the lines:

> The T'ang Empire waxed and waned;
> The mountains and rivers of Hoan and Dien stand firm through the ages.[67]

While this inscription undoubtedly dates from the independence period, it articulates a frontier identity that lay at the core of the great movement led by Mai Thuc Loan.

T'ang authority in Hoan was secure as late as 705–6, when Shen Ch'üan-ch'i, one of whose poems we have read earlier in this chapter, was exiled there. Sometime within the next fifteen years, however, T'ang administration began to disintegrate as the frontier developed a political

---

64. *CL*, 99.

65. Georges Coedes, *The Indianized States of Southeast Asia*, pp. 81–86, 93–95.

66. Tran Ba Chi, "Mai Thuc Loan va cuoc khoi nghia cua ong," pp. 50–53. H. Maspero, "Etudes d'histoire d'Annam," 18: 29.

67. Tran Ba Chi, p. 51.

momentum of its own. Mai Thuc Loan built his citadel and directly challenged the imperial world. In 722, Thuc Loan rallied the people of thirty-two provinces, as well as contingents from Lin-i, Chen-la in the lower Mekong, an unknown kingdom named Chin-lin ("Gold Neighbor"), and other unnamed kingdoms; calling himself the Black Emperor, presumably because of his dark complexion, he led a multitude numbering four hundred thousand and seized all of An-nam.

The thirty-two provinces mentioned in the records undoubtedly included a large number of "halter provinces," which in reality consisted of mountain tribes that had recognized T'ang overlordship. As we have noted above, at one time twenty-seven such provinces were under the jurisdiction of Phong; several were also attached to Hoan. This curious union of foreigners, mountain tribespeople, and lowland peasants under the leadership of a man from a coastal village on the frontier poses questions to which there can be no documented answers.

What was the nature of the Black Emperor's appeal to his followers? For the foreigners and the mountain dwellers, plunder was surely the chief motivation. Peasants may have rallied to the Black Emperor as a welcome alternative to the heavy hand of T'ang; yet if the plundering that drew their ostensible allies against their oppressors was unrestrained, they would suffer as grievously as under a corrupt imperial administration, perhaps more.

The Black Emperor's "multitude" of four hundred thousand was clearly not a disciplined army, but was rather disparate bands of hungry people eating their way through the countryside, toppling established authority yet offering no guarantee of peace or security to the population. The peasant population probably rallied to the Black Emperor, at least initially; but the spectacle of a man from the far south leading a horde of foreigners could not have been viewed with total equanimity by a people already possessing a strong and ancient identity of its own.

Did the Black Emperor identify himself with the traditions of Giao, or did he simply preside over a collection of flotsam that had drifted across the frontier as the opening wedge for the forces of anarchy? This question cannot be answered with certainty, but the Black Emperor never came to occupy a prominent place in the traditions of the Vietnamese people. We do not know whether this is because his power was too ephemeral to make a lasting impression or because he was perceived as some kind of exotic hero.

Kuang Ch'u-k'e, the protector general, had escaped north and was eventually joined by cavalry commander and imperial chamberlain Yang Ssu-hsü. Ssu-hsü was himself from Lo Province in what is now western Kuang-tung. Using his relatives as officers, he raised an army of one hundred thousand, including a "multitude" of mountain tribesmen who had remained loyal to T'ang. Without delay, he marched directly along the coast, following the old road built by Ma Yüan. The sudden appearance of Ssu-hsü took the Black Emperor by surprise, and he had no time to plan a response before it was too late. The corpses of the Black Emperor and his followers were piled up to form a huge mound.[68]

The Black Emperor's mercurial career must have fed the imaginations of indigenous leaders to the north, for in the following years Yang Ssu-hsü had his hands full putting down rebellions.[69] In 724, he quelled a rebellion in modern Kuei-chou. He spent the entire year 726 putting down a rebellion by a Lao leader in modern Kuang-hsi; over thirty thousand rebels were captured and beheaded. In 728, three Lao leaders in modern Kuang-tung seized more than forty walled towns. One of these men proclaimed himself emperor; another called himself the king of Nan Yüeh. Ssu-hsü beheaded some sixty thousand rebels before this uprising was crushed. After this, the south settled down somewhat as the reign of Emperor Hsüan Tsung (713–55) provided a new era of stability.

In contrast to the rebellion of 687, which had been an internal affair of the Vietnamese peasantry, the uprising of Mai Thuc Loan was based on a flood of aliens breaching the T'ang frontier. It is therefore comparable to the seaborne invasion of the K'un-lun and She-p'o in 767, which we will consider in the next section. This consideration highlights the basic strategic interest of T'ang in An-nam.

From the middle of the eighth century until the end of the dynasty, T'ang faced a constant threat from the kingdom of Nan-chao in Yün-nan. Furthermore, as we will have occasion to note in the next chapter, ninth-century T'ang officials in An-nam tried to stop the commerce in horses and weapons with the Khmers. The border between the Vietnamese and the rest of Southeast Asia was essentially a defensive military line, and it was maintained only with considerable expense and effort. Such had been the case since the expedition of Ma Yüan, nearly seven centuries before the Black Emperor's northward march. Moreover, under Chinese leadership, the Vietnamese had been battling with Lin-i for centuries.

This military border, maintained by Chinese imperial interests, was an important factor in shaping the Vietnamese view of the rest of Southeast Asia. As we will see in the next chapter, the most promising attempt by the

68. According to CL, 98, Kuang (the CL has Yüan by mistake) Ch'u-t'e was appointed protector general of An-nam at the beginning of the K'ai-yüan period (713–41). The detail of Ssu-hsü's rallying a "multitude of southern barbarians" is found only in TCTC, 212, vol. 11, 826. The primary source for the events of 722 is Yang Ssu-hsü's biography (HTS, 207, 1b). TCTC, 212, vol. 11, 826, and TT, 5, 4b, are varying abridgements of the account in this biography. CL, 98, and the imperial annals (HTS, 5, 7b, and CTS, 8, 11a) contain very brief notices. CL, 98, also contains a short notice about an exile in Chu-dien District, Giao Province, during the K'ai-yüan period (713–41), named Sung Chih-t'i, who distinguished himself against "barbarians who seized Hoan Province."

69. HTS, 207, 1b, and 41, 13a; TCTC, 212, vol. 11, 854, 858, and 213, vol. 11, 870, 871.

Vietnamese to join with their neighbors against the Chinese failed in part because the Vietnamese realized that they could tolerate the avarice of their Chinese patrons more easily than they could the violence and unreliability of their non-Chinese allies.

The Mid-T'ang Crisis

The reign of Hsüan Tsung has been called the "golden age" of the T'ang dynasty. Literature and art flourished, and imperial armies marched out in all directions. Aside from the population statistics that we have already examined, the only surviving information on An-nam between the years 722 and 751 is a tradition preserved in Vietnam about a protector general named Lu Yü. Yü resided in the village of An-vien, a short distance west of Tu-thanh. He was so pleased with the scenery around An-vien that he moved his entire government to a hamlet of the village. In the midst of his newly constructed official compound, he built a shrine to the spirit of Emperor Hsüan Tsung and the current imperial reign period, K'ai-yüan (713–41). The shrine was clearly intended to celebrate the power and prosperity of the empire under Hsüan Tsung during the K'ai-yüan era and to popularize the name of the imperial reign title among the people. Yü also erected an inscribed tablet proclaiming the merit of "K'ai-yüan Son of Heaven," which meant the emperor of the K'ai-yüan period, Hsüan Tsung. He further dedicated a statue of the local earth spirit inscribed with a poem praising the beauty of the place. It was duly recorded that prayers at this shrine were speedily answered and that the incense there never ceased burning.[70]

The association of a scenic spot in the protectorate with the reigning emperor in this manner reflects an effort to provide an alternative to traditional objects of veneration. Lu Yü's shrine became a cult center that fed on the prestige of Hsüan Tsung's reign; it drew the religious sentiments of the people away from traditional heroes and fixed them instead on the empire itself.

The tradition of Lu Yü and his shrine bears witness to the impact of T'ang on Vietnamese society during the reign of Hsüan Tsung. It may also reveal that T'ang administrators felt a need to win the confidence of the people after the rebellion of 687 and the uprising of Mai Thuc Loan. The emperor was placed on the cultic level of local heroes and deities, on which he could be understood by the people. This represented a Vietnamization of imperial ideology, which implies more concrete measures taken to reshape

70. *VDULT*, 34. The text identifies Lu Yü as a "former governor of Kuang Province" and says An-vien was located between the district of Tu-liem and Long-do. Long-do was a popular name for Thang-long (Hanoi) in the independence period. Tu-liem was a T'ang district west of modern Hanoi.

Vietnamese society. As we will have occasion to note near the end of this chapter, evidence from the mid-eighth century shows that provisions of T'ang law designed to uphold the Chinese-style family system were applied in the protectorate. Such specific measures probably could not have been contemplated without an effort to provide cultural symbols linking the Vietnamese to the imperial world. A cult center featuring both a local earth spirit and the spirit of the reigning emperor reflects such an attempt.

During the first century and a half of T'ang, the Vietnamese appear to have been passive in the face of imperial power. Aside from the rebellion of 687 and the uprising of Mai Thuc Loan in 722, there is no surviving evidence of local political activity. The last century and a half of T'ang was very different, because of the great crisis through which T'ang passed in the mid eighth century and T'ang's loss of strategic momentum. Military defeats in Yün-nan signaled the arrival of this new era for An-nam.

During the second quarter of the eighth century, T'ang officials attempted to open a direct route from northern China to An-nam through Ssu-ch'uan and Yün-nan. For a short time, most of the proposed route was actually garrisoned. The rise of the kingdom of Nan-chao in Yün-nan was in part a result of this project, for T'ang cultivated the power of Nan-chao, hoping to gain an ally that could pacify the many mountain chiefs along the southern portion of the route. As the strength of Nan-chao increased, however, relations with T'ang deteriorated, resulting in open warfare.[71]

In 751, the protector general of An-nam, a man from Kuei named Ho Li-kuang, led an army into Yün-nan. He captured An-ning, a stronghold in east-central Yün-nan, and erected a pair of bronze pillars to mark the frontier in the style of Ma Yüan. This was only part of a larger T'ang campaign against Nan-chao, however, and the main T'ang armies suffered a serious defeat as they approached the center of the Nan-chao realm some two hundred miles west of An-ning. Two years later, Li-kuang participated in a second campaign against Nan-chao at the head of armies from all over the south. In 754, Nan-chao again sent the T'ang armies reeling.[72]

These defeats were part of a general failure of T'ang arms on all the imperial frontiers. In 751, nomadic tribesmen defeated a T'ang army in southern Manchuria. In the same year, Chinese power in Central Asia began to unravel at a battle near Samarkand in which an alliance of Arabs and Turks turned back the T'ang tide.

Behind these reverses lay a central government greatly weakened by the growing power of military governors who controlled the northern and

71. *MS*, 1, contains an itinerary from the capital of An-nam through Yün-nan. Also see Wilfred Stott, "The Expansion of the Nan Chao Kingdom between the Years A.D. 750–860 and the Causes That Lay behind It as Shown in the T'ai-Ho Inscription and the *Man Shu*," pp. 197–200, and Harold Wiens, *Han Chinese Expansion in South China*, pp. 152–59.

72. *CL*, 99; *HTS*, 5, 15a–b; *TCTC*, 216, vol. 11, 1024, 1042.

western frontiers. In 755, one of these military governors on the Manchurian frontier, An Lu-shan, rebelled. An Lu-shan's rebellion struck the empire a blow from which it never fully recovered.[73]

The death of An Lu-shan in 757 did not end the rebellion, for the trouble afflicting the empire went deeper than the ambitions of any one man. In the half century that followed, northern China was ravaged by repeated rebellions, while Tibetans and Uighurs broke through the western frontier. When T'ang began to recover near the end of the century, it did so from a new social and economic base.

The crippling of imperial power was felt immediately in the south. In the heat of crisis, regular administration was superseded by newly appointed military governors. In 756, a military governor was appointed in Hu-nan. He forthwith marched north against An Lu-shan with an army of fifty thousand, which included imperial units from the south. In the same year, Ho Li-kuang was named military governor of Ling-nan, a jurisdiction covering modern Kuang-tung and Kuang-hsi.[74]

As imperial garrisons were withdrawn to the north, the mountain tribesmen of Kuei, Yung, and Jung, in modern Kuang-hsi and western Kuang-tung, seized population centers and proclaimed at least seven independent kingdoms, forcing T'ang administrators out of the area and closing all land communication between An-nam and the empire. It was not until two years later, in 758, that a T'ang counteroffensive materialized, and then only partial and temporary success was achieved. In that year, the name *An-nam*, "Pacified South," was changed to *Tran-nam*, "Guarded South," and the protector general was given the status of a military governor.[75]

The situation in the provinces directly north of the protectorate remained precarious throughout the 760s. Modern Kuang-tung and Kuang-hsi were divided by T'ang into the four central administrations of Kuang,

---

73. Edwin Pulleyblank, *The Background of the Rebellion of An Lu-shan*, p. 1.

74. *TCTC*, 217, vol. 11, 1082, and 218, vol. 11, 1095, 1120.

75. *HTS*, 222c, 20a–b; *VSL*, 1, 10a, follows the geographic sections of the *HTS* (43a, 9a) and the *CTS* (41, 43a), as well as *YHCHC*, 1082, in dating the name change from An-nam to Tran-nam in the year 757. *TT*, 5, 4b, dates it in 758. It is very likely that the name change was officially made in 757, for *TCTC*, 220, vol. 11, 1201, dates the change from An-hsi, "Pacified West," to Chen-hsi, "Guarded West." in 757. Yet, considering the conditions in the south, it is reasonable to associate the effective name change with the appointment of a military governor in An-nam, which did not occur until 758, according to *TCTC*, 220, vol. 11, 1219, and *HTS*, 69, 5a. *YHCHC*, 1082, places the naming of a military governor in 757, although it is likely that this is simply the date when the official decision to do so was recorded. In 757, land communication between An-nam and the empire was cut by rebellious Lao tribespeople (*HTS*, 6, 2a); it is unlikely that any major administrative change was undertaken until the following year, when T'ang arms reopened the land route. In 758 jurisdictions in the protectorate were restored to provincial status; in 742 they had all been reduced to prefectural status (*CTS*, 41, 42b–46b). It is reasonable to associate this reform with the name change and the appointment of a military governor.

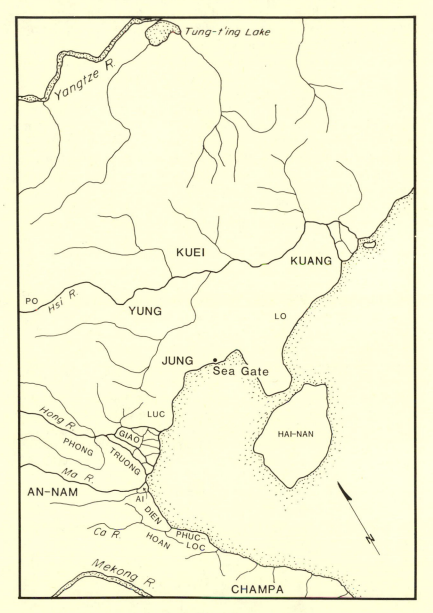

Map 8. The South during the T'ang Dynasty

Kuei, Jung, and Yung. In 760 and 762, rebellious Lao tribespeople in Kuei were defeated, but in 767 they forced T'ang officials to flee the area. Yung and most of Jung remained in the hands of rebels throughout the decade. In 763, an official in Kuang rebelled and chased out the military governor. Order was finally restored in Kuang and Kuei in 769, and by 771 it was safe for T'ang officials to return to Jung.[76]

The protectorate escaped most of these difficulties. In 761, a Japanese named Abe-no Nakamaro was given charge of the protectorate; his Chinese name was Chao Heng. He had come to China from Japan in 717 at the age of nineteen to study and subsequently spent his life as an official of the empire. In 753 he had attempted to return to Japan, but his ship was struck by a storm and blown far to the south, where it eventually landed in Hoan. He immediately returned to the T'ang capital, but gave up hope of returning to his homeland. A few years later he was sent back south as protector general.[77]

The only trouble recorded during Nakamaro's tenure in the protectorate was with tribespeople on the Yün-nan frontier. In 766 he pacified them and received an imperial commendation.[78] It was during his governorship that Dien was detached from Hoan, perhaps to deal more effectively with restive peoples in the mountains.

In 767, Nakamaro was replaced by Chang Po-i, the son of a former protector general.[79] Whereas his colleagues to the north were occupied with threats from the mountains, Po-i was challenged from the sea. In 767, the protectorate was overrun by seaborne invaders called K'un-lun and She-p'o.[80] K'un-lun was a name used by the Chinese to refer to inhabitants of the coasts and islands of Southeast Asia in general, and She-p'o referred to Java in particular.[81]

It was about this time that Chinese records began speaking of Huan-wang in place of Lin-i; Huan-wang was centered further south than Lin-i had been, in the vicinity of the modern cities of Phan-rang and Nha-trang. In 774 and 787, Huan-wang suffered maritime invasions similar to that in the protectorate. Scholars generally believe that these events were related to the rise of the Śailendra dynasty in Java.[82]

The K'un-lun and She-p'o captured Tu-thanh and plundered the

76. *TCTC*, 221, vol. 12, 28; 222, vol. 12, 64; and 224, vol. 12, 157, 186; *CTS*, 11, 13a, and 157, 1a–b; *HTS*, 6, 8b, 10b, 11a, and 222c, 19a.

77. On Nakamaro, see Pierre Daudin, "Un Japonais a la cour des T'ang," pp. 223–32.

78. *CL*, 99.

79. *VSL*, 1, 10a. Chang Po-i was the son of Chang Shun, a protector general during the reign of Hsiao Tsung (756–62).

80. The only source for this invasion is *TT*, 5, 4b–5a.

81. *HTS*, 222c, 2b, 3b.

82. Coedes, *Indianized States*, pp. 87–93, 95.

lowlands at will. Chang Po-i called for help, and Kao Cheng-p'ing, a military official further north, sent soldiers, who defeated the intruders and sent them fleeing.

Following this episode, Chang Po-i abandoned the site of Tu-thanh. He built a new capital nearby and surrounded it with a rampart. In T'ang times, a rampart of this kind was called a *lo-ch'eng*, and the new citadel was accordingly known as La-thanh (Chinese Lo-ch'eng).[83] Tu-thanh had been overrun in 687, 722, and 767. The building of outer fortifications was intended to prevent future disasters of this kind.

The construction of La-thanh was followed by an effort to restore the official status of the protectorate as it had existed before the An Lu-shan emergency. In 768, the name of the protectorate was changed back to An-nam, and the protector general thereafter bore the concurrent title of imperial commissioner rather than military governor.[84]

A system of military governors was nevertheless institutionalized throughout much of the empire, particularly in the north, where major rebellions continued through the 780s. This meant that the central government and its imperial army was simply one of several rival power centers, and imperial administration depended on shifting alliances among these centers. The arena of conflict was northern China; the south remained ostensibly loyal to the central government or, if rebellious, at least did not participate in the struggles further north. Still, the south could not help but be affected by the prevailing centrifugal forces. In 773, a governor in Kuang killed the military governor at Canton and united large areas of the south under his authority.[85] This rebellion was put down in 776, but it demonstrated the underlying instability of the south.

From the time of An Lu-shan's rebellion, T'ang power began to ebb from the south. As imperial soldiers garrisoned in the south were withdrawn north, mountain tribesmen ventured forth for plunder, undermining the established order and encouraging rebellion. Yet, for twelve years after An Lu-shan's rebellion, the protectorate remained politically stable and at peace, even when the land routes connecting it with the rest of the empire were temporarily severed. It was not until after the maritime invasion of 767 that the protectorate became the scene of insurrection.

83. *TT*, 5, 4b–5a; *VSL*, 1, 10a; *CL*, 99; *YHCHC*, 1083.

84. On the restoration of the name An-nam, see: *HTS*, 43a, 9b; *VSL*, 1, 10a; *TT*, 5, 5a. On the name change and the title change, see: *YHCHC*, 1082; *TPHYC*, 170, 3a. The *Fang-chen* section of the *HTS* (69, 5b–6a) dates the change from An-nam to Tran-nam in 764 and the restoration of An-nam in 766; these must be errors. The *Fang-chen* section dates the first use of the title imperial commissioner in An-nam in 751 (*HTS*, 69, 4a). It was changed to military governor in 758 (*HTS*, 69, 5a), and the title military governor was changed to "Great Defense Inspector and Imperial Commissioner" in 764 (*HTS*, 69, 5b). The date 764 must be an error.

85. *HTS*, 138, 5b.

The inherent stability of the protectorate was probably enhanced by the leadership of men whose families had been active in the south for more than one generation. Ho Li-kuang, the protector general during the Nan-chao campaigns of the 750s and later the military governor at Canton, was a native of the south, as had been Yang Ssu-hsü, who marched against Mai Thuc Loan in 722. Chang Po-i was apparently from the south, for his father had also been protector general. Kao Cheng-p'ing, who came to Po-i's rescue in 767, spent his career in the south and later became protector general. The one man during this time who was clearly not from the south, the Japanese Nakamaro, was nevertheless a man of outstanding ability.

The shock of 767 is difficult to evaluate because little information survives. There was undoubtedly extensive destruction, for the old government seat was abandoned for a newly fortified site. The fact that soldiers had to be called in from outside suggests that the protectorate lay prostrate before the invader. Although the episode appears to have been rather brief, the following quarter century saw a breakdown of T'ang control in An-nam. This breakdown was initially heralded by incidents of mutiny and rebellion among the soldiers, which implies that the events of 767 had dealt civil administration a severe blow, opening the way for military adventurers. The personal ambitions of T'ang officers, however, were quickly superseded by the rise of local leaders with roots in the village politics of Vietnamese society.

Phung Hung

As the emerging system of military governors gained ground, the prestige and effectiveness of civil administration declined throughout the empire. In An-nam, beginning in the Ta-li period (766–78) the military began to assert itself in acts of insubordination and open rebellion.[86]

The earliest specific information comes from 782. In that year a military commander of Dien Province named Ly Manh Thu and the governor of Phong, Bi An, raised armies and rebelled. Ly Manh Thu claimed the title An-nam military governor; both men were captured and beheaded by Protector General Fu Liang-chiao.[87]

A short time later, An-nam Imperial Commissioner Chang Ying died

---

86. *TT*, 5, 6a, is based on *VDULT*, 6, which cites the *Chiao chou chi* of Chao Ch'ang, the protector general who restored T'ang authority in 791.

87. *HTS*, 7, 3b, says that Dien Province commander Ly Manh Thu and Phong Province Governor Bi An rebelled and were suppressed. *TCTC*, 227, vol. 12, 239, mentions only Ly Manh Thu, but records that he claimed the title An-nam military governor and was beheaded by Protector General Fu Liang-chiao. *CL*, 99, combines all of this information into a single account, and records Bi An's name as Ly Bi An.

in office; his assistant, Ly Nguyen Do, led soldiers and, "gathering provinces and districts, became a treacherous rebel." T'ang general Li Fu "admonished and captured" Nguyen Do, and "the southern frontier was accordingly respectful."[88] From these events it is clear that T'ang power in An-nam had greatly diminished. Individual officials acted on their own initiative when they could, and, rather than ruling the southern frontier, T'ang officers were content to elicit formal respect. It was in these years that an indigenous Vietnamese leader appeared.

Phung Hung was from a wealthy, prestigious family established on the right bank of the Hong River near Mount Tan-vien, west of modern Hanoi, in Phong.[89] Trung Trac had come from this area, and it was not far from where the Hung kings are reported to have ruled. The Phung family bore the hereditary title *quan-lang*, which, according to Vietnamese tradition, was held by sons of the Hung kings.[90] In the independence period, this title was used among the Muong, upland cousins of the lowland Vietnamese, where it survived into the twentieth century.[91] A Vietnamese linguist has suggested that this term may be indigenous to Vietnam and was later borrowed by Chinese.[92] In any case, the term *quan-lang* embodied a traditional concept of authority related to the Hung kings. The Phung family thus claimed political leadership on the basis of an ancient hereditary right predating the Chinese provincial regime.

In the parlance of imperial administration, however, Phung Hung was a "frontier garrison barbarian leader." This implies official recognition in exchange for assistance in securing the lowlands against incursions from the mountains. Hung was famed for his physical strength and bravery. He is reported to have attacked a tiger with his bare hands and to have wrestled an ox. He had a younger brother named Hai who was a veritable Atlas. It was claimed that Hai could lift rocks weighing over a thousand pounds and carry them for several miles. It is recorded that Lao tribesmen dwelling in the mountains were in great awe of Hai's strength.

88. *CL*, 99. According to table C appended to the surviving portions of the *MS*, 336, Chang T'ing was protector general in 788 and a certain P'ang Fu was protector general in 789; perhaps *Chang T'ing* is an error for *Chang Ying* and *P'ang Fu* is an error for *Li Fu*. I do not know the origin of this table. Parts of it are reliable, but there are several inconsistencies between it and other sources. For example, it assigns four different men to the year 819, the year of a major rebellion; the events of this rebellion as recorded in other sources deny the possibility of four separate protector generals, unless these be merely paper appointments. For the period prior to 791, I am not convinced of its reliability. It does not mention Fu Liang-chiao, whose tenure in 782 is attested by other sources; rather, it has a certain Wu Ch'ung-fu as protector general from 777 to 787.

89. See Appendix J for a discussion of the sources for the Phung Hung era.

90. *LNCQ*, 6; *VDULT*, 6; *TT*, 1, 3a.

91. Tran Quoc Vuong, "Ve Danh Hieu 'Hung Vuong,'" p. 354.

92. Hoang Thi Chau, "Nuoc Van-lang qua tai lieu ngon ngu," pp. 41, 46–47.

When civil administration began to give way before the ambitions of military men in the 770s, Hung and Hai went from village to village, establishing their authority wherever they went. The rebellions of Ly Manh Thu and Bi An in 782 and that of Ly Nguyen Do, shortly after, opened the way for the Phung family. As ambitious officials challenged an increasingly embattled central administration, villages were left unattended, and the Phung brothers stepped in.

It is recorded that after Hung "achieved his ambition," he changed his name to "Great Venerable"; at the same time, Hai changed his name to "Great Strength." These names suggest a partnership of brains and brawn that may have described the relationship between the brothers. This theme is further pursued in the Vietnamese sources, which say that Hung styled himself "Metropolitan Lord" (*Do Quan*) and Hai styled himself "Metropolitan Guardian" (*Do Bao*). These titles were added by later Vietnamese historians interested in literary allusions. "Metropolitan Lord" is a title used in classical texts for the wise and filial Emperor Shun of Chinese mythology.[93] "Metropolitan Guardian," on the other hand, was a military position created by Wang An-shih's reforms in Sung China during the eleventh century.[94]

Although Hung may have already "achieved his ambition," he was unavoidably drawn into a situation of expanding possibilities as T'ang authority ebbed from the protectorate. Do Anh Han, a warrior from the same district as the Phung family, was employed by the brothers as a military advisor. Do Anh Han raised an army and began to patrol an ever-widening region encompassing the western half of the Hong River plain from Phong to Truong. As the people readily submitted to the Phung family, Hung's prestige soared throughout the protectorate, and he made it known that he intended to enter La-thanh.

The protector general at this time was Kao Cheng-p'ing, the military official who had sent soldiers against the maritime invasion of 767. When the Vietnamese army under Do Anh Han appeared before La-thanh, Cheng-p'ing sallied forth and attacked. He was defeated, however, and retreated behind the city walls where, it is recorded, he developed an ulcer from exasperation and died.

After Cheng-p'ing's death, the city gates were opened. Hung entered peacefully and took control of the government. Vietnamese sources assign a reign of seven years to Hung. Since the same sources say that his successor ruled for two years until 791, this reign would have begun in 782, the year of the military rebellions put down by Protector General Fu Liang-chiao. This was before Hung could have entered La-thanh, so the seven-year reign

93. Morohashi Tetsuji, *Dai Kanwa Jiten*, 11, 279.
94. Ibid., 11, 284.

appears to represent his larger career as a popular leader, perhaps dating from the time he "achieved his ambition."

After Hung's death in 789, the people reported supernatural events and attributed them to his spirit. It was popularly believed that Hung appeared in dreams to announce especially felicitous events. A temple was erected for his spirit west of La-thanh, where prayers for rain obtained results. Whenever there was some calamity or unhappy affair, it is recorded that all the people would gather at the temple and make a sacrifice, calling out for Hung to mediate between them and the forces of evil. The people would swear an oath before Hung and would immediately obtain an omen to guide future conduct. It is further recorded that traders and merchants prayed to Hung for large profits and received them, that daily sacrifices of thanksgiving were offered to Hung, that the roads leading to Hung's temple were thronged with supplicants, and that incense never ceased burning there. The flourishing of Hung's posthumous cult reveals the mark his life left on the minds of the Vietnamese.

An eighteenth-century Vietnamese commentator wrote:

> Metropolitan Lord Phung was an extraordinary man; an extraordinary man must have extraordinary circumstances, and extraordinary circumstances must wait for an extraordinary man. Mark his strength, able to attack a tiger bare-handed, and his spirit, hungry enough to swallow an ox in one gulp; he simply made the people submit out of awe. If he did not have talent beyond ordinary men, how could he have accomplished what he did? When Cheng-p'ing's death was announced, he leisurely entered the capital, gathered the banners of seventy strongholds, and grasped thousands of miles with his heroic majesty. He was of upright countenance and boundlessly self-confident; he held fate in his hand. He rose up just like Trieu and Ly; how can the Black Emperor, merely a one-of-a-kind chief who seized a single province, be compared with him?[95]

Regardless of the historical accuracy of this commentary, it gives us an idea of how Phung Hung was viewed by later Vietnamese historians in comparison with other national leaders during the Chinese provincial period. The reference to Trieu and Ly is to Trieu Quang Phuc and Ly Phat Tu; both, like Phung Hung, had their roots in the Hong River plain. The idea that these three men "rose up just like" one another implies an eighteenth-century criterion for national leadership that each of these men met. All three were associated with the pre-Chinese political traditions of Lac society: Trieu Quang Phuc and Ly Phat Tu by the claw myth, and Phung Hung by the title *quan-lang*. On the other hand, Mai Thuc Loan, the Black Emperor, had no connection with these traditions. He came from a frontier district far to the south and led a horde of aliens. Phung Hung was

95. *VDULT*, 7.

recognized by later Vietnamese historians as one of their own heroes with a legitimate place in the mainstream of their national heritage.

Phung Hung was clearly more than an ordinary rebel playing opportunistic politics. The Phung were more than a military family; they used the military skills of other men. They bore a hereditary title connected with the earliest traditions of the Vietnamese people; their success came from their ability to focus the indigenous culture in a political arena. Phung Hung succeeded where isolated imperial officials or military commanders had failed because his was a broadly based peasant movement that rose out of village politics rather than the politics of military adventurers. Hung and his brother Hai were both known for their great physical strength, a quality respected by peasants. His posthumous cult bears witness to the powerful image his career left in the minds of the people.

After Hung's death, the popular sentiment was to raise his brother Hai to succeed him. However, Hai was opposed by his chief assistant, a man from the Phung family's home district named Bo Pha Lac. Bo Pha Lac is reported to have been of surpassing strength, bravery, and stubbornness; it was rumored that he could push over mountains and lift huge bronze cauldrons. Pha Lac championed the cause of Hung's son An and rallied the people against Hai, who was forced to flee into the mountains, where he disappeared.

Phung An honored his father with the posthumous title "Great *Bo Cai* King" (*Bo cai dai vuong*). In eighth-century Vietnamese, according to the *Viet dien u linh tap*, *bo* was the word for "father" and *cai* was the word for "mother"; the title thus means "Great Father and Mother King," or "The Great King Who is the Father and Mother of His People."[96]

The idea of a good ruler's being "the father and mother of his people" is found in the writings of Mencius, the ancient Chinese philosopher. Educated Vietnamese in T'ang times were certainly familiar with Mencius. In Mencius they could find authoritative statements condemning the kind of misgovernment they experienced under Chinese rule. For example, in one passage Mencius asks a ruler, "Is there any difference between killing a man with a sword and killing him with a method of government?" When the ruler affirms that there is no difference, Mencius goes on to declare:

> There is fat meat in your kitchen and there are fat horses in your stable but your people bear the mark of famine and in the fields are those who have starved to death, which is an encouragement for beasts to devour men. . . . If

96. Haudricourt's idea that *bo cai* should be interpreted as *vua cai*, "great king" (John DeFrancis, *Colonialism and Language Policy in Vietnam*, p. 22) is reasonable and appealing, but it overlooks the fact that in the text of the *VDULT* the term is explicitly explained: "Because, according to local usage, father was called *bo* and mother was called *cai*" (*VDULT*, 6).

you, being the father and mother of your people, cannot administer your government without encouraging the beasts to devour men, how can you be called the father and mother of your people?[97]

Many Vietnamese may have felt that under the T'ang regime they were being "killed by a method of government." They probably witnessed the kind of conditions that Mencius denounced here. The idea that a good ruler is "the father and mother of his people" consequently held a special appeal for them.

This theme is elaborated in another passage from Mencius:

[When a ruler,] being the father and mother of his people, causes the people to wear distress on their face by making them toil all year without being able to feed their parents and making them borrow for their livelihood with the result that the old people and children are left to die in the gutters and ditches, how can he be called the father and mother of his people?[98]

A passage such as this probably came close to the experience of Vietnamese who resented the greedy practices of Chinese officials and the effects of these practices on the life of the people. Mencius's strong moral tone legitimized the grievances of the Vietnamese with the authority of an established classical text.

A third passage from Mencius clearly defines the theory that the ideal ruler is in a parental relation to his subjects:

Since the birth of mankind, no one has ever succeeded in leading children to attack their parents. Considering this, [he who is regarded as a father and mother by the people] will have no enemy in all the realm. He who has no enemy in all the realm is none other than the minister of Heaven. In such a case it has never happened that such a one did not become king.[99]

The idea that the good ruler is in a parental relation with his people appears to have held a special significance for the Vietnamese during the Chinese period. We have already noted that it is recorded how, on the death of T'ao Huang, an especially humane and able governor in the late third century, the Vietnamese mourned for him "as if for a parent." Phung Hung's posthumous title suggests that this theory of parental kingship was well known among the people, for *bo* and *cai* are indigenous Vietnamese words represented by phonetically appropriate Chinese characters. This is the earliest surviving example of Vietnamese character writing, called *nom*, meaning "southern script."

The term *nom*, rendered by combining the Chinese characters for

97. *MT*, 12.
98. Ibid., 114–15.
99. Ibid., 77.

"south" and "mouth," refers to the earliest surviving system for transcribing the Vietnamese language; *nom* comprises both standard Chinese characters selected for their phonetic value and freshly coined characters that include Chinese characters selected for their meaning. The oldest extant piece of literature in *nom* does not date before the thirteenth century, but it is clear that by then *nom* had already gone through several centuries of development. In chapter 7, we will see an example of *nom* used in the tenth century. It is reasonable to assume that Chinese characters were used to render Vietnamese words as early as the eighth century. The Chinese characters used to represent *bo* and *cai* are unrelated to the Vietnamese meaning, but are faithful phonetic transcriptions.

The expression *bo cai*, meaning "father and mother," is no longer used in modern Vietnamese; it is an old expression that apparently was current in the eighth century. Although *bo* can still be used to mean "father," *cai* has evolved to mean simply "female" and is usually applied to animals.[100] This may reflect the erosion of maternal rights through later centuries of patriarchal influence.

Phung Hung was not remembered as the "Great *Fu Mu* King," *fu mu* being "father and mother" in Chinese. He was remembered with an expression embedded in the vernacular usage of the Vietnamese people. This could mean that some of the teachings of Mencius had been popularized among educated Vietnamese. But it could also mean that educated Vietnamese found in Mencius a textual authority to confirm ideas that were already part of their cultural heritage.

The Vietnamese word for "king," *vua*, means a ruler who governs according to the established customs and traditions of the people. It is an intimate word, suggesting a close relationship between ruler and people. On the other hand, the words of Chinese origin for "king," *vuong*, and "emperor," *de*, are more ceremonial and imply, at least for the Vietnamese, a commission to rule from above, without any sympathetic link to the people themselves. Phung Hung's posthumous title contains the Sino-Vietnamese appellation *vuong*; the term *vua* did not appear until the independence period. The expression *bo cai* in a political context nevertheless reflects a phase in the development of the concept of *vua* that appeared in later centuries. This is clear from the *nom* character for *vua*, which combines the Chinese character for *vuong* with the *nom* character for *bo*, thus meaning "father king."

In 1329, King Tran Minh-tong listened to an official advise against a dangerous expedition against marauding mountain tribesmen in favor of an attack on Champa, which the official believed would be less risky and more profitable; the king admonished the official by saying:

100. *Tu dien tieng Viet*, p. 137.

I am the father and mother of my people. If the people are in distress, I am bound to help them. How can I compare the easy with the difficult, the advantageous with the unprofitable?[101]

Minh-tong brushed aside mundane considerations by invoking an ideal of the king as a protecting parent. This ideal was expressed as a legitimizing principle to justify the king's authority. The same ideal is exemplified in the posthumous title assigned to Phung Hung, where it reflects a Vietnamese response to the experience of T'ang rule.

In 791, Emperor Te Tsung of T'ang ordered the formation of an army named Jou-yüan Chun, "Army to Overcome Distant Places with Gentleness," and appointed Chao Ch'ang as protector general of An-nam. As Ch'ang crossed the An-nam border with this army, he sent envoys offering ceremonial presents and giving advance notice to Phung An. An arranged for a peaceful transfer of power, and the Phung family dispersed.

The Phung Hung era was a turning point in the history of T'ang Vietnam. The experience of watching imperial authority fade and then raising a home-grown hero was not lost on the Vietnamese people. T'ang officials would never again be able to pursue exploitative policies with impunity. The Vietnamese had lost their fear of imperial might and thereafter demanded greater recognition as a separate people. T'ang officials, for their part, were generally willing to accord this recognition, for the empire would never again be strong enough to assert the alternative. Throughout the ninth century, T'ang officials were repeatedly given the choice of accommodating local sensibilities or fleeing north for safety.

During the seventh and eighth centuries, the Vietnamese experienced an unprecedented demonstration of imperial power. In 687 this power provoked and crushed a peasant rebellion; in 722 it successfully countered restless forces breaking through the frontier. The decline of T'ang power during the second half of the eighth century, however, opened the way for champions of the indigenous culture. Once again, imperial authority faded to reveal local concepts of authority.

Phung Hung, the "Great Father and Mother King," was quite different from the sixth-century "King of Night Marsh," Trieu Quang Phuc. He did not brandish ancient symbols or bestir hoary spirits. Instead, he commanded respect by his awesome physical presence; the relationship between him and his followers was idealized as that between parent and child. After experiencing a century and a half of T'ang rule, the Vietnamese people were no longer inspired to action by appeals to mythical traditions; all they wanted was a father and a mother to care for and protect them. Anything in Vietnamese culture that did not directly buttress resistance to

101. *TT*, the year 1329.

northern domination became largely superfluous by the end of T'ang. At the same time, aspects of Chinese civilization that strengthened local sensibilities were incorporated into the indigenous perspective. Thus, claw myths were abandoned for the moralistic teachings of Mencius on good government.

The Phung Hung era witnessed a new flourishing of maritime commercial contacts in An-nam. Canton's position as the major port on the South China Sea was eclipsed in the mid-eighth century by An-nam. This was to some extent due to the abusive policies of officials in Canton toward foreign merchants doing business there. With imperial control weak, local strong men preyed on international trade. In 758, Canton was sacked by its large community of Arabs and Persians in retaliation for the blood-sucking practices of Chinese officials.[102]

In 792, after the reestablishment of T'ang authority in An-nam, the military governor at Canton reported: "Recently, the merchant vessels with rare goods have shifted to the markets of An-nam; I request a judgment to close the An-nam markets; please send a legate to deal with this matter." The court was about to comply when a high minister advised;

> The merchants of distant kingdoms only seek profit. If they are treated fairly they will come; if they are troubled, they will go. Formerly, Kuang Province was a gathering place for merchant vessels; now, suddenly they have changed to An-nam. If there has been oppressive misappropriation over a long period of time, then those who have gone elsewhere must be persuaded to return; this is not a matter for litigation but of changing the attitude of officials.[103]

By the early ninth century, Canton had recovered its position as the preeminent southern port. However, the fact that An-nam had attracted a dominant share of the maritime commerce when it was most free of imperial authority is a significant indication of the place occupied by the Vietnamese in the world of Southeast Asia. Contact between the Vietnamese and the south seas was a natural pattern, which reasserted itself whenever imperial control was weak. Considering this, it is easy to understand why traders and merchants prayed to Phung Hung's spirit for large profits and were not disappointed. The Phung Hung era was a time of prosperity for the Vietnamese.

T'ang-Viet Society, Economy, and Culture

Although evidence is slight, some general conclusions can be drawn about social, economic, and cultural development in

102. Schafer, *Vermilion Bird*, p. 28.
103. *TCTC*, 234, vol. 12, 596.

Vietnam during the T'ang era. This period can be analyzed in three phases. In the first phase, during the seventh century, the regional ruling class was neutralized and swallowed up by T'ang administration. In the second phase, during the eighth century, T'ang administration broke down, and popular local leadership briefly appeared under the Phung family. In the third phase, during the ninth century, T'ang cultivated the revival of a new regional ruling class, which promptly divided over the issue of T'ang overlordship, producing a prolonged confrontation. This confrontation was eventually resolved in favor of T'ang, but by then T'ang was fading from the scene, so a pro-T'ang regional ruling class led Vietnam into the independence era. Now, we will look more carefully at each of these three phases.

As we have noted earlier, the Han dynasty fell because of the centrifugal influence of powerful landlord families who controlled vast estates and maintained private armies. The question of how to curb the power of these great families and reestablish the imperial regime was not answered until the sixth century, when Sui began to apply a system of land distribution, developed by earlier northern dynasties, to all of China. This so-called "equal-field" system was a way for rulers to keep land and taxpaying farmers from falling under the control of great landowners.

The basic idea of the "equal-field" system was to assign a certain amount of state land to able-bodied adults for the duration of their lifetimes. This slowed the drift of free, taxpaying farmers off the tax rolls into the great private estates and insured a stable source of state revenue. T'ang integrated the great families into the "equal-field" system by assigning them permanent holdings of a specified size, theoretically no more than one hundred times the amount assigned to a free farmer. Great families might also be assigned certain lands according to the governmental positions held by their members.[104] These reforms were the basis of the expansion of T'ang power in the seventh century.

There is no direct evidence that the "equal-field" system was applied in Vietnam, but there are indications that it was. One consideration is the development of the Hanoi area under Sui and T'ang. The "equal-field" system was often applied to lands newly opened up for cultivation. By placing the administrative center of Vietnam south of the Hong River for the first time, Sui and T'ang may have been seeking to establish a new base of power outside of the traditional provincial heartland, where great families presumably were entrenched. By extending the diking system down the Hong River from Hanoi, new lands were made available for assignment to free farmers. An important feature of the "equal-field" system under T'ang was that the free farmers were given military training and organized into militia units. The Hanoi area seems to have been developed by T'ang as a

104. Edwin Reischauer and John Fairbank, *East Asia, The Great Tradition*, pp. 158–61.

source of revenue and military power to counter the great families and to serve as a pillar of regional authority.

We have looked at the tradition of the K'ai-yüan cult established by a T'ang official during the reign of Hsüan Tsung in the second quarter of the eighth century; this cult associated the emperor with a local earth spirit of the Hanoi area. After the ravages of the seaborne invasion of 767, a new city with defensive ramparts was built here. In the ninth century, repairing or enlarging the walls of this city and building outer fortifications was a persistent concern of T'ang officials. This suggests that defense of the Hanoi area was crucial to T'ang authority in Vietnam, which may have resulted from its being the area most affected by land-distribution policies initiated in the seventh century. A relatively large population of free, taxpaying farmers organized in militia units may have been an important feature of the area where T'ang authority in Vietnam was based.

We have previously referred to the so-called "southern selection" that is mentioned in 676. Let us look at this more closely. On the seventh day of the eighth month of 676, an imperial order went out to the governor generals of Kuei (Kuang-hsi), Kuang (Kuang-tung), Ch'ien (Kuei-chou), and Giao:

> In recent years there have not been very many petitions to select aboriginal leaders for official positions. From now on, let it be authorized according to the old regulations, one time in four years, to distinguish the energetic, intelligent, pure, and upright and to select them to fill up the vacancies of the fifth grade and above. Once again, the censorate is ordered to investigate this.[105]

This reveals that, for some time before 676, there had been a policy of selecting local men for official positions, but that this policy had not been satisfactorily implemented. Mention of the censorate suggests that the policy had been facing obstruction somewhere along the line. Perhaps T'ang officials in the south were reluctant to risk sharing the administration with great local families until land reforms had established a solid base for their authority. Although there is no further information about the "southern selection" in Giao, after 676 a reasonably strong effort must have been made to bring powerful local families into the administrative system and to force them to identify more closely with the T'ang structure of government.

The great families continued to exist, but no longer as an autonomous regional ruling class. Members of these families became magistrates and officials; their power and influence was no longer based on control of land and the regional economy, but was rather an aspect of their being part of the T'ang system of government. Their activities were formally restricted to

105. Tsang Wah-moon, p. 49.

their official duties. The trend of the seventh century, then, was to absorb the great families of the regional ruling class into the administration, thereby rendering lower-class people more vulnerable to the policies of T'ang government.

This situation is illuminated by the rebellion of 687. The doubling of taxes that provoked this rebellion was imposed on the lower classes (*li hu*), and it was lower-class people who led the uprising. This is the only documented "peasant rebellion" in the entire history of the Chinese provincial period in Vietnam. The reason for this seems to be that the lower classes were deprived of upper-class mediators between themselves and Chinese officials, for upper-class people were apparently neutralized by the T'ang policy of absorbing them into officialdom.

The story of the "kingdom-protecting spirit" from the 650s may suggest the changing perspective of old ruling-class families. As we have noted earlier, this story explains how the "local magistrate" spirit prevailed over the "great lord" spirit to become the "kingdom-protecting spirit." The old class of "great lords," families with private power bases, was being transformed into a new class of "local magistrates," men who were servants of the empire.

In the eighth century, T'ang lost the momentum of its initial expansion and began to fall into a defensive posture. This was particularly true after An Lu-shan's rebellion at mid-century, when T'ang soldiers were withdrawn north. Although the stability of Hsüan Tsung's reign made it possible for T'ang administration in Vietnam to recover from the violence of 722, it seems that the administration was demoralized and broken by the seaborne invasion of 767. Attempts to recover from this episode appear to have had little effect beyond the Giao heartland. Rebel leaders soon appeared in Phong and Dien, and the general weakness of T'ang permitted central authority to unravel until Phung Hung marched into the capital with an army recruited in Phong and Truong.

The events of the eighth century show that the old regional ruling class of great families no longer played a significant independent political role. The governor of Phong, Bi An, the military commander of Dien, Ly Manh Thu, and the imperial assistant, Ly Nguyen Do, who rebelled in the 780s, were probably men from powerful local families who had made careers in T'ang administration. Their leadership seems to have evoked little popular response, however, and they were quickly eliminated by T'ang officials. On the other hand, Phung Hung led a popular insurrection that grew from the perspective of village politics.

The Phung can also be interpreted as being a "great family," but they were not in the same class as the great families who were incorporated into the T'ang system of government. In the eyes of T'ang, Phung Hung was a "frontier garrison barbarian leader." "Barbarian" probably meant that he maintained a non-Chinese cultural outlook. He came from an area adjacent to where the Muong now live, so we can surmise that he was from the sector of Vietnamese society that escaped heavy Chinese cultural influence.

That a man like Phung Hung should gain supreme power in Vietnam at this time raises the question: Where were all the great old landowning families that had dominated Vietnam since the fall of Han? The answer to this seems to be that they had been swallowed up by T'ang government and had lost their roots in the local society. When T'ang government disappeared from Vietnam in the last half of the eighth century, these families went with it. Thus, there was room for the ascendance of relatively more indigenous forms of leadership. The Phung brothers, Do Anh Han, and Bo Pha Lac, the major figures of the Phung Hung era, were all from Phong.

This naturally raises the question of what was going on in the agrarian heartland of Giao. The answer to this appears to lie in the growth of Buddhism. Vinitaruci's chief disciple, Phap Hien, instructed over three hundred disciples before his death in 626. The next major Buddhist figure of whom information has survived is Thanh Bien (died 686). When he was twelve years old, Thanh Bien entered monastic life at Pho-quang Temple. After the death of his teacher, Phap Dang, he spent eight years studying the *Vajra-prajñaparamita-sutra* (*Kim cuong kinh*), the Treatise on the Great Perfection of Wisdom, translated by Kumarajiva in 405 at Ch'ang-an.[106]

Beginning as early as the Han dynasty, a number of "perfection of wisdom" sutras were translated into Chinese. These sutras reached a peak of influence in China during the fourth century under the Chin dynasty. Their basic idea is the "emptiness" (*sunyata*) of "reality" (*dharma*), meaning that all of reality is "conditioned," or without its own self-existent nature. This idea leads to the belief that there is no individual entity and that to attempt to assert one's own will is to attempt the impossible; consequently, these sutras preach an attitude of nonassertion. This attitude was very close to the Neo-Taoist ideal of nonaction, which gained widespread popularity after the fall of Han. During the Chin dynasty, several *Prajña*, or "Wisdom," schools of Buddhism appeared under the inspiration of these sutras and both influenced and were influenced by Neo-Taoist thought.[107]

The appearance of a *Prajña* sutra in seventh-century Vietnam implies that this kind of thought was of some importance among educated people there. After studying the sutra for eight years, Thanh Bien went to Sung-nghiep Temple to discuss it with the Buddhist master Hue Nghiem. Later, he established himself at Kien-duong Temple, where he taught until his death in 686.[108] We can assume that these monks, like monks in China,

106. Tran Van Giap, "Bouddhisme," p. 237; K. Ch'en, *Buddhism in China*, p. 83.
107. K. Ch'en, pp. 58–67.
108. Tran Van Giap, "Bouddhisme," p. 237.

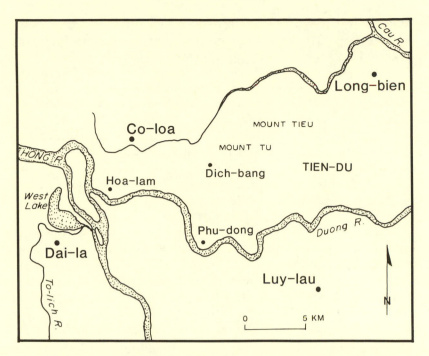

Map 9. The Heartland of Provincial Vietnam

generally came from prominent families, for their family names have been preserved; both Phap Hien and Thanh Bien bore the surname Do.[109] Phap Hien is said to have come from Chu-dien District,[110] which is where the Do family that ruled Vietnam at the turn of the fifth century had settled. The sixth- and seventh-century monks may have been related to this family. The disappearance of the great families from political life in the seventh and eighth centuries suggests that they turned their creative energies elsewhere. While some became T'ang administrators, others retreated to the temples. It is possible that the demoralizing effects of being pressed into T'ang government provoked a distaste for public affairs among some members of the great families, and that this mood found expression through an interest in the *Prajñā* sutras, which were close to the spirit of Neo-Taoist escapism.

All of the temples mentioned above were located in the agrarian heartland of Giao, north of the Hong River. This area was the cradle of Vietnamese Buddhism and until recent centuries maintained a stronger Buddhist character than other areas in Vietnam. Nearly all of the major Vietnamese Buddhist figures during the Chinese provincial period came

109. Ibid., pp. 236–37.
110. Ibid., p. 236.

from this region. When the Phung brothers gathered the leaderless villages of Phong and Truong and besieged the capital, Giao may have been governed by Buddhist leaders through village temples.

The only known Buddhist figure in eighth-century Vietnam was Dinh Khong. He was born in 729 at Co-phap, in the midst of the Buddhist heartland of Giao. He resided at Thien-chung Temple in the village of Dich-bang, a short distance east of Co-loa. During the Chen-yüan period (785–805), he founded Quynh-lam Temple in his native village. Dinh Khong is reported to have been a popular figure among the people, who called him "the old one." After his death in 808, his disciple Thong Thien built a stupa near Luc-to Temple on Mount Tieu, a few miles northeast of Dich-bang, and dedicated it to his memory with an inscription of his last words.[111]

From the career of Dinh Khong, we can surmise that Buddhism continued to prosper in Giao throughout the Phung Hung era. Numerous village temples and a large monkhood imply that the economy and society of Giao were organized to serve the interests of Buddhist institutions. There is nothing essentially new about this in the T'ang period, for Buddhism seems to have been entrenched in the area since the early third century. But in the seventh and eighth centuries, as upper-class people were under pressure to stand with T'ang, the monkhood was an attractive alternative for people who did not wish to enter imperial service.

In times of tranquillity, the number of Chinese monks was limited, and their activities were closely supervised by T'ang officials. But the Vietnamese monkhood was far from major T'ang centers of power, and it is unlikely that the degree of government control over the monkhood in Vietnam was equal to what it was in China. In Vietnam, it seems reasonable to view temples as a new form of the great estates. Great families could turn their lands over to temples where their sons, or adopted clients, presided.

There is an example of this in the early ninth century. The Nguyen family of Phu-dong turned their residence into the Kien-so Temple and invited a monk named Cam Thanh to come and live there. In 820, Cam Thanh welcomed an old Chinese monk from the north at this temple, and together they established a new Buddhist sect that appears to have served a political role on behalf of local families who favored T'ang against local rebel leadership; this sect will be discussed in the next chapter.[112]

During the seventh and eighth centuries, great landowning families in Giao seem to have contributed to both the Buddhist establishment and T'ang officialdom. The failure of T'ang power in the late eighth century probably encouraged Vietnamese monasteries to take a more direct interest

111. Ibid., pp. 237–38.
112. Ibid., p. 244.

in political affairs, at least on a local level. During the confrontation of the ninth century, the monkhood appears to have been a partisan of T'ang. The great families who supported monasteries and temples were probably the same families who contributed sons to T'ang government.

By the end of the eighth century, the difference between Buddhist Giao and the more rustic frontier jurisdictions was well established, and, during the ninth century, this difference was clearly revealed by the course of events. Although Giao was willing to cooperate with T'ang, the other provinces were a constant source of insurrection. All of the major rebel figures of the ninth century came from Hoan, Ai, or Phong.

During the brief T'ang revival that followed the Phung Hung era, T'ang officials encouraged the emergence of a new regional ruling class of powerful local families to govern the area. A formal administration was organized, but T'ang was too weak to dominate it. Local men appeared as governors of provinces and frequently became rebel leaders. T'ang authority was even challenged by soldiers stationed in the Hanoi area.

The rise of a new class of great landlord families at the turn of the ninth century was encouraged by the so-called "double tax" reform that was adopted by T'ang in 780. Before this, Chinese dynasties collected most of their tax revenue on a per capita basis. Farmers who became tenants on great estates were not counted for taxation, for they were considered as part of the estate; this is why the "equal-field" system had attempted to keep farmers in a free, taxpaying status. Now, for the first time, land rather than people became the major basis of taxation. The "equal-field" system of land distribution, which had limited the growth of private estates, was abandoned, and there was now no legal barrier to the accumulation of land by men of wealth.

We can only conjecture to what extent the social effects of the "double tax" reform were felt in Giao, but we know that the "double tax" was collected in Vietnam in the ninth century, and it is reasonable to see the sudden appearance of powerful local families at that time as a result of this new T'ang tax policy, which removed all restraints on the accumulation of land. The effect of this reform seems to have been greater in the frontier areas than in Giao, probably because more land was available there to be opened up for cultivation. In Giao, patterns of land ownership may have been institutionalized as temple estates; the temples, in any case, would seem to have been the chief beneficiaries of the new policy there.

From what kind of people did this new class of landowners come? The first major rebel leader of the ninth century was Duong Thanh. According to a Vietnamese source, his forebears had served as governors of Hoan Province since the K'ai-yüan period (713–41).[113] This suggests that the

---

113. *TT*, 5, 7a–b.

Duong family was established in Hoan in the wake of Mai Thuc Loan's uprising in 722. We might conjecture that one of Duong Thanh's ancestors was a Chinese official who came to Hoan with the T'ang army that pacified this uprising. In subsequent generations, the family was Vietnamized, although it retained its status in T'ang government. Thus, we can surmise that some members of the new landlord class were Chinese immigrants of the early T'ang period who were in the process of being assimilated into the local society.

As we have already noted, census statistics suggest rather significant Chinese immigration during the first half of the eighth century. An explanation for this may lie in the T'ang army that entered Vietnam in 722. This army is reported to have comprised one hundred thousand men, most of whom were recruited in the area of modern Kuang-tung and Kuang-hsi. Such a large army was apparently called for because of the size of Mai Thuc Loan's following, said to number four hundred thousand, mainly comprising armed groups from the mountains and from beyond the southern frontier. The violence and destruction in 722 was undoubtedly much greater than that of 687. In 687, peasant armies besieged and captured the capital and were subsequently defeated. In 722, alien marauders appear to have ravaged at will. After 722, T'ang soldiers may have been settled in Vietnam to assist in rebuilding the local economy and administration. A large number of these soldiers were surely placed in Hoan, where the trouble of 722 had started, to guard the volatile southern frontier. The Duong family was prominent in Hoan from this time.

A second family of importance in the ninth century was the Do. In the 850s, Do Ton Thanh and his son Do Thu Trung were prominent anti-T'ang leaders. Both were executed by the Chinese. Do Ton Thanh, the governor of Ai, earned the hatred of Chinese officials by maintaining friendly relations with tribal peoples in the mountains who were hostile to T'ang. According to a Chinese source, the Do family had been powerful in Vietnam since the Ch'i and Liang dynasties (479–556).[114] We probably cannot identify this family with the Do who ruled Vietnam at the turn of the fifth century, but we can nevertheless surmise that this was a Chinese immigrant family, for a Chinese source makes a point of dating the beginning of its fortunes in Vietnam. The example of this family suggests that some members of the new landlord class were old great families from the pre-T'ang era who reemerged as important regional leaders.

Duong Thanh was from Hoan. The Do were from Ai. In the 820s, the governor of Phong, Vuong Thanh Trieu, rebelled and was eventually captured and killed. Although nothing else is known of this man, we can imagine that, like the Duong and the Do, his was a family of Vietnamized

114. *TCTC*, 249, vol. 13, 559.

Chinese immigrants. All of these families were from the southern or frontier jurisdictions. The only explicit example of a Chinese immigrant in the Giao heartland is Wu Hun, a protector general in the 840s, who was chased out by an uprising but later returned to settle permanently in Vietnam, thus founding a family that became prominent under Vietnamese dynasties of later centuries. Wu Hun settled in eastern Giao, where there seems to have been a strong Chinese community.[115] This suggests that, while other provinces were chafing at what they regarded as the T'ang leash, Giao was relatively tranquil behind what it may have regarded as the T'ang shield.

After the Nan-chao War of the 860s, which saw the final assertion of this "T'ang shield," Chinese soldiers and officials drifted back north as T'ang authority disappeared, leaving Vietnam in the hands of the Khuc family. The Khuc were from eastern Giao, where Wu Hun settled, and, although there is no direct evidence, their behavior in the tenth century, discussed in chapter 7, indicates that they were also a recently arrived Chinese immigrant family.

In addition to military men and administrators, many Chinese merchants also settled in Vietnam. There is no evidence of their becoming politically prominent until the tenth century, when four men from Chinese merchant families briefly emerged as local "warlords" in the transition to an independent Vietnamese monarchy.

We can imagine that a number of Chinese Buddhist monks also came to live in Vietnamese temples. In 820, the Chinese monk Vo Ngon Thong came to Vietnam and founded a new sect. Other Chinese monks probably came either with him or at other times. Buddhist monks also became politically prominent in the tenth century, but the contribution of Chinese immigrants to the Vietnamese monkhood cannot be stressed for lack of evidence.

One of the more famous Chinese immigrant families in Vietnam, from the Chinese point of view, was the Khuong family (Chinese Chiang). Khuong Cong Phu (Chinese Chiang Kung-fu) became a member of the Han-lin Academy and briefly rose to the position of premier under Emperor Te Tsung (780–804).[116] His younger brother Khuong Cong Phuc (Chinese Chiang Kung-fu) became a high minister at the T'ang capital.[117] The brothers were studious and have left essays composed during their careers.[118] According to surviving information, there is little to associate

115. Vu Phuong De, *Cong du tiep ky*, 1: 1.

116. *CTS*, 138, 8a–9a; *HTS*, 132, 2b–3a.

117. *CTW*, 622.

118. *CTW*, 446, contains two essays by Khuong Cong Phu. *CTW*, 622, contains one essay by Khuong Cong Phuc. See Tran Nghia, "Mot so tac pham moi phat hien co lien quan toi giong van hoc Viet bang chu Han cua nguoi Viet thoi Bac Thuoc," pp. 86–88, 90–91, for discussions of these essays.

these men with Vietnam aside from the biographical information that they came from Ai. Their careers were made at the T'ang court; they gained high positions not only because they were intelligent, but also because of influential family connections.[119]

Their grandfather, Khuong Than Duc (Chinese Chiang Shen-i) is identified as a man from Ai, but the only other information about him is that he served as governor of Shu Province, in modern An-hui.[120] Their father is supposed to have been a district magistrate, but where he served is uncertain.[121] One of Khuong Cong Phu's biographers did not know where his home district was.[122] Another identified him as an "Ai Province, Nhat-nam man."[123] His brother Cong Phuc was identified as a "T'ien-shui man who changed his residence to Cuu-chan."[124] T'ien-shui was in Kan-su, in northwest China. Cong Phu died in 805 as he was about to take up his duties as governor of Chi Province, in Chiang-hsi.[125]

Considering the evidence, we can imagine that the Khuong family may have had some attachment to Ai, perhaps having served there at one time and thereafter maintaining some kind of residence, perhaps as absentee landlords. But it is clear that the family was entrenched in officialdom and had contacts ranging from one end of the empire to the other, and that their connection with Vietnam was of no major significance.

The Khuong family was not typical of people in Vietnam. In 845, a T'ang official reported to the throne: "An-nam has produced no more than eight imperial officials; senior graduates have not exceeded ten."[126] Outside of the Khuong family, the name of only one *chin shih* ("doctorate") degree holder from Vietnam has survived. This is Lieu Huu Phuong. We know of him because he wrote a poem preserved by Chinese anthologists. He wrote the poem under circumstances that offer a clue to the mood of aspiring scholars from Vietnam. Here is how he described the experience:

> In 815, I failed the examinations [at Ch'ang-an, the T'ang capital in northern China]. I traveled in the west and came to the Precious Chicken Inn. There I was surprised to hear the sound of someone groaning. I inquired about that person's distress. He replied: "I have toiled through many examinations but have not yet found favor." Then he knocked his head on the floor. I talked with him for a long time. His replies were prompt and bitter. Unable to say more, he suddenly leaned to one side and died. I immediately sold my horse to a village notable and bought a coffin for his burial. Alas, I did not even know

119. Tran Nghia, p. 86, n. 3.
120. *CL*, 144; *CY*, 178
121. Tran Nghia, p. 86, n. 3.
122. *CTS*, 138, 8a.
123. *HTS*, 152, 2b.
124. *CTW*, 622, 16b.
125. *HTS*, 152, 3a; *CTS*, 138, 9a.
126. *CL*, 153.

his name! I took a path through the mountains and sadly laid him to rest. Later, I returned with an inscription:

> Alas, the gentleman died; reduced to extremities, he abandoned the world.
> How many rules weary the heart; brush, ink, the examination yard.
> But briefly acquainted, I offer a little sadness,
> Without knowing where his family's village stands.[127]

This poem is entitled: "On a Stranger's Coffin: A Poem Engraved on the Occasion of Burying a Scholar at Precious Chicken Inn." Lieu Huu Phuong's sympathetic attitude toward this unfortunate was clearly based on his own frustration in the examination yard. But he surmounted his disappointment. In the following year, 816, he passed the exams, earning the *chin shih* degree, and received an appointment at court as a collator of books. He took the honorific style of "Wandering Gentleman."[128]

Lieu Huu Phuong was from Giao Province. To go from Giao to Ch'ang-an in T'ang times, it was usual to embark and sail 250 miles downriver and along the coast to Sea Gate, the port in western Kuang-tung where the land route began. From there to the capital, a horse would have had to cover 1,200 miles. By the time Lieu Huu Phuong had received his *chin shih* degree, he truly was a "wandering gentleman."

When an aspiring scholar in Vietnam made the decision to go north and seek fame and fortune through the examination system, he was, for all practical purposes, turning his back on his native land. There was very little chance of his returning in any official capacity; either his career would be made in the north or he would disappear somewhere along the way, for not many would have wanted to face the disgrace of returning in failure. We do not know the number of young men who made this decision, but it may well have been greatly out of proportion to the number who actually succeeded. Those aspiring to careers in officialdom generally needed the assistance of influential patrons. Not many people from Giao, far from the T'ang capital, would have enjoyed this kind of advantage. The fate of the poor wretch laid to rest by Lieu Huu Phuong may have been common among aspiring candidates from Giao, and this circumstance may have been the source of Lieu Huu Phuong's solicitous care for the deceased. A Vietnamese scholar has recently written: "In mourning for this man, Lieu Huu Phuong mourned for all the talented men of Vietnam who were ignored or who disappeared while pursuing civil service examinations under the northern regime."[129] We can only conjecture to what extent this evaluation is correct.

We can nevertheless assume that the number of literate people in

127. *ChTS*, 490, p. 5550.
128. *ChTS*, 490, p. 5550.
129. Tran Nghia, p. 89.

Vietnam at this time was significant. The greatest number of Chinese loan words in Vietnamese are of a literary character and date from the T'ang epoch. Unlike the mainly administrative terms brought in during Han, which retained the old pronunciation of the Han era, these T'ang words were adapted to the Vietnamese tongue, undergoing a process of elaboration or simplification that incorporated them into the vocabulary of educated Vietnamese.[130]

At this time, the Vietnamese also began to experiment with using Chinese characters to write their own language. The earliest example of Vietnamese character writing, as we have noted earlier, is for the words *bo* and *cai* in the posthumous title given to Phung Hung. Although Vietnamese character writing was eventually developed for literary purposes from the thirteenth through the eighteenth centuries, it was generally viewed with suspicion by Vietnamese dynasties. Their view of the national language as a language of subversion was probably rooted in the T'ang experience.

Educated men who went north to compete in the examinations must have spent a large part of their youth studying the Chinese classics. This implies that there was a social basis in Vietnam for the cultural outlook expressed by this literature. The earliest surviving evidence for the propagation of Chinese-style family ethics in Vietnamese society comes from the eighth century.

According to a Chinese source, the mother of a rebel leader in Annam constantly admonished her wayward son to be a loyal citizen. Seeing that the young man was obstinate, she disowned him and refused him rice from the family fields and cloth from her spinning wheel. All her neighbors were so impressed by this upright behavior that they also began to respect the laws. At the beginning of the Ta-li reign period (766–79), her meritorious conduct was recognized by an imperial decree assigning two *ting-shih* to support her.[131]

The assignment of *ting-shih*, or "men servants," was part of the *shih-ting* system, an aspect of family organization as established by T'ang law. Old and feeble people of merit were assigned able-bodied men to care for them. These men were then exempted from corvée obligations.

From this example it is clear that the *shih-ting* system was applied in Vietnam, at least in the secure portions of the plains. We do not know if the woman in this episode was Vietnamese, a Chinese immigrant, or something in between. Still, we can assume that Chinese-style family values were publicized, officially encouraged, and established by law, although they were not firmly established even in the society of southern China until the eleventh century.[132]

130. Vuong Loc, "Glimpses of the Evolution of the Vietnamese Language," pp. 16–18.
131. *HTS*, 205 (Katakura, p. 32).
132. Miyakawa Hisayuki, "The Confucianization of South China," pp. 40–41.

The law codes of later Vietnamese dynasties were strongly influenced by T'ang law. However, it is significant that the portions of the T'ang legal system retained by the Vietnamese were chiefly about court etiquette, loyalty to the ruler, the behavior of officials, public order, and such administrative procedures as census registration and taxation. On the other hand, portions of T'ang law dealing with criminal justice, marriage, inheritance, and other aspects of family organization and customary usage were replaced or significantly altered by distinctive Vietnamese provisions.[133] From this we can assume that T'ang efforts to reform Vietnamese society were not very successful, and legal provisions such as the *shih-ting* system may in fact have been applied only among immigrant Chinese.

We can nevertheless be sure that Vietnamese culture and society were to some degree modified by nearly three centuries of T'ang rule. It was during this time that the Vietnamese language was enriched with Chinese literary terms, suggesting a significant knowledge of classical learning and an ability to apply it to popular forms of expression. During this time were also formed certain legal and administrative habits that became characteristic of Vietnamese government during the independence period.

Still, by the middle of the ninth century, Vietnam "had produced no more than eight imperial officials, and senior graduates had not exceeded ten." We should not overestimate the significance of classical studies in T'ang-Viet society. Although Giao was relatively docile under the T'ang regime, the more traditional Vietnamese society of Phong, Ai, and Hoan produced a succession of rebel leaders who turned much of the ninth century into a prolonged and violent confrontation. The events of the ninth century brought the long period of Chinese hegemony in Vietnam to an end. Although the spirit of Vietnamese independence was temporarily lost in the larger violence of T'ang's southern frontier, the ninth-century T'ang-Viet confrontation was a harbinger of the tenth century, when that spirit ultimately prevailed.

133. Yu Insun, "Law and Family in Seventeenth and Eighteenth-Century Vietnam," pp. 56–80.

6

The
T'ang-Viet
Confrontation

The T'ang Revival

By the turn of the ninth century, the political situation in China had stabilized, and T'ang enjoyed an era of relative peace during the reign of Hsien Tsung (806–20). Hsien Tsung achieved some success in reducing the power of military governors and enforced his authority over much of the empire. During his reign, strong protector generals developed Vietnam's potential as a regional power center. Bridging the gap between the Phung Hung period and this new imperial era was Chao Ch'ang.

Chao Ch'ang governed Vietnam for fifteen years. Rather than attempt to suppress or to interfere with the awakening of indigenous sensibilities that occurred in the Phung Hung period, he seems to have legitimized his own authority in the context of those sensibilities.

According to a Vietnamese source, Ch'ang frequently traveled about the countryside familiarizing himself with local customs and cults. One of his favorite places was the village of Tu-liem, a short distance west of La-thanh. Tradition identified this place as the natal village of Ly Ong Trong, a giant who was supposed to have battled the Hsiung-nu on China's northern frontier during the reign of Ch'in Shih Huang Ti (246–10 B.C.). Ch'ang took a special interest in Ong Trong. During one of his visits to Tu-liem, Ch'ang claimed to have been visited by the giant in a dream; together they discussed the *Ch'un ch'iu* (Spring and Autumn Annals), a text from ancient China, and the question of how best to govern the people. Ch'ang subsequently searched out Ong Trong's birthplace, where he built a shrine and presented ceremonial offerings to the giant's spirit. The prosperity of Ong Trong's cult dates from this time.[1] As a local hero who made a career of defending the empire, Ong Trong was an appropriate cult figure for a protector general to patronize.

Mention of the *Ch'un ch'iu* brings to mind the exetical interest in the

---

1. *VDULT*, 15–16.

Ch'un ch'iu that was popular among critical T'ang scholars at this time. This interest stemmed from a skeptical attitude toward traditional interpretations of the classics and a desire to rediscover their original meaning; these scholars were sometimes led to champion the wisdom of "village elders" over the orthodox tradition of classical scholarship.[2] Chao Ch'ang's interest in the *Ch'un ch'iu* may reflect an unorthodox outlook and helps explain his appreciation for folklore.

Chao Ch'ang collected Vietnamese folk traditions and compiled them in a book entitled *Chiao chou chi* (Vietnamese *Giao chau ky*; Records of Giao Province). This book is the only source of information on Phung Hung and on the tradition of Li Ch'ang-ming in the 650s. The book no longer exists in its original form, but portions of it are preserved in a fourteenth-century work.[3]

After serving in An-nam for ten years, Chao Ch'ang was over seventy years of age; complaining of a bad leg, he requested retirement. In the summer of 802, a member of the Imperial Academy named P'ei T'ai was sent to replace Ch'ang.[4] No sooner had Ch'ang departed, however, than Vietnam was rocked by invasion and rebellion.

At the end of 802, Huan-wang seized Hoan and Ai. Two months later, a general named Vuong Quy Nguyen led an uprising that chased P'ei T'ai out of the protectorate. This rebellion came after an order by P'ei T'ai to strengthen the fortifications surrounding La-thanh; the protector general may have been personally odious to the local officials, or his conscripting labor to repair the walls may have provoked resistance.

Vuong Quy Nguyen was promptly defeated by Military Legate Chao Chün, but Emperor Te Tsung was sufficiently shaken by these events to summon Chao Ch'ang for a report on affairs in Vietnam. The emperor was so pleased by the clarity and intelligence of Ch'ang's report, which has

2. William Nienhauser, *P'i Jih-hsiu*, pp. 19, 45, 66.

3. See appendix J and Émile Gaspardone, "Bibliographie annamite," p. 129. According to a tradition appended to the *VDULT* during the reign of Minh Mang, in the first half of the nineteenth century, Chao Ch'ang established the Eastern Local School, in eastern Giao, about twenty-five miles east of La-thanh; within a short time, this place became famous as a center of learning and was crowded with students. A village developed around the school. Many of its graduates went on to successful careers as government officials. After his death, Ch'ang was honored at the school by the building of a shrine and the maintenance of a cult (*VDULT*, 52–53). In the independence period, the area where the school was supposed to have been located became a major center of classical learning and produced a disproportionately large number of scholars and officials in Vietnamese government. The eighteenth-century *Cong du tiep ky*, by Vu Phuong De, largely consists of family and local traditions from the area extolling the careers of scholars and officials; among the many prominent statesmen to come from this place was Pham Cong Tru, who dominated Trinh government for over twenty years in the mid seventeenth century.

4. *CTS*, 13, 19b, and *HTS*, 170, 8b–9a.

unfortunately not been preserved, that he requested the old official to return to his post. When Ch'ang returned to Vietnam early in 804, it is recorded that the people "congratulated one another and rebellion ceased immediately." [5]

Ch'ang's popularity in Vietnam was a tribute to his skill as an administrator and must surely have been based on an overt sense of sympathy between him and the Vietnamese people. He was an old man and was not interested in lining his pockets or in brandishing imperial authority; it is clear that the local population trusted him. What was unusual was that such a man was also trusted by the imperial court. When he returned to Vietnam in 804, he bore the full title "An-nam Protector General, Doctor of the Censorate, Resident Imperial Commissioner." While most protector generals in the ninth century would also carry the title "Resident Imperial Commissioner," Chao Ch'ang was the only one to be distinguished as a "Doctor of the Censorate," a title that suggests he enjoyed discretionary powers ordinarily retained by the court.

It is characteristic of the post–Phung Hung era that a wise old man rather than an army was sent to calm a rebellion in Vietnam. Whatever the fate of Vuong Quy Nguyen, the Vietnamese clearly felt that they had won a contest with the T'ang court. They rejoiced to see the return of an old friend. Chao Ch'ang could easily have cultivated an image as the "father and mother of the people." The brash newcomer, P'ei T'ai, apparently expected the Vietnamese to follow orders, not realizing that his predecessor had won back the protectorate only through laying aside his imperial habits and gaining the confidence of the people by entering their cultural world.

Ch'üan Te-yü, the T'ang poet, was a high court official at this time.[6] He wrote a poem to commemorate P'ei T'ai's escape from Vietnam. It expresses the frustration of Chinese attempts to absorb the Vietnamese:

> Hastily secure the seal of Giao Province;
> Take leave of officials at successive halting places.

5. On the Huan-wang invasion, see HTS, 7, 10a. The annals of the CTS (13, 20b) simply say that P'ei T'ai was chased out by provincial general Vuong Quy Nguyen. Chao Ch'ang's biography includes the same information without naming Vuong Quy Nguyen (HTS, 170, 9a). The annals of the HTS (7, 10a) add the information that Military Legate Chao Chün defeated the rebel general. TCTC, 236, vol. 12, 698, expands this to say that Chao Chün beheaded Vuong Quy Nguyen and reinstated P'ei T'ai. CL, 99, says only that Vuong Quy Nguyen chased out P'ei T'ai. VSL, 1, 10b, contains a garbled account saying that P'ei T'ai was killed by Vuong Quy Nguyen and Chao Chün was then appointed protector general. TT, 5, 6b–7a, mentions neither Chao Chün nor P'ei T'ai's reinstatement, but does provide a reason for the rebellion. According to the TT, P'ei T'ai filled in the water courses that pierced the city walls to form an unbroken wall; this defensive measure, perhaps stimulated by the loss of Hoan and Ai, was interpreted by the local people as a provocation. On Chao Ch'ang's recall to An-nam, also see CTS, 13, 21a.

6. Ch'üan Te-yü's biographies are in CTS, 148, 8a–11a, and HTS, 165, 8b–10a.

Do not speak of serving in distant lands;
One's lot includes both pleasure and unhappiness.
Wind down the Chu-dien route,
Escorted by wheeling flocks of kingfishers;
Sail by war boat over the Chang Sea,
Banners furling in the swirling mists.
Raise the curtain of this remote frontier;
Fires along the valleys send up an excellent fragrance.
Remember when the north was on good terms with the Yüeh;
For a long time both were nourished by the southern fragrance.
Alas, there was no meeting of minds!
How happy to see the end of a strange affair!
No desire remains at the time of returning;
Perhaps the gentleman was annoyed by grass seeds.[7]

"Wind down the Chu-dien route" refers to the sinuous river channels leading to the sea through Chu-dien District. The Chang Sea was the Gulf of Tonkin. The "excellent fragrance" and the "southern fragrance" suggest nostalgia for the luxury goods of the south, among which were incense and aromatic woods. There is regret that nothing more had come of the relationship between "north" and "south," but mainly there is relief that the "strange affair" was over. The last line suggests that P'ei T'ai had provoked the Vietnamese with an exaggerated reaction to local conditions or, perhaps, that China's attempt to rule the Vietnamese produced nothing more than petty vexation and was not worth the trouble.

Chao Ch'ang returned to a difficult situation. In addition to soothing the ruffled feelings of the momentarily rebellious provincials, something had to be done about Hoan and Ai, which had fallen under the control of Huan-wang. Ch'ang apparently realized that a younger and stronger hand was needed for the tasks that lay ahead, and in 806 he returned north after entrusting An-nam to the care of his able subordinate, Deputy Imperial Commissioner Chang Chou.[8]

Chou was immediately appointed protector general and resident imperial commissioner, thereby avoiding the mistake of 802, when P'ei T'ai was sent fresh from the capital. The most pressing need was to rebuild the military forces of the protectorate so that Hoan and Ai could be recovered. Chou could expect no assistance from the north, for at this moment the "Yellow Grotto Barbarians" in modern Kuang-hsi were in rebellion and were absorbing all the attention of officials there.[9]

Chang Chou began by enlarging the wall constructed by Chang Po-i

7. *CL*, 157.

8. *HTS*, 170, 9a; *CTS*, 14, 10b. Chao Ch'ang served as the military governor at Canton before returning north, where he died at the age of eighty-five.

9. *CTS*, 14, 8a; *TCTC*, 237, vol. 13, 19, 31.

in 768. Chao Ch'ang had repaired Po-i's wall, La-thanh, after his arrival in 791. Now, Chou built a larger wall, called Dai-la, "Great La." This wall was twenty-two feet high and contained a total of eleven gates, five on the south, three on the east, and three on the west. Watchtowers were built over the gates, and ten new public buildings were constructed within.[10]

In three years, Chou expanded the army from eight thousand regulars to a force that, with militia units and tribal levies, mustered three hundred thousand men; thirty new arsenals were built to supply this army. The navy was expanded from ten old-fashioned slow boats to thirty-two fast boats manned by twenty-five warriors, twenty-three oarsmen, and two cross-bowmen apiece.[11]

In 809, Chou marched south. He defeated the Huan-wang army and captured more than thirty thousand of the enemy in battle. Among those captured were the Cham king's son and fifty-nine of his officers. Chou also seized the "false governors" of Hoan and Ai, who had collaborated with Huan-wang. Finally, he rebuilt the citadels of Hoan and Ai that had been destroyed by Huan-wang. In recognition of this new assertion of imperial power on the frontier, envoys from Huan-wang and Chen-la arrived at Dai-la to demonstrate their good will.[12]

Chang Chou's efforts represented the first effective reassertion of T'ang power in the protectorate since the rebellion of An Lu-shan half a century earlier. Chao Ch'ang had ruled, not from a position of strength, but rather in a spirit of cooperation with local interests. This had been a necessary transitional phase after the affirmation of local feeling in the Phung Hung era. The Phung family had been intelligent enough to realize that they could not win a military contest with a reviving T'ang. But Chao Ch'ang also realized that the Vietnamese could no longer be easily pushed about. As the imperial recovery progressed, however, the strength of T'ang relative to local interests increased, and, under the pressure of foreign invasion, the Vietnamese acquiesced in a major expansion of imperial might in their midst. Nevertheless, as the "false governors" of Hoan and Ai imply, all Vietnamese were not whole-hearted partisans of the T'ang revival; in any case, the T'ang revival in Vietnam was dependent on the continued cooperation of local interests.

The labors of Chao Ch'ang and Chang Chou provided a good foundation for T'ang-Viet relations. They had achieved a viable balance between imperial authority and local feeling. Chou's successor, Ma Tsung, did nothing to endanger this balance.

10. *TT*, 5, 6b, 7a; *CL*, 99–100.
11. *CL*, 100, is the principal source for Chang Chou's military reforms. *TT*, 5, 7a, mentions only the naval details and says three hundred new boats in place of thirty-two.
12. *CTS*, 14, 15a; *HTS*, 7, 13a, and 222c, 16a–b; *TCTC*, 238, vol. 13, 47; *CL*, 100; *TT*, 5, 7a.

Ma Tsung arrived in the autumn of 810. He claimed to be a descendent of Ma Yüan, who conquered the Vietnamese in A.D. 42–43. The memory of Ma Yüan was still potent among the people, and Ma Tsung exploited the reputation of the ancestor he claimed to garnish his own prestige among the Vietnamese. Like Ma Yüan, Tsung erected a pair of bronze pillars to symbolize the southern frontier of the empire. It is recorded that he was honest and did not trouble the people. A poem associated with his rule includes the following lines: "The red banner [symbolizing imperial authority] flies brilliantly on the sea, / Bringing law and order to the southern frontier."[13] This suggests a peaceful time.

In the autumn of 813, Tsung was transferred northward and replaced by Chang Mien. However, Mien was too old to assume his duties, and within a month he had been replaced by P'ei Hsing-li,[14] whose uncompromising outlook ended an era of good feeling.

Of P'ei Hsing-li's rule it is recorded that previous protector generals had been tolerant and lax; consequently the people and officials had accumulated undisciplined habits and were difficult to govern. When one of the military commanders ignored a warning to forgo his frequent swimming excursions, P'ei Hsing-li beheaded him and replaced him with his son. After this, it is said that authority prospered and stern majesty prevailed. This legalistic attitude extended to foreign relations as well. When a rebel from Huan-wang arrived requesting aid, his head was promptly returned to the Cham court.[15]

These policies provoked resentment and disaffection among the class of native officials upon which T'ang power now depended. This class had risen under the guidance of Chao Ch'ang and Chang Chou; it had prospered under the symbolic imperialism of Ma Tsung. The legalism of P'ei Hsing-li, however, tore the benevolent mask from T'ang rule and exposed the underlying conflict between imperial ideology and the indigenous way of life. A violent reaction waited only for an opportune moment.

Duong Thanh and Vo Ngon Thong

T'ang's brief recovery from the disruptions of the An Lu-shan era was drawing to a close, and the empire was beginning its long final decline. Accompanying and hastening this trend on the southern frontier was an increasingly militant attitude among tribal mountain chiefs, which was related to the growing power of the kingdom of Nan-chao in Yü-nan. In 794, Chao Ch'ang had obtained a treaty with Nan-chao, and

---

13. *CTS*, 14, 17a; *CL*, 100.
14. *CTS*, 15, 4a–b.
15. *CL*, 100.

relations with the mountains remained peaceful until after the difficulties provoked by P'ei T'ai's arrival in 802–3. From that time, the "Yellow Grotto Barbarians" periodically raided the valleys of what is now western Kuang-hsi.[16]

In late 817 or early 818, P'ei Hsing-li was transferred to Kuei, where he joined with other officials of the area in requesting authority at attack the "Yellow Grotto Barbarians." The military governor at Canton, K'ung K'uei, warned against the project, saying. "This matter has not been sufficiently discussed." His advice was ignored, however, and Hsing-li was authorized to begin operations. Hsing-li and his associates advanced into the mountains with a large army, but the campaign soon bogged down with incompetence and malaria.[17] Hsing-li's group had bled its jurisdiction white to support the ill-fated project and, with conditions of distress undermining authority in the rear of the beleaguered army, potential rebels in An-nam were inspired to believe that the empire was on the verge of collapse.

P'ei Hsing-li's successor in An-nam was a member of the imperial family named Li Hsiang-ku. It is recorded that Hsiang-ku was avaricious and disregarded the law, thus provoking popular resentment and fostering the spirit of rebellion. His protagonist was Duong Thanh, whose forebears had served as governors of Hoan since the K'ai-yüan period (713–41). Duong Thanh was a local leader of some stature. Hsiang-ku felt sufficiently threatened by his reputation to deprive him of his governor's seat in Hoan and to make him a petty military commander at the capital.

Thanh grew frustrated and melancholy; he became increasingly attentive to the popular anger directed against Hsiang-ku's high-handed rule. Desiring to get Thanh completely out of the way, Hsiang-ku gave him three thousand soldiers and ordered him to go to the assistance of P'ei Hsing-li's army, pinned down in the mountains to the north. Burning with ambition, Thanh turned about at night and, gaining access to the unsuspecting city, put Hsiang-ku and over one thousand of his family, servants, and personal retainers to death.[18]

---

16. *MS*, 267–68.

17. *TCTC*, 239, vol. 13, 125, and 241, vol. 13, 187. The date of P'ei Hsing-li's appointment as governor general of Kuei is approximately dated by the appointment of K'ung K'uei as military governor at Canton in the autumn of 817 (*CTS*, 15, 12b). K'ung K'uei was military governor at the time of P'ei Hsing-li's activities as governor general at Kuei.

18. The information that Duong Thanh's ancestors served as governors of Hoan Province beginning in the K'ai-yüan period is peculiar to the *TT* (5, 7a–b). The fullest account of Duong Thanh's uprising is in Hsiang-ku's biography (*HTS*, 80, 12a), which is closely followed by *TCTC*, 241, vol. 13, 187, and *TT*, 5, 7a–b; a shorter version is in *CL*, 100. Simple notices of Hsiang-ku's death appear in the *CTS* (15, 19a), the *HTS*(7, 16b), and the *VSL*(1, 10b). The *CTS* says the An-nam army rebelled; the *HTS* attributes Hsiang-ku's death to "An-nam General Duong Thanh"; the *VSL* merely identifies Duong Thanh as an "official."

Duong Thanh was convinced that the T'ang Empire had come to an end as far as An-nam was concerned. And, indeed, it might well have been so had he been capable of rallying the protectorate behind him. However, he was not an inspiring leader. It is recorded that his churlish temperament led him to acts of harshness bordering on cruelty, which alienated his followers.

T'ang authorities, realizing the impossibility of immediate military action, attempted to deflect Duong Thanh's ambition by pardoning him and appointing him to a governor's seat on Hai-nan Island. But Duong Thanh was not interested, and when the newly appointed protector general, Kuei Chung-wu, attempted to enter An-nam, Thanh sealed the border.

Camped on the border, Chung-wu resorted to secret negotiations with Thanh's subordinates. After several months, Chung-wu's emissaries gained the support of a growing number of rebel officials, including the commanders of seven thousand soldiers. The imperial court, however, decided that Chung-wu was moving too slowly and, early in 820, appointed P'ei Hsing-li to replace him. But before Hsing-li could arrive on the scene, Chung-wu's efforts bore fruit. A group of generals broke with Duong Thanh, seized Dai-la, and welcomed Chung-wu. Duong Thanh and his family were put to death. P'ei Hsing-li had meanwhile died at Sea Gate, and Chung-wu's appointment was subsequently reconfirmed.[19]

Kuei Chung-wu's mobilization of certain Vietnamese leaders against Duong Thanh seems to have been assisted by elements of the Vietnamese Buddhist community. This assistance was signaled by the inauguration of a new Thien sect by a monk from China, perhaps sent at Chung-wu's instigation.

In 820, a Chinese monk arrived in An-nam. He was originally from Kuang Province, and his family name was Cheng, but he has been remembered by his Vietnamese name, which was bequeathed to the sect he founded in Vietnam: Vo Ngon Thong. He began his studies at Shuang-lin Temple, in modern Che-chiang, and subsequently studied under Patriarch

---

19. Hsiang-ku's biography (*HTS*, 80, 12a) provides the basic narrative of these events and is followed by *TCTC*, 241, vol. 13, 195, which adds the detail of seven thousand soldiers. These events are noted in the imperial annals of the *CTS* as follows: in the sixth month of the year, Chung-wu reported the execution of Duong Thanh and the restoration of the protectorate of An-nam (16, 3a); in the eighth month of the year, Chung-wu sent Duong Thanh's head to the capital (10, 4a). *CL*, 100, simply says that Chung-wu pacified Duong Thanh's rebellion. *TT*, 5, 7b–8a, contains a different version, according to which Duong Thanh successfully resisted not only Chung-wu but two later protector generals as well and was actively in rebellion as late as 828. As we will see, the lingering state of rebellion that characterized the following decade was a heritage of Duong Thanh's uprising and was undoubtedly inspired by memories of him. However, the evidence shows that Duong Thanh was beheaded in 820. P'ei Hsing-li's reappointment to An-nam is dated in the second month of 820 by *CTS*, 16, 2a. The court learned of Hsing-li's death in the seventh month of the year (*CTS*, 16, 4a).

Ma in Chiang-hsi. Patriarch Ma's mentor and predecessor had been a disciple of Hui Neng, the first patriarch of the so-called "Southern School" of Chinese Ch'an Buddhism. Hui Neng was himself considered to be the third in a line of transmission from Seng Ts'an, the patriarch who had sent Vinītaruci south in the sixth century.

After the death of Patriarch Ma, Vo Ngon Thong continued to study under Patriarch Ma's famous disciple Huai Hai, who invigorated the Chinese monkhood. After Huai Hai's death 814, Vo Ngon Thong remained in the company of Huai Hai's disciples and assisted in the education of the monk Hui Chi, who later founded the Kuei-yang School of Ch'an, a minor school that did not survive the T'ang dynasty.

In 820, Vo Ngon Thong was an old man. When he arrived in Vietnam he was received by the Vietnamese monk Cam Thanh at Kien-so Temple in Phu-dong Village. There he practiced "wall meditation." Vo Ngon Thong died in 826, after passing on the teachings of Huai Hai to Cam Thanh; Cam Thanh died in 860. The Vo Ngon Thong sect, like the Vinītaruci sect, endured into the thirteenth century.[20]

The founding of the Vo Ngon Thong sect at this time certainly held political implications. As rival factions maneuvered for power at Dai-la and T'ang agents shuttled in and out of the protectorate, the arrival of this monk was surely more than coincidental. He was already an old man at the time and did not come in search of a teacher or of a quiet place to retire. We can reasonably imagine that the Vo Ngon Thong sect mobilized the monastic communities of Giao on behalf of pro-T'ang interests. The monastic communities had important ties to Chinese culture and probably looked askance at Duong Thanh's revolutionary schemes.

The Vo Ngon Thong sect seems to have been a response of the agricultural areas to the more volatile political ambitions of those who guarded the mountain frontiers. Duong Thanh's rebellion initially owed little, if anything, to the civil officials who administered the agricultural communities of Giao; many of these officials were undoubtedly closer in outlook to their Chinese overseers than to the less literate society of the frontier districts, where military men made their careers. The coup that removed Duong Thanh most likely resulted from civil officials in the Buddhist heartland of Giao mobilizing their strength against what they considered to be irrational extremism. They would benefit by the extremist threat in their dealings with the Chinese only so long as they were in a position to control it.

Duong Thanh was clearly a hothead. His career was made in Hoan, where a fluid border and a large tribal population produced chronic hostil-

20. On the establishment of the Vo Ngon Thong sect, see Tran Van Giap, "Le Bouddhisme en Annam des origins au XIIIe siècle," pp. 243–44.

ities. He slaughtered over a thousand people to revenge himself against Li Hsiang-ku; then he sealed the border as if he could defy the T'ang Empire. To many, he must have appeared both cruel and stupid.

This is not to discount the broader validity of Duong Thanh's movement. His actions occurred against a background of popular resentment of arbitrary misgovernment; this resentment must have extended to the civil officials in Giao as well. But while the civil officials may have welcomed the protectorate's flexing its new-found political power, they assuredly did not want this power in the violent hands of military men who had more in common with mountain chiefs, among whom they wielded their authority, than with themselves, men whose outlooks were conditioned by agriculture, administration, and literature.

During the T'ang revival, a new class of officials rose up to meet the needs of local administration. We know that the local army was greatly expanded under Chang Chou; this, as well as the building and stocking of arsenals, the repair of citadels, and the renovation of the navy, could not have been accomplished without a thorough effort to register the population, to collect revenue, and to administer laws and regulations.

The growth of administration during this period significantly altered the relationship of the agricultural population to the adjacent frontiers. The values of a clearly defined agricultural way of life were henceforth articulated with greater precision, authority, and intolerance. Duong Thanh's leadership attracted untamed elements from the frontier and embittered elements from officialdom, but it could not hope to overcome educated officials who had learned to work in concert through administrative procedures and whose skills provided manpower and supplies for the military.

The strength of the rebel faction was that it could fall back upon the frontier areas, where a less regimented population furnished ready manpower for political adventures. Rebel elements unseated in 820 apparently did just that. The political instability that characterized the next four decades and culminated in the Nan-chao War can be traced to conflicting perspectives. These perspectives grew out of the administrative expansion of the preceding decades, which nurtured a cooperative attitude on the plains and provoked an attitude of resistance on the frontier.

Resistance to T'ang was probably not entirely a matter of regional perspective. We can assume that those who opposed the Chinese came from all parts of Vietnamese society, for the persistence of resistance in the ninth century implies the latent support of the society at large. It is nevertheless true that the frontier offered greater opportunities to develop revolutionary movements and that those who chose to stay in the security of the Giao heartland took a more passive view.

This was an overwhelmingly illiterate society. Public sentiments were for the most part expressed by a minority of monks, civil officials, and military officers. Many of the monks and some of the civil officials were undoubtedly men of culture and learning; most could at least read and write for practical affairs. Some military officers, on the other hand, were probably barely literate. Merchants surely had a certain specialized literacy.

Since the formal educational process inevitably inculcated the imperial point of view, it would not be far wrong to assert that the most highly educated tended to be the most pro-Chinese. Yet, there was an alternative sphere of thought for educated Vietnamese. We have seen how Chinese characters were used to express the Vietnamese term *bo cai*, the earliest surviving example of *nom*.

Educated Vietnamese were not isolated from their society. We can assume that many of them cultivated a feeling of sympathy with the preliterate culture of their compatriots, and some of them apparently expressed this sympathy by developing the native idiom through the use of *nom*. It is clear from the events of the ninth century that some of them also expressed this sympathy by resorting to violence against their T'ang overlords.

From 820 until the resolution of the Nan-chao War nearly half a century later, T'ang policy toward the protectorate had to take into account an evaluation of Vietnamese officialdom and its loyalty to the empire. This troubled half century brought the history of T'ang Vietnam to a head. Duong Thanh may have been an uninspiring leader, but he was a portent of things to come.

Confrontation

Although Kuei Chung-wu had regained possession of Dai-la, there was no mistaking that T'ang power in the south had received a deadly blow. The "Yellow Grotto Barbarians" were momentarily forgotten in the urgency of the An-nam situation. P'ei Hsing-li's disastrous campaign against them nevertheless provoked increasingly serious uprisings in following years. The center of trouble was the jurisdiction of Yung, north of An-nam, which T'ang authorities were finally forced to abandon to the "Yellow Grotto Barbarians."

In 822, the assistant legate of An-nam, Ts'ui Chieh, was named imperial commissioner of Yung and was charged with reestablishing imperial authority there.[21] Within a few months, his place in Yung was taken by Kuei Chung-wu. Chung-wu's replacement in An-nam was originally Wang Ch'eng-pien, but before the end of the year Ch'eng-pien was replaced by Li Yüan-hsi.[22] These rapid changes in personnel reflect an attempt

---

21. *CTS*, 16, 16a; *TCTC*, 242, vol. 13, 239, 240.
22. *CTS*, 16, 13a, 17a, 18a.

to reorganize the shattered southern frontier. During the following decade, frontier difficulties combined with a simmering state of rebellion in An-nam to keep T'ang officials on the defensive.

At the beginning of summer in 823, Li Yüan-hsi reported that the Lao peoples of Luc Province had attacked and plundered agricultural settlements.[23] A few months later, the "Yellow Grotto Barbarians" attacked and plundered Yung,[24] and the following autumn they attacked and plundered An-nam.[25] In the next year, the "Yellow Grotto Barbarians" carried out devastating raids in all directions. The military governor at Canton reported that they killed one of his generals.[26] In the autumn of 824, they again invaded and plundered An-nam. This time a seaborne contingent from Huan-wang joined them, and together they seized Luc Province and killed the governor.[27] These aggressions were encouraged and assisted by rebellious survivors of Duong Thanh's group.[28]

The trials and tribulations of Li Yüan-hsi in the midst of these depredations are vividly symbolized by his abandonment of Dai-la. In 825, he reported that he had moved his government to the north bank of the Hong River. According to Vietnamese records, Dai-la was destroyed by local rebels. Yüan-hsi apparently moved to Long-bien, but his stay there was brief, for in addition to what was taken as an inauspicious river current at the north gate of the city, the protector general "feared numerous persons who harbored the spirit of rebellion" and shortly returned to the vicinity of Dai-la. After erecting a small citadel, he was openly ridiculed by some, who are reported to have said, "Your strength is not equal to the construction of a large citadel."[29]

23. *TCTC*, 243, vol. 13, 250.
24. Ibid., 243, vol. 13, 251.
25. *HTS*, 8, 3b; *TCTC*, 243, vol. 13, 253.
26. *TCTC*, 243, vol. 13, 256.
27. *HTS*, 8, 4a; *CTS*, 17a, 4b; *TCTC*, 243, vol. 13, 263.
28. *TT*, 5, 7b.
29. *CTS*, 17a, 6a, and *CL*, 100, cite Li Yüan-hsi's report that he moved his government north of the river; the river is not identified but the only plausible interpretation is that it was the Hong River. According to *TT*, 5, 7b, Duong Thanh had found refuge among the Lao barbarians, instigated rebellion, and succeeded in destroying Dai-la; this then led to the aggression of the Yellow Grotto Barbarians and Huan-wang. The earliest source on Long-bien in the context of these events is the *Chiao chou chi*, cited in *VDULT*, 18; this was not the work by Chao Ch'ang but rather a book of the same title by Tseng Kun, a T'ang official who was in An-nam from 865 to 880; see Gaspardone, "Bibliographie," p. 127. The *TT* (5, 7b), the *VSL* (1, 10b), and other Vietnamese sources (see Cao Huy Giu, trans., and Dao Duy Anh, annotator, *Dai Viet su ky toan thu*, 1: 325, n. 19) use essentially the same information, while adding the detail of rebellion to that of the inauspicious current. The inauspicious current must have been at Long-bien, as *VDULT*, 18, clearly says, for Dai-la had no north gate and was located on the north bank of the To-lich River, a confluent of the Hong; see H. Maspero, "Le Protectorat general d'Annam sous les T'ang," pp. 555–56. *TT*, 5, 7b, dates the return of the government to

The building of this citadel, again called La-thanh, has been re-membered in a story, which associates it with a local spirit. This story is derived from a book written no more than half a century later, which allows us to place some confidence in its historical value.[30]

According to this tradition, Li Yüan-hsi's citadel was double-walled and circular; it contained a jumble of hastily constructed buildings. Yüan-hsi was persuaded that the place he had chosen to build his citadel was the birthplace of a powerful local spirit, who would have to be propitiated if future trouble were to be averted. The spirit belonged to a certain To Lich, who had been a local magistrate during the Chin dynasty.

According to surviving tradition, To Lich's family had not been wealthy or powerful, but it was extremely virtuous; To Lich was a second-degree graduate and earned an imperial commendation, which was posted at the gate of his house. When he died, a hamlet and a river were named after him.

The region drained by the To-lich River, which flows through Hanoi to this day, became politically important starting in the sixth century. It became popularly known as the "dragon's belly," and represented the geographical and spiritual center of the Vietnamese realm; To Lich, the spirit of this place, was inevitably identified with local concepts of kingship. In an effort to gain the good will of To Lich's spirit, Li Yüan-hsi embarked on a series of activities designed to advertise his compliance with indigenous customs.

First, Yüan-hsi held a feast. Then, he built a shrine. Finally, he built a temple and held another feast, accompanied by elaborate ceremonies, music, and dancing. After the festivities, Yüan-hsi was awakened from his sleep by a strong wind that blew sand through his window, shook the bamboo blinds, and caused his table to tremble. The spirit of To Lich appeared as an old man astride a white stag. The old man exhorted the protector general to be a good ruler. Yüan-hsi replied that he would be.

This tradition suggests that Yüan-hsi was dependent on local advisors, who encouraged him to adjust his authority to the cultural and political realities of the protectorate. He apparently achieved a working relationship with some of the local officials. Yet the situation increasingly progressed out

---

the vicinity of Dai-la in the eleventh month of 824; *VDULT*, 18, only mentions the year of Li Yüan-hsi's appointment, 822. *HTS*, 43a, 9b, dates the shifting of the government back to the vicinity of Dai-la in 825; *CTS*, 17a, 6a, dates the abandonment of Dai-la in the fifth month of 825. For the quotation mocking Yüan-hsi's new citadel, see *TT*, 5, 7b, and *VSL*, 1, 10b. The full quotation includes a prophecy that fifty years later a man of the Kao family would come to build a real city at the spot; this reference to Kao P'ien suggests that the entire quotation may date from the end of the century.

30. *VDULT*, 18; from Tseng Kun's *Chiao chou chi*.

of his hands, for early in 827 Han Yüeh was appointed to replace him because "Giao-chi was in rebellion." Standing at the head of the rebels was the governor of Phong, Vuong Thanh Trieu; in the summer of 828, Han Yüeh captured and beheaded him.[31]

Han Yüeh's appointment was accompanied by a simplification of the protectorate's administration. "Provincial inspectors" were discontinued, and their powers were concentrated in the hands of the protector general. This was probably done because "provincial inspectors" became superfluous as T'ang authority remained on the defensive. Han Yüeh was nevertheless successful in asserting his control over enough territory so that with heavy taxation he was able to fill the treasury and to accumulate a personal fortune. This undoubtedly explains why in the autumn of 828 the local army rebelled and chased him out of An-nam.[32]

There followed a three-year interval from which there is no information. Then, in 831, Cheng Ch'o was named protector general.[33] Nothing further is known of this man. In 833, the military governor at Canton reported that official positions throughout the southern frontier had not been filled for one to two years and requested that new officials be sent.[34] In the following year, Han Wei was appointed protector general.[35] Nothing further is known of him. We can assume that administrative neglect in the south encouraged the development of local political initiative, while T'ang officials were inhibited by conflicts between emerging factions.

In 835, Protector General T'ien Tsao attempted to build a system of hedgerows and wooden palisades to keep raiders from penetrating the capital area; funds were lacking, however, and the project was not completed.[36] Either the political difficulties of the protectorate invited these incursions or, more probably, they were simply an aspect of the internal political situation.

T'ien Tsao's palisade nevertheless signaled a more determined T'ang effort to bring the southern frontier back under control. In 835, the court sent three generals into sensitive frontier provinces. Two were sent into the mountains of modern Kuang-hsi, and a certain Yang Ch'eng-ho was sent to "pacify and establish" Hoan Province,[37] implying that Hoan was in a state

31. *CTS*, 17a, 12a, provides the date of Han Yüeh's appointment. Han Yüeh's biography (*HTS*, 179, 10a) says: "Giao-chi rebelled; [Han Yüeh was] entrusted with the Protectorate of An-nam." On Vuong Thanh Trieu, see *TCTC*, 243, vol. 13, 293; *CL*, 100; *TT*, 5, 8a.

32. On "provincial inspectors," see *VSL*, 1, 10b. On Han Yüeh's financial accomplishments, see *HTS*, 179, 10a. On the rebellion of 828, see: *CTS*, 17a, 15a; *HTS*, 8, 5b; *TCTC*, 243, vol. 13, 294; *TT*, 5, 8a; *CL*, 100.

33. *CTS*, 17c, 6a.

34. The military governor's report of 833 is in *CTS*, 17c, 8b.

35. Ibid., 17c, 14a.

36. *HTS*, 167, 9b; *CL*, 101.

37. *TCTC*, 245, vol. 13, 356.

of rebellion. In the following year, a military governor who had arrogated a title in excess of his authority was exiled to Hoan,[38] perhaps to lend assistance to Ch'eng-ho.

While military men were sent to the southern border in Hoan to insure basic frontier security, a new approach was taken in the agricultural heartland of An-nam. Faced with stubborn resistance by the taxpaying peasantry, T'ang reverted to a conciliatory policy. A decree dated in the fourth month of 836 said:

> As for the taxation of distant peoples, every year when we go to collect what is due, the people speak out their suffering and hardship, so let the taxes be temporarily remitted. As for An-nam, it is altogether fitting to remit this year's autumn tax; we order Protector General T'ien Tsao to gather the people and announce this remission lest the garrisons be cut off and starved out.[39]

The decree went on to provide for the financial needs of the protectorate's administration by having money sent down from the imperial treasury. Although An-nam had become a financial liability, T'ang was determined to maintain its control there for strategic reasons. With an expansionist Nan-chao looking out from Yün-nan, the protectorate had become the keystone of the southern frontier. The realization of this basic strategic fact lay behind a strong, though brief, T'ang initiative to win back the loyalty of the Vietnamese. The man sent to implement this new program was Ma Chih, who replaced T'ien Tsao in the ninth month of 836.

The decree of 836 cited above reveals that there was open hostility between T'ang garrisons in An-nam and the surrounding population, and that the garrisons were actually in danger of being besieged. This consideration seems to have been the immediate cause for remitting taxes. It also seems to have prompted the appointment of Ma Chih, a man of particular talent.

It is recorded that Ma Chih was educated, skilled in public administration, cultured, chaste, and refined to the point of stylishness. These attributes earned him the respect and cooperation of the Vietnamese. His rule was "correct and honest"; he did not trouble the people with vexing regulations or harsh taxes. Most remarkable, however, was that all the tribal leaders in the mountainous hinterland submitted to him; they sent their sons and younger brothers with tribute, requesting authority to collect taxes and rule their localities. Chih reestablished Luc Province, which had been in administrative limbo since 824, when the governor was killed by a combined force of "Yellow Grotto Barbarians" and raiders from Huang-wang; Chih named a local leader as governor. As a general indication of well-

38. CTS, 17c, 20a.
39. See Katakura Minoru, "Chugokū Shihaika no Betonamu," p. 35.

being, it is recorded that oyster ponds that had been unproductive for years began to produce pearls again.[40]

Ma Chih presided over a return to peace and prosperity that temporarily suspended the political troubles that had absorbed the protectorate since Duong Thanh's rebellion. Evidence suggests he enjoyed and profited from his time in Vietnam.[41] Peaceful administration in the protectorate, however, was heavily dependent upon the personality of the protector general and his ability to adjust imperial ideals to indigenous reality. Ma Chih was exceptional. After his departure, relations between the protectorate and the empire rapidly deteriorated again.

The conciliatory policy of the 830s came during the reign of Wen Tsung (827–40), who implemented sensible policies and appointed honest officials. After the death of Hsien Tsung in 820, Wen Tsung was perhaps the last T'ang emperor noted for presiding over a rational regime. Ma Chih brought this brief, enlightened era to Vietnam. Both he and the policy he was called upon to implement went against the prevailing trend of confrontation.

Ma Chih's successor was Wu Hun. In 843, Hun ordered the local generals to repair the walls of La-thanh. They mutinied, burned the watchtower, and plundered the storehouse. Hun fled north. Tuan Shih-tse, the military overseer, persuaded the generals against further resistance.[42] This episode was similar to the uprising of 803, when P'ei T'ai ordered a strengthening of the city walls, and demonstrates how fragile the relationship between T'ang officials and local leaders continued to be.

The most effective argument for accepting T'ang overlordship must have been the increasing seriousness of predatory incursions from the mountains. This problem slipped out of the control of local officials in 846, when T'ang general P'ei Yüan-yu arrived with an army and expelled the raiders.[43] These raiders were very likely allies of rebel elements in An-nam. Some officials in Giao seem to have been increasingly determined to live with T'ang authority out of a sense of necessity, while others began to think of an alliance with the mountain chiefs as a means of driving out the Chinese once and for all.

40. The primary source is Ma Chih's biography (HTS, 184, 1a), of which CL, 101, is an abridgment.

41. Tran Nghia, "Mot so tac pham moi phat hien co lien quan toi giong van hoc Viet bang chu Han cua nguoi Viet thoi Bac Thuoc," pp. 96–97.

42. HTS, 8, 10a, and CL, 101, contain brief notices on the uprising. TCTC, 247, vol. 13, 460, and TT, 5, 8a, contain fuller versions. VSL, 1, 11a, simply cites Wu Hun as a protector general during the reign of Wu Tsung (841–46).

43. HTS, 8, 11a, says that barbarians from Yün-nan invaded An-nam but were defeated by Imperial Commissioner P'ei Yüan-yu. TT, 5, 8a, says that P'ei Yüan-yu was sent to deal with the situation at the head of soldiers from neighboring jurisdictions. VSL, 1, 11a, simply lists P'ei Yüan-yu as an official during Wu Tsung's reign (841–46).

A description of An-nam from the mid-ninth century has been preserved; contained in a document recorded at the T'ang court, it begins by
saying that the importance of the protectorate was to

> defend the land routes and prevent the Khmers from coming to buy weapons
> and horses; in the ravines dwell savage and stubborn people who must be
> repressed. . . . Once every three years soldiers are sent to patrol and repress,
> then the situation is reported to the throne. All frontier officials must concern
> themselves with befriending local leaders and teaching them the proper way
> to behave. An-nam has less than three hundred cavalrymen. . . . There are
> strong clans and aboriginal tribes; a question of prime importance is the
> distribution of military equipment. If there are any fathers or elder brothers of
> good character with literary and martial talents, each year their names are
> recommended for official positions.[44]

This description is most apt for those considerable portions of the
protectorate situated beside or within the mountainous hinterland. The basic
problem was frontier security. The selection of local leaders and the cultivation of their loyalty, as well as the fundamental matter of weapons
control, were the most important considerations.

The passage provides a glimpse of the frontier situation that became so
explosive in the 850s. There was apparently a great deal of coming and going
between the lowland agricultural areas and the mountains. Merchants in
salt, cattle, horses, and weapons were fanning out through a mountain
population in the process of being galvanized by the powerful leadership of
Nan-chao. Even the Khmers in the Mekong basin beyond were drawn into
the trade. This undoubtedly stirred memories of the Black Emperor's horde
in 722 among T'ang officials familiar with the south. An-nam had become a
soft frontier that threatened to undermine the integrity of T'ang government. Constant vigilance was required; patrolling and repressing became
standard operating procedure.

In the agricultural heartland of Giao, a more settled existence obtained. This is clearly demonstrated by the posterity of Wu Hun, the
protector general driven out of An-nam by the mutiny of 843. Originally
from Fu-chien, Hun returned to An-nam and settled in eastern Giao.
According to one of his descendents, a Vietnamese scholar-official writing in
the eighteenth century, Hun liked An-nam. The region in which Hun
settled was located where the sea route from China entered the zone of
settled habitation. It remained a center of Chinese influence during the
centuries of Vietnamese independence, and starting in the fourteenth century the descendents of Wu Hun became prominent officials in Vietnamese
government.[45]

Although Wu Hun may not have ventured back until the end of the

44. *CL,* 153.
45. Vu Phuong De, *Cong du tiep ky,* 1: 1.

Nan-chao War, we should be cautious about making any sweeping statements about oppression and resistance. T'ang's impact was uneven, and this unevenness underlay the political difficulties of the mid-ninth century. It gave rise to a polarization of sentiment within the protectorate, with one side drawing closer to the imperial world, while the other side drew closer to potential anti-T'ang allies in the mountains. This polarization did not fail to stimulate the interest of Nan-chao.

During the second quarter of the ninth century, the rising power of Nan-chao encouraged a confrontation between pro-T'ang and anti-T'ang leaders in the protectorate. Many educated Vietnamese undoubtedly found no difficulty in choosing alliance with the empire over the unknown dangers of alliance with a "barbarian kingdom." The idea of independence was ill defined after more than two centuries of T'ang rule. Still, a strong movement of resistance to T'ang thrived on the fringe of settled life. This movement was led by military families and disaffected officials, and it placed its hopes increasingly on Nan-chao as a counterweight to T'ang pressure. Thus, the scene was set for one of the most prolonged and devastating wars during Vietnam's history as a Chinese province.

The Nan-chao War

Two of P'ei Yüan-yu's successors in the late 840s and early 850s, T'ien Tsai-yu and Ts'ui Keng, seem to have enjoyed relatively stable conditions during their short stays in the protectorate. Of T'ien Tsai-yu, it is simply recorded that he "did good work on the frontier." In 852, Ts'ui Keng erected a memorial stele for the famed calligrapher Ch'u Sui-liang, who in 658 had died in the protectorate after being unjustly accused of treason and exiled. Aside from this, there is no substantive information until 854, when Protector General Li Cho presided over the disintegration of An-nam's frontier defenses.[46]

Li Cho has been remembered as the most infamous of all protector generals, for the local people resented his harsh rule and the Chinese later blamed him for causing the Nan-chao War. He was known for his greed and his violent temper, which drove him to acts of cruelty. His greatest mistakes, however, were in his dealings with the mountain chiefs.

There was a trade between the mountain chiefs and the protectorate. The mountain chiefs bartered horses and cattle for salt. Li Cho changed the terms of the trade so that the chiefs received only one peck of salt for each head of livestock. Since he controlled the collection of salt from villages on the tidewaters, Cho hoped to obtain a large number of horses, which he

---

46. See *CL*, 101, for T'ien Tsai-yu and Ts'ui Keng. According to the *MS* chart, p. 336, P'ei Yüan-yu departed in 848; T'ien Tsai-yu is listed for the years 849–50 and Ts'ui Keng for 851–52; Li Cho's dates are given as 853–55.

could then sell to accumulate a fortune. The mountain chiefs, however, attempted to force Cho back to the original arrangement, the details of which have not been recorded. They raided the lowlands and attacked Cho's garrisons. Too proud to back down, Cho ordered his men to force the chiefs into submission. Within a short time, over half of Cho's soldiers were dead from fevers contracted during campaigns into the mountains. The survivors were exhausted from continual fighting, and supplies were running out.

The most ominous development, however, was that the mountain chiefs placed themselves under the protection of the king of Nan-chao and allied themselves with rebellious elements in An-nam. This combination of anti-imperial interests grew rapidly under Cho's inept rule.

Do Ton Thanh was the governor of Ai and a military commander. According to Chinese records, his family's power in Vietnam dated from the Ch'i and Liang dynasties (479–556), and subsequent Chinese regimes could not dislodge it. The Do family was established in Ai, beyond the direct purview of T'ang officialdom. When Li Cho provoked war with the mountains and began to suffer reverses, Do Ton Thanh allied himself with the tribal chiefs against Cho. He may have done this in order to preserve the position of his family when Chinese administration began to break down as a result of Cho's military failures, or he may in fact have been actively pursuing an anti-T'ang policy. In any case, Cho succeeded in having Do Ton Thanh killed. However, this deed only added fuel to the fires of resistance.[47]

Warfare was heaviest in Phong Province, where the Hong River and its tributaries enter the plains. Phong was defended by a local general named Ly Do Doc, who was assisted by seven commanders called "Lords of the Ravines." During the winter season, the season for warfare, they were supported by an army of six thousand men called the "Winter Garrison." The civil official in charge of Phong seems to have sympathized with the anti-T'ang cause; he requested that the Winter Garrison be dismissed from Phong. He apparently hoped to shift the theater of war from his own province to areas deeper in the protectorate, where hostilities might more effectively undermine Li Cho's authority and provide an opportunity to chase him out. Plagued by problems of supply and manpower, and unfamiliar with the intricacies of protectorate politics, Cho approved the request.

Without the Winter Garrison, Ly Do Doc's position was untenable. The king of Nan-chao sent a "Trustee of the East" among the chiefs opposing Do Doc, for An-nam lay on Nan-chao's eastern frontier. The Trustee of

47. The information that Do Ton Thanh was governor of Ai and a military commander and that Li Cho had him killed because he allied himself with the Lao is cited from the *Shih lu*, "Authentic Records," in a note to *TCTC*, 250, vol. 13, 587. Elsewhere Do Ton Thanh is simply identified as a "barbarian leader." On the background of the Do family, see *TCTC*, 249, vol. 13, 559.

the East sent a letter to Do Doc soliciting his submission. Do Doc was amenable, so the Trustee of the East sent one of his daughters, who was then married to Do Doc's eldest son. In this way, Do Doc and the seven Lords of the Ravines became vassals of Nan-chao. All the mountain chiefs who up to this time had accepted T'ang overlordship now went over to Nan-chao. The year was 854, and this was the beginning of the Nan-chao War.[48]

Large Nan-chao armies did not appear in An-nam until 858. In the meantime, local chiefs led raids that brought warfare to villages in the heart of the protectorate. In 857, a T'ang general named Sung Ya was sent to deal with the situation, but he was in An-nam less than two months before a rebellion in Jung prompted his recall north.[49]

After Sung Ya's departure, control of An-nam fell into the hands of a local general named La Hanh Cung, who had two thousand well-trained soldiers at his command. He collected taxes and ignored the protector general, Li Hung-fu, who could only muster a bodyguard of a few hundred poorly equipped imperial troops. When Li Hung-fu's replacement, Wang Shih, arrived with reinforcements in the spring of 858, La Hanh Cung was flogged and banished.[50]

Wang Shih was one of T'ang's best generals. His first measure was to complete the fortifications that had been started by T'ien Tsao in 835. He surrounded La-thanh with a high wooden palisade some five miles in circumference; it was built to last for decades. Outside the palisade, he dug a moat and filled it with flowing water; beyond the moat he planted a barrier of thorny bamboo. Raiders could not casually penetrate these defenses. Shih then selected and trained new officers and men.[51]

When a large Nan-chao reconnaissance force entered the protectorate

---

48. Li Cho is a shadowy figure; Ssu-ma Kuang commented on the difficulty of identifying Cho with persons of that name who appear in other sources (*TCTC*, 249, vol. 13, 558). The significance of his disastrous rule was not realized until later, after the situation had evolved into a major crisis and historians began to look for the cause of the trouble. Thus, the events of 854 are included under the year 863 in *CTS*, 19a, 4a, and under the year 858 in *TCTC*, 249, vol. 13, 558, and *TT*, 5, 8b–9a; in these sources the information is presented by way of explaining the origins of the situation obtaining in later years. *HTS*, 22b, 1a, dates these events to the Ta-chung period (847–59), whereas the more detailed account in *MS*, 4, 87–88, and 107–8, provides the date of 854 as the time of Li Cho's dismissal of the Winter Garrison and the commencement of full-scale warfare. The *CL*(101, 110–11) summarizes the events.

49. *CTS*, 18c, 15a; *TCTC*, 249, vol. 13, 551, 552; *TT*, 5, 8a–b. All these sources date Sung Ya's appointment to the protectorate in the fourth month of the year. The Jung army rebelled and chased out the resident imperial commissioner in the fifth month (*HTS*, 8, 13a). Sung Ya was sent to Jung to deal with the rebels in the sixth month (*CTS*, 18c, 15b).

50. Wang Shih replaced Li Hung-fu in the third month of the year (*CTS*, 18c, 18a–b). The information about La Hanh Cung is in: *TCTC*, 249, vol. 13, 556; *TT*, 5, 8b; and *CL*, 101.

51. The palisade was twelve *li* in circumference and was made of trees levied from the markets of An-nam, according to Wang Shih's biography (*HTS*, 167, 9b). According to *TCTC*, 249, vol. 13, 555, the palisade was made of jujube wood, from a fruit tree that grows as tall as fifteen feet.

in midsummer of 858, Wang Shih sent an interpreter to read them a statement declaring the pros and cons of their departing immediately. They left the same night, sending their apologies and the explanation that they had come looking for some Lao rebels and had no hostile intentions. Soon after, an invasion led by local mountain chiefs was defeated.[52] Within a few months, Shih had dramatically changed the situation.

Although Wang Shih had improved T'ang's position in An-nam, authority was being challenged throughout the southern half of the empire. In the single year 858, serious rebellions broke out in Kuang, Hu-nan, Chiang-hsi, and again in Jung.[53] The situation in Jung held the threat of severing land communication between An-nam and the empire, so a special army was established there to deal with rebels and to insure communications. This army was called the Yellow Head Army, for the soldiers wore yellow bands around their heads.

It is recorded that "in An-nam were traitorous persons who often rebelled"; in early autumn of 858, these persons were agitated by a rumor that the Yellow Head Army had embarked to attack them by surprise. One evening they surrounded La-thanh and demanded that Wang Shih return north and allow them to fortify the city against the Yellow Head Army. Shih was eating his evening meal when this commotion broke out. It is reported that, paying no heed to the mutineers, he leisurely finished his meal. Then, dressed in his battle gear, he appeared on the wall with his generals and admonished the crowd of rebels, who dispersed. The next morning, Shih's troops captured and beheaded some ringleaders of the affair.[54]

According to Chinese sources, Do Ton Thanh's son, Do Thu Trung, was involved in this mutiny. Thu Trung was probably nursing revenge for the death of his father at the hands of Li Cho four years earlier. Wang Shih was unable to lay hands on Thu Trung, so he attempted to sow dissention among Thu Trung's followers,[55] an expedient without long-range effect. This episode reveals that An-nam continued in a state of political turmoil, even during the relatively successful rule of a talented general.

For six years, ever since the beginning of Li Cho's rule, no taxes had been sent from An-nam to the T'ang capital, and soldiers in the protectorate had not received the bonuses they would have been given according to usual practice. In the two years he was in An-nam, Wang Shih succeeded in doing

52. For these events, see: Wang Shih's biography (HTS, 167, 9a–b); TCTC, 249, vol. 13, 555–56; TT, 5, 8b–9a; CL, 101. The invasion by the mountain chiefs is dated in the sixth month of the year by: CTS, 18c, 19b; HTS, 8, 13b; TCTC, 249, vol. 13, 558.

53. HTS, 8, 13a–b.

54. Ibid., 167, 9b; TCTC, 249, vol. 13, 559; TT, 5, 9b.

55. See TCTC, 249, vol. 13, 559, for the link between Do Thu Trung and the mutiny; the TCTC states that Wang Shih succeeded in alienating Thu Trung from his family and followers, forcing him to flee and causing his death, but Ssu-ma Kuang, in a later note (vol. 13, 588), calls this a confusion in the light of firmer evidence that Thu Trung was later killed by Li Hu.

both. In addition to momentarily intimidating the spirit of rebellion in the protectorate and its potential ally Nan-chao, Shih's reputation also drew envoys from the Chams and the Khmers. If Shih had remained in An-nam, the worst of the Nan-chao War might have been avoided, but early in 860 he was recalled to put down a rebellion elsewhere in the empire.[56]

Wang Shih's successor, Li Hu, inherited a seemingly stable situation. Yet, within one year, Hu's rash deeds undid all that Shih had accomplished. His first mistake was to execute Do Thu Trung. The death of Thu Trung's father at the hands of Li Cho had contributed to the outbreak of warfare in 854, and the Do family was clearly recognized by Chinese officials as a threat to their authority. Li Hu inflamed the situation by having Thu Trung killed, thereby alienating many of the powerful families in An-nam.

Li Hu's second mistake was to depart the protectorate in search of military glory. One month before his arrival in An-nam, Nan-chao had seized Po Province, in modern Kuei-chou. Anxious to make a name for himself, Hu led an army to retake Po. In his absence, the Do family gathered a great host, thirty thousand men in all, which included contingents from Nan-chao. Hu returned from his successful adventure in Po to find that An-nam had slipped from his control. In the last month of 860, La-thanh fell, and Hu fled north to Yung.[57]

In the first month of 861, the garrisons in Yung and neighboring jurisdictions were ordered into An-nam. By the middle of the year, Li Hu had recaptured La-thanh, but Nan-chao forces simply moved around to his rear and seized Yung. Hu was banished to Hai-nan Island for incompetence and was replaced by Wang K'uan.[58]

Unlike Li Hu, whose desire for acclaim had prompted him to storm mindlessly from one place to another, K'uan attempted to effect a policy of conciliation. Recognizing the power of the Do family, the court decided to seek its cooperation; an edict was sent to K'uan granting a posthumous title to Do Ton Thanh along with an apology for the deaths of both him and his son and an admission that Li Hu had exceeded his authority.[59] This conciliatory policy was an expedient arising from a position of weakness.

Very little is known of the Do family, although its role in these years

56. *HTS*, 9, 1a, and 167, 9b; *TCTC*, 249, vol. 13, 559, and 250, vol. 13, 572; *TT*, 5, 9b–10b.

57. The fall of Po to Nan-chao is dated in the twelfth month of 859 by *HTS*, 9, 1a, and *TCTC*, 249, vol. 13, 569. Li Hu retook Po Province in the tenth month of 860 and was forced to flee from An-nam in the twelfth month, according to *HTS*, 9, 1b, and *TCTC*, 250, vol. 13, 580–81. These events are also cited in: *HTS*, 222b, 1b; *CL*, 101; *VSL*, 1, 11a; and *TT*, 5, 9b–10a. On the role of the Do family and its alliance with Nan-chao, see *TCTC*, 250, vol. 13, 581, 587, and *TT*, 5, 10a.

58. *TCTC*, 250, vol. 13, 586, 588; *TT*, 5, 10a; *VSL*, 1, 11a. *HTS*, 9, 1b, dates Wang K'uan's appointment in the sixth month of the year. On Li Hu's banishment, see *TCTC*, 250, vol. 13, 587, and *VSL*, 1, 11a.

59. *TCTC*, 250, vol. 13, 587.

was evidently of great importance. A prominent family in Vietnam for nearly four centuries, it was apparently the prime mover of the alliance between anti-T'ang Vietnamese and the peoples of the mountains. The fact that leaders of this family in two successive generations were beheaded by the Chinese suggests that they were perceived by T'ang officials as serious threats. The Do had actively resisted Li Cho, Wang Shih, and Li Hu. Now, the T'ang court hoped that if the Do could be placated, peace would ensue. However, events had evolved beyond the control of either the Vietnamese or the Chinese; the choice of war or peace now lay with Nan-chao.

Up to this time, Nan-chao had followed a cautious policy of probing raids and joint operations with allies inside An-nam. Early in 862, the character of the war changed when Nan-chao launched a full-scale invasion of its own. Wang K'uan sent repeated pleas for reinforcements, but he was replaced by Ts'ai Hsi, who arrived with a newly assembled army of thirty thousand men. Within a few months, Hsi had stalled Nan-chao's offensive; the war subsided to raids and skirmishes as the opposing generals assessed the situation.[60]

As a result of the war, T'ang authority in the south was reorganized. Ts'ai Ching was named to a newly established military governorship with headquarters in Yung. Ching's jurisdiction included An-nam. He was jealous of Ts'ai Hsi and feared that Hsi's success would overshadow his own reputation. In the summer of 862, Ching reported that Nan-chao had withdrawn into the mountains and that there was no threat of further warfare; he recommended that the army sent into An-nam with Hsi be retired. The T'ang court approved this recommendation, and Hsi's army was ordered to return.

Hsi responded with a report that not only had the enemy not withdrawn, but hostilities were continuing, while his men were exhausted and short of supplies; he submitted a list of ten points to support his declaration that withdrawal of the army was a matter of life or death for him. The court ignored his appeal and stood by the recommendation of his superior. The army was withdrawn, and Hsi was left to face the enemy forces with only a small imperial guard and the local army.[61]

Ts'ai Ching had meanwhile alienated his subordinates with his corrupt habits, and, in the autumn of the year, he was driven out of Yung by the army stationed there. He was banished to Hai-nan Island, but immediately returned without authorization and was forced to commit suicide.

Emboldened by the withdrawal of the imperial army and the confusion of the Ts'ai Ching affair, Nan-chao returned to the offensive at the end

60. CTS, 19a, 2b, 3b; HTS, 9, 1b; TCTC, 250, vol. 13, 590–91; TT, 5, 10b; VSL, 1, 11b; CL, 101. The TCTC and the TT, which follows it, contain the fullest accounts.

61. TCTC, 250, vol. 13, 592; TT, 5, 10b–11a; VSL, 1, 11b.

of the year with an army of fifty thousand. Hsi called for reinforcements, and a force of five thousand was hastily assembled at Yung, but it was feared that Nan-chao would strike Yung if this reserve force should advance into An-nam, so Hsi was ordered to retreat to Sea Gate. However, Hsi was by this time already besieged in La-thanh, and an emergency force of one thousand failed to reach him.[62]

In the first month of 863, La-thanh fell after a siege of twenty-four days. Wounded by an arrow in his left shoulder, Hsi managed to escape to the Hong River. His boat, however, capsized in midstream, and he drowned. When the rear guard of four hundred men reached the river, there were no boats left. The commanding officer roused his men to the glory of their hopeless situation, and they fought their way back into the citadel, killing, it is said, two thousand of the enemy before succumbing. It is recorded that a total of one hundred fifty thousand T'ang soldiers were killed or captured by Nan-chao during 862 and 863; of course, many of these were men levied in An-nam. It would be more than two and a half years before a T'ang army was ready to challenge Nan-chao again. In the meantime, the armies from the mountains spread over the protectorate to reap the benefits of conquest.[63]

Nan-chao left an occupying force of twenty thousand in An-nam under the command of General Yang Ssu-chin at La-thanh. Anti-T'ang Vietnamese may have welcomed Nan-chao's intervention to begin with, but they were pushed aside by the great hosts pouring out of the mountains. The population was scattered, and their homes plundered. It is recorded that

> Many refugees dwelt in the caves and ravines of An-nam, and the number of [refugee] civil and military officials constantly arriving at Sea Gate was not small.... military leaders appeared in the caves and ravines of An-nam, leaders who enjoyed popular confidence and governed even while the barbarians plundered; they assumed command of fortified towns and stood up as local heroes, individually defending the frontier lands according to their reputations. In the caves and ravines, all was confusion.[64]

This passage, with its stress on a refugee population living in "caves and ravines," gives an idea of the great impact of the war on Vietnamese society. Popular leaders stood up to defend the people against the reign of plunder. The passage implies that villages were emptied and the population scattered far and wide.

This was a painful moment in Vietnamese history. Anti-T'ang leaders

---

62. On the Ts'ai Ching affair and the Nan-chao offensive, see: *HTS*, 9, 1b–2a; *TCTC*, 250, vol. 13, 594–95; *TT*, 5, 11a.

63. *HTS*, 9, 2a; *TCTC*, 250, vol. 13, 597–98; *TT*, 5, 11a–12a; *VSL*, 1, 11b; *CL*, 101–2; *MS*, 101.

64. *CTS*, 19a, 4a.

had been betrayed by their ostensible allies, and the pro-T'ang faction had been let down by their patron. The anguish of this experience extended far into China as well, for thousands of Chinese soldiers perished in Vietnam, provoking the poet P'i Jih-hsiu to risk his career in officialdom by publicly denouncing T'ang policy there.[65]

Nan-chao followed its conquest of An-nam with major raids into Yung as had been feared. In the summer of 863, ten thousand soldiers were rushed to Sea Gate, where K'ang Ch'eng-hsün assumed the position of military governor with responsibility for the Nan-chao problem. A government-in-exile for the protectorate was established at Sea Gate with Sung Jung in charge; ten thousand new troops were raised in Shan-tung and placed under his command.

With soldiers from all over the empire concentrating at Sea Gate, the problem of supply became acute. A system of supply by sea was soon organized, using a fleet of one thousand ships to bring grain from Fu-chien, a journey of less than a month. Although there was great abuse as officials confiscated merchant vessels and dumped their cargoes, then forced ship-owners to make good losses occasioned by shipwreck, still the armies were fed.[66]

At the beginning of 864, Sung Jung was replaced by the imperial commissioner at Sea Gate, Chang Yin. Yin was given command of twenty-five thousand soldiers and ordered to retake An-nam. However, K'ang Ch'eng-hsün was engaged in heavy fighting with Nan-chao in Yung during the first half of the year, and Yin dared not advance; consequently, he was replaced by Kao P'ien at the beginning of autumn.[67]

Kao P'ien was a general who had made his reputation fighting Turks in the north. A man of great pride and ability, he considered preparation the key to success in any enterprise. After his arrival at Sea Gate, month after month passed as he trained his men and gathered intelligence. Li Wei-chou, the military governor at Sea Gate, envied P'ien's command and repeatedly accused him of moving too slowly. The two men did not get along. When P'ien finally sailed for the protectorate in the summer of 865, Wei-chou remained behind in command of the reserve force.

P'ien arrived in the protectorate by sea with only five thousand men. His move was well planned, however, for he surprised a Nan-chao army of fifty thousand as it lay scattered over the landscape collecting rice from the

---

65. See Appendix N.
66. *TCTC*, 250, vol. 13, 598–600; *TT*, 5, 12a–b; *CL*, 102; *VSL*, 1, 12a.
67. *TCTC*, 250, vol. 13, 603, 604, 605; *TT*, 5, 12b; *HTS*, 9, 2a, and 224c, 3b; *VSL*, 1, 12a. *CTS*, 19a, 4b, confuses K'ang Ch'eng-hsün's campaign in Yung with Kao P'ien's later campaign in An-nam.

villages. Completely routing the foe, P'ien captured large quantities of rice, which he used to feed his army.[68]

When the report of P'ien's victory reached Sea Gate, Wei-chou did not forward it to the imperial court. After several months had passed, the court sent an inquiry. Wei-chou's reply accused P'ien of stalling before the enemy. The court accordingly sent a general named Wang Yen-ch'üan to replace P'ien.

In the meantime, P'ien had been reinforced by seven thousand men who arrived overland under the command of Wei Chung-tsai. In the spring of 866, P'ien defeated a fresh Nan-chao army and chased it into the mountains. Then, he turned to deal with enemy forces now cut off in the plains. By the fall of the year, P'ien was preparing the siege of La-thanh, where the last of the enemy had taken refuge.[69]

It was at this time that P'ien learned of Wei-chou's intrigue and of the appointment of Yen-ch'üan. He accordingly sent his aide-de-camp Tseng Kun to travel directly to the capital and report the true situation; Wang Hui-tsan, an official on Chung-tsai's staff, accompanied Kun. As Kun and Hui-tsan sailed through the Bay of Along, they were forced to hide on an island to avoid a fleet bringing Wei-chou and Yen-ch'üan to the protectorate. P'ien was ten days into the siege of La-thanh when he heard of the approach of Wei-chou and Yen-ch'üan. Leaving his army in the hands of Chung-tsai, P'ien took one hundred men and departed overland for Sea Gate.

When Wei-chou and Yen-ch'üan arrived in An-nam, all military activity ceased. Yen-ch'üan lacked imagination and left all decisions to Wei-chou; Wei-chou was quick-tempered and alienated the officers of P'ien's army. Refusing to cooperate with the new commanders, the officers lifted the siege, and more than half of the trapped enemy escaped to the mountains.

After reaching the capital and making their report, Kun and Hui-tsan hastened back to Sea Gate with P'ien's reinstatement. P'ien immediately returned to the protectorate, renewed the siege, and beheaded thirty thousand enemy who had remained in La-thanh.[70]

The striking contrast between the rancorous years leading up to the

---

68. *TCTC*, 250, vol. 13, 608; *TT*, 5, 13a–b; *CL*, 102. *CTS*, 19a, 6b, makes this a victory over "Lin-i." The *CTS* likewise attributes an invasion of An-nam to "Lin-i" in the ninth month of 861 (19a, 2b) and the fall of the protectorate in 863 to "Lao who induced Lin-i barbarians to attack An-nam" (19a, 4a). These are confusions, for the name Lin-i is incongruous in the context of the ninth century. It can be assumed, however, that the Chams did not neglect this opportunity to extend their influence northward; they were aware of events in An-nam, as demonstrated by their sending envoys to Wang Shih. Nan-chao occupied the Hong River plain; as for Ai and Hoan, there is no information, but the Chams may well have moved in.

69. *TCTC*, 250, vol. 13, 610–11; *TT*, 5, 13b–14a.

70. *HTS*, 224c, 3b; *VSL*, 1, 12a–b; *TCTC*, 250, vol. 13, 611–12; *TT*, 5, 14a–b; *CL*, 102.

Nan-chao War and the era of peace that followed suggest that the war saw important changes in Vietnamese political life. The anti-T'ang elements that had solicited Nan-chao's intervention are not heard of again. We can reasonably assume that the anti-T'ang leadership was either destroyed or permanently forced into the mountains by the end of the war.

The confrontation that culminated in the Nan-chao War reveals two opposing cultural currents in ninth-century Vietnam. The T'ang-Viet culture of Giao was heavily Buddhist and depended on T'ang to maintain order. In the frontier areas, it is appropriate to speak of a Muong-Viet culture, a culture of resistance to T'ang. The thirty thousand men beheaded by Kao P'ien when he captured La-thanh surely included an important part of the local anti-T'ang leadership. More than half of the besieged, however, had escaped to the mountains during P'ien's brief absence from the protectorate. The retreat of anti-T'ang forces into the mountains at this time may well have sealed the separation of Muong from Vietnamese, which linguistic evidence suggests took place at the end of T'ang.[71]

The ninth century appears to have been a particularly formative era in Vietnam. Whether this is simply a reflection of the relative abundance of information from that time or whether it represents deeper currents of national experience is difficult to say. The ninth century was a time of greatly diminished imperial power. Consequently, the Vietnamese were much freer in their reaction to imperial authority, both in a positive and in a negative way.

The Vietnamese reacted with some interest to the enlightened rule of Chao Ch'ang, Chang Chou, and Ma Tsung, and actively participated in the government. The more repressive and unreasonable rule of P'ei Hsing-li and Li Hsiang-ku, however, provoked violence and prolonged instability. The troubled years that followed Duong Thanh's uprising and culminated in the Nan-chao War were filled with tension between anti-T'ang and pro-T'ang groups. Protector generals were either killed or chased out in 803, 819, 828, 843, 860, and 863. Only the rule of Ma Chih provided a much-needed respite in the 830s.

T'ang attempts to collect taxes seem to have been viewed by the Vietnamese as a provocation. When Han Yüeh successfully collected enough taxes to replenish the local treasury in 828, he was driven out. The decree of 836 cited popular disaffection and the danger that T'ang garrisons might be overrun as reasons for remitting the autumn tax of that year, and money was sent down from the north to provide for government expenses. In 858, Wang Shih finally managed to collect taxes, after six years during which T'ang officials had been unable to collect anything. A decree of 863 remitted

---

71. Nguyen Linh and Hoang Xuan Chinh, "Dat nuoc va con nguoi thoi Hung Vuong," pp. 103–4.

the "double tax" and all other obligations for a period of two years.[72] This, of course, was when Nan-chao was in control of An-nam. After the Nan-chao War, grain and other supplies were sent from China to Vietnam to meet postwar needs. It is doubtful that T'ang collected any more taxes from this time on.

The war ended with the formal reassertion of T'ang rule over Vietnam. But T'ang was already far down the road to collapse, and the regime that emerged from the postwar reconstruction was the first of a number of transitional regimes that finally led to the establishment of an independent Vietnamese monarchy.

If T'ang had failed to win the war, it is difficult to imagine how Vietnamese society would have developed. As it happened, the outcome of the Nan-chao War affirmed Vietnam's long-standing ties to Chinese civilization. This was as much a decision of the Vietnamese as it was of T'ang, for many Vietnamese seem to have viewed Kao P'ien as a liberator who freed them from Nan-chao's reign of plunder.

Yet, T'ang was now too weak to dominate Vietnam. T'ang, in its weakness, finally gave the Vietnamese what in its strength it was too proud to grant. The Vietnamese now had the benefits of an imperial umbrella without the unhappiness of direct imperial rule. Postwar Vietnamese leaders maintained formal allegiance to the theory of Chinese empire long after the collapse of T'ang dynastic power, which may illustrate how attractive a culture can look when it is not politically threatening.

72. *CTS*, 19 (Katakura, p. 35).

7
Independence

Reconstruction

Kao P'ien earned a good reputation among the Vietnamese, and his efforts to rebuild the war-torn land were praised by later Vietnamese historians.[1] One of the first tasks taken up by P'ien was rebuilding the capital city. The new city was called Dai-la,[2] and it remained the political center of Vietnam for nearly eighty years.

The wall of the new city was twenty-five feet high and about four miles in circumference. Guard posts, courtyards, roads, a water-drainage system, and several thousand buildings were constructed within the wall, which was ringed by a dike some fifteen feet high.

1. *TT*, 5, 14b–15a, 16a–b.
2. In my narrative, I have referred to three cities, all in the vicinity of modern Hanoi. The first was Tu-thanh, built by Ch'iu Ho in 618. In 768, Chang Po-i built the first La-thanh; the walls of this La-thanh were repaired by Chao Ch'ang after 791 and were enlarged to form the first Dai-la by Chang Chou between 806 and 809. In 825, this Dai-la was abandoned, apparently because it was dismantled by rebels, and Li Yüan-hsi built a second La-thanh, which was rebuilt by Kao P'ien to form the second Dai-la. This interpretation is essentially the same as that of H. Maspero, "Le Protectorat general d'Annam sous les T'ang," pp. 553–56, and is sufficient for the purposes of this narrative. There are enough obscurities in the sources, however, to warrant further study of the question. *MS*, 92–93, 97, and 101, speaks of four cities in the year 863: Tu-thanh, To-lich Old City, Giao Province City, and East La-thanh. Nguyen Phuc Long, "Les Nouvelles Recherches archéologiques au Vietnam," pp. 24–25, has argued that the terms *la-thanh* and *dai-la* (*thanh*) should not be used as proper names, for they simply refer to a certain kind of wall, or outer fortification, and not to the city itself. The same can be said to apply to *tu-thanh*, which, strictly speaking, refers to a kind of inner citadel. Despite the logic of this argument, I think there is good reason to believe that these terms gained common currency in Vietnam as proper names. The edict cited in the following note reveals that a Vietnamese king in 1010 considered Dai-la to be the proper name of the city built by Kao P'ien. Nguyen Phuc Long wants to call this city Tong-binh, after the name of the district where it was located, but there is no evidence that it was ever called by that name. The four cities mentioned by the *MS* can be conceived as parts of a single metropolis, with Tu-thanh being the inner citadel, Giao Province City the city in general, East La-thanh a suburb along the eastern ramparts, and To-lich Old City another suburb. The *MS* narrative nevertheless implies that these were distinct places. Of Kao P'ien's city, *TCTC*, 250, vol. 13, 612, says the wall was three thousand paces in circumference; *TT*, 5, 14b–15a, says 1,982 *chang*, 5 *ch'ih*; *VSL*, 1, 12b, says 1,980 *chang*, 5 *ch'ih*. H. Maspero, "Le Protectorat general," p. 557, discusses these measurements. *VSL*, 1, 12b, says the new city contained five thousand buildings. *TCTC*, 250, vol. 13, 612, and *TT*, 5, 14b–15a, say four hundred thousand buildings; H. Maspero, "Le Protectorat general," p. 558, n. 1, believed this to be an error. The height of the dike was 1 *chang*, 5 *ch'ih*, according to *TT*, 5, 14b–15a, and *VSL*, 1, 12b.

Almost a century and a half later, after Dai-la had been abandoned for over fifty years, the founder of the Ly dynasty moved his capital to this place and built Thang-long, the city that eventually became Hanoi. In a proclamation announcing the move, the Ly monarch criticized the narrow view of his predecessors, who had ruled from a mountain fortress, and then went on to cite Kao P'ien's precedent:

> It is especially impossible for me not to move when there exists the old capital of King Kao at Dai-la, between heaven and earth, where the dragon can coil and the tiger is able to sit, in the midst of north and south and east and west, with a good view of the mountains behind and the river in front, where the earth is spacious and flat and high and clear, where the inhabitants are not oppressed by flooding, where the earth is fertile and prosperous, a site overlooking the entire land of Viet; it is the best spot imaginable, where the four directions meet, the location for a capital that will last ten thousand ages.[3]

This proclamation reveals a happy memory of Kao P'ien's city capable of recommending the site to later Vietnamese kings. The dragon and tiger were symbols of power. The so-called "Dai-la era" of the late ninth and early tenth centuries was a period of peace and prosperity, and it was Kao P'ien, remembered as "King Kao," who laid the foundations for this auspiciously recalled regime.

It is recorded that P'ien constructed roads, bridges, and public inns throughout the protectorate. Dikes and canals were built and repaired. The terrain was inspected and mapped out. Spirit shrines, Buddhist and Taoist temples, and a temple to the God of Thunder were constructed.[4]

The God of Thunder was associated with P'ien himself, for when P'ien sent a crew to dredge the sea approaches to An-nam and to remove hidden obstructions, two stubborn rocks resisted all drills and chisels until a sudden thunder storm broke them off. The clearing of these dangerous waters had been attempted for centuries; P'ien's success with the aid of what was perceived to be supernatural power was taken as a sign of his virtue.[5]

Before he left An-nam, Kao P'ien ordered his bookkeepers to write down all that had been accomplished. The officials who supervised this program of public works further requested that their labors be commemorated with the erection of a stele. In 870, a tablet was set up in Kao P'ien's name with the following inscription:

3. *TT*, under the year 1010 (*Ban ky*, 2, 2a).

4. *CL*, 104.

5. *HTS*, 224c, 3b–4a; *CTS*, 19a, 7b; *TCTC*, 250, vol. 13, 615; *VSL*, 1, 12b–13a; *CL*, 103–4; *TT*, 5, 15b–16a. The theme of abolishing navigation hazards with supernatural assistance through a violent storm is shared with Wang Shen-chih, who founded the empire of Min in the tenth century; see Edward Schafer, *Empire of Min*, pp. 102–3.

Heaven and earth are boundless;
Man's strength is but a trifle.
Banish distress by bringing food;
Prosperity comes riding in boats.
Breaking free of this strange affair,
Not just defeat but prolonged destruction,
I devised plans against civil disorder,
For excavating mountains and splitting rocks,
For meritoriously caring for those in need,
Thus rousing the power of thunderbolts,
Causing the sea to form a channel,
Where boats can pass in safety,
With the deep sea stretching out peacefully,
A highway of supply for our city.
The way of Heaven is the foundation of prosperity;
The majesty of the spirits supports and maintains.[6]

The inscription suggests that Kao P'ien's first concern was to feed the people. Judging from the lines "Banish distress by bringing food; / Prosperity comes riding in boats" and the reference to the sea route from China as "a highway of supply for our city," we can assume that considerable assistance was sent from the north. In the last two lines, the "way of Heaven," which sanctioned imperial authority, and the "majesty of the spirits," which presided over the local culture, are cited as complementary powers working for the good of the people. This is an indirect reference to a cultural revival in Vietnam that accompanied the material reconstruction.

Like Chao Ch'ang seventy years earlier, Kao P'ien familiarized himself with the indigenous culture. According to tradition, P'ien was fond of the spiritual arts. It is said that, after setting up camp when he first arrived in An-nam, he erected an altar and offered sacrifices, calling on the local spirits. One night a spirit spoke to him in a dream and encouraged him in his efforts to bring peace and good government to the land. He responded by erecting a shrine to the spirit.[7]

The spirit of Ly Ong Trong, which had been sought out and worshipped by Chao Ch'ang, was thought to have been of great assistance to P'ien in his battles with Nan-chao; P'ien had a statue carved of the ancient giant and sacrificed to it. The spirit of To Lich, which had appeared to Li Yüan-hsi in 825, also appeared to P'ien; P'ien worshipped it and declared it the protective spirit of Dai-la. On one occasion, P'ien was visited by the spirit of Shih Hsieh; they reportedly discussed the history of the Three

6. *CL*, 104.
7. *VDULT*, 40–41.

Kingdoms, and P'ien later commemorated the meeting with a four-line poem.[8]

According to another tradition, P'ien was visited by the spirit of Cao Lo, the man who had constructed the crossbow with the turtle-claw trigger for King An Duong in the third century B.C. P'ien had heard that Lo was slandered by the Lac lords, who thereby obtained his execution; he asked the spirit why he was so hated by the Lac lords. Lo's reply reveals that he was an outsider of northern origin and, for that reason, was not tolerated. This association of P'ien with Lo and the nature of their conversation seem to express P'ien's own sense of his position as an outsider. P'ien commemorated his interview with Cao Lo by composing the following poem:

> The land of Giao Province is beautiful;
> So has it been from eternity.
> The worthy men of old extend their welcome;
> Then one is not ungrateful to the spirits.[9]

This poem suggests that P'ien's interest in the scenery and cultural heritage of Vietnam was more than casual.

The tradition explaining P'ien's departure from Vietnam is also linked to the spirit world. One morning at the break of dawn, P'ien was strolling outside the gates of Dai-la. Pausing on the bank of the river, he stood gazing into the water. Suddenly a great wind arose, and the water erupted in billowing waves. The sky was darkened by clouds, and swirling mists covered the land. Then, P'ien saw an extraordinary man, more than twenty feet tall, standing on the water; the man wore a yellow robe and a purple hat, and held a gold document in his hand. P'ien was greatly alarmed at this apparition and decided to exorcise it.

That night as P'ien slept, the apparition appeared to him in a dream and said:

> Do not try to exorcise me. I am the spirit of the Dragon's Belly, first among the supernatural powers of this land; I heard that you came to build a city here and, since we had not yet met, I came to see you; if you resort to exorcism, I am not worried.

In the independence period the term "Dragon's Belly" (*Long-do*) became synonymous with the capital city; it connoted the realm's spiritual center of gravity.

In spite of this warning, P'ien built an altar and arranged bronze and iron to exorcise the spirit. But the metals burned to ash in the midst of a violent thunderstorm. Seeing this, P'ien said:

8. On Ly Ong Trong, see *VDULT*, 16, and *LNCQ*, 19. On the protective spirit of Dai-la, see *VDULT*, 19, and *LNCQ*, 34. On Shih Hsieh, see *VDULT*, 2.

9. *VDULT*, 29.

This place has a spirit with unusual powers; it will not be possible for me to remain here very long without meeting misfortune. I must return north as soon as possible.[10]

The tradition of P'ien and the spirit of the land became a popular tale, and to this day it is used to inspire and to express patriotic sentiment against foreign domination.

The Protectorate of An-nam was officially abolished at the end of 866 after Kao P'ien's victory over Nan-chao. It was replaced by the Peaceful Sea Army, commanded by a military governor.[11] This was the beginning of a new era in Vietnamese history. Not much is known of the government established by Kao P'ien. Although T'ang officials remained until 880, centralized dynastic power was no longer strong enough to have any impact on Vietnam, and a new regional ruling class appeared.

Judging from the people holding power when T'ang finally disappeared, we can surmise that this new ruling class was rooted in great landowning families of the Giao agricultural heartland. These people governed Vietnam for nearly a century before giving way to forces that moved steadily toward full independence from the Chinese political realm. The post-T'ang ruling class was independent in fact, yet it was limited by the cultural assumptions of T'ang civilization. The gradual weaning of the Vietnamese from the symbols and concepts of T'ang authority began under the leadership of Kao P'ien's two successors, his grandson Kao Hsün and his aide-de-camp Tseng Kun.

It is sometimes imagined that Vietnamese independence appeared as the result of so-called "indigenous" forces breaking through a superficial crust of Chinese influence, and to some degree this is accurate. But we must also accept Kao P'ien's role in Vietnam as an indigenous factor. What he did could not have been accomplished without broad Vietnamese support, and the way he was remembered reveals that his labors represented what the Vietnamese themselves wished for their land.

The art and architecture that began to flourish at this time have been called the "Dai-la style," an early type of what became standard Vietnamese styles in later centuries.[12] This was a time of peace and prosperity. The passing of the T'ang dynasty went virtually unnoticed as a stable regional political system emerged to replace the protectorate. The preceding half

10. *LNCQ*, 34–35. A less detailed and slightly different version of the story appears in *VDULT*, 32–33.

11. On the abolition of the protectorate, see: *HTS*, 224c, 3b; *TCTC*, 250, vol. 13, 612; *LNCQ*, 34; *TT*, 5, 14b–15a; *VSL*, 1, 12b; *CL*, 102.

12. On the "Dai-la style," see L. Bezacier, *L'Art vietnamien*, p. 199. This term is no longer favored by Vietnamese scholars; see Nguyen Phuc Long, p. 25.

century of political violence was, in effect, the shaking off of direct T'ang rule.

Shortly after the end of the Nan-chao War, T'ang began its final slide into ruin. The first overt sign of this in the south was the revolt of P'ang Hsün in 868. Among the soldiers levied in 862 and sent to deal with the Nan-chao invasion was a contingent from what is now Chiang-su, at the mouth of the Yangtze River. For six years the soldiers of this unit had been garrisoned in Kuei; their repeated demands to be returned to their homes were ignored because the government could not afford the expense of sending them back. At the end of summer in 868, they rebelled under the leadership of a minor official named P'ang Hsün and marched back to their home districts, plundering as they went and defeating all who resisted them. This uprising attracted thousands of adherents and was not put down for more than a year.[13]

P'ang Hsün's rebellion was simply a sign of the times, and a man of Kao P'ien's ability could not be spared to idle away his time in a quiet corner of the empire. At the beginning of autumn in 868, P'ien was recalled to the north; he recommended that his grandson Kao Hsün succeed him as military governor at Dai-la.[14]

Nothing is known of Kao Hsün, though it can be assumed that he continued the successful policy of his grandfather. Somewhat more is known of Tseng Kun, who succeeded Hsün in the late 870's, for he collected local traditions and recorded them in a book that was used by later Vietnamese historians. Tseng Kun was remembered by the Vietnamese as a good and humane ruler; it is recorded that the people called him "Minister Tseng."[15]

Although Kun's book no longer exists, portions of it have been preserved in later Vietnamese works. Some of the traditions connected with Kao P'ien are derived from his book, as was the tradition of Li Yüan-hsi and the spirit of To Lich. The ancient Vietnamese myth of the battle between the Mountain Spirit and the Water Spirit, a theme reminiscent of the Nan-chao War, was also included in the book. In a prologue to this myth, Kun described in some detail how the ancient Hung kings of Vietnam were

---

13. *TCTC*, 251, vol. 13, 619–20; Robert des Retours, "La Revolte de P'ang Huin (868–869)," pp. 229–40.

14. *HTS*, 224c, 4a; *TCTC*, 251, vol. 13, 620; *VSL*, 1, 13a; *CL*, 105; *TT*, 5, 16b–17a.

15. *CL*, 105, dates Tseng Kun's appointment in 877. *TT*, 5, 16b–17a, says that Kao P'ien and Kao Hsün governed a total of thirteen years: P'ien from 866 to 874, and Hsun from 875 to 878. The *TT* erroneously assumes that P'ien was not succeeded by Hsün until his appointment as military governor in Ssu-ch'uan at the beginning of 875 (*TCTC*, 252, vol. 13, 685). He was in fact succeeded by Hsün in 868 (*TCTC*, 251, vol. 13, 620). On Tseng Kun, see also *VSL*, 1, 13a.

bound to follow the advice of the Lac lords.[16] That situation probably approximated the relationship existing between the military governor and local leaders in Kun's own time. The revival of indigenous culture encouraged by Kao P'ien and his successors must surely have had its political corollary. The Vietnamese no longer thought of rebellion because they were given no excuse to do so.

Some poetry has survived from the brush of Tseng Kun. It reflects the new spirit prevailing among the Vietnamese. The first two lines of one poem place the empire in the more ancient context of the local scene:

> The mountains and rivers of the realm of Viet are old;
> The men of the House of T'ang are new.[17]

These lines seem to view the local culture as being on a level comparable with that of T'ang civilization. They also suggest that, while dynastic fortunes rise and fall, the cultural habits of a people, rooted in their land of birth and hardened by generations of usage, are among the more indestructible features of historical experience.

In the following poem, the relationship between the "Dragon Spirit" of the imperial throne and the Vietnamese realm, prophetically referred to as the "Southern Kingdom," is one of harmony and benefit:

> The mountains and rivers of the Southern Kingdom are beautiful;
> The place where the Dragon Spirit dwells is blessed.
> Giao Province has ceased to be pressed down;
> From now on there will be peace and prosperity.[18]

The reason the Vietnamese had "ceased to be pressed down" was that the Chinese were now too occupied with their own political problems to do any "pressing." T'ang was dying.

The End of T'ang

In 875, a rebellion broke out in northern China that, during the following decade, ravaged the entire empire and rendered the already faltering T'ang court virtually powerless. In 879, this rebellion spilled into the south when rebel leader Huang Ch'ao sacked Canton and put its inhabitants to the sword. The military governor at Canton, Li T'iao, was forced by Ch'ao to request imperial recognition of Ch'ao's authority in the south, including An-nam. This was refused, and T'iao was soon after killed

16. *VDULT*, 36–37.
17. Ibid., 29.
18. Ibid., loc cit.

by Ch'ao. In 880, after an epidemic had carried off 40 percent of his men, Ch'ao returned north by way of Kuei.[19]

The march of the rebel army westward from Canton and north through Kuei swept away the last vestiges of T'ang control over the Vietnamese. Only a few years earlier, in 876 and 877, soldiers withdrawn from Dai-la to Kuei had mutinied and were not brought under control for six months.[20] Huang Ch'ao's passage left surviving T'ang forces in the south stunned and demoralized. In 880, the T'ang garrison at Dai-la mutinied, forcing Tseng Kun to flee north. Thereafter, T'ang troops returned north in small groups on their own initiative.[21] Effective T'ang rule was accordingly finished in Vietnam.

At the end of 880 and the beginning of 881, Huang Ch'ao captured both T'ang capitals, forcing the emperor to flee to Ssu-ch'uan. Uncertain relations with Nan-chao added to the fears of T'ang officialdom in the south.[22] Huang Ch'ao was finally defeated in 884, but thereafter northern China fell prey to the ambitious men who would shortly usher in the so-called Five Dynasties period. Southern China, for the most part, remained aloof from the struggles in the north, maintaining a superficial loyalty to the T'ang court while awaiting the outcome of events.

There were ostensibly three military governors in the south: one at Canton, one of West Ling-nan, in modern Kuang-hsi, and one at Dai-la.

The military governorship at Canton developed into a regional power center under the leadership of Liu Yin. Yin's father had started the family's rise to power as a provincial commander in the wake of Huang Ch'ao's tour of the south.[23] In 897, Liu Yin quelled a rebellion against the military governor,[24] and in 898 he defeated an attempt by Tseng Kun, at this time a provincial governor in Kuei, to seize Canton.[25] When the military governor died at the end of 901, Yin was recognized as his acting successor.[26]

In 904, the T'ang court sent an official named Ts'ui Yüan to be military governor at Canton. However, Yin refused to receive him. Yüan feared to advance into the south, and the court accordingly recalled him. Yin thereupon sent gifts to Chu Ch'üan-chung, who shortly thereafter founded the Later Liang dynasty; Ch'üan-chung recognized Yin as military gover-

19. *TCTC*, 253, vol. 13, 729; *HTS*, 9, 6a, 6b; Howard Levy, trans. and annotator, "Biography of Huang Ch'ao," pp. 17–19.

20. *TCTC*, 252, vol. 13, 698, 705.

21. Ibid., 253, vol. 13, 736; *TT*, 5, 17a.

22. *CL*, 105.

23. Edward Schafer, "The History of the Empire of Southern Han," p. 347.

24. *TCTC*, 260, vol. 13, 1023. Schafer, "Southern Han," p. 348.

25. *TCTC*, 261, vol. 13, 1050.

26. Ibid., 262, vol. 13, 1097.

nor at Canton.[27] Liu Yin's family eventually founded the Southern Han dynasty.

The military governorship of West Ling-nan lacked a stable power base. This jurisdiction lay between the larger centers of Canton and Hu-nan. It had been created on the frontier in 862 during the Nan-chao emergency. In 882, the military governor of West Ling-nan was driven out when the army stationed in Kuei rebelled, and the imperial commissioner of Jung was named to replace him.[28] From 891 to 893, West Ling-nan was held by a military governor in Hu-nan, who subsequently rebelled and was beheaded.[29] In 895, Kuei fell under the control of an emerging power center in Hu-nan.[30] West Ling-nan was subsequently partitioned between the Hu-nan group and Canton, though as late as 900 a military governor was busy dealing with mutinous soldiers in Yung.[31]

The third military governorship in the south was assigned to the Peaceful Sea Army at Dai-la; after 880, this became an empty title. There is no clear evidence that anyone held the title of Peaceful Sea Army military governor from 880 to 901.[32] From 901 to 905, this title appeared in connection with three men, only one of whom may possibly have tried to go to Dai-la.

In the first month of 901, Sun Te-chao was appointed Peaceful Sea Army military governor; five days later he was named "Military Governor of An-nam."[33] At the same time, two other men were named military governors in Jung and Yung. These appointments were made by Chu Ch'üan-chung to dispose of undesirable officials left over from the powerless T'ang court; it is certain that none of these men ever went south.

The one man who may have at least attempted to go to Dai-la was Chu Ch'üan-yü, Ch'üan-chung's elder brother. In the second month of 905 he was dismissed from his position as "Military Governor of An-nam" by his younger brother because he was "stupid and without ability." The Chu

---

27. Ibid., 265, vol. 13, 1177.

28. *HTS*, 9, 9a; *TCTC*, 255, vol. 13, 791.

29. *TCTC*, 258, vol. 13, 938, and 259, vol. 13, 974–75.

30. Ibid., 260, vol. 13, 1010.

31. Ibid., 262, vol. 13, 1062.

32. The chart in *MS*, 336, lists three men during this period: one in the year 882, one in 884, and one for the years 897–900. These men do not to my knowledge appear in the dynastic histories. *CL*, 105, lists two men after Tseng Kun but without dates; one is identified as a governor of Ai, the other as an "An-nam Protector General" whose son-in-law obtained the governorship of Hoan, where he governed avariciously, cruelly, and without restraint. The *CL* often lists men out of chronological order; the title "An-nam Protector General" was defunct after 866. The last recorded exiles were casualties of court intrigues during the reign of I Tsung (860–73); in 869 one man was sent to Ai, and in 870 two men were sent to Hoan (*TCTC*, 251, vol. 13, 650, and *CL*, 111).

33. *CTS*, 20a, 23a.

family was of peasant stock, and Ch'üan-yü was an acknowledged rustic. If Ch'üan-yü did indeed travel south, it was certainly after the alliance between Ch'üan-chung and Liu Yin in Canton was concluded; this was not until the last month of 904. Therefore, Ch'üan-yü would have had two months at most between his appointment and his dismissal. Either he did not go south, or else he attempted to but failed because of the political situation at Dai-la.[34]

In the third month of 905, Tu-ku Sun was appointed to succeed Ch'üan-yü. Ch'üan-chung was now in the final stages of eliminating untrustworthy holdovers from the old T'ang court. Tu-ku Sun was such a person, as was Ts'ui Yüan, who had been turned back from Canton by Liu Yin the previous year. Sun's and Yüan's careers were henceforth parallel. In the fifth month of the year, a mere fifty-six days after Sun's appointment as military governor at Dai-la, both men were named to governorships in Shantung; eight days later they were exiled to the south, Sun to Hai-nan Island, Yüan to the adjacent mainland; seven days later they were ordered to commit suicide. It is doubtful that either of these men ever stirred from the capital during this time.[35]

In the first month of 906, a man from Giao named Khuc Thua Du obtained appointment as military governor at Dai-la. A year and a half later, Thua Du died, and his son Hao was confirmed as his successor.[36] The process by which the Khuc family rose to power is unclear, but it was almost certainly peaceful. Later Vietnamese historians cited "unofficial records"

---

34. On Chu Ch'üan-yü's dismissal, see *TCTC*, 265, vol. 13, 1181, and *TT*, 5, 17a. The *VSL* (1, 13a) cites Ch'üan-yü as Tseng Kun's successor. On the alliance between Chu Ch'üanchung and Liu Yin, see *TCTC*, 265, vol. 13, 1177. Chu Ch'üan-yü's biography in *WTSC*, 13, 5b, says that Ch'üan-yü was "Shan-nan Western Circuit Military Governor"; no date is supplied. Shan-nan was a T'ang jurisdiction in Hu-pei, and it was divided into eastern and western circuits. Likewise, Ling-nan was divided into eastern and western circuits; East Lingnan was the official title of the military governorship at Canton. Shan-nan, "South of the Mountains," was sometimes used colloquially for Ling-nan, "South of the Passes," so the reference in Ch'üan-yü's biography could conceivably be to West Ling-nan. Such, indeed, is the interpretation of Tran Quoc Vuong in his translation of the *Viet su luoc*, p. 38, n. 3. If this were the case we might surmise that Ch'üan-yü traveled as far as the border between West Ling-nan and An-nam; however, I strongly suspect that Hu-pei is what is intended in the passage and that Ch'üan-yü never ventured into the south.

35. On Tu-ku Sun's appointment to succeed Chu Ch'üan-yü, see *CTS*, 20c, 4a–b, and *TCTC*, 265, vol. 13, 1181–82. On the final days of Tu-ku Sun and Ts'ui Yüan, see: *HTS*, 10, 9b–10a, 10b; *CTS*, 20c, 7a, 7b–8a; and *TCTC*, 265, vol. 13, 1183. *VSL*, 1, 13a–b, cites Tu-ku Sun as the successor of Chu Ch'üan-yü and adds the curious information that he was called the "Prison Minister." Perhaps this means that he was in prison during the time of his appointment as military governor at Dai-la.

36. On Khuc Thua Du'a appointment, see *TCTC*, 265, vol. 13, 1199. On Khuc Hao's appointment, see *TCTC*, 266, vol. 14, 13. Khuc Hao was appointed in the seventh month of 907, forty days after his father's death.

stating that the Khuc family was from an area in eastern Giao; the "unofficial records" further contained the following information on Khuc Thua Du:

> Thua Du was kindly and loving toward others; he was accordingly raised up by the esteem of the people; when Tseng Kun abandoned the city, Thua Du proclaimed himself military governor; he requested authority from the imperial court and the T'ang emperor conferred it.[37]

Since the authenticity of this information is not known, firm conclusions cannot be drawn from it. Yet, it is the only surviving account of the manner in which the Khuc rose to power.

When Tseng Kun fled northward in 880, followed by the remaining T'ang soldiers garrisoned at Dai-la, someone must have taken control. Since there is no indication of any struggle or political conflict from 880 to 906, when Khuc Thua Du first appears in Chinese records, it is reasonable to assume that the Khuc family was in control throughout these years. Thua Du died in 907 and was succeeded by his son; this suggests that the family was already well established by this time, for otherwise such a transition might not have been so casual. If the Khuc were indeed from eastern Giao, their prominence seems to indicate the power of interests associated with the imperial world. This is the area where Wu Hun, a protector general in the 840s, had settled; there was probably a strong Chinese community here. It is reasonable to view the Khuc as growing naturally out of the political system established by Kao P'ien and his successors.

The generation that lived through the Nan-chao War probably considered the peace established by Kao P'ien too precious to be thoughtlessly thrown away for personal ambition or political intrigue. The process of reconstruction after the war was not simply a matter of material well-being; it also required time to heal the wounds of the spirit. In such a time, the statement that Khuc Thua Du earned the esteem of his countrymen by his kindly and loving attitude toward others takes on significance.

The Khuc family ruled Vietnam until 930. They posed as loyal representatives of the Chinese imperial order. We can surmise that they represented the landowning class of Giao, which took advantage of Kao P'ien's victories to consolidate its hold over the frontier areas.

According to a seventeenth-century Chinese source, Khuc Hao "changed all districts and villages into sections [*chia*: that is, groups of ten households] and appointed an assistant to collect taxes."[38] This passage is of doubtful value, for the use of "sections" (*chia*) in local administration was

---

37. The "Unofficial Records" (*Da su*) were cited in the *Dai Viet su ky* of the late eighteenth century; see Yamamoto Tatsurō, "Annan ga Dokuritsu-koku o Keiseishitaru Katei no Kenkyū," p. 62.

    38. *CY*, 180–81.

not widespread in China until the eleventh century.[39] We can reasonably
surmise that some adjustments in local administration were made after the
departure of T'ang officials, though what these adjustments may have been is
a matter of conjecture. The idea of "sections" suggests a concept of community responsibility. This is the only source to mention abandonment of
the system of "prefectural and district administration," which had theoretically prevailed since the time of the Former Han.

The events of the tenth century indicate a revival of village politics as
an alternative to the old imperial administration. The Hoa-lu monarchy that
appeared in the 960s seems to have grown out of village politics. The Khuc
presided over an early phase of this process.

Khuc Thua My

As we have seen, Khuc Thua Du obtained imperial
recognition as military governor at Dai-la in early 906, and, when he died a
year and a half later, his son Hao was formally recognized in his place. At this
time T'ang was being superseded by the Later Liang dynasty of Chu
Ch'üan-chung. The new dynasty's accession posed a challenge to the Khuc
family, for new groups of men were coming into power in the north. Old
relationships that had been cultivated under T'ang were no longer politically useful, and the Khuc faced the danger of becoming outsiders in the new
system taking shape.

Although Later Liang endured for less than twenty years and as time
went on exerted less and less influence outside northern China, it was
originally viewed by contemporary observers as T'ang's legitimate heir, as
well as the potential restorer of imperial law and order. As it grew increasingly clear, however, that Later Liang was not able to perform this task,
powerful regional families proclaimed their independence, ushering in the
so-called Five Dynasties period of Chinese history, named after the five
dynasties that ruled northern China in less than sixty years. One of these
regional powers was the Liu family of Canton that claimed imperial status in
917. The Khuc quickly realized that the Liu posed a strong threat to their
position and consequently followed a policy of friendship with Later Liang
in the hope that it would restore the imperial peace.

Liu Yin had allied himself with Chu Ch'üan-chung as early as 904. So
when Ch'üan-chung took the throne in 907, the Khuc were anxious to have
their authority confirmed by the new dynasty. This became urgent in 908
when Khuc Hao died, for his appointment as military governor then
reverted to the imperial court, which was free to assign it to anyone of its
choice.

39. Morohashi Tetsuji, *Dai Kanwa Jiten*, 7, 1068.

Khuc Thua My was Hao's son. Hao had earlier sent him to the Canton area to gather information on the Liu family. There he was alerted to the ambitions of the Liu. However, when his father died, Thua My, at Dai-la, was cut off from the Later Liang court, and Liu Yin was able to gain appointment as military governor at Dai-la.[40]

Liu Yin was nevertheless unprepared to enforce his authority over the Vietnamese, and Thua My maintained effective control at Dai-la. When Liu Yin died in 911, Thua My sent gifts to the Later Liang court by an envoy from Fu-chien. As a result, the double assignment of Canton and Dai-la was broken up. In the fifth month of the year, Liu Yin's brother and successor was named military governor at Canton only. In the last month of the year, an imperial envoy arrived at Dai-la to confirm Thua My as military governor there.[41]

Thua My's success apparently lay in an alliance with Wang Shen-chih, who was in control of Fu-chien. Shen-chih and Thua My cultivated diplomatic relations with Later Liang for a similar reason: fear of their neighbors. Shen-chih maintained contact with the Later Liang court by sea to northern Shan-tung, then overland to the captial at K'ai-feng. Given the anarchy of the time, it was a perilous journey, and four-fifths of Shen-chih's tribute to Later Liang was lost en route to shipwreck, pirates, bandits, or rival powers. Shen-chih reportedly nurtured foreign trade and had dealings with "southern barbarian merchants," so it was natural for Thua My and Shen-chih to be in contact. Since merchants could easily pass political frontiers, they were often employed for diplomatic work.[42] It seems that one such merchant-envoy from Fu-chien successfully pled Thua My's case at the Later Liang court.

Thereafter, Thua My developed close relations with Later Liang as the Liu family advanced their regional ambitions. In 917, the Liu claimed imperial status, and soon afterward they founded the Southern Han dynasty. Thua My responded by drawing diplomatically closer to Later Liang. In 918 he obtained a new series of titles from Later Liang to reinforce his legal position.[43]

Later Liang, however, was a weak reed to lean on, and in 923 it fell. Thua My could no longer look north for legal and moral support. By this time the empire had been partitioned into eight domains, each claiming imperial status. The T'ang political heritage had finally crumbled, to be replaced by predatory regional powers. The Southern Han at Canton controlled all of the Hsi River basin; they were eager to add the Vietnamese

40. Yamamoto, "Annan," pp. 8, 14. The Chinese and Vietnamese sources for the tenth century have been studied in detail by Yamamoto, Sugimoto, and Kawahara. I therefore forgo discussing the textual problems of these sources.

41. Yamamoto, "Annan," p. 9.

42. Schafer, *Min*, pp. 13–15, 75–78.

43. Yamamoto, "Annan," pp. 9–10.

lands to their realm and to reassemble the ancient inheritance of Chao T'o's kingdom of Nan Yüeh.

Thua My's ally, Wang Shen-chih, was dead, and his realm in Fu-chien fell apart in civil war during 930 and 931.[44] This is perhaps what prompted Liu Kung of Southern Han to send an army to Dai-la in the fall of 930. Khuc Thua My was captured and taken to Canton, where he was allowed to live out his days quietly. The Chinese army apparently took Dai-la with ease, for no battles are recorded; the capture of Thua My is the only detail remembered from the campaign. It is likely that many members of the local ruling class, particularly in the Hong River plain, were not opposed to pledging allegiance to Southern Han. They had been raised on the assumptions of T'ang civilization, and looking north for political and cultural leadership was for them a venerable habit. Many were undoubtedly attracted by the regional brilliance of the aspiring imperial court at Canton. Some may simply have preferred a peaceful transition, not being emotionally or physically prepared to offer more than token resistance.

It is recorded that Liu Kung had Khuc Thua My brought before him, and they discussed the vagaries of fate. Kung said: "An imperial court of law would consider me a false sovereign, but now the tables are turned and it is you who stand accused." By way of reply, Thua My simply bowed his head in submission.[45]

Liu Kung was an adventurer rather than an imperialist. He did not believe in the imperial mandate of Heaven, for he admitted that the law of such a mandate would in fact find him guilty of treason. For him, success was the prize of those who were strong and clever. Khuc Thua My had no taste for this view of the world. He preferred an empire to serve, if only in theory. He was a diplomat in a world of soldiers. While Kung represented the disorderly forces of the new age, Thua My revealed a lingering desire for the law and order of the T'ang peace.

The Khuc family gave the Vietnamese a half century of prosperity and tranquillity. Culturally, the Vietnamese enjoyed a revival of T'ang civilization. Buddhism and Taoism flourished, as did classical studies. The ruling class turned to easy living, and the martial arts were neglected. The dearth of information from this time suggests a time of peace. Yet, beneath the surface, important changes were taking place.

The basis of Vietnamese identity as it developed in the tenth century was a denial and an affirmation: "We are not Chinese; we are Viet." For some ruling-class people, this denial and affirmation was personally demoralizing. For the people as a whole, however, the choice was less difficult. People simply began to "act natural."

The Vietnamese learned to use chopsticks from the Chinese, but they

44. Schafer, *Min*, p. 38.
45. Yamamoto, "Annan," p. 16.

also persisted in chewing betel. Chewing betel was an indigenous socializing skill important for extending hospitality and for family-to-family relations. The arbitrariness of patriarchal authority was not congenial to a people who valued not only the role of women in society but also the gloss of friendship experienced while chewing betel.

The political importance of marriage alliances and bilateral kinship ties surfaced among ruling-class Vietnamese in the tenth century. Royal polygamy, the practice of having more than one queen, was a natural development of this trend, as was the marriage of a new king to one of his predecessor's queens. Rulers buttressed their authority by contracting marriage alliances with powerful families in the realm and by treating the women obtained from these families as queens of equal status.

Vietnamese kingship grew out of peasant life and village politics. The royal style developed rapidly in the eleventh century, but the major kings of the tenth century were rustics. Culturally, we can speak of a kind of primitive strength, such as that expressed in the "animal art" of Hoa-lu and the monumental stone lion, horse, rhinoceros, and elephant at Van Phuc Temple.[46] These artifacts suggest a time when village life turned to itself for inspiration and when "ordinary things" were elevated to a new status as "significant symbols."

At a more coherent and discernible level, Vietnamese Buddhism helped foster stable dynastic institutions that gave political shape to the new Vietnamese identity. The increasingly visible role of the Buddhist hierarchy in society and politics is a major theme in the history of tenth- and eleventh-century Vietnam.

At the same time, popular Vietnamese Taoism prospered as an expression of ancient animist beliefs, much like Japanese Shintoism. In the absence of Chinese authority, the skills of indigenous geomancers, astrologers, sorcerers, and sorceresses filled a need for guidance in human affairs. Prophesies, riddles, signs, and slogans all had a role in the propagandizing of political change in tenth- and early eleventh-century Vietnam.

The appearance of Vietnamese independence in the tenth century represented the ascendance of indigenous tradition at the expense of China's imperial claims. But it is not easy to define what this "indigenous tradition" was in specific terms, for the indigenous content had been transformed during the centuries of Chinese rule. By the tenth century there is no more talk of claw myths, and levirate had surely been stamped out. On the other hand, *nom* was used to express native concepts of kingship in terms advanced by the Chinese classics.

Perhaps one of the more significant T'ang-Viet developments for later Vietnamese kingship was the emergence of the "Dragon's Belly," *Long-do*, the area of modern Hanoi, as the legitimate center of the Vietnamese realm,

46. Nguyen Phuc Long, p. 30, figs. 285–90.

and the elaboration of this theme in the spirit cult of To Lich. This super-seded not only the old provincial centers of Luy-lau and Long-bien but also the pre-Chinese centers of Co-loa and Me-linh. Co-loa enjoyed a brief revival in the tenth century, but the ancient seat of the Hung kings was never reoccupied. The kings who actually established the new Vietnamese throne ruled from a hitherto insignificant place, Hoa-lu. But there was no stable monarchy until the throne was placed at the Dragon's Belly. This was, of course, a matter of geography and demography, but it nevertheless indicates the scope of change experienced by Vietnamese society since the days when it was ruled from Me-linh by the legendary Hung kings.

It was during the rule of the Khuc family that the Vietnamese began to sense the possibilities of a new age. The process of pursuing these possibilities was a drawn-out affair covering several generations. The earlier of these generations had no clear idea of how the process would end, but they consis-tently resisted northern soldiers, and this, more than anything else, kept them on the road to independence.

Duong Dinh Nghe

Following the capture of Khuc Thua My, a South-ern Han general named Liang K'e-chen led an army down the coast to the Cham capital, near modern Da-nang. In a quick raid, he entered the city, seized a load of treasure, and hastened back north. He was then charged with the defense of Dai-la. At the same time, a Southern Han official named Li Chin was appointed "Governor of Giao Province" and was given full administrative responsibility for the Hong River plain. Liu Kung is said to have remarked: "The people of Giao Province often rebel; but still it is possible to control them, and it shall be done."[47] In spite of this determined attitude, the Southern Han occupation was very brief.

Although Southern Han apparently met little resistance in the Hong River plain, it made no effort to rule Ai or Hoan. These southern areas remained in the hands of one of Khuc Thua My's generals, a native of Ai named Duong Dinh Nghe. Southern Han conferred a rank of nobility on Dinh Nghe, hoping thereby to encourage his cooperation, but otherwise left him alone. Dinh Nghe was nevertheless determined to drive the Chinese out.

Whereas Khuc Thua My had pursued an idealized vision of T'ang civilization, Duong Dinh Nghe was willing to enter into the reality of regional power politics. He presided over the first awakening of "Viet-namese power" in the tenth century. Because he was a son of Ai, his respect for Chinese civilization was less than Thua My's had been, and in building up an indigenous power base to resist Southern Han he opened the way for a

47. Yamamoto, "Annan," pp. 17–18.

rapid evolution of Vietnamese national feeling that gained momentum through three wars against the Chinese during the next half century.

Duong Dinh Nghe gathered and trained an army of three thousand men in Ai. Hearing of this, Li Chin offered him a bribe to disband his soldiers. Dinh Nghe refused. In the last month of 931, Dinh Nghe marched against Dai-la. Southern Han sent a general named Ch'eng Pao with reinforcements, but the city fell before he could arrive. Liang K'e-chen and Li Chin fled; when Ch'eng Pao reached Dai-la, Dinh Nghe attacked and killed him in battle. Li Chin reached Canton, only to be beheaded for incompetence. Dinh Nghe promptly named himself military governor, and Southern Han later recognized him as such.[48]

Dinh Nghe ruled from Dai-la for six years. No information survives from these years. It is nevertheless clear from later events that this was a time of political ferment. Dinh Nghe had come out of Ai to push the Chinese from Giao. Those who had collaborated with Southern Han were probably done away with, disinherited, or otherwise penalized. Powerful landlord families in Giao, where there were many schools and Buddhist temples, may well have regarded Dinh Nghe as a rural rustic and perhaps had difficulty comprehending the forces he represented. Dinh Nghe, riding the crest of a popular revival of Vietnamese identity, probably saw Giao as gravely contaminated with northern influence.

Although Dinh Nghe stood but briefly on the stage of Vietnamese history, he was considered by the Vietnamese of that time to be an important figure, and his family continued to exert a strong, though indirect, influence on Vietnamese politics for the rest of the century. As we will see, his son later attempted to rule during a period of spreading anarchy. More significant was that marriage to a woman from the Duong family became a criterion for establishing one's claim to the soon-to-be-established Vietnamese throne. Each of the three major kings of the tenth century married a Duong woman. For two of these kings, it was the same woman, and she played an important role in the succession. We can surmise that Dinh Nghe was viewed as a founder of the Vietnamese monarchical tradition, and an association with him through marriage with a member of his family became a means of legitimizing one's possession of political power.

In the third month of 937, Dinh Nghe was assassinated by Kieu Cong Tien. Identified in Chinese records as "a petty military officer," Cong Tien was, according to Vietnamese records, a member of a prominent local family established in Phong. Cong Tien attempted to replace Dinh Nghe and to steer a pro-Chinese course. Although Giao was apparently quiescent, he was undone by an army marching out of Ai led by Ngo Quyen.[49]

48. Ibid., pp. 18–23.
49. Ibid., pp. 24–25.

Ngo Quyen

Kieu Cong Tien represented pro-Chinese interests in the Hong River plain. Faced with Ngo Quyen leading an army from Ai, he sent envoys to Southern Han to request assistance. From this it is clear that he was unable to rally sufficient support among the Vietnamese. Giao was unwilling to defend itself against the much smaller but more militant Ai and Hoan. The people of Giao may have regarded the army from Ai as more legitimate than the Chinese interlopers and their local clients. Giao, with its temples and schools, cities and markets, paddy and population, was very desirable. Southern Han yearned for it mightily, but Ai, a country cousin, defended its honor.

Liu Kung, the Southern Han ruler, jumped at the chance to intervene in Vietnam again. He had been foiled by Duong Dinh Nghe in 931, but now that Dinh Nghe was dead, he thought the time was ripe for another try. He placed his own son, Liu Hung-ts'ao, in command of the expedition, naming him "Peaceful Sea Military Governor" and "King of Giao." He hastily assembled an army at Sea Gate, where he personally took charge of the reserve force. One of his court ministers advised restraint, saying, "Rain has been accumulating continuously for ten days now; the sea route is long and dangerous; Ngo Quyen is a treacherous adversary, he cannot be treated lightly." However, Kung was too eager for victory and ignored this warning. He ordered Hung-ts'ao to embark the army and sail to Giao.

Ngo Quyen's father, Ngo Man, had been a provincial magistrate on the right bank of the Hong near Mount Tan-vien, in Phong. Phung Hung, the eighth-century national leader, came from this area, which was associated with the oldest traditions of the Vietnamese people. Although Kieu Cong Tien came from the same general region, his loyalties, unlike those of Ngo Quyen, were apparently not rooted in the area's heritage.

According to Vietnamese tradition, at birth Ngo Quyen was bathed in a strange luminosity and three black moles were discovered on his back. These were taken as signs of his future greatness, and, in anticipation of this, he was named Quyen, meaning "authority and power." He is said to have grown into an unusually fine-looking and stalwart young man with eyes like lightning and a measured step like that of a tiger. He was noted for his wisdom, bravery, and physical strength.[50]

Quyen became a general of Duong Dinh Nghe. In 931, when Dinh Nghe defeated Southern Han, Quyen was thirty-three years old. Dinh Nghe gave him one of his daughters in marriage and placed him in charge of Ai Province. Ai was Dinh Nghe's birthplace and base of power. His giving command of this region to Quyen is an indication of Quyen's quality as a

50. Ibid., p. 30.

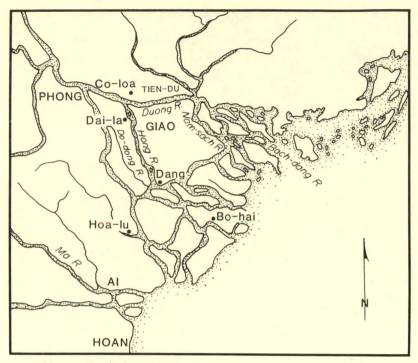

Map 10. Tenth-Century Vietnam

subordinate. When Dinh Nghe was killed by Kieu Cong Tien in the spring of 937, Quyen mobilized an army and marched north to avenge the death of his patron. Once this was accomplished, he unavoidably became the leader of the Vietnamese battle against the Chinese.

By the time Liu Hung-ts'ao arrived in Vietnamese waters with the Southern Han expedition, Ngo Quyen had already put Kieu Cong Tien to death and was prepared to meet the Chinese assault. Hung-ts'ao's plan was to ascend the Bach-dang River and to place his army in the heart of Giao before disembarking; the Bach-dang was the major riverine route into the Hong River plain from the north. Quyen anticipated this plan and brought his army to the mouth of the river. He had his men plant a barrier of large poles in the bed of the river. The tops of the poles reached just below the water level at high tide and were sharpened and tipped with iron. When Hung-ts'ao appeared off the mouth of the river, Quyen sent out small, shallow-draft boats at high tide to provoke a fight and then retreat upriver, drawing the Chinese fleet after in pursuit. As the tide fell, the heavy Chinese warboats were all caught on the poles and lay helplessly trapped in the middle of the river. Quyen attacked vigorously. More than half the Chinese were drowned, including Hung-ts'ao. When news of the battle reached Sea Gate with the survivors, Liu Kung wept openly. He collected what remained of his army and returned to Canton.[51] Southern Han never attacked the Vietnamese again.

The Battle of Bach-dang River took place in the autumn of 938. It has been remembered by the Vietnamese as an important milestone on their path to national independence. It had a powerful effect on the people of the time, as well, for it directly led to the abandonment of T'ang-style political titles and to the proclamation of the first Vietnamese "king" of the tenth century.

In the spring of 939, Ngo Quyen took the title of king. Duong Dinh Nghe had dared aspire to nothing more than the title of military governor. With the Battle of Bach-dang River, however, the national feelings of the Vietnamese people began to blossom. The mass of the population may have seen the battles of 931 as simply quarrels between rival warlords. The Battle of Bach-dang River and the rise of Ngo Quyen, however, had a stirring effect on the people. It was now possible for them to imagine a Vietnamese king.

Vietnamese tradition attributed the victory at Bach-dang River to the supernatural intervention of Phung Hung. According to a fourteenth-century Vietnamese source:

> When the first lord of Ngo established the nation, northern soldiers invaded for plunder. The first lord was distressed about this. Then suddenly in the middle of the night he saw in a dream a hoary-headed old man in formal dress with a dignified and refined bearing holding a feathered fan and a bamboo staff. The old man announced himself [as Phung Hung] and said: "I will personally lead ten thousand ranks of immortal soldiers to occupy a strategic position and make ready an ambush. You, sir, advance your soldiers rapidly to resist the enemy. I will give you secret assistance. There is no need for worry." At the time of the Bach-dang River victory, the sounds of horses and chariots could be heard in the air. This battle was accordingly a great victory. [The first lord] proclaimed and established temples and shrines, added to and strengthened old rituals, and also provided feathered accessories, yellow banners, brass gongs, and deerskin drums for all the ancient dances with sword and battle axe [as well as] the sacrificial ox to convey thanks [to Phung Hung]. Through the successive changes of different dynasties [these observances] have gradually become ancient custom.[52]

Ngo Quyen's patronage of Phung Hung's cult was based on the fact that both he and the eighth-century hero came from the same district. The idea of supernatural intervention was an acceptable way to link Quyen with

51. Ibid., pp. 27–28.
52. *VDULT*, 6–7.

independence movements of the past. By reaching back to Phung Hung, Quyen was laying claim to a local tradition of kingship. The passage quoted above implies that Quyen buttressed his royal claim with appropriate obeisance to indigenous perceptions of political authority.

Ngo Quyen abandoned Dai-la and established his capital at Co-loa, the ancient city built by King An Duong in the third century B.C. This reveals a deep understanding of Vietnamese identity. Dai-la had been built by the Chinese and had served as an imperial administrative center. On the other hand, Co-loa echoed the greatness of Vietnamese kingship before the coming of the Chinese. This change of capital symbolized a change in popular attitudes toward political authority. A Vietnamese king ruling from Co-loa evoked cultural memories embedded in myths and legends passed down from generation to generation. The Vietnamese people were treading on what for centuries had been forbidden ground.

The court that Ngo Quyen established was based on traditional Chinese etiquette, even to the regulation of the color of garments to be worn by officials. Although Quyen had moved closer to local sensibilities, he nonetheless remained a member of an upper class that knew no alternative to the forms of Chinese civilization. Quyen continued to look north for concepts of authority and legitimacy. This was a fatal limitation, and the throne he founded grew increasingly isolated from Vietnamese society in the years following his death.

The Duong family continued to exercise influence. Ngo Quyen's wife, a daughter of Duong Dinh Nghe, was proclaimed queen. With its home in Ai, the Duong family was less committed to Chinese civilization than the landlords of the Hong River plain. While these landlords had reason to fear the growing cultural and political awareness of the Vietnamese people, the Duong family was prepared to benefit from it. The Ngo monarchy was a temporary alliance between natural antagonists made possible only by the personality and accomplishments of a single man.

Ngo Quyen died in 944 at the age of forty-seven. Le Van Huu, a prominent thirteenth-century historian, wrote:

> King Ngo was able to take soldiers freshly recruited from our land of Viet and defeat Liu Hung-ts'ao's multitude of ten thousands; he raised up the country and established a kingdom; he made it so the northerners dared not come back again.[53]

Le Van Huu nevertheless did not consider Ngo Quyen to be in the same class as Dinh Bo Linh, who ruled twenty years later and was the first Vietnamese leader of the tenth century to claim imperial status.[54] When

53. *TT*, 5, 21a.
54. *TT, Ban ky*, 1, 2b–3a.

Ngo Si Lien compiled his national history near the end of the fifteenth century, he cited Ngo Quyen's reign as the beginning of the independence period. Early in the sixteenth century, the historian Vu Quynh returned to Le Van Huu's preference for Dinh Bo Linh; this interpretation prevailed throughout all later historical writing and reflected a perception of Ngo Quyen as a transitional figure not fully representative of the Vietnamese political tradition.[55] Ngo Quyen's death opened an era of anarchy that was eventually brought to a close by the rise of Dinh Bo Linh.

Duong Tam Kha and the Ngo Brothers

When he died, Ngo Quyen left four young sons. Two, who were still children, remained in the care of the queen. The other two were older but still immature. It is recorded that, on his deathbed, Quyen charged Duong Tam Kha with the task of supporting and advising his young heirs. Duong Tam Kha was a son of Duong Dinh Nghe, a brother of the queen. After Quyen's death, he usurped the throne and proclaimed himself the "King of Peace" (*Binh Vuong*).[56]

The title "King of Peace" suggests that Tam Kha saw himself as a man of the hour stepping in to keep the peace at a time of potential disturbance. However, either he was an uninspiring, inept leader or the problems he faced were insurmountable, for his sphere of authority shrank progressively during the six years of his attempted reign. In fact, after Quyen's death, the ruling class began to break up into an anarchic system of local heroes. This trend was undoubtedly encouraged by the appearance of a usurper with roots outside the Hong River plain.

The eldest of the Ngo brothers, Xuong Ngap, feared for his life when Tam Kha took the throne, and managed to escape to the Nam-sach River, a channel in eastern Giao. This area was the main center of Chinese settlement and influence in Vietnam. Here Xuong Ngap found refuge with a local noble of the Pham family. Since Tam Kha was strongly anti-Chinese by virtue of his father's career, those who opposed him found natural allies in the sinophile community of Giao.

According to traditions recorded in temple documents,[57] the Pham family was powerful in the lower Hong River plain. The most prominent member of this family was Pham Bach Ho. Bach Ho was born into a family of merchants. It is recorded that, before he was born, his mother was caught in a downpour and took shelter in a temple. While waiting for the rain to stop, she was terrified by the supernatural appearance of a white tiger. She

55. Sugimoto Naojirō, *Tōnan Ajiashi Kenkyū*, pp. 88–90.

56. Yamamoto, "Annan," p. 32.

57. Translated excerpts from temple biographies in Tran Quoc Vuong's translation of *Viet su luoc*, notes on pp. 46 and 47.

later gave birth to her famous son and consequently named him Bach Ho, meaning "White Tiger." The tiger spirit was the most potent in the pantheon of popular Vietnamese Taoism. This birth story is typical of a local hero and was meant to account for the man's greatness in terms of prevailing ideas about supernatural intervention in human affairs.

According to temple biographies, Bach Ho followed Ngo Quyen against Kieu Cong Tien and participated in the Battle of Bach-dang River. Then, when Tam Kha took the throne, Bach Ho helped Xuong Ngap escape to the Nam-sach River.

The blood relationship, if any, between Bach Ho and the local noble who protected Xuong Ngap is unknown, although their surnames were the same. They in any case shared political interests. Bach Ho was from a place called Dang along the Hong River a little more than halfway from Co-loa to the sea. Dang was on the southern edge of the agricultural heartland of Giao and faced the swampy seacoast and Ai Province. After Ngo Quyen's death, Bach Ho followed a policy of opposing the development of any single power center in Giao. A man like him, on the fringe of the heartland, could best maintain his position if political power was diffuse.

A second man who, according to temple biographies, joined the conspiracy to help Xuong Ngap escape from Tam Kha was Kieu Cong Han of Phong Province. Cong Han was a member of the same family as Kieu Cong Tien, who had killed Duong Dinh Nghe in 937. He and his younger brother Thuan were in control of most of Phong. The Kieu family and the Duong family were irreconcilable because of the events of 937.

Another man listed by temple biographies as having aided Xuong Ngap's escape was Do Canh Thac. The Do family was established on the Do-dong River west of Dai-la. Historical records identify Do Canh Thac as a military commander who, along with a certain Duong Cat Loi, was sent by Tam Kha to capture Xuong Ngap. Three times Canh Thac and Cat Loi were sent to get Xuong Ngap, and three times they returned empty-handed. When Tam Kha learned that Xuong Ngap had been hidden in a cave in the mountains, he sent them a fourth time, to no avail. Canh Thac was a half-hearted follower of Tam Kha.

Tam Kha attempted to control Ngo Quyen's second son, Xuong Van, by adopting him as his own heir and encouraging him to participate as a member of the court. In 950, Tam Kha sent Xuong Van along with Do Canh Thac and Duong Cat Loi in an expedition against a pair of villages on the border of Phong.

It is recorded that while the expedition was enroute Xuong Van found a favorable moment to approach the two commanders. He boldly made his complaint:

> Our first king's virtue was that he was in harmony with popular feeling; all who received his commands were happy to comply. Unfortunately, all of his

officers have now been discarded. The King of Peace has unrighteously set himself up and snatched away the inheritance belonging to me and my brothers; is there any crime greater than this? Now he again sends us to attack an innocent district. If by luck we succeed, then that's that; but if they do not submit, then what will we do about it?[58]

The commanders answered, "Your wish is our command." Xuong Van then said, "I want to return to the capital city to seize the King of Peace and restore the inheritance of our first king; can it be done?" The two men replied, "We approve."

This short dialogue reveals that Tam Kha had been a disappointment to those who had served Ngo Quyen. Quyen's men had all been "discarded." These men probably included Pham Bach Ho and perhaps even Kieu Cong Han. These "discarded" men had gone back to their home districts and barricaded themselves against Tam Kha. Those whom Tam Kha sent out against these local powers were secretly in sympathy with them.

Xuong Van and the two commanders returned to Co-loa and deposed Tam Kha. It is recorded that there was a popular clamor for Tam Kha's death, but Xuong Van refused, saying, "The King of Peace has been kind to me; how can I bear to have him killed?" Tam Kha was given an estate to support his retirement on the Hong River a short distance downriver from Dai-la.[59]

Xuong Van declared himself "King of Southern Chin" (*Nam Tan Vuong*). This was in imitation of the local dynasties prevailing in China at that time. The Later Chin dynasty had ruled northern China from 936 to 946, during the time of Ngo Quyen's reign. Xuong Van probably hoped to lend a broader sense of legitimacy to his authority by associating himself with the postimperial political system of China.

In 951, a year after the removal of Tam Kha, Xuong Van sent messengers to his elder brother inviting him to share the throne. Xuong Ngap came and declared himself "King of the Heavenly Plan" (*Thien Sach Vuong*). The brothers attempted to cooperate in a two-headed government, but the experiment soon failed. Xuong Ngap "usurped authority and took the law into his own hands," forcing Xuong Van to retire from public affairs. There is no information from the few years of Xuong Ngap's reign, but we can assume that he was no more successful than Tam Kha had been in arresting the trend toward political disorder.

The royal titles taken by aspiring monarchs during this period, "King of Peace," "King of Southern Chin," and "King of the Heavenly Plan," suggest a search for legitimacy. These men seem to have come from a landowning class with little idea of how to inspire royal awe.

58. *TT*, 5, 22b.
59. Yamamoto, "Annan," p. 32.

In 954, Xuong Ngap died, and Xuong Van again took the throne. During the few years of his forced retirement, Xuong Van must have decided that the disintegrating political situation called for some new initiative. In the month that he returned to the throne, Xuong Van declared himself a vassal of Southern Han and sent envoys to Canton bearing tribute and requesting credentials. Southern Han sent Supervising Censor Li Hsü to proclaim its authority among the Vietnamese and to welcome the allegiance of Xuong Van, naming him "Peaceful Sea Military Governor."

Xuong Van soon realized that he had made a mistake, however, and sent messengers to intercept Li Hsü and stop him from coming with the excuse that "pirates are in rebellion and the way is not clear." Li Hsü consequently turned back. The idea of seeking protection under the Southern Han banner probably grew from the assumption that local leaders would respect the representative of a relatively well-established Chinese dynasty. This assumption, perhaps based on Xuong Van's Sinitic education, was false, however, and Xuong Van soon discovered that there was no way to avoid the hard work of political survival.

No information survives from the period between 954 and 963, the year of Xuong Van's death. During this time, the inheritance of Ngo Quyen grew increasingly fragile as local leaders continued to pursue their individual ambitions. Xuong Van eventually turned to armed coercion in an attempt to enforce his authority. In 963, he campaigned against a pair of villages on the border of Phong. While observing the battle from a boat in the river, he was shot and killed by a crossbowman lying in ambush. Upon his death, there was a rush for power as strong men contended for supremacy, the most prominent being Kieu Cong Han, Do Canh Thac, Ngo Xu Binh, and Duong Huy, the last two cited only in Chinese records.[60]

The few chaotic years that followed have traditionally been called the Period of the Twelve Warlords. In addition to Kieu Cong Han, his brother Thuan, Do Canh Thac, and Pham Bach Ho, eight other men are listed as comprising the twelve warlords.

According to temple biographies, three of these men were brothers, sons of a Chinese immigrant merchant who adopted the family name of their Vietnamese mother. Nguyen Thu Tiep, the second eldest, had made a career as a military commander on the southern frontier with Champa.[61] After Xuong Van's death, he established himself at Tien-du, just east of Co-loa. His elder brother, Khoan, set himself up on the eastern border of Phong, while his younger brother, Sieu, established himself at Dai-la. Two other men, of whom nothing is known, held the heavily populated area south of the Duong River; their names were Ly Khue and Lu Duong. On the

60. Ibid., pp. 34–38, 46.
61. Tran Quoc Vuong, *Viet su luoc*, p. 47.

southern coast of the Hong River plain, an immigrant Cantonese named Tran Lam was in control of Bo-hai, a seaport at the mouth of the Hong River. This man became an important ally of Dinh Bo Linh and will be discussed in the next section. Leadership of the Ngo family after Xuong Van's death devolved upon Ngo Nhat Khanh, listed among the twelve warlords in possession of the Ngo home district. Finally, there is a name that is differently recorded but is identified by fifteenth-century Vietnamese historians as Ngo Xuong Xi. Supposedly Xuong Xi was a son of Xuong Ngap. This identification was a convenient historiographical device that allowed historians to regard the period of the twelve warlords as the reign of Ngo Xuong Xi, thus providing unbroken dynastic continuity.[62] The name of the place cited as this man's headquarters is obscure.

Dinh Bo Linh, who ultimately united the Vietnamese, was not included among the twelve warlords. He represented an attitude incompatible with the political system inherited by Ngo Quyen. The men listed among the twelve warlords all at one time participated in that system. Dinh Bo Linh was a different sort of man. He was a popular leader rising out of peasant society.

The two decades from Ngo Quyen's death to the rise of Dinh Bo Linh witnessed the progressive erosion of political values imported from China. Ruling-class people saw a gulf open between the narrow world of their Sinitic education and the dangerous path of power in a Vietnamese society rediscovering its own heritage. The political assumptions that for centuries had tied the Vietnamese to China had been weakening ever since the fall of T'ang, fifty years before. By the time of Ngo Xuong Van's death, these assumptions had been thoroughly discredited. Dinh Bo Linh led the inevitable change.

Dinh Bo Linh

Dinh Bo Linh's father, Dinh Cong Tru, had served both Duong Dinh Nghe and Ngo Quyen as governor of Hoan on the Cham border in the south. According to Chinese records, Bo Linh succeeded his father as governor of Hoan and from this base eventually united all the Vietnamese lands.[63]

Vietnamese historians recorded several stories about Dinh Bo Linh. These stories are to some extent hagiographical, so, while the general circumstances described in them may be authentic, many details are later elaborations.

Bo Linh was born at Hoa-lu, in a narrow valley running into the

62. Yamamoto, "Annan," pp. 41–43.
63. Ibid., p. 49.

Hong River plain from the south, some thirty miles from the sea. He lived with his mother, a concubine of Dinh Cong Tru, beside the temple of a mountain spirit. His father was absent and so, apparently, were all other able-bodied men. Bo Linh was born in 923, so it is possible that the stories of his youth date from either the years 930–31, when Duong Dinh Nghe mobilized an army against Southern Han, or, more likely, the years 937–38, when Ngo Quyen marched against Kieu Cong Tien and fought the Battle of Bach-dang River. It is also possible that for reasons no longer clear Bo Linh and his mother remained in Hoa-lu while Cong Tru was occupied with affairs in Hoan.

It is recorded that the village children were responsible for tending the water buffaloes and that Bo Linh was recognized as their leader. The youngsters liked to play at imperial ritual and paraded about with Bo Linh in the role of emperor. On holidays, Bo Linh often led his followers against the youth of neighboring villages and always won the fray. His followers competed in gathering firewood and providing personal services for him. Seeing this, and feeling proud of it, Bo Linh's mother cooked a pig and laid a feast.

All of this impressed the old men of the village, who took counsel together: "This boy's behavior is extraordinary; he will be able to benefit his generation and bring peace to the people. If we do not support him now, we will certainly regret it later." Consequently the village acknowledged him as its leader and built him a palisade. Only a younger brother of his father refused to follow him and established a separate palisade.

Bo Linh led a band against his uncle but was repulsed. As Bo Linh fled, a bridge collapsed, and he fell in the mud. His uncle rushed up, intending to stab him, but was astonished to see two yellow dragons appear and hover over the boy in protection. Realizing that Bo Linh possessed supernatural qualities, the uncle submitted.[64]

This story describes a village society in the absence of authority. As Chinese hegemony faded and the men were absorbed in urgent struggles against its resurgence, village life was left open to the ambitions of a buffalo boy. Gaining the loyalty of his peers, Bo Linh advertised his pretensions with mock processions and battles. Supported by his mother, who distributed food in his honor, he gained the respectful attention of the old men in charge of village affairs. A stubborn uncle was won over by the miraculous appearance of two dragons, symbols of sovereign power.

The anarchic conditions of the times are clearly exposed in this story. Political power was reduced to its most primitive elements: a charismatic leader, public displays of power, the cultivation of prestige by feasting loyal followers, the possession of a palisade, the belief in the inevitability of success

64. Ibid., p. 48; *TT, Ban ky,* 1, 1a–b.

guaranteed by supernatural intervention. Bo Linh's appeal as a leader was based on the values of peasant society.

The date of Dinh Cong Tru's death is not recorded, but it appears that sometime during the reign of Duong Tam Kha, Dinh Bo Linh gained control of Hoan and Ai. Hoa-lu was well placed for observing the Hong River plain and defending the routes leading south. It is recorded that in 951, when the two Ngo brothers were attempting to rule together, Dinh Bo Linh, trusting to strongly defended mountain passes, refused to recognize their suzerainty. As the two kings prepared to march against Hoa-lu, Bo Linh sent his son Lien as a hostage of good faith. The Ngo brothers responded by denouncing Bo Linh for not coming in person, securing Lien, and proceeding to attack Hoa-lu. After a month of fruitless hostilities, the kings suspended Lien from a pole in plain view of Bo Linh and shouted that he would be killed unless Bo Linh submitted. Bo Linh angrily replied, "How can a great man compromise a great affair simply because of his son?" Bo Linh ordered more than ten arrows shot in Lien's direction. The Ngo brothers were astonished at this and, not knowing what else to do, abandoned the campaign. Lien subsequently escaped and returned to Hoa-lu.[65]

This story portrays Bo Linh as a strong, heroic figure, who viewed the traditional ruling class with contempt.[66] He nonetheless moved into the Hong River plain with caution. His first move was an alliance with Tran Lam.

Tran Lam was of Cantonese origin.[67] He presided over Port Bo-hai near the mouth of the Hong River, where the inland trade met the south-bound seaborne trade. He apparently recognized the Ngo monarchy, for he is listed among the twelve warlords. He probably did this to facilitate commerce. His position on the coast was relatively secure from land-based threats, for the coast was at this time swampy and undeveloped. Furthermore, because he controlled a major international entrepôt he was largely immune to political intrigues; all factions probably wanted to be on good terms with him for reasons of trade.

As relations with China declined during the tenth century, the Sino-Vietnamese border became a bandit lair. As we have mentioned, Vietnamese messengers dissuaded a Southern Han envoy from proceeding south in 954 with the excuse that the route was infested with bandits. The envoy's ready

65. Yamamoto, "Annan," p. 34; *TT*, 5, 23b–24a.

66. Yamamoto, "Annan," pp. 51–52, doubted the authenticity of this story because it seems to imply that the Ngo brothers marched all the way down to Hoan to confront Bo Linh. This interpretation mixes Chinese and Vietnamese sources. Only Chinese sources refer to Bo Linh as succeeding his father as governor of Hoan. Vietnamese sources mention only Hoa-lu as the scene of Bo Linh's activities. I think the story represents some actual event involving Bo Linh and the Ngo brothers, although we can assume that it has been elaborated.

67. Tran Quoc Vuong, *Viet su luoc*, pp. 46–47.

acceptance of this excuse implies that such a circumstance was not considered unusual at that time and place. Thus it was that, with a disunited and potentially hostile China discouraging contacts northward, Port Bo-hai, oriented toward the southern coast, grew in importance from year to year. This economic reorientation toward the sea routes leading south paralleled the rising power of Dinh Bo Linh in the south, and an alliance between the two centers of Hoa-lu and Port Bo-hai, one political and the other commercial, was a natural step toward the unification of the Vietnamese lands.

The alliance between Dinh Bo Linh and Tran Lam was accomplished by the expedient of adoption. Tran Lam, known for both wealth and virtue, had no heir. Bo Linh accordingly presented himself to Lam and expressed a desire to serve him. It is recorded that Lam, "seeing that he was of a stalwart appearance and had natural ability, adopted Bo Linh as his own son, loved, entertained, and favored him daily with increasing generosity." Lam eventually entrusted Bo Linh with his army.[68] Lam financed Bo Linh's ambitions, and Bo Linh guaranteed the security of Lam's market.

When he learned of the alliance between Bo Linh and Lam, Pham Bach Ho quickly surrendered to Bo Linh with all his soldiers. Pham Bach Ho was at Dang, the next political center upriver from Port Bo-hai. As the middleman for moving trade up and down the Hong, Bach Ho was economically dependent on Tran Lam. Bo Linh rewarded Bach Ho's prompt submission by appointing him commander of his bodyguard.[69]

Once he had gained the support of Tran Lam and Pham Bach Ho, Bo Linh was ready to challenge the lords of the upper plains. The anarchy that followed the death of Ngo Xuong Van in 963 gave him the opportunity to do so. The forces at Bo Linh's disposal were ample. In addition to his own army, probably recruited in Ai, and the armies of Tran Lam and Pham Bach Ho, Chinese records speak of an army of thirty thousand recruited in Hoan and led north by his son Lien.[70] Furthermore, strong local forces organized by individual villages for self-defense came to Bo Linh's aid.

Bo Linh's pacification of the Hong River plain was accomplished in three steps. The first step was to subdue the Ngo family warriors, who mobilized at Do-dong River with the apparent intention of advancing against Hoa-lu. The Ngo seem to have been enfeebled by the chronic hostilities of the preceding years and mustered only a few more than five hundred men. They probably hoped to catch Bo Linh off guard with a surprise attack. However, as they passed through a village named O-man, they were defeated and turned back by a local villager bearing the title assistant commissioner. It is not clear whether this titleholder was a sub-

68. Yamamoto "Annan," pp. 50–51.
69. Ibid., p. 51.
70. Ibid., pp. 49. 53.

ordinate of Bo Linh or not, but when Bo Linh heard of the battle at O-man
he mobilized an army and marched against Do-dong River. There he
defeated the assembled forces and secured the submission of Ngo Nhat
Khanh, the surviving leader of the Ngo family.[71]

Bo Linh followed up this victory by marching against Phong and
defeating Kieu Cong Han. According to temple biographies, Cong Han
escaped with a few hundred men and looked for Ngo Nhat Khanh, hoping
to join forces with him. However, when he heard that Nhat Khanh had
already surrendered, he fled south along the coast and disappeared.[72]

Finally, according to temple biographies, Bo Linh sent Nguyen Bac,
one of his assistants, against Nguyen Thu Tiep in Tien-du. Thu Tiep was
defeated and fled south to the Cham frontier, where he died.[73]

With these victories, all major centers of resistance to Bo Linh were
broken. Conditions were far from settled, however, for the effects of two
decades of anarchy could not be erased at once. Bo Linh had to build his
kingdom from the ground up.

The first decision facing Bo Linh was where to establish his capital.
The old political centers of Dai-la and Co-loa were unsuitable for two
reasons. First, they were located in the heartland of Chinese influence and
were for that reason inhospitable to the revival of Vietnamese sensibilities
taking place around Bo Linh. Second, situated in the plains, they were
difficult to defend against the inevitable reactions, both domestic and foreign, that could be expected to test Bo Linh's revolutionary regime. It is
recorded that Bo Linh selected for his capital a village named Dam, which
seems to have been the home of his mother's family. Dam was soon
abandoned because it "lacked the advantage of protection by narrow
passes," and the capital was "returned" to Hoa-lu.[74]

Hoa-lu was virtually impregnable. It lay in a narrow valley whose
entrance was guarded by easily defended passes, and it could be conveniently
reinforced from Ai and Hoan to the rear. It stood like a sentinel watching
over the plains to the north. For forty years Hoa-lu would watch the Hong
River plain and the Chinese frontier beyond as the Chinese-influenced
culture of Giao was impregnated with a new sense of national awareness and
a Chinese invasion was repulsed. After centuries of imperial control, the new
Vietnamese kingdom needed time to find its feet. To have settled in the
plains where Chinese officials had ruled for so many years would have risked
stunting a fragile, newborn national spirit. Bo Linh chose to stay at Hoa-lu,
waiting and watching. China was in the process of reunification, and the

71. Ibid., p. 51.
72. Tran Quoc Vuong, *Viet su luoc*, p. 46.
73. Ibid., p. 47.
74. *TT, Ban ky*, 1, 2a–b.

inevitable attempt to reimpose the provincial regime once this process was completed would be only a matter of time and opportunity. Bo Linh had the political wisdom of a peasant. He would not expose himself unnecessarily.

Survivors of the old royal family, led by Ngo Nhat Khanh, had surrendered to Bo Linh. Nhat Khanh was a kinsman of Ngo Quyen, although their exact relationship is not revealed in the sources. Bo Linh was interested in winning Nhat Khanh over to his side and attempted to unite the Ngo and Dinh families by multiple marriage alliances. Bo Linh took Nhat Khanh's mother in marriage and made her a queen. Then he married Nhat Khanh's younger sister to his son Lien. Finally, he gave Nhat Khanh one of his own daughters in marriage, because, in the words of the chronicler, he "still feared some rebellion would arise."

After this, "Nhat Khanh showed a cheerful exterior but was not at peace within himself"; consequently, he took his wife and fled south. At the Cham frontier he drew his sword and slashed his wife's face; scolding her, he said, "Your father took advantage of and coerced my mother and sister. How can I, simply on your account, forget the wickedness of your father? You go back. I will go a different way and look for those who can help me." He went to Champa. More than ten years later Nhat Khanh would attempt to revenge himself on the Hoa-lu throne with Cham assistance.[75]

We can assume that the bitter resistance of Nhat Khanh to Bo Linh was duplicated on a smaller scale in many other episodes. Banditry and insubordination were Bo Linh's chief concerns in the first years of his rule. Bo Linh's response to the situation was unequivocal. In the palace courtyard he displayed a big kettle and a tiger in a cage. He decreed that "those who violate the law will be boiled and gnawed." It is recorded that "all were afraid and submitted; no one dared violate his commands."[76] The anarchy of the preceding years prompted Bo Linh to grasp his kingdom with a firm hand.

In 965, two years after the death of Ngo Xuong Van, Bo Linh proclaimed himself "Great Vanquishing King" (*Dai Thang Vuong*). At the same time, he honored his son Lien with the old T'ang title "Peaceful Sea Military Governor." He informed Southern Han of Lien's appointment, and the Canton court formally acknowledged it. In this way, Bo Linh was able to maintain proper relations with the north according to established usage while at the same time putting himself diplomatically beyond the reach of the Chinese.

Bo Linh went a step further the following year, 966, when he proclaimed himself emperor. Now there could be no doubt that he was claiming genuine independence from China. According to Chinese political theory, there could by definition be only one true emperor on earth. By

75. *TT*, *Ban ky*, 1, 8b.
76. Yamamoto, "Annan," p. 51.

assuming this supreme title, Bo Linh asserted political equality between Vietnam and China.

At the same time, Bo Linh published the name of his kingdom as Dai Co Viet. *Dai* is a word of Chinese origin meaning "great." *Co* is a Vietnamese word, written with a phonetically appropriate Chinese character, also meaning "great."[77] The name Dai Co Viet endured until 1054, when the word *co* was removed by the third king of the Ly dynasty. This hybrid expression for "great," *dai co*, is peculiar to the early independence period and reflects a creative development of the vernacular idiom for political purposes. The use of a Chinese character to render the Vietnamese word *co* is another early example of *nom*, Vietnamese character writing.

In 967, Bo Linh assigned his son Lien the title "King of Nam Viet."[78] This title had been held by Chao T'o during the Former Han dynasty and carried a heritage of resistance to northern hegemony.

Not until 970 did Bo Linh officially open his reign by entitling it "Great Peace" (*Thai-binh*). Until this time he was apparently busy bringing order to his new realm. In the same year, he established five empresses.[79] The titles he assigned to his empresses provide hints of the cultural perspective of Hoa-lu.

The first empress was entitled "Cinnabar Wedding" (*Dan-gia*). Cinnabar was a prime ingredient of the Taoist elixir of immortality. This title suggests a virgin whose companionship was thought to induce longevity. This is a popular Taoist idea. Likewise, the second empress's title, "Pure and Bright" (*Trinh-minh*), expresses Taoist sentiments.

Popular Taoism was very close to the traditional animist beliefs of the Vietnamese. Its interest in astrology, geomancy, and sorcery was simply a technical addition to fundamental beliefs held by the people since prehistoric times. The appearance of Taoist-inspired titles at the Hoa-lu court suggests an interest in the indigenous spirit world similar to Shinto in Japan. Such an interest surely would have been an encouragement to the flowering of an independent Vietnamese identity.

The titles of the third and fourth empresses, "National Reformation" (*Kieu-quoc*) and "National Vigilance" (*Co-quoc*), strike political themes. Reformation and vigilance were the main orders of business for the Hoa-lu throne. Portions of Vietnamese society had to be weaned from the cultural assumptions of imperial China and reformed according to more indigenous patterns of thought. The political pitfalls of this process as well as the perennial threat of foreign aggression made vigilance a way of life.

77. *Tu dien tieng Viet*, 188.

78. The events I have described as occurring in 965–67 are placed by traditional chronology in 967–69; see Kawahara Masahiro, "Tei Buryō no Sokui Nendai ni Tsuite," pp. 32–37.

79. *TT*, *Ban ky*, 1, 2b.

The fifth empress was entitled "Singing Gentleman" (*Ca-ong*). This title has no particular significance that I can think of.

In 971, Bo Linh officially published his appointments to the chief court positions.[80] Nguyen Bac was placed at the head of the nobility, with the title "Nation-Establishing Duke" (*Dinh Quoc Cong*). As we have seen, according to temple biographies, Nguyen Bac had been entrusted with the task of pacifying the old provincial heartland of Giao. Judging from his actions after the death of Bo Linh, we can assume that he was in control of the day-to-day activities of the court. The expression "to establish the nation" used in this title comes from the *Tso-chuan*, one of the Chinese classics.[81]

A certain Luu Co was named "Judge of the Protectorate" (*Do-ho-phu Si-su*).[82] Henri Maspero believed that the expression "Protectorate" here refers to the locale of the government of the T'ang-era protectorate at Dai-la.[83] But judging from the use of this title in the eleventh century, it appears that *protectorate* was an administrative rather than a geographical term and may perhaps be more meaningfully rendered as "central government." In the eleventh century, "Judges of the Protectorate" were responsible for administering justice at the capital, as well as for overseeing the prison system.[84] We can surmise that Luu Co dispensed justice at Hoa-lu.

Le Hoan, a native of Ai and a protégé of Dinh Lien, was named "General of the Ten Circuits" (*Thap-dao Tuong-quan*). This title refers to the division of the T'ang empire into ten circuits. Bo Linh seems to have organized his control over the Hong River plain by dividing it into ten circuits. Use of T'ang-inspired titles and organization is not surprising, considering that T'ang administration ruled the Vietnamese for nearly three centuries. These titles do not necessarily mean that the Vietnamese were emulating the Chinese, but more probably indicate that they were using well-known concepts of government for their own purposes.

Ngo Chan Luu, a Buddhist priest holding the title "Buddhist Unifier" (*Tang-thong*), was named "Great Teacher for Correcting and Sustaining Viet" (*Khuong Viet Dai-su*). The title "Buddhist Unifier" dates from the Northern (Later) Wei dynasty in the fifth century, when it was given to priests assigned the task of reforming and unifying the Buddhist church.[85] Ngo Chan Luu apparently possessed this title prior to the rise of Bo Linh. He has been remembered as a patriarch of the Vo Ngon Thong sect and was probably a prominent leader of the Buddhist community in Giao. The title

80. Ibid., 1, 3b.
81. Morohashi, 3, 977.
82. *TT*, Ban ky, 1, 3b; *si su* is a Chou-period title for a judge. *VSL*, 1, 17a, says *thai su*; I believe this is an error.
83. H. Maspero, "Etudes d'histoire d'Annam," 16: 28.
84. *TT*, Ban ky, 2, 25a–b, and 3, 4a.
85. Morohashi, 1, 931.

"Great Teacher" that Bo Linh gave to him originated after 860 with T'ang emperors, who gave it as an honorific to "profound and virtuous" priests.[86] Ngo Chan Luu, as "Corrector and Sustainer of Viet," probably rallied the Buddhist leadership behind the Hoa-lu throne. This was an important task, for Buddhist monastic interests comprised the only supralocal organization capable of challenging the authority of Hoa-lu. In fact, after only forty years the Buddhist leadership did absorb the Hoa-lu monarchy and moved the central government back to the northern plain, where it could be surrounded with temples. Ngo Chan Luu's appointment was a recognition of Buddhist power and influence by a group of peasant soldiers.

Truong Ma-ni, also a Buddhist priest, received the title "Buddhist Priest Overseer" (*Tang-luc Dao-si*). This title first appeared in the late 830s for a T'ang official in charge of temples.[87] Truong Ma-ni was apparently responsible for administering temple affairs and perhaps also for providing scribes to the court.

Dang Huyen Quang, a Taoist priest, was given the title "Noble and Upright Majesty" (*Sung-chan-uy-nghi*). The role of Taoism at Hoa-lu is not explicitly known, although the skills of astrologers, geomancers, and sorcerers were presumably in demand, and such persons would have been proficient in the lore of popular Taoism. From a broader philosophical viewpoint, Taoism reinforced indigenous animist beliefs and buttressed Hoa-lu's rejection of the established centers of power. Judging from the role of Taoist priests at the Vietnamese court in the eleventh century, we can surmise that so-called Taoism in Vietnam was similar to what is called Shinto in Japan, and that so-called Taoist priests were custodians of spirit cults associated with the local terrain and with local heroes.

Finally, a younger brother of Tran Lam, named Tran Thang, was married to a Dinh princess and promoted to be "Commandant of the Spare Horses" (*Pho-ma Do-uy*). In early Han times, this title was assigned to the man responsible for the emperor's spare chariot. In Wei and Chin times, it was specifically applied to the husband of a princess.[88] What duties, if any, Tran Thang may have held at Bo Linh's court are unknown, although as a kinsman of one of Bo Linh's early collaborators we can assume he was a trusted subordinate.

Through these appointments, the general shape of Bo Linh's court can be seen: an emperor, five empresses, a king, a duke, a judge, a general, two Buddhist priests, a Taoist priest, and a son-in-law. It was a rudimentary government, preoccupied with basics. However, already at this early point and in spite of certain continuities, there were important departures from the

86. Ibid., 3, 404.
87. Ibid., 1, 932.
88. Ibid., 12, 514.

Chinese usages learned during the provincial era. The most significant was imperial polygamy. A Chinese emperor could have countless concubines but only one empress.

Bo Linh had five empresses. We know that one of his empresses was chosen from the once royal Ngo family. As we shall see, another empress was from the once powerful Duong family. Bo Linh may have selected an empress from each of the powerful Vietnamese families to unite potential factions behind his throne. A. Thomas Kirsch, discussing bilateral kinship in early Khmer society, recently wrote about "the institution of royal polygamy" and "the role of the king's harem as an integrating mechanism in Khmer society" in the context of "efforts to mobilize political support through emphasizing a ramifying network of kinship to a number of powerful families."[89] As we have seen, the pattern of bilateral kinship also existed in early Vietnamese society. Royal polygamy was an early aspect of Vietnamese kingship that came from the local society. It was continued by Vietnamese rulers for two centuries, although later Vietnamese historians condemned it as immoral and divisive.

Bo Linh surrounded himself with strong personalities like himself. His court retained something of the atmosphere of a military camp and partook of the rustic setting of Hoa-lu.

It is recorded that Bo Linh established shrines to the gods of the earth and of agriculture.[90] The term used refers to a practice recorded in ancient Chinese texts in connection with the worship of two deities named Coiled Dragon (*Chü-lung*) and Grain Sovereign (*Hou-chi*). Coiled Dragon is simply geomancer's shorthand for the spiritual powers of the earth. Grain Sovereign was the minister of agriculture under the mythical Emperor Shun and subsequently became popularly known as the god of agriculture. According to the *Viet dien u linh tap*, a shrine to Grain Sovereign (Vietnamese *Hau Tac*) was built in the Hanoi area in T'ang times.[91] According to ancient Chinese texts, a feudal lord would raise shrines to the two deities, Coiled Dragon and Grain Sovereign, when he built his palace, and, since these shrines would be maintained only as long as the lord's realm endured, they became synonymous with the concept of state or nation.[92] What veneration of these deities meant to Bo Linh cannot be known for sure, but it is reasonable to assume that they were intended to be national gods symbolizing the fertile power of the earth both agriculturally and politically.

Geomancy was a popular art in tenth-century Vietnam. Its basic idea is that human events are affected for good or ill by the spiritual powers of the

89. A. Thomas Kirsch, "Kinship, Genealogical Claims, and Societal Integration in Ancient Khmer Society," p. 201.

90. *VSL*, 1, 17a.

91. *VDULT*, 10.

92. Morohashi, 8, 418.

earth, and if one would benefit from these powers one must understand and respect them. Applied to national affairs, this theory implies that a society can flourish only if it is in harmony with the elemental forces of the land, which include the generative process of agriculture. Relying on the Taoist notion of harmony with nature, Bo Linh turned his back on the unharmonious cultural edifice of provincial Vietnam and instead struck deep roots into the indigenous soil.

During the years that Bo Linh was uniting the Vietnamese and organizing his kingdom, the new Sung dynasty was consolidating its control over northern China and conquering the kingdoms in southern China. In 971, Sung armies conquered Southern Han. A united China posed a great danger to the young Vietnamese realm. Judging from past experience, the Vietnamese could expect the reborn empire to claim their lands. This in fact happened, but not for another decade. The Sung were momentarily busy with more urgent affairs in the north, and this gave the Vietnamese time to prepare. Bo Linh followed a policy of maintaining correct diplomatic relations with Sung while training a large standby army.

In 973, after Southern Han had been completely pacified, Bo Linh sent envoys to Sung. These envoys officially went under the authority of Dinh Lien as "Peaceful Sea Military Governor," a title that had been confirmed by Southern Han and now belonged to Sung by right of conquest. The envoys brought tribute and requested that Lien's title be confirmed by the new dynasty. Sung quickly approved. The edict granting the title praised the Dinh family for having "suppressed rebels and plunderers in an entire region." The edict went on to cite the distance of the Vietnamese lands from the imperial court and the difficulty of ruling such remote areas; finally, it justified the favorable judgment "because [Lien] signaled [his intention] to serve in agreement [with us]."[93]

The prompt Sung approval was based on expedience, for the Chinese were not yet ready to go back into Vietnam. The decision was all the easier for Sung because the Vietnamese were united under able leadership that both kept the peace and performed traditional diplomatic amenities.

In addition to "Peaceful Sea Military Governor," Sung conferred several other titles on Lien, including "An-nam Protector General" and the rank of duke. The Sung envoys who arrived in Hoa-lu with these titles were surely aware that Bo Linh was the real ruler, but there is no evidence that they objected to the situation. The first diplomatic contact with Sung having been a success, Bo Linh felt encouraged to regularize his own position in the eyes of the empire.

In 975, envoys were again sent north in Lien's name, bearing gifts and "asking for favor." The favor being asked for is not explicitly recorded, but

93. Yamamoto, "Annan," pp. 56–57.

it is clear from the Sung response that Lien was asking for an imperial edict on behalf of his father. Sung again sent envoys to Hoa-lu, this time bearing the title "King of Giao-chi Prefecture" for Bo Linh. This strange title had no precedent; it was coined for the occasion. The reason for this may have been that all the traditional titles had already been given to Lien. But it is more likely that Sung did not perceive Bo Linh as conforming to any previously known pattern.

The edict granting this title to Bo Linh stated:

> For generations [yours has been] an honorable family, capable of protecting a distant region, inclined to advance Chinese culture, and often paying consideration to the imperial court. [When] the Nine Provinces [meaning China proper] were united into one and beyond the Five Passes all was peaceful and quiet, [you] accordingly notified [us] without delay and, furthermore, paid the required tribute.[94]

The edict went on to describe the relationship between Bo Linh and the Sung emperor as that between an obedient son and a beneficent father.

Bo Linh's diplomatic status opened a new era in the long history of Sino-Vietnamese relations. Sung was in effect recognizing the Vietnamese kingdom on two levels. One was the traditional relationship with Bo Linh's son. Bo Linh himself never communicated directly with the imperial throne; all contact with Sung was made in the name of his son, who held the customary titles. For example, in 977, when Sung T'ai Tsu died and was succeeded by T'ai Tsung, congratulatory tribute was sent to the new emperor in the name of Dinh Lien as "Peaceful Sea Military Governor."[95]

On the other hand, Sung recognized Bo Linh with an irregular title that carried no traditional diplomatic responsibilities. As "King of Giao-chi Prefecture," he was not obliged to send congratulatory tribute on the accession of T'ai Tsung, as was the "Peaceful Sea Military Governor." Thus, Bo Linh succeeded in translating a degree of distance into a diplomatic relationship with Sung that lent weight to his claim of true independence. Sung was too busy to split hairs and was content to vaguely idealize the relationship in terms of the clichéd concept of filial piety, while maintaining proper diplomatic contact with his son. According to Vietnamese records, "in relations with Sung, Lien was considered to be the ruler."[96]

The title "King of Giao-chi Prefecture" (*Giao-chi Quan-vuong*), which Bo Linh elicited from Sung, became the standard way for Sung to recognize Vietnamese kings until the mid-twelfth century, when Sung officially changed the name of Vietnam from Giao-chi Prefecture to An-nam Kingdom and began to recognize Vietnamese kings with the title "King of the

94. Ibid., p. 57; *TT, Ban ky*, 1, 4a–b.
95. Yamamoto, "Annan," p. 60.
96. *TT, Ban ky*, 1, 4b.

An-nam Kingdom" (*An-nam Quoc-vuong*).[97] Bo Linh thus set a diplomatic precedent that lasted nearly two centuries.

Bo Linh must have realized that this double relationship was unstable and would not endure, that it was only a matter of time before Sung would begin to put pressure on the southern frontier. The major achievements of his reign were the establishment of a diplomatic basis for Vietnamese independence and the laying of foundations for universal military mobilization.

In the spring of 974, Bo Linh published an organizational plan for an army of one hundred thousand men. This army was called the Ten Circuit Army. It was a territorial militia organized in ten circuits, or geographical districts. Each circuit held ten armies, and each army was composed of ten brigades. Each brigade had ten companies, each company had ten squads, and each squad had ten men. This army was in addition to Bo Linh's personal troops and those of his trusted followers, who were probably recruited mainly from Ai and Hoan. It was designed to mobilize the peasant manpower of the Hong River plain. The men of the Ten Circuit Army were distinguished by the hats they wore. Their hats were square, with the four sides of the brim coming to a point at the top; the exterior was covered with leather. This style of military hat was still used in the Vietnamese army as late as the fifteenth century.[98]

The significance of this army continues to the present day. National defense is a major theme in Vietnamese history, and it is no accident that one of Bo Linh's major accomplishments was to organize a large peasant militia. A country the size of Vietnam could not hope to resist the military pressure of a neighbor like China without mobilizing the entire population. Such a broadly based army also reveals the popular support that Bo Linh enjoyed.

It is recorded that, in 976, "merchant boats from different nations beyond the sea arrived and presented the goods of their countries."[99] The political unity and stability achieved by Bo Linh made large regional markets possible. This encouraged commercial expansion and attracted foreign merchants. The Hoa-lu court provided a new market for the luxury goods in which foreign merchants specialized.

In an edict of 975, Bo Linh prescribed the types of clothing to be worn by civil and military officials at the court.[100] The envoys sent to China in that year bore gifts of gold, rhinoceros horn, and elephant tusks. In addition to these ceremonial goods, military expenditures must have been considerable; weapons and special leather hats were made for one hundred

---

97. See the *TT* under the years 993, 1007, 1010, 1029, 1055, 1073, 1130, and 1164.
98. *TT, Ban ky*, 1, 4a.
99. Ibid., 1. 4b.
100. Ibid., loc. cit.

thousand men. The Vietnamese economy was transformed to serve the needs of a strong king ruling from a hitherto insignificant place.

Dinh Lien had assisted his father from the beginning. He led soldiers during the war years and later stood at the head of the kingdom in relations with China. At the Hoa-lu court, he was second only to his father, being Bo Linh's only adult son. In spite of this, in the first month of 978, Bo Linh designated his infant son Hang Lang heir apparent. Lien did not consent to this arrangement. In the month of Hang Lang's elevation, an earthquake is recorded. A hailstorm is recorded the following month, and drought is recorded the ensuing summer.[101] According to traditional historiographical practice, domestic political troubles were often expressed as natural calamities. The earthquake, hailstorm, and drought of the chronicler can thus be taken as indications of dissention in the court.

It is recorded that Bo Linh established Hang Lang as his heir because of his "extreme love" for the infant.[102] Hang Lang's exact age is not known, but he was younger than Bo Linh's four-year-old second son, Toan. It seems curious that Bo Linh would pass over his experienced eldest son for a mere babe simply as an affectionate whim. It is reasonable to assume that factions were contending for supremacy at the court. Bo Linh was not a sophisticated man. He had led an active life and was now in his mid-fifties. It is conceivable that he was manipulated by certain people, perhaps through Hang Lang's mother, to disinherit Lien. Who these people were and what interests they represented are not explicitly known. Lien was closely associated with his father's rustic origins and may have been opposed by the landowning and ecclesiastical leaders of Giao. In any case, Lien was not about to let his inheritance be stolen. Early in 979 he sent an assassin, who did away with Hang Lang. Several months later, near the end of the year, an official named Do Thich killed both Bo Linh and Lien as they slept off their drunkenness in a palace courtyard after a feast.[103]

Do Thich was a so-called "imperial attendant" with the rank of marquis. It is recorded that he had formerly been a customhouse officer, and that one night, laying down to sleep on the bridge where the customhouse was located, he had dreamed that a meteor fell from the sky into his mouth. Taking this to be an auspicious sign, he accordingly sprouted a regicidal heart.[104] This story may explain Do Thich's predilection for slaying his lords, but it tells us little else. There is no evidence to suggest that he was part of a conspiracy involving other persons. It is nevertheless likely that his deed was related to the succession trouble of the previous two years. After the

101. Ibid., 1, 4b–5a.
102. Ibid., 1, 5a.
103. Ibid., 1, 5a–6a; *VSL*, 1, 17b.
104. *TT, Ban ky*, 1, 5b–6a; *VSL*, 1, 17b.

deaths of Bo Linh and Lien, the single surviving male member of the Dinh family was the child Toan, whose mother was from the Duong family. Whether or not Do Thich considered himself a partisan of the Duong family can only be conjectured. In the absence of information we cannot guess his motivation.

After killing the two rulers, Do Thich climbed up and hid under the eaves of the palace. After three days of this he grew very thirsty, and when it rained he reached out his hand to catch some water. This was seen by a kitchen maid; she informed Nguyen Bac, who was in command of the palace. Bac sent men to fetch Do Thich down and had him beheaded. The assassin's corpse was cut into small pieces and distributed among the populace to be eaten. It is recorded that "there were none who did not strive to eat of him."[105]

A common belief in some premodern societies was that a murderer acquired the power and virtue of his victim. Bo Linh had been a great national hero who was popularly believed to possess supernatural power. The virtue stored up by Bo Linh in a lifetime of incomparable success was transmitted to his assassin. By devouring Do Thich, people seem to have hoped to acquire some of Bo Linh's virtue.

Bo Linh's murder was accounted for in a number of ways. The official chronicle records that in 974 Bo Linh had received a prophecy that he would be assassinated.[106] However, the prophecy, as it has been preserved, contains riddles that allude to later Vietnamese dynasties, so it cannot be regarded as authentic. Furthermore, the founder of the Ly dynasty, whose rise to power is an important part of the prophecy, was born in 974, so the dating of the prophecy to this year certainly occurred after he took the throne, thirty years after Bo Linh's death.

The official chronicle further tells a story, claiming to date from the early years of Bo Linh's career, that carries a hint of foreboding. According to this story, Bo Linh was, in his early days, a humble fisherman who often cast his net in Giao-thuy River, an estuary of the Hong near the sea. One day he pulled in a large jade tablet but accidentally broke off a corner when it knocked against the prow of his boat. That night he stayed at Giao-thuy Temple and put the tablet in a fish basket when he went to sleep. During the night a bright light emanated from the fish basket. The temple priest awoke and asked the reason for the light. Bo Linh showed him the tablet. When the priest saw the tablet, he sighed and said: "My son, you will someday be prosperous and respected; I cannot say why, but unfortunately your good fortune will not last long."[107]

105. *TT, Ban ky,* 1, 6a; *VSL,* 1, 18a.
106. *TT, Ban ky,* 1, 6a–b; *VSL,* 1, 17b.
107. *TT, Ban ky,* 1, 6a–b; *VSL,* 1, 17b.

This story seems to be inspired by the outlook of later Vietnamese literati. The jade tablet symbolizes the mandate of Heaven that Bo Linh received to rule his people. His manner of obtaining it suggests that the mandate originated from the land itself, as opposed to being conferred by a distant imperial throne. But in damaging the tablet Bo Linh revealed his own flawed, or untutored, character, and spoiled the full measure of benefit from the mandate. This fits the view of later Vietnamese scholars who saw Bo Linh as a great national leader but as uneducated and lacking the necessary knowledge to rule properly.[108]

An eighteenth-century Vietnamese scholar recorded a folk tradition that explains Bo Linh's greatness and death in terms of popular animist and Taoist beliefs. According to this tradition, Bo Linh's father was a huge otter, which coupled with his mother as she bathed in a pond. Dinh Cong Tru, whose concubine she was, died a few years later without knowing that he was not the boy's father. Bo Linh grew into an agile lad, skilled in swimming and diving. When his mother heard that the villagers had caught and eaten the otter, she gathered the otter's bones from the rubbish heap, put them in a funerary container on a shelf over her hearth, and told Bo Linh, "Here are your father's remains."

Later, a Chinese geomancer arrived in the area. He had been following "dragon's veins." Geomancers were experts in studying terrain to apprehend its spiritual nature. They believed that supernatural power originated in the highlands of Tibet and flowed down along mountain ranges through "dragon's veins." These "dragon's veins" branched out carrying spiritual energy to all parts of the earth. The power was not evenly distributed, however, and the peculiarities of terrain produced spots where it collected, which became resting places for powerful spiritual beings. It was generally believed that a person could obtain special powers in pursuing his ambitions if he buried his ancestors at such a place. This was the object of the Chinese geomancer who arrived at Hoa-lu. According to the "dragon's vein" theory, Hoa-lu was situated at a critical point along the uplands separating the Hong and Ma river plains.

One night the geomancer saw a brilliant red light issue from the depths of the pond where Bo Linh had been conceived and shoot up into the sky, where it struck the Heavenly Horse Star. Since the Heavenly Horse Star symbolized the steed that bore the emperor, the geomancer realized that there was a powerful supernatural being living at the bottom of the pond. He accordingly advertised for someone to dive down and take a look. Bo Linh took the job and found a stone horse standing at the bottom of the pond. After he reported to the geomancer, the geomancer had him go back down with a handful of grass and offer it to the horse to see what would

108. For example, see Le Van Huu's comments in *TT, Ban ky*, 1, 3a–b.

happen. When Bo Linh reported that the horse had snapped at the grass, the geomancer understood that this was an auspicious burial site. He paid Bo Linh for his services, then hastened back to China to get his father's bones.

Being a bright lad, Bo Linh had surmised what the geomancer was up to, and so he wrapped the otter's bones in a bundle of grass, dived down, and fed them to the horse at the bottom of the pond. He subsequently became a powerful leader. Some years later the Chinese geomancer finally came back with his ancestral bones, but, seeing that Bo Linh was now a great hero, he immediately realized that his burial site had been stolen. Intent on revenge, the geomancer went to Bo Linh and congratulated him on his cleverness in burying his father in the pond. He then gave Bo Linh a precious sword and urged him to go down and hang the sword on the horse's neck in order to make the burial complete and to insure that no enemy could ever stand against him. This seemed reasonable to Bo Linh, so he dived down and placed the sword on the horse's neck.

Bo Linh later united the country and founded a kingdom, but suffered an untimely death at the hands of an assassin. Consequently it was rumored that he had fallen into the geomancer's trap, for in geomancy there is a maxim that says: "When a horse's head carries a sword, it produces a homicidal effluvium."[109]

This story contains two basic themes. One is the idea that Bo Linh's father was an otter. The significance of this is that it links Bo Linh with the ancient belief that kingship derives from water spirits, that children of the "water clan" become kings. Lac Long Quan, the original Vietnamese culture hero and father of the Hung kings, was a prince of the watery realm. King An Duong received his mandate to rule from a turtle. Trieu Quang Phuc became king with the blessing of a dragon that appeared to him in the midst of a vast swamp. Dragons were considered to be the most powerful of all water spirits. In the story of Bo Linh's boyhood that we have already considered, he is protected by two dragons. The otter is also a water creature. As the son of an otter, Bo Linh had a mandate to rule in terms of indigenous cultural beliefs. For the Vietnamese, this mandate superseded the heavenly mandate of Chinese imperial ideology. The idea that kingship derived from water spirits was common throughout most of Asia, including China. In Vietnam, it became particularly important as an alternative to the claims of Chinese imperialism.[110]

The second theme of the story centers around the geomancer. The philosophical outlook that encompasses "dragon's veins" and auspicious burial sites is essentially Taoist, as is the astrological implication of the red

109. Matusmoto Nobuhiro, "Rō Dacchi Densetsu no Annan Iden," pp. 3–4.

110. Yamamoto Tatsurō, "Ōken no Hongen o Monogataru Indoshina no Kazukazu no Setsuwa ni tsuite," pp. 925–38.

light from the pond shooting toward the Heavenly Horse Star. Both the Heavenly Horse and the horse at the bottom of the pond can be regarded as forms of dragons, for horses and dragons were often interchangeable in popular lore. The dragon symbolized power, immortality, and imperial sovereignty. The geomancer believed he had found a burial site befitting the ancestors of an emperor. Moreover, it was believed that if anyone should succeed in burying the bones of his ancestors at this site, he would indeed become an emperor. The implication of Bo Linh's usurping such a site from a Chinese is that he deprived China of its presumed right to rule the Vietnamese. The Chinese gained revenge by tricking Bo Linh into tarnishing the benefits of the burial site. This is an allegory of subsequent Sino-Vietnamese relations. The Vietnamese gained their independence, but were repeatedly challenged by Chinese aggression. The Chinese geomancer was outsmarted, but he made sure that his antagonist paid for it.

The otter story is not unique. It is almost identical to a story accounting for the rise of the Manchu dynasty in Manchuria that Japanese scholars reported early in this century from oral traditions in Korea.[111] The coincidence does not necessarily mean that one of the stories derived from the other, for behind the specific significance of the story's being attached to Bo Linh and to the Manchus is the broader environment shared by peoples on a receding imperial frontier. The basic elements of the story are common to most of East and Southeast Asia. Its importance is that it explains the displacement of imperial authority by more indigenous concepts of sovereignty.

Vietnamese historians in later centuries held a high opinion of Bo Linh. In the thirteenth century, Le Van Huu wrote:

> The first emperor, with a gifted brilliance beyond ordinary men and a courageous strategy that overshadowed his age, at a time when our land of Viet was masterless, being hacked in pieces and occupied by a crowd of strong men, struck a single blow causing all twelve warlords to submit, founded the kingdom, built a capital, changed his title to emperor, appointed all the officials, established the six armies, almost completely put in order the laws and administration; was it not the will of Heaven that caused our land of Viet to bring forth a wise and virtuous man to receive the succession of King Trieu?[112]

These words were echoed in the fifteenth century by Ngo Si Lien:

> The emperor, with a gifted brilliance beyond ordinary men and a courageous strategy that overshadowed his age, exterminated the whole crowd of strong

111. Matsumoto, "Rō Dacchi Densetsu," pp. 1–5.
112. TT, Ban ky, 1, 2b–3a.

men and carried forward the succession of Martial [Emperor] Trieu; but he neglected to take precautions and did not secure a full lifespan.[113]

Trieu is Vietnamese for Chao, and these passages refer to Chao T'o, the Chinese official who proclaimed the kingdom of Nan Yüeh at Canton near the end of the third century B.C. In telling their national history, Vietnamese scholars wanted to emphasize the legal and historical basis of their independence, because China posed a constant threat of intervention. The earliest recorded example of a southern ruler successfully resisting northern aggression was Chao T'o. In 185 B.C. he reacted to Han hostility by proclaiming himself emperor and manning his frontier with a large army. Han was forced to back down, and as a result Chao T'o's name rang through the centuries. In Vietnamese mythology he gained possession of King An Duong's magic turtle claw and thereby became the last ruler legitimized by local cultural symbols before the Chinese provincial regime was introduced. Thus, Chao T'o was both an end and a beginning. He represented the end of the pre-Chinese indigenous royal succession; he also represented the beginning of imperial succession in an age when the concept of kingship became more firmly associated with the ability to resist Chinese aggression. This is what Le Van Huu had to say about Chao T'o:

> Martial Emperor Trieu, succeeding in opening up and developing our land of Viet, named himself emperor of the nation, and, contending with Han, published a letter proclaiming himself emperor, thereby originating the imperial inheritance in our land of Viet; his achievement can be said to be great. If those who later were emperors in the land of Viet could have emulated Martial Trieu in carefully guarding the frontier, establishing the army and the nation, and keeping friendly relations with neighboring countries in order to preserve the throne with humanity, then the borderlands would have been protected in perpetuity and the northerners would not again have been able to stare arrogantly at us.[114]

The historiographical connection made by Vietnamese historians between Chao T'o and Dinh Bo Linh was useful in buttressing the Vietnamese claim to independence in relations with China. The Vietnamese considered their kings to be in a line of succession that began before the provincial era. Although Chao T'o was not Vietnamese by birth, Vietnamese historians recognized in him the spirit of their political survival and on that account claimed him as their own.

Chao T'o was a regular fixture in the historical self-image of the south from the time of Han. Vietnamese historians inherited this self-image in the

---

113. Ibid., 1, 1a.
114. *TT*, 2, 8a–b.

same way that they inherited Chinese characters and the literature that came with them. The Wu prefect, Hsüeh Tsung, in his memorial of 231, and the T'ang exile, Shen Ch'üan-chi, in his poem quoted in an earlier chapter, both routinely cited Chao T'o as a founding father of the south. These two examples are typical of the way Chao T'o thrived in the educated imagination of southern literati.

Aside from his literary fame, Chao T'o also left a political legacy of anti-imperialism on the southern frontiers. As we have seen, in 728 a rebellion in the Canton area was led by a man who styled himself the "King of Nan Yüeh." We do not know what Bo Linh had in mind when he gave this title to his son, but he probably knew that the Chinese considered it subversive, although Sung later conferred it posthumously on Vietnamese kings.

The lingering heritage of imperial insubordination probably encouraged Le Van Huu's projection of Chao T'o as the original prototype of a good Vietnamese ruler and the political forerunner of Dinh Bo Linh. Later Vietnamese historians enlarged Chao T'o's historical image to envision a golden age of Vietnamese independence in antiquity that could reinforce their continuing resistance to northern pressure.[115] Although they were primarily interested in interpreting the past to meet contemporary needs, their selection of Bo Linh as Chao T'o's successor reveals something of their perception of Bo Linh in his own right.

Bo Linh established an imperial tradition recognized by all later Vietnamese kings. He was designated by later historians as the heir of what they considered to be the ancient foundations of their nation. He earned this distinction largely by virtue of having "exterminated the crowd of strong men" who had "hacked in pieces" the Vietnamese lands, thereby securing the conditions necessary for a stable, united kingdom that could concentrate its energy against foreign threats.

Bo Linh nonetheless remained a controversial figure in Vietnamese history. In 1683, Samuel Baron wrote the first detailed description of Vietnam in the English language. His father was a Dutch merchant who had lived in Hanoi for several years, and his mother was Vietnamese. He himself became a British citizen. He was a keen observer, and his familiarity with Vietnamese society and government was sufficiently intimate that we can regard his descriptions of contemporary affairs as accurate. When he discusses Vietnamese history, we can assume that he is reflecting popular opinion on the subject. This is what he wrote about Bo Linh:

> after their [the Chinese] departure Ding [Baron's spelling for *Dinh*] was king. Now, whether they made him so, or whether he usurped the regality, by the

115. See O. W. Wolters, "Historians and Emperors in Vietnam and China."

assistance of great numbers of vagabonds, and other scum of the nation, is differently delivered. They say, that King Ding had enjoyed the scepter but a small time before the great ones murmured against him.[116]

This seems a strange commentary on a man portrayed in the official history as a great national hero. Baron's discussion of Vietnamese history contains many errors of unknown origin, as well as suppositions that he supplied to provide a plausible narrative. But when he speaks of the versions of Bo Linh's rise to power as being "differently delivered" and cites "they say" as a source of information, we can assume that he is reporting interpretations current among the Vietnamese of his time. Prior to the passage quoted above, Baron says:

> They [the Vietnamese] pretend they have had the use of the Chinese characters amongst them before the reign of Ding, one of their first kings, according to their best historians.[117]

Elsewhere in his account, Baron shows remarkable knowledge of and sympathy with classical studies, as well as knowledge of the steps in the careers of scholar-officials, so it is not unreasonable for him to be familiar with the opinions of the "best historians."

Nevertheless, his comments are unaccountable unless we assume that Bo Linh had somehow become entangled in the social contradictions of the seventeenth century. If we bear in mind that the otter story was recorded half a century after Baron's account, this is a strong probability. With the otter story, the peasantry could claim Bo Linh as one of its own. The ruling class of the seventeenth century could likewise project its social perspective into the past by identifying with the "great ones" who considered Bo Linh to be a leader of "vagabonds and other scum of the nation." Social problems of the seventeenth century may in this way have been reflected in Baron's knowledge of Bo Linh.

Bo Linh occupied a sensitive spot in national memory. He was a rustic who founded a kingdom. Ruling-class Vietnamese of later centuries had difficulty identifying with him in social terms, although his political achievement was a cornerstone of their national heritage. Bo Linh swept out the upper-class T'ang residue of the tenth century. This social upheaval laid the foundation for Vietnamese independence. Educated Vietnamese of later centuries could afford the luxury of cultivating a taste for Chinese civilization, but this luxury had been purchased for them by such men as Dinh Bo Linh, who saw China as primarily a threat and a potential adversary.

---

116. Samuel Baron, "A Description of the Kingdom of Tonqueen," p. 19.
117. Ibid., loc. cit.

Conclusion

As we have seen, the regime established in Vietnam by Kao P'ien after the Nan-chao War endured well into the tenth century. However, it never surmounted its ideological dependence on the imperial world. The Co-loa monarchy founded by Ngo Quyen was little more than a feeble imitation of the regional domains existing in China at the time, and after Quyen's death it simply mirrored the progressive deterioration of the upper-class position in Vietnam.

The ruling class in Vietnam initially began to falter under the pressure of Southern Han aggression. The Battle of Bach-dang River put an end to that threat, and thereafter the Giao landowners fell prey to newly-awakened domestic forces. The rise of Dinh Bo Linh was a reaction against the anarchy of the ruling landlord class and an affirmation of village cultural values.

The death of Dinh Bo Linh was followed by a brief civil war, during which the commander-in-chief of the army, Le Hoan, took the throne. An important reason for his success was that the Sung dynasty was finally ready to claim China's presumed right to rule Vietnam, and he was the senior military leader at Hoa-lu. Hoping to benefit from Bo Linh's assassination, Sung launched an invasion, but Le Hoan rallied the Vietnamese and defeated the Chinese expedition. This victory gave the Vietnamese nearly a century of relief from northern pressure. During that century, institutional foundations were laid that would serve as the basis of Vietnamese independence until the end of the fourteenth century.

During the quarter century of Le Hoan's relatively tranquil reign, the Buddhist interests of Giao infiltrated the Hoa-lu court. In 1009, four years after Hoan's death, Ly Cong Uan, a temple orphan and commander of the palace guard, was raised to the throne, thereby founding the Ly dynasty, which endured for more than two centuries.

Ly Cong Uan abandoned Hoa-lu and established his capital on the site of Dai-la, naming it Thang-long. This city, now called Hanoi, remained the capital of Vietnam until the nineteenth century, when the Nguyen dynasts of Hue gained control of the country.

The first three kings of the Ly dynasty were capable rulers. They established a Buddhist monarchical tradition that had ideological affinities with other Southeast Asian kingdoms. When the last of these kings died in 1072, he left a stable throne to his seven-year-old son. Four years later, in 1076, the Vietnamese defeated a second Sung invasion. This was the last war with China until the Mongol-Yüan invasions two hundred years later.

Early in the fifteenth century, China attempted to reestablish its ancient hegemony. The Ming dynasty occupied Vietnam for twenty years, but was finally pushed out by a determined national liberation movement. An important result of this crisis was the decline of Vietnamese Buddhism and its replacement at court by Neo-Confucian currents of thought as defined by Ming orthodoxy. Thus, many of the Chinese-inspired aspects of traditional Vietnamese government and culture that are often attributed to the so-called "thousand years of Chinese domination" were in fact not introduced until the fifteenth century or after by Vietnamese kings trying to establish greater control over their realm.

This change came at a time when the Vietnamese were expanding southward and regional loyalties posed new challenges to the historical unity of the nation. The disciplined sense of national identity that is second nature among the Vietnamese of the northern plains has to varying degress been modified in the lands conquered from the Chams and Khmers. The necessity of dealing with China was a central element of Vietnamese national experience, but was confined to the northern frontier. Facing the north, the Vietnamese needed fixed concentration, steady nerves, and unfathomable resolve. However, when they turned south, it was possible to relax somewhat and to indulge the senses.

Beginning in the seventeenth century, the Vietnamese of the southern frontier began to develop a more autonomous point of view. For them, the threat of China was less urgent. The south stretched out before them, theirs for the taking. The two poles of Vietnamese national character in modern times grew out of the experience of the two national frontiers. They are complementary. This combination of northern resolve and southern release is a source of both irritation and creativity.

A strong, united China has historically posed a problem to Vietnam. Chinese policy has traditionally been either to dominate Vietnam or, if that be impossible, to keep Vietnam weak and divided. As a result of their imperial legacy, the Chinese instinctively perceive a strong, united Vietnam as a special, almost domestic, problem.

Sino-Vietnamese relations have traditionally been expressed in terms of vassalage. Only in recent years have the Chinese and Vietnamese begun to speak of their relationship in terms of theoretical equality. Making this new relationship effective will require a large adjustment in the view each nation has historically had of the other. Chinese pressure of any kind is instinctively felt by the Vietnamese as a threat to their national survival. On the other hand, the assertion by Vietnam of its national interests other than in deference to Chinese policies is instinctively felt by the Chinese as impertinence bordering on insubordination. Perhaps an inevitable result of the difference in size between the two countries, these feelings lie at the root of Sino-Vietnamese relations today as they did two thousand years ago.

The impact of Chinese civilization on Vietnam during the period discussed in this book was large. But the Vietnamese capacity developed at that time for receiving selected elements of Chinese civilization was at least as important as the specific items absorbed, since Chinese influence on

Vietnamese society in the independence period was as great as it was under Chinese provincial government. Vietnamese kings could foster Chinese ways of doing things with more success than could Chinese officials, for they generally knew how much of what their people would tolerate.

The habit of looking to China was nevertheless involuntarily imposed by a simple fact of life. China was big and Vietnam was small. The Vietnamese grasped Chinese ways of doing things as a means of survival. Whether on the level of an exchange of poems between Vietnamese and Chinese diplomats or on that of an exchange of sword strokes between Vietnamese and Chinese warriors, the Vietnamese had to show that they were equal to the test. Consequently, the Vietnamese invested a great deal of effort in acquiring and maintaining technical, administrative, and cultural skills simply to hold the line against "the arrogant stare of the northerners." Whether consciously or not, the creative powers of the Vietnamese were to a significant degree absorbed in this endeavor. We only need compare Dong-son art with Vietnamese art of later centuries to realize this sobering fact. The cheerful grace and originality of Dong-son art gave way to Vietnamized renderings of Chinese styles. This is why the Vietnamese value their independence so highly. It is one thing they have managed to preserve.

Chinese contributions to Vietnam cover all aspects of culture, society, and government, from chopsticks wielded by peasants to writing brushes wielded by scholars and officials. But generally speaking, Chinese influence was most strongly felt at the highest levels of government and society. Chinese concepts of law and administration became important elements of Vietnamese government in the independence period, for they contributed to the ability of Vietnamese leaders to consolidate their power and resist external threats, in particular the Chinese threat. Scholarship and literature were unavoidably impregnated with the classical heritage of China; Chinese was the language of administration and scholarship, as Latin was in pre-modern Europe. The ability of Vietnamese envoys at the Chinese court to express themselves fluently in terms of Chinese language and culture was an important way to demonstrate that Vietnam was a "civilized" country and did not need the "civilizing" care of Chinese tutelage. The necessity of maintaining this "civilized" face toward China resulted in a neglect of vernacular Vietnamese culture, which was but gradually remedied through the centuries.

Upper-class Vietnamese imbibed the ideology of the Chinese classics and formally recognized the patriarchal family system of China as the ideal basis for organizing society. This ideal penetrated Vietnamese society, but only as an ideal; it was to a degree realized only among upper- or middle-class Vietnamese who aspired to prominent roles in government or society.

The Vietnamese ability to absorb Chinese influence brings to mind the legend of Lac Long Quan and Au Co, discussed in chapter 1, which exemplifies the theme of Vietnam's neutralizing the threat of northern domination by appropriating the source of northern legitimacy. In the independence period, ruling-class Vietnamese learned to pose as disciples of classical civilization, thereby overcoming their "barbarism" and removing any pretext for China to exercise its "civilizing" mission in their land.

Why did China's impact on Vietnam fall short of turning the Vietnamese into Chinese? The Vietnamese clearly did not want to become Chinese, and this surely lies at the root of their continuing existence as a separate nation. Furthermore, unlike Kuang-tung and Kuang-hsi, Vietnam was on the border. Contact with Chams and Khmers, both having a high level of non-Chinese culture, was relatively intimate, and this reinforced Vietnam's separate identity. In the Chams and Khmers, the Vietnamese witnessed alternatives to Chinese civilization; although these alternatives were less viable for the Vietnamese than for their Southeast Asian neighbors, they nevertheless broadened the cultural perspective of ruling-class Vietnamese.

Unlike Nan-chao in Yün-nan, and other upland kingdoms on the periphery of China, Vietnamese society rested firmly on the foundation of lowland wet-rice agriculture; this lowland society was culturally buttressed with strong prehistoric traditions. Unlike landlocked Ssu-ch'uan, Vietnam was far from the centers of Chinese power and on an international trade route that brought stimulating contact with other peoples and civilizations.

Patterns of Chinese immigration and settlement had, by the end of the T'ang period, determined that Vietnam lay beyond the absorbing powers of Chinese society. From the beginning, Chinese interest in Kuang-tung, Kuang-hsi, and northern Vietnam was primarily commercial; the Chinese wanted a port on the South China Sea. It was necessary that the Vietnamese be conquered because they demographically dominated the shores of that sea. By T'ang times, Canton had been sufficiently built up by Chinese immigration as a counterweight to the Vietnamese that the necessity of ruling Vietnam became less urgent.

Table 7 shows a comparison of registered households in Kuang-tung and Kuang-hsi with those in Vietnam from the four dynasties for which statistics are available. According to Han statistics, registered households in Kuang-tung and Kuang-hsi in the first century were only half the number in Vietnam. By the fourth century, registered households in Kuang-tung and Kuang-hsi were more than one and a half (1.68) times the number in Vietnam. In the fifth century, they were nearly five (4.85) times more. In the eighth century, registered households in Kuang-tung and Kuang-hsi were well over five (5.36) times the number in Vietnam.

Tsang Wah-moon discussed these demographic patterns in the context of what he called "the centricity of development of Ling-nan [Kuang-tung, Kuang-hsi, and northern Vietnam] during the T'ang dynasty." He has

Table 7. Registered Household Statistics from Kuang-tung, Kuang-hsi, and Vietnam

	Kuang-tung and Kuang-hsi	Vietnam
Han (A.D. 2)	71,805	143,643
Chin (fourth century)	43,120	25,600
Sung (fifth century)	50,664	10,453
T'ang (742)	219,430	40,963

shown that the rise of Canton as an international port was accompanied by the rapid commercial and demographic development of towns and cities on major routes connecting Canton with the north.[118] The implication of this is that, in terms of maintaining China's commercial interests on the South China Sea, Canton became the end of the road. There was no urgent necessity to go any further south.

If it had been able to control Vietnam without constantly sending soldiers, China would have enjoyed certain strategic advantages, particularly as long as Yün-nan remained unconquered. But with the passing of each century, Chinese rule in Vietnam drifted further away from the real interests of the empire. Ruling Vietnam became a luxury that China could not afford. Han had ruled Vietnam, so every succeeding dynasty thought it should also. By the tenth century, however, ruling Vietnam had become for China a costly habit.

For their part, the Vietnamese retained their own language and, with it, memories of their pre-Chinese civilization. The survival of the Vietnamese language is extremely significant, for it means that whatever the Chinese did in Vietnam was conditioned by a cultural realm that remained distinct and separate from the Chinese sphere of thought. The Vietnamese never lost their taste for local heroes, such as the Trung sisters, Lady Trieu, Trieu Quang Phuc, and Phung Hung. What China had to say to them was bent through the prism of their own language and culture.

As a result of their experience under Chinese rule, the Vietnamese developed a sharp awareness of Chinese intentions. Living in the shadow of a large empire, they necessarily became expert survival artists. An interesting statement of the Vietnamese attitude toward China and of how Vietnamese leaders were expected to respond to the constant threat of northern aggression comes from Ngo Si Lien, the fifteenth-century historian. Commenting on the surrender of Ly Phat Tu to Liu Fang in 602, he wrote:

118. Tsang Wah-moon, *T'ang-tai Ling-nan fa-chan ti heh-hsin hsing.* pp. 14–23.

South and North, when strong or when weak, each has its time. When the North is weak, then we are strong, and when the North is strong, then we become weak; that is how things are. This being so, those who lead the country must train soldiers, repair transport, be prepared for surprise attacks, set up obstacles to defend the borders, use the ideas of a large country with the warriors of a small country. Days of leisure should be used to teach loyalty and respect for elders, so the people will clearly know their duty toward superiors and be willing to die for their leaders. If an invasion is imminent, take words and negotiate, or offer gems and silk as tribute; if this does not succeed, then, though danger flood from every side, man the walls and fight the battles, vowing to resist until death and to die with the fatherland; in that case one need be ashamed of nothing. But imagine someone who sees the enemy arrive on the border and, without a battle, grows afraid and begs to surrender! The king was a coward and none of his officials spoke up; it can be said that there was no one in the country at the time.[119]

Ngo Si Lien admits the danger of having China for a neighbor: "That is how things are." But he quickly gets down to business with practical measures for making the best of the situation. The birth of Vietnam was the birth of a spirit of resistance to the universal claims of Chinese power. It represented the collective decision of a society to risk danger for the sake of preserving its heritage. Vietnamese independence is the result of commitments made by successive generations.

119. *TT,* 4, 22a–b.

Appendix A

The Legend of Lac Long Quan and Au Co

The legend of Lac Long Quan and Au Co is recorded in the *Linh-nam chich quai* and the *Dai Viet su ky toan thu*. The *Dai Viet su ky toan thu* version is a slight modification of the *Linh-nam chich quai* account. According to the *Linh-nam chich quai* (*LNCQ*, 5), Au Co was the wife of the interloping king. The *Dai Viet su ky toan thu* (*TT*, 1, 2a), however, makes her his daughter, apparently for moralistic reasons, for Lac Long Quan would then not be guilty of taking another man's wife.

According to the *Linh-nam chich quai* (*LNCQ*, 6), one hundred sons were born from a single egglike sack; Lac Long Quan took fifty sons with him to the sea, leaving the other fifty with Au Co on Mount Tan-vien, among whom the most courageous was selected to become the first of the Hung kings. The *Dai Viet su ky toan thu* (*TT*, 1, 2a), however, makes the first of the Hung kings one of those who followed the father, thus stressing patriarchal values. This is remembered differently among the upland Muong, who, like the modern Vietnamese, are descendents of the ancient Vietnamese. According to the Muong, there were fifty sons and fifty daughters instead of one hundred sons; half followed their mother to the mountains and became the ancestors of the Muong, while half followed their father to the sea and became the ancestors of the Vietnamese (Nguyen Linh and Huang Xuan Chinh, p. 103).

The genealogy of the Hung kings occurs in both sources (*LNCQ*, 5–6, and *TT*, 1, 1b–2a). Lac Long Quan and De Lai, the interloping monarch from the north and husband of Au Co, were cousins. They represented two branches of a single family originating with the mythical Chinese ruler Yen Ti Shen Nung (Vietnamese Viem De Than Nong). Shen Nung was an agricultural deity with roots in Tibetan culture who first appeared among the Chinese in northern Hu-pei and southern Ho-nan, where the ancient Pa and Thai cultures mingled. His followers came from the south and were foreign to the ancient Chinese. They were wet-field peasants, and Shen Nung's cult was connected with systems of agricultural settlement (Eberhard, pp. 219–21, 229).

In Chinese mythology, Shen Nung is regarded as the second of the so-called Three Sovereigns, the third being Huang Ti, who was supposedly the first of the legendary Five Emperors. Shen Nung could thereby be said to predate the founding of the imperial tradition in China.

The two branches of the family represented a northern, continental, imperial branch, whose scions all bore the title "emperor" (*de*), and a southern branch associated with the sea:

Viem De Than Nong (Yen Ti Shen Nung)
|
|
|
? = De Minh = Vu Tien Nu   Dong Dinh Quan
| | |
De Nghi   Kinh Duong Vuong = Than Long Nu
| |
De Lai = Au Co = Lac Long Quan
| |
De Du   Hung Kings

Lac Long Quan's mother was a "Lady Dragon Spirit" (Than Long Nu), who was a daughter of the "Lord of Tung T'ing Lake" (Dong Dinh Quan) in the basin of the Yangtze River; his father, the Kinh Duong king (Kinh Duong Vuong), ruled a land south of the "Five Passes" named the "Kingdom of Red Devils" (Xich Qui Quoc). Kinh Duong Vuong's mother was Vu Tien Nu, a constellation in the heavens overlooking northern Vietnam (see the *Han shu* reference in Aurousseau, p. 205), who was encountered by De Minh, Kinh Duong Vuong's father, as he traveled in the southern regions. De Minh was the reigning emperor in the third generation from Shen Nung. The northern branch came to an end when De Lai's son and successor, De Du, was defeated by Huang Ti, the "Yellow Emperor."

The northern branch of this family, as well as its claimed progenitor, can be relegated to a late recension; its only function is to claim a more ancient lineage for the Hung kings than that of China's first emperor, Huang Ti. The southern branch, however, displays enough geographical and cultural detail to make more plausible the idea that it is based on ancient traditions.

Kinh Duong Vuong's mother was the stellar constellation corresponding to northern Vietnam, and Kinh Duong Vuong ruled a kingdom with the barbaric designation (at least in the Chinese context) of "Red Devils"; he married a "Lady Dragon Spirit" from Tung T'ing Lake (perhaps an oblique reference to the ancient state of Ch'u) and had a son who became the culture hero of the ancient Vietnamese. C. Madrolle (p. 268) reported that something supposed to be Kinh Duong Vuong's tomb could be found in the vicinity of Luy-lau.

The idea of a royal genealogy with a northern and a southern branch may express the political dimension of Vietnam's geographical position in ancient times. As the corridor between the Yün-nan, and by extension the Tibetan, plateau to the west and the sea to the east, the Hong River plain was the place of maximum strategic pressure in prehistoric times between "northern" and "southern" peoples of East and Southeast Asia. In terms both of the genealogy and of Vietnam's historical experience, the Vietnamese considered themselves to be a "southern" people as distinct from the "northern" Chinese. The genealogy could thus be a literary elaboration of ancient traditions, of subsequent historical experience, or of both.

In a recent article, Nguyen Thi Hue discusses the legend of Lac Long Quan and Au Co as it is preserved among Vietnamese peasants today.

Appendix B

Hung *and* Lac *in the Sources*

In 1918, Henri Maspero ("Etudes," 18: 1–10) decided that *Hung* was an error for *Lac* and that *Van-lang* was an error for *Yeh-lang*, the name of an ancient kingdom in Kuei-chou; Maspero believed that these errors occurred in Chinese sources no later than the fifth century and were picked up and elaborated by Vietnamese scholars. Thus, Maspero concluded that there never were Hung kings and there never was a kingdom of Van-lang; these were simply clerical mistakes.

In 1955, Émile Gaspardone ("Champs Lo," pp. 474–77) examined the paralled sources in which *Hung* and *Lac* are found and discovered that they can be shown to belong to two separate traditions. While the *Lac* tradition stemmed from a Chinese perception of the tidal paddy fields of ancient Vietnam, a separate tradition reflected the penetration of the term *Hung* into Chinese sources and an attempt to explain it in terms of the Chinese character used to transcribe it phonetically. Gaspardone found occurrences of *Hung* as a family name and a toponym in ancient Yün-nan and Kuei-chou and concluded: "Thus, the name is well attested in the southwest [of China], and Maspero's casual correction belongs to the heroic age of Indochinese philology" ("Champs Lo," p. 471, n. 1). Gaspardone similarly regarded Maspero's correction of *Van-lang* to *Yeh-lang* as unwarranted ("Champs Lo," p. 470, n. 4).

Gaspardone's conclusions were supported by a 1973 article of Tran Quoc Vuong, according to which *Hung* derives from a Mon-Khmer title of chieftainship and *Van-lang* from an ancient Vietnamese name for the mythical bird thought to have been the clan totem of the Hung kings ("Ve Danh Hieu 'Hung Vuong,'" pp. 354–55). With regard to *Van-lang*, in 1969, Hoang Thi Chau proposed that it derives from a word shared by Austroasiatic and Austronesian languages meaning "people" and, by extension, "nation" (pp. 40–42).

Jao Tsung-i ("Wu Yüeh," p. 628) conjectured that *Hung* is a corruption of its Chinese homophone *hsiung*, the clan name of the kings of the ancient state of Ch'u in the central Yangtze. This possibility makes Maspero's idea of a scribal error for *Lac* less tenable. We cannot dismiss *Hung* simply on the basis of its late appearance in Chinese sources without also dismissing the arguments of Gaspardone and Tran Quoc Vuong, which suggest a cultural and linguistic origin for the term beyond the purview of Chinese scholarship. Jao Tsung-i's theory of a connection to the name of the

Ch'u royal clan lends credence to the authenticity of *Hung*, for it raises the possibility that *Hung* shares its linguistic origin with a tradition that came to be included within the domain of Chinese scholarship.

The problem of the Hung kings has been compounded by national pride. Chinese historians dismiss the Hung kings as a scribal error or a textual corruption; they take a conservative view that rejects anything that cannot be confirmed by their own scholarly tradition. On the other hand, Vietnamese historians have made the Hung kings the cornerstone of their national history, relying on their own historical tradition and on recent linguistic research. While Vietnamese historiography is to a large degree indebted to the tradition of Chinese scholarship, we cannot deny that important aspects of Vietnamese history are not accounted for by that tradition, else there would be no such thing as a Vietnamese nation today.

I personally want to study this question more than I have before committing myself on it; in the meantime, I use the term *Hung* as it has traditionally been used by Vietnamese historians.

Chinese texts that cite the Lac lords date no earlier than the Han dynasty and propose to describe the Hong River plain at some time after the imposition of Chinese suzerainty in 111 B.C. but before the defeat of the Lac lords in A.D. 42–43; this is clear from the detail that the Lac lords governed by the authority of "copper seals with green ribbons," a symbol of investiture used by Ch'in and Han (Gaspardone, "Champs Lo," pp. 473–74).

The earliest passage, from the *Kuang chou chi*, makes no mention of a king but simply states that there were Lac fields where the water rose and fell with the tides, and those who lived from the produce of these fields were called "Lac marquis," while those who ruled "districts" called themselves "Lac generals" and held copper seals with green ribbons (Gaspardone, "Champs Lo," p. 469).

The recensions of the *Chiao chou wai yu chi* and the *Nan Yüeh chi*, both dating from the third to the fifth century, speak of a king and a people in addition to the lords (marquis and generals) and seem to reflect the filtering of Vietnamese legendary traditions into Chinese literary sources during the time of Wu in the third century (Gaspardone, "Champs Lo," pp. 574–75; Jao Tsung-i, "An Yō Ō," pp. 36–37). While the *Chiao chou wai yu chi* follows the information of the *Kuang chou chi* with the additional mention of a Lac people and a Lac king, the *Nan Yüeh chi* is based on an entirely different source.

The *Nan Yüeh chi* makes no mention of tidal paddy fields or of copper seals with green ribbons; rather, this source emphasizes fertile soil and a fierce climate, thereby phonetically explaining the name *Hung* in terms of the Chinese language (Chinese *hsiung*, meaning "strong, virile") and expanding it to Hung fields, Hung people, Hung king, Hung marquis, and Hung generals (Gaspardone, "Champs Lo," pp. 467–70).

The *Nan Yüeh chi* citation, which could be based on information earlier than that of the *Kuang chou chi* inasmuch as there is no mention of copper seals with green ribbons, takes the fierce tropical climate to be the most distinctive attribute of ancient Vietnam in order to explain the title of the ancient kings, a title that is then extended to be the name of the land, the people, and the lords. The *Kuang chou chi* takes the tidal paddy fields to be the most distinctive attribute of ancient Vietnam; these fields are called Lac, thus accounting for the Lac lords who ruled over them by virtue of their copper seals with green ribbons. The *Chiao chou wai yu chi* simply extends the name *Lac* to include a king and the people.

The *An-nam chi luoc* provides a paraphrase of the *Chiao chou wai yu chi*, which it specifically cites as its source (*CL*, 24–25). The *Viet su luoc* makes no mention of the Lac lords. The *Dai Viet su ky toan thu* follows the *Linh-nam chich quai*, which says that the Hung kings sent their younger brothers to govern "provinces," whereas those of "secondary rank" were appointed to "civil" and "military" duties, and were called respectively "Lac marquis" and "Lac general" (*TT*, 1, 3a; *LNCQ*, 6).

The Lac lords appear twice in the *Viet dien u linh tap*. In each instance they are portrayed in the role of powerful advisors capable of imposing their will on the throne. The *Viet dien u linh tap* quotes Tseng Kun's ninth-century *Chiao chou chi* in an instance demonstrating that the Lac lords could dictate to the Hung king about the eligibility of prospective husbands for a royal princess, as well as the method of final selection (*VDULT*, 36–37). Also, the *Viet dien u linh tap* cites the *Giao-chi ky* from Do Thien's *Su ky* as the source for a story from the time of King An Duong, the conquerer who brought the line of the Hung kings to an end yet who came to terms with the Lac lords. According to this story, the Lac lords forced King An Duong to put one of his most talented generals to death because he was of northern origin (*VDULT*, 29).

While the Chinese sources and the *An-nam chi luoc*, which follows them, reflect Chinese perceptions of ancient Vietnam, the *Viet dien u linh tap* and the *Linh-nam chich quai* reflect the mainstream of indigenous tradition. The *Viet dien u linh tap* is the most reliable source, for its information is derived from identifiable works of earlier centuries and is relatively free of detectable revision. The *Linh-nam chich quai*, on the other hand, cites no prior sources and appears to be a rationalization of legendary traditions in accordance with Chinese political, administrative, and historical concepts.

I have chosen to use the expression "Lac lords" to identify this ancient ruling class. The terms translated "marquis" and "general" reflect Chinese perceptions, and although they may correspond to distinctions that did exist within the Lac ruling class, there is no way to analyze such distinctions without excessive conjecture.

Appendix C

The Rise of the Hung Kings
in the Viet su luoc

Ngo Si Lien's fifteenth-century *Dai Viet su ky toan thu* dates the rise of the Hung kings in 2879 B.C. in order to predate the mythical emperors of China, thereby claiming historical equality with China (*TT*, 1, 5b). Vietnamese historians were apparently not concerned with establishing chronological equality with China until after the Ming occupation of the early fifteenth century. The *Viet su luoc*, written earlier, contains an account of the rise of the Hung kings that is aimed more at the internal Vietnamese intellectual world than at the arena of Sino-Vietnamese relations:

> In the time of King Chuang of Chou [696–682 B.C.], in Gia-ninh, there was an extraordinary man who was able to cause the submission of all the aboriginal tribes by using the magical arts. He styled himself Hung king, established his capital at Van-lang, and named his realm the kingdom of Van-lang. He used simplicity and purity as the basis for customs and knotted cords for government. The realm was handed down through eighteen generations and each ruler styled himself Hung king. (*VSL*, 1, 1a)

The *Viet su luoc* apparently dates the rise of the Hung kings in the reign of King Chuang of Chou to accommodate an inherited tradition that there were eighteen generations of Hung kings and that their line extended down to "the end of Chou"; eighteen generations of the Chou royal family held the throne from King Chuang to the end of the dynasty.

The toponym *Gia-ninh* refers to the old Me-linh area at the head of the Hong River plain, where the Hong is joined by its three major tributaries. This was supposedly the seat of the Hung kings (see Le Tuong and Nguyen Loc; also Van Lang). Gia-ninh itself was an administrative subdivision established during the Wu dynasty that became the headquarters of Phong Province during T'ang. The use of a T'ang era toponym in reference to an event in antiquity is characteristic of Vietnamese historical geography. The traditional fifteen "provinces" of the kingdom of Van-lang were compiled no earlier than the last half of the T'ang dynasty (H. Maspero, "Études," 18: 4–7). These "provinces" were compiled in at least three separate lists comprising a total of twenty-two toponyms. Of these, three are of unknown origin, two probably originated in pre-Chinese traditions, two were

Ch'in jurisdictions in southern China, four date from the Han dynasty, five are from Wu, one from Chin, one from Liang, and four from T'ang. Having inherited the idea that Van-lang comprised fifteen "provinces," Vietnamese historians drew on a mixed collection of toponyms with which they were familiar.

The title *Hung* and the name *Van-lang* pose problems addressed elsewhere (see Appendix B). Here it is useful to note that, aside from a poem that probably dates from the 1360s (Wolters, "Assertions," 11: 74), the *Viet su luoc* is the earliest surviving Vietnamese source to use the name *Van-lang*. The only earlier mention of this name occurs in certain T'ang texts (H. Maspero, "Études," 18: 1–10). The significance of this may be related to the two items that follow in the passage: simple and pure customs and the use of knotted cords.

O. W. Wolters has recently discussed this passage in connection with poems by fourteenth-century Vietnamese writers who were concerned about the weakening of family ties and the spreading social disorder of their day. The expressions "simple and pure customs" and "knotted cords" evoked the well-regulated harmony of the classical golden age as described in ancient Chinese texts. "Simple and pure customs" recalled a peaceful time when rulers enforced proper rules of social intercourse, while "knotted cords" were reportedly used by the mythical Three Emperors of China's golden age to carry on their government. These and other classical allusions were cited by Vietnamese writers to lend textual authority to their call for a reformation of Vietnamese society in the late fourteenth century. Van-lang became important as a Vietnamese golden age that could be made to exemplify the qualities to which the fourteenth century writers wanted to return (Wolters, "Assertions," 10: 445–50). In this light, our passage is more important as a document of Vietnamese intellectual history in the fourteenth century than it is as a record of the rise of the Hung kings.

We are left with an "extraordinary man" who used the "magical arts." Both of these expressions are imprecise, which could mean that they were used in lieu of more specific, but perhaps obscure or unpalatable, details from oral tradition. The "magical arts" could be taken as the invocation of supernatural sanctions for administering oaths of loyalty. More broadly, the reference can be related to the general theme of supernatural intervention in human affairs that prevails in Lac mythology.

In the words of Professor Wolters, our passage

> reads like a Chinese text on ancient Chinese civilization. The chronological precision, dynastic content, and description of good government are Chinese in vocabulary. The Van-lang rulers exercised the prerogatives of the Chinese sage-rulers. Yet the setting is Vietnamese. The view of the past is, in effect, a "Vietnamization" of Chinese materials, and it is not the only instance of this phenomenon in the fourteenth century. ("Assertions," 11: 81)

The *Viet su luoc* contains the earliest surviving account of the establishment of the kingdom of Van-lang, but this account is heavily weighted with the ideological baggage of the fourteenth century. Consequently, we must be careful about drawing any conclusions about antiquity from the account.

On the other hand, the author of the *Viet su luoc* took a conservative view of early Vietnamese history. Except for this and two related passages, all of the *Viet su luoc*'s information on the pre-tenth-century period is derived from identifiable Chinese sources. That Van-lang was an ancient kingdom in Vietnam is attested as early as T'ang, and that *Hung* was the title of a line of kings is attested as early as Chin. The golden age affirmed by the fourteenth-century writers was probably based on a well-established, although perhaps poorly articulated, oral tradition rooted in the prehistoric culture of the Hong River plain. Elaborated themes of this tradition appear in two other fourteenth-century works, the *Viet dien u linh tap* and the *Linh-nam chich quai*.

Appendix D

The Archeological Record of Dong-son

In the past twenty-five years, Vietnamese archeologists have brought to light enough information to provide our first coherent view of Vietnamese prehistory. Vietnamese archeologists see a pattern of continuous development from the Paleolithic Age to the Neolithic Age through the Son-vi, Hoa-binh, and Bac-son cultures. They consider the newly discovered Son-vi culture to belong to the late Paleolithic Age and early Mesolithic Age, Hoa-binh to be a Mesolithic culture, and Bac-son to be an early Neolithic culture. According to carbon-14 tests, the transition from Son-vi to Hoa-binh appears to have been around 9,000 B.C., and the Son-vi culture was in existence at least six or seven thousand years before then. (Pham Huy Thong, "Muoi nam xay dung," p. 5; Ha Van Tan and Nguyen Khac Su, pp. 46–50.)

The cultural progression leading directly to Dong-son began during the third millennium B.C. with the Phung-nguyen culture in the Hong River valley. Phung-nguyen was a fully developed Neolithic culture with sophisticated pottery and ornaments. In the view of Vietnamese scholars, Phung-nguyen was the beginning of the Bronze Age in Vietnam. By the middle of the second millennium B.C., Phung-nguyen had evolved into the Dong-dau culture, which Vietnamese archeologists regard as Middle Bronze Age. By the turn of the first millennium B.C., Dong-dau, in turn, evolved into the Go-mun culture, which was the peak of Bronze Age culture in Vietnam.

In the Ma River valley, further south, parallel and related cultures evolved in a similar direction, although at a more rudimentary level. The Dong-khoi culture, contemporaneous with Phung-nguyen, developed through the Thieu-duong half-level into the early grave level of Dong-son. There were other localized cultures along the coasts to the north and the south, but, because of their locations in fertile plains, the Phung-nguyen and Dong-khoi cultures acquired common elements and became two related cultural zones. There was a measure of contact and exchange between the two zones, but each area maintained distinctive features. For example, pottery in the Hong valley, fired with high heat, was smooth, diversified, and grey-white with evolved decorative patterns; on the other hand, pottery in the Ma valley, fired with low heat, was coarse, simple, and dark red with cord patterns. Bronze artifacts from the Hong valley include arrowheads, javelin points, butchering implements, fishhooks, sickles, and a statue of a chicken; in the Ma valley, the only bronze artifacts are simple blades.

Around the seventh century B.C., Go-mun gave rise to the Dong-son culture, which spread to encompass the Ma valley and neighboring areas north and south. Dong-son was the culmination of the Bronze Age and the opening stage of the Iron Age. (For more details, see: Pham Huy Thong and Nguyen Duy Ty, pp. 39–52; Nugyen Duy Ty, pp. 77–84; Hoang Xuan Chinh, pp. 119–26; Hoang Xuan Chinh and Bui Van Tien, pp. 40–48; Pham Huy Thong and Chu Van Tan, pp. 37–44.)

The Dong-son culture is still the subject of research and speculation. Scholars have traditionally traced its bronze-casting technology to northern China (Chikamori, pp. 65–96). This theory was based on the assumption that bronze casting in eastern Asia originated in northern China; however, this idea has been discredited by recent archeological discoveries in northeastern Thailand. In the words of one writer, "bronze casting began in Southeast Asia and was later borrowed by the Chinese, not vice versa as the Chinese scholars have always claimed" (Neher, p. 186). The implications of the Thai excavations have not yet been fully explored, but if initial indications are reliable and bronze-casting technology spread from Southeast Asia to China rather than from China to Southeast Asia or, at least, developed independently in Southeast Asia and in China, then the Dong-son bronze technology probably developed from local or regional industries rather than from imported Chinese skills.

Such an interpretation is supported by the work of modern Vietnamese archeologists. They have found that the earliest bronze drums of Dong-son are closely related in basic structural features and in decorative design to the pottery of the Phung-nguyen culture. They further suggest that the Dong-son culture of northern Vietnam had important links with Tibeto-Burman cultures in Yün-nan, with Thai cultures in Yün-nan and Laos, and, especially, with Mon-Khmer cultures in Laos, particularly on the Tran-ninh plateau (Tran Manh Phu, pp. 286–87, 289–92). The Tran-ninh plateau, or "Plain of Jars," is the most natural route from northern Vietnam to northeastern Thailand.

Aside from technical aspects, Dong-son culture was strongly influenced by seaborne contacts. The distinctive figures and decorative designs on the Dong-son drums are generally believed to "express one phase of maritime art" (Chikamori, p. 90). Boats filled with oarsmen and warriors surrounded by seabirds and other forms of maritime life unmistakably testify to the ascendancy of sea-based power (Bezacier, *Manuel*, figs. 75–78, 104–5, 109–10, 113–15).

Most scholars agree that "the formation of the Dong-son bronze culture was deeply related to the people of the Hong River plain" (Chikamori, p. 90). It is reasonable to assume that, conversely, an early stage in the formation of the Vietnamese people was related to the emergence of the Dong-son bronze culture.

Appendix E

The Yüeh Migration Theory

The rise of a Yüeh ruling class along the coasts and up the valleys of southeastern China after Ch'u's conquest of Yüeh in 333 B.C. gave rise to Leonard Aurousseau's ill-fated theory that the origin of the Vietnamese people lay in the migration of the refugee population of Yüeh (Aurousseau, pp. 245–64). Of this theory, Henri Maspero simply wrote, "It is best, I believe, to let it pass in silence" ("Bulletin," p. 393, n. 1). Perhaps because of its simplicity, this theory has nevertheless continued to attract attention.

Claude Madrolle, in his 1937 article, which Émile Gaspardone has referred to as "article appliqué mais peu sur" (Gaspardone, "Champs Lo," p. 467, n. 1), rejected Aurousseau's theory on the basis that it "took account neither of the difficulties of a route across basins placed perpendicular to the ocean, nor of the reactions of the indigenous people in the path of these vagabond and desperate groups" (Madrolle, p. 310), only to replace it with his own modified seaborne version, according to which the Lac people were the ancient Hoklos of Fu-chien who, in the role of coastal corsairs, penetrated the Hong River plain and created a political system to rule the tidal populations there (Madrolle, pp. 313–25).

Madrolle's theory, while certainly worth consideration, is not solidly based on evidence, but is rather a spiderweb of texts, proper names, and outright conjectures in an apparent effort to salvage something of Aurousseau's idea.

While Aurousseau's reputation has suffered as a result of his outlandish theory on the origin of the Vietnamese people, and even more as a result of his temerity in challenging Henri Maspero's work on the location of the ancient prefecture of Hsiang (H. Maspero, "Études," 16: 49–55; Aurousseau, pp. 153–244; H. Maspero, "Bulletin," pp. 373–93; Gaspardone, "Champs Lo," p. 465, n. 1), we need not on that account regard everything he wrote as unworthy of notice; the seeming brashness of his general conclusions was nonetheless based on a careful study of the sources, and if he is to be faulted it is because of an overregard for detail rather than inattention to the evidence. He is the only investigator to attempt to view Vietnamese origins from the perspective of political events occurring in southeastern China prior to the Ch'in invasions.

Aurousseau, like other scholars of his generation, thought that the migration of a ruling group necessarily implied the concurrent migration of the people they ruled. Historians now recognize that in ancient times a predatory princely retinue could impose its name on the people it succeeded in conquering regardless of that people's true origin. A documented example of this is the ascendance of the Iranian Croats and Serbs over the Slavic peoples of the Balkans in the seventh century A.D. (Dvornik, pp. 268–304). Once this is understood, Aurousseau's essay on the origins of the Vietnamese people takes on new significance.

Aurousseau chronicled the fortunes of the short–lived kingdoms in the southern path of Ch'in and Han expansion. The ancient Vietnamese stood at the end of this path. There is no question of denying the Vietnamese their roots in the plains of northern Vietnam, for we need not speak of the wholesale movement of populations, as Aurousseau unfortunately did. But as the imperial tide flowed south, it pushed a crest of disinherited ruling-class people ahead of it. These people exerted a political and cultural influence out of proportion to their numbers, for they were militarily superior to the societies they encountered as they marched south.

Appendix F

The Legend of the Turtle Claw

The legend explaining the victory of Chao T'o over King An Duong by his possession of the turtle claw apparently entered Chinese sources during the Wu dynasty by means of the *Jih-nan chuan* (Jao Tsung-i, "An Yō Ō," pp.36–37). It subsequently appeared in the *Chin T'ai K'ang ti chi*, the *Chin liu hsin ch'i Chiao chou chi*, and the *Chiao chou wai yu chi*, all from the Chin dynasty period (Jao Tsung-i, "An Yō Ō," pp. 34–35, 37, 38). On the Vietnamese side, the *An-nam chi luoc* (*CL*, 24–25) and the *Viet su luoc* (*VSL*, 1, 1b) accounts are based on the *Chiao chou wai yu chi*, while the *Linh-nam chich quai* version (*LNCQ*, 23–24), incorporated into the *Dai Viet su ky toan thu* (*TT*, 1, 8b–10b), was independently preserved in Vietnam.

For the man who constructed the magic crossbow with the turtle-claw trigger, all the Chinese sources use the name Cao Thong, and nearly all identify him as a "holy man" who abandoned King An Duong after making the crossbow because the king did not recognize his spiritual nature and treated him improperly. Of the Chinese sources, only the *Chin liu hsin ch'i Chiao chou chi* identifies him in secular terms as an "assistant" of King An Duong. On the Vietnamese side, the *An-nam chi luoc* and the *Viet su luoc* likewise identify him as a "holy man," but whereas the *An-nam chi luoc* remains faithful to the *Chiao chou wai yu chi* in all details, the *Viet su luoc* uses the name Cao Lo, which is peculiar to Vietnamese sources, and, like the *Chin liu hsin ch'i Chiao chou chi*, says nothing of his being improperly treated or of his departure.

The *Linh-nam chich quai* identifies Cao Lo as a "minister" of King An Duong and says nothing of his departure. The *Viet dien u linh tap* does not contain the turtle-claw legend, but it does contain a separate tradition about Cao Lo. Making no mention of the crossbow, it describes him as follows:

> In ancient times he supported King An Duong as a great general with high merit against the enemy; later, because of the slander of high ministers who were Lac lords, he was killed. (*VDULT*, 29).

This passage is quoted in the *Dai Viet su ky toan thu* (*TT*, 1, 7b). Cao Lo's untimely end is explained by the fact that he was a "Giap Mao Stone Dragon" (*Giap Mao Thach Long*) spirit. The Lac lords were "White Monkey" spirits, and King An Duong was a "Golden Chicken" spirit. Although the chicken and monkey were "mutually compatible," the dragon was "opposed to both" (*VDULT*, 29). This suggests that Cao Lo was of Chinese origin, for the "Giap Mao Stone Dragon" appears to be an appellation of Sinitic origin, in contrast to the indigenous chicken and monkey.

The sources differently record the entrance of Shih Chiang into King An Duong's court as follows. The *Chin T'ai K'ang ti chi*: "[The King of Nan] Yüeh sent his heir apparent named Shih Chiang to serve King An Duong; [Shih Chiang] pretended to be a loyal subject and served [King An Duong]" (Jao Tsung-i, "An Yō Ō," p. 37). The *Chin liu hsin ch'i Chiao chou chi*: "Pretending to be a traveler, [Shih Chiang] subsequently gained the confidence of King An Duong's daughter My Chau" (Jao Tsung-i, "An Yō Ō," p. 38). The *Jih-nan chuan*: "Shih [Chiang] was handsome and sober; King An Duong's daughter My Chau was pleased with his appearance and became his mistress" (Jao Tsung-i, "An Yō Ō, p. 36). The *Linh-nam chich quai*: "[Chao] T'o sent his son to enter [the court of King An Duong] for a night's lodging; [his son] asked to marry the king's daughter My Chau; the king did not suspect the conspiracy between T'o father and son" (*LNCQ*, 24). While the Chinese sources emphasize the romantic side of the episode, the Vietnamese version stresses the conspiratorial undercurrent.

Chinese sources do not mention the turtle claw but simply say that Shih Chiang rendered the crossbow useless: "stole and sawed in half the magic crossbow" (*Jih-nan chuan*, Jao Tsung-i, "An Yō Ō, p. 36); "stole the crossbow and sawed it in half thus making an end of it" (*Chin T'ai K'ang ti chi*, Jao Tsung-i, "An Yō Ō," p. 37; and *Chiao chou wai yu chi*, as quoted in *SCC*, 37: 7a); "broke in half the stringed weapon" (*Chin liu hsin ch'i Chiao chou chi*, Jao Tsung-i, "An Yō Ō," p. 38). On the Vietnamese side, the *Viet su luoc* follows the Chinese: "destroyed its trigger" (*VSL*, 1, 1b). The *An-nam chi luoc* says: "changed the trigger of the crossbow" (*CL*, 25); this comes closer to the indigenous version, which emphasizes that Shih Chiang gained possession of the turtle claw: "stealthily took the magic-triggered crossbow, secretly made another trigger and exchanged it with the turtle claw, [which he] took" (*LNCQ*, 24). The indigenous Vietnamese version thereby stresses the transfer of sovereign power embodied in the turtle claw.

There is a tradition that King An Duong fled south to the modern province of Nghe-an, where he built a new citadel and ruled until his death (Bui Van Nguyen in Tran Quoc Vuong and Do Van Ninh, p. 381).

J. Pryzluski pointed out that this legend is associated with myths from many parts of Southeast Asia that derive from maritime culture (Pryzluski, pp. 278–80). Preserved by Chinese sources in the guise of a romance, this legend seems to have expressed potent political truths in the symbolic language of ancient Vietnamese culture.

Events in the sixth century were also remembered in terms of this legend (*VDULT*, 7–10). The question arises whether this was merely a historiographical device or whether it was a genuine reflection of cultural sentiments existing in the sixth century.

To begin with, the legend, as it pertains to King An Duong and Chao T'o, was established in Chinese sources no later than the fourth century, so we can assume that it was known to educated Vietnamese of the sixth century, leaving aside the question of its currency among the general population as a popular tradition. Ly Bi's advisor Tinh Thieu was a man of letters who had served at the Liang capital with Ly Bi. Ly Bi's establishment of a ritually correct imperial court implies the skills of more than a few literate assistants; it would be unusual if some of these men did not also serve Trieu Quang Phuc and/or Ly Phat Tu. So we can conclude that the claw myth as a rationalization for the transfer of sovereignty was known to men who were involved in the process of royal succession during the sixth century.

Did these men in fact use the myth to propagandize political change among the people of their day? If they did not, then someone else before the twelfth century connected the myth with the sixth-century figures, for the *Viet dien u linh tap* cites Do Thien's *Su ky* for the myth in its sixth-century context. Who did link the myth with the sixth-century figures and for what reasons? There are no likely candidates for this task between the sixth and twelfth centuries. If the myth had also been applied to tenth-century figures, say to the Ngo family and Dinh Bo Linh or to the Le family and Ly Cong Uan, then it would be easier to assume that Trieu Quang Phuc and Ly Phat Tu were drawn into the myth retrospectively to lend weight to its legitimizing power in the tenth century. But since this is not the case, and we furthermore cannot associate the myth with the heavily edited traditions of the *Linh-nam chich quai*, which were not fixed before the fourteenth, perhaps even the fifteenth, century, it is difficult to explain what the myth could possibly have meant to Vietnamese of the twelfth century.

Trieu Quang Phuc and the myth in its sixth-century context are not mentioned in the *Viet su luoc*, and Le Van Huu commented on neither. Ngo Si Lien's comment on the myth in its sixth-century context shows that he received it as an established historical tradition and did not particularly care for it, for he expressed surprise that, after the marriage of Ly Phat Tu's son and Trieu Quang Phuc's daughter, the new husband stayed on in his father-in-law's household and did not immediately bring his bride back to his own father's house. This suggests that the sociological basis of the myth had eroded by the fifteenth century, and we can imagine that it had indeed done so much earlier, perhaps as early as T'ang, when we hear of the *shih-ting* system based on Chinese-style family values being applied in Vietnam by law.

Since historians in later centuries seem disinterested in, or even perplexed by, the myth, we are led to wonder why men like Ngo Si Lien ever bothered with it; the answer to this seems to be that they could not avoid it because their knowledge of the sixth century was embedded in it. Knowledge of Trieu Quang Phuc and of the rise of Ly Phat Tu first appears in connection with the myth (Do Thien's *Su ky* via *VDULT*), so it is reasonable to assume that this knowledge was preserved from the beginning in the form of the myth, which means that these figures were associated with the myth during or shortly after their lifetimes.

If this was so, then the question of why the myth was applied to these men in the sixth century arises. It is difficult to avoid concluding that those who wielded the myth in the name of the sixth-century heroes did so for practical reasons linked to the events of the time rather than as a posthumous historiographical rationalization. For with the advent of Sui and T'ang, the literate class had no discernible incentive to glorify the sixth-century figures in terms of a barbarian myth, unless it was to culturally discredit them in the context of Chinese thought, a very curious possibility given the Chinese preference for officially ignoring local heroes, as in the case of Phung Hung (see Appendix J). It appears more probable that the myth was in fact used during the sixth century by the class of men directly involved in Vietnam's political life for propaganda purposes, specifically to legitimize Ly Phat Tu's ascendance over Trieu Quang Phuc. And if this was so, then we must assume that they did so in the knowledge that by evoking the myth they would elicit a desired response from the populace, in which case we cannot avoid the conclusion that lower-class people were familiar with, and understood the meaning of, the myth.

Appendix G

Textual Problems Related to
Ly Bi's Background

The *Dai Viet su ky toan thu* reads:

The king's family name was Ly; [his] personal name was Bi; [he] was from Thai-binh in Long-hung. [His] ancestors were northerners; at the end of Western Han [they] were placed in distressing circumstances as a result of warfare; [they] fled and dwelt in the south; after seven generations [they] thereupon became southerners. The king was talented in both the literary and military arts. (*TT*, 4, 14b)

There are two problems in this passage: first, the place names *Thai-binh* and *Long-hung*; second, the "seven generations." The latter problem has arisen because Maurice Durand miscorrected "Western [Former] Han" to "Eastern [Later] Han" and misinterpreted the phrase "[Ly Bi's ancestors] thereupon became southerners" as "[Ly Bi] consequently was a southerner."

The administrative history of Vietnam under the different Chinese dynasties is complex. Perhaps because of this, Vietnamese historians developed a set of historical toponyms, based mainly on T'ang usage, which they indiscriminately applied to all earlier periods. These toponyms were often contaminated with names and geographical associations that appeared after the end of T'ang.

In chapter 4, I describe "Thai-binh in Long-hung" in the context of the early sixth century as "on the north bank of the Hong River in Vu-binh near Tan-xuong, in the shadow of Mount Tam-dao." *Tan-xuong* was the Chin dynasty name for old Me-linh of Han, at the head of the Hong River plain. During the course of the sixth century, the name *Tan-xuong* was changed, first to *Hung*, by Ch'en Pa-hsien, and then to *Phong*, by Ling-hu Hsi of Sui. The name *Phong* endured into the independence period.

Vu-binh was the prefecture established east of Tan-xuong and north of Giao-chi by T'ao Huang in the late third century. Located along an upland frontier, it disappeared as an administrative entity during the sixth century (*YHCHC*, 38, 1083–84). At the end of the century, Sui designated what had been the headquarters of Vu-binh as Long-binh District (*SuiS*, 31, 12b). In 621, T'ang raised Long-binh to provincial status and subdivided it into three prefectures. Six years later, one of these prefectures was separated and assigned to Phong, while Long-binh was reduced to district status again. Finally, in 714, the name *Long-binh* was changed to *Thai-binh* (*HTS*, 43a, 9b).

The name *Long-hung* in reference to Ly Bi's home district is an error arising from postindependence usage. *Long-hung* first appeared in the second quarter of the thirteenth century as the name of a circuit in the lower central plain of the Hong; originally part of what became the province of Son-nam, it was incorporated into the province of Hai-duong in the sixteenth century (Buu Cam et al., pp. 194–95). This error seems to have derived from the proximity of Long-hung to a postindependence jurisdiction on the coast named Thai-binh (Ton Nu Thuong Lang and Ta Quang Phat, part 1, 4: 1b–2a).

The citation of "Thai-binh in Long-hung" should be understood as the T'ang period Thai-binh District, located in what, at the time of Ly Bi, was Vu-binh Prefecture, but which Sui named Long-binh (H. Maspero, "Le Protectorat general," pp. 579–80; M. Durand, "La Dynastie," p. 438, n. 4, also discussed this problem but made use of misinformation about the names *Hung* and *Phong*).

In 1960, Tran Quoc Vuong and Ha Van Tan found confirmation of this localization in the style adopted by a tenth-century lord established at the place; Nguyen Khoan, situated on the north bank of the Hong River at Nguyen-gia-loan, called himself Nguyen Thai-binh. In a recent article, Do Duc Hung rejected this idea in favor of a location on the south bank of the Hong River in the vicinity of modern Quoc-oai, a localization first proposed in 1957 by Dao Duy Anh (See Do Duc Hung). Do Duc Hung cited the presence of spirit shrines associated with Ly Bi in the vicinity of Quoc-oai, although he dismissed the shrines to Ly Bi at the downriver site, where the name *Thai-binh* has been applied in more recent centuries. As Appendix H demonstrates, the locations of spirit shrines are poor evidence for localizing toponyms because people move from one place to another and take their favorite spirits with them.

Do Duc Hung's strongest argument is based on an episode in 950, when Duong Tam Kha sent Ngo Xuong Van and two generals against a pair of rebellious villages in Thai-binh. Duong Tam Kha's capital was at Co-loa, and Nguyen-gia-loan lay on the same side of the Hong River, a short distance upstream. Yet, the expedition went by way of Tu-liem, located south of the Hong River near modern Hanoi, which was on a more direct route to Quoc-oai. Do Duc Hung asks why the expedition should have crossed the river when a short, direct route lay along its north bank.

An answer to this may be that the expedition crossed the river to attack Thai-binh from some unexpected quarter, for surely the land route, hemmed in between Mount Tam-dao and the river, was well defended. It is also possible that the generals crossed the river to get their soldiers, for one of the generals had home estates in the area, and he may have gone there to augment the expedition with his private army. Furthermore, the expedition may have been waterborne and the river itself the route of attack; in 963, Ngo Xuong Van was killed while attacking the same two villages by boat.

Do Duc Hung favors the Quoc-oai location because it is where the home estates of the Ngo family were located. He surmises that the Ngo resisted Duong Tam Kha's authority and that the expedition was sent against this resistance. But it is unlikely that Duong Tam Kha would have sent Ngo Xuong Van to attack his kinsmen. Furthermore, in 963 Ngo Xuong Van died while fighting against Thai-binh, long after Duong Tam Kha was out of the picture, and there is no reason to believe that the Ngo family was warring against itself.

Turning to the second problem, there is some obscurity in the idea that Ly Bi's ancestors became "southerners" after seven generations in the south; why seven generations? M. Durand solved this problem rather too hastily by changing the time of the Ly family migration from the Wang Mang disorders at the end of Western (Former) Han, as stated in the text, to the disorders at the end of Eastern (Later) Han; this allowed him to assume that the seven generations were what separated Ly Bi from his ancestral migration, and it was Bi who was consequently a "southerner" (Durand, "La Dynastie," p. 438).

There are two reasons why Durand's interpretation is unacceptable. First, if we allow that the character for "west" is a mistake for "east," then we should be prepared to allow that the number "seven" might be a mistake for some larger number more in conformity with the passage of five centuries. Second, and more fundamentally, it is clear from the context of the passage that the phrase about "becoming southerners" refers to Ly Bi's ancestors and not to himself.

In the passage cited at the beginning of this appendix, there are three grammatical parts. The subject of the first part is "the king," and it tells his name and where he was from. The subject of the second part is the king's "ancestors," and it tells of their origin, when and why they came south, and when they "became southerners." The third part goes back to "the king" and begins to enumerate his qualities.

It is clear from the context of the passage that the seven generations separate the southward migration of the Ly family from the time they "became southerners" and does not refer to the time separating Ly Bi from his ancestral migration. So there is no need to be concerned that seven generations are too few to span the five centuries from the end of Western Han to Ly Bi and to thereupon decide that "Western Han" is a mistake for "Eastern Han."

The question remains, however, what happened in the seventh generation to warrant the memory that at that particular time the family became "southern." Suppose we assume that the text is correct and that the Ly family came south at the same time as the Shih family, during the Wang Mang era. We know that Shih Hsieh was in the sixth generation after this migration and that he lived to the age of ninety. The seventh generation of the Ly family was probably contemporaneous with Shih Hsieh. From what we know of the time of Shih Hsieh and of the flowering of political consciousness among immigrant Chinese in the south at that time, it is reasonable to assume that the seventh generation of the Ly family experienced a new awareness of itself as a leader in the arena of southern political life, and that a basic part of that awareness as remembered by later family members was that they were "southerners."

One might be tempted to theorize that Ly Ton of the late fourth century and the family of Ly Truong Nhan and Ly Thuc Hien of the late fifth century were related to the family of Ly Bi, but there is no evidence for this.

Considering that certain details about Ly Khai and his faction of the early sixth century are peculiar to the *Dai Viet su ky toan thu*, one might surmise that information on this man and his family was preserved together with Vietnamese records on Ly Bi, stimulating the possibility of blood relationship. Only the *Dai Viet su ky toan thu* records a middle name for Ly Khai. Furthermore, only the *Dai Viet su ky toan thu* records that the "rebel" killed by Ly Tac in 516 was a member of Ly Khai's clique and bore the Ly surname; Chinese records give his surname as Nguyen.

However, if one were interested in relating Ly Bi to earlier provincial leaders bearing the Ly surname, Ly Tac, and not his discredited rivals, would be the most likely candidate. Ly Tac was in control of the province as late as 516, and it was at that time or thereabouts that Ly Bi served at the Liang capital. One might conjecture that Bi was a close relative of Tac and went to the capital as a token of Tac's loyalty. But there is no evidence for any of these speculations.

The Ly (Chinese Li) surname was politically potent in early Vietnam. Why this was so is not clear from the sources. Perhaps it derived from the expression *hsing-li*, meaning baggage, which in ancient times meant a traveler or those who served in the retinue of an official. When such persons from the north, or their descendents, eventually decided to "become southerners," they may also have changed their surname to remove themselves from the imperial gaze, particularly if they had come south to escape some public humiliation or political intrigue. By taking the Ly (Li) surname they may have gained a certain anonymity in the eyes of officialdom, while setting themselves apart from the local society as families of northern origin.

Appendix H

The Location of Chu-dien

Chu-dien was among the first districts established by Han in the Hong River plain. It endured as an administrative toponym for more than a thousand years. It is known in history as the home of Trung Trac's husband, Thi Sach, in the first century, of the Do family of the fourth and fifth centuries, and of Trieu Quang Phuc in the sixth century. It was also the site of the first battle between Ly Bi and Ch'en Pa-hsien in 545.

Henry Maspero ("Le Protectorat general," pp. 580–84) examined the Chinese sources on the location of Chu-dien and found them too contradictory to yield a solution. He then turned to Ch'en Pa-hsien's campaign of 545, which consisted of three engagements. First Pa-hsien defeated Ly Bi in Chu-dien. Bi then retreated to the vicinity of modern Hanoi, where he constructed fortifications. Defeated a second time, he retreated to the fortress of Gia-ninh at the head of the plain. Defeated at Gia-ninh after a siege, Bi further retreated into the mountains. Maspero concluded that Chu-dien must have been in the lower plain, and that Pa-hsien arrived either by sea or by marching along the coast. This would explain a three-step retreat by Bi toward and into the mountains. Maspero found corroboratory evidence for this localization in other Chinese sources.

In 1954, Maurice Durand ("La Dynastie," pp. 441–42) cited "the traditional Vietnamese localization" to place Chu-dien north of the Hong River at the head of the plain and went on to elaborate his interpretation of Pa-hsien's campaign. This was unfortunate, for his uncritical acceptance of traditional Vietnamese historical geography led him to propose an impossible scenario for the events of 545.

Placing Chu-dien at the head of the plain, Durand was led to assume that Pa-hsien arrived by way of the mountains rather than by sea or along the coast. This in itself is geographically and tactically implausible. Pa-hsien set out from Kuang-tung, and his army rendezvoused in Kuang-hsi. During the entire history of Sino-Vietnamese relations in premodern times, there is no evidence that any Chinese army ever set out from this direction and then swung through the mountains in a needlessly circuitous route to emerge at the head of the plain. To do so would invite ambush and encirclement. The Vietnamese would not have waited quietly for the Chinese to come out of the mountains, but would have taken full advantage of the upland terrain. The movements of any Chinese army marching through Kuang-tung and Kuang-hsi would have been watched at every step of the way by Vietnamese spys. That is why, if water transport was available, Chinese generals preferred the sea route, for that was the only way to achieve enough speed for surprise.

Durand cites the route through Yün-nan taken by Sui general Liu Fang in 602, which indeed emerged at the head of the plain, but Liu Fang came directly from Ch'ang-an, in northern China, via Ssu-ch'uan, and the route through the mountains by way of Yün-nan was the most direct in that case; furthermore, the reason for Liu Fang's success was that the Vietnamese did not know where he was until it was too late. Fang left most of his army in Yün-nan and pushed ahead with his vanguard in order to reach the Vietnamese before they learned of his whereabouts. The element of surprise that played such an important part in Liu Fang's campaign would have been impossible for any army traveling the traditional route through Kuang-tung and Kuang-hsi.

If Pa-hsien took the traditional land route from Kuang-hsi, he would have emerged from the uplands, not at the head of the plain, in the northwest, but rather in the northeast, before Long-bien, which does not figure in the campaign of 545.

Considering that Ly Bi certainly would have had his northern border well guarded, it is most reasonable to assume that Pa-hsien embarked at Ho-p'u and sailed into the Hong River plain, hoping to benefit by the strategy used by Lü Tai in 226 and T'ao Huang in 271. In A.D. 42, Ma Yüan had planned to use this strategy, but lack of water transport forced him to march along the coast instead. In 722, a T'ang army used Ma Yüan's coastal road as it marched against the Black Emperor. In 865, the sea route was used to advantage by Kao P'ien. It is significant that the Vietnamese victory in 938 over a Chinese invasion by sea has been popularly regarded as the beginning of independence. Pa-hsien had enough boats to embark his army at the battle on Lake Dien-triet.

Assuming, however, that Pa-hsien entered the plain from the mountains and fought his first battle with Ly Bi at the place proposed by Durand, the next phase of the campaign becomes even more implausible, for Durand would have Ly Bi retreating into the plain toward the sea. This is inconceivable from a military point of view, for Bi would be cutting himself off from any means of escape; he would be placing himself between the Chinese and the sea. Durand explains this by citing the traditional view of Vietnamese historians that Long-bien was on the site of modern Hanoi. Here Durand ignores the Chinese sources that localize Long-bien elsewhere (see H. Maspero, "Le Protectorat general," pp. 509–75). Furthermore, the sources do not mention Long-bien in Pa-hsien's 545 campaign. The site of the second battle is simply described as at the mouth of the To-lich River, which is where Hanoi now stands. There is no evidence that this was a place of political importance before the seventh century. Just before the battle in 545, Ly Bi built fortifications at the spot; this would not have been necessary if a walled city had already stood there. Durand assumes that Long-bien was Ly Bi's capital, and so he went there to defend it. In fact, we do not know where Ly Bi's capital was. Judging from the campaign of 545, it is reasonable to think that Gia-ninh, near his family estates, may have been his capital, for it is the only city that he attempted to defend.

Nevertheless, even if we assume that Durand's interpretation is correct up to this point, the final phase of the campaign becomes impossible, for after his second defeat, Bi would have had to retreat through the Chinese ranks in the direction of his first defeat. Furthermore, he would have had to secure the fortress of Gia-ninh after it had presumably been lost to the Chinese in the wake of the first battle, for Gia-ninh was in the immediate vicinity of Durand's localization for Chu-dien.

Durand's localization of Chu-dien, as well as his localization of Long-bien, is based on theories developed by Vietnamese historians in the in-dependence period. In a recent article, Dinh Van Nhat surmised that Vietnamese scholars in the fifteenth century located Chu-dien north of the Hong River on the basis of spirit temples to Thi Sach situated there; he furthermore finds evidence to suggest that the location of these temples can be attributed to inhabitants of Chu-dien resettled north of the Hong River by Ma Yüan after the Trung sisters were suppressed (Dinh Van Nhat, "Dat Me-linh," 190: 49–51). The traditional Vietnamese localization of Chu-dien is thus an error.

The name *Chu-dien* probably originated in the western part of the plain between the Hong and Day rivers. It seems to have shifted downriver with the Hong River diking system and eventually included a large area comprising most of the plain south and west of the Thai-binh River below Hai-duong. Chu-dien was principally composed of swampy tidelands and was distinguished by its proximity to the sea.

Perhaps the most direct confirmation of H. Maspero's localization for Chu-dien can be found in a poem, translated in its entirety in chapter 6, written to commemorate the forced departure of an unpopular T'ang offi-cial in 803. By this time, a city in the vicinity of modern Hanoi was the capital of the Vietnamese lands. The unlucky official fled downriver from this city to the sea by boat. Four pertinent lines read:

> Wind down the Chu-dien route,
> Escorted by flocks of kingfishers;
> Sail by war boat over the Chang Sea [Gulf of Tonkin],
> Banners furling in the swirling mists.
>
> (*CL*, 157)

The line "Wind down the Chu-dien route" suggests floating down the sinuous river channels to the sea through Chu-dien. This poem implies that a battle fought in Chu-dien would be against a seaborne intruder.

Appendix I

An-vien, Duong-lam, Phuc-loc

One problem in early Vietnamese history is posed by the toponyms in the title of this appendix. According to Chinese sources, *An-vien*, *Duong-lam*, and *Phuc-loc* are T'ang toponyms dating from the seventh century and refer to an area in the region of the Ca River. According to Vietnamese sources and tradition, these names refer to an area in the northwestern part of the Hong River plain. It is clear that the T'ang toponyms as used in Chinese sources refer to the southern location. It is equally clear that the traditional Vietnamese use of these toponyms refers to the northern location. Frankly, I do not know how to account for this, but since it has been customary among modern scholars to follow the traditional Vietnamese localization, I think it would be good to lay out the Chinese sources to show how I have followed them for the T'ang period.

An-vien first appeared during the Sui dynasty as a district name in what was at that time called Nhat-nam Prefecture, formerly Cuu-duc Prefecture (*SuiS*, 31, 13a). In 622, T'ang included An-vien District in what was called Duc Province; Duc became Hoan in 627 (*HTS*, 43a, 10b, and *CTS*, 41, 46a). Some time between 639 and 669, An-vien was discontinued as a district under Hoan and was joined with a new Duong-lam District to form Duong-lam Province. In 669, a Phuc-loc District was added to Duong-lam, and the provincial name was changed to Phuc-loc (*HTS*, 43a, 10b–11a; *CTS*, 41, 45a–b; *TPHYC*, 171, 10b–11a).

According to the *T'ai P'ing huan yu chi*, Phuc-loc lay 102 *li* east of Hoan "along the sea" (*TPHYC*, 171, 6a); the *T'ung tien* says that the Phuc-loc border was 100 *li* east of the Huan provincial seat (*T'T*, 174, 50b). According to an itinerary compiled during the Chen-yüan period (785–805), An-vien District in Duong-lam lay two days east of the Hoan provincial seat, and Huan-wang (Champa) lay a two-day journey south of An-vien (Pelliot, "Deux Itineraires," p. 184). This places An-vien in what is now southern Ha-tinh, in the vicinity of the Hoanh-son massif, on the Cham frontier.

According to the *Chiu T'ang shu* and the *Hsin T'ang shu*, the history of Phuc-loc Province after its establishment in 669 is as follows: (1) in 742, Phuc-loc was reduced to prefectural status as part of a general reform affecting all provinces in the empire (in place of this, the *Hsin T'ang shu* contains a garbled citation about Phuc-loc's being changed to "An-vu

Province" in an indecipherable year; this is an error); (2) in 757, the name Phuc-loc Prefecture was changed to Duong-lam Prefecture; (3) in 758, the old name of Phuc-loc Province was restored as part of a general reform affecting all prefectures in the empire (*CTS*, 41, 45a–b; and *HTS*, 43a, 10b–11a).

The *T'ung tien*, a source dating from the mid-eighth century, says only that Phuc-loc Province became Phuc-loc Prefecture in 742 (*T'T*, 174, 50b). The *Yüan Ho chün hsien chih*, a source dating from the early ninth century, simply cites Duong-lam Province and ignores the name *Phuc-loc* (*YHCHC*, 38, 1091). It seems that the names *Phuc-loc* and *Duong-lam* were to some extent interchangeable.

The *Hsin T'ang shu*, which gives the most information on the formation of Phuc-loc Province in the seventh century and which demonstrates a basic desire to give a proper accounting of T'ang era toponyms, is the only source to include a Phuc-loc District in Phuc-loc Province. All other sources cite only two districts in this province: Duong-lam and An-vien, or its variant Nhu-vien. The *Hsin T'ang shu* and the *Chiu T'ang shu* state that the district name *An-vien* was changed to *Nhu-vien* in 757; at the same time *Duong-lam* briefly superseded *Phuc-loc* as the prefectural name. The *T'ung tien* cites the two districts of Duong-lam and Nhu-vien, but then incongruously states that the government of Phuc-loc Province was located in An-vien District. The *Yüan Ho chün hsien chih* lists *Duong-lam* and *An-vien* as the district names for Duong-lam Province. From this it is clear that the toponym *Duong-lam* was more firmly established as a specific locality than was *Phuc-loc*; it can also be conjectured that *An-vien* and *Nhu-vien* were variants for what was probably the provincial or prefectural seat, for this was the oldest district in the jurisdiction, dating from Sui.

Considering the above information from Chinese sources, we can see that, in the initial period of establishing the T'ang regime in the seventh century, Phuc-loc Province was developed on an expanding administrative frontier along the coast south of the Ca River. An-vien District was detached from the jurisdiction of Hoan to become the nucleus of a new jurisdiction facing toward a region occupied by nomadic tribespeople; according to the sources, "uncivilized Lao" had migrated here in the sixth century and the establishment of the new jurisdiction was part of a policy of "beckoning and soothing" these people. The jurisdiction grew to include a new district named Duong-lam and finally to include a third district named Phuc-loc. Each time the jurisdiction was enlarged, its name was changed to that of the newest district, clearly a policy of "beckoning and soothing" newcomers by granting the most formal prestige to the most recent members.

In the eighth and ninth centuries, Phuc-loc District disappeared from the records; *Phuc-loc* as a provincial or prefectural name was temporarily replaced by *Duong-lam* in the mid eighth century and permanently replaced by *Duong-lam* no later than the early ninth century. This was probably due to the abandonment of Phuc-loc District as T'ang power declined; Phuc-loc District was the last to be added and the first to go, for it was probably an unstable outpost. Duong-lam District was more enduring and gained added adminstrative recognition when Phuc-loc faltered. The fortunes of these district names, insofar as they were given formal recognition as the name of a larger jurisdiction, were probably based on the political loyalties of their inhabitants.

Beginning in the eighth century, An-vien District was also known as Nhu-vien District. These two names may have derived from rival localities, or factions within the same district, and their successive fortunes may have been based on their relative status in the eyes of the empire. *An-vien* can be translated "to pacify distant places" and implies a certain militancy; on the other hand, *Nhu-vien* can be translated "to overcome distant places by gentleness" and implies a more passive attitude. These names may in fact have derived from contrasting policies followed in establishing and maintaining the new jurisdiction. For example, the name *An-vien* was changed to *Nhu-vien* in 757, when Phuc-loc was briefly lost; this was when T'ang power was crippled by the rebellion of An Lu-shan and frontier adminstration was forced into a defensive, conciliatory posture. The T'ang army sent to reestablished order in Vietnam in 791 was named the Jou-yüan (Vietnamese Nhu-vien) Army, and it achieved success without a battle simply by relying on persuasion.

By the tenth century, after the fall of T'ang, the application of these toponyms was strangely distorted. Their connection with the southern frontier was lost, and instead they were applied to one of the most venerable regions in Vietnamese history, along the right bank of the Hong near the head of the plain.

According to later Vietnamese historians, both Phung Hung and Ngo Quyen, independence leaders from the eighth and tenth centuries respectively, were from Duong-lam. In the eighteenth century, Cao Huy Dieu commented on Phung Hung's birthplace:

> It has been said that Duong-lam was the same as present day Phuc-loc; Saint Phung is currently the guardian deity of Mong-phu village. I do not yet know what is correct. (*VDULT*, 7)

In the independence period, *Phuc-loc* was the name of a jurisdiction a short distance west of Hanoi on the right bank of the Hong (Buu Cam et al., pp. 22, 24, 53, 119, 190, 207). Vietnamese historical tradition has fixed Phung Hung's birthplace in this area at a village presently named Cam-lam, where a temple to Phung Hung has survived to this day (Cao Huy Giu and Dao Duy Anh, p. 324, n. 14; Ton Nu Thuong Lang and Ta Quang Phat, part 1, 4: 26;

Tran Trong Kim 1: 60; Le Thanh Khoi, p. 124; Uy Ban Khoa Hoc Xa Hoi, 1: 130; *TT*, 5, 6a). According to the *Viet dien u linh tap*, Phung Hung's cult developed after his death around a temple built west of modern Hanoi (*VDULT*, 6). It is reasonable to assume that this temple was built near Phung Hung's birthplace. The source for Phung Hung, Chao Ch'ang's *Chiao chou chi*, passed through the *Viet dien u linh tap*, so it is not surprising that the geographical details were preserved according to Vietnamese tradition.

Beginning with Ngo Quyen in the tenth century, Vietnamese sources use *Duong-lam* as a toponym for this Hong River location. Later in the independence period, *Phuc-loc* became an established jurisdictional name in this place. Vietnamese historians also used the name *An-vien* in the same vicinity. According to the *Viet dien u linh tap*, a protector general in the eighth century resided at An-vien village, a short distance west of modern Hanoi (*VDULT*, 34). Whether or not this instance has any connection with our discussion is a matter for speculation, for here An-vien is a village name rather than a district name, as in the Chinese sources, yet the village it names is located in the general area in which Vietnamese sources place Duong-lam and Phuc-loc.

The problem of relating the Chinese and Vietnamese sources on these toponyms remains unsolved. They are not the only Chinese-period toponyms to survive into the independence era in a different geographical location; they are only the most curious combination of such toponyms, and they also happen to concern two important Vietnamese leaders in the T'ang and immediate post-T'ang era. The manner in which the Vietnamese discarded, changed, or rearranged toponyms from the Chinese provincial period after independence does not reflect any readily perceivable pattern. Perhaps subsequent investigation will prove more fruitful.

Appendix J

Sources for the Phung Hung Era

The primary source on the Phung family is the *Chiao chou chi*, "Records of Chiao Province," attributed to Chao Ch'ang, the protector general who reestablished T'ang authority in Vietnam in 791. Ch'ang was one of the few Chinese officials in Vietnamese history to gain a measure of acceptance among the people. He was an old man who understood the difference between the form and the substance of power; he nurtured imperial rule without severely offending local sensibilities. He served in Vietnam for twelve years, and when his replacement ran into trouble he briefly returned to set things straight. According to Vietnamese sources, he was interested in the local culture and frequently traveled about familiarizing himself with village customs and cultic traditions. His book undoubtedly came from firsthand experience in talking with the Vietnamese people and observing their way of life.

Chao Ch'ang's *Chiao chou chi* was not preserved in China, and it has not survived in its original form even in Vietnam. The *Viet dien u linh tap* specifically cites it for two accounts: the "kingdom-protecting spirit" patronized by Li Ch'ang-ming in the 650s and Phung Hung. The accounts from Ch'ang's book preserved in the *Viet dien u linh tap* contain toponyms and titles peculiar to Vietnamese historiography in the independence period, so it is clear that the surviving portions of the book have been incorporated into the Vietnamese historical tradition.

The *Viet dien u linh tap* account for Phung Hung (*VDULT*, 6) mainly explains the origin and development of Hung's cult. It begins by citing historical details from Chao Ch'ang's *Chiao chou chi*. It is not clear whether the portion of the *Viet dien u linh tap* text describing the development of Hung's posthumous cult is based on Ch'ang or on popular traditions locally preserved. The final items in the text about the development of the cult in the tenth and thirteenth centuries are of course not attributable to Ch'ang.

The historical part of the *Viet dien u linh tap* text, about the actual careers of Phung Hung, his brother, and his son, is clearly based on Ch'ang. Since most of this information does not exist elsewhere, it is important to consider the other sources and, in particular, to understand how Chinese historians dealt with the period.

The events of the Phung Hung era posed a problem to Chinese historians; they lacked specific information on the actual course of events and consequently used what details they possessed to reconstruct a reasonable account consonant with their imperial perspective.

The annals of the *Chiu T'ang shu* say that in the fourth month of 791, An-nam leader Do Anh Han rebelled and attacked the capital city of the protectorate; Protector General Kao Cheng-p'ing died of melancholy; in the fifth month, the Jou-yüan Army was established for the Protectorate of An-nam; in the seventh month, Chao Ch'ang was appointed protector general of An-nam and imperial commissioner with the title "Proclaiming and Punishing Legate" (*CTS*, 13, 6a).

The annals of the *Hsin T'ang shu* only state that in the fourth month of 791 An-nam leader Do Anh Han rebelled and was suppressed (*HTS*, 7, 7b).

Chao Ch'ang's biography says that An-nam "Lao leader" Do Anh Han rebelled and Protector General Kao Cheng-p'ing died of melancholy; when Ch'ang was appointed protector general, "the barbarians scattered" as Ch'ang "encouraged and influenced" them such that they "did not dare to make trouble" (*HTS*, 170, 8a).

Ssu-ma Kuang uses all of the above information but adds certain interpretive details; he begins by stating that An-nam Protector General Kao Cheng-p'ing doubled taxes; then, in the fourth month (791), the "barbarian leader" Do Anh Han raised soldiers and besieged the capital city; Cheng-p'ing died, and when the "barbarian multitude" heard of this they returned to T'ang allegiance; in the fifth month the Jou-yüan Army was established in An-nam; in the seventh month, Chao Ch'ang was appointed protector general, and the "barbarian multitude" submitted (*TCTC*, 233, vol. 12, 587).

Unlike the Chinese sources, which possess only a few isolated details, Chao Ch'ang's account in the *Viet dien u linh tap* presents a coherent narrative that seems to be derived from firsthand witnesses. The Chinese sources are oblivious of Phung Hung, his brother, and his son; they know only of the military commander Do Anh Han, who led an army against Kao Cheng-p'ing. Either the Chinese were ignorant of the true nature of the movement opposing them or else they desired to expunge the name of Phung Hung from history.

The dating of Do Anh Han's offensive and Kao Cheng-p'ing's death in 791, only three months prior to Chao Ch'ang's pacification of the protectorate, is suspicious. According to Chao Ch'ang's account, Phung Hung entered the city after Cheng-p'ing's death, and Hung's subsequent death was followed by the two-year reign of his son An prior to Chao Ch'ang's arrival. Thus, Cheng-p'ing's death could not have been after 789. The *Chiu T'ang shu* states that Chao Ch'ang was given the title "Proclaiming and Punishing Legate," and a contemporary source, the *Yüan Ho chün hsien chih*, dates the creation of a "Proclaiming and Punishing Department" with a special legate for An-nam in 790 (*YHCHC*, 38, 1082).

Ssu-ma Kuang's account demonstrates the elaborating influence of imperial ideology in constructing the official historical version. The idea that Kao Cheng-p'ing provoked the rebellion by doubling taxes surfaces for the first time with Ssu-ma Kuang. Either the real origin of the situation was unknown or information about it had been suppressed. The rebellion of 687 had followed the doubling of taxes, and this thereby became a reasonable explanation for what was regarded as a rebellion in 791, although the doubling of taxes at this time is improbable considering T'ang weakness in the south. Furthermore, whereas the *Chiu T'ang shu* and *Hsin T'ang shu* identify Do Anh Han as an "An-nam leader" and Chao Ch'ang's biography calls him a "Lao leader," Ssu-ma Kuang calls him a "barbarian leader" and elaborates the events of the rebellion as an uprising of barbarians. This reflects a hardening of imperial ideology that belies an impatience with rebellion and a lack of interest in what motivates it so long as it is suppressed.

The *Viet su luoc* only says that Chao Ch'ang replaced Kao Cheng-p'ing (whom the *Viet su luoc* dates to the reign of Tai Tsung, 763–79) and in 791 requested the formation of the Jou-yüan Army (*VSL*, 1, 10a). The *An-nam chi luoc* account is taken directly from Chao Ch'ang's biography (*CL*, 99). The *Dai Viet su ky toan thu* combines Chao Ch'ang's account from the *Viet dien u linh tap* with Ssu-ma Kuang, while squeezing it all into Ssu-ma Kuang's chronology (*TT*, 5, 6a–b).

Two final considerations lend credence to Chao Ch'ang's account. The details of the power struggle following Phung Hung's death suggest an actual sequence of events; if the account was fabricated, there would be no reason to include such an affair. And the 792 report from the military governor at Canton requesting that the international markets in An-nam be closed down (see chapter 5) implies that there had been no effective imperial authority in An-nam for a significant period of time; international trade had shifted to An-nam from Canton against the wishes of T'ang authorities, so An-nam must have been beyond their control.

Appendix K

The Trung Sisters in the Literature
of Later Centuries

Vietnamese scholars of the independence period, educated in a patriarchal mold, were as much astonished by the fact that Trung Trac and Trung Nhi were women as they were by what these women actually did. In the thirteenth century, historian Le Van Huu wrote:

> Trung Trac and Trung Nhi were women; they gave one shout and all the prefectures of Cuu-chan, Nhat-nam, and Ho-p'u, along with sixty-five strongholds beyond the passes, responded to them, and, establishing the nation, they proclaimed themselves queens as easily as turning over their hands, which shows that our land of Viet was able to establish a royal tradition. What a pity that, for a thousand years after this, the men of our land bowed their heads, folded their arms, and served the northerners; how shameful this is in comparison with the two Trung sisters, who were women! Ah, it is enough to make one want to die! (*TT*, 3, 1b)

In this comment, Le Van Huu reveals his characteristic interest in establishing the pre-Chinese "royal tradition" in Vietnam, although he refrains from including the sisters in the Vietnamese "imperial tradition," which he sees exemplified by Chao T'o and Dinh Bo Linh. He also expresses deep anguish over what he interprets as male passivity and female initiative.

A fifteenth-century poet echoed this feeling of shame that it was the women rather than the men who had led the nation in such a time of crisis:

> All the male heroes bowed their heads in submission;
> Only the two sisters proudly stood up to avenge the country.
> (Dang Thanh Le, pp. 46–47)

In the same vein, a popular historical poem of the seventeenth century declared:

> The Han emperor was extremely furious:
> This insignificant speck of a Giao-chi!
> And it was not even a man,
> But a mere girl who wielded the skill of a hero!
> (Dang Thanh Le, p. 51)

By the nineteenth century, the sentiment had become even sharper:

A woman proudly led a young nation;
Even the Han emperor heard of it and was terrified.
                    (Dang Thanh Le, p. 50)

The inevitable literary effect of this exaggeration of the Trung sisters'
femininity was to romanticize the marriage of Trung Trac and Thi Sach.
The seventeenth-century historical poem cited above elaborates their courtship and marriage, using romantic images of the time. Trac's motive for
rebellion is portrayed as a mixture of revenge for the death of her husband at
the hands of the Han governor and a desire to free her compatriots from a
foreign yoke. This combined ideal of romantic love and patriotism became
important in Vietnamese thought in recent centuries. It appeared during the
Tay-son peasant rebellion of the eighteenth century and has been widely
expressed in patriotic literature since 1945 (Dang Thanh Le, pp. 47–48).

The woman who fights for her country while mourning the battle-
field death of her husband or lover is a compelling image in modern
Vietnam, for it portrays the experience of many Vietnamese in recent years.
However, this image and this experience are not new in Vietnamese history.
At their source lies the eternally attractive figure of Trung Trac, "cloud of
hair, snow-white shoulders, fragrant breath, skin of ivory . . . a smile more
joyous than a blossoming flower," leading her army against the Chinese
(Dang Thanh Le, p. 44).

Even Chinese writers could not resist this image as an exotic embellish-
ment of their poetic skills. The Sung poet and calligrapher, Huang T'ing-
chien (1054–1105), celebrating the exploits of heroes on the southern frontier, compared Trung Trac with Lü Chia, who resisted Han Wu Ti's armies
in the name of Nan Yüeh in 111 B.C.:

Lü Chia refused treasonous bribes;
Trung Trac raised her shield to resist oppressors.
                    (Dang Thanh Le, p. 47)

There is evidence that the Trung sisters became cultic figures in parts
of China in later centuries. The fifteenth-century *Dai Viet su ky toan thu*
reports in a note the existence of a shrine to the Trung sisters at Canton
(*Ngoai ky*, 3, 3b). A Vietnamese envoy to China in 1793 reported seeing a
shrine to the Trung sisters in Hu-nan, on the south shore of Lake Tung-t'ing
(see Nguyen Tuan Luong). His account, however, sounds suspiciously like a
confusion with the twin goddesses of the Hsiang, legendary consorts of
Shun, whose cult was established on the shores of Lake Tung-t'ing no later
than Han times (see Schafer, *Divine Woman*, pp. 38–42, 57–69, 93–103,
137–45).

For the Vietnamese themselves, the importance of the Trung sisters in
later centuries became closely associated with the sisters' spirit cult and with

their prominent position in the pantheon of national spirits able to give supernatural aid in time of need. Ngo Si Lien, the fifteenth-century historian, expressed an appreciation of their posthumous role:

> Trung Trac, angry with the tyrannical Han governor, raising her hand and giving a shout, all but united and restored our country. Her heroic courage was not limited to her lifetime achievements of establishing the nation and proclaiming herself queen, but after her death she also resisted misfortune, for, in times of flood or drought, prayers to her spirit have never gone unanswered. And it is the same with her younger sister. Because they had both the virtue of scholars and the temperament of warriors, there are no greater spirits in all of heaven and earth. Should not all great heroes nurture an attitude of upright hauteur such as they had? (*TT*, 3, 2a)

The Trung sisters' posthumous cult was popular in the independence period. It is recorded that, during a drought, King Ly Anh-tong (1138–75) went to the Trung sisters' ancestral temple and ordered Buddhist priests to pray for rain. The prayers were soon answered. As it rained, the king fell asleep and dreamed of "two pretty-faced women with willowy eyebrows wearing green robes over red garments with red crowns and sashes, astride iron horses, passing by with the rain." Astonished, the king asked the women who they were, and they replied, "We are the two Trung sisters; we have been sent from Heaven to bring rain." When the king awoke, he immediately ordered repairs to their ancestral temple and established rituals for offering sacrifices. At the same time, he sent officials back to the capital with orders to erect a temple on the north side of the inner citadel for use as a sacrificial center to the "Rain Maidens." He later built another temple in a hamlet outside the city walls and issued posthumous imperial appointments to the "Pure Spirit Ladies." Kings of the Tran dynasty also honored the Trung sisters with posthumous imperial appointments in the thirteenth and early fourteenth centuries (*VDULT*, 11).

A commentary on the Trung sisters survives from Cao Huy Dieu, a scholar writing in 1715:

> The imperial court was far away; local officials were greedy and oppressive. At that time the country of one hundred sons was the country of the women of Lord To. The ladies used the female arts against their irreconcilable foe; skirts and hairpins sang of patriotic righteousness, uttered a solemn oath at the inner door of the ladies quarters, expelled the governor, and seized the capital—the territories from Cuu-chan to Ho-p'u again saw the light of day. Were they not grand heroines?
>
> From antiquity, women have played a conspiratorial role. For example, Empress Lü of Han and Empress Wu of T'ang were able to command China with loud threatening noises, like wind and thunder, but the rightful heirs of the one great heritage of the everlasting First Emperor [Ch'in Shih Huang Ti] were cheated, taken advantage of, treated contemptibly, and

ridden roughshod over by women using deception and intimidation, who, in the end, were simply criminals, "gone forever."

On the other hand, our two ladies brought forward an army of all the people, and, establishing a royal court that settled affairs in the territories of sixty-five strongholds, shook their skirts over the Hundred Yüeh. In the south, they were proclaimed sovereign lords, in the same class as Martial Emperor Trieu [Chao T'o] and Southern Emperor Ly [Ly Bi], inspiring later generations to call them queens. Still, they did not follow the advice of others. They died at the defeat of Cam-khe in the spirit of uprightness and in purity of mind, towering in the midst of the vast universe, bringing men to their feet sighing affectionately over their memory. Were those hens that crowed at dawn during Han and T'ang even worthy of being the hibiscus-capped, green-gowned attendants of our two Trung ladies?

Today, their temple is at An-hat in Phuc-loc. The temple hall is majestic and well cared for. People enter with dignity and depart with reverence. On festival days for welcoming the spirits, the local people perform in battle array with elephants and horses; their bearing is truly frightening. An-lang and Ha-loi also observe ceremonial sacrifices to the spirits of the Trung ladies, using imperially appointed implements. The ancestral images in these places are magnificent. Travelers passing by these shrines stop and visit. Literary men and poets, coming and going like the shuttle of a loom, spontaneously intone the theme [of their heroism]; thus, the two immortal ladies will never die.

Now, in these days, there are the Chaste Widow of Trao-nha and the Pure Wife of Ty-ba who are unanimously acclaimed for their uprightness and for whom the whole nation laments! It was the same kind of resolute appeal that pushed out the borders of the Trung queens' territory. It cannot be denied that this appeal, beginning in Me-linh, swallowed Chu-dien, echoed through Nhat-nam, and cleared accounts at Lang-bac; was not this an affair of "lifting the heavens and pulling up the earth"? (*VDULT*, 11–12)

This commentary contains several items of interest. It is written in a cliché-ridden style characteristic of educated Vietnamese in the early eighteenth century. It begins with the familiar formula of "distant imperial court, greedy local officials" that became the standard explanation for uprisings in Vietnam during the period of Chinese rule. The Vietnamese realm is identified as the "country of one hundred sons" in reference to the myth of Lac Long Quan and Au Co, whose one hundred sons supposedly gave rise to the Vietnamese race.

The time of the Trung sisters is described as an era when the country belonged to "the women of Lord To." Lord To refers to To Lich, the man who, according to tradition, gained eminence during the fourth century as the owner of estates located where the capital city that became Hanoi was eventually built. This area was popularly known as the "Dragon's Belly" (*Long-do*), the geographical and spiritual center of the Vietnamese realm. The spirit of To Lich was invoked by two T'ang governors who built cities

on the site and by Vietnamese kings in the eleventh, thirteenth, and fourteenth centuries. To Lich was regarded as the guardian spirit of the capital
city and, by extension, of the entire kingdom. His posthumous cult was
maintained by ruling-class people, particularly by those seeking to rule from
the "Dragon's Belly" (*VDULT*, 18–19).

The eighteenth-century commentator used the curious expression
"women of Lord To" as a euphemism for "queens." It was apparently the
most convenient means he could devise for bringing the strongly matrilineal
society of the Trung sisters into congruence with the mentality of educated
men in his day. This is the only known reference to To Lich in connection
with events prior to the fourth century.

One can sense the commentator's patriotic spirit overcoming his
patriarchal puritanism as he wrote of "skirts and hairpins," a cliché for
women, becoming "grand heroines." He indulged his instinctive prejudice
against female rulers while discussing the Chinese empresses, then indulged
his instinctive patriotism when he praised the virtues of the Trung sisters.

As a good moral historian, the commentator could not resist offering
the usual explanation for failure: "They did not follow the advice of others."
Scholar-officials, and their ideals, thrived only when rulers followed their
advice; consequently, this is a typical comment, which was also an admonition to rulers in the writer's day.

The commentator compared the Trung sisters with Chao T'o,
"Martial Emperor Trieu," and the sixth-century independence leader Ly Bi,
"Southern Emperor Ly." He thereby placed them in what was, in the
eighteenth century, a conventional category for legitimate Vietnamese
sovereigns. This distinguished them from the "gone forever" Chinese
empresses, who were thought of as usurpers.

Cam-khe was cited by the commentator as the traditional name of the
Trung sister's natal village. This was where the sisters made their last stand.
(See Dinh Van Nhat, "Dat Cam-khe.")

The description of how the Trung sisters' posthumous cult flourished
in the eighteenth century is a vivid indication of how the sisters fared in the
popular culture of later centuries. The commentator compared this with
two exemplary women who achieved fame in the society of his time. He
implies that a certain kind of ideal woman exerted a powerful appeal in
Vietnamese society.

The Trung sisters were leaders of a ruling class and of the society
dominated by this class. They thereby became the symbolic guardians of the
cultural heritage of the society. The significance of their guardianship has
grown with the passing centuries. In 1975, Pham Huy Thong, director of
the Archeological Institute in Hanoi, wrote:

> The greatness of the two women from Me-linh, and of all the brave
> people of the year 40, was in their realization that thousands of ancient

customs and habits carried the soul of the nation; they thereupon arrived at a time when a question fraught with responsibility was placed before all the people and before history; was this life of the people, together with independence and freedom, worth defending with flesh and blood? People of the four directions, from the territories of the old Hung kings, seizing their weapons and standing up as one, answered—answered for themselves and for all later generations.

In the end, the uprising failed. Ancient Viet civilization was destroyed. But this was a "death that did not become death," as history eventually saw. Even if the ancient Viet people had not risen up in the year 40, Dong-son culture still would not have survived, whether by enticement or coercion. It would have faded and fallen into ruin by degrees. At the same time, the memory of the Hung kings and the idea of a common Viet people would have melted away. But Dong-son culture poured itself out in the towering, flaming tongue of a courageous struggle. Along with resentment, the memory of this was deeply engraved in the feelings of the people. That is the secret of a miraculous phenomenon not easy to see in history: though oppressed by a foreign country for a thousand years, the will that "we are we" among our people was not something that could be shaken loose. (Pham Huy Thong, "Ba lan," p. 67)

This statement shows how contemporary Vietnamese evaluate the Trung sisters. It implies that if the Trung sisters had not resisted, there would be no Vietnamese nation today, that the uprising of A.D. 40 effectively "froze" the Dong-son heritage in a moment of heroic courage, insuring that it would not degenerate and invite the scorn of later generations. The Trung sisters were the last of the pre-Chinese popular leaders; their deeds echoed across the centuries of Chinese rule, calling the Vietnamese back to an ancient inheritance.

Appendix L

*Li Ku's Seven-Point Memorial on
the Rebellion of 136*

If the Provinces of Ching [Hu-nan and Hu-pei] and
Yang [Chiang-hsi, Che-chiang, and Fu-chien] were peaceful, raising troops
there would be possible, but at this time they are infested with rebels and
bandits; furthermore, the barbarian peoples there are not at peace. Soldiers
have been raised from Chang-sha and Kuei-yang [in Hu-nan] many times
already; if we again attempt to conscript troops from these provinces, there
will be trouble. This is the first point.

If we propose to send men from the Provinces of Yen [Shan-tung]
and Yü [Ho-nan] to a distant frontier thousands of miles away without hope
of return, there will be mutiny and desertion. This is the second point.

The climate in the southern provinces is hot, and there are epidemics
that will cause the death of four or five out of every ten men. This is the third
point.

The soldiers will have to march for thousands of miles, and by the time
they arrive in the south they will be too exhausted to fight. This is the fourth
point.

It will take three hundred days to march an army from the provinces
of Yen and Yü to Nhat-nam. During this time the army will consume six
hundred thousand pecks of rice, not to mention provisions for the officers,
their staffs, and the horses. Such expenditure is out of the question. This is the
fifth point.

By the time the army reaches the south, so many men will have died of
illness that it will be ineffective in battle, and more men will have to be sent,
resulting in great disaffection. This is the sixth point.

Cuu-chan is only a few hundred miles from Nhat-nam, yet the
soldiers conscripted there refused to march south; now how can we expect to
send soldiers thousands of miles to do what they would not? This is the
seventh point.

Some time ago, General Yin Chiu campaigned against the Ch'iang
tribes of I Province [Ssu-ch'uan]. The people of I Province said: "When the
bandits came we could survive, but when Yin came, he ruined us." Later,
Chiu was recalled and his military command was given to the governor,
Chang Ch'iao. Using his own generals, Ch'iao destroyed the bandits in less

than a month. This shows that sending generals is not as effective as relying on good local officials.

I advise selecting men of ability and humanity to fill the administrative positions in Giao-chi; ordering the isolated soldiers in Nhat-nam who lack supplies and are too few for battle to take their people north to Giao-chi; issuing proclamations to the barbarians inciting them to attack one another; supplying our officials with gold and rice; and rewarding rebel leaders who surrender with their followers by conferring titles and grants of land.

Formerly, Chu Liang was governor at Chang-sha; he is a man of high spirit and great courage. Also, Chang Ch'iao showed his ability in destroying the Ch'iang of I Province. I recommend using these men. (*HHS*, 116, 11b–13a; slightly abridged versions can be found in *CL*, 69–70, and *TT*, 3, 5a–b.)

Appendix M

T'ao Yüan and the King of Dao-lang

Citing the twelfth century *Su ky* of Do Thien, the *Viet dien u linh tap* says:

> Ly Phat Tu was a junior kinsman of Ly Bi. When Bi died, he followed Bi's elder brother Thien Bao who, with an army of thirty thousand, fled among the Lao barbarians; [Ch'en] Pa-hsien offered a reward for them without success. Thien Bao arrived at the spring at the source of the Dao River in Da-nang grotto. He saw that the place was beautiful, that fertile soil yielded abundant produce, that the land was rich and vast, so he built a city and dwelt there. Those who gathered in that place increased daily in number; wisdom and ability were felt far and wide. The kingdom of Da-nang was accordingly established, and the people elected Thien Bao to be king of Dao-lang. Shortly after, he died without an heir. The people deliberated and elected Phat Tu as king. When Ch'en Pa-hsien returned north, Phat Tu led soldiers down east. His counselors advised him to proclaim himself emperor. Phat Tu followed their advice and styled himself Emperor of the South. (*VDULT*, 8)

Da-nang grotto, at the source of the Dao River, brings to mind T'ao Yüan, the secluded paradise of Chinese utopians popularized by the Chin dynasty author T'ao Yüan-ming. T'ao Yüan-ming imagined T'ao Yüan as a place blessed with happiness and prosperity reached through a cavelike tunnel at the source of a river. *Dao* is Vietnamese for *t'ao*, meaning "peach," and the meaning of *yüan* is "source." It seems the Ly family chose to remember its sojourn in the mountains in terms of the idyllic scenario of Chinese utopians. The name *Da-nang* is unknown elsewhere, but may in fact have been the name of a valley where the Ly found temporary refuge.

There are several reasons why T'ao Yüan, the classical Chinese utopia, was associated with the Ly family during the time its fortunes were at a low point. The Ly fled into the mountains and disappeared from the lowland political scence for a time. They naturally had to have an acceptable explanation for where they had been before they could claim to reenter lowland political life. A place corresponding to the established educated concept of an ideal realm not only would have been a good explanation, but also would have had positive propaganda value.

T'ao Yüan was a place of social harmony, peace, and prosperity, located at the source of a river; it was a temporary abode for an outsider who, after departing, could not find it again. By describing Da-nang valley at the source of the Dao River in nearly identical terms, the Ly implied that this place was outside normal experience and denied responsibility for its precise location.

Furthermore, T'ao Yüan and the kingdom of Da-nang were myths of good government. This not only served to advertise the monarchical skills of the Ly, but also appealed to a Vietnamese desire to escape the heavy hands of Chinese dynasties. The inhabitants of T'ao Yüan had found their secluded paradise after escaping from the disorders of Ch'in; they had never heard of Han or later dynasties. They were beyond the reach of the Chinese imperial system and its greedy officials. By associating themselves with this utopian tradition, the Ly were claiming separation from the Chinese dynastic world.

Finally, more than simply a Ly family myth of good government, the kingdom of Da-nang was a way of transmitting the legitimate succession from Ly Bi through Ly Thien Bao to Ly Phat Tu. This was an important matter, for when Ly Phat Tu emerged from the mountains to challenge Trieu Quang Phuc, he did so as Ly Bi's political heir.

It is conceivable that the connection with T'ao Yüan was not made by the Ly themselves but was instead a later elaboration by Vietnamese historians who thereby thought to fill a gap in their historical knowledge. The literary nature of the association and the probability that T'ao Yüan meant very little, if anything, to ordinary Vietnamese in the sixth century lends credence to such an idea. But it is more likely that this literary association was understood by important members of the ruling class of the time and that it embodied a special kind of appeal to those both educated and politically aware.

Finally, the title "King of Dao-lang" is reminiscent of the title *quan-lang* attributed to sons of the Hung kings and held by Phung Hung in the eighth century. If, as one modern Vietnamese linguist has proposed (Hoang Thi Chau, pp. 41, 46–47), *lang* is a term indigenous to the Austroasian (Austronesian and Austroasiatic) cultural world, which was later borrowed by China, we can surmise that it embodied some local concept of authority.

Appendix N

P'i Jih-hsiu and the Nan-chao War

P'i Jih-hsiu was a prominent T'ang poet of the late ninth century. He became famous for his so-called "New Music Bureau" verse, which was didactic, concerned with social injustice, and critical of authority. New Music Bureau poetry had a strong moral tone and was meant to be sung in public as a way of circumventing traditional means of addressing the emperor (Nienhauser, pp. 20, 37, 46). P'i Jih-hsiu was alert to social injustice and was not afraid to openly criticize the government (Nienhauser, pp. 35–37, 43–44, 53, 64). He followed the new trend of critical scholarship, which rejected traditional interpretations of the classics in favor of efforts to penetrate their true, original meaning (Nienhauser, p. 66). He was especially fond of Mencius and the Mencian idea that the people have the right to revolt if the country is ruled improperly (Nienhauser, p. 26). He cited Mencius on the theory of parental kingship and in Mencius found authority for his strong personal distaste for the military and his conviction that military prowess was a criminal offense (Nienhauser, p. 65). According to William H. Nienhauser, Jr., who recently published a study of P'i Jih-hsiu, Jih-hsiu "stresses especially the unfairness of the North's hegemony over the South during his lifetime" (p. 81), and was interested in "appeals from regions not normally heeded by the central government" (p. 83).

In 865, after wandering about the Yangtze basin for two years, P'i Jih-hsiu traveled to Ch'ang-an, the T'ang capital, to take the civil service examination (Nienhauser, pp. 26–27). On his way, he stopped in the city of Hsü (variously Hsü-ch'ang or Hsü-ch'uan), located on the Ying River in modern Ho-nan, about two hundred miles southeast of Lo-yang. In 862, two thousand men from Hsü had been drafted for the T'ang army sent to Vietnam against the Nan-chao offensive of that year. Here is how P'i Jih-hsiu's visit to Hsü is recorded in the *Ch'üan T'ang shih*:

> Jih-hsiu was staying at an inn in Hsü-ch'uan. He suddenly heard the sound of wailing outside the city walls and inquired of people passing in the street. They said: "Southern barbarians besieged our Giao-chi. An imperial order was received to levy two thousand Hsü soldiers to attack them. They attacked again and again, and they all died in battle. Those who weep are the families of those soldiers. Alas! There is no news from Yang-tzu because contact with Chu-yai has been broken. Our armies are advancing over the dead bodies of

our own men, for otherwise the 'little fish' will scorn our Central kingdom; is not that how it is said?" [On "little fish" as a term for "barbarians," see Morohashi, 1, 595.] Sir P'i, walking among them, said: "There is nothing I can do to help this situation; I cannot even complete my degree. Furthermore, my hands will not lift sticks to beat drums, and I hate weapons of war. I just quietly follow my own nature, quietly follow my own pleasure. But I am also quilty of the Hsü warriors' fate [not having done anything to prevent it] and will compose a poem to mourn for them." (*ChTS*, 608)

Yang-tzu was the main T'ang port at the mouth of the Yangtze River. Chu-yai was on the north coast of Hai-nan Island. The T'ang army in Vietnam was being supplied by sea; Yang-tzu and Chu-yai were major ports along the supply route. In the summer of 865, Kao P'ien was heavily engaged against Nan-chao in Vietnam, and a jealous official was intercepting battlefield reports before they could reach Chu-yai. After several months of silence, the T'ang court finally sent an inquiry. P'i Jih-hsiu seems to have been in Hsü at this time.

The soldiers from Hsü were probably lost when Nan-chao crushed T'ang forces in Vietnam early in 863. The news of that defeat, or at least news of the Hsü soldiers' fate in it, apparently reached Hsü while Jih-hsiu was there.

P'i Jih-hsiu's poem to mourn the Hsü warriors is the second of his "Three Poems of Shame" (see Nienhauser, pp. 76–77, for a translation of the third). It is preserved in *Ch'uan T'ang shih*, as follows:

1   The south was neglected, officials were not selected,
      Causing the overthrow of our Giao-chi,
      Which, for three or four successive years,
      Has drifted away, bringing disgrace to the empire.
5   The timid yield readily in battle;
      The warlike revel in their weapons.
      Soldiers fill the empire,
      Battle leaders accumulate treasure;
      Exactions reduce the common people to misery,
10   In order to distribute the wages of valiant men.
      Brave Hsü-ch'ang warriors,
      Their loyalty and daring brought honor to their families;
      They went with the wind of myriad galloping horses,
      They ceased in a river of flesh.
15   Yesterday morning the defeated troops returned;
      There is weeping at a thousand gates and ten thousand hearths.
      The sound of wailing echoes through the village streets;
      Resentment spreads over the mountains and valleys.
      Who can listen to wardrums in the daytime,
20   And not suffer the sight of metal arrowheads?
      I have a plan for victory,

Though irregular and considered worthless by others.
I store it in my mind and heart;
I am ashamed to see the families of the Hsü warriors.
25   I lament those thoughtless ones,
Who simply follow the steps of their ancestors.
My family does not produce grain for the army;
I am not familiar with military affairs.
Yet I wear the same kind of clothing as the Hsü warriors,
30   And I eat the same kind of food as the Hsü warriors.
Now I know that the teachings of the Ancients
Are already enough to shelter me.
To whose shame is this song sung?
The Ying River flows far and green.

                                                    (*ChTS*, 608)

In the first four lines, Jih-hsiu blames the loss of Giao-chi on administrative neglect. He was apparently well informed, for this seems to have been a large factor in the Vietnamese situation as perceived by T'ang officials. In 833, the military governor at Canton had complained that new officials had not been appointed on the southern frontier for as long as two years (*CTS*, 17c, 8b). In 857–58, Vietnam fell into the hands of a powerful local general because the senior T'ang administrator had no soldiers to enforce his authority (*TCTC*, 249, vol. 13, 556). The events of the Nan-chao War reveal that factionalism and incompetence were characteristic of T'ang officialdom on the southern frontier.

Lines 5 and 6 suggest that "timid," or unqualified, officials in the south were an encouragement to the warlike among the population there. In lines 7 through 10, Jih-hsiu discloses his strong antimilitary outlook. Then, in lines 11 through 14, he portrays the soldiers from Hsü as innocent men who were caught up in forces beyond their control and ended in a pile of dead bodies, "a river of flesh." In lines 15 through 18, he expresses the grief of the dead soldiers' families. The rhetorical question in lines 19 and 20 seems to say that those who yield to the excitement of war must expect to suffer the consequences.

In lines 21 through 24, Jih-hsiu introduces himself into the picture. His "plan for victory" is clearly a plan for morally responsible government, which would avoid the extremity of war and the "shame" of grieving widows and orphans. Lines 25 and 26 depict the fate of the Hsü warriors as the result of "thoughtlessly" following authority. In lines 27 through 30, Jih-hsiu implies his feeling of shame at having fared better than the Hsü people although he is in fact no different from them, wearing the same kind of clothing and eating the same kind of food.

In lines 31 and 32, Jih-hsiu states that, far from trusting in weapons of war, he rests his heart in "the teachings of the Ancients." The "shame" in line 33 belongs to a government that did not select good officials in the south, thereby provoking a war that sent thousands of innocent men to their deaths in a distant land. The "shame" is also shared by Jih-hsiu, who could do nothing to prevent the situation, and perhaps even by "the Ancients," whose teachings have done nothing to help the common man.

The reference to the Ying River in the last line recalls a tale about the mythical Emperor Yao, who wanted to bequeath his realm to the hermit Hsü Yu. When Hsü Yu heard of this, he was so repulsed that he went to the Ying River and washed out his ears (Morohashi, 10, 408). When the hermit Ch'ao Fu later came to the Ying River during the course of his travels, he found that it was still dirty from Yu's ears, and he went back rather than contaminate himself by crossing it (Morohashi, 4, 339). This tale would have appealed to P'i Jih-hsiu; it portrays ruling-class pretensions as a kind of pollution. The last line is an enigmatic response to the question raised in the preceding line.

P'i Jih-hsiu arrived in Ch'ang-an too late to take the civil service examination in 865, and he failed the examination of 866 (Nienhauser, p. 27). He finally passed the exams in 867, perhaps with the help of an influential patron; but he passed near the bottom of the list and certain people, including his examiner, ridiculed him (Nienhauser, p. 29). After failing a higher-level examination in 868, he left Ch'ang-an in disappointment, without having received a position in the capital bureaucracy (Nienhauser, p. 30).

P'i Jih-hsiu's failure in Ch'ang-an seems to have been related to his outspoken, critical attitude toward the government. A line in a later poem of his says: "After writing those pieces that caused my failure in the examinations" (Nienhauser, p. 76). One of the "pieces" referred to here was probably the poem inspired by the mourners in Hsü, for *Ch'uan T'ang shih* (*ChTS*, 784) cites Sun Kuang-hsien's (d. 968) *Pei-meng so yen*, the earliest source for Jih-hsiu's poetry (Nienhauser, p. 109), for "A Poem Criticizing Affairs in An-nam," by a supposedly anonymous "examination candidate during the reign of I Tsung [860–73]." The *Ch'uan T'ang shih* quotes from the *Pei meng so yen* as follows:

> During the reign of I Tsung, An-nam was lost from our tender care, causing great trouble for soldiers on the frontier. An examination candidate heard that two thousand Hsü soldiers were killed in a barbarian village; he wrote a critical poem and sang it. He knew he would ruin his chance for employment; for the sake of the country he created a disturbance. (*ChTS*, 784)

The poem cited here is the same as the poem cited above from *Ch'uan T'ang shih*, 608, except that lines 21 through 32, lines directly identified with P'i Jih-hsiu's personal outlook, are omitted.

An-nam chi luoc (*CL*, 157) cites the poem as it exists in *Ch'uan T'ang shih*, 784, but attributes it to P'i Jih-hsiu; character variations suggest that Le Tac also consulted the poem as it is preserved in *Ch'uan T'ang shih*, 608.

Li Cheng-fu (p. 176) and Lü Shih-p'eng (p. 137) cite the poem from *Ch'uan T'ang shih*, 784, and say that the author must have been a Vietnamese, presumably in China to take the civil service examination. This idea has been endorsed by a modern Vietnamese scholar, Tran Nghia (pp. 97–99).

But evidence suggests that the poem belongs to P'i Jih-hsiu, and that Jih-hsiu eschewed a career in officialdom in order to protest T'ang policy in Vietnam. The poem he wrote about his experience in Hsü seems to have been popularized in a shorter version that was preserved separately.

Appendix O

Sources for Early Vietnamese History

Chinese dynastic histories and related writings are an indispensable group of source materials for early Vietnam. In most cases, they are the only source of information on Vietnam up to the tenth century; later Vietnamese works rely heavily on them for this period.

The dynastic histories were compiled from official documents and archives. They contain biographies, geographical and administrative data, and a chronological record of major events in the realm. The history of each dynasty was, as a rule, written by the succeeding dynasty.

The tradition of writing dynastic histories was inspired by the *Shih chi* of Ssu-ma Ch'ien (149–90 B.C.), which is itself a valuable source for early Vietnamese history (see Watson; also Aurousseau, pp. 175–201). The *Huai nan tzu* of Liu An (died 123 B.C.) complements some information in the *Shih chi* (Aurousseau, pp. 169–78).

Much of our information on early Vietnam is from the biographies of Chinese officials who served in Vietnam. This is especially true for such political events as rebellions, invasions, or frontier expeditions. The "Southern Barbarian" sections in each dynastic history contain general descriptions of events on the frontier.

The dynastic histories also contain a wealth of administrative data, such as jurisdictional organization, geographical information, and census records. This kind of data is often difficult to interpret. It is therefore useful to compare it with other collections of administrative records, such as the *T'ung tien*, compiled in the mid eighth century, the *Yüan Ho chün hsien chih*, compiled in the early ninth century, and the *T'ai P'ing huan yu chi*, compiled in the late tenth century (H. Maspero, "Le Protectorat general," pp. 546–49).

A particularly valuable source for early Vietnam is Li Tao-yuan's *Shui ching chu* from the early sixth century (Stein, pp. 1–3). Much of the value of this source lies in its citations from earlier, nonextant works. Similarly, a number of important citations from nonextant works appear in Ssu-ma Chen's eighth-century annotations to Ssu-ma Ch'ien's *Shih chi* and in two tenth-century works, *T'ai P'ing huan yu chi* and *T'ai P'ing kuang chi* (Gaspardone, "Champs Lo," p. 467).

Liu Hsi, a scholar who resided in Vietnam for a decade at the end of Han, wrote the *Shih ming*, which contains at least one clue to social patterns in early Vietnam (Gotō, p. 160; also Ming dynasty Ou Ta-jen, *Pai Yüeh hsien*

hsien chih, chapter 3, Liu Hsi section, and Ching dynasty Yeh Te-hui, *Liu Hsi shih chi kao*).

The *Man shu*, written by a ninth-century T'ang official who served in Vietnam, contains firsthand descriptions of communication routes, peoples, and events in both the mountains and plains of northern Vietnam (for an English translation, see Luce).

The *Ch'uan T'ang wen* and *Ch'uan T'ang shih* contain prose and poetry from the T'ang period that was written in Vietnam, about Vietnam, or by people from Vietnam. This literature contains clues to the way educated people perceived Vietnam or were influenced by residence in Vietnam.

In the eleventh century, Ssu-ma Kuang compiled the *Tzu chih t'ung chien*, a chronological survey based on the dynastic histories, as well as archival materials that were not used in the histories. Heavily edited, it contains some material no longer found elsewhere.

Turning from the Chinese sources, we come to five Vietnamese sources that survive from the fourteenth and fifteenth centuries. Written in Chinese, the language of scholarship, these works are based on earlier records and writings, Vietnamese as well as Chinese, most of which no longer exist. Four works from the fourteenth century reflect four different perspectives that were synthesized in the fifteenth century. Introducing these five sources will show the kind of information available from the Vietnamese side.

The first was written by Le Tac, a Vietnamese official who submitted to the Yüan (Mongol) dynasty of China during its 1285 invasion of Vietnam. He wrote the *An-nam chi luoc* (Annals of An-nam) in China, where he remained in exile for the rest of his life. This work is arranged topically in twenty chapters and was first published in 1340 or thereabouts. (A collated edition of the *An-nam chi luoc* with Vietnamese translation and introductory essay was prepared under the supervision of Ching-ho A. Ch'en and published by the University of Hue in 1961; on the date of this work, see pages vii-xii of the introductory essay.)

Except for items dating from Le Tac's lifetime, the *An-nam chi luoc* is derived almost entirely from Chinese records; it contains a certain amount of information no longer found elsewhere. As the title indicates, it was written with a Chinese bias, for *An-nam*, "pacified south," was the Chinese name for Vietnam during the T'ang dynasty.

It may not be correct to call the *An-nam chi luoc* a Vietnamese source, for Le Tac was an expatriate. However, he was born and raised in Vietnam and served the Vietnamese court; his formative years were spent in the Vietnamese environment. Furthermore, some of his material about "rebels" is not what one would expect of a Chinese historian. For example, his is the earliest surviving source to mention Lady Trieu, a third-century Vietnamese heroine who died in battle fighting the Chinese.

In contrast with the *An-nam chi luoc*, which was written in exile, the second work, the *Viet su luoc*, is in the tradition of official Vietnamese historiography. At present little is known of official historiography at the Vietnamese court in the four centuries following independence. During the Ming occupation of Vietnam in the early fifteenth century, books, libraries, and archives were taken away and subsequently lost in China. One work that has survived under Chinese custodianship is the *Viet su luoc* (Historical Annals of Viet). (A Vietnamese translation of the *Viet su luoc* with copious notes and an introduction by Tran Quoc Vuong has been published in Hanoi. The original title was *Dai Viet su luoc*. *Dai Viet*, "Great Viet," had been the official name of Vietnam since 1054. The Chinese abbreviated the title to suit their own notions of propriety and historical tradition.)

The *Viet su luoc* has three chapters. The first chapter begins with earliest antiquity and ends in the year 1009, when the Ly dynasty was founded. The second and third chapters cover the period of the Ly dynasty, ending in 1225. Appended to these chapters is a list of the kings of the Tran dynasty with the dates of their respective reign periods, ending with the "present king," whose date of accession is given as 1377; thus, the work appears to date from the reign of Tran Phe De (1377–88). (The Tran reign list appears between chapters 2 and 3 in the *Shou shan ko ts'ung shu* edition; see also Gaspardone, "Bibliographie," p. 2, n. 4.)

The *Viet su luoc* appears to be based on the *Dai Viet su ky* (Historical Records of Great Viet), which was presented to King Tran Thanh-tong by historian Le Van Huu in 1272. The *Dai Viet su ky* no longer exists in its original form, but in the fifteenth century it was incorporated into the *Dai Viet su ky toan thu*, which will be discussed presently. According to the *An-nam chi luoc*, Le Van Huu "revised" a *Viet chi* (Annals of Viet) which was written by Tran Pho, an official who had served King Tran Thai-tong, who reigned from 1225 to 1258 (*CL*, 146; Cadiere and Pelliot, pp. 623–24). Le Van Huu's *Dai Viet su ky* started with the beginning of recorded history in the third century B.C. and stopped with the end of the Ly dynasty in 1225, thereby coinciding with the *Viet su luoc* in chronology (Gaspardone, "Bibliographie," p. 49). Professor Yamamoto Tatsurō ("Esshiryaku") suggested that the *Viet su luoc* is a condensed version of Le Van Huu's *Dai Viet su ky* prepared in the late fourteenth century. Its treatment of the pre-Chinese period reflects the intellectual outlook of that time (see Wolters, "Assertions," 11: 76, and Appendix C). Ching-ho A. Ch'en ("Daietsu," pp. 7–8) conjectured that the *Viet su luoc* is in fact Tran Pho's *Viet chi*, with the Tran reign list having been added at the end of the fourteenth century, but there is no evidence for this.

Apart from its treatment of the pre-Chinese period, the *Viet su luoc* is based on Chinese sources up to the middle of the tenth century. The compiler was mainly interested in the Ly dynasty (1009–1225). Little interest is shown in the Chinese provincial period other than to lay out a bare narrative derived from Chinese records; there is no perception of how this period was experienced by the Vietnamese.

Tran Pho had been chancellor of the prestigious Han-lam Academy, modeled on the Han-lin Academy of China; Le Van Huu had been a member of the Han-lam Academy, as well as a senior compiler at the National Board of History. Furthermore, Le Van Huu's *Dai Viet su ky* was completed in response to a royal order. In contrast to these men, who filled prominent positions at the Vietnamese court in the thirteenth century, was Ly Te Xuyen, whose position as custodian of the Buddhist scriptures was similar to that of a head librarian (Le Huu Muc's introduction to his translation of the *VDULT*, pp. 16–18; also Durand, "Recuil," pp. 5–6).

Ly Te Xuyen "compiled" a book entitled *Viet dien u linh tap* (Compilation of the Departed Spirits in the Realm of Viet) (Gaspardone, "Bibliographie," pp. 126–28; Durand began to collate available texts of this work, but did not continue beyond a first installment, "Recuil"—a text with Vietnamese translation, notes, and an introduction by Le Huu Muc was published in 1960 in Saigon). In 1329, Ly Te Xuyen wrote the following preface (translated from p. 229 of Le Huu Muc's edition):

> The ancient sages said: "Intelligence and upright conduct are necessary for one to be named a godly being; depraved divinities, evil spirits, and wild demons cannot be so called." The godly beings dwelling in our realm of Viet since ancient times, worthy of being worshipped with temples and sacrifices, are indeed many! But how many are able to perform great achievements that are a mystery to living men? Certainly, those from past to present are not equal in their merit. Some are the spiritual essence of mountains and rivers; some are the heroic spirits of people that soared with heavenly breath power in their own time and have stood prominently as valorous spirits through succeeding ages. If their deeds are not authentically recorded, then it is difficult to distinguish between those of small merit and those of great merit. Therefore, according to the shallow perception of my mind, I have applied brush, ink, and paper to the mysterious affairs of the spirits. If by this lowly means is obtained something good, learned and accomplished, suited to the vast horizons of a wise man, then I will have hit my mark; such is my hope.

The *Viet dien u linh tap* contains twenty-seven tales arranged under three headings: "sovereigns," "ministers," and "superhuman powers." The seventeen tales included under the first two headings are about actual historical persons whose lives sufficiently stirred the people that their spirits posthumously became objects of popular veneration.

As he indicates in his preface, Ly Te Xuyen wanted to present as factual an account as possible to ascertain the relative merits of these departed spirits. Thus, for the first departed spirit, that of Shih Hsieh, who ruled the Vietnamese for forty years at the turn of the third century, the compiler cites

Shih Hsieh's biographical information from the *San kuo chih* (History of the Three Kingdoms), a Chinese dynastic chronicle. Next, he cites a work entitled *Bao cuc truyen* (Records Declaring the Unfathomable) (Gaspardone, "Bibliographie," p. 127, n. 1; variously *Bao duc truyen*) for the information that, about 160 years after Shih Hsieh's death, his tomb was opened by invaders from Lin-i, who were astonished to find the corpse perfectly preserved and with a countenance as if still alive; the people thereafter built a shrine and worshipped his spirit. This is followed by the story of a visit Shih Hsieh's spirit made to Kao P'ien, a ninth-century T'ang general who achieved fame among the Vietnamese; the story closes with a poem that P'ien wrote to commemorate the occasion. Finally, the entire account ends with an enumeration of titles conferred on Shih Hsieh's spirit by the Vietnamese court in the years 1285, 1288, and 1313.

This is typical of the way each tale in the *Viet dien u linh tap* is arranged. First, some historical source is cited for information about the actual life of the individual; second is recorded information about the development of a spirit cult after the person's death; finally, official titles conferred on the departed spirit at the end of the thirteenth and beginning of the fourteenth century are listed.

The significance of these titles is that they came during and after the Mongol invasions; the titles were conferred in recognition of what was believed to have been assistance rendered by the departed spirits during a national emergency. Since every account contains these titles, we can reasonably assume that the *Viet dien u linh tap* was in some way related to the process of identifying departed spirits worthy of being so honored, or those considered sufficiently powerful and loyal to Vietnamese heroes to have been efficacious against the Mongol foe. These titles were not conferred indiscriminately; they were surely based upon information about the deeds of the departed spirits. This is clear from Ly Te Xuyen's preface: "If their deeds are not authentically recorded, then it is difficult to distinguish between those of small merit and those of great merit."

Le Quy Don, a prominent eighteenth-century scholar, praised the historical authenticity of the *Viet dien u linh tap* and considered Ly Te Xuyen to have been a "good historian" (Gaspardone, "Bibliographie," p. 128; H. Maspero's translation of Le Quy Don's comments, "Etudes," 16: 13, appears to be in error). This is probably because Ly Te Xuyen cited prior sources for virtually everything he wrote. By the time of Le Quy Don, all of these earlier works, with the exception of one Chinese source, the *San kuo chih*, had already been lost (Gaspardone, "Bibliographie," p. 127).

However, the authors of three of these sources are known. Two T'ang administrators in Vietnam during the ninth century wrote books with an identical title: *Chiao chou chi* (Vietnamese *Giao chau ky*, Records of Giao Province—*Giao* was a name given to Vietnam by the Chinese). These men were Chao Ch'ang, who ruled the Vietnamese from 791 to 806, and Tseng Kun, who served in Vietnam from 866 to 880. Both men were popular among the people and took an interest in the local culture. Whether there were two books or whether Tseng Kun simply added to Chao Ch'ang's edition is not clear, but Ly Te Xuyen cites the authors as if these were two separate works. A third source used by Ly Te Xuyen is the *Su ky*, "Historical Records," written by Do Thien, an official of the Ly dynasty during the first half of the twelfth century (Gaspardone, "Bibliographie," p. 55, n. 2, and p. 127; H. Maspero's dating of Do Thien, "Etudes," 16: 13, is based on a misconception about the text). Do Thien, in turn, cites a *Giao-chi ky* (Records of Giao-chi) of which nothing is known. Little is known about the *Bao cuc truyen*, mentioned earlier in connection with Shih Hsieh. In addition to references to these written works, the *Viet dien u linh tap* cites "tradition" for some information.

Because of its reliance on documentation, the *Viet dien u linh tap* is believed to have survived through the centuries with a minimum of change (Gaspardone, "Bibliographie," p. 126). The fact that virtually the entire work comprises quotations taken from earlier sources would have discouraged revision, addition, or correction. It is true that information quoted from sources written before the tenth century is sometimes given with titles and toponyms from the tenth and eleventh centuries, but these discrepancies undoubtedly appeared before the time of Ly Te Xuyen.

Nguyen Van Trat, a fifteenth-century literatus, supplemented the *Viet dien u linh tap* with four new tales. A number of additional supplements were subsequently added, and an eighteenth-century scholar, Cao Huy Dieu, wrote a commentary (Gaspardone, "Bibliographie," pp. 127–28).

The *Viet dien u linh tap* is an important source for the early history of Vietnam. In addition to preserving traditions that reflect the cultural flavor of different eras during the Chinese provincial period, it also contains much information of more specific value; in particular, it is the earliest surviving record of two indigenous leaders of independence movements: Trieu Quang Phuc in the sixth century and Phung Hung in the eighth century (Durand, "La Dynastie," pp. 447–49, and "Recuil," pp. 27–29).

The *Viet dien u linh tap* reflects elements of popular culture that were officially recognized by the royal court during the Ly and Tran Dynasties. Fifteen of the spirits in the work were either Ly dynasty figures or were honored by Ly kings. All of the spirits received posthumous titles from the Tran court.

On the other hand, our fourth work from the fourteenth century, the *Linh-nam chich quai*, seems not to have gained favor among ruling-class people until the fifteenth century, when portions of both it and the *Viet dien u linh tap* were incorporated into the official court history.

Linh-nam chich quai can be translated as "Wonders Plucked from the Dust of Linh-nam" (a text with Vietnamese translation and an introduction by Le Huu Muc was published in Saigon in 1961; on the translation of the title, see pp. 7–9 of the introduction). *Linh-nam*, "South of the Passes," is a geographical term that has been differently applied through the centuries but here refers to the Vietnamese lands.

In 1492, scholar-official Vu Quynh wrote a preface to the work; following are excerpts (translated from *LNCQ*, 1–2):

In ancient times there were not yet books of history to record the facts; therefore nearly all of the old affairs have been forgotten and lost. Fortunately, there still exist some items that were not neglected, having been passed down from mouth to ear among persons of special ability.... Now, as for this work of handed-down tales, I do not know in which dynasty it was written or by whom. My opinion is that it was initially drafted in rough form by an eminent scholar of broad learning during the Ly or Tran dynasty [1009–1400], then enriched and adorned by learned and accomplished gentlemen of the present day. ... This material, although wonderful, does not reach the point of extravagance, and this literature, although unorthodox, does not reach the point of fantasy; although passed down through an unverified tradition, not being found in the classics, it still has something that can be relied on, namely to warn against evil and to exhort the people to reform, to discard the false and to follow the true, thereby encouraging public morality. ... Alas! The wonders of Linh-nam are differently reported; These tales have not been engraved in stone or recorded in books, but have been kept in the hearts of the people and inscribed on the tongues of men. The leader able to do what is proper cherishes and admonishes the young and the old alike, so their deeds will be bounded by principles and rules and enclosed within public morality. Is there not some small use in this? I first encountered this manuscript in the spring of 1492. I opened it up and carefully read it. It did not lack confusions caused by clerical errors and obscure meanings. So, setting aside the low and vulgar, I revised and corrected it, arranged it in three chapters, and entitled it *Linh-nam chich quai liet truyen*, "Tales of Wonders Plucked from the Dust of Linh-nam." I kept it in my home to read it at my leisure and to improve it with a view toward publishing it. I enriched and adorned it so that it might be brought to perfection; I examined its characters, refined its phrases, and expanded its meaning. All this I did for the benefit of future scholars fond of the past; is it possible that there will be such persons? Thus I have written this preface; autumn, 1492.

The work that Vu Quynh edited in 1492 and entitled *Linh-nam chich quai liet truyen* was used by Ngo Si Lien in compiling the *Dai Viet su ky toan thu* in 1479. He was therefore dealing with a source that was well known to the historians of his day but was apparently in need of revision to make it palatable to the reading public. This task was carried a step further in the following year, 1493, when Kieu Phu, an official several years senior to Vu Quynh, wrote a preface that includes the following comment (translated from Gaspardone, "Bibliographie," p. 130):

> I compared manuscripts, added my own ideas, made changes and corrections;
> I ascertained past errors in order to avoid ridicule in the future; I also expunged
> what was tedious and wrote it more concisely so that it can be conveniently
> kept in a hand-sized treasure box for reading.

This kind of editing, expunging, and augmenting is characteristic of the manner in which the *Linh-nam chich quai* has survived through the centuries. In the sixteenth century, a supplement, mainly comprising extracts from the *Viet dien u linh tap*, was added. There were further additions in the eighteenth century. It is therefore not surprising that there came to be some confusion about the original author of the work. It has been attributed to Vu Quynh, to Kieu Phu, and to both (Gaspardone, "Bibliographie," pp. 128–30). Yet Vu Quynh stated in his preface that he did not know who the author was, although he suspected that the author lived during the Ly or Tran dynasty. Vu Quynh seems to have worked from only one manuscript; on the other hand, Kieu Phu had several manuscripts, which he compared. It would seem that at least one of these manuscripts carried the name of Tran The Phap, for in the 1520 preface to his *Viet giam vinh su thi tap* (Compilation of Verse Reflecting the History of Viet) Dang Minh Khiem cited the "*Linh-nam chich quai* by Tran The Phap" as a work held in the bureau of History (Gaspardone, "Bibliographie," p. 109). This preface was apparently the source of Le Quy Don's statement about the *Linh-nam chich quai*: "Author unknown; according to tradition it was Tran The Phap" (Gaspardone, "Bibliographie," p. 128). Beyond this, nothing is known of Tran The Phap.

The problem of dating the *Linh-nam chich quai* remains unsettled. The tale of O Loi, cited in Vu Quynh's preface as being contained in the manuscript he used, cannot date before 1370, for O Loi was Duong Nhat Le, who briefly occupied the throne in 1369–70 (Le Huu Muc's introduction, pp. 13–15). However, if the tale of O Loi is regarded as a later addition to an already existing manuscript, then it is possible to date the original work any time after the early twelfth century (Gaspardone, "Bibliographie," p. 130). On the other hand, it is difficult to date it any later than towards the end of the Tran dynasty in 1400 (Le Huu Muc's introduction, pp. 13–15).

The contents of this work suggest that the date 1370–1400 may be artificial. Rather than emphasize a single author and a single date, it might be more appropriate to see a process of collecting and revising that extended over several generations. Although this view has the virtue of caution, there are nevertheless good reasons why a work such as this might have been compiled in the period 1370–1400. This was a time of crisis and self-doubt among officials. The throne stood powerless while the Hinduized kingdom of Champa, lying to the south of Vietnam on the sea, repeatedly marched north to sack the capital and plunder the countryside; no effective resistance was offered to these depredations. The Tran dynasty was crumbling to ruin, and the only strong leader was a nephew of two queens who had insinuated himself into the royal clan. This was a time when educated men were searching for some new source of national vitality. The *Linh-nam chich quai* bears witness to such a search: "Wonders Plucked from the Dust of Linh-nam," treasures that had been previously ignored and perhaps scorned but that now gave a renewed sense of identity to a people adrift in a stormy era.

The importance placed on the traditions recorded in the *Linh-nam chich quai* appears to be related to the experience of national humiliation at the hands of Cham aggressors and Ming invaders. The old order was being swept away. A usurper seized the throne and withdrew to a fortress in the mountains. Then the Chinese came and imposed a bitter occupation of two decades. Independence was regained only after a long and spirited struggle.

There was now a deeper awareness of what it meant to be Vietnamese. Historians began to "pluck wonders from the dust"; they began to take note of those things "passed down from mouth to ear among persons of special ability." The popularity of this kind of writing is demonstrated in Kieu Phu's statement that he is interested in making the work sufficiently concise "to be conveniently kept in a hand-sized treasure box for reading."

The core of the *Linh-nam chich quai* comprises traditions about the Hung kings of the pre-Chinese period, which were surely transmitted during the Chinese period. These traditions concerned, among other things, cultural attributes of the Vietnamese that distinguish them from the Chinese, such as chewing betel. We can assume that existing texts of the *Linh-nam chich quai* were considerably modified after the fifteenth century; yet the value of these traditions does not lie in the authenticity of their details but rather in their appeal to a special sense of moral authority within the Vietnamese heritage. Thus, Vu Quynh wrote of traditions preserved in the hearts of the people that were an encouragement to "public morality." Certainly, these tales were edited by ruling-class people to propagate prevailing ideas of proper behavior; the "principles and rules" cited by Vu Quynh refer to the "great way" of social order as defined in the Chinese classics (Morohashi, 8, 1099).

However, this does not mean that these traditions were without historical background, or that they are simply didactic tales fabricated in the name of Vietnamese culture. In fact, they fit within the outline of recorded history, as represented by Chinese texts, and reflect the oldest articulated cultural perspective of the Vietnamese people.

This perspective was officially adopted by the Vietnamese court in the fifteenth century with the *Dai Viet su ky toan thu* (Gaspardone, "Bibliographie," 51–76; Tran Van Giap, "Tim Hieu Kho," pp. 64–90; Ching-ho A. Ch'en, "Daietsu"—I have used a Tōyō Bunko "mixed copy," which is a nineteenth-century reprint of the original 1697 Chinh-hoa edition, but Professor Ch'en has recently discovered an original copy of the

Chinh-hoa edition). We have already referred to the *Dai Viet su ky* of Le Van Huu, completed in 1272, which chronicled events to the end of the Ly dynasty in 1225. In 1455, King Le Nhan-tong charged Phan Phu Tien with the task of compiling a history of the period from 1225 to 1428, when the Ming occupation ended. Phan Phu Tien was a member of the Royal Academy and director of the Bureau of History. His work was called *Dai Viet su ky tuc bien* (Continued Compilation of the Historical Records of Great Viet) (Gaspardone, "Bibliographie," p. 50).

In 1479, the two works of Le Van Huu and Phan Phu Tien were combined into the *Dai Viet su ky toan thu* (Complete Book of the Historical Records of Great Viet), by Ngo Si Lien. Ngo Si Lien was appointed to the Bureau of History in 1473. This was during the reign of Le Thanh-tong, a strong king who patronized a thriving community of scholars. According to Ngo Si Lien's preface, Le Thanh-tong ordered a thorough examination of all historical records in the Quang-thuan period (1460–69). While the official product of this research was locked up and subsequently disappeared, Ngo Si Lien, who had participated in the endeavor, later wrote the *Dai Viet su ky toan thu*, on his own initiative, and presented it to the throne (Gaspardone, "Bibliographie," pp. 51–54).

Ngo Si Lien's work is modeled on Ssu-ma Kuang's *Tzu chih t'ung chien* in its chronological method and its adherence to orthodox rules for establishing legitimacy (Gaspardone, "Bibliographie," pp. 56–58). However, the *Dai Viet su ky toan thu* was unprecedented in that it incorporated into its narrative the traditions found in the *Viet dien u linh tap* and the *Linh-nam chich quai*; Ngo Si Lien brought together for the first time the traditions from the Chinese and the Vietnamese sides to form a single account of the preindependence period.

A second innovation was the division of Vietnamese history into *Ngoai Ky* (Peripheral Records) up to the time of independence and *Ban Ky* (Basic Records) for the independence period. Ngo Si Lien divided the peripheral and basic records at the rise of Ngo Quyen in 938. In 1511, Vu Quynh, whose preface to the *Linh-nam chich quai* we have already noted, completed the *Viet giam thong khao* (Complete Study of the History of Viet), which was a reorganization of Ngo Si Lien's work that divided the peripheral and basic records at the rise of Dinh Bo Linh, thirty years later (Gaspardone, "Bibliographie," pp.58, 76–77). All subsequent editions of the *Dai Viet su ky toan thu* followed this change. Ngo Quyen, although he dropped the T'ang titles used by his predecessors and proclaimed himself a king, nevertheless tried to establish a Chinese-style royal court. His death was followed by anarchy until the country was unified by Dinh Bo Linh, who claimed imperial status. Vu Quynh's revision seems to have been a return to the outlook of Le Van Huu, who faulted Ngo Quyen for not proclaiming himself emperor and praised Dinh Bo Linh for standing in the Vietnamese "imperial" tradition. By beginning the basic records with Dinh Bo Linh's reign, Vietnamese historians apparently wished to emphasize the importance of national unity for the independence of the country, as well as to stress the "imperial" status of Vietnamese kings.

Vu Quynh's *Viet giam thong khao* was only the first of several revisions and continuations through which Ngo Si Lien's work was carried forward to become the official court history of Vietnam. In 1514, a summary of the *Viet giam thong khao* entitled *Viet giam thong khao tong luan* (General Summary of the Complete Study of the History of Viet) was prepared by Le Tung in response to an order by King Le Tuong Duc, who desired an abridged version of Vu Quynh's work (Gaspardone, "Bibliographie," pp. 77–78). This summary survives in the form of an introduction to the existing *Dai Viet su ky toan thu*.

In 1665, the *Dai Viet su ky toan thu tuc bien* (Continued Compilation of the Complete Book of the Historical Records of Great Viet) was completed under the supervision of Pham Cong Tru, the foremost scholar and statesman of his generation; this "continued compilation" ends with the year 1662 (Gaspardone, "Bibliographie," pp. 59–61). In 1697, scholar-official Le Hi supervised the completion of a supplement for the years 1663–75. The entire work from Ngo Si Lien through the last installment to 1675 was then engraved on woodblocks and printed for the first time, thereby fixing the *Dai Viet su ky toan thu* as it exists today.

The *Dai Viet su ky toan thu* is an indispensable source for Vietnamese history from the tenth century through the seventeenth century. For the Chinese period, it contains some information that seems to be original and may result from giving events recorded in Chinese sources a more acceptable rendering from the Vietnamese point of view; it is basically a synthesis of the Chinese sources, the *Viet dien u linh tap*, and the *Linh-nam chich quai*.

One nineteenth-century work should be mentioned. The *Kham dinh Viet su thong giam cuong muc* (Imperially Ordered Annotated Text Completely Reflecting the History of Viet) was initially assembled in 1856–59 and thereafter revised and annotated in 1871, 1872, 1876, and 1878 (Cadiere and Pelliot, p. 639). In his annotations of this text, the bookish monarch Tu-duc (1847–83) set down his convictions on government and public morality. Up to the seventeenth century, the *Kham dinh Viet su thong giam cuong muc* generally covers the same ground as the *Dai Viet su ky toan thu*, although it reflects a more extensive knowledge of Chinese sources for the pre-independence period; it also has extensive annotations containing geographical and biographical information of uneven quality.

Glossary

H. Maspero ("Le Protectorat general," p. 549) proposed a set of rules for transcribing proper names and titles in early Vietnamese history. I follow these rules except in two points. I have decided to transcribe all place names in Vietnam during the period of Chinese rule in Vietnamese, for they are firmly attached to the Vietnamese landscape and have become an integral part of Vietnamese history. The first section of the glossary contains the characters for these names; names associated with Chinese provincial administration are shown with Chinese in parenthesis. I have translated official titles and administrative jurisdictions of the provincial period into English; Vietnamese and character equivalents are in the second portion of the glossary, followed by personal names in the third. Other terms and expressions can be found in the final section.

Complete Vietnamese readings, including diacritical marks, are provided for all names and terms introduced in the main text and for those mentioned in the footnotes. The arrangement is alphabetical, but not in standard Vietnamese fashion (i.e., broken down by diacritical markings, multiple-letter initial consonants, etc.), since this might be too confusing to some readers. Only one non-English initial consonant demands differentiation in the alphabet here: Đ (in lower case, đ), which follows D.

Characters are provided for all names and terms that appear in the primary sources.

Place Names

Vietnamese

Ái (Ai) 愛
An-hát 安喝
An-lãng 安朗
An-nam (An-nan) 安南
An-viên (An-yüan) 安遠
An-vũ (An-wu) 安武
Bạch-đằng 白藤
Bô-hải 布海
Câm-Khê 禁溪
Câm-lâm

Chu-diên (Chu-yüan) 朱鳶
Cư-phong (Chü-fêng) 居風
Cửu-chân (Chiu-chên) 九眞
Cửu-đức (Chiu-tê) 九德
Cổ-loa 古螺
Cổ-pháp 古法
Dã-năng 野能
Dịch-bảng 驛榜
Diễn (Yen) 演
Đà-năng
Đại-la (Ta-lo) 大羅

Đàm   潭

Đằng   藤

Điển-triệt (Tu-lung; third century) 典澈

Đô-long (Tu-lung; third century)
都龐

Đô-long (Tu-lung; sixth century)
都隆

Đỗ-động   杜洞

Đức (Tê)   德

Đường-lâm (T'ang-lin)   唐林

Gia-ninh (Chia-ning)   嘉寧

Giang

Giao (Chiao)   交

Giao-chỉ (Chiao-chih)   交趾

Giao-thủy   膠水

Hạ-lôi   夏雷

Hà-nội

Hà-tĩnh

Hải-dương   海陽

Hoa-lư   華閭

Hoài-hoan (Huai-huan)   懷驩

Hoan (Huan)   驩

Hoàng (Huang)   黃

Hoành-sơn   橫山

Huê

Hưng (Hsing)   興

Khu-túc (Ch'ü-su)   區粟

Khuất-liệu   屈獠

Kinh (Ching)   景

La-thành (Lo-ch'êng)   羅城

Lâm (Lin)   林

Lãng-bạc   浪泊

Lĩnh-nam   嶺南

Lô-dung (Lu-jung)   盧容

Long-bien (Lung-pien)   龍編

Long-hưng (Lung-hsing)   龍興

Lục (Lu)   陸

Luy-lâu (Lui-lou)   贏陞

Lý (Li)   利

Mê-linh (Mi-ling)   麋泠

Minh (Ming)   明

Mông-phụ   蒙阜

Nam-sách   南册

Nam Việt (Nan Yüeh)   南越

Nguyễn-gia-loan   阮家鸞

Nha-trang

Nhật Dạ Trạch   一夜澤

Nhật-nam (Jih-nan)   日南

Nhu-viên (Jou-yüan)   柔遠

Ô-diên   烏鳶

Ô-man   烏蠻

Phan-rang

Phô-dương (P'u-yang)   浦陽

Phong (Fêng)   峯

Phong-khê (Fêng-ch'i)   封溪

Phù-đổng   扶董

Phù-nghiêm (Fu-yen)   扶嚴

Phúc-lộc (Fu-lu)   福祿

Sơn (Shan)   山

Sơn-nam   山南

Tân-hưng (Hsin-hsing)   新興

Tản-viên   傘圓

Tân-xương (Hsin-ch'ang)   新昌

Tây-vu (Hsi-yu)   西于

Thạch-kỳ (Shih-ch'i)   石碕

Thái-bình (T'ai-p'ing)   太平

Thăng-long   昇龍

Tiên-dư   仙遊

Tiêu   蕉

Tô-lịch   蘇歷

Tống-bình (Sung-p'ing)   宋平

Trà-kiêu

Trấn-nam (Chên-nan)   鎮南

Trấn-ninh

Trảo-nha   爪牙

Tri (Chih)   智

Trường (Chang)   長

Tự-liêm (Tz'u-lien)   慈廉

Tứ-thành (Tzǔ-ch'êng)   子城

Tương-lâm (Hsiang-lin)   象林

Tỳ-bà   琵琶

Văn-lang   文郎

Việt-thường (Yüeh-shang)   越裳

Vọng-hải (Wang-hai)   望海

Vũ-bình (Wu-p'ing)   武平

Vũ-ninh (Wu-ning)   武寧

Chinese

An-ning 安寧
Chan-ch'êng 占城
Chang (Sea) 漲海
Chên-la 眞臘
Ch'ên-liu 陳留
Ch'eng-tu 成都
Chi 吉
Chiao 交
Chiao-chih 交趾
Chin-lin 金鄰
Chu-yai 朱崖
Fên-shui 分水
Fu-nan 扶南
Hêng 衡
Ho-ling 訶陵
Ho-p'u 合浦
Hsiang 鄉
Hsin 新
Hsü 許
Hsü-ch'ang 許昌
Hsü-ch'uan 許傳
Huan-wang 環王
Jung 容
Kao 高

Kuang 廣
Kuei 桂
Lin-i 林邑
Ling-nan 嶺南
Lung-men 龍門
Nan-chao 南詔
Nan-hai 南海
Nan Yüeh 南越
Ning-p'u 寧浦
Shih-hsing 始興
Shu 舒
T'ang-ming 堂明
T'ien-shui 天水
Ting 定
Ts'ang-wu 蒼梧
Tung-kuan 東莞
Yang-tzu 揚子
Yeh-lang 夜郎
Yeh-t'iao 葉調
Ying 潁
Ying-ch'uan 潁川
Yung 邕
Yü-lin 鬱林
Yüeh 越
Yüeh-shang 越裳

Administrative Jurisdictions and Titles from the Provincial Period

Jurisdictions

Central Administration
    Tổng Quản Phủ 總管府
Circuit
    Bộ 部
District
    Huyện 縣
General Government
    Đô Đốc Phủ 都督府
Halter Province
    Cơ Mi Châu 羈縻州

Prefecture
    Quận 郡
Protectorate
    Đo Hộ Phủ 都護府
Province
    Châu 州

Titles

Administrator
    Tổng Quản 總管

Commandant
    Đô Úy 都尉
Commissioner
    Úy 尉
Governor
    Thứ Sử 刺史
Governor General
    Đô Đốc 都督
Imperial Commissioner
    Kinh Lược Sử 經略使
Legate
    Sử 使
Magistrate
    Linh 令
Military Governor
    Tiêt Độ Sử 節度使

Military Legate
    Binh Mã Sử 兵馬使
Military Overseer
    Giám Quân 監軍
Prefect
    Thái Thú 太守
Protector General
    Đô Hộ 都護
    (6th century: Đôc Hộ 督護)
Senior Clerk
    Trưởng Sử 長史
Superintendent
    Giám 監
Viceroy
    Mục Bá 牧伯

Personal Names

Vietnamese

An Dương 安陽
Âu Cơ 嫗姬
Bì An 皮岸
Bồ Phá Lặc 蒲破勒
Cam Lễ 甘醴
Cảm Thành 感誠
Cao Huy Diệu 高輝耀
Cao Lỗ 高/皋/皋 · 魯
Cao Thông (Kao T'ung)
    皐/皋/皋 · 通
Cảo Nương 杲娘
Chu Đạt 朱達
Chử Đồng Tử 褚童子
Dương Cát Lợi 楊吉利
Dương Đinh Nghệ 楊廷藝
Dương Huy 楊暉
Dương Nhật Lễ 楊日禮
Dương Tam Kha 楊三哥
Dương Thanh 楊清
Đại-thặng-đăng 大乘燈
Đặng Huyền Quang 鄧玄光
Đặng Minh Khiêm 鄧鳴謙

Đê Du 帝楡
Đê Lai 帝來
Đê Minh 帝明
Đê Nghi 帝宜
Đinh Bộ Lình 丁部領
Đinh Công Trứ 丁公著
Đinh Hạng Lang 丁項郎
Đinh Kiên 丁建
Đinh Liễn 丁璉
Đinh Toàn 丁璿
Đinh Khong 定空
Đỗ Anh Hàn 杜英倫
Đỗ Bảo 杜寶
Đỗ Cánh Thạc 杜景碩
Đỗ Hoằng Văn 杜弘文
Đỗ Thích 杜睪
Đỗ Thiện 杜善
Đỗ Thú Trừng 杜守澄
Đỗ Tôn Thành 杜存誠
Đỗ Tuệ Độ 杜慧度
Đỗ Viện 杜瑗
Động Đình Quân 洞庭君
Hoàn Lân 桓鄰

Hoàn Trị　桓治
Hoàng Ngô　黃吳
Hồ Tông Thốc　胡宗鷟
Hồ Triệu　胡肇
Huệ Diệm　慧琰
Huệ Nghiêm　惠嚴
Khâu Đà La　丘陀羅
Khúc Hạo　曲顥
Khúc Thừa Dụ　曲承裕
Khúc Thừa Mỹ　曲承美
Khương Công Phu　姜公輔
Khương Công Phục　姜公復
Khương Thần Dực　姜神翊
Khuy Sung　窺冲
Kiều Phú　喬富
Kiều Công Hãn　矯公罕
Kiều Công Tiễn　矯公羨
Kiều Thuận　矯順
Kinh Dương Vương　涇陽王
La Hành Cung　羅行恭
Lạc Long Quân　貉龍君
Lê Hi　黎僖
Lê Hoán (third century)　黎晃
Lê Hoàn (tenth century)　黎桓
Lê Nhân-tông　黎仁宗
Lê Qúy Đôn　黎貴惇
Lê Tắc　黎崱
Lê Thánh-tông　黎聖宗
Lê Tung　黎嵩
Lê Tương-dực　黎襄翼
Lê Văn Hưu　黎文休
Liêu Hưu Phương　廖有方
Lữ Đường　呂唐
Lữ Hưng　呂興
Lương Kỳ　梁奇
Lương Long　梁龍
Lương Thạc　梁碩
Lưu Cơ　劉基
Lý Anh-tông　李英宗
Lý Bí　李賁
Lý Công Uẩn　李公蘊
Lý Do Độc　李由獨
Lý Đại Quyền　李大權

Lý Hữu Vinh　李幼榮
Lý Khải　李凱
Lý Khuê　李圭
Lý Manh Thu　李孟秋
Lý Nguyên Độ　李元度
Lý Nhiếp　李弈
Lý Ông Trọng　李翁仲
Lý Phật Tử　李佛子
Lý Phổ Đỉnh　李普鼎
Lý Phục Man　李服蠻
Lý Tắc　李裔
Lý Tê Xuyên　李濟川
Lý Thiên Bảo　李天寶
Lý Thiệu Long　李紹隆
Lý Thoát　李脫
Lý Thúc Hiến　李叔獻
Lý Thường Kiệt　李常傑
Lý Tộ　李祚
Lý Tôn　李遜
Lý Trương Nhân　李長仁
Lý Tự Tiên　李嗣先
Lý Xuân　李春
Mai Thúc Loan　梅叔鸞
Man Nương　蠻娘
Mộc-xoa-đề-ba (Mokṣadeva)　木叉提婆
My Châu　眉珠
Ngô Chân Lưu　吳眞流
Ngô Mân　吳旻
Ngô Nhật Khánh　吳日慶
Ngô Sĩ Liên　吳仕連
Ngô Quyền　吳權
Ngô Xử Bình　吳處玶
Ngô Xương Ngập　吳昌岌
Ngô Xương Văn　吳昌文
Ngô Xương Xí　吳昌熾
Nguyễn Bặc　阮匐
Nguyễn Khoan　阮寬
Nguyễn Lang　阮朗
Nguyễn Siêu　阮超
Nguyễn Thủ Tiệp　阮守捷
Nguyễn Văn Trât　阮文質
Nhã Lang　雅郎

Ô Lôi   烏雷
Ông Gióng (Dóng)   翁董
Phạm Bạch Hổ   范白虎
Phạm Công Trứ   范公著
Phạm Tu   范修
Phan Huy Chú   潘輝注
Phan Phu Tiên   潘孚先
Pháp Đăng   法燈
Pháp Hiền   法賢
Phật Quang   佛光
Phục Đăng Chi   伏登之
Phùng An   馮安
Phùng Hãi   馮駭
Phùng Hưng   馮興
Quan Duyên   觀緣
Thanh Biện   清辨
Thần Long Nứ   神龍女
Thi Sách   詩索
Thông Thiên   通善
Thục Phán (An Dương)
   蜀泮(安陽)
Tiên Dung   僊容
Tính Thiều   井/幷・紹/韶
Tô Lịch   蘇歷
Tông Lịnh Vọng   宋令望
Trần Lãm   陳覽
Trần Minh-tông   陳明宗
Trần Phê Đế   陳廢帝
Trần Phổ   陳普
Trần Thái-tông   陳太宗
Trần Thăng   陳升
Trần Thánh-tông   陳聖宗
Trần Thế Pháp   陳世法
Trí Hành   智行
Triệu Ẩu (Lady)   趙嫗
Triệu Chí   趙祉
Triệu Quang Phục   趙光復
Triệu Túc   趙肅
Trưng Nhị   徵貳
Trưng Trắc   徵側
Trường Liên   張璉
Trường Ma-ni   張痲尼
Tu Định   修定

Tự-đức   嗣德
Vận Kì   運期
Viêm Đê Thần Nông   炎帝神農
Vô Ngôn Thông (Chêng)
   無言通(鄭)
Vũ Quỳnh   武瓊
Vụ Tiên Nứ   婺僊女
Vương Qúy Nguyên   王季元
Vương Thành Triều   王昇朝

Chinese

An Lu-Shan   安祿山
Ch'ai Che-wei   柴哲威
Chang Ch'iao   張喬
Chang Chin   張津
Chang Chou   張舟
Chang Hui   張恢
Chang Mien   張勔
Chang Mu-chih   張穆之
Chang Po-i   張伯儀
Chang Shou-chieh   張守節
Chang Yin   張茵
Chang Ying   張應
Chao Ch'ang   趙昌
Chao Chün   趙均
Chao Hêng   朝衡
Chao T'o   趙佗
Ch'ao Fu   巢父
Chih I   智顗
Chên Wu   鎮武
Ch'ên Fa-wu   陳法武
Ch'ên Pa-hsien   陳霸先
Ch'ên Po-shao   陳伯紹
Ch'ên Shih   陳時
Ch'ên Wên-chieh   陳文戒
Chêng Ch'o   鄭綽
Ch'êng Pao   程寶
Chia Ch'ang   賈昌
Chia Tsung   賈琮
Chiang Chuang   姜壯
Chih Hung   智弘
Ch'iu Ho   丘和

Chou Ch'ang　周敞
Chou Ch'êng　周乘
Chou Yung　周隅
Chu Chih　朱治
Chu Ch'üan-chung　朱全忠
Chu Ch'üan-yü　朱全昱
Chu Chüan　朱儁
Chu Fan　朱藩
Chu Fu (second–third centuries)　朱符
Chu Fu (fourth century)　朱輔
Chu Liang　祝良
Ch'u Sui-liang　褚遂良
Ch'ü Lan　曲覽
Ch'üan Tê-yü　權德興
Fan Fu　范佛
Fan Fu Lung　范扶龍
Fan Hsiung　范熊
Fan Hu Ta　范胡達
Fan I　范逸
Fan P'i Sha　范毗沙
Fan Yang Mai　范陽邁
Fan Yen　樊演
Fang Fa-ch'êng　房法乘
Fang I-ai　房遺愛
Fang T'ai　方泰
Fêng Ang　馮盎
Fêng Yüan-ch'ang　馮元常
Fu Chien　苻堅
Fu Liang-chiao　輔艮交
Han Ssǔ-yen　韓思彦
Han Wei　韓威
Han Yüeh　韓約
Ho Li-kuang　何履光
Hou Ching　侯景
Hou Fu　侯輔
Hsi Kuang　錫光
Hsia Fang　夏方
Hsia-hou Lan　夏侯覽
Hsiao Ching-hsien　蕭景憲
Hsiao Hsien　蕭銑
Hsiao Po　蕭勃
Hsiao Tzǔ　蕭諮

Hsiao Yung　蕭暎
Hsieh Cho　謝擢
Hsiu Chan　修湛
Hsiu Tsê　修則
Hsü Yu　許由
Hsüeh Tsung　薛綜
Huai Hai　懷海
Huan Hung　桓閎
Huan Shen　桓深
Huang Ch'ao　黃巢
Huang Kai　黃蓋
Huang T'ing-chien　黃庭堅
Hui Chi　慧寂
Hui K'o　慧可
Hui Ming　慧命
Hui Nêng　慧能
Hui Ning　會寧
Huo I　霍弋
I Ching　義淨
I Hsü Sung　譯吁宋
Jên Yen　任延
Kan Ting　甘定
K'ang Ch'êng-hsün　康承訓
K'ang Sêng Hui　康僧會
Kao Chêng-p'ing　高正平
Kao Hsün　高潯
Kao Pao　高寶
Kao P'ien　高駢
Kao Shih-lien　高士廉
Ko Ch'i　葛祇
Ko Yu　葛幽
Kou Chien　勾踐
Ku Pi　顧秘
Ku Shou　顧壽
Ku Ts'an　顧參
Kuan Sui　灌邃
Kuang Ch'u-k'ê　光楚客
Kuei Chung-wu　桂仲武
K'ung K'uei　孔戣
Lai Kung　賴恭
Lan Ch'in　蘭欽
Lan Yü　蘭裕
Lang She-ch'ing　郎余慶

Li Ch'ao　李巢
Li Ch'ang-ming　李常明
Li Ch'êng-ch'ien　李承乾
Li Chi　李勣
Li Chin　李進
Li Ch'ien-yu　李乾祐
Li Ching-yeh　李敬業
Li Cho　李涿
Li Fu　李復
Li Hsiang-ku　李象古
Li Hsü　李嶼
Li Hu　李鄂
Li Hung-fu　李弘甫
Li I-fu　李義府
Li Ku　李固
Li Kuang-shih　李光仕
Li Shan　李善
Li Shou　李壽
Li Tao-hsing　李道興
Li Tao-yen　李道彥
Li T'iao　李迢
Li Wei-chou　李維周
Li Yu　李友
Li Yüan-hsi　李元喜
Liang K'ê-chên　梁克貞
Li Shih-hung　林士弘
Ling-hu Hsi　令狐熙
Liu Ch'ên　劉沉
Liu Chün　劉俊
Liu Fang　劉方
Liu Hsi　劉熙
Liu Hsin-ch'i　劉欣期
Liu Hsiung　劉雄
Liu Hung-ts'ao　劉弘操
Liu K'ai　劉楷
Liu Kung　劉龑
Liu Mu　劉牧
Liu Pei　劉備
Liu Piao　劉表
Liu Po　劉勃
Liu Shan-ming　劉善明
Liu Tzǔ-ch'i　劉子奇
Liu Yen　劉龑

Liu Yen-yu　劉延祐
Liu Yin　劉隱
Liu Yu　劉祐
Liu Yü　劉裕
Liu Yüan-yen　劉元偃
Lu (Superintendent)　祿
Lu Hsün　盧循
Lu I　陸裔
Lu Po-tê　路博德
Lu Tsu-shang　盧祖尙
Lu Tzǔ-hsiung　盧子雄
Lu Yin　陸胤
Lu Yü　盧魚
Lu Yun　陸允
Lü Chia　呂嘉
Lü Tai　呂岱
Ma Chih　馬植
Ma Tsung　馬揔
Ma Yüan　馬援
Mêng Ch'ang　孟嘗
Mêng Kan　孟幹
Ming Yüan　明遠
Mou Po　牟博
Ni Shih　倪式
Ning Ch'ang-chên　寧長眞
Ning Mêng-li　寗猛力
Ou K'uei　區逵
Ou Lien　區連
Ou Ta　區達
Ou Ta-jen　歐大任
Ou-yang He　歐陽紇
Ou-yang Sheng　歐陽盛
Ou-yang Wei　歐陽頠
P'ang Hsün　龐勛
P'ei Ch'ien-t'ung　裴虔通
P'ei Hsing-li　裴行立
P'ei T'ai　裴泰
P'ei Yüan-yu　裴元祐
P'i Jih-hsiu　皮日休
Pu Chih　步隲
Sêng Ts'an　僧璨
Shen Ch'üan-ch'i　沈佺期
Shen Chün-kao　沈君高

Shen Hsi-tsu   申希祖
Shen Huan   沈煥
Shen K'o   沈恪
Shen Liang-tê   沈諒德
Shih Chiang   始降
Shih Hsieh   士燮
Shih Hsin   士廞
Shih Hui   士徽
Shih I   士壹
Shih K'uang   士匡
Shih Ssŭ   士賜
Shih Wu   士武
Shih Yü   士鮪
Shun   舜
Su Ting   蘇定
Sun Ch'iung   孫冏
Sun Ch'üan   孫權
Sun Hsü   孫謂
Sun Kuang-hsien   孫光憲
Sun Tê-chao   孫德昭
Sung Jung   宋戎
Sung Tz'ŭ-ming   宋慈明
Sung Ya   宋涯
Ssŭ-ma Kuang   司馬光
Tai Huang   戴晃
Tai Liang   戴良
Tan Mêng   儋萌
T'an Ch'ien   曇遷
T'an Ho-chih   檀和之
T'an Jun   曇閏
T'ao Chi   韜戢
T'ao Hsieh   陶協
T'ao Huang   陶璜
T'ao K'an   陶侃
T'ao Wei   陶威
T'ao Yüan-ming   陶淵明
Têng Hsün   鄧荀
Têng Jang   鄧讓
T'êng Chün   滕畯
T'êng Han   藤含
T'êng Tun-chih   騰遯之
T'ien Tsai-yu   田在宥
T'ien Tsao   田早

Ting Kung   丁宮
Ts'ai Ching   蔡京
Ts'ai Hsi   蔡襲
Ts'ai Ning   蔡凝
Ts'ai Tsun   蔡樽
Tsang Ling-chih   臧靈智
Ts'ao Hsüan-ching   曹玄靜
Tseng Kun   曾袞
Ts'ui Chieh   崔結
Ts'ui Kêng   崔耿
Ts'ui Yüan   崔遠
Tsung Ch'üeh   宗愨
Tu Chêng-lun   杜正倫
Tu Hung   杜洪
Tu Ming-chü   杜明舉
Tu Shen-yen   杜審言
Tu T'ao   杜弢
Tu Tsan   杜讚
Tu-ku Sun   獨孤損
T'u Sui   屠睢
Tuan Shih-tsê   段士則
Tung Yüan   董元
Wan Pei   萬備
Wang An-shih   王安石
Wang Ch'êng   王澄
Wang Ch'êng-pien   王承弁
Wang Chi   王幾
Wang Fu-shih   王福時
Wang Hsü   王項
Wang Hui   王徽
Wang Hui-tsan   王惠贊
Wang K'uan   王寬
Wang Liang   王諒
Wang Lin   王琳
Wang Mang   王莽
Wang Po   王勃
Wang Shen-chih   王審知
Wang Shih   王式
Wang Yen-ch'üan   王晏權
Wei Chung-tsai   韋仲宰
Wei Lang   魏朗
Wei Ts'an   韋粲
Wên (King of Lin-i)   文

Wên Fang-chih　溫放之

Wu Hsing　無行

Wu Hun　武渾

Wu Yen　吳彥

Yang Ch'an　揚孱

Yang Ch'êng-ho　楊承和

Yang Chi　楊稷

Yang Chien　楊堅

Yang Chin　楊縉

Yang Hsiu-p'u　楊休浦

Yang Hsiung-chên　楊雄箋

Yang P'iao　揚膘

Yang P'ing　楊平

Yang Ssŭ-chin　楊思縉

Yang Ssŭ-hsü　楊思勖

Yang Su　楊素

Yao　堯

Yeh Tê-hui　葉德輝

Yen Shan-ssŭ　嚴善思

Yin Chiu　尹就

Yüan Ching-chung　元景仲

Yüan Cho　阮卓

Yüan Fang　沅放

Yüan Fu　阮敷

Yüan Mi-chih　阮彌之

Yüan T'an-huan　袁曇緩

Yüan Yen　阮研

Sanskrit

Bodhidharma (Bồ-đế-đạt-ma)
　菩薩達摩

Jīvaka (Kì-vực)　耆域

Kalyāṇaruci　疆梁婁

Saṃghavarma (Tăng-cà-bạt-ma)
　僧伽跋摩

Vinītaruci (Tỳ-ni-đa-lưu-chi)
　毘尼多流支

Terms and Expressions

Vietnamese

An-nam Quốc-vương　安南國王

Âu　甌

Âu Lạc　甌駱

Bắc-sơn

Bản Ký　本紀

Báo Cực Truyện　報極傳

Báo Đức Truyện　報德傳

biêt

Bình Vương　平王

bèo

bố cái　布蓋

Bố cái đại vương　布蓋大王

bố-chính　蒲正

bọt

Ca-ông　歌翁

chét　札

chó　獠

Chúng-thiện　衆善

cơ mi châu　羈縻州

Cổ-quốc　蔞國

con

Da sử　野史

Đại Cồ Việt　大瞿越

Đại Thắng Vương　大勝王

Đại Việt sử ký　大越史記

Đại Việt sử ký toàn thư tục biên
　大越史記全書續編

Đại Việt sử ký tục biên　大越史記
　續編

Đào-lang　桃郎

đằm/đầm

Đan-gia　丹嘉

đế　帝

Định Quốc Công　定國公

Đô Bảo　都保

Đô-hộ-phủ Sĩ-sư　都護府士師

Đô Quan　都君

đồng

Đông-đậu

Đông-khôi

Đông-sơn

Giao châu ký 交州記

Giao-chỉ ký 交趾記

Giao-chỉ Quan-vương
交趾郡王

Giao-thúy 膠水

Giáo-tôn 教宗

Giáp Mão Thạch Long
甲卯石龍

Gò-mun

Hòa-bình

hồn

Hùng 雄

kè (fish)

kẻ (locality)

Khâm Định Việt Sử Thông Giám
 Cương Mục 欽定越史通鑑綱目

Khuông Việt Đại-sư 匡越大師

Kiên-dương 建陽

Kiên-sơ 建初

Kiểu-quốc 矯國

Kim Cương Kinh 金剛經

Lạc 貉／駱／雒

Lĩnh-nam chích quái liệt truyện
 嶺南摭怪列傳

Long-độ 龍度

Lục-tổ 六祖

mị-nương 媚娘

Mường

Nam Cương

Nam Tấn Vương 南晉王

Nam Việt 南越

Ngoại Ký 外紀

nôm 喃

Nùng

Pháp-điện 法電

Pháp-lôi 法雷

Pháp-vân 法雲

Pháp-vũ 法雨

Phò-mã Đô-úy 駙馬都尉

Phổ-quang 普光

phụ-đạo 父道

Phúc-nhan 福嚴

Phùng-nguyên

quan-lang 官郎

Quang-thuận 光順

Quỳnh-lâm 瓊林

sam

sĩ sư 士師

Sơn-vi

sông

Sùng-chân-uy-nghi 崇眞威儀

Sùng-nghiệp 崇業

Tây

Tăng-lục Đạo-sĩ 僧錄道士

Tăng-thống 僧統

Thái-bình 太平

thái-phó 太傅

thái-sư 太師

Thập-đạo Tướng-quân
 十道將軍

Thiền 禪

Thiền-chúng 禪衆

Thiên-đức 天德

Thiên Sách Vương 天策王

Thiệu-dương

Trinh-minh 貞明

Văn-lang 文郎

Vạn Phúc 萬福

Vạn Thọ 萬壽

Vạn Xuân 萬春

Việt giám thông khảo 越鑑通考

Việt giám thông khảo tổng luận
 越鑑通考總論

Việt giám vịnh sử thi tập
 越鑑詠史詩集

vua 喣

xảo

Xích Qúi Quốc 赤鬼國

Chinese

Ch'an 禪

chang 丈

Chên-yüan 貞元

chia 甲

chiang 江

Chiao chou chi 交州記

Chiao chou wai yu chi 交州外域記

ch'ih 尺

Chin liu hsin ch'i Chiao chou chi
   晉留心奇交州記

chin-shih 進士

Chin T'ai K'ang ti chi
   晉泰康遞記

Chü-lung 句龍

Ch'ü-lien 區憐

ch'ü-she 曲赦

Ch'un ch'iu 春秋

chün-i-kuan 君宜官

fu-t'ou 夫頭

fu mu 父母

Hou-chi (Hậu Tắc) 后稷

hsing-li 行李

hsiung 雄/熊

Hsiung-nu 匈奴

Huai nan tzŭ 淮南子

Huang Ti 黃帝

Jih-nan chuan 日南傳

Jou-yüan Chün 柔遠軍

K'ai-yüan 開元

Kuang chou chi 廣州記

Kuei-yang 潙仰

K'un-lun 崑崙

lang 郎

Lao 獠

Li 俚

li hu 俚戶

Liu Hsi shih chi kao 劉熙事蹟考

mao-ts'ai 茂才

Nan Yüeh chih 南越志

niang 娘

Ou 甌

Pai Yüeh hsien hsien chih
   百越先賢志

Pei mêng so yen 北夢瑣言

San kuo chih 三國志

Shê-p'o 闍婆

Shih chi 史記

Shih lu 實錄

Shih ming 釋名

shih-ting 侍丁

Shuang-lin 雙林

T'ao Yüan 桃源

T'ien T'ai 天台

ting-shih 丁侍

Tso chuan 左傳

Bibliography

Primary Sources

Vietnamese

CL: Lê Tắc 黎崱, *An-nam chí lược* 安南志略. Hue, 1961.

LNCQ: Trần Thế Pháp 陳世法, *Lĩnh-nam chích quái* 嶺南摭怪. Saigon, 1961.

TT: Ngô Sĩ Liên 吳仕連, *Đại Việt sử ký toàn thư* 大越史記全書 (Tōyō Bunko manuscript). All *TT* references are to the *Ngoại ký* 外紀 unless identified as *Bản ký* 本紀.

VDULT: Lý Tê Xuyên 李濟川, *Việt Điện u linh tập* 越甸幽靈集. Saigon, 1960.

VSL: *Việt sử lược* 越史略, in *Shou shan ko ts'ung shu* 守山閣叢書. Taipei, 1968.

Chinese

Dynastic Histories

All histories referred to are in *Pai na pen erh shih ssu shih* edition (Shanghai, 1930–37).

CS: *Chin shu* 晉書

ChS: *Ch'ên shu* 陳書

CTS: *Chiu T'ang shu* 舊唐書

HHS   *Hou Han shu* 後漢書

HS: *Han shu* 漢書

HTS: *Hsin T'ang shu* 新唐書

LS: *Liang shu* 梁書

NCS   *Nan Ch'i shu* 南齊書

NS: *Nan shih* 南史

SC: *Shih chi* 史記

SKC: *San kuo chih* 三國志

SS: *Sung shu* 宋書

SuiS: *Sui shu* 隋書

WTSC: *Wu tai shih chi* 五代史記

Other

CTW: *Ch'üan T'ang wen* 全唐文. Taipei, 1961.

ChTS: *Ch'üan T'ang shih* 全唐詩. Peking, 1960.

CY: *An Nan chih yüan* 安南志原, *Collection de textes et documents sur l'Indochine*, vol. 1. École Française d'Extrême-Orient: Hanoi, 1932.

HYKC: *Hua Yang kuo chih* 華陽國志. Shanghai, 1922.

LC: *Li chi* 禮記. Taipei, 1975.

MS: *Man shu* 蠻書. Peking, 1962.

MT: *Mêng tzǔ* 孟子. Taipei, 1974.

MoT: Sun Hsing-yen 孫星衍 (1753–1818), ed, *Mou tzǔ* 牟子. Taipei, 1970.

SCC: *Shui ching chu* 水經注. Shanghai, 1929.

SM: Liu Hsi 劉熙, *Shih ming* 釋名, in *Han Wei ts'ung shu* 漢魏叢書, compiled by Wang Mu 王謨 (preface dated 1792).

TCTC: Ssǔ-ma Kuang 司馬光, *Tzǔ chih t'ung chien* 資治通鑑. Taipei, 1970.

TPHYC: *T'ai P'ing huan yu chi* 太平寰宇記. Taipei, 1963.

T'T: *T'ung tien* 通典. Shanghai, 1902.

YHCHC: *Yüan Ho chün hsien chih* 元和郡縣志. Shanghai, 1935–37.

Secondary Sources

Asami Shōzō. "Kōshi to iu Koshō." *Rekishi* 18 (1943): 64–67. On the origin of the term *Giao-chi*.

Aurousseau, Leonard. "Le Premier Conquete chinoise des pays annamites." *Bulletin de l'École Française d'Extrême-Orient* 23 (1923): 137–264. A pioneer study whose general conclusions are largely in error, but still a useful reference work.

Baron, Samuel. "A Description of the Kingdom of Tonqueen." In *A Collection of Voyages and Travels*, edited by Awnsham Churchill, 6: 1–40. London, 1732. The earliest detailed description of Vietnam in the English language; written half a century before it was published.

Bayard, D. T., "Comment." In *Early South East Asia: Essays in Archeology, History, and Historical Geography*, edited by R. B. Smith and W. Watson, pp. 278–80. New York, 1979. A comment on H. L. Shorto's essay.

Bezacier, L. *L'Art vietnamien*. Paris, 1955.

———. *Manuel d'archéologie d'Extrême-Orient. Première Partie: Asie du sud-est*. Vol. 2, *Le Vietnam*. "Première Fascicule: de la Préhistoire a la fin de l'occupation chinoise." Paris, 1972. A summary of French scholarship; ignores archeological work since 1954.

Bielenstein, Hans. "The Census of China during the Period 2–742 A.D." *Bulletin of the Museum of Far Eastern antiquities* 19 (1947): 125–63.

Bui Quang Tung. "Le Soulevement des Soeurs Trung." *Bulletin de la Société des Études Indochinoises* 36 (1961): 78–85.

Bửu Cam et al. *Hồng Đức bản đồ.* Saigon, 1962.

Cadiere, L., and Pelliot, P. "Premièr Étude sur les sources annamites." *Bulletin de l'École Française d'Extrême-Orient* 4 (1904): 617–71.

Cao Huy Đinh. "Hình tượng khổng lồ và tập thể anh hùng dựng nước, giữ nước trong truyền cổ dân gian Việt Nam." In *Truyền thống anh hùng dân tộc trong loài hình tự sự dân gian Việt Nam*, pp. 65–99. Hanoi, 1971.

Cao Huy Giu, trans., and Đào Duy Anh, annotator. *Đại Việt sử ký toàn thư.* 2d ed. Vol. 1. Hanoi, 1972.

Chavannes, Edouard. "Les pays d'Occident d'après le *Heou Han Chou.*" *T'oung Pao* 8 (1907): 149–234.

———. "Seng Houe." *T'oung Pao* 10 (1909): 199–212.

Ch'ên, Ching-ho A. "An Yō Ō no Shutsuji ni tsuite." *Shigaku* 42 (1970): 1–12. A companion essay to Jao Tsung-i, "An Yō Ō."

———. "Daietsu Shiki Zensho no Senshū to Denpon." *Tōnan Ajia: Rekishi to Bunka*, no. 7 (December, 1977), pp. 3–36. A study of the *Đại Việt sử ký toàn thư.*

Ch'en, Kenneth. *Buddhism in China.* Princeton, N. J., 1972.

Chêng Tê-k'un. *Archeological Studies in Szechwan.* Cambridge, 1957.

Chikamori Masashi. "Don Son Seidōki Bunka no Kigen ni kansuru Ichi Shiron." *Shigaku* 35 (1962): 65–96. A dated study of the Đông-sơn bronze culture; a good review of traditional theories.

Chử Văn Tân. "Cây lúa và nghề trồng lúa xưa ở Việt Nam." *Khảo cổ học* 33 (February 1980): 43–51.

Coedès, Georges. *The Making of Southeast Asia*, translated by H. M. Wright. Berkeley, 1967.

———. *The Indianized States of Southeast Asia*, translated by Susan Brown Cowing. Honolulu, 1968.

Cuisinier, Jean. *Les Muong.* Paris, 1948.

Đặng Thanh Lê. "Văn học cổ với nữ anh hùng Trưng Trắc." *Tập chí văn học* 5 (1969): 42–57.

Đặng Văn Lung. "Thành Cổ Long-biên." *Nghiên cứu lịch sử* 160 (1975): 72–74.

Daudin, Pierre. "Un Japonais a la cour des T'ang." *Bulletin de la Société des Études Indochinoises* 40 (1965): 215–80.

Davidson, Jeremy H. C. S. "Archeology in Northern Vietnam since 1954." In *Early South East Asia: Essays in Archeology, History, and Historical Geography*, edited by R. B. Smith and W. Watson, pp. 98–124. New York, 1979.

de Crespigny, Rafe. "Prefectures and Population in South China in the First

Three Centuries A.D." *Bulletin of the Institute of History and Philology, Academia Sinica* 40 (1968): 139–54.

DeFrancis, John. *Colonialism and Language Policy in Vietnam*. The Hague, 1977.

des Retours, Robert. "La Revolte de P'ang Huin (868–869)." *T'oung Pao* 56 (1970): 229–40.

Diệp Đình Hoà. "Tính độc đáo của người Việt cổ qua việc khảo sát những lưỡi rìu Đông-sơn." *Khảo cổ học 34 (May 1980): 48–60*.

Đinh Văn Nhật. "Đất Cẩm-khê, căn cứ cuối cùng của Hai Bà Trưng trong cuộc khởi nghĩa Mê-linh nam 40–43." *Nghiên cứu lịch sử* 148 (1973): 26–34; and 149 (1973): 31–40.

———. "Vùng Lãng-bạc về thời Hai Bà Trưng." *Nghiên cứu lịch sử* 156 (1974): 44–59.

———. "Vết tích của những ruộng Lạc đầu tiên quanh bờ Hồ Lãng-bạc và trên đất quê hương của Phù-đổng Thiên Vương." *Nghiên cứu lịch sử* 187 (July–August 1979): 24–37.

———. "Đất Mê-linh—trung tâm chính trị, quân sự và kinh tế của huyện Mê-linh về thời Hai Bà Trưng." *Nghiên cứu lịch sử* 190 (January–Feburary 1980): 35–53; and 191 (March–April 1980): 35–49.

Đỗ Đức Hùng. "Về tên đất Thái-bình, quê hương của Lý Bôn trong cuộc khởi nghĩa chống quân Lương." *Nghiên cứu lịch sử* 191 (March–April 1980): 63–65.

Đỗ Văn Ninh. "Về một vài khia cạnh của văn hóa vật chất thời kỳ An Dương Vương." In *Hùng Vương dựng nước*, edited by Ủy ban khoa học xã hội, 3: 389–94. Hanoi, 1973.

Dubs, Homer H. "A Military Contact between Chinese and Romans in 36 B.C." *T'oung Pao* 36 (1940): 64–80.

Dumoutier, Gustave. *Le Grand Buddha de Hanoi*. Hanoi, 1888.

———. "Choix de legendes historique de l'Annam et du Tonkin." *Révue d'ethnographie* 8 (1890): 159–91.

———. "Étude historique et archeologique sur Co-loa, capital de l'ancien royaume de Au Lac (reunion de Thuc et de Van Lang), 255–207 av. J.C." *Nouvelles Archives des Missions Scientifiques et Litteraires* 3 (1892).

———. "Étude historique sur Trieu-vo-de (Tchou-wou-ti) et sa dynasty." *T'oung Pao* 7 (1906): 413–36.

Durand, Maurice. "Recuil des puissances invisibles du pays de Việt de Lý Tê Xuyên." *Le Peuple vietnamien* 3 (1954): 3–44.

———. "La Dynastie des Lý anterieurs d'après le *Việt diện u linh tập*." *Bulletin de l'École Française d'Extrême-Orient* 54 (1954): 437–52.

Dvornik, Francis. *The Making of Central and Eastern Europe*. London, 1949.

Eberhard, Wolfram. *The Local Cultures of South and East China*. Leiden, 1968.

Fang, Achilles, trans. and annotator. *Chronicle of the Three Kingdoms* (from Ssu-ma Kuang's *Tzu chih t'ung chien*). Vol. 1. Cambridge, Mass., 1952.

Gaspardone, Émile. "Materiaux pour servir a l'histoire d'Annam." *Bulletin de l'École Française d'Extrême-Orient* 29 (1929): 63–106.

———. "Bibliographie annamite." *Bulletin de l'École Française d'Extrême-Orient* 34 (1934): 1–172. A useful reference work.

———. "L'Histoire et la philologie indochinoise." *Révue historique* 71 (July–September 1947): 1–15.

———. "Champs Lo et Champs Hiong." *Journal asiatique* 243 (1955): 461–77. A densely argued but important essay on early Chinese texts that describe ancient Vietnam.

Gerini, G. E. *Researches on Ptolemy's Geography of Eastern Asia*. London, 1909.

Gotō Kimpei. *Betonamu Kyūgoku Kōsō Shi*. Tokyo, 1975. A fine study of early Vietnam based on a broad knowledge of the sources.

Gourou, P. *Les Paysans du Delta Tonkinois*. Paris, 1936.

Hà Văn Tấn and Nguyễn Duy Hinh. "Kinh tê thời Hùng Vương." In *Hùng Vương dựng nước*, edited by Ủy ban khoa học xã hội, 3: 143–59. Hanoi, 1973.

Hà Văn Tấn and Nguyễn Khắc Sử, "Văn hóa Sơn-vi mười năm sau khi phát hiện." *Khảo cổ học* 28 (October 1978): 37–50. An evaluation of the newly discovered Sơn-vi Stone Age culture.

Hejzlar, J. *The Art of Vietnam*. Prague, 1973. Very fine photographs.

Hoàng Thị Châu. "Nước Văn-lang qua tài liệu ngôn ngữ." *Nghiên cứu lịch sử* 120 (1969): 37–48. A linguistic study of terms found in legendary traditions recorded in the fifteenth century.

Hoàng Xuân Chinh. "Quá trình hòa hợp thống nhất văn hóa khảo cổ ở Miền Bắc Việt Nam và cương vục nước Văn Lang." In *Hùng Vương dựng nước*, edited by Ủy ban khoa học xã hội, 3: 119–26. Hanoi, 1973.

Hoàng Xuân Chinh and Bùi Văn Tiến. "Văn hóa Đông-sơn và các trung tâm văn hóa trong thời Đại Kim Khí ở Việt Nam." *Khảo cổ học* 31 (August 1979): 40–48.

Holmgren, Jennifer. *Chinese Colonisation of Northern Vietnam: Administrative Geography and Political Development in the Tongking Delta, First to Sixth Centuries A.D.* Canberra, 1980.

Hsu Cho-yun. *Ancient China in Transition*. Stanford, Calif., 1965.

Hucker, Charles O. *China's Imperial Past*. Stanford, Calif., 1975.

Hùynh Sanh Thông, ed. and trans. *The Heritage of Vietnamese Poetry*. New Haven, Conn., 1979.

Jao Tsung-i. "Wu Yüeh wen-hua." *The Bulletin of the Institute of History and Philology, Academia Sinica* 41, part 4 (1969), pp. 609–36.

———. "An Yō Ō to Nichinanden ni tsuite." Translated by Ching-ho A. Ch'ên. *Shigaku* 42 (1970): 33–40. A study of early texts that mention King An Dương.

Katakura Minoru. "Chūgoku Shihaika no Betonamu." *Rekishigaku Kenkyū*

380 (January 1972): 17–26; and 381 (February 1972): 28–35. A study
of law and taxation in Vietnam under Chinese rule.

Kawahara Masahiro. "Tei Buryō no Sokui Nendai ni tsuite." *Hōsei Daigaku Bungakubu Kiyō* 15 (1970): 29–46. Revises the traditional chronology of tenth-century Vietnam.

Khổng Đức Thiên. "Từ sự tham gia của nhân dân Vũ-ninh vào cuộc khởi nghĩa Hai Bà Trưng." *Nghiên cứu lịch sử* 161 (1975): 54–59.

Kirsch, A. Thomas. "Kinship, Genealogical Claims, and Societal Integration in Ancient Khmer Society: An Interpretation." In *Southeast Asian History and Historiography*, edited by C. D. Cowan and O. W. Wolters, pp. 190–201. Ithaca, N.Y., 1976.

Lapique, P. A. "Note sur le canal de Hing-ngan." *Bulletin de l'École Française d'Extrême-Orient* 11 (1911): 425–28.

Lê Hữu Mục, trans. *Việt điện u linh tập.* Saigon, 1960.

———. *Lĩnh-nam chích quái.* Saigon, 1961.

Lê Thanh Khoi. *Le Viet-Nam.* Paris, 1955.

Lê Tượng and Nguyễn Đình Ái. "Qúa trình hình thành khu di tich lịch sử thời Vua Hùng trên Núi Hùng." *Nghiên cứu lịch sử* 160 (1975): 66–71.

Lê Tượng and Nguyễn Lộc. "Về kinh đô Văn-lang." *Nghiên cứu lịch sử* 185 (March–April 1979): 34–45.

Lê Văn Lan. "Tài liệu khảo cổ học và việc nghiên cứu thời kỳ Hai Bà Trưng." *Nghiên cứu lịch sử* 148 (1973): 35–40.

Levy, Howard S., trans. and annotator. *Biography of Huang Ch'ao.* Chinese Dynastic Histories Translation, no. 5. Berkeley, 1961.

Li Chêng-fu. *Chün-hsien shih-tai chih An-nan.* Shanghai, 1945.

Lü Shih-p'êng. *Pei-shu shih-chi ti Yüeh-nan.* Hong Kong, 1964.

Luce, G. H., trans. *The Man Shu: Book of the Southern Barbarians.* Data Paper 4, Southeast Asia Program, Cornell University. Ithaca, N.Y. 1961.

Mabbett, I. W. "The Indianization of Southeast Asia." *The Journal of Southeast Asian Studies* 8 (1977): 1–14 and 143–61.

Madrolle, Claude. "Le Tonkin ancien." *Bulletin de l'École Française d'Extrême-Orient* 37 (1937): 263–333. Ambitious but not very reliable.

Maspero, Georges. *Le Royaume de Champa.* Paris, 1928. Many errors of interpretation, but useful for reference.

Maspero, Henri. "Le Protectorat general d'Annam sous les T'ang." *Bulletin de l'École Française d'Extrême-Orient* 10 (1910): 539–682.

———. "Études d'histoire d'Annam." *Bulletin de l'École Française d'Extrême-Orient* 16 (1916): 1–55; and 18 (1918): 1–36:

    I. "La Dynastie des Lí anterieurs." 16: 1–26.

    II. "La Geographie politique de l'empire d'Annam sous les Lí, les Trần et les Hô." 16: 27–48.

    III. "La Commanderie de Siang." 16: 49–55.

    IV. "Le Royaume de Văn-lang." 18: 1–10.

V. "L'Expedition de Ma Yüan." 18: 11–28.

VI. "La Frontiere de l'Annam et du Cambodge du VIIIe au XIVe Siecle." 18: 29–36.

————. "Bulletin critique." *T'oung Pao* 23 (1924): 373–93.
With few exceptions, H. Maspero's work has stood the test of time remarkably well.

Matsumoto Nobuhiro. "Rō Dacchi Densetsu no Annan Iden." *Minzokugaku* 5 (December 1933): 1010–19. Cites the Manchu otter story from oral lore gleaned in Korea and compares it with the Vietnamese story.

————. "Religious Thoughts of the Bronze Age Peoples of Indochina." In *Folk Religion and the Worldview in the Southwestern Pacific*, edited by N. Matsumoto and T. Mabuchi, pp. 141–57. Tokyo, 1968.

Miller, J. Innes. *The Spice Trade of the Roman Empire*. New York, 1969.

Miyakawa Hisayuki. "The Confucianization of South China." In *The Confucian Persuasion*, edited by Arthur Wright, pp. 21–46. Stanford, Calif., 1960.

Morohashi Tetsuji. *Dai Kanwa Jiten* (Shukusha ban). 12 vols. Tokyo, 1966–68.

Neher, Clark D., ed. "Area News: Southeast Asia; Research Notes: The Bronze Drum Tradition." *Asian Studies Professional Review* 4 (Fall-Spring 1974–75): 186.

Nguyễn Đình Chiên and Ngô Thê Long. "Tâm bia đời Trân Du Tông mới phát hiện ở Hà-tuyên." *Khảo cổ học* 31 (August 1979): 64–74.

Nguyễn Đình Thực. "Cuộc khởi nghĩa Bà Triệu." *Nghiên cứu lịch sử* 147 (1972): 47–55.

Nguyễn Duy. "Cư dân ở Việt Nam trước, trong, và sau thời Hùng Vương." *Khảo cổ học* 30 (June 1979): 1–24. A physical anthropological study of prehistoric and early historical Vietnam.

Nguyễn Duy Chiêm. "Tìm dâu vết của An Dương Vương trên đất Cổ Loa." In *Hùng Vương dựng nước*, edited by Ủy ban khoa học xã hội, 3: 387–88. Hanoi, 1973.

Nguyễn Duy Hinh. "Nghề trồng lúa nước thời Hùng Vương." In *Hùng Vương dựng nước*, edited by Ủy ban khoa học xã hội, 3: 172–83. Hanoi, 1973.

Nguyễn Duy Tỷ. "Niên đại văn hóa Đông Sơn." In *Hùng Vương dựng nước*, edited by Ủy ban khoa học xã hội, 3: 77–84. Hanoi, 1973.

Nguyễn Khắc Đam, "Cuộc nổi dậy chống nhà Han của Lã Gia." *Nghiên cứu lịch sử* 149 (1973): 55–62.

Nguyễn Khắc Tụng. "Nghiên cứu văn hóa vật chật các dân tộc ở nước ta." *Khảo cổ học* 28 (October 1978): 77–81.

Nguyễn Khắc Xương. "Về cuộc khởi nghĩa Hai Bà Trưng qua tư liệu Vĩnh Phú." *Nghiên cứu lịch sử* 151 (1973): 41–49.

Nguyễn Linh and Hoàng Xuân Chinh. "Đất nước và con người thời Hùng Vương. In *Hùng Vương dựng nước*, edited by Ủy ban khoa học xã hội, 3: 91–112. Hanoi, 1973.

Nguyễn Lộc. "Bước đầu tìm hiểu mối quan hệ Hùng Vương và Thục Vương." *Nghiên cứu lịch sử* 137 (1971): 54–60.

Nguyễn Ngọc Chương. "Bước đầu giới thiệu một số nguồn tư liệu xung quanh de tích lịch sử thuộc về cuộc khởi nghĩa Hai Bà Trưng." *Nghiên cứu lịch sử* 146 (1972): 23–27.

Nguyễn Phuc Long. *Les Nouvelles Recherches archéologiques au Vietnam*. Arts asiatiques, 31. Paris, 1975. A critique of Bezacier, *Manuel*; summarizes recent archeological work in Vietnam.

Nguyễn Thị Huê. "Người dân Hà Bắc kể chuyện Lạc Long Quân—Âu Cơ." *Tạp chí văn học* 4 (1980): 102–7.

Nguyễn Tuân Lương. "Thêm một tư liệu về khởi nghĩa Hai Bà Trưng trên đất Lĩnh Nam." *Nghiên cứu lịch sử* 190 (January–February 1980): 81.

Nguyễn Văn Huyên. "Contribution a l'étude d'un génie tutelaire annamite Lí Phục Man." *Bulletin de l'École Française d'Extrême-Orient* 38 (1938): 1–110.

Nguyễn Việt. "Bước đầu nghiên cứu phương thức gặt lúa thời Hùng Vương." *Khảo cổ học* 34 (May 1980): 11–30.

Nienhauser, William H., Jr. *P'i Jih-hsiu*. Boston, 1979.

Norman, Jerry, and Mei, Tsu-lin. "The Austroasiatics in Ancient South China: Some Lexical Evidence." *Monumenta Serica* 32 (1976): 274–301. Suggests a reevaluation of the relationship between Chinese and neighboring southern languages.

Ozaki Yasushi. "Gokan no Kōshi Shishi ni tsuite—Shi Shō o meguru Sho Seiryoku." *Shigaku* 33 (1961): 139–66. A fine study of the era of Shih Hsieh.

Pearson, Richard. "Dong-son and Its Origins." *Bulletin of the Institute of Ethnology, Academia Sinica* 13 (1962): 27–53.

Pelliot, Paul. "Deux Itineraires de Chine en Inde a la fin du VIIIe siècle." *Bulletin de l'École Française d'Extrême-Orient* 4 (1904): 131–413. A good study that is still useful.

———. "Meou-tseu ou les doutes leves." *T'oung Pao* 19, no. 5 (December 1919): 255–433.

———. "Artistes des Six Dynasties et des T'ang." *T'oung Pao* 22, no. 4 (October 1923): 215–91.

Phạm Huy Thông. "Ba lần dựng nước." *Học tập* 21, no. 237 (September 1975): 63–72, 76. A new synthesis of Vietnamese history inspired by recent archeological discoveries.

———. "Mười năm xây dựng và phát triển ngành Khảo Cổ Học." *Khảo cổ học* 28 (October 1978): 3–11. An overview of archeological work in Vietnam in the decade 1968–78.

Phạm Huy Thông and Chử Văn Tấn. "Thời Đại Kim Khí ở Việt Nam và 'Văn Minh Sông Hồng': Văn Hóa Đông Sơn." *Khảo cổ học* 30 (June 1979): 37–44. A general summary of current ideas about the Bronze Age in Vietnam.

Pryzluski, Jean. "La Princesse a l'odeur de poisson et la Nagi dans les traditions de l'Asie oriental." In *Études Asiatique*, Publications, École Française d'Extrême-Orient, vols. 19–20, 2: 265–85. Paris, 1925.

Pulleyblank, Edwin G. *The Background of the Rebellion of An Lu-shan*. New York, 1955.

Reischauer, Edwin O., and Fairbank, John K. *East Asia, The Great Tradition*. Tokyo, 1970.

Roth, Henry Ling. *The Natives of Sarawak and British North Borneo*. Kuala Lumpur, 1968, reprint.

Sakurai Yumio. "Rakuden Mondai no Seiri." *Tōnan Ajia Kenkyū* 17, no. 1 (June 1979): 3–57.

Schafer, Edward H. "The History of the Empire of Southern Han." In *Silver Jubilee Volume of the Zinbun-Kagaku-Kenkyushu*, edited by Kaizuka Shigeki. Kyoto, 1954.

———. *Empire of Min*. Tokyo, 1954.

———. *The Vermilion Bird*. Berkeley, 1967.

———. *The Divine Woman*. Berkeley, 1973.

Seidel, Anna K. "The Image of the Perfect Ruler in Early Taoist Messianism: Lao-tzu and Li Hung." *History of Religion* 9 (November 1969–February 1970): 215–47.

Shorto, H. L. "The Linguistic Protohistory of Mainland South East Asia." In *Early South East Asia: Essays in Archeology, History, and Historical Geography*, edited by R. B. Smith and W. Watson, pp. 273–78. New York, 1979.

Stein, Rolf A. "Le Lin-i." *Han Hiue*, Bulletin du Centre d'Études Sinologiques de Pekin, vol. 2, fasc. 1–3. Peking, 1947. A fine study of the southern frontier of early Vietnam; clarifies many obscurities.

Stott, Wilfrid. "The Expansion of the Nan Chao Kingdom between the Years A.D. 750–860 and the Causes That Lay behind It as Shown in the T'ai-ho Inscription and the *Man Shu*." *T'oung Pao* 50 (1963): 190–220.

Sugimoto Naojirō. *Tōnan Ajiashi Kenkyū*. Vol. 1. Tokyo, 1956:

    I. "Shin Kan Ryōdai ni okeru Chūgoku Nankyō no Mondai." 1: 1–42.

    II. "Godai Sō Sho ni okeru Annan no Dogō Goshi ni tsuite." 1: 43–91. An evaluation of Wu policy toward Vietnam in the third century.

    V. "Sangoku Jidai ni okeru Go no Tainansaku." 1: 417–526. A good study of the sources for the tenth century Ngô family.

Tan Vu. "Tư tưởng chủ yếu của người Việt thời cổ quá những truyền đứng đầu trong thần thoại và truyền thuyết." In *Truyền thông anh hùng dân tộc trong loài hình tự sự dân gian Việt Nam,* pp. 100–19. Hanoi, 1971.

Taylor, K. W. "Madagascar and the Ancient Malayo-Polynesian Myths." In *Explorations in Early Southeast Asian History: The Origins of Southeast Asian Statecraft,* Michigan Papers on South and Southeast Asia, no. 11, edited by K. R. Hall and J. K. Whitmore, pp. 25–60. Ann Arbor, 1976.

———. "An Evaluation of the Chinese Period in Vietnamese History." *The Journal of Asiatic Studies* (Korea University) 23 (January 1980): 139–64.

Tôn Nữ Thương Lãng, trans., and Tạ Quang Phát, annotator. *Khâm định Việt sử thông giám cương mục.* Saigon, 1974.

Trần Bá chí. "Mai Thúc Loan và cuộc khởi nghĩa của ông." *Nghiên cứu lịch sử* 68 (1964): 50–57.

Trần Mạnh Phú. "Nghệ thuật tạo hình Đông Sơn: bản chất, diễn biến và ảnh hưởng." In *Hùng Vương dựng nước,* edited by Ủy ban khoa học xã hội, 3: 286–93. Hanoi, 1973.

Trần Nghĩa. "Một số tác phẩm mới phát hiện có liên quan tới giòng văn học Việt bằng chữ Hán của người Việt thời Bắc Thuộc." *Tạp chí văn học* 4 (1975): 84–99.

Trần Trọng Kim. *Việt Nam sử lược.* 2 vols. Saigon, 1971.

Trần Quốc Vượng. "Về danh hiệu 'Hùng Vương.'" In *Hùng Vương dựng nước,* edited by Ủy ban khoa học xã hội, 3: 353–55. Hanoi, 1973.

———. "Từ tư duy thần thoại đến tư duy lịch sử." In *Hùng Vương dựng nước,* edited by Ủy ban khoa học xã hội, 3: 402–5. Hanoi, 1973.

———. trans. and annotator. *Việt sử lược.* Hanoi, n.d..

Trần Quốc Vượng and Đỗ Văn Ninh. "Về An Dương Vương." In *Hùng Vương dựng nước,* edited by Ủy ban khoa học xã hội, 3: 362–82. Hanoi, 1973.

Trần Văn Giáp. "Le Bouddhisme en Annam des origines au XIIIe siècle." *Bulletin de l'École Française d'Extrême-Orient* 32 (1932): 191–257. A study of early Vietnamese Buddhist texts.

———. *Tìm hiểu kho sách Hán Nôm.* Vol. 1. Hanoi, 1970. A bibliography of Vietnamese works written in Chinese.

Trịnh Sinh. "Vài nét về giao lưu văn hóa ở thời Đại Kim Khí trong bối cảnh lịch sử Đông Nam Á." *Khảo cổ học* 31 (August 1979): 49–63. A study of Bronze Age artifacts from Vietnam and other parts of Southeast Asia.

Trương Hoàng Châu. "Phát biểu thêm về niên đại Cổ-loa." In *Hùng Vương dựng nước,* edited by Ủy ban khoa học xã hội, 3: 383–86. Hanoi, 1973.

Tsang Wah-moon. *T'ang-tai Ling-nan fa-chan ti heh-hsin hsing.* Hong Kong, 1973. A study of economic and demographic development in southern China during T'ang.

Từ điển tiếng Việt (Dictionnaire vietnamien francais). 2 vols. Paris, 1977.

Twitchett, Denis. "Some Remarks on Irrigation under the T'ang." *T'oung Pao* 48 (1960): 175–94.

Ủy Ban Khoa Học Xã Hội Việt Nam. *Lịch sử Việt Nam*. Vol. 1. Hanoi, 1971. A major interpretation of premodern Vietnam by contemporary scholars.

Văn Lang. "Đất tổ đền Hùng." *Nghiên cứu lịch sử* 185 (March–April 1979): 76–77.

Vũ Phương Đê. *Công dư tiệp ký*. 3 vols. Saigon, 1961.

Vũ Tuân Sán. "Cuộc khởi nghĩa Hai Bà Trưng tại thủ đô Hà-nội *Nghiên cứu lịch sử* 149 (1973): 41–50.

Vương Lộc. "Glimpses of the Evolution of the Vietnamese Language." *Linguistic Essays* (*Vietnamese Studies*, 40), pp. 9–30. Hanoi, 1975.

Wang Gung-wu. "The Nanhai Trade: A Study of the Early History of Chinese Trade in the South China Sea." *Journal of the Malayan Branch of the Royal Asiatic Society* 31 (June 1958): 1–135.

Watson, Burton. *Ssu-ma Ch'ien, Grand Historian of China*. New York, 1958.

Wiens, Harold J. *Han Chinese Expansion in South China*. Hamden, Conn., 1967.

Wolters, O. W. *Early Indonesian Commerce*. Ithaca, N.Y., 1967.

———. "Historians and Emperors in Vietnam and China: Comments Arising Out of Lê Văn Hưu's History, Presented to the Trần Court in 1272." In *Perceptions of the Past in Southeast Asia*, edited by Anthony Reid and David Marr, pp. 69–89. Singapore, 1979.

———. "Assertions of Cultural Well-being in Fourteenth-Century Vietnam." *Journal of Southeast Asian Studies* 10 (September 1979): 435–50; and 11 (March 1980): 74–90.

Woodside, Alexander B. *Vietnam and the Chinese Model*. Cambridge, Mass., 1971.

Wright, Arthur F. *The Sui Dynasty*. New York, 1978.

Yamamoto Tatsurō. "Ōken no Hongen o Monogataru Indoshina no Kazukazu no Setsuwa ni tsuite." In *Katō Hakase Kanreki Kinen Tōyōshi Shūsetsu*, edited by Katō Hakase Kanreki Kinen Rombunshū Kankōkai, pp. 924–44. Tokyo, 1941.

———. "Annan ga Dokuritsu-koku o Keiseishitaru Katei no Kenkyū." *Tōyō Bunka Kenkyū-jo Kiyō* 1 (1943): 1–90. A good study of the texts on tenth century Vietnam.

———. "Esshiryaku to Daietsu Shiki." *Tōyō Gakuhō* 32 (1949): 433–56. On the *Việt sử lược* and the *Đại Việt sử ký toàn thư*.

———. "Myths Explaining the Vicissitudes of Political Power in Ancient Viet Nam." *Acta Asiatica* (Bulletin of the Institute of Eastern Culture, Tokyo) 18 (1970): 70–94.

———. ed. *Betonamu Chūgoku Kankei Shi*. Tokyo, 1975.

Yang Lien-sheng. "Notes on the Economic History of the Chin Dynasty." *Harvard Journal of Asiatic Studies* 9 (1946): 107–86.

Yu Insun. "Law and Family in Seventeenth and Eighteenth-Century Vietnam." Ph.D. dissertation, University of Michigan, 1978.

Yü, Ying-shih. *Trade and Expansion in Han China: A Study in the Structure of Sino-Barbarian Economic Relations.* Berkeley, 1967.

Index